CASSELL

Dictionary of Norse Myth and Legend

CASSELL

Dictionary of Norse Myth and Legend

Andy Orchard

CASSELL

This edition first published in the UK 1997 by

CASSELL

Wellington House, 125 Strand, London WC2R 0BB

Copyright © Andy Orchard 1997

Distributed in the United States by
Sterling Publishing Co., Inc.
387 Park Avenue South, New York, NY 10016–8810

A British Library Cataloguing in Publication Data block for this
book may be obtained from the British Library

ISBN 0 304 34520 2

Typeset by Bibliocraft, Dundee
Printed and bound in Great Britain by The Bath Press

Contents

Preface

This is a book about the changing range of myths and legends current among the Germanic peoples of Northern Europe over more than a millennium. Its focus is mainly – though not exclusively – literary, and seeks to represent the primary evidence both by illustration and, more pertinently, by quotation. It is symptomatic of the subject that the majority of the illustrations offered here should relate to material from before around 1000, and the majority of the 350 or so quotations cited should recount matter from the eleventh century on. The year 1000 around which the evidence is spread is not in itself significant, except in so far as it coincides with the traditional date of the conversion to Christianity of Iceland (although some prefer to place the conversion in the previous year, 999), but it is worth noting that this pivotal year in terms of data (if not precise dates) falls towards the end of the so-called Viking Age, generally dated $c.800-1100$. This is not, then, primarily, or even mainly, a book that is simply about Vikings and Norsemen. It is also to some extent about their ancestors in the continental Germanic homelands, their cousins in Anglo-Saxon England and, most especially, their descendants, who settled widely in Scandinavia and beyond.

That so much of the purely literary evidence for the myths and legends of the North should stem from the post-conversion period does not of itself negate its value. In many cases Christian authors took great care to transmit their heathen inheritance intact, or inadvertently preserved much useful material in parody. Throughout the book, moreover, it will be seen that certain myths and legends kept their essential shape across the centuries, being dimly recalled by classical ethnographers, carved in stone in an age when the written record had barely begun, celebrated in skaldic verse and eddic song, and finally set down in sagas towards the end of the medieval period. But it is also true to say that few aspects of the myths and legends kept their

shape for so long, and it is part of the aim of the book to trace the development of individual notions throughout the period, as well as the kaleidoscopic variety of so much of the material.

Within a book of this limited size, the coverage is necessarily somewhat truncated and diffuse, and in many cases I have merely attempted to suggest the bare outline of what is known, pointing instead to the wealth of further material available for study. Nonetheless, it is hoped that by offering some 750 main entries (each with references to a supplementary bibliography), together with more than 300 other headwords and literally thousands of cross-references, some conception might be given of the vast range of material involved and disciplines implied in any serious study of the myths and legends of the North.

Each headword is presented in **bold** type, with all names rendered in a simplified spelling and followed, where feasible and appropriate, by a translation. After each main article there follow references to individual entries in the bibliography of suggested further reading, which contains around 900 items and which is divided into general surveys, primary texts, translations and secondary criticism. Cross-references are indicated in the text by the use of SMALL CAPITALS.

In truncating and doubtless over-simplifying what are in many cases extremely complex questions and issues, I am quite aware that I risk offending those more scholarly readers who may be disappointed at the dearth of academic debate offered here. I have tried in the references, which often signal competing attitudes, to present some sense of the richness and vigour of the current critical wrangling in an area in which very little can be considered truly settled. A book of this size cannot hope to do more than introduce the uninitiated to the range and variety of the tales once told and beliefs once held, and perhaps to offer a fresh perspective to those who are familiar with those tales and beliefs in a

Preface

particular form. In compiling this book in this rather haphazard fashion, I have had to try to tread the narrow path between the demands of modern scholarship and the pleasures of medieval story-telling, and have therefore taken some comfort in the words of the eddic poem *Hávamál*:

Each man should be only middling-wise,
never over-clever:
a wise man's heart is seldom glad,
if he is truly wise.

There is certainly much wisdom in many of these narratives, far deeper than I could hope to fathom or present here, but there is also (and more importantly, perhaps) much wonder and delight. With this book I should hope to whet the appetites of readers to look beyond its limitations and to explore further the rich legacy that still survives. For, after all, the myths and legends of the North have gladdened not only my heart since childhood, but many wiser hearts, in many lands and across many centuries.

Andy Orchard

EMMANUEL COLLEGE, CAMBRIDGE

Introduction: The Nature of the Sources

Norse myths and legends are found in a bewilderingly wide array of sources from different periods and places, reflecting hugely varying views. The sources themselves, moreover, have survived only sporadically and cannot be taken to represent anything other than a rather random sample. Such a background necessarily implies that a fully rationalized and comprehensively cohesive account of the myths and legends of the North is neither possible nor (perhaps) desirable, and that instead the best that can be produced is a somewhat fractured and kaleidoscopic picture. As in any mosaic, it is the most striking and cohesive fragments that command attention, and so it is that the often splendid literary material, with its dazzling narratives and starkly vivid verse, has greatly overshadowed other kinds of evidence in the eyes of most observers. But quite apart from the ample testimony of the literary record, whether in the form of praise-poems by named (and even dateable) poets, anonymous mythological verses of uncertain age or the prose accounts of later antiquarian authors, other kinds of evidence, whether from runes, archaeology or onomastics (the study of place- and personal names) must be weighed against the accounts of more-or-less hostile outsiders, pouring out a steady stream of propaganda, reproach and, occasionally, praise. The great diversity of sources stems directly from the huge spans of chronology and geography throughout which traces of the myths and legends of the North survive, beginning from the time when classical ethnographers described the customs and beliefs of the ancestral continental Germanic peoples and continuing through to an age of Scandinavian exploration and settlement some ten centuries later, which saw Norsemen as far west as North America and east as far as Uzbekistan.

The picture is complicated still further by periodic attempts by authors and antiquarians of differing abilities and eras to synthesize and integrate the material then at hand. On one level this book can be considered just such another attempted overview, although here it is acknowledged from the outset that the search for any single solution to the various problems of meaning and interpretation raised by the material is inevitably doomed. Instead it is hoped that by considering the variety of complementary and contradictory witnesses available, readers will be encouraged to go further in engaging and examining the sources themselves, whether through the filter of translation or in the original, and to weigh the developing opinions of successive scholars striving to interpret the evidence. To that end the extensive (but by no means exhaustive) bibliography is intended more as a spur to further exploration than a simple list of references cited. Given, however, the great diversity of the primary material available for study, it seems most helpful in a general Introduction to offer a brief summary of the main types of evidence and of some of the individual sources concerning which more information is given within the main body of the book.

In view of its comparative antiquity and (to the uninitiated) apparent impenetrability, it seems appropriate to begin by noting the existence of a large body of epigraphic, linguistic and non-literary evidence, including that of runes and picture-stones, some of which provide the illustrations. Such evidence requires careful exposition, and it is symptomatic of both kinds of material that the interpretations of individual scholars will vary – sometimes wildly. Although often clearly more ancient (and often considered more 'authentic') than the literary evidence, runic inscriptions and picture-stones are no less prone to 'imaginative' readings. Similar difficulties beset the interpretation of archaeological finds, such as, for example, boat burials, bog corpses and burial mounds. Much exciting evidence for ritual and practice can be deduced from such finds, however, and some sites in particular –

Introduction

Gokstad, Jelling, Oseberg, Uppsala and, in Anglo-Saxon England, Sutton Hoo – have proved particularly fruitful. Much useful work has also been done in the field of onomastics, considering the personal and place-name evidence that attests to cult activity. Such evidence has proved particularly useful in assessing the cults not only of such well-known figures as the gods Odin and Thor, but also of more obscure deities, such as Forseti or Ull.

The non-epigraphic written evidence can be considered under a number of headings. Distinctions between what can be termed 'literary' and what 'historical' are not always easy to maintain. Following in the tradition of first-century classical historians and ethnographers, writing in both Greek and Latin, such as Strabo and Tacitus, there came a whole series of contemporary chroniclers who give an insight (and usually a Christian gloss) into the beliefs and legends of the Germanic world from the sixth century on, including such figures as Paulus Diaconus, Paulus Orosius, Procopius and Sidonius Apollinaris. Later Christian writers who came into contact with Vikings were still less generous in their assessment, and often, as in the case of the Anglo-Saxons Ælfric and Wulfstan, had to measure their contempt for the raiders with the knowledge that they shared a common Germanic heritage, of a kind witnessed in earlier works, such as the writings of Bede or the Old English poem *Beowulf*. Less partial (but equally astonished) testimony to the activities of the Scandinavians abroad is offered by non-Germanic contemporaries, such as Ibn Fadlan. As the Viking Age drew to a close, Christian writers from nearer home, such as Adam of Bremen, cast a baleful eye on the customs of their neighbours. What such authors offered was the perspective of the outsider, although in every case the view offered could hardly be described as objective; religious and racial considerations conspired to create a picture that was distinctly distorted. Later Scandinavian writers, looking back at the myths and legends of their ancestors and purporting to give a historian's (or antiquarian's) perspective on the pagan past, might occasionally offer a more rose-tinted (but not necessarily more objective) view. Modern scholarship has repeatedly shown that the confident pronouncements of Saxo Grammaticus and Snorri Sturluson need to be considered with caution, notwithstanding their greater proximity to the sources and their undoubted access to material long since lost.

Snorri and Saxo were themselves much exercised by the problems of interpreting the written evidence then extant, and indeed some of the material they used still survives. Such evidence, predominantly literary in character, continues to offer difficulties of interpretation of various kinds. In the case of skaldic poetry a primary problem has been simply understanding the verses, a question intensified by the highly allusive nature of skaldic diction, with its poetic periphrases or kennings, and frequent use of poetic synonyms or *heiti*. A further difficulty surrounds the attribution of the texts themselves, ostensibly to named poets from the ninth century on, since in some cases the accuracy of the ascription is far from secure; in the main body of the book consideration is given to skaldic verse that has been attributed with varying degrees of confidence to a wide range of poets, including Bragi Boddason inn gamli, Eilíf Godrúnarson, Eyvind Finnsson skáldaspillir, Hallfred Ottarsson vandrædaskáld, Kormák Ögmundarson, Sighvat Thórdarson, Thjódólf of Hvín, Thorbjörn dísarskáld, Thorbjörn hornklofi and Úlf Uggason.

The verses of some of these poets are preserved in Icelandic sagas composed sometimes four centuries after the alleged dates of their supposed authors, and such sagas have often been taken to contain other ancient lore. Such a supposition is deeply problematic, given the innately retrospective nature of the sagas, celebrating as they do for the most part events from a distant past when Iceland was newly settled. Nonetheless, such sagas certainly offer a picture at times remarkably consistent with what can be deduced from other and much older sources, as well as bearing witness to the extraordinarily vigorous tradition of story-telling in the North, and in the pages that follow evidence is offered from the late witness of a number of these Icelandic sagas, specifically *Egils saga Skalla-Grimssonar*, *Eiríks saga rauda*, *Eyrbyggja saga*, *Gísla saga*, *Grettis saga Ásmundarsonar*, *Hallfredar saga*, *Hrafnkels saga Freysgoda*, *Kormáks saga*, *Laxdæla saga*, *Njáls saga* and *Viga-Glúms saga*. Some of the great manuscripts containing these works, notably Flateyjarbók, also preserve other traditions of doubtful date and authenticity, which have been taken by some to reflect much earlier narratives and beliefs, and some of these tales, too, have been considered below. The famously direct and understated style of the Icelandic sagas is, of course, no guarantee of the truth of the traditions recorded, although some have certainly been seduced into thinking that the evidence offered in so casual and apparently artless a fashion must of necessity carry some weight. More obviously fictitious are the so-called *fornaldarsögur*, which are positively teeming with supernatural and improbable features. Nonetheless, it is quite clear that amid all the monster-slaying and shape-changing there can be found traces of much earlier mythical and legendary material. The problem lies in deciding how to determine what can be considered genuinely old. Of the large numbers of such legendary sagas still extant, only a handful have been considered here, including *Gautreks saga*, *Hervarar saga*, *Hrólfs saga kraka*, *Örvar-Odds saga*, *Thidreks saga* and *Völsunga saga*.

Still more can be deduced about the myths and legends of the North from the Poetic Edda, a collection of poems mostly preserved in a single manuscript, the Codex Regius, which offers a marvellously vivid and detailed (if sometimes contradictory) picture of mythical and legendary lore. Many of the poems were clearly plundered for their own purposes by later writers, notably Snorri Sturluson and the author of *Völsunga saga*, and the broad term 'eddic poetry' is used to cover a great range of styles and genres of verse evidently composed over a period of centuries. The clear differences in tone that mark out, say, the stark heroism of *Atlakvida*, a grim tale of legendary heroes, from the slapstick buffoonery of *Thrymskvida*, a comic romp among the gods, should give any reader pause in supposing that such witnesses should be given equal weight. The difficulty lies in attributing to either work a date that can be agreed. Current suggestions offer leeway of around three centuries, with varying degrees of chronological difference between the texts. The dangers of synthesizing such disparate material are evident to even the most casual reader of eddic verse, and it is ironic that undoubtedly the most influential single figure in terms of the modern perception of the myths

and legends of the North, namely the Icelander Snorri Sturluson, did just that in compiling the compendious work known as *Snorra Edda*, which also makes copious use of skaldic sources. This largely coherent overview of mythology and legendary history, which Snorri put together in the thirteenth century as a largely antiquarian exercise to help his countrymen preserve a centuries-old heritage of verse inextricably bound by its diction to a body of mythical and legendary lore, is a masterpiece of humorous and vivid composition, and it is sometimes difficult to see beyond the punchy and memorable scenes depicted. Yet it is quite clear that in some instances Snorri misunderstood, manipulated or simply manufactured material to suit himself and that *Snorra Edda*, although invaluable, is not a source above suspicion.

Such a brief survey of the nature of the sources available to those interested in the myths and legends of the North will inevitably focus on the hazards of interpreting a disparate body of material. The weight to be attached to each type of witness remains a matter for vigorous (and sometimes vicious) debate. A book of this size can aim only to indicate the main areas of discussion and to offer an outline of the great range of material that might be considered. Each kind of evidence has its own problems of interpretation, but together the various types of witness provide a compelling (if necessarily incomplete) picture of a vibrant tradition of myth and legend lasting more than a millennium.

Spelling and Pronunciation

Norse (and Anglo-Saxon) spelling is notorious: there are a number of models for transliteration available, each of which is prone to local misconstruction. Here I have chosen in the main body of the dictionary to adopt the spellings of 'standard' Old Norse (basically Old Icelandic), but to remove the final consonant marking the nominative singular (generally - *r*, - *n* or - *l*), except where it follows a vowel. I have retained the digraphs æ and Œ, as well as accents, but have levelled the less familiar ǫ to ö. In the same way I have chosen to simplify the unfamiliar consonants ð and þ to d and th respectively; the corresponding capitals Ð and Þ are found as D and Th. A few examples will illustrate usage: Bǫlþorn appears as Bölthorn, Þrúðgelmir as Thrúdgelmir, Starkaðr as Starkad, and Geirvimull as Geirvimul. Some words, like Glæsivellir, therefore appear unchanged. In a number of cases, notably Odin and Thor, I have retained the form most familiar to the general reader; to insist upon the more accurate Ódin and Thór might have seemed pedantic. The hawk-eyed will doubtless spot other inconsistencies; I can only observe that they will be similarly displeased with the spellings in many of the items listed in the Bibliography.

This is not the place to offer a comprehensive guide to Norse pronunciation, itself a topic fraught with perils. Suffice it to say that the acute accent on vowels is a mark of length, not stress; most Norse words are stressed on the first syllable. It may be helpful to note that, in Modern Icelandic pronunciation, the unfamiliar characters þ/Þ and ð/Ð are pronounced 'th', as in 'thin' and 'the' respectively, while the vowels æ and ö/ǫ are pronounced as in 'eye' and 'turn' respectively.

List of Illustrations

List of Illustrations

Oseberg The ship from the burial mound at Oseberg, Vestfold, Norway, reproduced courtesy of Universitetet i Oslo.

Ratatosk An illustration from the manuscript AM 738 4to of *Snorra Edda*, reproduced courtesy of Stofnun Arna Magnússonar, Reykjavik.

Regin Detail of the Rasmundsberget runestone from Jäder, Södermanland, Sweden, reproduced courtesy of York Archaeological Trust.

Runes Detail from an Anglo-Saxon manuscript, St John's College, Oxford, MS 17, reproduced courtesy of The President and Scholars of St John's College, Oxford.

Sigurd Detail of the portal from the church at Hylestad, Setesdal, Norway, reproduced courtesy of Universitetet i Oslo.

Snorra Edda An illustration from the fourteenth-century manuscript, Uppsala University Library, Delagardie 11, reproduced courtesy of Uppsala University Library.

Sutton Hoo The helmet from Sutton Hoo, copyright British Museum.

Thor Copper alloy figure from Eyrarland, Iceland, reproduced courtesy of Ívar Brynjólfsson, National Museum of Iceland.

Valhall Picture stone from Tjängvide, Gotland, Sweden, reproduced courtesy of Gunnel Jansson, ATA, Stockholm.

Valkyries Silver figures from Birka, Björkö, Uppland, Sweden, reproduced courtesy of ATA, Stockholm.

Vídar Detail from the late tenth-century Gosforth Cross, Cumbria, England, drawn by Collingwood.

Völsunga saga Detail of the portal from the church at Hylestad, Setesdal, Norway, reproduced courtesy of Ove Holst, Universitetet i Oslo.

Völund The Franks casket, copyright British Museum.

The Dictionary

A

Adal *see* RÍGSTHULA.

Adam of Bremen

Author of the *Gesta Hammaburgensis ecclesiae pontificum* ('Deeds of the Bishops of the Church of Hamburg-Bremen'), composed after he arrived in Bremen in 1066 or 1067 to act as adviser to Archbishop Adalbert (1043–72). Adam took a particular interest in missionary activities, and consequently the *Gesta* contains a good deal of useful information (as well as considerable speculation) about the customs of the neighbouring pagan Germanic and Scandinavian peoples. Perhaps his best known set-piece description is that of the great pagan temple at UPPSALA, although it is unclear to what extent his description has a basis in historical fact rather than lurid fiction.

B48, 70; C47; D221, 280

Adils

A legendary king of Sweden, married to Yrsa, the mother of the mighty king HRÓLF KRAKI, who features in several tales. The quarrel between Adils and his stepson is described in detail in a number of literary sources, including SNORRA EDDA.

B24, 28, 35, 40, 50; C5, 9, 48

Ægir ('sea', 'sea-giant')

The Norse god of the sea, also known as HLÉR and GYMIR, whose wife is RÁN, and whose nine giant daughters are waves, named Bara (or Bára; 'wave'), BLÓDUGHADDA ('bloody hair'), Bylgja ('billow'), DÚFA ('dipping'), Hefring ('raising'), Himinglæva ('heaven-bright'), HRÖNN ('wave'), Kólga ('cool wave') and Unn (or Ud; 'wave'); in other lists the name DRÖFN ('foaming sea') is found in place of Bara.

Ægir appears in a number of poems in the POETIC EDDA, most notably in LOKASENNA, in which the feast to which he invites the ÆSIR and for which he provides the ale forms the backdrop to the slanging-match that follows. The tale of how the god THOR acquired a kettle large enough for Ægir to brew ale for the Æsir is given in another eddic poem, HYMISKVIDA. The notion that Ægir hosts feasts for the Æsir is also made explicit in both GRÍMNISMÁL and skaldic verse, while in SNORRA EDDA, in what is presumably a deliberate inversion of the motif, a figure called Ægir or Hlér is introduced by the thirteenth-century Icelander SNORRI STURLUSON at the beginning of SKÁLDSKAPARMÁL as a wanderer invited to a feast by the Æsir; there he is given an exposition of much mythological lore by BRAGI, the god of poetry, including (appropriately enough) an account of the winning of the MEAD OF POETRY. According to Snorri:

> There was a figure called Ægir or Hlér; he lived on an island, which is now called Hléysey [identified with modern-day Læssø in Kattegat, Denmark]. He was very crafty in magic. He set off to visit ÁSGARD, and when the Æsir realized he was coming, he was given a splendid welcome, although many things were not as they seemed; and in the evening, when they were about to begin drinking, ODIN had swords brought into the hall, which were so bright that light shone from them, and no other light was used when they were drinking . . . Everything there seemed to Ægir to be splendid to look at; the walls were all hung with magnificent shields. The mead there was also strong, and vast quantities were drunk. Next to Ægir was seated Bragi, and they drank and talked together; Bragi told Ægir many of the deeds in which the Æsir had been embroiled.

The magnificent martial setting of the hall described here has much in common with other descriptions of VALHALL, while the general scenario, of a wanderer received among the Æsir and told tales of their deeds, consciously echoes the deluding of King GYLFI also told by Snorri in his GYLFAGINNING.

Ælfric

In several mnemonic name-lists or THULUR, Ægir is given as the name of a giant, and, given both the description of his daughters as giants, and, at least in some sources, his own descent from the giant FORNJÓT, it may well be that Ægir's adoption into lists of the Æsir is a late development.

B12, 14, 23, 24, 28, 30, 35, 39, 40, 45, 50, 56, 59, 62, 73, 83, 87, 90; C2, 5, 9, 13, 16, 17, 24, 33, 46, 48; D541

Ælfric

Celebrated Anglo-Saxon abbot of Eynsham, who died in 1010 after a long career as a composer of homilies, saints' lives and a whole range of other pedagogical and didactic material. As an author whose chief concern was orthodoxy, Ælfric was unremittingly scathing about all aspects of paganism, whether from the classical past or the heathen present, and in particular his *De falsis deis* ('On False Gods'), an Old English rendering of a much earlier Latin discussion by the sixth-century Visigothic archbishop, Martin of Braga, contains a number of close comparisons between the pagan deities of the classical past, witnessed by literary sources, and the gods worshipped by the invading Danes. Part of Ælfric's *De falsis deis* was reworked by his contemporary, Archbishop WULFSTAN, who produced a still pithier comparison between the classical and pagan gods of his acquaintance.

B67; D572

Æsir ('gods')

The generic name given to the Norse gods (the singular form is Ás), although some sources seek to make a distinction between two groups of deities, the Æsir and the VANIR, who, as we learn from the eddic poem VÖLUSPÁ, once fought a mighty war. In general, the Æsir are associated with war, death and power, the Vanir with growth and fertility, although the distinction is often far from clear. According to the thirteenth-century Icelander SNORRI STURLUSON, there are thirteen male Æsir, which he lists in the following order: ODIN, THOR, NJÖRD, FREY, TÝR, HEIMDALL, BRAGI, VÍDAR, VÁLI, ULL, HŒNIR, FORSETI and LOKI. In the same place Snorri also lists eight goddesses, known as ÁSYNJUR, although elsewhere he gives a quite different list of no fewer than sixteen. Moreover, Snorri's effort to produce a list of thirteen Æsir, of whom one (Loki) was to prove a traitor, looks suspiciously like an attempt to align the Æsir with the disciples of Christ and may account in part for his inclusion of some figures (notably Forseti) who are seldom heard of elsewhere.

A similar motivation to explain away the deities of the pagan past surely lies behind the elaborate EUHEMERISM exhibited by Snorri and the early thirteenth-century Danish historian SAXO GRAMMATICUS in their attempts to explain the term Æsir as related to Asia, whence the (on this view wholly human) Æsir are said to have come. In this way, the myths and legends of the north could be aligned with those of classical Greece and Rome, just as, say, the Middle English Arthurian poem *Gawain and the Green Knight* begins by describing Troy. Such a notion is purely the product of an impulse to 'dignify' indigenous vernacular tales by linking them to the illustrious world of Latin learning. By contrast, cognate forms of the term Æsir are well attested in other Germanic languages and help to testify to its antiquity: Old English speaks of *esa gescot* ('shot of the Æsir'; cf. *ylfa gescot* 'shot of the elves'), while Gothic contains references to divinities known as *ansis*, a form which is also recorded by the sixth-century historian JORDANES.

Snorri provides a wealth of trivial information about the Æsir, including lists of the names of their horses: Falhófnir, Gils, Glad, Glær, Gulltopp, GYLLIR, Léttfeti, Silfr(in)topp, Sinir, Skeidbrimir and finally SLEIPNIR, Odin's own horse. Such information, matched with other details about their daily dealings that can be gleaned from the POETIC EDDA, lends a familiar and almost homely air to many of the actions of the Æsir, of whose ultimate doom in the apocalyptic events of RAGNARÖK we are continually assured.

B12, 14, 23, 24, 28, 30, 35, 40, 50, 55, 56, 59, 64, 73, 87, 90; C2, 5, 7–9, 17, 24, 31, 33, 46, 48; D49, 115, 120, 439, 443, 504

Æthelweard *see* SCEAF.

Ætternisstapi ('family drop')

According to the legendary GAUTREKS SAGA, a huge cliff over which members of a particular family fling themselves in times of crisis, as a voluntary form of euthanasia. King Gauti stumbles across their dwelling while lost hunting, and he forces his way in past a servant. As one of the young girls in the family rather jauntily explains:

> There's a cliff near the farm called Gilling's Bluff, and we call its highest point Ætternisstapi. The fall is so steep that no creature on earth could ever survive it. It's called Ætternisstapi because we use it to cut down the size of our family whenever something remarkable happens. In this way our elders are permitted to die without delay, and suffer no sicknesses, and go straight to ODIN, while their children are spared all the trouble and expense of being forced to look after them. Everyone in our family is free to take advantage of the facility provided by the cliff, so that there is no need for any of us to live in famine or poverty or endure any other difficulties that may arise. I hope you realize how remarkable my father

2

thinks your arrival at our house; it would have been extraordinary for any stranger to take a meal with us, but it really is a marvel for a king to come cold and naked to our house. Such a thing has never happened before. So my mother and father have decided to divide the inheritance tomorrow between my brothers and sisters and me, then take the servant with them and go over Ætternisstapi to VALHALL. My father reckons that the least he can do for the servant in return for trying to stop you coming in is to allow him to share his happiness. Besides, he's quite certain that Odin won't ever accept the servant unless he goes with him.

The references to Odin and Valhall may suggest that behind this undoubtedly jocular tale there lurks the shadow of an authentic tradition of human SACRIFICE, although such fantastic episodes are relatively commonplace in the world of the FORNALDARSÖGUR.

B69; C35, 38; D376

Afi *see* RÍGSTHULA.

Agnar Audabródir

According to the eddic poem SIGRDRÍFUMÁL, the king to whom the Valkyrie SIGRDRÍFA gives the victory in a battle against one HJÁLMGUNNAR, who is the favourite of the god ODIN. In revenge, Sigrdrífa is stripped of her status as a Valkyrie and struck with a sleepthorn, to await the arrival of the hero SIGURD, who will wake her from slumber. In another eddic poem, HELREID BRYNHILDAR, the fierce and proud heroine BRYNHILD identifies herself as Agnar's champion, and so as Sigrdrífa, while the legendary VÖLSUNGA SAGA transfers the entire account to her.

B12, 25, 30, 42, 56, 65, 68, 73, 79, 87, 90; C1–3, 6, 17, 24, 33, 46

Agnar Geirrödsson *see* AGNAR HRAUDUNGSSON.

Agnar Hraudungsson

According to the eddic poem GRÍMNISMÁL, the elder of the two sons of King HRAUDUNG. On their return from an unintentional stay with a mysterious elderly couple (later identified as the gods ODIN and FRIGG), Agnar, Frigg's favourite, is cast adrift by his brother, GEIRRÖD, and apparently ends his days living with a witch in a cave. Looking down from his lofty vantage-point of HLIDSKJÁLF, Odin chides his wife that while his adopted son, Geirröd, is a king, hers has had a disreputable and sorry end. Frigg challenges Odin to test the hospitality of his favourite, with predictably grim results: Geirröd has Odin tied up and tortured between two blazing fires for eight nights. Throughout his ensuing ordeal, Odin is aided only by Geirröd's young son, who, ironically enough, is named Agnar after his uncle,

and is the same age that his namesake had been at his betrayal.

B12, 30, 56, 73, 87, 90; C2, 17, 24, 33, 46

Ái ('great-grandfather')

(1) A dwarf, according to the catalogue in the eddic poem VÖLUSPÁ. (2) Presumably a quite separate character, who forms, together with his wife Edda ('great-grandmother'), the first couple visited by the mysterious wanderer RÍG on his travels, according to the eddic poem RÍGSTHULA. The couple invite Ríg to share both their hospitality and their bed, and nine months later Edda gives birth to Thræl ('slave'), from whom the whole race of slaves is descended.

B12, 30, 56, 59, 73, 87, 90; C2, 17, 24, 33, 46

Albruna ('elf-confidante')

According to the Roman historian TACITUS, one of the women venerated by the continental Germanic tribes in the first century AD, in accordance with a custom that he describes as follows:

> We saw how during the reign of the deified Vespasian, one VELEDA was long reckoned by many as a divine presence; but formerly [the Germanic tribes] venerated Albruna and many others, not in adulation nor as if they were making them goddesses.

It seems likely that Albruna was viewed as a kind of wise-woman or seer, although it is quite possible that she was part of the so-called cult of matrons (most of whom are, like Albruna, now little more than names) witnessed by more than 500 inscriptions on the western bank of the Rhine between the first and fifth centuries AD. Because a number of later commentators have made much of Albruna's name, it is worth pointing out that most manuscripts in fact call her Aurinia; the (highly appropriate) name Albruna rests solely on the emendation of a modern scholar.

B2; C29

Alcis ('elks'?, 'protectors'?)

Twin gods who, according to the Roman historian TACITUS, were venerated during the first century AD in a sacred grove of an otherwise unknown Germanic tribe called the Nahanarvali or Naharvali:

> Among the Nahanarvali [or Naharvali] there is revealed a grove of ancient worship; a priest in women's clothes presides, and they commemorate, according to the Roman interpretation, the gods Castor and Pollux, or at least their godhead, 'Alcis' by name: there are no idols or any trace of foreign superstition; they are worshipped as young brothers.

If the etymology 'elks' is correct, it is possible that the

Álf Hjálpreksson

Alcis were twin equine deities, perhaps analogous with the horse-named twins HENGEST and Horsa of Anglo-Saxon mythical history.

B2; C49; D606

Álf Hjálpreksson

The son of King HJÁLPREK of Denmark. His wooing and winning of the beautiful HJÖRDÍS, widow of the mighty SIGMUND, is told in the legendary VÖLSUNGA SAGA. Hjördis is already pregnant with SIGURD, Sigmund's son, but Álf brings up young Sigurd as his own and supports him in his expedition to avenge his dead father.

B25, 42, 65, 68, 79; C1, 6

Álf Hringsson inn gamli *see* HÖDBRODD.

Álf Hrodmarsson

A king, who, according to the eddic poem HELGAKVIDA HJÖRVARDSSONAR, rather rashly challenges the mighty hero HELGI HJÖRVARDSSON to a duel and is duly killed.

B12, 30, 56, 73, 87, 90; C2, 17, 24, 33, 46

Álf Hundingsson *see* HELGI SIGMUNDARSON HUNDINGSBANI.

álfablót ('elves' sacrifice')

Evidently a SACRIFICE to appease harmful ELVES or to request healing or other benefits. Literary evidence for such a practice is extremely scanty, and it is far from clear how widespread the custom was and whether it was an annual or simply casual event. The earliest secure reference to the custom is found in the so-called *Austfararvísur* ('verses on a journey east'), composed by the poet SIGHVAT THÓRDARSON to commemorate a trip to West Gautland, probably in the autumn of 1018. Several skaldic stanzas describe how he was refused entry to a number of houses because a sacrificial ceremony was taking place:

'Come in no further,
wretched fellow', said the dame,
'we're heathens here;
I'm scared of Odin's wrath.'
The grim crone that checked me,
firmly, as if I were a wolf,
said that inside the house
they were holding elf-sacrifice.

Apart from a general sense that some local heathen ceremony is occurring, there is little that can be gleaned here. To judge from his other stanzas, such a ceremony was taking place in more than one household, but if it was a regular sacrifice, clearly this is one whose timing is unfamiliar to the hapless Sighvat. Only marginally less baffling are the slightly fuller accounts to be found in later prose, for example in the probably thirteenth-century KORMÁKS SAGA, which describes the advice of a witch to a man whom Kormák has wounded just before going off to sacrifice a bull. The wounds are taking a long time to heal:

There is a mound not far from here, where the elves live. Now get hold of the bull that Kormák killed, and redden the outside of the mound with its blood and make a feast for the elves with its meat. Then you will be healed.

The cure is effective, but it is difficult to assess the importance to attach to the witness of the saga, even though the author demonstrates clear antiquarian interests elsewhere.

B39, 45, 62, 75, 83, 87; C16, 18

Álfheim ('elf-home')

The dwelling place of only one class of ELVES, according to the thirteenth-century Icelander, SNORRI STURLUSON:

There is a place called Álfheim, where live the folk called LIGHT ELVES, but BLACK ELVES live underground and are quite different in appearance, and still more different in character. Light elves are fairer to look upon than the sun, but black elves are darker than pitch.

From this distinction it would appear that black elves were little different from DWARFS, who were thus excluded from Álfheim itself.

B24, 28, 35, 40, 50; C5, 9, 48

Álfhild

According to the prose preface to the eddic poem HELGAKVIDA HJÖRVARDSSONAR, one of the four wives of King HJÖRVARD, and the mother of HEDIN, whose fateful vow to win the Valkyrie SVÁVA, the beloved of his own brother, HELGI, has dire consequences. It is, presumably, a quite separate character called Álfhild who is described as the grandmother of the hero STARKAD.

B12, 30, 56, 73, 87, 90; C2, 17, 24, 33, 46

Álfrödul An alternative name for SÓL.

Ali, Áli

A puzzling character, identified by the thirteenth-century Icelander SNORRI STURLUSON variously with two members of the ÆSIR – VÁLI and VÍDAR – as well as (through EUHEMERISM) with the Trojan heroes

Helenus and Aeneas. Elsewhere, an Ali or Áli appears variously as a son of LOKI, a sea-king and a legendary king of Norway.

B24, 28, 35, 40, 50; C5, 9, 48

Alíus *see* ANNAR (2).

almáttki áss ('the almighty Ás')

Evidently one of the ÆSIR, invoked alongside NJÖRD and FREY (who are both VANIR in origin) in an oath apparently sworn on a TEMPLE RING, and recorded in both LANDNÁMABÓK and *Oláfs saga Tryggvasonar* in HEIMSKRINGLA. The precise identification of this *almáttki áss* is a matter of some debate. The gods ODIN, THOR, ULL and even TÝR have been suggested. Of these, Odin himself swears a ring-oath in HÁVAMÁL (which, however, he immediately breaks; as the poet notes: 'how can one trust his pledge?'), and Ull is invoked (alongside Odin) in a ring-oath in the eddic poem ATLAKVIDA, in which GUDRÚN reminds her cruel husband ATLI BUDLASON of his broken promises to her brother GUNNAR:

> 'May it go with you, Atli, according to those oaths
> you often swore to Gunnar, and invoked long ago:
> by the sun in the south and by Odin's rock;
> by the horse of sleep's bedding, and by Ull's ring.'

Thor, who is invoked by name in several sagas, is perhaps the most plausible candidate for the title *almáttki áss*, but the identification is far from certain.

B6, 12, 14, 20, 23, 30, 31, 56, 73, 86, 87, 90; C2, 17, 24, 33, 36, 46; D166, 450

Álof

According to the eddic poem HELGAKVIDA HJÖRVARDSSONAR, the daughter of the shape-changing Earl FRANMAR, and the wife of Earl ATLI IDMUNDSSON, who later becomes the companion-in-arms of the hero HELGIA HJÖRVARDSSON.

B12, 30, 56, 73, 87, 90; C2, 17, 24, 33, 46

Alsvid ('all-swift')

One of two horses – the other is ÁRVAK – who pull the sun, SÓL, across the sky, according to the eddic poem GRÍMNISMÁL. The alternative spelling Alsvinn is also attested. A further eddic poem, SIGRDRÍFUMÁL, which is also cited in the legendary VÖLSUNGA SAGA, adds the detail that there are RUNES cut into Alsvid's head. This detail may be related to the fact that the name Alsvid is also given to a giant, to whom, according to the eddic poem HÁVAMÁL, is imputed a deep knowledge of runes.

B12, 14, 23, 25, 30, 42, 56, 65, 68, 73, 79, 87, 90; C1–3, 6, 17, 24, 33, 46

Alsvid Heimisson

According to the legendary VÖLSUNGA SAGA, the son of HEIMIR and BEKKHILD BUDLADÓTTIR, the sister of the Valkyrie BRYNHILD. When SIGURD comes and professes his love for Brynhild, Alsvid vainly tries to dissuade him, saying:

> A man like you should not pay heed to a woman. It is bad to worry over what cannot be won.

Naturally, a hero like Sigurd is not to be swayed by such unheroic advice.

B25, 42, 65, 68, 79; C1, 6

Alsvinn *see* ALSVID.

Alsvinnsmál see KÁLFSVÍSA.

alu

The best attested of a range of apparently MAGIC words (others include *auja*, *laþu* and *laukar*) found inscribed in RUNES. Evidently the word invoked the suggestion of protection or luck, and often the objects on which it is inscribed appear to be AMULETS of some description. The precise meaning of *alu* is unclear, but it is evident that as time went on it became increasingly identified with the Germanic terms for 'ale' or 'beer'. The eddic poem SIGRDRÍFUMÁL speaks of *ölrúnar* ('ale-runes'), which may describe runes where *alu* is invoked, while the Old English poem BEOWULF describes grief or terror as *ealuscerwen* ('pouring away of *alu*'?), a unique word perhaps deliberately echoed (and misinterpreted?) by another Anglo-Saxon poet who uses the term *meoduscerwen* ('pouring away of mead') in a directly parallel context.

B44; C4; D236

Alvaldi ('all-powerful')

According to an ambiguous passage in the eddic poem HÁRBARDSLJÓD, the father of the giant THJAZI, whose eyes (like the frozen toe of AURVANDIL) THOR threw into the sky to form stars. The thirteenth-century Icelander Snorri Sturluson (who calls him Ölvaldi) gives a fuller account, having the god BRAGI recount the following:

> He was very wealthy in gold, and when he died and his sons had to split up their inheritance, they doled out the gold and divided it by taking a mouthful in turn, each receiving the same number. One of them was Thjazi, the second Idi, the third Gang; and so we use the expression that gold is 'the mouth-tally' of these giants, and we conceal it in opaque language or in

poetry, by calling it the 'speech' or 'words' or 'talk' of these giants.

B12, 14, 23, 24, 28, 30, 35, 40, 50, 56, 59, 73, 87, 90; C2, 5, 9, 17, 24, 33, 46, 48

Alvís ('all-wise')

The pale-nosed dwarf who engages in a nocturnal battle of wits with the god THOR, who is not otherwise known for his intellectual talents, according to the eddic poem ALVÍSSMÁL. At stake, we are given to understand, is the hand of an unnamed daughter of Thor (perhaps the same daughter elsewhere called THRÚD). Thor keeps Alvís preoccupied with a series of questions until sunrise, when (we must suppose) Alvís turns to stone, just like the hapless giantess HRÍMGERD, who is similarly delayed in the eddic poem HELGAKVIDA HJÖRVARDSSONAR. Thor's 'victory' is thus reminiscent of the equally sly and, one might think, underhand victories of ODIN in similar battles of wits with giants, such as that depicted in another eddic dialogue-poem, VAFTHRÚDNISMÁL.

B12, 30, 51, 56, 73, 87, 90; C2, 17, 24, 33, 46

Alvíssmál ('The Song of All-wise')

A versified wisdom contest between the god THOR and the knowledgeable dwarf ALVÍS ('all-wise'), probably composed in the twelfth century, and preserved in the POETIC EDDA alongside comparable dialogue-poems and gnomic verses such as VAFTHRÚDNISMÁL and GRÍMNISMÁL. Alvís comes to claim Thor's daughter as his wife, but is first challenged to a test of wisdom. Thor questions Alvís thirteen times about the names for various largely cosmological objects and concepts (earth, sky, moon, sun, clouds, wind, calm, fire, sea, wood, night, corn and beer) 'in all the worlds there are'. In reply, Alvís lists the various terms used by ÆSIR, men, VANIR, GIANTS, DWARFS and ELVES. Alvíssmál provides in effect a thesaurus of poetic and taboo terms, each characterized to some extent according to the perceived nature of their suggested user. So, for example, the words used by elves are rather dainty and delicate (the sky is 'fair roof' and night is 'sleep-joy'), while those used by giants sound suitably unimaginative (wood is 'kindling' and corn is 'food'). Apart from such basic characterization, there is little attempt at verisimilitude, and the practicalities of the verse-form dictate much of the content, leaving the Vanir, for example, with a vocabulary consisting entirely of words beginning with the letter v. The artificial nature of the debate is underlined by its abrupt conclusion: Thor tricks Alvís into continuing the contest after sunrise, when, we understand, the all-wise dwarf promptly turns to stone.

B12, 30, 51, 56, 73, 87, 90; C2, 17, 24, 33, 46; D208, 294, 381, 607

Alvitr see HERVÖR ALVITR.

Ambát see RÍGSTHULA.

Amma see RÍGSTHULA.

Ammianus Marcellinus see SACRAL KINGSHIP.

Amsvartnir ('pitch black')

According to the thirteenth-century Icelander SNORRI STURLUSON, the lake to which the ÆSIR enticed the wolf FENRIR, before binding him with the enchanted fetter, GLEIPNIR, which had been fashioned by DWARFS.

B24, 28, 35, 40, 50; C5, 9, 48

amulets

Objects worn as charms against disease, sorcery or any other ill, often inscribed with RUNES. Sometimes such amulets take the form of votive or cultic ornaments, such as the small hammers or axes (presumably invoking the protection of the hammer-wielding god THOR), which are often found in archaeological sites, or the tiny spears that are also attested. Only rarely do such amulets take the form of figurative depictions of the gods whose protection is being sought.

D195, 234

Andhrímnir ('sooty')

According to the eddic poem GRÍMNISMÁL, the person who cooks SÆHRÍMNIR, 'the best of meats' (and, according to the thirteenth-century Icelander SNORRI STURLUSON, a boar), in the pot ELDHRÍMNIR, so that it can be consumed every night in VALHALL by the hungry warriors known as the EINHERJAR.

B12, 14, 23, 24, 28, 30, 35, 40, 50, 56, 59, 73, 87, 90; C2, 5, 9, 17, 24, 33, 46, 48

Andlang see VINDBLÁIN.

Andvaranaut ('Andvari's heirloom')

According to a prose passage in the eddic poem REGINSMÁL, the cursed ring extracted from the dwarf ANDVARI by the cunning LOKI and used to complete payment to HREIDMAR in recompense for Loki's accidental killing of his son OTR. The legendary VÖLSUNGA SAGA goes further, making Andvaranaut the ring that the hero SIGURD gives to the Valkyrie BRYNHILD when they exchange vows and swaps for another from the dragon FÁFNIR's hoard when he crosses the wall of flickering flames in the guise of the young prince GUNNAR. It is the sight of Andvaranaut, triumphantly demonstrated to Brynhild by Gunnar's sister, GUDRÚN, that finally persuades Brynhild that she has been deceived by Sigurd and Gunnar, sparking off her dreadful vengeance.

B12, 25, 30, 42, 56, 65, 68, 73, 79, 87, 90; C1–3, 6, 17, 24, 33, 46

Andvari ('careful one')

A dwarf mentioned in the eddic poems VÖLUSPÁ and REGINSMÁL, whence he is also described by the thirteenth-century Icelander Snorri Sturluson, and in the mnemonic lists known as THULUR. In *Reginsmál* Andvari actually names himself as a son of ODIN (although it seems likely that this is a scribal error for the dwarf-name Óin), condemned by the NORNS to spend his life in the form of a pike, taking his food from a waterfall. LOKI caught Andvari and forced him to hand over all his gold, including a particular ring, ANDVARANAUT, which the dwarf attempted to keep back. When Andvari eventually surrendered the ring, he did so with a curse:

> Now the gold that belonged to GUST
> shall drive two brothers to their deaths,
> push eight princes to killing and strife;
> no one wins joy with my wealth.

The legendary VÖLSUNGA SAGA, drawing freely on *Reginsmál*, tells substantially the same story, but focuses the curse on Andvaranaut itself.

B12, 14, 23–5, 28, 30, 35, 40, 42, 50, 56, 59, 65, 68, 73, 79, 87, 90; C1–3, 5, 6, 9, 17, 24, 33, 46, 48

Angantýr

(1) One of the mighty warriors of the eddic poem HLÖDSKVIDA. (2) The name of the antagonist of Ottar in the eddic poem HYNDLULJÓD.

B12, 30, 32, 56, 73, 87, 90; C2, 17, 24, 33, 46; D421, 579

Angrboda ('harm-bidder')

A grim giantess on whom, according to the eddic poem HYNDLULJÓD, LOKI got the wolf FENRIR. The Icelander SNORRI STURLUSON goes further, making Angrboda also the mother of Loki's other terrible offspring, JÖRMUNGAND and HEL. Whatever the antiquity of the notion that these three monsters were born of Loki and a giantess, the name Angrboda seems to date from no earlier than the twelfth century.

B12, 14, 23, 24, 28, 30, 35, 40, 50, 56, 59, 73, 87, 90; C2, 5, 99, 17, 24, 33, 46, 48

Annar ('second', 'other')

(1) According to the thirteenth-century Icelander, SNORRI STURLUSON, the second husband of night, NÓTT. The name suggests a certain lack of imagination, if it is not indeed the result of an earlier misinterpretation. (2) Annar is also found as the name of a DWARF, alongside similar dwarf-names, such as the distinctly Latinate Alíus ('second', 'other').

B24, 28, 35, 40, 50; C5, 9, 48

Apollinaris *see* SIDONIUS APOLLINARIS.

Arastein ('eagle rock')

The place where, according to the eddic poem HELGAKVIDA HUNDINGSBANA I, the mighty hero HELGI SIGMUNDARSON HUNDINGSBANI killed in battle four sons of King HUNDING: Álf, Eyjólf, Hagbard and Hervard.

B12, 30, 56, 73, 87, 90; C2, 17, 24, 33, 46

Arfi *see* RÍGSTHULA.

Arinnefja *see* RÍGSTHULA.

Árvak ('early-riser')

One of two horses – the other is ALSVID – who pull the sun, SÓL, across the sky, according to the eddic poem GRÍMNISMÁL. A stanza from another eddic poem, SIGRDRÍFUMÁL, which is also cited in the legendary VÖLSUNGA SAGA, adds the detail that there are RUNES cut into Árvak's ear.

B12, 25, 30, 42, 56, 65, 68, 73, 79, 87, 90; C1–3, 6, 17, 24, 33, 46

Ás *see* ÆSIR.

Ása-Thor An alternative name for THOR.

Ásabrag An alternative name for THOR.

Ásabrú An alternative name for BIFRÖST.

Ásgard ('home of the Æsir')

Although universally used to describe the home of the ÆSIR, the name Ásgard in fact occurs only twice in the POETIC EDDA (in THRYMSKVIDA and HYMISKVIDA) and only once in a skaldic verse of the tenth century. The wide currency given to the name in modern sources arises almost entirely from its frequent use by the thirteenth-century Icelander SNORRI STURLUSON, who appears to envisage Ásgard as containing all the dwellings of the gods (as specified in the eddic poem GRÍMNISMÁL), as well as VALHALL and other specific sites, including HLIDSKJÁLF, VINGÓLF, GLADSHEIM and IDAVÖLL. It is difficult to determine the precise position of Ásgard from Snorri's account. At times it appears to be simply another region of MIDGARD, allowing the Æsir to travel to visit the world of men with ease, but separated from the outer world of ÚTGARD. On other occasions, however, Snorri appears to imagine Ásgard as a celestial dwelling, also called HIMINBJÖRG, that is linked to the other realms by the rainbow-bridge, BIFRÖST. At the moments when Snorri's antiquarian analysis tends towards EUHEMERISM, Ásgard is nothing more than the capital of Ásaland or Ásaheim, which Snorri identifies with Asia; at one point 'the ancient Ásgard' is even equated with Troy.

B12, 14, 23, 24, 28, 30, 35, 39, 40, 45, 50, 56, 59, 62, 73, 83, 87, 90; C2, 5, 9, 13, 16, 17, 24, 33, 46, 48; D181, 574

Ask ('ash tree')

According to the eddic poem VÖLUSPÁ, Ask and EMBLA are the first two human beings, created by the god ODIN and his two companions, HŒNIR and LODUR, from two tree trunks they found by the shore of the circling sea. In the thirteenth century the Icelander SNORRI STURLUSON repeats the tale but credits Odin's brothers, VILI and VÉ, with accompanying him. The fact that Anglo-Saxon genealogy of the kings of Kent is traced to one Æsc ('ash tree'), listed as a son of HENGEST, is sometimes held to suggest that the Norse accounts are not the result of later mythography, although the argument is far from conclusive.

B12, 14, 23, 24, 28, 30, 35, 40, 50, 56, 59, 73, 87, 90; C2, 5, 9, 17, 24, 33, 46, 48

Áslaug

According to the legendary VÖLSUNGA SAGA, the daughter of the doomed heroic couple BRYNHILD and SIGURD; Áslaug also plays a minor role in the legendary *Ragnars saga lodbrókar* ('saga of Ragnar hairy-breeches').

B25, 42, 65, 68, 79; C1, 6

Ásynja *see* ÁSYNJUR.

Ásynjur

The name given to the goddesses or female ÆSIR; the singular form is Ásynja. According to the thirteenth-century Icelander Snorri Sturluson, there are eight Ásynjur, whom he lists in the following order: FRIGG, FREYJA, GEFJON, IDUN, GERD, SIGYN, FULLA and NANNA. Elsewhere, however, Snorri gives a quite different list of no fewer than sixteen Ásynjur: Frigg, SÁGA, EIR, Gefjon, Fulla, Freyja, Sjofn, LOFN, VÁR, VÖR, Syn, HLÍN, SNOTRA, GNÁ, SÓL and BIL. The omission from this list of a number of the wives of important gods, especially SIF (the wife of THOR and mother of ULL) and SKADI (the wife of NJÖRD) is particularly noteworthy. While Skadi was of giant-descent, it might seem unlikely that the wife of Thor, the chief scourge of the giants, should come from like stock.

B12, 14, 23, 24, 28, 30, 35, 40, 50, 55, 56, 59, 64, 73, 87, 90; C2, 5, 7–9, 17, 24, 31, 33, 46, 48; D49, 115, 120, 439, 443, 504

Atlakvida ('the poem of Atli')

One of the earliest of the poems in the POETIC EDDA, although of uncertain date. A close relationship is implied with the poetry of THORBJÖRN HORNKLOFI, who composed HRAFNSMÁL around the turn of the tenth century, and it has even been suggested that Thorbjörn was the author of *Atlakvida* itself. *Atlakvida* makes use of a number of different metres, and some scholars have thought that they could detect different layers of composition, although none has managed to put forward an entirely convincing case. In the CODEX REGIUS some connection with Greenland is stated (the poem is subtitled 'from Greenland'), despite that fact that Greenland was not settled until after 985. It is more likely that ATLAMÁL, the poem's companion-piece in the manuscript (and which is given the same subtitle), derives from Greenland, but that *Atlakvida* itself was composed in an earlier period.

Atlakvida describes a key episode in the VÖLSUNG-cycle, namely that in which the hero GUNNAR and his brother HÖGNI GJÚKASON are lured to their deaths by the Hunnish lord ATLI BUDLASON, who has married GUDRÚN, their sister, and covets their gold, acquired after the death of the valiant SIGURD. In the poem, Atli's invitation to the two brothers to visit him in his stronghold is accompanied by a ring, which Gudrún has sent, wound round with a wolf's hair, to warn of her husband's treachery. When this warning is spotted by Högni, it serves only to increase Gunnar's rash determination to make the trip. The brothers are duly captured, after a particularly stout resistance by Högni, who kills or injures no fewer than nine of his assailants, and Atli attempts to make the brothers reveal the treasure's whereabouts. Gunnar appears to relent, but claims that he will not speak until Högni is dead and demands that Högni's heart be placed in his hands. A substitute is offered, which Gunnar scorns as the heart of the craven HJALLI, but eventually Högni's heart is brought, and Gunnar praises it lovingly and reveals his own deception: when they both lived he worried that one of them might be forced to reveal the secret. Now he alone is left, they could do what they liked – he would never say where along the Rhine the treasure lay. Atli's punishment is swift and terrible: Gunnar is cast into a snake-pit, where he perishes, still playing his harp. Gudrún's response to the killing of her brothers is equally grim: she slaughters her own two sons, Atli's dear boys, and serves them to their father at a feast. When he is drunk, she tells him the truth and stabs him in their marital bed before burning the place down.

With its taut style (the whole tale takes some forty-four stanzas) and stark subject-matter, *Atlakvida* is a highly dramatic and wonderfully charged piece, containing many memorable scenes. The gruesome episode of the cutting-out of Högni's heart is a case in point, where we are told that:

Then Högni laughed
when they sliced to his heart,
still living, the wound-smith;
least of all did he reckon to sob.

Famed Gunnar spoke,
the spear-Niflung:
'Here I hold the heart
of Högni the bold,
unlike the heart
of Hjalli the craven;
it quivers little
as it lies on the plate:
it quivered still less
when it lay in his chest.'

The economy of style compares very favourably with
that of the clearly derivative *Atlamál*, which directly
follows *Atlakvida* in the Codex Regius manuscript.

B12, 20, 25, 30, 31, 42, 56, 65, 68, 73, 79, 87, 90; C1–3, 6, 17, 24, 33, 46; D8, 13,
109, 130, 155, 192, 299, 491, 556, 569

Atlamál ('the lay of Atli')

At the end of ATLAKVIDA a note in the CODEX REGIUS
manuscript records that 'the tale is told more clearly
in the Greenlandic *Atlamál*'. The poem that follows
certainly recounts essentially the same narrative as
Atlakvida in more than twice as many stanzas (103 as
against the 44 of *Atlakvida*), but many commentators
have considered the much younger *Atlamál* (perhaps
composed in the twelfth century) a decidedly inferior
piece. Many of the gruesome elements of *Atlakvida*
are rendered still more gruesome, even bizarre: the
idea that GUNNAR played the harp in the snake-pit,
mentioned in two lines in *Atlakvida*, is developed into
an entire stanza in *Atlamál*, and the author, doubtless
recalling that we have already been told that Gunnar
was bound, has him play with his toes instead:

Gunnar took a harp,
strummed it with foot-twigs,
he knew how to play,
so that women wept,
and men sobbed,
who could hear it clearly.
He announced the affair to the powerful lady:
the rafters burst apart.

Likewise in *Atlamál*, GUDRÚN does not simply caution
her recently arrived brothers about their impending
capture, she actively fights, sword in hand, to prevent their being taken, slicing away the leg of ATLI
BUDLASON's brother and killing another of her husband's men. The poet's evident desire to expand or
extrapolate what are mere hints in the earlier poem is

typified by the nature of her original warning to Gunnar
and HÖGNI GJÚKASON not to accept Atli's invitation:
in *Atlakvida* she laconically twists a wolf's hair round
a ring; in *Atlamál* she literally spells it out in runes. In
much the same way, *Atlamál* considerably extends the
list of characters depicted, including several unmen-
tioned in *Atlakvida*: so, for example, Högni is given
a wife, KOSTBERA, whose skill at reading Gudrún's
runic warning and foreboding dreams (including one
interpreted by her husband as a polar bear, perhaps
an indication of the Greenlandic origin of the poem
which the manuscript asserts) cannot prevent Gunnar
and Högni from undertaking their doomed expedition.
Sometimes the richness and baroque adornment of the
narrative spills over into comedy, as in the case of the

*Atlamál Detail of the doorway from Hylestad church,
Setesdal, Norway, depicting the tragic hero Gunnar in
the snake-pit, playing the harp with his toes in the
manner described in the eddic poem* Atlamál.

coward HJALLI, who remains a cipher in *Atlakvida* but whose whole character is laid bare in *Atlamál*:

> The saucepan-keeper panicked,
> he didn't hang around:
> he knew how to blub,
> and climbed into every cranny.
> He called himself a victim of their war
> repaying all his effort:
> it was a sad day for him,
> to die and leave the pigs,
> all the resources,
> which he had owned before.

Such explicit description of essentially unheroic emotion is quite alien to the highly charged, economic and allusive style that the poet of *Atlakvida* had so evidently mastered.

B12, 20, 30, 31, 56, 73, 87, 90; C2, 17, 24, 33, 46; D13, 81, 109, 155, 192, 299, 491

Atli An alternative name for THOR.

Atli Budlason ('the fearsome one')

The Norse name for the character history records as Attila the Hun. Atli is one of the major figures of early Germanic legend, and features prominently as a cruel and ruthless king in several poems of the POETIC EDDA, notably those of the so-called VÖLSUNG-cycle, alongside his sister, the Valkyrie BRYNHILD, and GUDRÚN, his (eventual) wife. His name then becomes linked in skaldic verse with poetic periphrases or KENNINGS for any king. The notion, vividly developed in the eddic poems ATLAKVIDA and ATLAMÁL, that Atli died in his bed besides his blood-stained wife, after an evening of excessive feasting and drinking is strikingly supported by the sixth-century description of the death of Attila by the historian JORDANES, who claims at this point to be citing the (now-lost) contemporary account of the Greek historian Priscus; Jordanes depicts Attila's demise as follows:

> As the historian Priscus relates, around the time of his death Attila married an extremely beautiful girl called Ildico, after numerous other wives, as was the custom of his people. At his wedding he over-indulged in celebration and lay down on his back, heavy with wine and sleep. A stream of blood, which would normally have run out of his nose, was prevented from its normal course: it flowed on a fatal path into his throat and killed him. So drunkenness brought a shameful end to a king famed in war. The next day, when a great part of the day had passed, the king's servants suspected something amiss and, after a great outcry, broke down the doors. They found Attila dead, with no wounds. He had died from an excessive nosebleed, and the girl, with head bowed, sobbed under her veil.

Apart from his central role in the two eddic poems that bear his name (*Atlakvida* and *Atlamál*), Atli appears as a cruel and brooding presence in other eddic poems, notably GUDRÚNARKVIDA I – III and ODDRÚNARGRÁTR. All the aforementioned versified accounts are clearly used by the anonymous author of the legendary VÖLSUNGA SAGA, who provides Atli with a strangely stilted death-scene, bickering to the end with Gudrún, who has just stabbed him with the help of the son of her brother HÖGNI GJÚKASON:

> King Atli woke up at the wound and said: 'There's no need for bandages or nursing. Who gave me this wound?' Gudrún said: 'It was partly my doing, partly Högni's son.' King Atli said: 'It wasn't right for you to do it, even though you have some cause; you were married to me with your kinsmen's consent, and I paid out a bride-price for you of thirty fine knights and comely maids and many other folk. But you wouldn't behave yourself properly unless you took control of all the lands that Budli owned, and you often made your mother-in-law cry.' Gudrún said: 'Much of what you have said is false, but I don't care. My temperament was often brusque, but you made it much worse. There's often been discord here in your court: friends and kinsmen often fought and provoked each other. We had a better life, when I was with Sigurd. We killed kings and took what they had and gave quarter to those who sought it. Leaders put themselves in our hands, and we gave riches to anyone who sought them. Then I lost him, and it was a little thing, to be called a widow; but what grieved me most was that I came to you, when I had been married to the finest of kings. You never came back from a battle without having been beaten.' King Atli said: 'That's not true, but such wrangling doesn't help either of us; I'm finished. Act properly towards me now and grant me a splendid funeral.' She said: 'I'll do that. I'll have a fine burial prepared and a magnificent stone casket made; I'll wrap you in beautiful sheets and see to your every need.' Then he died, and she did what she promised. Then she set fire to the hall. When the retainers awoke in fear, they couldn't stand the flames and hacked at one another and so died. There ended the lives of Atli and all his retainers.

Even through the rather awkward prose the description of Atli's essentially pathetic and unworthy demise mirrors precisely the impression gleaned from eddic verse. Atli is a character overshadowed by almost everyone around him, whether it is his sister, Brynhild, his wife, Gudrún, the men he murders, GUNNAR and Högni, and especially the noble hero, SIGURD, whose wife he inherits, but whose standards of magnificence he can never attain.

B12, 20, 25, 30, 31, 39, 42, 45, 55, 56, 62, 65, 68, 73, 79, 83, 87, 90; C1–3, 6, 13, 16, 17, 24, 31, 33, 46

Atli Hringsson *see* HÖDBRODD.

Atli Idmundsson ('the fearsome one')
One of the key figures in the eddic poem HELGAKVIDA HJÖRVARDSSONAR. After overhearing a bird describing the beauty of the young maiden SIGRLINN, Atli informs King HJÖRVARD and is instrumental in winning her for him. When Hjörvard and Sigrlinn are married, Atli marries ÁLOF, the daughter of Sigrlinn's foster-father. After HELGI, the product of the union between Hjörvard and Sigrlinn, grows up to prove a fearsome hero, Atli acts as his loyal companion, and when Helgi is harassed by HRÍMGERD, the daughter of the giant HATI, whom he has killed, it is Atli who engages Hrímgerd in a vicious battle of words or FLYTING, delaying her until sunrise, when, like (we assume) the dwarf ALVÍS in ALVÍSSMÁL, she promptly turns to stone. As the poem moves on to consider Helgi's love-match with SVÁVA, who is a Valkyrie, Atli understandably fades from view.

B12, 30, 56, 73, 87, 90; C2, 17, 24, 33, 46

Aud *see* NÓTT.

Audabródir *see* AGNAR AUDABRÓDIR.

Audhumla ('hornless and fecund'?)
According to the thirteenth-century account of the Icelander SNORRI STURLUSON in GYLFAGINNING, the primeval cow, who licked BÚRI, the ancestor of the ÆSIR, free from the salty blocks out of which he emerged and whose four streams of milk provided YMIR, the first GIANT, with nourishment. It is sometimes suggested that Snorri's description of the four streams of milk deliberately echoes the four rivers of Paradise mentioned in the Book of Revelations and in many patristic commentaries on the Bible.

B24, 28, 35, 40, 50; C5, 9, 48

auja see ALU.

Aurboda ('gravel-bidder')
(1) A giantess, the wife of GYMIR and the mother of the beautiful GERD, whom, according to the eddic poem SKÍRNISMÁL, the god FREY loved and wooed. (2)

The name of a handmaid of the giantess MENGLÖD in another eddic poem, FJÖLSVINNSMÁL.

B12, 30, 56, 73, 87, 90; C2, 17, 24, 33, 46

Aurgelmir ('gravel-yeller')
A GIANT, perhaps to be identified with YMIR, since, according to the eddic poem VAFTHRUDNISMÁL, he is the father of the primeval giant THRÚDGELMIR and grandfather of BERGELMIR.

B12, 30, 51, 56, 73, 87, 90; C2, 17, 24, 33, 46

Aurinia An alternative name for ALBRUNA.

Aurvandil ('gravel-beam'?)
Husband of the witch GRÓA, who caused the shattered fragment of whetstone, which had lodged in THOR's head after his battle with the giant HRUNGNIR, to loosen. In gratitude, Thor described how he carried Aurvandil in a basket on his back while wading over the frozen river ÉLIVÁGAR when he returned from a trip to JÖTUNHEIM. Aurvandil's toe, which had been poking out from the basket, had frozen stiff, so Thor broke it off and threw it into the sky (as he had done with the giant THJAZI's eyes), where it still remains, as a star.

The Old English poem *Christ III* contains an invocation to 'Earendel, brightest of angels', a figure who appears to be the personification of the North Star. The early thirteenth-century Danish historian SAXO GRAMMATICUS describes one Horwendillus as the father of Amlethus, the figure who later emerges as Hamlet.

B24, 28, 35, 40, 50, 64; C5, 7–9, 48

Aurvang *see* AURVANGAR.

Aurvangar ('wet-gravel plains')
According to the eddic poem VÖLUSPÁ, the aptly descriptive name of the place where the DWARFS live. The catalogue of dwarfs in the same poem includes one Aurvang ('wet-gravel plain').

B12, 30, 56, 59, 73, 87, 90; C2, 17, 24, 33, 46

Austri ('East')
According to the thirteenth-century Icelander SNORRI STURLUSON, one of the four DWARFS set by the sons of BOR to support the skull of the primeval giant YMIR, whom they had killed, which was to form the sky. The other three dwarfs, unsurprisingly enough, are named Nordri ('North'), Sudri ('South') and Vestri ('West').

B24, 28, 35, 40, 50; C5, 9, 48

B

Bældæg (Old English: 'bright day', 'fire-day')

The name of Bældæg figures in a number of Old English genealogies as a son of WODEN, and has naturally prompted comparison with the Norse figure of BALDR, the son of the god ODIN. Such a comparison is only heightened by the fact that Æthelweard, the tenth-century Anglo-Saxon chronicler, actually substitutes the names Baldr at the appropriate place in the genealogies, while the thirteenth-century Icelander SNORRI STURLUSON mentions among the Saxons one 'Beldegg, whom we call Baldr'. That the Old English word *bealdor* means 'lord' or 'leader' only increases the confusion and has led some to suppose that the Norse name Baldr hides an honorific title. A similar suggestion is prompted by the Old English word *frea*, which also means 'lord' and which corresponds to the Norse name FREY.

D424

Bakrauf ('arse-hole')

The name of a troll-wife, found in the name-lists or THULUR. This rather strikingly lowbrow name may in fact reflect a 'learned' Latin pun: many troll-wives are depicted as ugly witches or wizened crones, and the Latin word *anus* means both 'old woman' and 'anus'.

D396

Baldr

The story of the death of the beautiful god Baldr is among the best known of all Norse myths, and the thirteenth-century Icelander SNORRI STURLUSON devotes a considerable part of his SNORRA EDDA to the tale. Snorri's initial description of the character of Baldr is of a beautiful but ineffective cipher, introduced after the mighty god THOR, who is himself depicted as 'the most outstanding' of the ÆSIR:

> ODIN'S second son is Baldr, and there are good things to be said of him; he is best, and everyone praises him. He is so fair in appearance and so brilliant that all light flashes from him, and there is a plant so white that it is named after Baldr's brow [the ox-eye daisy]. It is the whitest of plants, and by this you can tell the beauty both of his hair and form. He is the wisest of the Æsir, and has the most mellifluous voice, and is the kindest, but

it is one of his characteristics, that none of his decisions have effect. He lives in a place called BREIDABLIK, which is in heaven, and where nothing impure is allowed.

Baldr's wife is NANNA and his son is FORSETI, neither of whom plays more than a minor role in the extant literature. Snorri goes on to describe in detail how, when Baldr was troubled by disturbing dreams of his own demise (which also provide the impetus for the eddic poem BALDRS DRAUMAR), his mother, FRIGG, extracted solemn promises from fire, water, metals, stones, trees, diseases, beasts, birds, poisons and snakes that they will not harm him. A game grew up among the Æsir to have him stand up at their gatherings while they threw weapons or stones at him with no effect. But out of spite LOKI, in the guise of a woman, asked Frigg if there was anything she had spared from taking the oath and was told that the delicate sapling of the mistletoe had been exempted for its tender age. Shortly afterwards, Loki plucked a wand of mistletoe and gave it to HÖD, the brother of Baldr, who had been excluded from the game because of his blindness. Loki guided him to shoot the dart at Baldr:

> The dart flew through him, and he fell dead to the ground, and that was the greatest mishap ever caused among gods and men. After Baldr fell, the power of speech failed all the Æsir, as did the power of their hands to take him up; each of them looked at the others, and they were all of one mind towards the one who had done the deed, though they could not take revenge, it was so great a place of sanctuary. When the Æsir tried to speak, the first thing to happen was that sobbing broke out, and none of them could express to each other in words their grief. But Odin took the loss the hardest, since he knew most clearly how great a damage and deprivation there was for the Æsir in Baldr's death.

We are to understand from both Snorri's account and the allusions to the death of Baldr in the eddic poem VÖLUSPÁ that Baldr's demise heralds the beginning of the destruction of the Æsir in the fateful conflict at RAGNARÖK. Snorri tells how, as preparations for Baldr's funeral take place, another of Odin's sons, HERMÓD, is sent to HEL, the kingdom of the dead, to attempt to ransom Baldr back. The funeral itself is a suitably sumptuous affair, as Baldr is sent off in his flaming ship, HRINGHORNI, accompanied in a ritual of SUTTEE by his wife, Nanna, and (inadvertently, perhaps echoing a tradition of SACRIFICE), by a dwarf named LIT. The pyre had been consecrated by Thor, with his hammer MJÖLLNIR, and the ship was launched by the giantess HYRROKKIN. As Snorri continues, apparently basing his account on the description of the poet ÚLF UGGASON in HÚSDRÁPA:

> Many kinds of being came to this burning: Odin (first to tell), accompanied by Frigg and Valkyries and his ravens; Frey in a chariot with the boar called GULLINBORSTI or Slídrugtanni; HEIMDALL rode the horse called Gulltopp; FREYJA came with her cats; there also came a great company of frost-giants and mountain-giants.

Meanwhile, Hermód managed to extract an undertaking from Hel to release Baldr if everything in the world wept for him. In a deliberate echo of the list of things that had earlier vowed not to harm Baldr, Snorri describes how men and animals, earth, stones, trees and metals all wept. But a certain giantess called THÖKK, suspected to be Loki in disguise, apparently refused to weep, quoting a bitter verse. In the eddic poem LOKASENNA Loki boasts that he is responsible for Baldr's no longer being alive, although this could refer to his role in Baldr's death rather than to his thwarted

return. According to *Völuspá*, however, both Baldr and his killer, the hapless Höd, who was himself killed in revenge by VÁLI, will return after Ragnarök to inhabit the reborn world.

B12, 14, 23, 24, 28, 30, 35, 40, 50, 56, 59, 73, 87, 90; C2, 5, 9, 17, 24, 33, 46, 48; D100, 104, 122, 281, 288, 383, 390, 510, 514, 601

Baldrs draumar ('Baldr's dreams')

A poem usually counted among those of the POETIC EDDA, perhaps composed in the twelfth century and preserved only in the single manuscript AM 748 I 4to.

SOUTH   WEST   NORTH   EAST

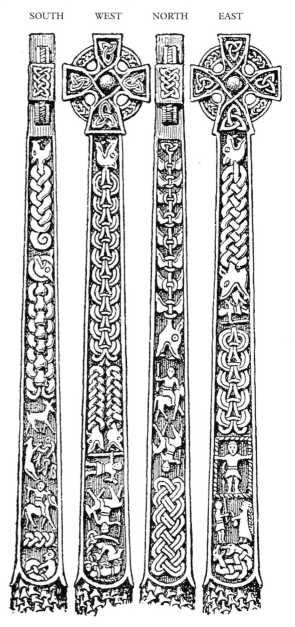

Baldr The carvings on a late tenth-century Anglo-Saxon stone cross from Gosforth, Cumbria, England have been interpreted as focusing on scenes from the life of the god Baldr, here evidently being identified with Christ. The southern panel, with its supposed depictions of the god Odin, complete with spear, and the stag Eikthyrnir atop a rather schematic representation of Yggdrasil, the world-tree, with Ratatosk, the squirrel, in attendance, would represent the world before Baldr's death; the west panel, with Loki bound in punishment for his part in the killing, soothed by Sigyn, whilst Odin and Heimdall (with his horn) stand against the monstrous powers, would signal the beginning of the end of the world at Ragnarök; the battle itself between gods and giants is supposedly represented on the north panel, whilst the east panel would then depict the slaying of the wolf, Fenrir, by Vidar, signaling the end of Ragnarök, after which Baldr would return. The evident identification of Baldr with Christ (here complete with pierced side, spearman, and a woman in the characteristic pose of a Valkyrie) is echoed elsewhere in Norse sources, notably Snorra Edda.

Bara, Bára

The poem describes how the god ODIN, calling himself Vegtam (hence the alternative title, *Vegtamskvida*), rides his eight-legged horse SLEIPNIR down to NIFLHEL to question a dead sibyl about some troubling dreams that his son BALDR has had. After reluctantly answering three questions about Baldr's imminent death at the hands of his brother, HÖD, and the subsequent killing of Höd by VÁLI in revenge, Odin asks an enigmatic fourth question – 'Who are those maids that mourn so much, and throw their sheet-corners into the sky?' – which in some way reveals his true identity to the sibyl. She refuses to answer further and in response to an insult from Odin, who calls her the mother of three monsters (a role usually associated with the giantess ANGRBODA), looks forward to RAGNARÖK, the freeing of LOKI and (implicitly) Odin's own death. The question-and-answer structure of the main body of the poem, together with the mythological subject-matter, resembles that of other eddic poems preserved in the CODEX REGIUS, such as VAFTHRÚDNISMÁL and ALVÍSSMÁL. In view of Odin's insult that the sibyl is the mother of three monsters, it has been suggested that she is Loki himself, in disguise. Certainly, Loki (who boasts of his role in Baldr's death in LOKASENNA) appears twice in female guise in the account of the death of Baldr by the thirteenth-century Icelander SNORRI STURLUSON, first, as a mysterious woman who prompts FRIGG to reveal that she failed to extract from the fatal mistletoe a promise not to harm her son, and second, as the bitter giantess THÖKK, whose refusal to weep causes Baldr to remain with HEL. Likewise the meaning of the last question posed by Odin in *Baldrs draumar* has exercised commentators, although no suggestion has met general approval.

B12, 14, 23, 24, 28, 30, 35, 40, 50, 51, 56, 59, 73, 87, 90; C2, 5, 9, 17, 24, 33, 46, 48; D100, 157, 236, 256, 452, 514, 601

Bara, Bára *see* ÆGIR.

Barn *see* RÍGSTHULA.

Barnstokk ('offspring-trunk')

According to the legendary VÖLSUNGA SAGA, the mighty tree that stands in the centre of King VÖLSUNG's hall:

> It is said that King Völsung had a built a splendid palace in the following manner: a mighty tree stood with its trunk in the hall, and its branches, with beautiful blossoms, stretched out through the roof. They called the tree Barnstokk.

In an episode reminiscent of King Arthur's drawing of the sword Excalibur, *Völsunga saga* reports how the hero SIGMUND alone was able to draw a sword embedded in Barnstokk by a mysterious figure whose description fits that of the god ODIN himself:

> Now it is said that when people were sitting by the fires in the evening a man entered the hall. He was not known by sight to the men. He was dressed as follows: he wore a mottled cloak with a hood; he went barefoot, with linen breeches tied about his legs. As he approached Barnstokk he held a sword in his hand, and over his head his hood hung low. He was very tall and grey, and one-eyed. He brandished the sword and thrust it into the trunk as far as the hilt. No one welcomed him. Then the man began to speak: 'Whoever pulls this sword from the trunk shall have it from me as a gift, and he shall prove that he never wielded a better sword than this.' Then the old man went out of the hall, and no one knew who he was or where he went. They leapt up, and there was no discussion whether or not to grab the sword; everyone reckoned that whoever reached it first would do best. The most noble men approached it first, and then the others in turn, but no one who approached could shift it, whatever they tried. Then Sigmund, King Völsung's son, approached. He took the sword and drew it from the trunk, as if the sword became loose for him. The weapon seemed so splendid to everyone that no one could remember seeing a better.

The role and placement of the legendary Barnstokk as a mighty tree, supporting and sprouting through the roof of Völsung's hall, clearly parallel on a mythological plane those of the world-tree YGGDRASIL, especially with regard to Yggdrasil's position in relation to the mighty hall of VALHALL.

B25, 42, 65, 68, 79; C1, 6

Bar(r)i ('barley-island'?, 'cornfield'?, 'coniferous'?)

According to the eddic poem SKÍRNISMÁL, Barri is the windless grove where the god FREY and the giantess GERD meet to consummate their love-match. In his account, the thirteenth-century Icelander SNORRI STURLUSON spells the place 'Barrey', a place-name reflected in the Hebridean isle of Barra, once Barrey. All the proposed etymologies suit a site fitting for the love-rites of a fertility deity, although the common noun *barri* also has the sense 'fool', and, as such, a DWARF with the (to English ears) perhaps unromantic name of Barri appears in the eddic poem FJÖLSVINNSMÁL.

B12, 14, 23, 24, 28, 30, 35, 40, 50, 56, 59, 73, 87, 90; C2, 5, 9, 17, 24, 33, 46, 48

barrow *see* BURIAL MOUNDS.

Baugi

A giant, the brother of SUTTUNG, and the hapless victim of the god ODIN's wiles in his search for the MEAD OF POETRY. The thirteenth-century Icelander SNORRI STURLUSON provides the most detailed account. After he has caused Baugi's nine slaves to hack each other to death with scythes, Odin, travelling under the assumed name of Bölverk ('evil-worker'), offers to do the work of all nine in exchange for a drink of Suttung's mead. Baugi agrees to help Odin acquire a draught, and bores a hole through a mountain to reach the chamber where the mead is kept, watched over by GUNNLÖD, Suttung's daughter. When Odin changes into a snake and disappears through the hole, Baugi realizes rather too late what he has done and unsuccessfully attempts to spear the departing god with his auger, which Snorri names RATI.

B24, 28, 35, 40, 50; C5, 9, 48; D282

bauta(r)stein ('driven stone')

Large upright stone monument, particularly common in Sweden and Denmark, used to mark burial sites from the Iron Age on; in the Viking Ages such monuments were frequently inscribed with RUNES.

B4, 36, 46, 49, 54, 57, 89

Beaduhild The Anglo-Saxon name for BÖDVILD.

Bede

Anglo-Saxon monk of Wearmouth-Jarrow, who died in 734. His *Historia ecclesiastica gentis Anglorum* ('Ecclesiastical History of the English People'), completed in 731, contains several references to pagan practices. Perhaps most fascinating is his account of the conversion of King Edwin of Northumbria in 627; the vivid speech put into the mouth of one of Edwin's counsellors is justly famous:

> My lord, when we compare the present life of man on earth with that time about which we have no knowledge, it seems to me like the fleeting flight of a single sparrow through the banquet-hall where you sit to dine on a winter's day with your thegns and counsellors. In the middle is a comforting fire to warm the hall; outside, the storms of winter rain or snow are raging. This sparrow flies swiftly in through one door of the hall, and out through another. While it is inside, it is safe from the winter storms, but after a few moments of comfort, it disappears from sight into the wintry world from whence it came. Just so, man appears on earth for a brief space; but of what went before this life, or of what follows, we know nothing. Therefore, if this new teaching has brought any more certain knowledge, it seems only right that we should follow it.

The doubts expressed about the uncertainties of what happens to the soul before life and after death are closely echoed by what is said in the Anglo-Saxon poem BEOWULF about the BOAT BURIAL of SCYLD, who arrived mysteriously from across the water, and is committed after death to an equally doubtful trip:

> Men cannot truly tell, warriors under the heavens, counsellors in hall, who received that cargo.

In Bede's account of the conversion of Edwin, the king turns to his pagan high priest, Coifi:

> And when he asked the high priest who should be the first to profane the altars and shrines of the idols, together with the enclosures that surrounded them, Coifi replied: 'I shall do it myself; for now that the true God has granted me knowledge, who more suitably than I can set a public example and destroy the idols that I worshipped in folly?' So, he formally renounced his idle superstitions, and asked the king to give him arms and a stallion (for up until then it had been forbidden to the high priest to carry arms or ride anything but a mare), and, fitted-out in this way, he set out to destroy the idols. Girt with a sword, and with a spear in his hand, he mounted the king's stallion and rode up to the idols. When the crowd saw him, they thought he was in a frenzy; but without delay, immediately he reached the temple, he cast into it the spear that he carried and so profaned it. Then, full of joy at his knowledge of the true God, he told his companions to set fire to the temple and its enclosures and destroy them. The site where these idols once stood is still shown, not far east of York, beyond the river Derwent, and is known today as Goodmanham. Here it was that the high priest, inspired by the true God, desecrated and destroyed the altars that he had himself dedicated.

Bede's description of an event that apparently occurred over a century before he completed his *Historia ecclesiastica* cannot, of course, be considered an eyewitness account, but nonetheless a number of the incidental details of Bede's account can be paralleled elsewhere: taboos on horses and weapons, the sanctity not merely of the temple itself but of its surrounding enclosure, the worship of idols, an act of desecration involving casting a spear and even the notion that a priest might appear frenzied all echo material found in other sources. The literary nature of Bede's account, is, however, certain. Even his description of Coifi desecrating and destroying the altars that he himself had dedicated has a close verbal parallel in Vergil's description in his *Aeneid* of the fate of the pagan priest Laocoön, entwined in the mighty coils of a serpentine monster (itself perhaps a metaphor in Bede's mind for Coifi's previous involvement in paganism), who pol-

Beiti

luted with his own blood the altars where he used to perform blood sacrifice.

B15, 44; C4, 51; D28

Beiti

According to the eddic poem ATLAMÁL, the steward of the powerful King ATLI BUDLASON. It is he who suggests that the heart of the cowardly scullion HJALLI be cut out in place of that of the heroic HÖGNI GJÚKASON:

Beiti spoke,
he was Atli's steward:
'Let's grab Hjalli,
and let's spare Högni;
let's complete a task half-done:
he's ripe for death.
However long he lives,
he'll always be called a clot.'

B12, 20, 30, 56, 73, 87, 90; C2, 17, 24, 33, 46

Bekkhild Budladóttir

Daughter of King BUDLI and sister of the Valkyrie BRYNHILD; Bekkhild is also the wife of HEIMIR and mother of ALSVID, according to the legendary VÖLSUNGA SAGA. While her sister took up mail-coat and helmet and went off to war, Bekkhild apparently 'stayed at home, and learned needlework and other womanly skills'.

B25, 42, 65, 68, 79; C1, 6

Beli ('roarer')

A giant whom the god FREY, at this point apparently weaponless, meets and slays, according to the thirteenth-century Icelander SNORRI STURLUSON, with a stag's antler. The eddic poem VÖLUSPÁ describes Frey simply as 'Beli's slayer'. Snorri links the fact that Frey has no weapon in the contest with his gift of his sword and horse, as described elsewhere in the POETIC EDDA in SKÍRNISMÁL, to his servant SKÍRNIR, in order to persuade him to press his master's suit on the reluctant giantess GERD. Elsewhere in *Skírnismál*, it is clear that Gerd's reluctance to accept Frey's favours is based in no small part on her grief for her unnamed brother, whom Frey has killed. It is therefore possible that Beli is the brother of Gerd, although Frey's traditional weaponlessness, most tellingly at RAGNARÖK against SURT, render the identification uncertain.

B12, 14, 23, 24, 28, 30, 35, 40, 50, 56, 59, 73, 87, 90; C2, 5, 9, 17, 24, 33, 46, 48

Beow (Old English: 'barley')

In Anglo-Saxon royal genealogies, one of the descendants of WODEN. In the Old English poem BEOWULF, the name Beowulf appears in the place in royal line of the Danes where one would expect Beow, perhaps through confusion with the later eponymous hero of the poem. In the poem, this earlier Beowulf (presumably to be equated with Beow) is the son of the enigmatic SCYLD SCEFING, who appeared mysteriously from across the sea to save the Danish people. Beow's name may imply some link with a fertility figure.

B44; C4

Beowulf

An Anglo-Saxon poem of some 3,182 lines, preserved in the single manuscript British Library, Cotton Vitellius A. xv, which has been dated no earlier than around the turn of the eleventh century; most commentators believe that the poem, which depicts Scandinavian events from the far past (some of which appear to have occurred in the sixth century), was composed long before the manuscript was written. Other texts in the manuscript lay a heavy emphasis on the exotic and the monstrous, and it has been suggested that the poem itself, which is undoubtedly a masterpiece of poetic art, was largely preserved in its present context as the result of the manuscript compiler's interest in monsters. Certainly, the poem itself takes as its focus three encounters between the hero Beowulf and a succession of monsters: the huge man-shaped fiend GRENDEL, Grendel's mother (who has a number of bestial characteristics) and a mighty dragon, which Beowulf finally kills at the cost of his own life. This last episode has been thought by some to resemble the tale of the cataclysmic and mutually fatal encounter of the Norse god THOR with the MIDGARD-SERPENT, in the battle at RAGNARÖK, while the other monster-battles in the poem can be matched closely in several much later sagas; in particular it has been suggested that the huge and rapacious Grendel, who is impervious to weapons, resembles a specific kind of walking corpse known as a *draugr* (see DRAUGAR). Other episodes in the poem have also been considered to have reflexes in Norse myth, notably that of the accidental slaying of Herebeald by his brother Hæðcyn, as a result of which mishap Hygelac, Beowulf's lord, ascends the throne. The general circumstances surrounding the slaying seem close to those of the accidental death of BALDR (Here*beald*) at the hands of HÖD (*Hæð*cyn). Similarly, one might adduce broad parallels between the three types of creature fought by Beowulf – a giant with bestial qualities, a dread woman and a serpent – and the three monstrous offspring of LOKI – the monstrous wolf FENRIR, HEL and the Midgard-serpent. In the same vein, details in the narrative can be matched in Norse sources. The description of Grendel's *glof* ('glove', usually taken to be a bag) matches curiously what is said of the huge glove of the giant, SKRÝMIR.

Beowulf features explicitly many other legendary figures from the Germanic past, including Hrothulf (who
emerges in northern tales as HRÓLF KRAKI), Heremod
(Norse HERMÓD) and Sigemund (Norse SIGMUND),
among others, but was clearly composed by a Christian
poet, notwithstanding its evidently retrospective and at
times almost antiquarian interest. The poem's evident
regret at the passing of the old heroic world (albeit a
pagan one) is well captured by the framing effect of
the two funerals whose descriptions begin and end the
text. Both funerals have numerous parallels elsewhere
and represent the variety of BURIAL RITES practised in
the pagan past. The first funeral depicted is that of the
mysterious SCYLD, who had appeared, Moses-like from
across to water to help the Danes in their hour of need
and whose ultimate destination is equally uncertain:

> Then Scyld departed, at the appointed time,
> the bold one passed into the keeping of his lord;
> they bore him to the flood's edge,
> dear retainers, as he had himself ordained,
> friend of the Scyldings, when his words carried weight:
> the loved land-leader governed long.
> There stood at the harbour a ring-prowed ship,
> ice-covered, eager to be off, a prince's craft;
> then they laid the beloved lord,
> the giver of rings, in the bosom of the ship,
> the famed man by the mast. There was a host of
> 　　treasures,
> ornaments brought from distant trips;
> I never heard a ship adorned in more comely manner
> with war-weapons and battle-gear,
> swords and byrnies; they laid in its bosom
> a multitude of treasures which had with him
> to travel far into the flood's embrace.
> They decked him out with no lesser gifts,
> great treasures, than had those
> who at the start had sent him forth,
> alone, across the waves, a little lad.
> Further still, they set a golden sign
> high over his head, let the sea take him,
> gave him to the ocean. No men
> can truly tell, counsellors in hall,
> warriors under the heavens, who received that cargo.

Such a BOAT BURIAL shares several features with what is
found from other sources; some, indeed, have claimed
a particular connection with the boat burial at SUTTON
HOO. No less impressive is the description in *Beowulf*
of the burial rites accorded Beowulf himself by his own
people, the Geats, which takes up almost the last fifty
lines of the poem:

> Then the people of the Geats prepared
> a pyre on the earth, enormous,
> hung with helmets and battle-shields,

> bright corselets, just as he had asked.
> In the midst the grieving warriors laid
> their famous leader, their beloved lord.
> Then at the hilltop fighting-men began to light
> the greatest of pyres: wood-smoke ascended
> black over the flames, the roaring fire,
> mingled with weeping when the wind died,
> until it had broken down the house of bones,
> hot to the heart. Solemnly in thought
> they mourned with mind's cares their prince's death;
> likewise an aged crone sang a mournful dirge
> for Beowulf, with hair bound up,
> full of sorrow, said repeatedly,
> how she feared dire days of struggle for herself,
> a pile of slaughters, the terror of a warrior,
> humiliation and captivity: heaven swallowed the smoke.
> Then the people of the Weather-Geats built
> a mound on the slope, that was high and broad,
> visible from far off to seafaring men,
> and in ten days they had constructed
> the battle-hero's beacon: over the pyre's remains
> they built up a rampart, the most magnificent
> that men most prudent might devise.
> They placed in the barrow rings and gems
> all such baubles as had been removed
> from the dragon-hoard by hostile men:
> they let the earth keep the treasures of nobles,
> gold in the ground, where it still remains,
> as useless to people as it had been before.
> Then warriors rode around the mound, sons of princes,
> 　　twelve in all;
> they wished to grieve and remember their king,
> to craft a dirge, and speak about the man;
> they praised his nobility and his mighty deeds
> reckoned them highly. Just as it is fitting
> for a man to praise his dear lord with words,
> love him in one's heart when he must
> be led forth from the flesh,
> so did the people of the Geats bewail
> their lord's fall, the hearth-companions,
> said that he was of world-kings
> the mildest of men, and the most gracious
> the kindest to his people, the keenest for fame.

Rites similar to those in the first part of this ceremony are offered to the Danish king, Harald Hyldetan
(Harald Hilditönn), according to the early thirteenth-
century Danish historian SAXO GRAMMATICUS. After
dying in battle against his nephew Ring (Sigurd Hring),
apparently killed by his own weapon at the instigation
of the fickle god ODIN, Harald's corpse is recovered by
his enemy and given due burial:

> He raised a pyre, on which the Danes were to put their
> leader's golden ship to feed the fire. While the corpse,
> which had been placed on top, was being consumed by

the flames, [Ring] went around the mourning nobles and urged them all strongly to cast as kindling onto the pyre a vast amount of weapons, gold and treasure, in order to show respect to such a great king, who had earned so much from them all. He ordered that when the body was wholly burned, its ashes should be placed in an urn, taken to Lejre, and there buried with a regal funeral alongside his horse and his weapons.

Despite its unquestionable importance both as a literary piece and as a repository of ancient lore, it is important to stress that *Beowulf* was the work of a Christian author, displaying at times distinctly ambiguous attitudes towards the pagan heroes depicted; the final word of the poem, *lofgeornost* ('most eager for praise'), might be taken as symptomatic of those attitudes: the pride that in purely secular and heroic terms might well be seen as a positive social virtue was that which in Christian eyes deserved only the greatest contempt.

B34, 43, 44, 52, 53, 64, 88; C4, 7, 8, 13; D19, 37, 46, 68, 79, 80, 85, 86, 92, 110, 142, 143, 243, 244, 285–7, 321, 324, 357, 364, 424–6, 438, 440, 441, 468

Bera An alternative name for KOSTBERA.

Bergelmir ('mountain-roarer'?, 'bare yeller')
A giant, grandson of the primeval giant, YMIR (who was also called AURGELMIR), and son of THRÚDGELMIR. Bergelmir is mentioned twice in the eddic poem VAFTHRÚDNISMÁL, where he is described as 'wise', and is also listed among the giants in the name-lists or THULUR. According to the thirteenth-century Icelander SNORRI STURLUSON, when the sons of the giant BOR (including the god ODIN) killed Ymir, so much blood flowed that the entire race of frost-giants drowned, with the exception of Bergelmir, who escaped in what may be a boat (or perhaps a coffin or even a cradle) with his wife and re-founded the frost-giant race. The resemblance to the activities of Noah during the Flood is scarcely fortuitous; arguments have raged as to whether such a resemblance is the result of Christian antiquarianism or much older common inheritance.

B12, 14, 23, 24, 28, 30, 35, 40, 50, 51, 56, 59, 73, 87, 90; C2, 5, 9, 17, 24, 33, 46, 48

berserk ('bare-shirt', or perhaps 'bear-shirt')
A precociously fierce warrior, prone to a battle frenzy in which all thoughts of safety and survival are thrown to the wind. Berserks are particularly associated in the written record with the god ODIN and with shape-changing; reference is also made in the sources to figures known as ÚLFHEDNAR ('wolf-skins'), and in practice berserks are often compared both to wolves and bears. The confused etymology of the name has

also allowed room for artistic licence; in the first century AD the Roman historian TACITUS had described naked Germanic warriors, and later writers sometimes conflated several notions, depicting berserks as naked or lupine or ursine, or even all three. As the thirteenth-century Icelander SNORRI STURLUSON notes in his YNGLINGA SAGA:

Odin could make his enemies in battle blind, or deaf, or panic-struck, and their weapons so blunt that they could cut no better than a willow-wand; but his own men dashed forward without armour, and became as frenzied as dogs or wolves. They chewed their shield-rims, and became as strong as bears or bulls, and slaughtered people at a single stroke, but neither fire nor iron could touch them. It was called 'going berserk'.

Such 'going berserk' is specifically outlawed in a passage in the Icelandic law-code *Grágás*, parts of which may date back to the twelfth century, and indeed the same 'lesser outlawry' is set down both for anyone present who does not restrain the berserk and for other perceived crimes connected with heathenism, which is discussed in the same section of the laws. The col-

berserk *Copper alloy figure from Ekhammer, Kungsängen, Uppland, Sweden, of a horned warrior, perhaps a berserk, engaged in a ritual dance with spears.*

location is suggestive and is further emphasized by a tendency evident in the sagas to portray berserks as essentially outmoded or comic characters, yet to adjust to a civilized (which is to say Christian) way of life.

The earliest suggested witnesses to berserk activities, however, are not literary, but visual: a bronze matrix from Torslunda, perhaps dating to the sixth or seventh century, depicts a number of warriors in various animal guises. The oldest literary reference is contained in the skaldic poem HRAFNSMÁL, composed in the late ninth century, in which both berserks and *ulfhednar* are mentioned in the context of the battle of Hafrsfjörd. More often, berserks are depicted in the sagas as rather bullying or boorish types, generally found in pairs or groups of twelve when not alone, harrying the local population by demanding their wives or daughters, and simply an obstacle for the hero to sweep aside. Typical is the episode in GRETTIS SAGA ÁSMUNDARSONAR in which Grettir has been left behind with the womenfolk at the farmstead of Thorfinn, whom he is visiting and who has shown him no respect. A band of twelve berserks shows up and threatens to take over the place, including and especially Thorfinn's wife and daughters, but Grettir succeeds in locking them in a storehouse, where they begin to 'howl like dogs'. Despite their great strength, Grettir proceeds to dispatch them in pairs, until only two are left, running for their lives. Suffice it to say that berserks seldom feature as the heroes of a saga, although the hero of EGILS SAGA comes from a family of shape-changers and shows a particular devotion to Odin. Nonetheless, even Egil Skallagrímsson is depicted as a warrior who battles *against* berserks, albeit occasionally in a distinctly bestial mode, biting out the throat of one enemy in a manner more usually associated with WEREWOLVES. A more positive image is provided by the twelve berserks who serve King HRÓLF KRAKI in the legendary accounts, who act very much as largely sober (if fearsome) champions, serving their king with exemplary loyalty.

B2, 39, 41, 45, 58, 62, 82, 83, 87, 88; C10, 12, 16, 29, 37; D25, 38, 39, 87

Bestla ('wife'?, 'bark'?)
A giantess, daughter (according to SNORRA EDDA; granddaughter, according to the eddic poem HÁVAMÁL) of BÖLTHORN, wife of BOR, and so mother of ODIN, VILI and VÉ. Odin in particular is frequently described as 'Bestla's son' in both skaldic verse and in the poems of the POETIC EDDA.

B12, 14, 23, 24, 28, 30, 35, 40, 50, 56, 59, 73, 87, 90; C2, 5, 9, 17, 24, 33, 46, 48

Beyla ('cow-girl'?, 'bean-girl'?, 'little bee'?)
According to the eddic poem LOKASENNA, the wife of BYGGVIR. Both she and her husband are (as is appropriate to their names) servants of the fertility-god, FREY.

B12, 30, 56, 73, 87, 90; C2, 17, 24, 33, 46; D123

Bifröst ('shimmering path'?)
Also known as Ásabrú ('the bridge of the Æsir'), Bifröst (as the thirteenth-century Icelander SNORRI STURLUSON names it) is usually held to be the rainbow-bridge connecting the worlds of gods and men, ÁSGARD and MIDGARD, just as the bridge GJALLARBRÚ links Midgard to the Underworld. The god HEIMDALL is said to stand watch at the upper end of the bridge, at HIMINBJÖRG, and when the end of the world comes at RAGNARÖK, the hostile sons of MUSPELL will storm over Bifröst, and shatter it with their weight. In two sources from the POETIC EDDA, GRÍMNISMÁL and FÁFNISMÁL, the name of the bridge is given as Bilröst, the first element of which, *bil* ('a moment'), suggests the fleeting nature of the rainbow, just as the first element of Bifröst, from the verb *bifa* ('to shimmer', 'to shake') gives a sense of its lustrous sheen.

B12, 14, 23, 24, 28, 30, 35, 40, 50, 56, 59, 73, 87, 90; C2, 5, 9, 17, 24, 33, 46, 48

Bikki
The wicked counsellor of King JÖRMUNREKK, who is named once in the eddic poem SIGURDARKVIDA IN SKAMMA and whose tale is most fully told in the legendary VÖLSUNGA SAGA. When he accompanies Jörmunrekk's son, RANDVÉR, on a mission to woo the beautiful SVANHILD on Jörmunrekk's behalf, Bikki persuades Randvér to take Svanhild for himself, before betraying the young lovers to the aged king. Both Randvér and Svanhild are gruesomely killed, so launching the revenge described in the eddic poem HAMDISMÁL.

B12, 25, 30, 42, 56, 65, 68, 73, 78, 87, 90; C1–3, 6, 17, 24, 33, 46

Bil ('moment'?)
(1) According to the thirteenth-century Icelander SNORRI STURLUSON, one of the two children (the other is Hjúki) abducted by MÁNI, the moon, to be his companions. (2) Elsewhere, Snorri lists Bil as one of the goddesses of the ÁSYNJUR.

B12, 14, 23, 24, 28, 30, 35, 40, 50, 56, 59, 73, 87, 90; C2, 5, 9, 17, 24, 33, 46, 48

Billing ('twin')
Billing appears as the name of a dwarf in one version of VÖLUSPÁ, and as the father of a girl whom the god ODIN desires in the eddic poem HÁVAMÁL. Given Odin's propensity for lusting after the daughters of giants, such as GUNNLÖD or RINDA, it may be that the latter is a distinct figure, although (as is clear from Appendices

Bilröst

B and C) dwarfs and giants do share names. A single KENNING in skaldic poetry, describing poetry as the 'drink of Billing's son', seems to support the notion that Billing is a dwarf, given that dwarfs feature so heavily in kennings for poetry because of the role played by the dwarfs FJALAR and GALAR in the myth of the MEAD OF POETRY

B12, 14, 23, 30, 56, 59, 73, 87, 90; C2, 17, 24, 33, 46

Bilröst An alternative name for BIFRÖST.

Bilskírnir ('lightning-crack')
A hall that, according to the eddic poem GRÍMNISMÁL, has 540 doors and is the 'greatest of buildings'. The same number of doors is ascribed to VALHALL, the hall where ODIN marshals his dead, but, according to the thirteenth-century Icelander SNORRI STURLUSON, who is at this point following a KENNING from a tenth-century skaldic verse, Bilskírnir belongs instead to the god THOR.

B12, 14, 23, 24, 28, 30, 35, 40, 50, 56, 59, 73, 87, 90; C2, 5, 9, 17, 24, 33, 46, 48

Björn ('bear')
(1) The name used by the disguised god ODIN in *Hardar saga*, perhaps providing a connection between the god and his often bear-like warriors, the BERSERKS. (2) According to the thirteenth-century Icelander SNORRI STURLUSON, however, Björn is one of the titles of the god THOR.

B24, 28, 35, 40, 50; C5, 9, 48

black elves
A race of beings, distinct from LIGHT ELVES, according to the thirteenth-century Icelander SNORRI STURLUSON, who describes them as living underground and being darker than pitch. Although black elves might most logically be thought to be a category of elves, on both occasions when he mentions the place Svartálfaheim ('dwelling of the black elves'), it is clear that Snorri thought they were DWARFS.

B24, 28, 35, 40, 50; C5, 9, 48

Bláin ('corpse-blue')
Conceivably another name for the primeval giant YMIR (if the identification of Ymir with BRIMIR is allowed) or perhaps simply the name of a dwarf; certainly, however, Bláin is a figure who is intimately involved in the creation of the dwarfs. As the eddic poem VÖLUSPÁ says:

Then all the powers went to their judgement thrones,
the most holy gods, and took counsel on this:

that there should be shaped a troop of dwarfs
from Brimir's blood, and Bláin's bones.

B12, 30, 56, 59, 73, 87, 90; C2, 17, 24, 33, 46

Blíkjanda Böl *see* HEL.

Blind inn bölvísi ('Blind the mischief-maker')
According to the eddic poem HELGAKVIDA HUNDINGS-BANA II, one of King HUNDING's men, sent to flush out the eponymous hero HELGI when he is in hiding, disguised as a handmaid, at the court of HAGAL:

Then Blind spoke, the mischief-maker:
'Hagal's handmaid has piercing eyes;
no servant's son stands at the grinding mill:
the stones crumble, the stand shudders.
The prince has had a harsh turn of fate
when a chief must grind foreign barley.
That hand would hold more fitly
a sword-haft than a mill-handle.'

In classical legend there are similar tales about the hero Achilles, who is said to have disguised himself as a woman to escape the Trojan War; it seems possible that the motif has been borrowed here. Equally intriguing is the fact that both Blind's name and his epithet can be paralleled among the titles of the god ODIN. It may be that this episode is intended to suggest yet another case of the god's interference in the affairs of great heroes.

B12, 30, 56, 73, 87, 90; C2, 17, 24, 33, 46

blódörn see BLOOD-EAGLE.

Blódughadda ('bloody hair')
(1) According to the thirteenth-century account of SNORRI STURLUSON, one of the daughters of the sea-giant, ÆGIR. (2) The name also appears in the name-lists or THULUR as that of a giantess, perhaps the same figure.

B24, 28, 35, 40, 50; C5, 9, 48

Blódughófi ('bloody hoof')
According to a verse from the fragmentary poem KÁLFSVÍSA quoted by the thirteenth-century Icelander SNORRI STURLUSON, the name of the god FREY's horse.

B24, 28, 35, 40, 50; C5, 9, 48

blood-eagle
A barbaric form of slaughter, described in the literary sources, in which a living victim's ribs were forced apart and the lungs torn out to form the shape of eagle's wings. *Orkneyinga saga* is typical in its account of how Jarl Einar deals with the body of his sworn enemy, Hálfdan Longleg:

Einar had his ribs sliced from his spine with a sword, and his lungs dragged out through the slits in his back; he dedicated the victim to ODIN as a victory-offering.

The account of the same event by the thirteenth-century Icelander SNORRI STURLUSON is practically identical:

Then Jarl Einar approached Hálfdan, and carved an eagle on Hálfdan's back in the following way: he stuck his sword into the body next to the spine, cut away all the ribs down to the loins, and dragged out his lungs.

Although references to such a practice are widely scattered, being found in the POETIC EDDA in REGINSMÁL (where the hero SIGURD is supposed to have 'cut the blood-eagle' on the back of the killer of his father, SIGMUND), as well as in several sagas and in the Latin account of the early thirteenth-century Danish historian SAXO GRAMMATICUS, there is no indisputable evidence for the blood-eagle in Viking Age sources. It seems possible that the grisly descriptions of the practice are a product of an imaginative reconstruction, perhaps based on misinterpretation of earlier skaldic verse such as that of SIGHVAT THÓRDARSON, who says:

And Ívarr, who dwelt at York
caused Ella's back to be eagle-scored.

While the syntax of the verse certainly permits the view that Ívarr had Ella's back scored *with* an eagle, it seems at least as likely (and more natural, given the constant references in skaldic poetry to eagles as carrion birds) that Ívarr left Ella's corpse to be torn to pieces *by* an eagle. Saxo's version of the same event is as follows:

They ordered the figure of an eagle to be carved in his back, rejoicing to conquer their most savage foe by inscribing on him the cruellest of birds. Not satisfied with carving wounds, they salted the ragged flesh.

B12, 27, 30, 39, 45, 56, 62, 64, 73, 83, 87, 90; C2, 7, 8, 13, 16, 17, 24, 33, 46; D129, 171, 173, 369

blót see SACRIFICE.

boat burial

Boat burial or ship burial, often including cremation, is widely attested in both the archaeological and the literary records, and it appears to have taken several different forms. The inhumation of ships in large burial mounds, sometimes anchored by huge rocks, is witnessed, by, for example, the OSEBERG or GOKSTAD burials in Scandinavia or that at SUTTON HOO in Anglo-Saxon England on the one hand, and the funeral of

Thorgrím in Iceland, as described in GÍSLA SAGA on the other. Sometimes such buried ships were marked by standing stones, as in the moving account given by the thirteenth-century Icelander SNORRI STURLUSON of the burial of the old warrior Egil Ullserk by King Hákon the Good (935–960), after Egil had fallen in battle against the sons of Eirík Bloodaxe:

King Hákon took possession of those ships that had belonged to Eirík's sons and that had run aground; he had them hauled ashore. He had Egil Ullserk laid in a ship there, and beside him all those of their troop who had fallen there, and had earth and stones heaped over them. King Hákon had many other ships brought ashore, and the dead placed in them, and the mounds can be seen south of Fræðarberg . . . High memorial stones stand beside the grave of Egil Ullserk.

The archaeological record reveals numerous burials of a different but clearly related kind, in which a ship is not buried, but instead stones are laid around the grave (or sometimes cenotaph) in a ship-pattern. Well over 1,500 such ship-settings are recorded, notably in Denmark and Sweden.

More spectacular, but understandably unsubstantiated by the archaeological record, are those funerals in which a burning ship containing the dead is cast out to sea. Such a practice among tribes living on the North Sea coast is attested by the Greek historian PROCOPIUS from as early as the sixth century, and a similar kind of funeral is described at the beginning of the Old English poem BEOWULF. According to Snorri, the funerals of both Haki (a sea-king) and the god BALDR were of this type. The warrior Haki, mortally wounded in battle, supervises his own funeral:

He told them to take a warship that he owned, load it with dead men and weapons and launch it out into the open sea; he told them to ship the rudder, hoist the sail and set fire to the fuel, making a pyre within the ship. The wind was blowing out to sea. When Haki was laid on the pyre he was dead, or almost dead; then the ship sailed out to sea. This was celebrated for a long time afterwards.

Baldr's wife, NANNA, is said to have died of grief at her husband's funeral and to have been buried on the same pyre in a form of SUTTEE, while a female companion for the dead is provided by human SACRIFICE at a similar funeral among the so-called Rus' (who are sometimes thought to have been Scandinavians) by the Arab traveller and diplomat IBN FADLAN in the year 921 or 922. Here, however, the ship is burned and buried on land, a form of burial that is particularly well attested in Latin

Boddi

by the early thirteenth-century Danish historian SAXO GRAMMATICUS.
B37, 40, 64, 80; C7, 8, 19; D97, 150, 317, 343, 407, 434, 507, 536

Boddi *see* RÍGSTHULA.

Bodn *see* ÓDRERIR.

Bödvar Bjarki ('Bödvar little-bear'; 'little bear of battle')

One of the twelve BERSERKS of King HRÓLF KRAKI and, of all the berserks described in the literary sources, the one who most clearly exhibits bear-like traits. According to the legendary HRÓLFS SAGA KRAKA, a mighty bear appeared and fought alongside Bödvar's men as he slept; the bear vanished when he was woken. Clearly the bear is intended to signify Bödvar's own external soul or FYLGJA. Other aspects of the legends surrounding Bödvar Bjarki have close parallels in the Old English poem BEOWULF, whose own hero, Beowulf ('bee-wolf', 'bear') has a similarly ursine name.
B74; C20; D59, 438

Bödvild

Daughter of King NÍDUD, seduced by the legendary smith VÖLUND in revenge for his capture at her father's hands, according to the rather allusive account offered by the eddic poem VÖLUNDARKVIDA; from other sources, principally THIDREKS SAGA, we learn that the result of their union was the hero Vidja. It would appear that Bödvild developed a deep fascination for the mysterious and crippled smith whom her father had hamstrung and held captive on the island of SÆVARSTAD. Neither does she appear to realize that the ring that her father has given her had once belonged to Völund's beloved, the swan-maiden HERVÖR ALVITR. Völund has already begun his revenge on Nídud by slaughtering his two young sons and creating gems from their eyes for Nídud's queen and brooches from their teeth for Bödvild, when she coyly approaches with a request that the smith mend her by now broken ring:

> Then Bödvild began
> to praise the ring that had broken:
> 'I don't dare talk of it, except only to you.'
>
> Völund said:
> 'I'll repair the rent in the gold
> till it seems fairer to your father,
> much better to your mother,
> and the same as before to yourself.'
>
> He overbore her with beer, since he knew better,

so that on the seat she dropped off to sleep.
> 'Now I have avenged my grievances
> all except one, most malicious.
>
> 'If only', said Völund, 'I could get properly to my feet,
> of which Nídud's warriors have deprived me.'
> Laughing, Völund raised himself aloft;
> weeping, Bödvild departed the island:
> she loathed her lover's leaving and her father's wrath.

The audience is left to deduce that Bödvild has been violated and that Völund, who, as the prose sources tell us, has by this point made himself a pair of wings, has quite literally flown. After Völund lands to tell King Nídud precisely how he has wrought his revenge, the king is left bereft in the same way as his daughter, to whom he immediately turns for confirmation:

> Laughing, Völund raised himself aloft;
> full of sadness Nídud sat there afterwards.
>
> 'Stir yourself, THAKRÁD, best of all my servants;
> ask Bödvild, my white-browed maid,
> my beautiful girl, to come and converse with her father.
>
> 'Is it true, Bödvild, what I've been told:
> you and Völund, did you two spend time together on
>   the island?'
>
> 'It's true, Nithud, what he told you:
> Völund and I, we two spent time together on the island,
> a single tide's turn: it should never have been.
> I didn't have the wits to struggle against him;
> I didn't have the strength to struggle against him.'

Bödvild's tragedy was also well known in Anglo-Saxon England. The Old English poem *Deor* alludes to her misfortune (under the Anglicized name of Beaduhild), and it has even been thought that another Old English poem, *Wulf and Eadwacer*, which directly follows *Deor* in the Exeter Book manuscript, may be a dramatic monologue delivered by the unnamed Beaduhild in her grief.
B8, 12, 30, 31, 42, 56, 71, 73, 84, 87, 90; C2, 13, 15, 17, 21, 24, 25, 33, 44, 46

bog corpses

The generic name given to a group of remarkably well-preserved Bronze Age corpses found in bogs and marshes covering a wide geographical area, spanning from Britain, through Norway and southern Sweden, to Denmark and north Germany, where they are most frequent. Almost all have died a violent death, most frequently by strangulation or hanging. While it is possible that such corpses (whose preserved stomach-contents have been thought by some to contain the remains of a ritual meal) are the result of a practice of human SACRIFICE, it is tempting to connect the archaeological evidence with the testimony of the first-century Roman historian TACITUS, who notes that any cowardly or unmanly behaviour among the Germanic peoples was punishable by drowning the victims in a bog:

> Cowards, malingerers and sodomites are forced down beneath a wicker hurdle into the slippery mud of a bog.

The practical difficulties of differentiating between the practices of human sacrifice and judicial killing from purely archaeological evidence make any final judgement problematic.

B2; C29; D189

Böll *see* HVERGELMIR.

Bölthor An alternative name for BÖLTHORN.

Bölthorn ('evil-thorn')
According to the thirteenth-century Icelander, SNORRI STURLUSON, a giant, the father of BESTLA and therefore the maternal grandfather of the god ODIN. In the eddic poem HÁVAMÁL, Odin claims to have learned great magic from an unnamed son of the same giant, there called Bölthor:

> I had nine mighty songs from that famed
> son of Bölthor, father of Bestla,
> and one swig I snatched of that glorious mead
> drained from ÓDRERIR.

In claiming to have received wisdom from his maternal uncle, Odin is simply following an established pattern in Germanic myth and legend. The Roman historian TACITUS, writing in the first century AD, had already noted the importance of that particular family tie in Germanic society, and there are numerous examples of the closeness of male figures with their maternal uncles in the literary sources.

B2, 12, 14, 23, 24, 28, 30, 35, 40, 50, 56, 59, 73, 87, 90; C2, 5, 9, 17, 24, 29, 33, 46, 48

Bóndi *see* RÍGSTHULA.

Bor, Bur ('son')
According to the thirteenth-century Icelander SNORRI STURLUSON, the giant son of the primordial figure BÚRI, who was licked from salty blocks at the dawn of time by the mythical cow, AUDHUMLA. Quite how Búri produced Bor (whose name is also found as Bur) is unclear; no mother is mentioned. In his turn, Bor took as his wife the giantess BESTLA, daughter of BÖLTHORN,

and together they produced ODIN, VILI and VÉ, who are duly called 'Bur's sons' in the eddic poem VÖLUSPÁ.

B12, 14, 23, 24, 28, 30, 35, 40, 50, 56, 59, 73, 87, 90; C2, 5, 9, 17, 24, 33, 46, 48

Borghild
According to the poems HELGAKVIDA HUNDINGSBANA I and II of the POETIC EDDA and also the legendary VÖLSUNGA SAGA, the wife of the hero SIGMUND and mother of the warrior HELGI SIGMUNDARSON HUNDINGSBANI. Borghild eventually poisons SINFJÖTLI, her stepson, after he kills her brother when they both compete as rivals for the hand of a beautiful woman.

B12, 25, 30, 42, 56, 65, 68, 73, 79, 87, 90; C1–3, 6, 17, 24, 33, 46

Borgný
According to the eddic poem ODDRÚNARGRÁTR, the daughter of King HEIDREK. After she was made pregnant by her lover, VILMUND, she was unable to give birth until she was assisted by ODDRÚN, who uses magic to help her.

B12, 30, 56, 73, 87, 90; C2, 17, 24, 33, 46

bracteates
Medallions or coins, stamped on one side only, depicting a range of human or animal figures, including some from myth and legend, and often inscribed with RUNES.
D234

braga(r)ful ('chieftain's cup')
According to the thirteenth-century Icelander SNORRI STURLUSON, the toast drunk between that to the ÆSIR and that to the dead. The *bragaful* is then often connected to the formal boast or vow made at feasts. Such a series of toasts was thought particularly appropriate at SACRIFICES, as Snorri notes:

> Whoever was in charge of the sacrifice and was a GODI, blessed the full beakers and all the meat of the sacrifice. First, ODIN's beaker was drained for victory and power to his king; then beakers for NJÖRD and FREYJA, for peace and a fruitful harvest. Then it was a common custom to drain the *bragaful*, and then the guests drained a beaker in memory of their dead kinsmen, called the MINNI.

In YNGLINGA SAGA, Snorri outlines the practice of drinking a *bragaful* still further:

> At that time it was the custom that whoever gave an inheritance-feast for kings or earls and entered into their inheritance, should sit on the footstool in front of the high-seat, until the full beaker, known as the *bragaful*, was brought in. Then he should stand up, take the *bragaful*, make solemn pledges that he had to fulfill and drain the beaker. Then he should mount the high-

seat that his father had held and so come into the full inheritance of his father.

The absolute necessity, in heroic terms, of fulfilling such a formal vow or suffering disgrace naturally led to tragedy. An example of a foolhardy vow that has unfortunate consequences is found in the eddic poem HELGAKVIDA HJÖRVARDSSONAR, in which the warrior HEDIN HJÖRVARDSSON vows to take possession of the Valkyrie SVÁVA, the beloved of his own brother, HELGI. Hedin's vow is fulfilled, but only after Helgi is killed in battle.

B1; C22, 23

Bragi ('poetry', 'lord')

The thirteenth-century Icelander SNORRI STURLUSON names the god Bragi as the figure among the ÆSIR whose special concern was poetry, describing how:

> He is noted for wisdom, and particularly for eloquence and skill with words. He is especially knowledgeable about poetry, and because of him poetry is called *brag*, and from his name someone is called a *brag* ['chief', in its secondary meaning] of men or women, if they posses eloquence above others, whether they are a woman or a man.

Difficulties of interpretation emerge because of the existence of a body of skaldic verse (also preserved by Snorri) attributed to one Bragi Boddason inn gamli ('Bragi Boddason the old'), who was said to be the court poet of, among others, the Swedish King Björn at haugi, identified with the figure of King Bern of Birka, whom the missionary Anskar visited around 830. Bragi's skaldic verse is therefore among the earliest corpus of Norse poetry attributed to a named figure. The notion that a historical ninth-century figure somehow became transformed in later imagination into a divine character seems supported by his appearances outside Snorri's works. Bragi is found in VALHALL welcoming the chieftains Hákon the Good (who died in 961) and Eirík Bloodaxe (who died in 954) in the quasi-eddic poems HÁKONARMÁL and EIRÍKSMÁL, but earlier references are distinctly ambiguous, and in the eddic poem GRÍMNISMÁL, for example, it is unclear to which Bragi reference is made. By the twelfth century, Bragi appears in other poems of the POETIC EDDA such as SIGRDRÍFUMÁL and LOKASENNA, as well as in skaldic verses of the same date, for example in GRETTIS SAGA ÁSMUNDARSONAR. In the latter two examples, Bragi is named alongside IDUN, his wife, a connection that Snorri develops in several tales. Given that Bragi's main role in *Hákonarmál* and *Eiríksmál* is that of welcoming the dead kings to Valhall, it is intriguing to note that in *Lokasenna* Bragi is the first of the feasting figures to

address LOKI when he enters ÆGIR's hall and is singled out for special invective by Loki even in his opening speech to the assembled gods:

> 'Greetings, gods; greetings, goddesses,
> and all the most holy powers,
> except that one god, who sits furthest in,
> Bragi, at the benches' end.'

[Bragi said:]
> 'A horse and sword, will I give from my hoard,
> and Bragi will requite you with a ring,
> if only you'll check your malice at the gods:
> don't anger the Æsir against you!'

[Loki said:]
> 'As for horses and arm-rings,
> Bragi, you'll always lack both:
> of the Æsir and elves who are gathered here,
> you are the wariest of war,
> ever the most shy of shooting.'

[Bragi said:]
> 'I know, if only I were outside,
> as I'm inside Ægir's hall,
> I'd have your head held in my hand:
> I'll pay you back for that lie.'

[Loki said:]
> 'You're a soldier in your seat, but you can't deliver,
> Bragi, pretty boy on a bench:
> go and get moving if you're enraged:
> no hero takes heed of the consequences.'

Luckily for Bragi, one feels, his wife intervenes to spare his blushes at this point.

B12, 14, 23, 24, 28, 30, 35, 39–41, 45, 50, 56, 59, 62, 73, 83, 87, 90; C2, 5, 9, 12, 13, 16, 17, 24, 33, 46, 48; D476

Bragi Boddason inn gamli *see* BRAGI.

Bragi Högnason

According to the eddic poem HELGAKVIDA HUNDING-SBANA II, the son of the warrior HÖGNI, and brother of SIGRÚN and DAG. Bragi is killed alongside his father by the hero HELGI at the battle of FREKASTEIN.

B12, 30, 56, 73, 87, 90; C2, 17, 24, 33, 46

Brálund *see* HELGAKVIDA HUNDINGSBANA I.

Brattskegg *see* RÍGSTHULA.

Breid *see* RÍGSTHULA.

Breidablik ('broad-gleam')

According to the eddic poem GRÍMNISMÁL, the dwelling of the god BALDR, an association sustained by the thirteenth-century Icelander SNORRI STURLUSON, who adds that it is in heaven and that nothing impure is allowed there. Elsewhere, Snorri localizes Breidablik in ÁLFHEIM, the home of the ELVES, saying that there is no fairer place.

B12, 14, 23, 24, 28, 30, 35, 40, 50, 56, 59, 73, 87, 90; C2, 5, 9, 17, 24, 33, 46, 48

Brennu-Njáls saga see NJÁLS SAGA.

Brimir ('sea')

A giant in the eddic poem VÖLUSPÁ, perhaps an alternative name for the primeval giant YMIR, from whose blood the sea was created. The thirteenth-century Icelander SNORRI STURLUSON, presumably misinterpreting a verse from *Völuspá* that speaks of 'the beer-hall of the giant called Brimir', describes Brimir as a beer-hall where some folk will feast after the apocalyptic events of RAGNARÖK, and elsewhere, through a process of EUHEMERISM, goes so far as to identify Brimir's hall with the palace of King Priam at Troy.

B12, 14, 23, 24, 28, 30, 35, 40, 50, 56, 59, 73, 87, 90; C2, 5, 9, 17, 24, 33, 46, 48

Brísingamen ('necklace of the Brísings', 'flaming necklace'?)

A precious necklace, owned by the goddess FREYJA according to the thirteenth-century Icelander SNORRI STURLUSON and other late sources, notably the eddic poem THRYMSKVIDA. In his ninth-century skaldic poem HAUSTLÖNG, THJÓDÓLF OF HVÍN describes the god LOKI as 'the thief of Brísing's girdle', while a tenth-century skaldic poem, HÚSDRÁPA, appears to allude to a battle between Loki and the god HEIMDALL over some precious item of jewellery. Snorri, presumably synthesizing from these and other now-lost sources, recounts how Loki stole the Brísingamen from Freyja, but that Heimdall recovered it after he and Loki had fought in the shape of seals. A fourteenth-century source, SÖRLA THÁTTR, describes how Freyja acquired the necklace, which was made by four dwarfs, by spending a night with each in turn. According to *Sörla þáttr*, Loki stole the necklace at the request of the god ODIN, after changing himself into a fly, passing into Freyja's bedchamber through the keyhole and stinging the sleeping figure, who was lying on the necklace, to make her move. Only when Freyja causes an endless war between two kings (the so-called HJADNINGAVÍG) does Odin return her hard-won property.

The picture is somewhat clouded by the appearance of an equally precious item of jewellery, called *Brosinga mene* ('necklace of the Brosings') in the Old English poem BEOWULF, where it is carried off to 'the bright citadel' by one Hama, who is escaping the 'cunning hostility of Eormenric'. Attempts to rationalize the Old English and Norse evidence have been ingenious but so far fail to provide any clear solution.

B12, 30, 39, 45, 56, 62, 73, 83, 87, 90; C2, 13, 16, 17, 21, 24, 33, 46

Brokk ('blacksmith')

The dwarf who, according to the thirteenth-century Icelander SNORRI STURLUSON, gave the god LOKI his crooked smile. Loki had been to some other dwarfs known simply as ÍVALDI'S SONS to have a new head of hair made for SIF, the wife of the god THOR, after Loki had spitefully shorn her. These dwarfs had also made the magical ship SKÍDBLADNIR and the mighty spear GUNGNIR. As Snorri continues:

> Then Loki wagered his head with a dwarf named Brokk on whether his brother EITRI could make three treasures as fine as these. When they reached the forge, Eitri placed a pig-skin in the furnace and told Brokk to blow and not to stop until he removed what he had put into the furnace. But as soon as [Eitri] left the forge and [Brokk] was blowing, a midge landed on his arm and stung him, but he carried on blowing the same as before until the smith took the piece out of the furnace: it was a boar, with golden bristles. Then he placed some gold in the furnace and told Brokk to blow and not stop blowing until he returned, and then he went out. The midge came and landed on his neck and stung him twice as hard, but he went on blowing until the smith removed from the furnace a golden ring called DRAUPNIR. Then [Eitri] placed some iron in the furnace and told [Brokk] to blow, and said that it would not turn out well if there was any break in the blowing. Then the midge landed between [Brokk's] eyes and stung his eyelids, and when blood dribbled into his eyes so that he couldn't see, he swatted at it with his hand as quickly as he could while the bellows were deflating and swiped away the fly. When the smith returned he said that it was a near thing that the contents of the furnace had not been spoiled. Then he removed from the furnace a hammer and gave all the treasures to his brother Brokk and told him to take them to ÁSGARD and conclude the bet. When he and Loki produced the treasures, the ÆSIR sat on their judgement thrones, and the judgement declared by ODIN, Thor and FREY was to be final. Then Loki gave the spear Gungnir to Odin, the head of hair for Sif to Thor, and Skídbladnir to Frey, declaring the properties of each treasure: that the spear was never diverted from its thrust, that the hair took root in the flesh as soon as it was placed on Sif's head, and that Skídbladnir got a favourable wind as soon as its sail was hoisted, wherever it had to go, and could be folded up like a cloth and put in your pocket, if you wanted. Then Brokk produced his treasures. He gave the ring to Odin and said that every ninth night there would drop from it eight rings of the same weight. He gave the boar to Frey and said that it could speed across sea and sky at night faster than any steed, and it would never become so dark from night or in dim places that it was not bright enough wherever it

travelled, since so much light streamed from its bristles. Then he gave Thor the hammer and said that he would be able to strike as firmly as he wanted, whatever the target, and the hammer would not falter, and if he cast it at something, it would never miss, nor ever fly so far away that it would not find its way back to his hand, but if he wanted, it could be small enough to carry inside his shirt. But there was a blemish: the handle's end was slightly stunted. Their judgement was that the hammer was the greatest treasure, since it offered the best defence against frost-giants, and they decided that the dwarf had won his bet. So Loki offered to buy back his head, and the dwarf said there was no likelihood of that. 'So catch me,' said· Loki. But when Brokk attempted to catch him, he was far away. Loki had some shoes that allowed him to sprint over sea and sky. So the dwarf asked Thor to catch him, and he did. Then the dwarf was about to cut off Loki's head, but Loki said he could have the head but not the neck. Then the dwarf took a thong and a blade, and tried to put holes in Loki's lips, and was about to stitch up his mouth, but the blade would not bite. Then [Brokk] said it would be better if his brother's awl was there, and immediately he said that, an awl appeared and pierced the lips. [Brokk] stitched the lips together, but he tore the edges off. The thong that was used to stitch up Loki's mouth is called Vartari.

Neither Brokk nor his brother is witnessed elsewhere; it is possible that Snorri has simply confected the story himself.

B24, 28, 35, 40, 50; C5, 9, 48

Brot af Sigurdarkvidu ('fragment of a Sigurd-lay')

The fragmentary eddic poem found in the CODEX REGIUS manuscript, immediately following the now-lost portion of the manuscript known as 'the great lacuna'. Although the beginning of the poem has been lost, much of the content can be inferred from the legendary VÖLSUNGA SAGA. As the fragment opens, the heroes GUNNAR and HÖGNI GJÚKASON are recounting how they drove their brother GUTTHORM to kill SIGURD, the mightiest of all the heroes of the North. Gutthorm had been steeled to the task by eating the flesh of wolf and snake, although the dying Sigurd managed to kill him too, and Sigurd's horse, GRANI, is described mourning over his master's corpse. The poem closes with a bitter exchange between Gunnar and his wife, BRYNHILD, who had herself loved Sigurd greatly. Immediately following Brot af Sigurdarkvidu in the manuscript is a brief transitional passage in prose, recounting the variant traditions concerning Sigurd's death, including what is evidently a misunderstanding of a verse from GUDRÚNARKVIDA II:

It is said here in this poem about the death of Sigurd, and here it indicates, that he was killed outdoors. But some say that they killed him indoors, sleeping in his bed. But Germans say that they killed him in a forest. It says in the ancient Gudrúnarkvida, that Sigurd and the sons of Gjúki were riding to a meeting, when he was killed; but everyone agrees that they tricked him with cunning, and slew him unawares when he was lying down.

B12, 30, 56, 73, 87, 90; C2, 17, 24, 33, 46

Brúd see RÍGSTHULA.

Brunhild see BRYNHILD; NIBELUNGENLIED.

Brynhild ('bright battle')

According to a number of different sources, Brynhild is a VALKYRIE, identified with the figure of SIGRDRÍFA in the eddic poem SIGRDRÍFUMÁL. In the cycle of poems and legends associated with the VÖLSUNGS, she is described as a daughter of King BUDLI and sister of ATLI BUDLASON, first found asleep in her mail-coat, in a flame-encircled hall on a mountain-top. As befits such a proud and martial figure, she has sworn only to marry the man brave enough to dare the flames. The hero GUNNAR attempts to penetrate the flames but is turned back, and his (then) friend SIGURD, disguised as Gunnar, manages the deed and spends a night at Brynhild's side. Eventually released from her mountain-top hall, Brynhild marries Gunnar, while Sigurd marries GUDRÚN, Gunnar's sister. When Brynhild finds out, from a taunt by Gudrún, that it was Sigurd who had passed the flames and first spent the night with her, her vengeance is terrible: she brings about his death, Gudrún is married off to her brother Atli, and the cycle of revenge spins on.

Part of the flavour of her terrible wrath is captured in a lengthy exchange with Sigurd in VÖLSUNGA SAGA. This highly charged conversation occurs after she has taken to her bed in a brooding and silent protest at the revelation about the truth of her betrothal to Gunnar, and in it Brynhild emerges as the character with the greatest emotional depth, while Sigurd is depicted as rather brash and insensitive:

Sigurd went out and found the hall open. He thought that Brynhild was asleep, pulled back the bedclothes from her and said: 'Wake up, Brynhild. The sun is shining all over town, and you have slept enough. Shake off your sorrow and be happy.' She said: 'How smug of you to come and see me! In all this treachery no one has behaved worse to me than you.' Sigurd asked: 'Why won't you talk to people? What is the matter?' Brynhild said: 'I shall tell you of my anger.' Sigurd said:

'You're out of your mind if you think I think badly of you; you took as your husband the one you chose.' 'No,' she said, 'Gunnar didn't ride to me through the flames, nor did he pay my marriage settlement in slaughtered men. I marvelled at the man who came into my hall, and I thought I recognized your eyes, but I couldn't see clearly for the shroud that covered my face.' Sigurd said: 'I am no more noble than GJÚKI's sons; they killed the Danish king, and a mighty prince, King Budli's brother.' Brynhild answered: 'I have much to repay them for: don't remind me of my grief. Sigurd, it was you who slew the dragon and rode through the flames for my sake. Gjúki's sons did not do that.' Sigurd answered: 'I never became your husband, nor you my wife: a noble king paid your marriage settlement.' Brynhild answered: 'I have never glanced at Gunnar and been gladdened in my heart. I hate him, though I hide it from everyone else.' 'It is a terrible thing,' said Sigurd, 'not to love such a king. But what hurts you most? It seems to me that his love must be worth more to you than gold.' Brynhild answered: 'What hurts me most is that I can't make a sharp blade drip with your blood.' Sigurd said: 'Save your thoughts; there isn't long to wait before a sharp sword sticks in my heart, and you could't wish for anything worse for yourself, because you won't live long after me. After this, we two have few days to live.' Brynhild answered: 'Your words don't cause me great distress: since you tricked me of all happiness, I don't care about my life.' Sigurd said: 'Live, and love King Gunnar and me, and I shall give every treasure I own to stop your death.' Brynhild said: 'You don't know me at all. You exceed all other men, and yet no woman hates you more than I.' 'Something else would be closer to the truth,' replied Sigurd. 'I love you more than myself, although I was the instrument of the deception that cannot now be changed. Whenever I was in my right mind it hurt me that you were not my wife. But I put up with it as best I could while I lived in the king's hall; I was happy for us all to be together. It may be that what has been foretold must happen, but it is not to be feared.' Brynhild answered: 'You have taken too long to tell me that my pain hurts you; I can find no comfort now.' 'I want us both to share a bed,' said Sigurd, 'and you to be my wife.' Brynhild said: 'Don't say such things; I won't have two kings in a single hall: I'd sooner die than cheat King Gunnar,' – here she remembered their meeting on the mountain, and the oaths they swore – 'but now it is all changed, and I don't want to live.' 'I couldn't remember your name,' said Sigurd. 'I didn't know you until after you were married; that is what hurts me the most.' Then Brynhild spoke: 'I took a vow to marry the man who rode through my flickering flames, and to keep that vow or die.' 'Rather than let you die, I shall give up Gudrún and marry you,' said Sigurd; his sides swelled up so that the links of his mail-coat burst. 'I don't want you,' said Brynhild, 'or anyone else.'

A similar tone of thwarted petulance combined with brooding menace is found in many of the sources that deal with Brynhild; a striking example occurs in the final stanza of the eddic poem GUDRÚNARKVIDA I, which describes how Brynhild confronts the sight of the dead Sigurd:

> She stood by the pillar, summoned her strength:
> her eyes blazed, she exuded venom,
> Brynhild, Budli's daughter, when she gazed on Sigurd's wounds.

Her grief was such that she flung herself on Sigurd's pyre, usurping in death the wifely role she had been denied when she lived. Even the dead Brynhild excites animosity. The eddic poem HELREID BRYNHILDAR vividly describes an encounter between Brynhild and a giant witch on the road to HEL, when the ogress berates Brynhild for the sorrow she has caused. Unrepentant, Brynhild seeks only to justify her actions, and the poem closes memorably with the following grim and obsessive observation by the unbowed Brynhild:

> 'They must all too long
> in the face of great strife
> men and women
> be born and raised;
> we two shall share
> the rest of our time,
> Sigurd and I together:
> sink yourself, giantess-spawn!'

B12, 25, 30, 42, 56, 65, 68, 73, 79, 87, 90; C1–3, 6, 17, 24, 33, 46; D11, 469, 470

Budli

According to the tales associated with the VÖLSUNG-cycle, the father of both BRYNHILD and ATLI BUDLASON. The legendary VÖLSUNGA SAGA states that: 'he was more powerful than GJÚKI [the father of both GUNNAR and GUDRÚN, the hated rivals of Budli's offspring], although both of them were powerful.'

B12, 25, 30, 42, 56, 65, 68, 73, 79, 87, 90; C1–3, 6, 17, 24, 33, 46

Búi see RÍGSTHULA.

Bundinskeggi see RÍGSTHULA.

Bur see BOR; RÍGSTHULA.

Búri ('father', 'producer', 'inhabitant')

(1) According to the thirteenth-century Icelander SNORRI STURLUSON, the giant Búri was licked from the salty blocks of primordial ice over the course of three days by the mighty cow AUDHUMLA. Búri was the father of BOR and so grandfather of the god ODIN. No mention

is made of Búri in other sources. (2) A DWARF named
Buri (or perhaps Búri) is found in the catalogue of
dwarfs in the eddic poem VÖLUSPÁ.

B12, 14, 23, 24, 28, 30, 35, 40, 50, 56, 59, 73, 87, 90; C2, 5, 9, 17, 24, 33, 46, 48

burial customs *see* BURIAL RITES.

burial mounds (Old Norse *haugar*)

Burial mounds are found widely scattered throughout
Europe from the Neolithic period onwards and can
scarcely be described as specific to Germanic peoples,
but their popularity in Scandinavia in the late pagan
period is striking and is well attested in the archaeological and literary records. In addition to inhumation of
individuals or family groups, other forms of burial practice are often found in combination, such as cremation
or BOAT BURIAL within the mound. Such burials were
often a mark of high status, and many mounds contain
substantial quantities of treasure and grave goods –
for example, the impressive mounds at OSEBERG and
GOKSTAD both contain splendid ships. Occasionally the
mounds are as small as 2–3 metres (6–9 feet) across, as
at Ingleby in Derbyshire, but the enormous Raknehaug
in Norway is 19 metres (62 feet) high and 95 metres
(312 feet) in diameter. In the latter case, as with the
largest of the mounds at Jelling in Denmark, the mound
is entirely empty, although it has been suggested that
some structure for the dead may have been erected
at the top. Burial mounds are particularly associated
with the cult of the VANIR, and numerous magical
properties are attributed to them, typical of which is
the story told in FLATEYJARBÓK of Thorleif, who was
poetically inspired after sleeping on the mound of a
dead skald. Burial mounds are also considered to be the
home of the living dead or hostile ghosts (DRAUGAR),
who appear frequently in the Icelandic sagas. Several
Icelandic sources, notably LANDNÁMABÓK, NJÁLS SAGA
and EYRBYGGJA SAGA, also describe a clearly related
belief that the dead can inhabit mountains and live on
there in the company of their ancestors. Such occupied
mountains and mounds are often described as giving
off an eerie glow or light, as in the following description,
from *Njáls saga*, of what men saw when they rode past
the mound of the hero GUNNAR at Hlídarendi:

> It seemed to them that the burial mound was open and
> that Gunnar had turned himself in the burial mound
> and was gazing up at the moon. They thought that they
> saw four lights burning in the burial mound, and not a
> shadow anywhere. They saw that Gunnar was happy,
> with a face full of joy.

B6, 39, 45, 60, 76, 77, 83, 85–7; C116, 26, 36, 39; D65, 89, 132, 137, 201

burial rites

The Roman historian TACITUS, writing in the first

century AD, gives a bare account of the funerary obser-
vances of Germanic peoples in the first century in his
GERMANIA:

> There is no ostentation about their funerals; the only
> particular ceremony is that the bodies of famous men are
> burned with particular types of wood. When the pyre has
> been piled up, they do not throw cloths or spices onto
> it, only the dead man's weapons, and sometimes his
> horse as well, are consigned to the flames. The tomb is
> a raised mound of earth: they avoid showing honour by
> laboriously raising lofty monuments of stone, which they
> suppose would only lie heavy on the dead. Tears and
> wailing are soon left off; grief and sorrow less soon. It is
> proper for women to mourn, but for men to remember.

The thirteenth-century Icelander SNORRI STURLUSON
attempts to distinguish between the different kinds of
burial rites employed in Scandinavia in the prologue to
his YNGLINGA SAGA:

> The first age is called the Age of Burning; all the dead
> had to be burned, and memorial stones were raised over
> them. But after Frey had been placed in a burial mound
> in UPPSALA, many chieftains raised burial mounds as
> frequently as memorial stones in honour of their kin.
> But after Dan the Proud, the Danish king, had a burial
> mound raised for himself and ordered that he should
> be brought there after his death in his royal garb, with
> his weapons and horse and saddlery, and much treasure
> besides, many of his descendants acted likewise, and
> the Age of Burial Mounds began in Denmark, although
> among the Swedes and Norwegians the Age of Burning
> continued for a long time afterwards.

To compound his evident difficulties in distinguish-
ing the relative chronology of burial practices in the
Scandinavian homelands, Snorri gives a still more dis-
cursive account later in the same *Ynglinga saga*, in
which, however, he attributes common burial practice
to legislation established by none other than the god
ODIN himself:

> He laid down by law that all dead men should be
> burned, and their belongings placed with them on the
> pyre, and that the ashes should then be cast into the
> sea or buried in the ground. In this way, he said, every
> one will arrive at VALHALL with the treasures that ac-
> companied him on the pyre, and he would also enjoy
> whatever he had himself buried in the ground. For im-
> portant men a mound should be raised to their memory,
> and a standing stone for all other warriors who had been
> distinguished for bravery; and that custom remained
> long after Odin's day.

A similar distinction between various kinds of burial
rites can be observed in the varying descriptions of the

burial rites *A burial mound with satellite ship-settings at Anundshog, Badelunda, Västmanland, Sweden. Such sites demonstrate the range of burial rites employed during the period.*

funerals of SCYLD and Beowulf in the Anglo-Saxon poem BEOWULF, while numerous other detailed literary accounts of burial rites broadly sustain the thrust of Snorri's report, which gains still further support from the archaeological record.

B2; C29; D51, 132, 137, 196

Búseyra ('muddy-dwelling'?, 'big ears'?, 'house-saver'?)

According to a verse by the poet THORBJÖRN DÍSARSKÁLD, quoted by the thirteenth-century Icelander SNORRI STURLUSON, Búseyra was a giantess, one of a number killed by the god THOR.

B24, 28, 35, 40, 50; C5, 9, 48

Busiltjörn

According to the legendary VÖLSUNGA SAGA, the river into which the hero SIGURD drove his horse GRANI, at the instigation of the disguised god ODIN, in order to test his mettle:

> The following day Sigurd went into the forest and met an old man with a long beard; Sigurd did not know him. He asked where Sigurd was going. Sigurd answered: 'I am going to choose a horse; give me some advice.' The man replied: 'Let's drive them down to the river called Busiltjörn.' They drove the horses out into the deep river, and they all swam ashore except one; Sigurd took it. It was grey-coloured, young, large and handsome; no one had ever mounted it. The man with the beard said:

'This horse is descended from [Odin's horse] SLEIPNIR and must be brought up with care, because he is going to turn out better than any other horse.' Then the man disappeared. Sigurd called the horse Grani, and he was the finest horse that ever lived. Odin was the one Sigurd had met.

B25, 42, 65, 68, 79; C1, 6

Byggvir ('corn-boy'?)

According to the eddic poem LOKASENNA, Byggvir and his wife BEYLA are the (aptly named) servants of the fertility-god FREY. In *Lokasenna* Byggvir, outraged by the behaviour of LOKI, threatens to deal with him. Loki's answer is a masterfully sneering retort, putting the servant properly in his place:

> What's that little thing I see, wagging like a dog?
> You're always whispering in Frey's ears,
> twittering by the grindstone.

B12, 30, 56, 73, 87, 90; C2, 17, 24, 33, 46; D123

Byleist

According to the eddic poem VÖLUSPÁ, the brother of the mischievous LOKI. Byleist is named in several other sources, but always in poetic periphrases or KENNINGS for Loki.

B12, 30, 56, 59, 73, 87, 90; C2, 17, 24, 33, 46

Bylgja *see* ÆGIR.

Byrgir *see* MÁNI.

C

Codex Regius ('the royal manuscript')

A small Icelandic manuscript of some ninety pages, dated around 1270–80, and containing no fewer than twenty-nine poems of the POETIC EDDA. Perhaps sixteen further pages have been lost in what is often referred to as 'the great lacuna', the narrative content of which, in so far as it relates exclusively to a section of the manuscript dealing with the VÖLSUNG-cycle (the break in the text comes before the end of SIGRDRÍFUMÁL), can be reconstructed to some extent from the legendary VÖLSUNGA SAGA and from various other sources. The Codex Regius remains the sole surviving witness for much mythological material in verse. The next most important manuscript, AM 748 I 4to, by contrast, is fragmentary, and bears witness to only seven such poems.

There are, moreover, clear signs of careful arrangement of the poems in the Codex Regius: the first group of ten (that is, VÖLUSPÁ, HÁVAMÁL, VAFTHRÚDNISMÁL, GRÍMNISMÁL, SKÍRNISMÁL, HÁRBARDSLJÓD, LOKASENNA, THRYMSKVIDA, VÖLUNDARKVIDA and ALVÍSSMÁL) deal with mythological material, while the remaining nineteen (HELGAKVIDA HJÖRVARDSSONAR, HELGAKVIDA HUNDINGSBANA I, HELGAKVIDA HUNDINGSBANA II, FRÁ DAUDA SINFJÖTLA, GRÍPISSPÁ, REGINSMÁL, FÁFNISMÁL, SIGURDRÍFUMÁL, BROT AF SIGURDARKVIDU, GUDRÚNARKVIDA I, SIGURDARKVIDA IN SKAMMA, HELREID BRYNHILDAR, GUDRÚNARKVIDA II, GUDRÚNARKVIDA III, ODDRÚNARGRÁTR, ATLAK-VIDA, ATLAMÁL IN GRÆNLENZKU, GUDRÚNARHVÖT and HAMDISMÁL) are concerned with the heroic figures of Germanic legend. Even within these major groups, moreover, smaller patterns can be seen. The mythological group contains poems about the gods ODIN (*Völuspá*, *Hávamál*, *Vafdrúdnismál* and *Grimnismál*), FREY (*Skírnismál*) and THOR (*Hárbardsljód*, *Lokasenna*, *Thrymskvida* and *Alvíssmál*) seemingly carefully arranged, while the heroic group distinguishes the so-called Helgi-lays (*Helgakvida Hjorvardssonar*, *Helgakvida Hundingsbana I* and *Helgakvida Hundingsbana II*) from the poems of the VÖLSUNG-cycle. It seems highly probable that in compiling the SNORRA EDDA during the 1220s the Icelander SNORRI STURLUSON had access to texts from the same underlying tradition as that from which the Codex Regius was later copied.

Nothing is known of the precise provenance of the manuscript before 1641, when it came into the pos-

Codex Regius *The Codex Regius manuscript, opened at the end of the eddic poem* Völuspá, *and the beginning of the eddic poem* Hávamál.

session of Bishop Brynjólfur Sveinsson, who presented it (by this time lacking those pages that form the great lacuna) to the king of Denmark in 1662, and it remained in Denmark until 1972, when it was finally returned to Iceland.

B12, 14, 23, 25, 30, 31, 42, 51, 56, 59, 65, 68, 73, 79, 87, 90; C1–3, 6, 17, 24, 33, 46; D12, 327, 329

Coifi *see* BEDE.

cremation *see* BURIAL RITES.

D

Dag ('day')
(1) According to the eddic poem VAFTHRÚDNISMÁL, echoed in the thirteenth century by the Icelander SNORRI STURLUSON, Dag was the son of one DELLING and the personification of day. (2) Dag is also found in Snorri's account as the name of a legendary king, one of the sons of Halfdan.

B12, 14, 23, 24, 28, 30, 35, 40, 50, 51, 56, 59, 73, 87, 90; C2, 5, 9, 17, 24, 33, 46, 48

Dag Högnason
According to the eddic poem HELGAKVIDA HUNDINGS-BANA II, a son of the warrior HÖGNI and brother of SIGRÚN and BRAGI. After the hero HELGI kills his father and brother at FREKASTEIN, Dag wreaks his revenge, despite the fact that Helgi has gone on to marry his sister:

Helgi and Sigrún married and had sons. Helgi did not live to grow old. Dag, son of Högni, sacrificed to ODIN for help in avenging his father. Odin lent Dag his spear; Dag met Helgi, his sister's husband, at a place called Fjöturlund: he ran Helgi through with his spear. Helgi died there. Dag rode to the fells, and told Sigrún the news:

'Sister, I am sorry for what I must tell you,
I never meant to make you cry.
This morning at Fjöturlund there fell
the best of warriors in the world,
who put his heel on the necks of kings.'

B12, 30, 56, 73, 87, 90; C2, 17, 24, 33, 46

Dáin ('dead')
(1) According to the eddic poem HÁVAMÁL, an elf, or perhaps a kind of dwarf, with particular proficiency in RUNES. (2) The thirteenth-century Icelander SNORRI STURLUSON gives the name Dáin to one of the four stags that wander through the branches of the world-tree YGGDRASIL, grazing on its foliage.

B12, 14, 23, 24, 28, 30, 35, 40, 50, 56, 59, 73, 87, 90; C2, 5, 9, 17, 24, 33, 46, 48

Dáinsleif ('Dáin's heirloom')
According to the thirteenth-century Icelander SNORRI STURLUSON, the sword that the warrior HÖGNI drew in his battle against HEDIN HJARRANDASON, so precipitating the everlasting battle known as the HJADNINGAVÍG. The sword was drawn just before Hedin made Högni an offer of compensation for the abduction of his daughter HILD, but Högni answered:

'You have made this offer too late, for now I have drawn Dáinsleif, which the dwarfs made, which must be the death of some man every time it is unsheathed, and whose stroke never fails, and a wound from whose blow never heals.'

B24, 28, 35, 40, 50; C5, 9, 48

Dan
Along with one Danp, a splendid warrior whose heroic activities are commended as examples to the young prince Konung by a crow in a tree, according to the eddic poem RÍGSTHULA.

B12, 30, 56, 73, 87, 90; C2, 17, 24, 33, 46

Danp *see* DAN.

dark elves *see* BLACK ELVES.

Darradarljód ('pennant-song'?, 'song of Dörrud'?)
A poem, found only in NJÁLS SAGA, that celebrates the victory of a 'young king' over the Irish. The prose narrative of the saga describes the victory as that of Sigtrygg silkiskegg at Clontarf in 1014, but the identification is far from certain, and other possibilities have been suggested. The chief figures in the poem are depicted as VALKYRIES, and the battle is metaphorically portrayed as their weaving. As the prose text has it:

The heads of men were used instead of weights, and men's entrails instead of the warp and the woof; a sword ['spears' in the poem] was the treadle and an arrow the batten.

De falsis deis

In the saga an otherwise unattested character called Dorrud hears the Valkyries' song; more likely the KENNING *vefr darradar*, repeated as a refrain in three of the stanzas, refers to the 'weaving of the pennant(s)' that takes place on the battlefield as armies clash.

B76; C26; D263

De falsis deis *see* ÆLFRIC; WULFSTAN.

Delling ('shining one')

According to the eddic poem VAFTHRÚDNISMÁL, the father of DAG, the personified day. Elsewhere in the POETIC EDDA, in HÁVAMÁL, it is said that spells were recited by the dwarf Thjódrœrir, 'in front of Delling's doors'.

B12, 30, 51, 56, 73, 87, 90; C2, 17, 24, 33, 46

díar (Old Irish: 'gods')

The earliest recorded mention of the term *díar* is in a skaldic verse ascribed to the tenth-century Icelandic skald KORMÁK ÖGMUNDARSON, who describes the MEAD OF POETRY with a KENNING, *día fjǫrðr* ('fjord of gods'). The word appears to have derived from the Old Irish term *día* ('god') and may well have been introduced into Norse by Kormák himself, whose mother (if we credit the saga that circulated about him) was Irish, as indeed was his name. In the thirteenth century the Icelander SNORRI STURLUSON, who certainly knew and quoted the relevant stanza of Kormák's verse, used the term *díar* in YNGLINGA SAGA to describe the twelve priests, who, according to his euhemeristic analysis (*see* EUHEMERISM), ruled in ÁSGARD with ODIN.

B39, 45, 62, 75, 83, 87; C16, 18

Digraldi *see* RÍGSTHULA.

dísablót ('sacrifice to the *dísir*')

Evidently a SACRIFICE to the supernatural female figures known as the DÍSIR, first witnessed in the ninth-century poem YNGLINGATAL by THJÓDÓLF OF HVÍN. The much later (thirteenth-century?) evidence of EGILS SAGA and VÍGA-GLÚMS SAGA adds little except that the sacrifice appears to have taken place at the end of autumn or beginning of winter. A tale recorded in the late fourteenth-century manuscript FLATEYJARBÓK recalls how an eighteen-year-old Icelander named Thidrandi was apparently killed by *dísir* at a festival around the 'winter-nights'. Nine black-clad female riders, who are carrying swords, set upon and slay him as nine white-clad female riders struggle against them. The conflict between the various factions of supernatural women is held to mark the coming conversion to

Christianity. The thirteenth-century YNGLINGA SAGA similarly records how the legendary Swedish king ADILS perished at a *disablót* when he was thrown from his horse and his brains were dashed out.

B47, 58, 60, 81, 82, 85; C10, 30, 37

dísir ('goddesses')

The *dísir* are a group of supernatural female figures, whose precise attributes are unclear. Unlike VALKYRIES (who are associated with battle), NORNS (who are associated with destiny) or FYLGJUR (who are also associated with personal destiny), the *dísir* seem to have no definite role and occasionally appear to share the attributes of other female supernatural beings. Place-name evidence appears to suggest that the *dísir* were linked with fertility, as does one of the titles of the goddess FREYJA, who was known as *Vanadís* ('*dís* of the VANIR'), and there seems to have been a sacrificial festival known as DÍSABLÓT that, according to the thirteenth-century evidence of two Icelandic sagas (EGILS SAGA and VÍGA-GLÚMS SAGA), was celebrated during the autumn. Elsewhere, however, the *dísir* appear to be associated with the dead. In the eddic poem GUDRÚNARKVIDA I, Valkyries are described as 'the *dísir* of ODIN', and in the eddic poem ATLAMÁL, the *dísir* are simply called 'dead women'.

The situation is complicated still further by the fact that the simple noun *dís* ('lady', 'woman'; cf. Old English *ides*, Old High German *itis*, Old Saxon *idis*) is used in several KENNINGS, and the term therefore appears in descriptions and allusions to many of the female deities or ÁSYNJUR as well as to other female figures.

B12, 20, 30, 47, 56, 58, 73, 81, 82, 87, 90; C2, 10, 17, 24, 30, 33, 34, 37, 46; D198, 213, 561, 584

divination

The first-century Roman historian TACITUS gives a detailed account of the divinatory practices of the continental Germanic tribes:

> They retain the highest opinion for omens and the casting of lots. Their method of casting lots is always identical: they cut off a branch of a nut-bearing tree and cut it into strips, which they inscribe with various marks and cast entirely at random onto a white cloth. Then the public priest, if the deliberation is public, or the head of the family, if it is private, offers up a prayer to the gods and, gazing heavenwards, picks up three strips one at a time and interprets their meaning from the inscribed signs. If the lots proscribe any endeavour, there is no consultation that day on the matter; if they permit it, further confirmation is required by taking auspices. Although the normal method of

seeking indications from the calls and flight of birds is known among the Germans, they also have their own technique of trying to find omens and warning from horses. These horses are kept at the public expense in the aforementioned sacred woods and groves: they are pure white and unspoiled by any labour in man's service. The priest and the king, or the head of the people, yoke them to a sacred chariot and walk alongside, paying attention to their neighing and snorts. No kind of omen inspires greater faith, not only among the commoners, but even among the nobility and priests, who consider themselves merely servants of the gods, while the horses are privy to the counsels of the gods. There is still another sort of divination used to predict the outcome of serious wars. They devise a way of taking a prisoner from the tribe against which they are fighting, and match him against their own champion, while each of them is armed with his national weapons; the victory of one or the other is considered to predict the outcome of the war.

The description of the casting of inscribed wooden lots has given rise to speculation about the use of RUNES in such a manner, and indeed there are descriptions of runes being used in a prognostic fashion in some of the late legendary sagas. The mention of horses being used in a similar fashion is unsupported by the later written record, although there is certainly evidence that a number of taboos and cult practices centred on specific horses. In the late thirteenth-century Icelandic HRAFNKELS SAGA FREYSGODA, for example, Hrafnkel, who is a priest of the god FREY, has a horse dedicated to the god which he forbids anyone to ride. At the other end of the chronological spectrum, Tacitus includes accounts of the elaborate divinatory practices attributed to THORBJÖRG LÍTILVÖLVA in EIRÍKS SAGA RAUDA, and there is the hint in the eddic poem HYMISKVIDA that a particular kind of twig used at heathen SACRIFICES, the HLAUTTEIN, could also be used for the purposes of divination.

B2, 37, 38; C27, 29, 34, 42; D44, 75

Dómaldi

According to the ninth-century account of the poet THJÓDÓLF OF HVÍN, later elaborated by the thirteenth-century Icelander SNORRI STURLUSON, Dómaldi was an early king of the Swedish royal line of the YNGLINGS, who ruled at a time of famine and whom his own people chose to SACRIFICE in the hope of an improvement in harvests. Similar sacrifices of rulers are recorded of the Burgundians from the fourth century on. The Latin *Historia Norvegiae* adds the rather puzzling detail that Dómaldi was sacrificed by hanging to Ceres (presumably here representing the goddess FREYJA); while

Freyja is clearly linked with fertility, hanging is more normally associated with the god ODIN.

B1; C22, 23; D337

dragon

Although widely attested in art, most notably in the finely carved figureheads that adorned Viking ships, relatively few dragons are found in the literary sources, which, moreover disagree profoundly about such basic matters as the size and physical features of a dragon. Part of the confusion is one of nomenclature. The usual Norse word for a dragon, *dreki*, is often conflated in the sources with another word, *ormr* (literally 'worm'), and Norse 'dragons' often appear to be little more than mighty serpents. Flying dragons are mentioned in several sagas, but more usually the dragon is wingless and crawls. The most celebrated dragons of northern myth and legend are undoubtedly that slain by SIGURD (or, according to the Old English poem, BEOWULF, SIGEMUND, who would appear to equate better with Sigurd's father, SIGMUND; the NIBELUNGENLIED names the dragon-slayer differently again as Sifrit), and that slain by Beowulf himself. Sigurd's dragon (and its equivalents in *Beowulf* and the *Nibelungenlied*), named as FÁFNIR in Norse sources, is guardian to a fabulous hoard of treasure, as is Beowulf's, and the association of dragons and wealth is evidently ancient. It may also be relevant in this context to note that dragon-slaying is often attributed to the heroes of the legendary FORNALDARSÖGUR, and that the thirteenth-

dragon *Detail of the Rasmundsberget runestone from Jäder, Södermanland, Sweden, depicting the hero Sigurd piercing the belly of Fáfnir the dragon.*

century Icelander SNORRI STURLUSON also attributes the killing of a mighty dragon to the god THOR, in what is probably a euhemerized allusion to Thor's slaying of the MIDGARD-SERPENT during the apocalyptic events of RAGNARÖK.

B12, 14, 23, 24, 28, 30, 35, 40, 50, 56, 59, 73, 87, 90; C2, 5, 9, 14, 17, 24, 33, 46, 48; D46, 97, 293, 416, 459, 571

draugar ('ghosts'; 'walking dead')

The term 'ghost' is commonly used to translate the Icelandic word *draugr* (plural *draugar*), although the *draugr* is a much more physically robust and substantial figure, often inhabiting treasure-filled BURIAL MOUNDS – an alternative name for a *draugr* is *haugbúi* ('mound-dweller') – and able to inflict serious injury on property and people alike. Many *draugar* are simply dead pagans, whose corpses walk. Typical Icelandic examples are the heathen shepherd Glám in the early fourteenth-century GRETTIS SAGA ÁDMUNDARSONAR, whose eyes shine with a baleful light (and who is often compared with the monstrous figure of GRENDEL in the Old English poem BEOWULF), or Thorólf Crooked-Foot in the mid-thirteenth-century EYRBYGGJA SAGA, whose corpse, 'swollen to the size of an ox and as black as Hell', resists being transported to sacred ground for burial. In other respects the undead *draugar* are treated like any living pests; in EYRBYGGJA SAGA they are a rather sad band of drowned men who simply occupy their former dwelling, causing distress to their relatives but no real damage apart from their dripping clothes, and who have to be legally evicted. The only sure way to dispose of a *draugr* is decapitation, sometimes followed by the placing of the severed head on the corpse's buttocks, and cremation.

In the earliest skaldic poetry, including some that can be attributed to BRAGI Boddason in the ninth century, the term *draugr* is used exclusively of living pagan warriors, but this usage quickly dies out, and it may well be that after the introduction of Christianity these dead pagans in their barrows were demonized and transformed in popular myth into the dread figures who still haunt Iceland to this day.

B39, 41, 45, 62, 77, 83, 87; C12, 16, 39; D65, 83, 330, 415

draugr see DRAUGAR.

Draupnir ('the dripper')

(1) A fabulous gold arm-ring, from which eight equally heavy rings drip every ninth night, made, according to the thirteenth-century Icelander SNORRI STURLUSON, by the dwarfs BROKK and EITRI for the god ODIN at the same time as they forged other wondrous gifts for FREY and THOR. Odin placed Draupnir on his son

BALDR's funeral pyre, and it was returned by him to his father as a keepsake from HEL. In other sources similarly magical gold rings are mentioned but not named. A ring with identical properties appears in the eddic poem SKÍRNISMÁL, while the early thirteenth-century Danish writer SAXO GRAMMATICUS describes a gold ring that increased its owner's wealth in his own retelling of the tale of Baldr's death. Not surprisingly, therefore, Draupnir features in large numbers of poetic periphrases or KENNINGS for gold in skaldic verse.

(2) According to the catalogue in the eddic poem VÖLUSPÁ, Draupnir is also the name of a dwarf.

B12, 14, 23, 24, 28, 30, 35, 39, 40, 50, 56, 59, 62, 64, 73, 83, 87, 90; C2, 5, 7–9, 13, 16, 17, 24, 33, 46, 48

Dreng see RÍGSTHULA.

Drífa see FORNJÓT.

Dröfn ('foaming sea')

(1) According to the thirteenth-century account of the Icelander SNORRI STURLUSON, one of the daughters of the sea-god ÆGIR. In other lists she is replaced by Bara. (2) Dröfn appears in the name-lists or THULUR as the name of a giantess.

B24, 28, 35, 40, 50; C5, 9, 48

Drómi ('fetter')

According to the thirteenth-century Icelander SNORRI STURLUSON, the second of the fetters with which the ÆSIR attempt to bind the wolf FENRIR. Like its predecessor, LEYDING, Drómi is shattered, leading the Æsir to send SKÍRNIR, the servant of the god FREY, down to the BLACK ELVES to obtain the magical fetter GLEIPNIR, which eventually restrains the wolf.

B24, 28, 35, 40, 50; C5, 9, 48

Drösul ('horse')

According to a verse from KÁLFSVÍSA quoted by the thirteenth-century Icelander SNORRI STURLUSON, the horse belonging to the legendary hero DAG.

B24, 28, 35, 40, 50; C5, 9, 48

Drött see RÍGSTHULA.

Drumb, Drumba see RÍGSTHULA.

Dúfa ('dipping')

(1) According to the thirteenth-century account of the Icelander SNORRI STURLUSON, one of the daughters of the sea-giant ÆGIR. (2) The name also appears in the name-lists or THULUR as that of a giantess.

B24, 28, 35, 40, 50; C5, 9, 48

Dúneyr *see* YGGDRASIL.

Durathrór *see* YGGDRASIL.

Dvalar An alternative form of DVALIN.

Dvalin ('dawdler')
(1) A dwarf, according to the catalogue in the eddic poem VÖLUSPÁ, whose name also occurs in a number of other poems of the POETIC EDDA. (2) The thirteenth-century Icelander SNORRI STURLUSON gives the name Dvalin to one of the four stags who wander through the branches of the world-tree, YGGDRASIL, grazing on the foliage, although in another list the alternative form Dvalar is given.

B12, 14, 23, 24, 28, 30, 35, 40, 50, 56, 59, 73, 87, 90; C2, 5, 9, 17, 24, 33, 46, 48

dwarfs
Some of the primary material for assessing the attributes and characteristics of dwarfs is to be gleaned from the lists of their names, which occur in several sources and which are collected in Appendix B. Curiously, the notion of their small stature is not supported by the earliest sources, and few dwarf-names mention this characteristic. Much better attested are their wisdom and craftsmanship and their dwelling-place among the rocks and away from the light. Some dwarf-names – for example, BLÁIN, DÁIN, Náin and Nár – seem to speak for some association with the dead, although it may be that rather the names refer to the ghastly pallor induced by their subterranean abodes.

Accounts differ about the origin of the dwarfs. The eddic poem VÖLUSPÁ describes the dwarfs as having sprung from the blood of the primordial giant YMIR and from the bones of the giant Bláin, while the thirteenth-century Icelander SNORRI STURLUSON (who actually quotes the relevant passage from *Völuspá*) tells how:

> The dwarfs had first acquired form and life in the flesh of Ymir and were at that time maggots, but through a decision of the ÆSIR they acquired consciousness and wit and had the appearance of men, although they live in the ground and in rocks.

Elsewhere, Snorri appears to attribute to the shadowy figures known as BLACK ELVES many of the same characteristics generally associated with dwarfs, and it may well be that black elves and dwarfs are to be identified.

B24, 28, 35, 40, 50; C5, 9, 48; D193, 294, 338, 391, 392, 399, 492, 591

E

edda *see* RÍGSTHULA; SNORRA EDDA.

Eggthér ('edge-servant')
According to the eddic poem VÖLUSPÁ, the guardian of the giantess who lives in JÁRNVID and tends the wolf FENRIR. At RAGNARÖK, when the mighty conflict between the ÆSIR and their enemies will take place, he is described as sitting on a mound (perhaps a BURIAL MOUND), playing his harp with glee. The scene has a curious echo in the description of Gunnar, one of the heroes of the Icelandic NJÁLS SAGA, who is seen singing joyfully on top of his own burial mound. The formal parallel occasionally noted between Eggthér's name and that of Beowulf's father, Ecgtheow, as depicted in the Old English poem BEOWULF, is almost certainly a red herring.

B12, 30, 56, 59, 73, 76, 87, 90; C2, 17, 20, 24, 33, 46; D492

Egil
(1) According to the prose introduction to the eddic poem VÖLUNDARKVIDA, one of the brothers of the mighty smith VÖLUND and the husband of the Valkyrie ÖLRÚN. Other sources, notably the legendary THIDREKS SAGA, name him as an excellent archer, and it seems possible that one of the scenes on the eighth-century Franks Casket illustrates this. The RUNES on the casket clearly say 'æ g i l i', which some interpret as Egil; others, however, have suggested that the figure depicted is none other than Achilles.

(2) According to the eddic poem HYMISKVIDA, Egil is the name of the character who took care of the god THOR's goats while he was on his expedition to visit the giant HYMIR.

B8, 12, 30, 31, 42, 56, 71, 73, 84, 87, 90; C2, 13, 15, 17, 21, 24, 25, 33, 44, 36; D610

Egils saga Skalla-Grímssonar
A thirteenth-century Icelandic saga, sometimes held to have been composed by SNORRI STURLUSON, which gives an account of the life of the great tenth-century poet, Egil Skallagrímsson. Some of the finest and best wrought skaldic verse is preserved in the saga, which on one level chronicles the progressive deterioration of

relations between Egil and his god, ODIN, culminating in the trauma of Egil's loss of his own sons, movingly described in one of his greatest poems, *Sonatorrek* ('grievous loss of sons'). Egil himself is described as having descended from a line of shape-changers and WEREWOLVES, and his own grim and recalcitrant personality is implicitly ascribed to his ancestry, the more so when he battles against difficult or superhuman foes, especially BERSERKS, all of whom he overcomes by his own outstanding power.

B39, 45, 58, 62, 82, 83, 87; C10, 16; D30, 37, 98, 199, 218, 247, 432, 522, 542

Eikintjasna *see* RÍGSTHULA.

Eikthyrnir ('oak-thorny')
According to the eddic poem GRÍMNISMÁL, the hart that stands on top of the god ODIN's mighty hall VALHALL, and from whose dripping horns all rivers flow:

> Eikthyrnir the hart is called, standing on Herjafödr's
>   [Odin's] hall,
> who bites off LÆRAD's limbs;
> from his horns there drips into HVERGELMIR
> the source from which all rivers run.

It is intriguing to note that the vast Danish hall in which the main events of the first part of the Old English poem BEOWULF are set is called HEOROT ('hart'), ostensibly a reference to its wide gables.

B12, 14, 23, 24, 28, 30, 35, 40, 50, 56, 59, 73, 87, 90; C2, 5, 9, 17, 24, 33, 46, 48; D425

Eikthyrnir Detail from a late tenth-century carved cross from Gosforth, Cumbria, England, apparently depicting the stag Eikthyrnir atop a rather unconvincing depiction of the world-tree, Yggdrasil, being pestered by the squirrel Ratatosk, whilst the god Odin looks on. At the base of the cross lies the bound god Loki.

Eilíf Godrúnarson
A poet belonging to the court of the great Norwegian Jarl, Hákon Sigurdarson (who died around 995). All his extant work has been preserved through its quotation by the thirteenth-century Icelander SNORRI STURLUSON to illustrate points of skaldic diction or metre. Eilíf's most famous poem is the fiercely challenging THÓRSDRÁPA, which deals with the expedition of the god THOR to the home of the giant GEIRRÖD.

B24, 28, 35, 39, 40, 45, 50, 62, 83, 87; C5, 9, 16, 48; D172, 291, 609

Ein(d)ridi ('lone rider')
(1) One of the many names for the god THOR. (2) A name used by the thirteenth-century Icelander SNORRI STURLUSON in his account (*see* EUHEMERISM) of the ÆSIR to designate one of the descendants of TROR, a Trojan hero he equates with Thor.

B24, 28, 35, 40, 50; C5, 9, 48

einherjar ('lone fighters')
The dead warriors who inhabit the mighty hall VALHALL and who pass their time in feasting and continual fighting, as they wait for the final battle at RAGNARÖK, when they will turn out to fight on behalf of the ÆSIR against the gods' foes. They feast from the flesh of the ever-replenished boar SÆHRÍMNIR and drink mead from the udders of the goat HEIDRÚN, served to them by VALKYRIES. The notion that those *einherjar* who are wounded in their practice-battles are revived to fight the next day can be paralleled in the legend of the HJADNINGAVÍG, while other features of the *einherjar* can be matched elsewhere. In his first-century GERMANIA, TACITUS describes a fearsome tribe called the Harii (a name that some have suggested as related to that of the *einherjar*), who fight as a 'ghostly army':

> As for the Harii, quite apart from their strength, which exceeds that of the other tribes I have just listed, they pander to their innate savagery by skill and timing: with black shields and painted bodies, they choose dark nights to fight, and by means of the terror and shadow of a ghostly army they cause panic, since no enemy can bear a sight so unexpected and hellish; in every battle the eyes are the first to be conquered.

B2, 24, 28, 35, 40, 50; C5, 9, 29, 48

Eir ('help', 'mercy')
The name carried by a range of female figures, including the goddess or ÁSYNJA who is, according to the thirteenth-century Icelander SNORRI STURLUSON, most associated with healing, a VALKYRIE, and, according to the eddic poem FJÖLSVINNSMÁL, one of the servants of the giantess MENGLÖD. While the etymology of the

name would seem to fit the first and third of these roles most effectively, it should be remembered that among the attributes of the Valkyries was the power to waken the dead.

B12, 14, 23, 24, 28, 30, 35, 40, 50, 56, 59, 73, 87, 90; C2, 5, 9, 17, 24, 33, 46, 48

Eiríksmál ('the lay of Eirík')

A poem ostensibly composed on the death of Eirík Bloodaxe, who perished in battle in England in 954, of which a single stanza is cited by the thirteenth-century Icelander SNORRI STURLUSON. The whole poem (which even so may not be complete) is preserved in the manuscript now known as Fagrskinna, parts of which seem to date to the mid-thirteenth century. Despite the fact that Eirík was baptized a Christian, the poem is set in the pagan hall of the dead, VALHALL, and begins with the god ODIN discussing with the god BRAGI and the hero SIGMUND the imminent arrival of the dead king Eirík. Sigmund asks why Odin did not grant Eirík the victory, and his reply appears to hint at the imminence of the final battle at RAGNARÖK and the need for good men to serve in the army of EINHERJAR.

B39, 45, 62, 83, 87; D254, 347

Eiríks saga rauda

An Icelandic saga composed in the late thirteenth century and providing details of the early settlement in Greenland, together with an account of the exploration further west to Vinland, on the North American continent. Both topics are also covered in the earlier *Grœnlendinga saga*, which the author of *Eiríks saga* appears to have known. *Eiríks saga* contains a number of memorable set-piece scenes, notably a vivid description of the activities of a wandering witch and prophetess, THORBJÖRG LÍTILVÖLVA.

B38; C27

Eitil

According to the eddic poem ATLAKVIDA, one of the two sons of ATLI BUDLASON and GUDRÚN (the other is ERP ATLASON), murdered by his mother in retaliation for Atli's killing of her brothers GUNNAR and HÖGNI GJÚKASON. Both boys are also named elsewhere in the POETIC EDDA in HAMDISMÁL.

B12, 23, 30, 31, 56, 73, 87, 90; C2, 17, 24, 33, 46

Eitri ('poisonous')

According to the thirteenth-century Icelander SNORRI STURLUSON, a dwarf, brother of BROKK and the smith who forged three great gifts for the ÆSIR. These gifts went to the three most senior of the gods: GULLINBORSTI, the golden boar, to FREY; DRAUPNIR,

the golden ring, to ODIN; and MJÖLLNIR, the mighty hammer, to THOR.

B24, 28, 35, 40, 50; C5, 9, 48

Ekin *see* HVERGELMIR.

Elder Edda *see* POETIC EDDA.

Eldhrímnir ('fire-sooty')

According to the eddic poem GRÍMNISMÁL, the vast pot in which the cook ANDHRÍMNIR boils the great boar SÆHRÍMNIR, so that it can be consumed every night in the feasting in VALHALL by the hungry warriors of the EINHERJAR.

B12, 14, 23, 24, 28, 30, 35, 40, 50, 56, 59, 73, 87, 90; C2, 5, 9, 17, 24, 33, 46, 48

Eldir ('fire-stoker')

According to both the eddic poem LOKASENNA and the thirteenth-century Icelander SNORRI STURLUSON, one of the two servants of the sea-giant ÆGIR – the other is FIMAFENG – and the one who attempts to prevent the mischievous LOKI from entering the hall to abuse the feasting ÆSIR.

B12, 14, 23, 24, 28, 30, 35, 40, 50, 56, 59, 73, 87, 90; C2, 5, 9, 17, 24, 33, 46, 48

Éliúdnir ('rain-damp')

According to the thirteenth-century Icelander SNORRI STURLUSON, the livid hall in which HEL, the guardian of the dead, resides. As such, Éliúdnir functions as a kind of unheroic alternative to VALHALL and may perhaps be compared with the livid hall described elsewhere by Snorri, drawing on a description in the eddic poem VÖLUSPÁ:

> At NÁSTRANDIR there stands a mighty and evil hall, with its doors facing north. It is entirely woven from the spines of snakes, like a house with a wattle roof, and the heads of snakes face in, spitting venom, so that rivers of poison flow along the hall, in which oath-breakers and murderers wade.

B12, 14, 23, 24, 28, 30, 35, 40, 50, 56, 59, 73, 87, 90; C2, 5, 9, 17, 24, 33, 46, 48

Élivágar ('storm-waves')

According to the thirteenth-century Icelander SNORRI STURLUSON, partly drawing on details to be found in the eddic poems GRÍMNISMÁL and VAFTHRÚDNISMÁL, Élivágar is the collective name given to the eleven churning streams that flowed from the spring HVERGELMIR into the primordial void of GINNUNGAGAP, from whose coagulation grew the first giant, YMIR. Elsewhere, however, Snorri appears to conceive of Élivágar as a single stream separating JÖTUNHEIM from MIDGARD, and this also seems to be the sense of the eddic poem HYMISKVIDA, which describes the giant HYMIR as living to the east of Élivágar, on the edge of heaven.

B12, 14, 23, 24, 28, 30, 35, 40, 50, 51, 56, 59, 73, 87, 90; C2, 5, 9, 17, 24, 33, 46, 48; D238

Elli ('old age')

According to a description of the exploits of the god THOR at the court of the giant ÚTGARDALOKI, which is recounted only by the thirteenth-century Icelander SNORRI STURLUSON, Elli is an aged crone, whom Útgardaloki calls his wet-nurse and whom the increasingly humiliated Thor is invited to wrestle. Thor cannot throw her, and the contest is called off when she brings Thor to his knees. When a much chastened Thor has departed from Útgardaloki's house of illusions, it is revealed that Elli is the personification of old age, which no one can conquer and which can bring even the strongest to their knees.

B24, 28, 35, 40, 50; C5, 9, 48

elves

Norse myth and legend distinguish a number of varieties of elves, both helpful and harmful, fair and ugly, of which the broadest distinctions to be drawn are between the LIGHT ELVES and the BLACK ELVES (who may simply be DWARFS). Such essential ambiguity of nature is echoed in the evidence for elves from Anglo-Saxon England, where, for example, the positive nature of elves is underlined by their frequent occurrence in personal names (including that of King Alfred) or in the description of the biblical character of Judith as an 'elf-bright lady', while several charms are intended to ward off illness or ill-luck in the shape of 'elf-shot'.

B24, 28, 35, 40, 50; C5, 9, 48; D392, 578

Embla ('elm'?, 'vine'?)

According to the eddic poem VÖLUSPÁ, Embla was the name of the first woman, created alongside her male counterpart, ASK, from two tree trunks, which the god ODIN and two companions, HŒNIR and LODUR, found by the shore of the circling sea. The thirteenth-century Icelander SNORRI STURLUSON repeats the tale but names as Odin's companions his brothers, VILI and VÉ. Unlike Ask, which seems clearly to derive from the word for an 'ash tree', the etymology of Embla is obscure. Some see it as a distant form of the word for 'elm', while others have pointed out a similarity to the Greek word for 'vine' (ἄμπελος), a soft and inflammable wood, often used as a base into which a pointed stick of some harder wood such as ash is rubbed to produce fire. The psycho-sexual appeal of the latter interpretation will be clear.

B12, 14, 23, 24, 28, 30, 35, 40, 50, 56, 59, 73, 87, 90; C2, 5, 9, 17, 24, 33, 46, 48

Eostra

According to BEDE, writing in the early eighth century, the Anglo-Saxon name for April was Eosturmonath ('Eostra-month'), and many commentators have suggested on this basis the existence of a female deity with a festival during that month whose name was usurped to give that of the Christian festival of Easter.

B15; C41

eoten (Old English: 'eater?')

An Old English generic name for a GIANT, the Norse equivalent of which is JÖTUN. Both words appear to derive from the verb 'to eat', which may suggest that some giants (eotenas) at least, were associated with acts of devouring, presumably mankind. Certainly the monstrous GRENDEL, whose fearsome cannibalism is celebrated in the Old English poem BEOWULF and who is described as an eoten, would fit this bill.

B4; C44

Ermanaric An alternative name for JÖRMUNREKK.

Erna see RÍGSTHULA.

Erp Atlason

According to the eddic poem ATLAKVIDA, one of the two sons of ATLI BUDLASON and GUDRÚN – the other is EITIL – murdered by their mother in retaliation for Atli's killing of GUNNAR and HÖGNI GJÚKASON. As Gudrún gleefully reports to Atli, after she has served up their sons for his supper:

'Never again will you call to your knee
Erp or Eitil, an ale-merry pair;
never again will you see in the platform's midst
those givers of gold putting shafts to spears,
trimming manes, or trotting mounts.'

Both boys are also named elsewhere in the POETIC EDDA in HAMDISMÁL.

B12, 20, 30, 31, 56, 73, 87, 90; C2, 17, 24, 33, 46

Erp Jónakrsson

A legendary figure, son of King JÓNAK and half-brother of the heroes HAMDIR and SÖRLI, whom Jónak produced through his later marriage to GUDRÚN, the widow of the hero SIGURD. When Gudrún incites Hamdir and Sörli to avenge their half-sister SVANHILD, her only child by Sigurd, as is described in the eddic poems GUDRÚNARHVÖT and HAMDISMÁL, Erp attempts to join them, but in their folly they misconstrue his offer of help as insolence and kill him. Only later do they realize their folly, as they are overborne by

JÖRMUNREKK's men for want of an extra blade to finish off the maimed king.

B12, 30, 56, 73, 87, 90; C2, 17, 24, 33, 46

euhemerism

A system, named after the Greek philosopher Euhemeros of Messene, that seeks to explain gods and myths in terms of history. According to this notion, the great figures of the historical past come to be venerated by their descendants and, as the distance between the subjects and their worshippers increases, become progressively elevated to the status of gods. Such a system was used effectively by Christian authorities to downgrade pagan deities. Because Christianity was, it was argued, the one true religion, it naturally followed that worshippers of pagan deities were either simply mistaken or perversely deluded.

Many of the medieval authorities on whom we rely for our accounts of the myths and legends of the Germanic and Scandinavian pagan past offered euhemerized accounts, sometimes alongside more conventional narratives. So, for example, the Anglo-Saxon WULFSTAN, in his version of the polemical tract *De falsis deis* ('On False Gods'), traces the development of pagan belief to the fall of the Tower of Babel and the dispersal of nations through the world. First, he claims, the benighted wanderers adopted a form of animism:

> Through the devil's teaching they took it for wisdom to worship as gods the sun and the moon, because of their shining brightness, and through the devil's teaching they at last offered them sacrifices, and abandoned their Lord, who had shaped and created them. Some people also said of the shining stars, that they were gods, and they began to worship them eagerly, and some people also believed in fire for its sudden burning, some again in water, and some believed in the earth, because she feeds all things.

Only at a later stage, he continues, did the pagans begin to worship other gods in human form:

> But the heathens did not want to be restricted to as few gods as they had previously, but they began to worship various giants and fierce worldly men, who had become mighty in the pursuits of the world, and were awe-inspiring while they lived and foully followed their own desires.

Wulfstan goes on to name Saturn, Jove, Juno, Minerva, Venus and Mercury, whom he identifies with the Germanic god ODIN, adding that Odin's son THOR is also widely venerated among the contemporary pagan Danes.

A similar euhemerized scheme is offered by the thirteenth-century Icelander SNORRI STURLUSON in his YNGLINGA SAGA as he seeks to explain the origins of the ÆSIR and their dwelling of ÁSGARD:

> The land to the east of the Tanakvísl in Asia was called Ásaland, or Ásaheim, and the main city of that land was called Ásgard. In that city there was a chief called Odin, and it was a main site of sacrifice. It was the custom there that twelve temple priests should both direct the sacrifices, and pass judgement on the people. They were called *diar* ('gods') or *dróttnir* ('lords'), and all folk served and obeyed them. Odin was a mighty and much travelled warrior, who conquered many kingdoms and was so successful that in every battle the victory was his. When he sent his men into battle or off on any expedition, it was his habit first to lay his hand upon their heads and call down a blessing on them, and then they believed that their undertaking would succeed. Whenever they were in danger on land or sea, his people used to call on his name; and they reckoned that they always obtained comfort and assistance from it, for wherever he was, they thought help was at hand. Often he travelled so far that he spent many seasons on his travels.

An equally elaborate euhemerized account is offered by the early thirteenth-century Danish writer SAXO GRAMMATICUS:

> At that time there was a man named Odin, who was believed throughout Europe, albeit falsely, to be a god. He was accustomed to stay more frequently than anywhere at UPPSALA, deigning to stay there more constantly more because of the sloth of the locals than because of the beauty of the landscape. The kings of the north, keen to venerate his godhead with more zealous worship, had made a golden statue of him, with its arms weighed down with heavy bracelets, and in order to demonstrate their devotion they sent it with the greatest piety to him in Byzantium. Pleased by his fame, Odin eagerly accepted the homage of the donors. His wife, FRIGG, who wanted to go about better adorned, called in smiths to strip the statue of its gold. Odin had them hanged, set the statue on a pedestal and, by a wondrous piece of craftsmanship, caused it to respond to the human touch with speech. Frigg, valuing the divine honours paid to her husband less than her own adornment, submitted to the lust of one of her own servants, and by his craft the statue was destroyed and the gold that had been set up for public worship went to serve her personal enjoyment. This woman, unworthy of a husband who had been made a god, was not perturbed about submitting to illicit sex, if she could enjoy more quickly what she wanted. Do I need to ask whether such a god deserved such a wife? Men's sense was once made foolish by this kind of gullibility. As a result, Odin, wounded by both of his wife's crimes, brooded equally about the injury to his statue and the damage to his bed. Afflicted by this double humiliation, he went into exile, filled with

an honest shame, reckoning that by doing so he would remove the slur of his disgrace. A certain MITHOTYN, a renowned sorcerer, was stirred by his departure, as if by a divine gift, and seized the opportunity to affect divinity for himself. His reputation for sorcery clouded the minds of the barbarians with a new superstition, and caused them to perform sacred rites in his name. He claimed that the wrath of the gods and the desecration of their divine power could not be assuaged by chaotic and confused sacrifices; he arranged that they should not be prayed to together but that separate sacrifices should be offered to each deity. When Odin returned, the other character no longer practised his sorcery, but went off to hide in Fyn, where he was attacked and killed by the inhabitants. His foulness was even evident after his death; anyone approaching his tomb quickly died, and his corpse gave off such a foul pestilence that he almost appeared to offer worse tokens of himself dead than alive, as if he would wreak revenge on his murderers. The inhabitants, oppressed by this wickedness, disinterred the body, decapitated it and impaled it through the chest with a sharp stake; that was how people solved the problem. When his wife's death had allowed him to regain his reputation, and he had mended, as it were, the bad name of his godhead, Odin came back from exile and forced all those who in his absence had assumed the symbols of divine rank to renounce them, as though they had been borrowed. He scattered the groups of sorcerers that had sprung up, like shadows before the advent of his holy brightness, and halted them with an order not only to give up their feigned sanctity, but also to leave the country, reckoning that those who had so blasphemously thrust themselves into heaven deserved to be driven from the earth.

A key factor linking all three accounts – by Snorri, Saxo and Wulfstan – is the air of learned Christian antiquarianism; each author is seeking to downgrade and ridicule the systems of belief they seek to portray, although it is worth noting that each is in some sense captivated by the vividness of the narratives they travesty, and each offers a valuable witness to the pagan beliefs and customs they attempt to suppress.

B64; C7, 8

exposure of children

The right of fathers to expose unwanted children was evidently so ingrained in Norse culture that even after the conversion of Iceland around the turn of the eleventh century the custom was apparently still sanctioned in private (along with eating horse meat) for a short time. The practice was purely social and needs to be distinguished from that of human SACRIFICE, which is also recorded.

A132

Eyjólf Hundingsson *see* HELGI SIGMUNDARSON HUNDINGSBANI.

Eylimi

(1) According to the legendary VÖLSUNGA SAGA, drawing mainly on verses from the eddic poems REGINSMÁL and GRÍPISSPÁ, a 'powerful and famous' king who was the father of HJÖRDÍS and GRÍPIR. After his daughter chose the hero SIGMUND as her husband, Eylimi fought and died alongside his new son-in-law in a battle against her disgruntled suitor, LYNGVI, and his brothers. (2) The eddic poem HELGAKVIDA HJÖRVARDSSONAR names another Eylimi as the father of a single daughter, the Valkyrie SVÁVA, who becomes the beloved of the hero HELGI HJÖRVARDSSON.

B12, 25, 30, 42, 56, 65, 68, 73, 79, 87, 90; C1 – 3, 6, 17, 24, 33, 46

Eymód

According to the legendary VÖLSUNGA SAGA, one of the noble characters who are said to accompany the heroes GUNNAR and HÖGNI GJÚKASON on their mission to the court of King HÁLF, to reconcile themselves with their sister, GUDRÚN, after the killing of her husband, the mighty SIGURD.

B25, 42, 65, 68, 79; C1, 6

Eyrbyggja saga

One of the major Icelandic sagas, probably composed around the middle of the thirteenth century and purporting to depict events between the years 843 and 1031. The author shows considerable antiquarian interest in supernatural elements in his narrative in general and in the conflict between paganism and Christianity in particular. The saga contains an elaborate description of a pagan TEMPLE, albeit one drawn directly from the equally late account of the thirteenth-century Icelander SNORRI STURLUSON, as well as several scenes featuring witchcraft, MAGIC and the specific kind of Icelandic ghosts known as DRAUGAR. The author evidently structured a good part of the narrative around the conversion of Iceland, and clear parallels are drawn between episodes that are held to occur before and after that central event.

B77; C39; D114, 359, 365, 444

Eyvind Finnsson skáldaspillir ('the plagiarist')

A tenth-century Norwegian skaldic poet, two of whose poems, HÁKONARMÁL (composed after the death of King Hákon gódi in 961) and HÁLEYGJATAL (composed after 985 and tracing the ancestry of Earl Hákon back to the gods), are freely cited by the thirteenth-century Icelander SNORRI STURLUSON in his works.

B39, 45, 62, 83, 87; C16; D305, 619

F

Fadir *see* RÍGSTHULA.

Fáfnir ('embracer')

In the eddic poems of the VÖLSUNG-cycle, Fáfnir is the son of HREIDMAR and the brother of REGIN and OTR. Other versions of the tale are found in the legendary VÖLSUNGA SAGA, as well as in the retelling by the thirteenth-century Icelander SNORRI STURLUSON. When Otr (in the shape of an otter) is killed by the malicious LOKI, who is at that point accompanying ODIN and HŒNIR on their travels, recompense is paid in the form of a fabulous hoard of treasure, which, naturally, Fáfnir and Regin want for themselves. After murdering their father, the two brothers fall out, and Fáfnir drives Regin away and retires with his ill-gotten gains to Gníta-heath, where he promptly turns into a dragon. Eventually Regin, who has become a smith, persuades the hero SIGURD, by now his foster-son, to kill Fáfnir, whose last moments and final conversation with Sigurd are recorded in the eddic poem FÁFNISMÁL.

B12, 14, 23–5, 28, 30, 35, 40, 42, 50, 56, 59, 65, 68, 73, 79, 87, 90; C1–3, 5, 6, 9, 17, 24, 33, 46, 48

Fáfnir *Detail of the Rasmundsberget runestone from Jäder, Södermanland, Sweden, depicting the mighty hero Sigurd roasting the dragon Fáfnir's heart.*

Fáfnismál ('the lay of Fáfnir')

An eddic poem with prose passages, which, alongside REGINSMÁL, gives the fullest account of the slaying of the dragon FÁFNIR by the hero SIGURD. Both poems, together with their accompanying prose, are found in the same section of the late thirteenth-century manuscript known as the CODEX REGIUS, and they are probably intended to be read together; only later paper manuscripts (and still later editors) split the texts. *Fáfnismál* is largely concerned with the killing itself and its immediate aftermath. Much of the first part of the poem is taken up with a conversation between the dying Fáfnir and his slayer, in which the dragon initially attempts to discover the identity of his killer. A prose passage explains Sigurd's coyness:

> Sigurd hid his name because in olden days it was believed that the words of a dying man had great power if he cursed his enemy by name.

Nonetheless, he quickly reveals his identity and lineage, and the two then engage in a curious set of exchanges, which is part wisdom contest, part fatherly advice. Just before dying, the dragon warns Sigurd of the bad faith of REGIN, Sigurd's foster-father and Fáfnir's own brother. Such a warning is the more ironic in that Fáfnir had himself defrauded Regin of the treasure after killing their father, HREIDMAR. Regin approaches, cuts out the heart of his brother and drinks his blood. He intends to eat the heart, which he asks Sigurd to cook. When Sigurd does so and burns his thumb on the hot blood while testing the flesh, he finds that he is able to understand the language of birds. No fewer than seven, twittering in the branches above, warn him of Regin's perfidy; so Sigurd slays him. The birds further advise him to collect the dragon's treasure and head for the court of King GJÚKI, where he will find a bride. They describe how a shield-maiden (or VALKYRIE) called SIGRDRÍFA sleeps an enchanted sleep on a mountain-top, fenced in by flame, and Sigurd heads off to claim his prize, in an episode depicted in SIGRDRÍFUMÁL, which immediately follows in the Codex Regius.

B12, 30, 56, 73, 87, 90; C2, 17, 24, 33, 46; D301, 436, 466

Falhófnir

Falhófnir *see* ÆSIR.

Fallanda Forad *see* HEL.

Farbauti ('sudden-striker')

A giant and the father of LOKI, according to poetic periphrases or KENNINGS in the skaldic verse of THJÓDÓLF OF HVÍN and ÚLF UGGASON. The thirteenth-century Icelander SNORRI STURLUSON names two further sons, BYLEIST and HELBLINDI, but the little that is known of these figures from elsewhere inspires caution. A kenning in the eddic poem VÖLUSPÁ appears to refer to Loki as 'Byleist's brother' (and is presumably Snorri's source), but in a list of names in the eddic poem GRÍMNISMÁL, which Snorri actually cites, the god ODIN refers to himself as Helblindi.

B12, 14, 23, 24, 28, 30, 35, 39, 40, 45, 50, 56, 59, 62, 73, 83, 87, 90; C2, 5, 9, 13, 16, 17, 24, 33, 46, 48

Feima *see* RÍGSTHULA.

Fenja ('fen-dweller')

One of two prescient giantesses – the other is Menja – who, according to the eddic poem GROTTASÖNGR, works in a mill for the legendary King FRÓDI, milling gold. Her name appears frequently in KENNINGS for gold as well as (more surprisingly) a poetic term for 'arrow'.

B12, 30, 56, 73, 87, 90; C2, 17, 24, 33, 46

Fenrir ('fen-dweller')

The mighty wolf – hence the alternative name Fenrisúlf ('Fenrir's wolf') – that LOKI sired on the giantess ANGRBODA and therefore the brother of Loki's other monstrous offspring, the MIDGARD-SERPENT and HEL. According to the thirteenth-century Icelander SNORRI STURLUSON, the ÆSIR observed the growing size and strength of the young Fenrir with some horror, the more so when successive attempts to bind the wolf with the fetters LEYDING and DRÓMI proved futile. Eventually, the dwarfs were required to make a magically light and supple fetter called GLEIPNIR, which Fenrir viewed with (as it turned out) justifiable suspicion, refusing to be bound in it unless one of the Æsir should place their right hand in his mouth as a surety. Only TÝR was brave enough to do so. Snorri memorably describes the glee of the Æsir on discovering that Gleipnir was strong enough to contain Fenrir:

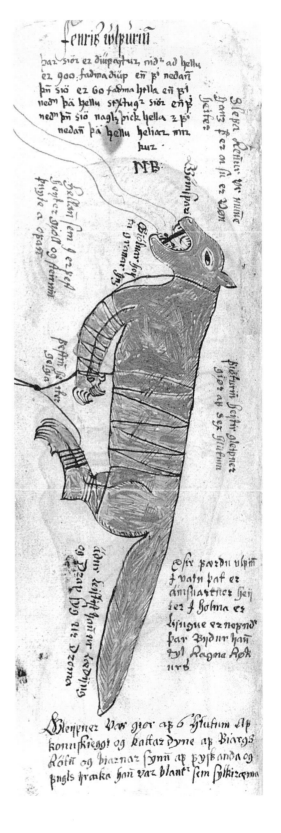

Fenrir Seventeenth-century manuscript illustration, depicting the monstrous wolf Fenrir breaking free of his bonds during the end of the world at Ragnarök.

And now, when the wolf kicked, the bond became firmer, and the more he struggled, the harder the bond became. Then they all laughed, except Týr. He lost his hand.

Fenrir is to remain bound, an upright sword thrust between his jaws, until the cataclysmic time of RAGNARÖK, when he will be freed, and when, in a final encounter, he swallows the god ODIN, who is in turn avenged by his son, VÍDAR.

Outside Snorri's works, references to Fenrir are far less clear. In the tenth century the Icelandic poet EYVIND FINNSSON SKÁLDASPILLIR alludes to Fenrir's sword-gag, while the eddic poem VÖLUSPÁ contains a reference to the rearing of Fenrir in the mysterious wood JÁRNVID, as well as to an unnamed wolf that devours Odin, and another (or perhaps the same) that swallows the sun and moon. *Völuspá* also mentions the breaking-free from chains of the hell-hound (or wolf), GARM. It is possible that all these wolves are one, namely Fenrir, but Snorri, characteristically, is careful to make distinctions, naming the wolves who devour the sun and moon as SKÖLL and HATI HRÓDVITNISSON respectively, and describing an encounter between Garm and Týr (who, one would have thought, might like to get his hand on Fenrir) at Ragnarök. Various visual representations of wolves are sometimes thought to depict Fenrir. From Anglo-Saxon England the so-called Gosforth Cross, which is certainly a product of the Danelaw, depicts a wolf with a sword between its jaws, while the tenth-century Thorvald Cross shows a lupine monster devouring a male figure.

Fenrir also occurs as a common noun for wolf and even as the name of a giant.

B12, 14, 23, 24, 28, 30, 35, 40, 50, 56, 59, 73, 87, 90; C2, 5, 9, 17, 24, 33, 46, 48; D207

Fenrisúlf *see* FENRIR.

Fensalir ('fen-halls')

According to the eddic poem VÖLUSPÁ, the name given to the dwelling of the goddess FRIGG. The thirteenth-century Icelander SNORRI STURLUSON simply describes the place as 'very splendid'.

B24, 28, 35, 40, 50; C5, 9, 48

Fimafeng ('quick service')

According to the prose introduction to the eddic poem LOKASENNA, one of the two servants of the sea-giant ÆGIR – the other is ELDIR. It is the killing of Fimafeng by LOKI that leads to his first expulsion from the feast of the ÆSIR, from which he returns to abuse the assembled company.

B12, 14, 23, 24, 28, 30, 35, 40, 50, 56, 59, 73, 87, 90; C2, 5, 9, 17, 24, 33, 46, 48

Fimbulthul ('mighty Thul')

(1) One of the many names of the god ODIN. (2) According to the thirteenth-century Icelander SNORRI STURLUSON, one of the rivers that flows from the horns of the hart EIKTHYRNIR, via the seething torrents of HVERGELMIR.

B24, 28, 35, 40, 50; C5, 9, 48

Fimbulvetr *see* FIMBUL-WINTER.

Fimbul-winter ('terrible winter')

According to the thirteenth-century Icelander SNORRI STURLUSON, the Fimbul-winter will consist of three harsh winters in a row, without any intervening season, heralding the beginning of the cataclysm of RAGNARÖK. During that time great battles will be fought and there shall be mighty kin-slayings, and all forms of vice and degradation will be rife.

B12, 14, 23, 24, 28, 30, 35, 40, 50, 56, 59, 73, 87, 90; C2, 5, 9, 17, 24, 33, 46, 48

Fitjung ('somebody')

An otherwise unknown person who appears in one of the gnomic or wisdom sections of the eddic poem HÁVAMÁL. The apparent meaning of the name does not inspire confidence that Fitjung is anything more than a cipher.

B12, 30, 56, 73, 87, 90; C2, 17, 24, 33, 46

Fjalar ('hider', 'deceiver')

As is perhaps appropriate for a character with such a deceptive name, there would appear to be more than one figure called Fjalar, and it is unclear what kind of creature is implied. The name occurs twice in the eddic poem VÖLUSPÁ, first in the catalogue of DWARFS, and then as that of a bright red cock, who sits near the giant EGGTHÉR and heralds the cataclysmic events of RAGNARÖK. In the name-lists or THULUR, Fjalar is given in a list of names of giants, and in the eddic poem HÁVAMÁL appears as a synonym for the giant SUTTUNG, who acquires the MEAD OF POETRY; elsewhere in the POETIC EDDA, in HÁRBÁRDSLJÓD, Fjalar appears to be another name for the giant SKRÝMIR. The usage in *Hávamál* is of particular interest, because the thirteenth-century Icelander SNORRI STURLUSON also connects the name with the tale of the mead of poetry, which he describes as being brewed from the blood of KVASIR by two dwarfs named Fjalar and GALAR. It is their subsequent (and rather unmotivated) murder of the giant GILLING and his wife that prompts the vengeance of their son, Suttung, and his consequent acquisition of the mead.

B12, 14, 23, 24, 28, 30, 35, 40, 50, 56, 59, 73, 87, 90; C2, 5, 9, 17, 24, 33, 46, 48; D492

Fjölnir

Fjölnir ('much-wise'?, 'concealer'?)

(1) According to SNORRI STURLUSON, writing in the thirteenth century, Fjölnir was a son of the god FREY and the giantess GERD. He is said to have ruled Sweden and drowned in a vat of mead at a feast. Snorri cites a supporting stanza of a ninth-century skaldic poem by THJÓDÓLF OF HVÍN.

(2) Fjölnir is frequently found as one of the many names for the god ODIN.

B24, 28, 35, 39, 40, 45, 50, 62, 83, 87; C5, 9, 16, 48

Fjölsvid, Fjölsvinn ('much-wise')

The name or title, variously spelled Fjölsvid or Fjölsvinn, given to a variety of characters, including the god ODIN, a dwarf and the eponymous giant of FJÖLSVINNSMÁL, who guards the beautiful MENGLÖD.

B12, 30, 51, 56, 73, 87, 90; C2, 17, 24, 33, 46; D139, 140, 393, 516

Fjölsvinnsmál ('the lay of Fjölsvinn')

One of two eddic poems – the other is GRÓAGALDR – that together tell the tale of the wooing of MENGLÖD by the legendary hero SVIPDAG. Both poems, which share similarities of metre and style, are often considered together, under the collective title SVIPDAGSMÁL.

Fjölsvinnsmál tells how Svipdag finally reaches the mountain-top castle of his intended bride, having presumably negotiated the encircling flames (in much the same way the hero SIGURD is urged to woo a woman in a similarly defended stronghold by the birds in FÁFNISMÁL). Svipdag find his way barred by the giant FJÖLSVINN (a name found also as one of the titles of ODIN), who demands to know his name. Svipdag hides his identity (again like Sigurd in *Fáfnismál*) and instead gives a number of aliases, before ascertaining that Menglöd is within. Then he questions the wise giant about a range of mythological issues, in a manner very similar to other eddic wisdom-poems, such as VAFTHRÚDNISMÁL or ALVÍSSMÁL. In somewhat the same way as in these two poems, the wisdom contest in *Fjölsvinnsmál* ends rather abruptly: Fjölsvinn is asked to reveal the name of Menglöd's intended, and when Svipdag hears his own name called, he reveals his true identity and is ushered into the presence of his beloved. Menglöd appears to be a spirited lass, who curses Fjölsvinn if he turns out to have been deceiving her:

'Mighty ravens shall peck out your eyes
as you swing high on a gallows tree,
if it proves a lie that from far away
the hero has come to my hall.'

Her mood soon softens when Svipdag announces himself:

'Welcome! My wish has been granted:
have a kiss to follow my greeting.
The sight of one's beloved gladdens all
who have felt yearning for another.

'Long have I sat on Lyfjaberg
I waited for you day after day;
Now what I longed for has come to pass,
hero: you have come to my hall.

'I had great yearning for your love
and you for my affection:
now it is true that we shall share
our lives and years together.'

B12, 30, 51, 56, 73, 87, 90; C2, 17, 24, 33, 46; D139, 140, 393, 516

Fjölvar

According to the eddic poem HÁRBARDSLJÓD, a companion of Hárbard (who is really the god ODIN in disguise) in some of his more riotous adventures:

I was with Fjölvar for five full years,
on that island they call All-green;
there we waged battles, piled up the dead,
passed many a test, tried many a maid.

While such activities are undoubtedly characteristic of what is known of Odin's various wanderings, and while Odin is often accompanied by characters such as HŒNIR or LOKI, the particular figure of Fjölvar (perhaps an alias for one of Odin's better known companions) is not attested elsewhere.

B12, 30, 56, 73, 87, 90; C2, 17, 24, 33, 46

Fjörgvin *see* FJÖRGYN.

Fjörgyn ('earth')

The mother of the god THOR. Fjörgyn is also called JÖRD, and so her name (also found in the form Fjörgvin) is occasionally used as a simple alternative for 'land', 'earth'. The masculine form of the name, also spelled Fjörgyn according to this system of transliteration, is that given to the father of the goddess FRIGG, according to the late witnesses of the thirteenth-century Icelander SNORRI STURLUSON and the eddic poem LOKASENNA.

B12, 14, 23, 24, 28, 30, 35, 40, 50, 56, 59, 73, 87, 90; C2, 5, 9, 17, 24, 33, 46, 48

Fjörm *see* HVERGELMIR.

Fjörnir

According to both the eddic poem ATLAKVIDA and the legendary VÖLSUNGA SAGA, the cup-bearer of the hero GUNNAR. As he and his brother HÖGNI GJÚKASON set out on their doomed journey to visit their sister GUDRÚN and her husband ATLI BUDLASON, Gunnar summons Fjörnir and says (according to *Völsunga saga*, drawing on *Atlakvida*):

> Get up and give us good wine to drink from great goblets, for it may be that this is our last banquet. If we die, the aged wolf will get the gold, and the bear will not delay to bite with battle-teeth.

B12, 20, 25, 30, 31, 42, 56, 65, 68, 73, 79, 87, 90; C1–3, 6, 17, 24, 33, 46

Fjósnir *see* RÍGSTHULA.

Flateyjarbók

The largest of all medieval Icelandic manuscripts, written between 1387 and 1394, and consisting of 225 sheets of parchment. Most of the material within the manuscript relates to the kings of Norway, but it includes a large number of tales about the alleged dealings of sundry Icelanders (both real and imagined) with the Norwegian crown. Flateyjarbók is an important witness in that it contains a number of more or less fanciful or legendary accounts that are either found elsewhere in quite different versions or are simply unique to the manuscript, including HYNDLULJÓD, NORNAGESTS THÁTTR and the narratives involving, for example, Thorleif and the BURIAL MOUND, Thidrandi and the DÍSIR (*see* DÍSABLÓT), and Gunnar helming and the priestess of the god FREY.

B60, 85; C21; D624

Fljód *see* RÍGSTHULA.

flyting (Old Norse *senna*)

A formalized contest of more or less ritualized abuse, witnessed in several texts in both prose and verse either as a prelude to physical combat or as a substitute for it. Much of the abuse centres on issues of alleged cowardice or sexual deviancy, often of a most bizarre kind. The lengthy flyting that takes place between ATLI IDMUNDSSON and the giantess HRÍMGERD in the eddic poem HELGAKVIDA HJÖRVARDSSONAR is a case in point, with the hero, HELGI HJÖRVARDSSON, occasionally joining in:

> [Hrímgerd said:]
> 'You would neigh, if you weren't a gelding:
> Hrímgerd tosses her tail;
> I think your heart is in your arse, Atli,
> though you have a stallion's voice.'

> [Atli said:]
> 'You'd soon learn what a stallion I was

in strength, if I stepped on shore:
> you'd take a great pasting, if I so wished,
> and lower your tail, Hrímgerd.'

> [Hrímgerd said:]
> 'Come ashore then, Atli, if you think you're up to it:
> I'll be waiting in Varin's Bay.
> You'll get your ribs crushed, warrior,
> if you come within reach of my claws.'

Elsewhere in the POETIC EDDA, entire poems, such as *Hárbardsljód*, are built on a slanging match between individuals, in this case the gods ODIN and THOR, but the most celebrated flyting of all occurs in the eddic poem LOKASENNA, in which the vicious LOKI abuses each of assembled ÆSIR in turn, broadly accusing the gods of the cowardice or unnatural sexual behaviour (or both), and the goddesses of unbridled sex, usually with him. The whole ritual of flyting, quite apart from its evident function of puncturing an individual's self-esteem, seems closely linked with the formal comparison between characters (Old Norse *mannjafnaðr*), which is such a notable feature of so many Norse texts.

B12, 30, 33, 56, 73, 87, 90; C2, 17, 24, 33, 46; D24, 78, 79, 225, 227, 354, 541, 568

Fólkvang ('field of the host')

According to the eddic poem GRÍMNISMÁL, the abode of the goddess FREYJA, who rides to battle from there and is allotted half the slain. The thirteenth-century Icelander SNORRI STURLUSON adds the detail that her hall in Fólkvang is called SESSRUMNIR and is 'large and fair'.

B12, 14, 23, 24, 28, 30, 35, 40, 50, 56, 59, 73, 87, 90; C2, 5, 9, 17, 24, 33, 46, 48

Fön *see* FORNJÓT.

För Scírnis *see* SKÍRNISMÁL.

fornaldarsögur ('sagas of bygone days')

The generic name usually given to a group of some thirty Icelandic sagas, dating from the late medieval period, which deal with the activities of a wide variety of legendary and heroic figures from days of yore. Their propensity to include bizarre and tawdry details of the pagan past makes them deeply problematic for use as witness to genuinely ancient traditions, but several of them unquestionably contain material that is far older than the supposed date of composition. Among the most celebrated of *fornaldarsögur* are VÖLSUNGA SAGA, GAUTREKS SAGA, HRÓLFS SAGA KRAKA and the vast and amorphous THIDREKS SAGA, all of which draw on a wide range of sources, including material from the POETIC EDDA, as well as other written and oral material.

B8, 25, 42, 65, 68, 69, 71, 74, 78, 84; C1, 6, 13, 15, 20, 21, 25, 35, 38, 44; D251, 252, 267, 270, 367, 379, 380, 414, 451, 471, 506, 532, 577, 581, 582, 605

Fornjót ('destroyer'?; 'ancient giant'?)

According to several mnemonic name-lists or THULUR, the name of a giant; the thirteenth-century Icelander SNORRI STURLUSON specifies that he is the father of the wind. Two further accounts place Fornjót at the head of a considerable genealogy of frost-giants: there his children are called HLÉR ('sea'), LOGI ('fire') and Kari ('wind'). Kari has a son called variously Frosti ('frost') or Jökul ('glacier'), who is the father of Snær ('snow') and grandfather of Drífa ('snow-flurry'), Fön ('snow-drift'), Mjöl ('powder-snow') and Thorri (one of the winter months).

B24, 28, 35, 40, 50; C5, 9, 48; D240, 278

Forseti ('chairman')

According to the thirteenth-century Icelander SNORRI STURLUSON, the son of the god BALDR and his wife NANNA. Forseti himself is numbered among the gods or ÆSIR by Snorri. Both his residence in GLITNIR, with its gold pillars and silver roof, and his remarkable powers of arbitration are mentioned in the eddic poem GRÍMNISMÁL, but his rather transparently suitable name (compare that of BRAGI) and the silence of other sources about him, have often been held to suggest that Forseti is a late and synthetic creation. However, the *Vita Sancti Willibrordi* of the great Anglo-Saxon scholar and cleric Alcuin, composed between 785 and 797, contains a reference to an island between Frisia and Denmark called Fositesland in honour of the god worshipped there and may preserve a distant memory of Forseti's cult.

B12, 14, 23, 24, 28, 30, 35, 40, 50, 56, 59, 73, 87, 90; C2, 5, 9, 17, 24, 33, 46, 48

Frá dauda Sinfjötla ('on the death of Sinfjötli')

The name given in the CODEX REGIUS manuscript to a brief passage in prose providing a narrative introduction to the eddic poems that celebrate the tragic events of the VÖLSUNG-cycle. The passage describes how the great hero SIGMUND witnesses the death of his son, SINFJÖTLI, the product of an incestuous union with Sigmund's own sister, SIGNÝ. After performing the burial rites for Sinfjötli (in which he appears to be aided by the god ODIN), Sigmund goes on to father another child, Sigurd, who grows up to be the greatest of the heroes of the North; as the passage concludes:

Sigmund and all his sons were far beyond all other men in strength, stature, bravery, and all accomplishments. But Sigurd was the most outstanding of them all, and everyone in the ancient tales says that he was the chief and noblest of fighting-kings.

B12, 30, 56, 73, 87, 90; C2, 17, 24, 33, 46

Franang

The waterfall in which, according to the thirteenth-century Icelander SNORRI STURLUSON, LOKI hid by assuming the shape of a salmon after his part in the killing of the god BALDR.

B24, 28, 35, 40, 50; C5, 9, 48

Franmar

According to the prose passages in the eddic poem HELGAKVIDA HJÖRVARDSSONAR, an earl at the court of the legendary King SVÁFNIR. As foster-father to the princess SIGRLINN and father of ÁLOF, Franmar tries to protect the young women by transforming himself into the shape of an eagle, but is speared by the warrior ATLI IDMUNDSSON, who takes both women away.

B12, 30, 56, 73, 87, 90; C2, 17, 24, 33, 46

Frea (Old English: 'lord')

(1) The Old English equivalent of the Norse god FREY, although the term is scarcely used in extant Anglo-Saxon records to refer to a pagan figure at all and, indeed, frequently occurs as an honorific title of the Christian god. Frea and other related terms do, however, occur in a number of royal Anglo-Saxon pedigrees alongside more clearly pagan figures such as WODEN.

(2) The late eighth-century Langobard historian PAULUS DIACONUS names as Frea a female divinity usually identified with the goddess FRIGG.

B9, 21; C11

Frekastein ('wolf stone')

The place where the heroes HELGI SIGMUNDARSON HUNDINGSBANI and SINFJÖTLI met to do battle with their enemies GRANMAR and HÖDBRODD, according to the eddic poems HELGAKVIDA HUNDINGSBANA I and II. The place-name is suitably portentous for a battle at which not only wolves, but other beasts of battle, such as eagles, might be busy. One might compare ARASTEIN, where Helgi was equally engaged.

B12, 30, 56, 73, 87, 90; C2, 17, 24, 33, 46

Freki ('wolf')

According to the eddic poem GRÍMNISMÁL, in a verse also cited by the thirteenth-century Icelander SNORRI STURLUSON, one of two wolves – the other is Geri –

to whom the god ODIN gives his food when he sits and feasts with the warriors of the EINHERJAR in VALHALL.
B12, 14, 23, 24, 28, 30, 35, 40, 50, 56, 59, 73, 87, 90; C2, 5, 9, 17, 24, 33, 46, 48

Frey ('lord')

Frey is the chief figure of the fertility-gods or VANIR, and, as the main figure associated with fertility, holds an important place in Norse myth. He is described as a son of NJÖRD and brother of the goddess FREYJA, who was also probably originally his wife. Together, the three dwell among the ÆSIR and are usually counted in their number. Frey's anguished wooing of the giantess GERD is described in detail in the eddic poem SKÍRNISMÁL, in which he appears to be punished for his presumption in mounting the panoramic high-seat HLIDSKJÁLF, usually the preserve of the god ODIN, as a result of the insatiable longing he feels for Gerd, of whom he catches sight from his lofty vantage-point. Only after long bargaining and cajoling (not to mention threatening) by Frey's servant SKÍRNIR, does Gerd consent to meet him. Frey is held to dwell in ÁLFHEIM, and among his prized possessions are the magic ship SKÍDBLADNIR and the golden boar GULLINBORSTI, which pulls his chariot. The thirteenth-century Icelander SNORRI STURLUSON describes him as follows:

> Frey is the noblest of the Æsir. He governs rain and sunshine, and so the produce of the earth, and it is good to pray to him for prosperity and peace; he also looks after the wealth of men.

According to the eddic poem VÖLUSPÁ, Frey meets the giant SURT in the cataclysmic battle at RAGNARÖK and is killed. Snorri links this fact with the assertion in *Skírnismál* that in order to persuade Skírnir to undertake to press his suit for him, Frey gives him a famous sword that will fight giants by itself. According to Snorri, it is at Ragnarök that the weaponless Frey regrets his gift, and Snorri even goes so far as to extrapolate from a simple description of Frey in *Völuspá* as a slayer of one BELI that the latter is a giant, slain by the swordless Frey with an antler. Given that in *Skírnismál* Gerd gives as one reason for her unwillingness to accept Frey's suit the fact that he had killed her brother, it seems possible that Beli (however he was killed) was the brother in question.

Several sources note the cultic importance of Frey in the Norse pantheon. In the late eleventh century ADAM OF BREMEN describes how a figure he names as Fricco is worshipped alongside THOR and WODEN in the great temple at UPPSALA; the fact that the statue of Fricco is depicted with an enormous phallus would suggest that

a fertility figure of some kind is intended, and an amulet with similar characteristics from Rällinge in Sweden is generally described as a statuette of Frey. The particular devotion of the Swedish royal house to Frey is enshrined in their very name, YNGLINGS, which is held to derive from a particular manifestation of the god as Yngvi or YNGVI-FREY. Outside Sweden, Icelandic sources mention several characters who carry the by-name *Freysgoði* ('priest of Frey'), and one such, Hrafnkel, has an entire saga, HRAFNKELS SAGA FREYSGODA, devoted to his gradual alienation from the god, which begins

Frey *Copper alloy figure from Rällinge, Södermanland, Sweden. The figure's prominent phallus may indicate that it depicts a fertility god; Frey has been suggested.*

with his dedication of a splendid horse to Frey and a fateful vow to kill anyone who rides it. Similarly, in GÍSLA SAGA it is said that the god will not permit frost or snow to fall on the BURIAL MOUND of his favourite, Thorgrím, while in the mid-thirteenth-century VÍGA-GLÚMS SAGA another of the god's priests, Thorkel, offers a sacrifice to Frey to prevent his rival, Víga-Glúm, from taking possession of the land of Thverá from which he has been driven:

> Before Thorkel went away from Thverá he went to Frey's temple, leading an old ox and said: 'Frey,' he said, 'you who for a long time has been my patron and have received many gifts from me, and repaid them well, now I offer you this ox, so that Glúm may not leave the land of Thverá any less reluctantly than I do now. Let a sign be seen, whether or not you accept this.' The oxen was so struck that it bellowed and fell down dead, and Thorkel reckoned that things had turned out well, and was more at ease, since he thought his offering had been accepted.

The fact that an almost identical scene, which seems suspiciously reminiscent of the sacrifice of the priest Chryses at the beginning of the *Iliad* (Latin accounts of which were certainly available in Iceland), is found elsewhere in Norse gives its inclusion here a distinctly literary feel, although the actual performance of sacrifices to Frey in the pagan period does not seem unlikely. A similarly intriguing tale from a late source is that of the fugitive Icelander Gunnar Helming, told in the late fourteenth-century FLATEYJARBÓK, in which the runaway takes refuge with a priestess of Frey processing through Iceland in a chariot. The subsequent pregnancy of the priestess is held by the local populace as an auspicious indication of the god's potency. Such a tale accords strikingly well with a description by the first-century Roman historian TACITUS, who notes that the fertility-goddess NERTHUS (usually identified with NJÖRD, the father of Frey) is similarly drawn in a chariot and attended by priests in a procession through the land.

B2, 12, 14, 23, 24, 28, 30, 35, 37, 40, 47, 50, 56, 59, 60, 73, 78, 81, 85, 87, 90; C2, 5, 9, 17, 19, 24, 29, 30, 33, 42, 46, 48; D34, 262, 544, 570, 583

Freyja ('woman')

Freyja is undoubtedly the most widely celebrated of the goddesses or ÁSYNJUR, even though Snorri places her second in rank below FRIGG, the wife of the god ODIN. She is the daughter of NJÖRD (and as such technically one of the VANIR), sister of FREY and lover of many. Her husband ÓD does not figure largely in the extant evidence, although she apparently wept golden tears for him when he left. It was, after all, apparently by

sleeping with four dwarfs in turn that she acquired her most treasured possession, the BRÍSINGAMEN. Several times she is sought after by giants, most notably by THRYM, by HRUNGNIR and by the anonymous MASTER BUILDER, a giant who undertakes to build ÁSGARD in the episode that ultimately leads to the birth of SLEIPNIR. Love and sex are her province (in the eddic poem LOKASENNA she is accused of being a whore), and her well-decked hall, SESSRUMNIR, and even her preferred mode of transport (carried in a chariot drawn by cats) attest to her quintessential femininity. Among her other possessions is a cloak made from falcon-feathers, which, according to the eddic poem THRYMSKVIDA, was employed by LOKI to find out who has stolen MJÖLLNIR, the hammer of the god THOR. An altogether darker side of her character is witnessed by her connection with battle, where she claims half the slain alongside Odin, and, like him, she is portrayed as engaged in a wisdom contest against a giantess in the eddic poem HYNDLULJÓD. Among the many names and titles recorded of Freyja are Gefn ('the giver'), Hörn ('flaxen'?), Mardöl ('sea-brightener'?), Skjálf ('shaker'), Thröng or Thrungva ('throng'), Vanadís ('the dís of the VANIR') and Sýr ('sow'). The last name connects Freyja with a pig-cult more usually associated with her brother Frey, and in *Hyndluljód* Freyja is even said to ride on a boar called Hildisvíni ('battle-swine'), presumably a counterpart to Frey's GULLINBORSTI.

B12, 14, 23, 24, 28, 30, 35, 40, 50, 56, 59, 73, 87, 90; C2, 5, 9, 17, 24, 33, 46, 48; D178, 404, 412, 413

Fricco see FREY; UPPSALA.

Frigg ('lady')

Frigg, as the wife of the god ODIN and mother of the tragic god BALDR, is the queen of the ÁSYNJUR. She has her own residence, FENSALIR, her own set of servants, FULLA and GNÁ, and plays an active maternal role in the story of Baldr's death, both in urging all creatures not to harm her son and, after his death, in sending HERMÓD to HEL to plead for his return. Often Frigg is found alongside Odin, taking an interest in the affairs of men, although each meddles on opposite sides. So much is clear not only from the prose introduction to GRÍMNISMÁL but also from the eighth-century Latin account of PAULUS DIACONUS, in which WODEN supports the Vandals, and his wife FREA (the Latin form of Frigg) supports the Langobards. Such squabbling strongly resembles what is told in Greek accounts of Zeus and Hera at Troy, or, perhaps more pertinently, of Jupiter and Juno in the *Aeneid*. A still less regal side to Frigg's nature is hinted at by SNORRI STURLUSON, who recounts in his YNGLINGA SAGA how during his exile Odin shared everything with his brothers, VILI and VÉ, including Frigg. In LOKASENNA, LOKI explicitly accuses her of sleeping with both brothers-in-law. The early thirteenth-century Danish historian SAXO GRAMMATICUS preserves a no-less shocking account of how Frigg, jealous of Odin's success, cuckolds him with a slave.

B9, 12, 14, 21, 23, 24, 28, 30, 35, 40, 50, 56, 59, 64, 73, 87, 90; C2, 5, 7–9, 11, 17, 24, 33, 46; D104, 463, 565

Frigida (Latin: 'cold', 'chilly')

According to the account (see EUHEMERISM) offered by the thirteenth-century Icelander SNORRI STURLUSON at the beginning of SNORRA EDDA, the 'historical' equivalent of the goddess FRIGG. Given the attempt to identify the descent of the ÆSIR from Asia, and specifically Troy, presumably the name of Frigida is intended to stand both for the chilly climate of the north and to recall the land of Phrygia, where Troy was to be found.

B24, 28, 335, 40, 50; C5, 9, 48

Friia see MERSEBURG CHARMS.

Fródi ('wise one')

Perhaps the most celebrated legendary king of Denmark, famed for the peace and stability of his rule. The so-called Peace of Fródi is alluded to in a skaldic poem from the very end of the tenth century, while the thirteenth-century Icelander SNORRI STURLUSON describes him as 'the greatest of all the kings of the lands of the north', and recounts the tale of him using the giantesses FENJA and Menja to grind out gold from a magical mill (as described in the eddic poem GROTTASÖNGR). Elsewhere he even goes so far as to identify him with the fertility-god FREY. Given the suc-

cess and stability of his reign, it is scarcely surprising that Fródi's achievements are celebrated widely. His Anglo-Saxon equivalent, Froda, appears in two Old English poems, BEOWULF and *Widsith*, while no fewer than five different kings, all called Frotho, are described by the early thirteenth-century Danish historian SAXO GRAMMATICUS.

B24, 28, 35, 40, 50, 64; C5, 7–9, 48

Frosti see FORNJÓT.

Fulla ('bountiful'?)

Named by the thirteenth-century Icelander SNORRI STURLUSON as one of the goddesses ÁSYNJUR and as a handmaid of the goddess FRIGG, Fulla is described as follows:

> She is a virgin, who goes about with flowing hair untied and wears a golden band about her head. She carries Frigg's basket, and takes care of her footwear, and is privy to her secrets.

A poetic periphrasis or KENNING in a tenth-century skaldic verse by the Icelander EYVIND FINNSSON SKÁLDASPILLIR describes gold as 'the falling sun of the plain of Fulla's brow'. It is likely that the figure named as Volla in the second MERSEBURG CHARM is to be identified with Fulla, whom the introductory prose to the eddic poem GRÍMNISMÁL simply names as one of Frigg's servants. The apparent appearance of Fulla alongside BALDR in the second Merseburg Charm is the more intriguing given that, according to Snorri, Fulla is one of three Ásynjur (the others are NANNA, his wife, and Frigg, his mother) to whom the dead Baldr sends gifts from HEL.

B12, 14, 23, 24, 28, 30, 35, 40, 50, 56, 59, 73, 87, 90; C2, 5, 9, 17, 24, 33, 46, 48

Fúlnir see RÍGSTHULA.

futhark, futhork

The names variously given to the alphabets of RUNES found amongst all the Germanic peoples; a distinction is made between the original continental Germanic runic alphabet or *futhark*, which developed in Scandinavia, and the Anglo-Saxon runic alphabet or *futhork* found in England.

A20, 88; B4, 18, 19, 29, 36, 46, 49, 54, 57, 66, 89; D48, 151, 161, 241, 326, 348, 386–8, 411, 445–7, 453, 577

fylgjur ('fetches')

Protective spirits (singular *fylgja*), which attach themselves to individuals, often at birth, and remain with them right through to death, when they may transfer

---

The Anglo-Saxon *futhorc* with some additional characters

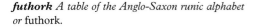

ᚠ	f	ᚻ	h	ᛏ	t	ᚪ	a
ᚢ	u	ᚾ	n	ᛒ	b	ᚫ	æ
ᚦ	th	ᛁ	i	ᛖ	e	ᚣ	y
ᚩ	o	ᛄ	j	ᛗ	m	ᛠ	ea
ᚱ	r	ᛃ	3	ᛚ	l	ᛣ	k
ᚳ	c	ᛈ	p	ᛝ	ŋ	ᚸ	ḡ
ᚷ	g	ᛉ	x	ᛟ	œ	ᛥ	k
ᚹ	w	ᛋ	s	ᛞ	d	ᛤ	st

futhork A table of the Anglo-Saxon runic alphabet or futhork.

their powers to another family member. Etymologically, the word is connected to that for 'follow', and some have even suggested a connection with another Norse word, *fylgja* ('afterbirth'). The idea that your *fylgja* is born alongside you and follows you through life seems to be reflected in the sources.

Often appearing in the form of an animal or woman, the *fylgjur* are usually visible only at times of crisis, both in waking and in dreams, either to the object of their protection or to others. The concept appears to be partly that of an externalized soul, but also an embodiment of personal luck or destiny, and it shares many of the attributes of the similar notion of HAMINGJA. A typical example of the form and function of the *fylgja* is found in the late thirteenth-century Icelandic NJÁLS SAGA:

> One day it happened that Njál and Thórd were outside; a goat used to wander round the yard, and no one was allowed to drive it away. Suddenly, Thórd spoke: 'That's odd,' he said. 'What do you see, that seems odd to you?' asked Njál. 'It seems to me that the goat is lying in the hollow here, all covered with blood.' Njál replied that there was no goat there or anywhere else. 'What is it then?' said Thórd. 'You must be doomed,' said Njál, 'and have seen your *fylgja*, so be careful.' 'That won't help me,' said Thórd, 'if I am doomed.'

Later on in *Njáls saga*, in the course of an account of the conversion of Iceland, Hall of Sída will consent to be baptized only if Saint Michael will be his *fylgjuengill* ('guardian angel'), a term that clearly owes something to the native conception of the *fylgja*.

futhark *A table of the Germanic runic alphabet or* futhark, *together with other tables illustrating the developing Norse* futhark.

The Germanic *futhark* (24 characters), c. 2nd–c. 7th century
* = *reconstructed form*

ᚠ	f	**fehu* 'livestock, wealth'
ᚢ	u	**ūruz* (?) 'aurochs'
ᚦ	th	**þurisaz* 'giant' or **þornaz* 'thorn'
ᚨ	a	**ansuz* '(pagan) god'
ᚱ	r	**raiðō* 'riding, journey, vehicle'
ᚲ	k	**kauna-*, **kēna-* (??)
ᚷ	g	**geƀō* 'gift'
ᚹ	w	**wunjō* 'joy'
ᚺ	h	**hagala-* 'hail'
ᚾ	n	**nauðiz* 'need'
ᛁ	i	**īsa-* 'ice'
ᛃ	j	**jǣra* 'year'
ᛇ	ï (?)	**ī(h)waz* 'yew'
ᛈ	p	**perþ-* (??)
ᛉ	R	**algiz-* (??)
ᛊ	s	**sōwil-* 'sun'
ᛏ	t	**tīwaz* '(the name of the god) Týr'
ᛒ	b	**berkana* 'birch-twig'
ᛖ	e	**ehwaz* 'horse'
ᛗ	m	**mannz* 'man'
ᛚ	l	**laguz* 'water'
ᛜ	ŋ	**ingwaz* '(the name of the god) Ing (Yngvi)'
ᛟ	o	**ōþilaz* 'inheritance, property'
ᛞ	d	**dagaz* 'day'

Scandinavian *futharks* (16 characters), c. 8th–c. 11th century

'Danish'	'Short-twig'	
ᚠ	ᚠ	f
ᚢ	ᚢ	u
ᚦ	ᚦ	th
ᚬ	ᚬ	ą
ᚱ	ᚱ	r
ᚴ	ᚴ	k
ᚼ	ᚽ	h
ᚾ	ᚿ	n
ᛁ	ᛁ	i
ᛅ	ᛆ	a
ᛋ	ᛌ	s
ᛏ	ᛐ	t
ᛒ	ᛓ	b
ᛘ	ᛙ	m
ᛚ	ᛚ	l
ᛦ	ᛧ	R

The Scandinavian medieval *futhark* with additional characters, c. 11th century onward

ᚠ	f
ᚢ	u
ᚦ	th
ᚬ	o
ᚱ	r
ᚴ	k
ᚼ	h
ᚽ	n
ᛁ	i
ᛆ	a
ᛌ	s
ᛐ	t
ᛒ	b
ᛚ	l
ᛘ	m
ᛦ	R/y
ᛅ	æ
ᚯ	ø
ᚤ	y
ᚵ	g
ᛑ	d
ᛕ	p
ᛍ	c

fylgja Stone 'hogback' grave-marker, from St Thomas's church, Brompton, North Yorkshire, England. This style of grave-marker is only found in the Norse-dominated areas of England; the 'end-beasts' are probably bears, and such representations may reflect the belief that, as in many sagas, an individual's personified destiny or fylgja might take the form of a bear.

In the legendary HRÓLFS SAGA KRAKA, a remarkable episode is described in which in the absence of the sleeping BERSERK, BÖDVAR BJARKI, a huge bear fights alongside his men, slaying the enemy with its paws and teeth and apparently invulnerable to weapons. When Bödvar is woken, the bear disappears and the tide of battle turns. Given that Bödvar Bjarki's name seems to mean 'little bear of battle', it seems likely that the bear depicted is indeed his *fylgja*, which disappears when the warrior himself comes on the scene.

The extent to which the *fylgja* was attached to a family, rather than an individual, can be seen in several sagas, most notably HALLFREDAR SAGA, in which Hallfred, newly converted to Christianity, and his two sons are on board ship one day, and see an extraordinary sight:

> They saw a woman walking behind the ship: she was tall, and wearing a mail-coat; she walked over the waves as if she was on dry land. Hallfred looked at her and saw that she was his *fylgja*-woman. 'I declare that everything between you and me is over,' he said. 'Will you accept me, Thorvald?' she asked. He said he wouldn't. Then the younger Hallfred said 'I'll accept you'. Then she vanished. Hallfred said: 'My son, I shall give you the sword that the king gave me; but you must place the other treasures beside me in my coffin, if I die on this ship.'

A rather similar scene is found in VÍGA-GLÚMS SAGA, where, however, it is the family *hamingja* that takes the form of an enormous woman.

B47, 74–6, 81; C3, 20, 26, 30; D408, 563, 587

G

Galar ('screamer')
(1) According to the name-lists or THULUR, the name of a GIANT. (2) In the account of the thirteenth-century Icelander SNORRI STURLUSON, Galar is also found as the name of one of the two dwarfs (the other is FJALAR) who murder both KVASIR and the parents of the giant SUTTUNG, and so acquire (and subsequently lose) the MEAD OF POETRY.
B24, 28, 35, 40, 50; C5, 9, 48

galdr ('chant', 'spell')
A chant or spell recited, rather than sung, as part of the practice of MAGIC, often associated with the particular form of magic known as SEID. The word is related to the verb *gala* ('to crow', 'to cry out'), a word used of cocks or crows. A description of the chanting of such *galdr* is apparently found in EIRÍKS SAGA RAUDA, in which a Christian woman named Gudrid is invited to chant a sequence of verses, which she calls *Vardlokkur* and which she claims to have learned from her foster-mother in Iceland, to assist the prognostications of the prophetess THORBJÖRG LÍTILVÖLVA:

> The women made a circle, and in the middle sat Thorbjörg on a special raised platform [*seiðhjalli*]. Gudrid recited the chants so beautifully and well that no one present thought they had ever heard more beautiful chanting. The prophetess thanked her for the chant; many spirits who thought the chanting beautiful had turned up 'who previously had avoided us and refused to give us any help; now many of those things are clear to me which had previously baffled both me and others'.

As a reward for her splendid rendition, Gudrid is rewarded by the prophecy that she will found a distinguished line in Iceland.

The existence of a specific (and particularly repetitive) poetic form known as *galdralag* ('*galdr*-metre') is noted by the thirteenth-century Icelander SNORRI

gambanteinn

STURLUSON, while other sources, notably GRETTIS SAGA ÁSMUNDARSONAR, seem to envisage spells of this kind being muttered as much as chanted; the term *galdrabók* ('book of chants') is given to any grimoire or book of spells.

B24, 28, 35, 38, 40, 41, 50; C5, 9, 12, 27, 48

gambanteinn ('magic wand')

A term used in two eddic poems, HÁRBARDSLJÓD and SKÍRNISMÁL, to denote a particular kind of magic wand. In *Hárbardsljód* the god ODIN boasts to THOR that he took a *gambanteinn* from the giant HLÉBARD, driving the giant into a frenzy (presumably by making use of the *gambanteinn*), while in *Skírnismál* SKÍRNIR, the servant of the fertility-god FREY, appears to make similar threat to the giantess GERD, namely that he will use his *gambanteinn* to drive her into a frenzy of wandering madness.

B12, 30, 56, 73, 87, 90; C2, 17, 24, 33, 46

Ganglati *see* HEL.

Gangleri *see* GYLFAGINNING.

Ganglöt *see* HEL.

Garm ('rag')

The greatest of dogs, according to the eddic poem GRÍMNISMÁL, while elsewhere in the POETIC EDDA the author of VÖLUSPÁ has Garm chained up and howling at the final cataclysm of RAGNARÖK. The identification of Garm with the dog found in HEL in the eddic poem BALDRS DRAUMAR is possible but far from certain. The thirteenth-century Icelander SNORRI STURLUSON elaborates considerably, making Garm the particular enemy of the god TÝR at Ragnarök, in a fight in which both protagonists perish. Such an account, which is not found elsewhere, may be a conscious attempt by Snorri to create a parallel between ODIN and Týr on (as it were) the one hand, and between Garm and FENRIR on the other.

B12, 14, 23, 24, 28, 30, 35, 40, 50, 56, 59, 73, 87, 90; C2, 5, 9, 17, 24, 33, 46, 48

Gaupnir

The name found in the legendary VÖLSUNGA SAGA for the rune-inscribed weapon of the god ODIN; presumably a scribal error for the famed spear GUNGNIR.

B25, 42, 65, 68, 79; C1, 6

Gaut, Gauti *see* GEAT.

Gautreks saga

One of the most celebrated of the so-called legendary sagas – FORNALDARSÖGUR – and preserved in around thirty manuscripts, dating from the beginning of the fifteenth century. Among the tales narrated in the course of the saga, which exists in two versions, is that of the peculiar practice of voluntary euthanasia associated with the ÆTTERNISSTAPI, and (in the longer version at least) the grisly sacrifice of King VÍKAR, betrayed by his foster-brother, the legendary and long-lived STARKAD.

B69; C35, 38; D252, 376

Geat

According to Anglo-Saxon royal genealogies, an ancestor of the god WODEN. In Norse sources the equivalent form, Gaut or Gauti, appears as a name for the god ODIN himself.

D424

Gefjon, Gefjun ('the giving one')

The thirteenth-century Icelander SNORRI STURLUSON describes Gefjon as one of the goddesses or ÁSYNJUR and tells a remarkable tale of how the legendary Swedish king GYLFI granted her some plough land, at which point she harnessed her four giant-born sons, transformed into oxen, and dragged Zealand into the sea from Sweden. In his GYLFAGINNING Snorri says of her 'she is a virgin, and is attended by all women who die virgins', although elsewhere, in his YNGLINGA SAGA, he claims that she was married to the legendary hero SKJÖLD, the son of the god ODIN. According to abuse from LOKI in the eddic poem LOKASENNA, Gefjon once gave her body to a 'bright white lad' in exchange for a bauble, and this has led some to identify Gefjon with the goddess FREYJA (one of whose names is Gefn), whose penchant for similar sexual currency is also claimed.

B12, 14, 23, 24, 28, 30, 35, 40, 50, 56, 59, 73, 87, 90; C2, 5, 9, 17, 24, 33, 46, 48; D476

Gefn An alternative name for FREYJA.

Geirmund

According to the eddic poem ODDRÚNARGRÁTR, it was while the unfortunate ODDRÚN was at the house of Geirmund, brewing beer, that her cruel brother ATLI BUDLASON put the hero GUNNAR into the snake-pit to die.

B12, 30, 56, 73, 87, 90; C2, 17, 24, 33, 46

Geirölul *see* VALKYRIES.

Geirröd ('spear-reddener')

(1) A king, son of HRAUNDUNG, and a figure who first

appears in the eddic poem GRÍMNISMÁL as the favourite of the god ODIN, but who betrays his elder brother, AGNAR HRAUDUNGSSON, in his desire to be king. When Odin visits his favourite in later years at the behest of his wife, FRIGG, he is held and tortured, helped only by Geirröd's young son, also called Agnar after his lost uncle. When Odin reveals his true identity, Geirröd's reaction, described in a prose epilogue to the poem, is too late to prevent Odin's terrible retribution:

> King Geirröd was sitting with a sword on his knee, half-drawn. When he heard that it was Odin who had come there, he stood up and wanted to take Odin away from the fires. The sword slipped out of his hand and turned hilt-down. The king stumbled and tripped forwards, and the sword went through him, and he got his death. Then Odin disappeared, and Agnar was king there for a long time afterwards.

(2) Geirröd is also the name of a GIANT, in visiting whom the god THOR had one of his most celebrated adventures, described in suitably oblique fashion by the late tenth-century Icelandic poet EILÍF GODRÚNARSON in his THÓRSDRÁPA. In the thirteenth century the Icelander SNORRI STURLUSON quotes a large number of stanzas of *Thórsdrápa* at the conclusion of his own retelling of the tale, which he presents as a story told by the god BRAGI to the sea-giant ÆGIR, in response to his question about Thor's activities against the giants, after hearing of his encounter with the mighty HRUNGNIR:

> Then Ægir said: 'Hrungnir appears to me to have been extremely powerful. Did Thor manage a mightier deed in his dealings with giants?' Then Bragi answered: 'The tale of how Thor visited the stronghold of Geirröd deserves recounting in full. At that time he didn't have with him the hammer MJÖLLNIR, nor the girdle of might, nor his iron gauntlets, thanks to LOKI. He accompanied him, since once it had happened that Loki had as a jest flown in the falcon shape of Frigg, and from curiosity had visited Geirröd's stronghold and, having spotted a large hall, had landed on a window-ledge and gazed in. But Geirröd caught sight of him and gave orders that the bird should be captured and brought to him. The person he sent managed to climb up onto the wall of the building only with difficulty, because it was so high; Loki was delighted that he was being put to such trouble to capture him, and intended to refrain from flying away until he had completed all of the dangerous climb. But when the man approached, he flapped his wings and hopped up smartly, but he found that his feet were stuck. Loki was then captured and taken to the giant Geirröd. When he looked at [Loki's] eyes, he sensed that it was somebody and demanded that he respond, but Loki stayed quiet. So Geirröd shut Loki up in a

chest and starved him there for three months. When Geirröd took him out and demanded that he speak, Loki told him who he was, and to ransom his life he swore oaths to Geirröd that he would cause Thor to come to Geirröd's stronghold without his hammer or girdle of might. Thor stayed for the night with the giantess GRÍD; she was the mother of VÍDAR the silent. She told Thor the truth about Geirröd, that he was a crafty giant and difficult to deal with. She loaned him another girdle of might, some iron gauntlets of her own and her staff, called Gríd's staff. Then Thor came to the river VIMUR, the most powerful of all rivers. Then he buckled on the girdle of might and put his weight down on Gríd's staff on the side furthest from the direction of the current, while Loki hung on under the girdle of might. But when Thor reached midstream, the river rose so high that it was washing up over his shoulders. So Thor said:

> 'Vimur, don't rise now,
> when I want to wade
> across to the stronghold of giants.
> Hear this: if you rise
> my Ás-strength will rise
> up as high as the sky.'

Then Thor saw that up in a gully Gjalp, Geirröd's daughter, was standing astride the stream, making it rise. So Thor picked a huge rock out of the river and threw it at her, saying: 'A river should be stemmed at its source.' He didn't miss what he aimed at, and then he found himself next to the bank and managed to get hold of a kind of rowan bush and pull himself out of the river. From this derives the expression that the rowan is Thor's deliverance. When Thor arrived at Geirröd's, he and his companion were first taken to the goat shed to stay, and inside there was a single seat to sit on, and Thor sat on it. Then he sensed that the seat was lifting up beneath him and heading for the ceiling, so he thrust Gríd's staff up into the rafters and forced himself back down onto the seat. Then there was a mighty crack, followed by a terrible scream: GJÁLP and Greip, Geirröd's daughters, had been underneath the seat, and he had broken both their backs. Then Geirröd had Thor summoned into the hall for some sporting contests. There were huge fires running the length of the hall, and when Thor entered the hall opposite Geirröd, Geirröd picked up a glowing lump of molten iron with some tongs and threw it at Thor, who caught it in his iron gauntlets and raised aloft the molten lump, while Geirröd ran behind an iron pillar for shelter. Thor threw the molten lump, and it smashed through the pillar, through Geirröd, through the wall, and so into the ground outside.'

This episode has many parallels with other tales that give further accounts of the trips of Thor or his counterparts into the abode of the giants. So, for example, Snorri describes in comic detail Thor's dealings with the mysterious ÚTGARDALOKI – when Thor is less than victorious in his sporting contests in the giant's hall – while the eddic poem HYMISKVIDA describes how Thor, on the advice of a friendly giantess, smashes the giant's goblet by flinging it at the giant's head. The early thirteenth-century Danish author SAXO GRAMMATICUS gives a number of clearly parallel accounts, in which Thor attacks one Geruthus and his daughters, or the heroic Thorkillus, whose exploits are certainly modelled on those of the god, experiences a number of adventures when visiting both Geruthus and the strikingly named Utgarthilocus. An Icelandic tale of uncertain date, *Thorsteins þáttr bæjarmagns*, preserved in a fifteenth-century manuscript, again transfers Thor's exploits to a fictional hero, and among the sporting contests in which Thorstein is involved at the hall of the giant-king Geirröd is one in which a red-hot seal's head weighing 440kg (200lb), which Geirröd describes as his 'golden ball', is thrown between the contestants.

B12, 14, 23, 24, 28, 30, 35, 40, 50, 56, 59, 64, 73, 87, 90; C2, 5, 7–9, 17, 24, 33, 46, 48; D477

Geirvimul *see* HVERGELMIR.

Geitir ('butt')

(1) According to the name-lists or THULUR, the name of a giant. (2) The name of the servant of GRÍPIR, the maternal uncle of the hero SIGURD. According to the eddic poem GRÍPISSPÁ, Geitir announces Sigurd's arrival and takes care of GRANI, his horse,

B12, 30, 56, 73, 87, 90; C2, 17, 24, 33, 46

Gelgja ('fetter')

According to the thirteenth-century Icelander SNORRI STURLUSON, a cord from the mythical fetter GLEIPNIR, by which the ÆSIR managed to secure the wolf FENRIR.

B24, 28, 35, 40, 50; C5, 9, 48

Gerd ('fenced-in')

The daughter of GYMIR the giant and the beloved of the fertility-god FREY. The wooing of Gerd is recounted in the eddic poem SKÍRNISMÁL. Elsewhere in the POETIC EDDA, the author of HYNDLULJÓD adds that Gerd's mother was called AURBODA, and the thirteenth-century Icelander SNORRI STURLUSON concurs, stating that she was a rock-giantess and that Gerd herself was 'the most beautiful of all women'. Her marriage to Frey elevates her to the status of one of the goddesses or ÁSYNJUR. Elsewhere, Snorri includes Gerd's name in a list of giantesses with whom the god ODIN had

sexually betrayed his wife FRIGG, although such a tale is alluded to nowhere else. It is possible that Odin's conquest was, in fact, the famously helpful giantess GRÍD, although elsewhere the god THOR is the beneficiary of her (non-sexual) attentions. It must remain at least a possibility that Odin's notorious appetites extended to Frey's beautiful wife, or perhaps that Snorri errs in naming Gerd as the rival of Frigg, rather than the goddess FREYJA, who, after the fashion of the fertility-gods or VANIR, may earlier have slept with her brother Frey herself.

B12, 14, 23, 24, 28, 30, 35, 40, 50, 56, 59, 73, 87, 90; C2, 5, 9, 17, 24, 33, 46, 48; D34, 397, 403

Geri *see* FREKI.

Germania

A treatise composed by the Roman historian TACITUS in AD 98 to bring the nobility and grandeur of the Germanic tribes to the attention of the (as Tacitus saw it) soft and decadent Roman citizenry. Despite its highly stylized and rose-tinted view of Germanic society and way of life, *Germania* remains an unquestionably valuable source for Germanic beliefs and customs in the first century.

B2; C29

Gersemi ('treasure')

According to the thirteenth-century Icelander SNORRI STURLUSON, a daughter of the fertility-goddess FREYJA.

B24, 28, 35, 40, 50; C5, 9, 48

Gesta Danorum *see* SAXO GRAMMATICUS.

Gesta Hammaburgensis ecclesiae pontificum *see* ADAM OF BREMEN.

Gestumblindagátur *see* GESTUMBLINDI.

Gestumblindi ('the blind guest')

The assumed name of the god ODIN as he engages in a riddling battle of wits, the so-called *Gestumblindagátur*, with King HEIDREK in the legendary HERVARAR SAGA OK HEIDREKS KONUNGS. As in his contest with the wise giant VAFTHRÚDNIR described in the eddic poem VAFTHRÚDNISMÁL, Odin rather unfairly ends the contest by asking an unanswerable question concerning the words that he had spoken in the ear of his dead son BALDR on the funeral pyre. At this point, both Heidrek and Váfthrúdnir guess the true identity of their mysterious opponent and concede defeat.

According to the early thirteenth-century Danish

historian SAXO GRAMMATICUS, there was a king of Gotland named Gestiblindus, whom some have identified with Gestumblindi, although the resemblance is not certain.

B12, 30, 56, 64, 73, 80, 87, 90; C2, 7, 8, 17, 21, 24, 33, 46

Getica see JORDANES.

ghosts see DRAUGAR.

giant builder

The story of the giant builder is told in full only by the thirteenth-century Icelander SNORRI STURLUSON, although the tale appears to be alluded to in the eddic poem VÖLUSPÁ, which elsewhere Snorri freely plunders as a source. After the ÆSIR had established MIDGARD and VALHALL, a builder approaches and offers to build in three seasons a citadel secure against the GIANTS; in return he asks for the fertility-goddess FREYJA, the sun and the moon. The Æsir, at the suggestion of LOKI, stipulate that he is to have only one season and must work unaided except for his stallion, SVADILFARI. Nonetheless, when progress is so rapid that the successful completion of the citadel seems assured, the Æsir resort to guile. Loki transforms himself into a mare and lures away Svadilfari, eventually giving birth to SLEIPNIR, who becomes the horse of the god ODIN. The builder, greatly handicapped by the loss of his stallion, fails to complete the contract, and when he flies into a giant-rage, the god THOR simply despatches him with his hammer MJÖLLNIR. The whole episode can hardly be said to reflect any credit on the Æsir, and it is strongly suggested by the allusion to the episode in *Völuspá* that the degeneration of the Æsir follows soon after.

B24, 28, 35, 40, 50; C5, 9, 48

giants

Giants play a central, if ambiguous, role in the mythology of the north, being presented on the one hand as primeval beings, from one of whose number, YMIR, the world is created and from whose seed the ÆSIR themselves ultimately sprang. On the other hand, giants are also presented as essentially inimical to both the Æsir and men, literal outsiders who inhabit the margins of the known world, dwelling in ÚTGARD. The blurring of interest between the giants and the Æsir is witnessed by the fact that two of the Æsir, FREY and NJÖRD (although it is intriguing to note that both are in origin VANIR), marry giantesses, GERD and SKADI, while a third, ODIN, devotes practically his entire energy as a serial adulterer to the seduction of giantesses, including GRÍD, GUNNLÖD, JÖRD, RIND and perhaps Gerd. In the same way, although with conspicuously

less success, a number of giants – HRUNGNIR, THJAZI, THRYM and the GIANT BUILDER (whose horse sires SLEIPNIR) – try to win the hearts and, more specifically, bodies of several of the goddesses or ÁSYNJUR, notably FREYJA, but also IDUN and SIF. While later legendary sources depict giants as essentially overgrown children, but with less sense and sensitivity, several giants – for example, MÍMIR or VAFTHRÚDNIR – are attributed with great wisdom, and are actively sought out by the god Odin in his quest for knowledge.

At the very beginning of *Gesta Danorum*, the early thirteenth-century Danish historian SAXO GRAMMATICUS famously asserts, on the evidence of megalithic monuments surviving into his own day, that Denmark had once been cultivated by giants:

> The fact that the land of Denmark was once inhabited by a race of giants is attested by the huge boulders found next to ancient burial mounds and caves. If anyone doubts whether or not this was carried out by superhuman power, let him ponder the heights of certain mounds and then say, if he can, who carried such huge rocks to their tops. Anyone considering this wonder must reckon it unthinkable that ordinary human strength could lift such bulk to that height. Even on a level plain it would be difficult, and perhaps beyond your strength, to shift it. There is not enough evidence to decide whether those who devised these works were giants who lived after the influx of the Flood or men of supernatural strength. Such creatures, as our compatriots maintain, are reckoned today to inhabit the rugged and inaccessible wasteland, which I discussed above, and to be endowed with transmutable bodies, so that they have the wondrous ability to appear and disappear, to be present and then suddenly somewhere else.

As the great range and variety of giant-names attests (*see* Appendix C), a large number of characteristics was associated with giants and the other creatures, such as TROLLS, *thursar* (*see* THURS) and *jötnar* (*see* JÖTUN), with which they are often conflated in the written record. There even seem to be distinctions drawn between kinds of giant, and texts often appear to distinguish, for example, frost-giants from rock-giants.

Although they are intimately associated with the distant past and with the beginnings of the world, perhaps the overriding characteristic of giants of all kinds is their essential hostility to gods and men, as witnessed most effectively by the enmity towards them of the chief defender of the gods (and chief giant-slayer), the god THOR, as well as by the fact that the giants fight on the 'wrong' side against both gods and men in the apocalyptic battle of RAGNARÖK.

B24, 28, 35, 40, 50, 64; C5, 7–9, 48; D71–3, 135, 199, 287, 395, 396, 398, 401, 402, 492, 550

Gilling

Gilling ('screamer')

A giant, according to the thirteenth-century Icelander SNORRI STURLUSON, and the father of SUTTUNG. He is drowned by FJALAR and GALAR, the two dwarfs who had previously slain KVASIR. It is in revenge for the murder of Gilling and, later, his wife (who has a millstone dropped on her head), that Suttung tortures the dwarfs into giving him the MEAD OF POETRY in recompense. So, in the late tenth century, a skaldic verse of EYVIND FINNSSON SKÁLDASPILLIR describes the mead of poetry as 'Gilling's recompense'.

B24, 28, 35, 40, 50; C5, 9, 48

Gils *see* ÆSIR.

Gimir *see* VINDBLÁIN.

Gimlé ('fire-proof'?)

A shining hall. The sibyl in the eddic poem VÖLUSPÁ, speaking of the great conflagration that will sweep the world after RAGNARÖK, says:

> I know a hall standing, more beautiful than the sun,
> better than gold, at Gimlé.
> Virtuous folk shall live there,
> and enjoy pleasure for all time.

The thirteenth-century Icelander SNORRI STURLUSON, who cites the particular version of the stanza from *Völuspá* quoted above, develops the inherent parallels with the Christian conception of heaven, in a discussion of the role of 'the highest and most ancient of gods', describing how he:

> Lives through all ages and governs his whole kingdom, and rules everything, great and small ... [who] made heaven and earth and the skies, and everything in them ... his greatest work is that he made man, and gave him a soul that shall live and never fail, though the body rot to dust or burn to ash. And all who are virtuous shall live and dwell with him himself in the place called Gimlé or VINGÓLF, but the wicked shall go to HEL and then to NIFLHEL, which is down in the ninth world.

Elsewhere, Snorri describes Gimlé as being in the third heaven and that up until the apocalyptic events of Ragnarök it is inhabited by LIGHT ELVES.

B12, 14, 23, 24, 28, 30, 35, 40, 50, 56, 59, 73, 87, 90; C2, 5, 9, 17, 24, 33, 46, 48

Gipul *see* HVERGELMIR.

Ginnungagap ('beguiling void')

The eddic poem VÖLUSPÁ places the beguiling void of Ginnungagap at the beginning of the world, in the time of the giant YMIR:

> It was the time when Ymir lived,
> there was no sand or sea, or cold waves;
> the earth could not be seen at all, nor high heaven,
> no sign of vegetation, but a beguiling void.

The thirteenth-century Icelander SNORRI STURLUSON, building on this account, makes Ginnungagap the primeval firmament, from which all things sprang.

B12, 14, 23, 24, 28, 30, 35, 40, 50, 56, 59, 73, 87, 90; C2, 5, 9, 17, 24, 33, 46, 48; D62, 593

Gísla saga

An Icelandic saga, perhaps dating to the thirteenth or fourteenth century, and purporting to give an account of the life of the great tenth-century outlaw, Gísli Súrsson. Unlike other outlaw-sagas, notably GRETTIS SAGA ÁSMUNDARSONAR, which was probably composed later, *Gísla saga* does not contain many descriptions of the hero's encounters with supernatural beings, although there is considerable emphasis on the power and workings of fate, and the latter part of Gísli's life is portrayed as beset with troubling dreams, with good and bad dream-women struggling over him in a manner not unlike that depicted of the supernatural female figures known as DÍSIR in other sources. Among many notable descriptions is a detailed account of a ceremony of blood-brotherhood, involving a ritual of passing under a strip of earth or JARDARMEN, in a doomed attempt to avert the course of fate.

B41, 78; C12, 19; D310, 586

Gjaflaug

According to the eddic poem GUDRÚNARKVIDA I, the sister of the legendary King GJÚKI and one of the women who attempts to console her recently widowed niece GUDRÚN by describing her own burden of grief:

> Then spoke Gjaflaug, Gjúki's sister:
> 'I think myself the world's most loveless:
> I've felt the loss of five husbands,
> three daughters, three sisters,
> eight brothers; but I live on.'

Gjaflaug's plight is by no means atypical of women in the legendary past, and she is strikingly unsuccessful in comforting the silently grieving Gudrún.

B12, 30, 56, 73, 87, 90; C2, 17, 24, 33, 46

Gjallarbrú ('bridge over the river Gjöll')

The name of a bridge over one of the rivers of the

Underworld called GJÖLL, according to the thirteenth-century Icelander SNORRI STURLUSON. An account is given of the ride of HERMÓD, the son of the god ODIN, down to HEL in search of the dead god BALDR. He has to pass over Gjallarbrú, which is 'covered with gold', and guarded by the giantess MÓDGUD (presumably he has already passed over BIFRÖST (Ásabrú), guarded by the god HEIMDALL).

B24, 28, 35, 40, 50; C5, 9, 48

Gjallarhorn ('yelling horn', 'horn of the river Gjöll'?)

The appropriately named 'yelling horn', which the god HEIMDALL sounds to mark the beginning of RAGNARÖK, according to the thirteenth-century Icelander SNORRI STURLUSON, who develops a notion found in the eddic poem VÖLUSPÁ, in which, however, the horn is unnamed. In the eddic poem GRÍMNISMÁL, Gjallarhorn is also mentioned in connection with Heimdall, but there the implication is that it is a drinking-horn, since we are told that Heimdall drinks good mead. With customary zeal to make use of every hint in his sources, Snorri also retains the notion that Gjallarhorn is a drinking-horn, naming it as the vessel from which the wise giant MÍMIR sups from his well and gains wisdom. It is possible that in the latter case the name Gjallarhorn is intended to signify 'horn of the river GJÖLL', since Gjöll is the name of one of the rivers of the Underworld, whence much wisdom is held to derive.

B12, 14, 23, 24, 28, 30, 35, 40, 50, 56, 59, 73, 87, 90; C2, 5, 9, 17, 24, 33, 46, 48; D435

Gjálp ('yelper')

According to the name-lists or THULUR, the name of a giantess. In the account of the thirteenth-century Icelander SNORRI STURLUSON, based largely on the skaldic poem THÓRSDRÁPA, she is specifically depicted as one of the two daughters of the giant GEIRRÖD – the other is Greip ('gripper') – who attempt to hinder the god THOR by urinating (or perhaps menstruating) into a river he is attempting to cross.

B24, 28, 35, 40, 50; C5, 9, 48; D477

Gjöll ('scream')

(1) According to the thirteenth-century Icelander SNORRI STURLUSON, one of the rivers that flows from the horns of the mythical stag EIKTHYRNIR, via the seething torrents of HVERGELMIR. (2) The name given by Snorri to the stone slab to which the wolf FENRIR is secured.

B24, 28, 35, 40, 50; C5, 9, 48

Gjúki

A powerful legendary king, husband of GRÍMHILD and father of three heroic sons – GUNNAR, HÖGNI GJÚKASON and GUTTHORM – as well as of the tragic heroine GUDRÚN. As the founder of the so-called dynasty of Gjúkings, Gjúki plays an important, if largely indirect role in the event surrounding the legendary VÖLSUNG-cycle. As the VÖLSUNGA SAGA has it:

> There was a king called Gjúki, whose kingdom was south of the Rhine. He had three sons, whose names were Gunnar, Högni and Gutthorm; Gudrún, his daughter, was the most famous of maids. They surpassed the children of other kings both in looks and in stature, and in every attainment. They were continually raiding, and accomplished many great feats. Gjúki was married to Grímhild, a woman well skilled in magic.

B25, 42, 65, 68, 79; C1, 6

Glad see ÆSIR.

Gladsheim ('bright home')

The hall where, according to the thirteenth-century Icelander SNORRI STURLUSON, the ÆSIR have their thrones, of which there are twelve, not including that of the god ODIN. As Snorri describes it:

> This building is the biggest and best that has been built in the world; both within and without it appears like nothing but gold.

B24, 28, 35, 40, 50; C5, 9, 48

Glær see ÆSIR.

Glæsivellir ('gleaming fields')

A legendary paradisal kingdom found in the northeast, according to the late witness of various FORNALDARSÖGUR, and ruled over by King GUDMUND, of whom the early thirteenth-century Danish historian SAXO GRAMMATICUS also speaks glowingly.

B64; C7, 8

Glasir ('gleaming')

According to the thirteenth-century Icelander SNORRI STURLUSON, a golden tree, 'the most beautiful tree among gods and men', which stands in front of the mighty hall VALHALL. Gold is accordingly described in a KENNING in a tenth-century skaldic verse as 'Glasir's glowing foliage'.

B24, 28, 35, 40, 50; C5, 9, 48

Glaumvör

The second wife of the legendary hero GUNNAR, according to the eddic poem ATLAMÁL (echoed in the legendary VÖLSUNGA SAGA). Glaumvör, like KOSTBERA,

Gleipnir

the wife of Gunnar's brother, HÖGNI GJÚKASON, has disturbing dreams before the two heroes set out on their doomed trip to visit their cruel brother-in-law ATLI BUDLASON. Gunnar's response to her flurry of ill omens is distinctly muted:

'I thought I saw a gallows prepared for you;
you went to be hanged,
worms ate you,
I lost you still alive:
RAGNARÖK has come.
Work out what that was!

'I thought I saw a bloody sword
pulled from your shirt:
dreadful to tell a dream like that
to a husband so close.
I thought I saw a spear stand
right through your middle;
wolves bayed at either end.'

'It must be dogs running,
howling loud;
often dogs' barking
signals the flight of spears.'

'I thought I saw a river running in
the whole length of the house;
it crashed with its current,
swelled over the benches,
broke the legs here
of both you brothers:
the water wouldn't stop.
It must stand for something.

'I thought I saw dead women
come here in the night:
they weren't badly dressed.
They wanted to pick you,
quickly called you
to their benches;
I reckon your DÍSIR
have been disarmed.'

B12, 20, 25, 30, 42, 56, 65, 68, 73, 79, 87, 90; C1 – 3, 6, 17, 24, 33, 46

Gleipnir ('open one')

According to the thirteenth-century Icelander SNORRI STURLUSON, the fetter with which the ÆSIR, after two failed attempts, finally manage to bind the wolf FENRIR. Gleipnir is described as 'smooth and soft as a silken ribbon', but it was strong enough. The god ODIN sent SKÍRNIR, the servant of the fertility-god FREY, to the dwarfs to have it made, and it was said to have been manufactured from the following six ingredients:

The sound of a cat's footfall, a woman's beard, a mountain's roots, a bear's sinews, a fish's breath and a bird's spit.

It is hardly surprising that Fenrir regarded the product of such rarities with suspicion, agreeing to be bound on condition that one of the Æsir place their right hand in his mouth. Only TÝR was brave enough – and Týr lost his hand.

B24, 28, 35, 40, 50; C5, 9, 48

Glen see SOL.

Glitnir ('shining one')

According to the eddic poem GRÍMNISMÁL, the silver hall with walls and pillars of gold belonging to the god FORSETI. The thirteenth-century Icelander SNORRI STURLUSON simply echoes *Grímnismál*. The name Glitnir also appears in the tenth-century YNGLINGATAL, but its function there is obscure.

B24, 28, 35, 40, 50; C5, 9, 48

Glóra see TROR.

Gná

Gná is known from the account of the thirteenth-century Icelander SNORRI STURLUSON, who describes her as one of the minor goddesses or ÁSYNJUR and depicts her in the role of FRIGG's messenger, riding a horse that can gallop across the sea and sky, called Hófvarpnir.

B24, 28, 35, 40, 50; C5, 9, 48

Gnipahellir ('overhanging cave'?)

According to the eddic poem VÖLUSPÁ, Gnipahellir is the place where the chained dog GARM sits barking before the apocalyptic events of RAGNARÖK. It is presumably through the association of Garm and the Graeco-Roman mythical dog Cerberus that Gnipahellir is sometimes situated at the entrance to HEL, although there is no external evidence to support this.

B12, 30, 56, 59, 73; C2, 3, 17, 24, 33, 46

Gnitaheid ('nit-heath')

The place where the dragon FÁFNIR lives and guards his treasure-hoard. In the legendary VÖLSUNGA SAGA Fáfnir's scheming brother REGIN tells SIGURD, his foster-son:

'When you get there, you'll say that you never saw more golden riches in a single place; and you won't need any more, even if you become the oldest and most famous of kings.'

B25, 42, 65, 68, 79; C1, 6

godi

An office, best attested in Iceland, denoting both social and sacral prominence. The holder of a *godord* served as both chieftain and priest. A handful of runic inscriptions, dating back to the fifth century, testify to the antiquity of the office, but it is the much later Icelandic sources that provide the best documented evidence for the activities of the *godi* (plural *godar*). In these sources, the *godar* appear for the most part in a purely secular context. Rarely is the devotion of an individual *godi*, whose legal obligation extended to the upkeep of a local TEMPLE and to presiding over sacrifices, stressed or even stated. An exception is HRAFNKELS SAGA FREYSGODA, a saga probably composed in the late thirteenth century that purports to tell the story of a chieftain named Hrafnkel, whose particular devotion to the god FREY manifests itself in the form of a sacred stallion, Freyfaxi, which Hrafnkel dedicates to Frey, vowing to kill anyone who rides him. The increasing secularization of the office is further witnessed by the account given in the mid-thirteenth-century EYRBYGGJA SAGA of the rights and duties of farmers and an individual *godi* with responsibility for a particular temple:

> Every farmer had to pay tax to the temple, and another of their duties was to support the temple *godi* in his duties, just as farmers these days have to support their chieftains. It was the duty of the temple *godi* to look after the temple and see to its proper upkeep at his own expense, as well as to hold sacrifices.

B37, 77; C39, 42; D457

Góin

According to the eddic poem GRÍMNISMÁL, in a verse cited by the thirteenth-century Icelander SNORRI STURLUSON, one of the snakes that slither at the foot of the world-tree YGGDRASIL.

B12, 14, 23, 24, 28, 30, 35, 40, 50, 56, 59, 73, 87, 90; C2, 5, 9, 17, 24, 33, 46, 48

Gokstad

A celebrated Viking Age BOAT BURIAL from Vestfold in Norway, conventionally dated around the turn of the tenth century. An elderly male, between sixty and seventy years old, has been placed in a burial chamber immediately aft of the mast, surrounded by grave-goods, including several fine strap-mounts, a finely wrought cauldron, a tub and a number of buckets. Buried along with the main ship, which is equipped for thirty-two oarsmen and appears to have been the private vessel of a powerful chieftain, are three smaller boats and a sledge. Animal remains suggest the sumptuous sacrifices made at the funeral – a dozen horses, half a dozen dogs and even a peacock.

D269, 536, 612

Göll *see* VALKYRIES.

Gömul, Göpul *see* HVERGELMIR.

Goti ('steed')

According to the legendary VÖLSUNGA SAGA, the horse belonging to the hero GUNNAR, which refuses to leap over the flames surrounding the sleeping Valkyrie BRYNHILD.

B25, 42, 65, 68, 79; C1, 6

Grábak *see* YGGDRASIL.

Grád *see* HVERGELMIR.

Grafvitnir *see* YGGDRASIL.

Grafvöllud *see* YGGDRASIL.

Gram ('wrath')

The mighty sword of the legendary hero SIGURD,

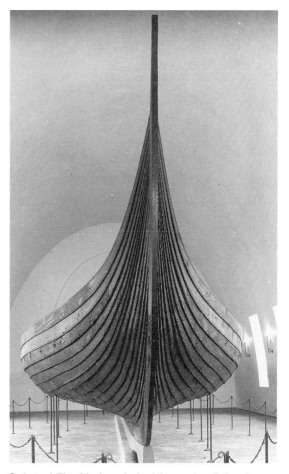

Gokstad The ship from the burial mound at Gokstad, Vestfold, Norway. Such boat burials are well-attested in both the literary and the archaeological evidence.

Gram *Detail of the portal from the church at Hylestad, Setesdal, Norway, showing the wicked Regin forging the great sword Gram for the mighty hero Sigurd, so that he can use it to kill Fáfnir the dragon and gain his fabulous hoard.*

forged by his foster-father REGIN from the broken remnants of his father SIGMUND's shattered blade. Using Gram, Sigurd avenged Sigmund and went on to kill both the dragon FÁFNIR and the dragon's brother, Regin. The legendary VÖLSUNGA SAGA adds a number of incidental details, namely that Gram was seven spans long and that when Sigurd, disguised as his eventual brother-in-law GUNNAR, first shared a bed with the Valkyrie BRYNHILD he placed the unsheathed Gram between them. *Völsunga saga*, drawing on a prose passage in the eddic poem REGINSMÁL, also contains the fullest account of the forging of Gram:

> Sigurd said: 'Now make a sword by your craftsmanship so that its equal has never been made. If you do this, I shall be able to do mighty deeds, if my courage holds, and if you want me to kill this dragon.' Regin said: 'Certainly I shall make it, and you will be able to kill Fáfnir with this sword.' Now Regin made a sword; he gave it to Sigurd, who took it and said: 'So much for your smithying, Regin.' Sigurd struck the anvil, and the sword shattered. He cast down the blade and told Regin to make another one better. Regin made a second sword and brought it to Sigurd. He looked it over. 'You'll like this one, though you are a difficult man to work for.' Sigurd tested the sword and shattered it just like the first one. Then Sigurd said to Regin: 'You are not to be trusted, just like your kin.' Then Sigurd went to

his mother; she gave him a good welcome. They talked together and drank. Then Sigurd said: 'Have I heard correctly that King Sigmund gave you the sword Gram in two pieces?' 'That is true,' she replied. 'Give it to me,' Sigurd said. 'I want to have it.' She said he was likely to win fame and gave him the sword. Then Sigurd met Regin and told him to make a sword worthy of these pieces. Regin became annoyed and went off to his forge with the pieces of sword; he thought that Sigurd was exacting in his metalcraft. Then Regin made a sword and when he drew it from the forge, it seemed to his helpers as if flames were playing about the edges. He told Sigurd to take hold of the sword and said that he was no swordsmith if this one shattered. Sigurd struck at the anvil and split it to its base. The blade did not break or fracture. He praised the sword highly and went to the river with a tuft of wool, which he threw in upstream; the sword sliced the wool in two when the tuft met the blade. Sigurd went home happy.

B12, 25, 30, 42, 56, 65, 68, 73, 79, 87, 90; C1–3, 6, 17, 24, 33, 46

Grani

The horse of the legendary hero SIGURD, selected, according to the legendary VÖLSUNGA SAGA, with the help of the god ODIN, who suggested that it be driven, along with other horses, into the river BUSILTJÖRN; only Grani did not turn back to shore. Grani is famously sensitive to his master's moods. For example, *Völsunga saga* reports how he moped around when Sigurd was first afflicted with love for the Valkyrie BRYNHILD, while, according to the eddic poem GUDRÚNARKVIDA II, Sigurd's widow GUDRÚN visits Grani first of all when she suspects that her brothers have slain Sigurd. As Gudrún explains:

> 'Grani galloped home: I heard his hoofs,
> though I could not see Sigurd himself.
> The saddle-horses were dark with sweat;
> they had hard work, to carry killers.
>
> 'I went in tears to talk to Grani;
> I asked him, weeping, what occurred.
> Grani sadly let his head droop down;
> the horse knew its master was gone.'

B12, 25, 30, 42, 56, 65, 68, 73, 79, 87, 90; C1–3, 6, 24, 33, 46

Granmar

Father of the legendary warrior HÖDBRODD. Granmar fights alongside his son against the heroes HELGI and SINFJÖTLI at the battle of FREKASTEIN. Granmar is chiefly remembered for the foul exchange of insults or FLYTING that he has with Sinfjötli just before the battle, according to the legendary VÖLSUNGA SAGA. In the eddic poem HELGAKVIDA HUNDINGSBANA I, which

Grani Detail of the Rasmundsberget runestone from Jäder, Södermanland, Sweden, depicting the splendid horse Grani tied to a tree full of birds. Grani's owner, the mighty hero Sigurd, who has drunk the blood of Fáfnir the dragon, can now understand the speech of birds.

is clearly the source for *Völsunga saga* at this point, it is his son GUDMUND, not Granmar, who has the battle of words.

B12, 25, 30, 42, 56, 65, 68, 73, 79, 87, 90; C1–3, 6, 17, 24, 33, 46

Greip *see* GJÁLP.

Grendel

The man-shaped monster whose battle with the poem's hero is celebrated in the Old English poem BEOWULF. He is said to have the strength of thirty men and (after the fashion of many TROLLS) inhabits a waterbound lair with his mother, an equally fearsome creature, who also battles against Beowulf. That similar creatures were attested in the north seems confirmed by the closeness of narrative structure of the monster-fights in *Beowulf* with episodes in some sagas, notably GRETTIS SAGA ÁSMUNDARSONAR. Some commentators have equated the depiction of Grendel with that of the Norse figures known as DRAUGAR, and the poem itself describes Grendel as a kind of giant.

B41, 44; C4, 12; D270, 324, 441, 508

Grettis saga Ásmundarsonar

An Icelandic saga of the early fourteenth century, purporting to give an account of the life of the outlaw Grettir Ásmundarson, who, unlike the heroes of other outlaw-sagas, notably GÍSLA SAGA, is depicted as an almost superhuman hero. Certainly, the saga makes extensive use of a number of supernatural motifs and figures, including BERSERKS, TROLLS, WITCHES and the specific kind of ghosts of walking dead known as DRAUGAR. In his successive battles against these and similar creatures the outlaw Grettir comes progressively to resemble the monsters he fights, and he is eventually killed in a manner traditionally associated with quieting *draugar*. The monster-fights in *Grettis saga* have been intensively studied for many years not only by Norse scholars but also by Anglo-Saxon critics because of a number of perceived close resemblances with the monster-fights in the Old English poem BEOWULF.

B41, 78, 88; C12, 19; D19, 71, 231, 270, 324, 358, 441, 464, 493

Gríd ('greed')

According to the thirteenth-century Icelander SNORRI STURLUSON, the helpful giantess who becomes the mother of VÍDAR, after sleeping with the god ODIN, and who assists the god THOR in his journey to the stronghold of the giant GEIRRÖD.

B24, 28, 355, 40, 50; C5, 9, 48

Grídarvöl *see* MEGINGJÖRD.

Grímhild

Wife of the legendary King GJÚKI and mother of several major figures, notably GUNNAR, GUDRÚN, GUTTHORM and HÖGNI GJÚKASON. Grímhild appears in a number of eddic poems, notably GRÍPISSPÁ and GUDRÚNARKVIDA II. The legendary VÖLSUNGA SAGA describes her as 'a woman well-versed in magic' and gives her a major role in contriving the marriage of the hero SIGURD and her daughter, Gudrún. First, she gives Sigurd a bewitched drink to make him forget his beloved, the Valkyrie BRYNHILD, and then she teaches Sigurd and Gunnar how to exchange shapes, so that Sigurd, in the shape of Gunnar, can win Brynhild for himself. Even after the deception has been discovered, Grímhild's wicked influence continues. She is instrumental in persuading Gutthorm to kill Sigurd, and she gives another bewitched drink to Gudrún to make her forget her grief afterwards and agree to marry the cruel ATLI BUDLASON. Only Brynhild appears to see through Grímhild's evil wiles: she predicts to Gudrún that Grímhild will administer her bewitched drink to Sigurd and blames her bitterly for the turn of events.

B12, 25, 30, 42, 56, 65, 68, 73, 79, 87, 90; C1–3, 6, 17, 24, 33, 46

Grímnir ('the masked one')

The suitably enigmatic name that the god ODIN assumes in the eddic poem GRÍMNISMÁL. As such, the name features in several KENNINGS for 'poetry' in the skaldic verses of, for example, ÚLF UGGASON and EILÍF GODRÚNARSON. In Eilíf's THÓRSDRÁPA the name Grímnir also occurs in a kenning for 'giant'. The simple term is also listed in the name-lists or THULUR with the same meaning. More startling, perhaps, is its appearance in a list of names for goats.

B12, 30, 56, 73, 87, 90; C2, 17, 24, 33, 46

Grímnismál ('the lay of Grímnir')

An eddic poem in a variety of metres, much echoed and quoted by the thirteenth-century Icelander SNORRI STURLUSON as a source for his mythological information and contained not only in the CODEX REGIUS but also in another manuscript, AM 748 I 4to. Snorri is not the only author to quote *Grímnismál*: the thirteenth-century Icelander Óláf Thórdarson cites part of a single stanza in the *Third Grammatical Treatise*.

The poem is transmitted alongside a prose introduction and conclusion that provide a narrative framework for the piece. The introduction describes how the two sons of the legendary King HRAUDUNG – AGNAR HRAUDUNGSSON and GEIRRÖD – are shipwrecked and given shelter over the winter by an elderly couple who 'adopt' one brother each; the old woman takes care of Agnar, the older brother, and the old man of Geirröd. In the spring the brothers sail away, but when they reach their father's port, Geirröd leaps out, thrusts the boat back and cries out to his brother: 'Be off with you, and may trolls take you.' When Geirröd walks up to the buildings, he is warmly welcomed: his father had died and he was now king. The scene now shifts to ÁSGARD, the home of the gods, where FRIGG and her husband ODIN, who had evidently been the old couple in question, are discussing the relative fortunes of the favourites. Odin points out that Agnar has ended up living in a cave, getting children on a witch; Frigg replies that Geirröd is stingy with food to his guests. When Odin disputes this, they make a bet. Odin,

calling himself GRÍMNIR, sets out to visit the court of Geirröd, and Frigg sends one of her handmaids, FULLA, to warn Geirröd to beware of a stranger whom his dogs would not attack. When Odin appears in a blue cloak and the dogs do not attack, Geirröd has him seized. Odin gives his name as Grímnir but refuses to say anything further, so Geirröd has him tortured, placing him between two fires for eight nights. At this point the king's son, Agnar, named after his uncle and at this time ten years old, the same age that the elder Agnar had been when shipwrecked, approaches Odin and hands him a horn of wine, saying that his father did wrong to torment him. Then Odin speaks the text of the poem, giving a lengthy recitation of mythological lore and concluding with an impressive list of his own titles, so gradually revealing his true identity. The prose conclusion describes Geirröd's desperate attempts to free Odin once he realizes his dreadful error, but he trips on his sword and perishes.

B12, 14, 23, 24, 28, 30, 35, 40, 50, 56, 59, 73, 87, 90; C2, 5, 9, 17, 24, 33, 46, 48; D160, 216, 467, 503, 513

Grípir

According to the large body of material circulating around the VÖLSUNG-cycle, a son of EYLIMI and the maternal uncle of the legendary hero SIGURD. The account of how he foretells Sigurd's fate is told in the eddic poem GRÍPISSPÁ.

B12, 25, 30, 42, 56, 65, 68, 73, 79, 87, 90; C1–3, 6, 17, 24, 33, 46

Grípisspá ('the prophecy of Grípir')

Also known as *Sigurdarkvida Fáfnisbana in fyrsta*, a poem of some fifty stanzas, and the first of a series of eddic poems in the CODEX REGIUS that deals with the life of the legendary hero SIGURD. *Grípisspá* was clearly composed somewhat later than some others of the eddic corpus that it echoes, but it must have been available to the Icelander Gunnlaug Leifsson, whose late twelfth-century *Merlínuspá* evidently borrows from it. The popularity of *Grípsspá* in the succeeding century is attested by a comment in *Breta saga*, perhaps composed in the mid-thirteenth century, and incorporating *Merlínuspá*, that asserts that many people had *Grípisspá* by heart.

The contents of the poem, which are often connected with the now-lost section of the Codex Regius containing SIGURDARKVIDA IN MEIRI, recount how Sigurd is given a prophetic account of his life by his maternal uncle, the prescient Grípir. As the brief prose preface has it:

> Grípir was the name of the son of EYLIMI, and the brother of HJÖRDÍS; this king was the wisest of men, and the best prophet.

Grípir's prophecy begins well enough, as he salutes his nephew:

You will be of men
the mightiest under the sun
the highest born
of any prince;
giving of gold,
a stranger to flight
glorious to gaze on,
and wise in words.

But as Grípir describes the forthcoming adventures of Sigurd's life, he becomes more and more tight-lipped about the impending tragedy. So, we hear about Sigurd's vengeance against the sons of the mighty warrior HUNDING; his killing of the dragon FÁFNIR and his own foster-father, REGIN, Fáfnir's brother; his acquisition of the dragon's hoard, his adventure with the king's daughter on the mountain-top; his meeting with the Valkyrie BRYNHILD; his trip to the court of King GJÚKI and marriage to Gjúki's daughter, GUDRÚN; his role in winning Brynhild for Gjúki's son, GUNNAR; and Brynhild's terrible vengeance when she finds out the truth. As Grípir describes the terrible grief of Gudrún, his final words to his nephew echo those with which he began his account:

So you must always consider,
war-band's leader,
that fortune must play a part
in a prince's life:
no nobler man
will walk the earth
under the expanse of the sky
than you, Sigurd, seem.

B12, 30, 56, 73, 87, 90; C2, 17, 24, 33, 46; D230

Gróa ('growing')

According to the eddic poem GRÓAGALDR, the dead mother of the hero SVIPDAG. As a sibyl or witch, she is able to offer him advice and teach him various helpful charms. The thirteenth-century Icelander SNORRI STURLUSON also makes her a sorceress but has her married to AURVANDIL, and tells the story of how she tried to remove a piece of whetstone that had lodged in the forehead of the god THOR after his encounter with the giant HRUNGNIR. She is apparently so entranced by Thor's account of how he threw Aurvandil's frozen toe into the sky, where it became a star, that she forgets to complete her spell; the whetstone remains in Thor's head.

B12, 14, 23, 24, 28, 30, 35, 40, 50, 56, 59, 73, 87, 90; C2, 5, 9, 17, 24, 33, 46, 48

Gróagaldr ('the spell of Gróa')

One of two eddic poems – the other is FJÖLSVINNSMÁL – that together tell the tale of the wooing of the beautiful MENGLÖD by the hero, SVIPDAG. Both poems, which share similarities of metre and style, are often considered together, under the collective title SVIPDAGSMÁL. The main body of the poem is taken up with the nine spells that GRÓA, a sibyl or witch, raised from the dead for the purpose, offers to help her son, Svipdag, who visits her grave to seek assistance in the dangerous quest he is about to undertake to seek the hand of Menglöd.

B12, 30, 56, 73, 87, 90; C2, 17, 24, 33, 46; D139, 140, 393, 516

Grottasöngr ('the mill's song')

A brief poem of some twenty-four stanzas preserved in some manuscripts of the thirteenth-century Icelandic treatise SKÁLDSKAPARMÁL, composed by SNORRI STURLUSON. According to the prose explanation offered by Snorri, King FRÓDI of Denmark, whose reign became a byword for peace and prosperity, bought two huge slave-girls – in fact, they were giantesses – called FENJA and Menja in Sweden, and set them to work a magic mill called GROTTI, which ground out whatever was wished. Fródi set them to grind out gold and prosperity, but granted them no rest, and eventually they ground out an army for the Viking Mysing, who killed Fródi and took possession of everything, including the mill. He set Fenja and Menja to grind salt, but he, too, omitted to grant them rest, and they churned out so much salt that Mysing's ships sank, the sea became salt and a whirlpool arose at the axis of the wheeling stones.

Like the weaving-poem DARRADARLJÓD, *Grottasöngr* appears to rely in part on the rhythms of the traditional work-song, although much of the poem is taken up with narrative stanzas. As soon as the two huge slave-girls start to speak, they rebuke Fródi for choosing them for their strength and looks, without asking after their ancestry. Then they mention some famous giants, beginning with HRUNGNIR and THJAZI, and ominously describe their lives as young giantesses and warrior-women, inciting slaughter. As they summon up images of chaos and death, the two giantesses grind on furiously. As the poem ends, it becomes clear that the mill itself is breaking up, a symbol of the ensuing catastrophe.

B12, 30, 56, 73, 87, 90; C2, 17, 24, 33, 46; D229, 580

Grotti

The hand-mill ground by the huge giantesses FENJA and Menja for the legendary king, FRÓDI, according to the eddic poem GROTTASÖNGR. Its special property, as explained by the thirteenth-century Icelander SNORRI

Gudmund

STURLUSON, was that it ground out whatever was wanted.

B12, 14, 23, 24, 28, 30, 35, 40, 50, 56, 59, 73, 87, 90; C2, 5, 9, 17, 24, 33, 46, 48; D580

Gudmund

(1) One of the sons of the ferocious warrior GRANMAR, and a character who features prominently in the eddic poems HELGAKVIDA HUNDINGSBANA I and II. In both poems Gudmund engages the hero SINFJÖTLI in a foul exchange of insults or FLYTING before the battle at FREKASTEIN, in which he is killed alongside his brothers.

(2) The name of the legendary king of GLÆSIVELLIR, according to the late witness of a number of sagas. Gudmund was held to be the neighbour, and, at least in several sources, the brother of the giant-king, GEIRRÖD.

B12, 30, 56, 73, 87; C2, 17, 24, 33, 46

Gudný

According to the thirteenth-century Icelander SNORRI STURLUSON, a daughter of the legendary king, GJÚKI, and so sister of the better attested GUNNAR, HÖGNI GJÚKASON, GUTTHORM and GUDRÚN. She does not appear in the other sources of the legendary VÖLSUNG-cycle.

B24, 25, 28, 35, 40, 42, 50, 65, 68, 79; C1, 5, 6, 9, 48

Gudrún

Daughter of the legendary king GJÚKI, and sister of the heroes GUNNAR, HÖGNI GJÚKASON and GUTTHORM. In the course of a long and tragic life she becomes wife in turn of the hero SIGURD and of the kings ATLI BUDLASON and JÓNAK, and so mother of a number of doomed figures of heroic legend, specifically SVANHILD, HAMDIR, SÖRLI, EITIL and ERP ATLASON. Gudrún is the quintessential tragic heroine, both the witness to, and the cause of, countless deaths of those connected to her by blood or marriage, and she makes an appearance in no fewer than a dozen eddic lays (REGINSMÁL, SIGRDRÍFUMÁL, BROT AF SIGURDARKVIDU, GUDRÚNARKVIDA I, SIGURDARKVIDA IN SKAMMA, HELREID BRYNHILDAR, GUDRÚNARKVIDA II, GUDRÚNARKVIDA III, ODDRÚNARGRÁTR, ATLAK-VIDA, ATLAMÁL, GUDRÚNARHVÖT and HAMDISMÁL), as well as in other works, notably the legendary VÖLSUNGA SAGA. In the beginning, she appears as little more than a helpless tool of the ambitions of her scheming mother, GRÍMHILD, who ensures by the use of a magic potion that the hero Sigurd forgets his love for the Valkyrie BRYNHILD and marries Gudrún instead. Gudrún's revelation to Brynhild of the circumstances of her be-

trothal to Gunnar seems prompted by simple jealousy, and in the cataclysmic events that follow, leading up to Sigurd's death at the hands of Gudrún's brothers, Gudrún is wholly eclipsed by her rival, even to the point that it is Brynhild who kills herself and occupies the wife's place on Sigurd's pyre.

Gudrún's reaction to Sigurd's death is characteristically passive; she takes herself off to the court of King HÁLF in Denmark, and passes the next seven seasons with THÓRA, Hákon's daughter, making an elaborate embroidery. Once again she becomes simply a bargaining-chip in her family's dynastic ambitions, as her mother employs a magic potion to make her forget her grief, be reconciled with her brothers and marry Atli, the brother of her hated rival, Brynhild. Having married unwillingly, Gudrún can only send an ineffectual warning to her brothers of Atli's wicked intentions when he extends to them an invitation to visit, and she has to watch helpless as her two brothers, Gunnar and Högni, are killed. Finally, provoked beyond endurance, Gudrún's reaction is swift and terrible: she kills her two sons by Atli, and cooks and feeds them to her despotic and drunk husband, before telling him what she has done. Before he can react, she kills him in their marital bed and sets his palace alight.

But her own suffering is not over. When she tries to drown herself, she is instead washed into the arms of King JÓNAK, who becomes her third husband. Together they have two sons, Hamdir and Sörli, but it is only when Svanhild, her much loved daughter by Sigurd, is killed by King JÖRMUNREKK, that Gudrún again asserts herself, driving her sons on to an ultimately fatal vengeance. It is characteristic of the essentially passive status of Gudrún throughout that after she has been deprived through violent death of two husbands, three brothers and at least five children, her own demise is not actually described, although the closing verses of *Gudrúnarhvöt* seem to suggest that after the deaths of her sons Hamdir and Sörli she simply casts herself on a pyre in grief.

Throughout the extant texts, two pictures of Gudrún remain in particular. The first is the description in the eddic poem *Atlakvida* of the manic and tearless Gudrún, wreaking terrible revenge on Atli for the murder of her brothers:

> A groaning grew on the benches,
> a dreadful dirge of men;
> a crying under rich cloaks:
> the Huns' children grieved,
> all except Gudrún
> who never grieved
> for her bearish brothers,
> for her sweetheart sons,

so young, so fresh,
whom she had borne to Atli.

Gosling-bright,
she scattered gold,
showered the servants
with red-gold rings.
She brought events to a head,
she poured out bright metal;
little did the lady
pay the temple-treasuries heed.

Unsuspecting, Atli
had drunk himself to a stop;
he had no weapons,
he did not shy from Gudrún;
often their sport was the sweeter,
when with many a kindly kiss
they often embraced
in front of noblemen.

With the point of a blade
she gave the bed a bloody drink,
with a Hel-keen hand,
and set the dogs free,
and woke the servants.
In front of the hall door
she flung a burning brand:
She paid them back for her brothers.

More representative, perhaps, are the various descriptions, scattered throughout the eddic poems, of Gudrún weeping for her lost loved ones. Typical is the way Gudrún mourns in *Gudrúnarkvida I*, when GULLRÖND, her sister, sweeps the covering from Sigurd's corpse:

Gudrún gave a single glance:
she saw the prince's hair drip blood,
the warrior's keen eyes dimmed,
the chieftain's mighty chest sword-rent.

Leaning, Gudrún bent low to the pillow
her hair came loose, her cheeks grew red,
raindrop tears ran down her knees.

Then Gudrún, Gjúki's daughter, grieved
and tears streamed through her tresses;
out in the yard, the geese began honking,
those famous fowl the lady owned.

Then said Gullrönd, Gjúki's daughter,
'I know that your love was greater
than any man's or woman's in the world;
you were never happy outside or in,
my sister, except by Sigurd.'

[Gudrún spoke:]
'Next to Gjúki's sons my Sigurd towered
like a leek that stands among grass,
or a dazzling gem on a string of beads,
a precious jewel among the princes.'

B12, 20, 25, 30, 31, 32, 42, 56, 65, 68, 73, 78, 87, 90; C1–3, 6, 17, 24, 33, 46

Gudrúnarhvöt ('Gudrún's incitement')

An eddic poem, one of the chain of poems in the CODEX REGIUS dealing with the tragic events surrounding the lives of the VÖLSUNG-cycle. As the poem opens, GUDRÚN is inciting HAMDIR and SÖRLI, her two sons by her third husband, JÓNAK, to avenge their sister SVANHILD; she had been killed by her husband JÖRMUNREKK, who had her trampled to death by horses for suspected adultery. The tale of their expedition is told more fully in the eddic poem HAMDISMÁL. She contrasts their indolence with the vigour of her own heroic brothers, GUNNAR and HÖGNI GJÚKASON, whom ATLI BUDLASON, her second husband, had slaughtered. Hamdir points out that these brothers had themselves been responsible for killing the hero SIGURD, her first husband, and that she had the blood on her hands of her own two sons by Atli, whom she killed in revenge for her brothers; but finally he agrees. Gudrún laughs and goes to fetch armour for her sons. As they depart, Hamdir prophesies their death. When her sons have left, Gudrún weeps, and, in a brief review of the tragic events surrounding her three marriages, she focuses on the happiness that her beautiful daughter Svanhild had given her and longs to return to her first love, Sigurd. She commands that a funeral pyre be built, to melt her sorrows for good:

'Nobles, pile up
the oaken pyre
let it be the highest, under heaven;
let the fire burn
my grief-filled chest,
forced from my heart,
let sorrows melt.'

B12, 20, 25, 30, 32, 42, 56, 65, 68, 73, 78, 87, 90; C1–3, 6, 17, 24, 33, 46; D518, 524

Gudrúnarkvida I–III ('the lay of Gudrún')

A group of three eddic poems found in the CODEX REGIUS, chronicling the life of the tragic heroine, GUDRÚN, after the killing of the hero SIGURD, her first husband, by her brothers, up to the point where she plots the murder of ATLI BUDLASON, her second husband, for his slaughter of those same brothers.

Gudrúnarkvida I is a brief poem of some twenty-seven stanzas, containing several elegiac passages of great beauty. The poem opens with a description of Gudrún sitting over the corpse of her beloved Sigurd, unable to weep. She is goaded by various noble ladies, each of whom describes their own grief in an effort to bring her to mourn. Finally, one sweeps off the sheet that covers Sigurd, revealing the dead hero, and Gudrún breaks down, mourning his fallen greatness and her own:

'Next to GJÚKI's sons my Sigurd towered
like a leek among grass,
or a dazzling gem on a string of beads,
a precious jewel among the princes.

'My lord's retainers once honoured me
more than any of ODIN's maids;
now I am as little as a winter-leaf
that clings to a willow, now the prince is dead.'

By contrast we are given a picture of Gudrún's rival, BRYNHILD (who, rather ironically, as a former Valkyrie was herself one of 'Odin's maids'). In the final stanza we see her, standing by a pillar and gazing at the wounds on Sigurd's body with blazing eyes.

Gudrúnarkvida II is separated from *Gudrúnarkvida* I in the Codex Regius by several other poems, and it contains a number of problematic passages. The forty-four stanzas effectively form an extended monologue by Gudrún, describing how she passed her time after Sigurd's death, until she was approached by emissaries from the court of Atli, the brother of Brynhild, evidently bringing an offer of marriage. Gudrún refuses, until she is given a potion of forgetfulness (whose extraordinary ingredients, including pig's blood, soot, sacrificial entrails and half-burned acorns, are duly listed). She foresees the killing of her brothers, GUNNAR and HÖGNI GJÚKASON, by Atli and her subsequent revenge on him. Nonetheless we infer that the match takes place, for Gudrún goes on to describe her soothing pillow-talk to Atli, distressed by foreboding dreams, which the audience is undoubtedly supposed to recognize as predicting Atli's death at the hands of Gudrún after she has slaughtered, cooked and served up to him their own two sons, in an episode portrayed more fully in the eddic poems ATLAKVIDA and ATLAMÁL. Gudrún's bland dismissal of Atli's worrying dreams is made to seem all the more chilling by her disturbing reaction once Atli's fears have been allayed:

'Then I lay awake,
not wishing to sleep,
nor to arise:
I remember it well.'

Gudrúnarkvida III, which immediately follows *Gudrúnarkvida* II in the Codex Regius, is a poem of only ten stanzas, describing what appears to be a peripheral episode, in which a previous mistress of Atli, HERKJA (1), accuses Gudrún of adultery with King THJÓDREK. She offers to undertake an ordeal by boiling water to clear her name and successfully does so; her accuser, Herkja, called to take the same ordeal, is badly scalded and exiled into a 'foul bog'.

B12, 30, 31, 56, 73, 87, 90; C2, 17, 24, 33, 46; D63, 82, 188, 527, 603, 618

Gullfaxi ('golden mane')

According to the thirteenth-century Icelander SNORRI STURLUSON, the swift horse ridden by the giant HRUNGNIR when he challenged the god ODIN (who was riding the eight-legged SLEIPNIR) to a race. After the god THOR killed Hrungnir, he gave Gullfaxi to his son MAGNI, much to Odin's chagrin.

B24, 28, 35, 40, 50; C5, 9, 48

Gullinborsti, Gullinbursti ('golden bristles')

According to the thirteenth-century Icelander SNORRI STURLUSON, the golden boar, also called Slídrugtanni ('sharp teeth'), which pulls the chariot of the god FREY. It seems likely that Snorri has extrapolated the name from a skaldic verse of the Icelander ÚLF UGGASON (who flourished around the year 1000), which describes Frey riding to the funeral pyre of the god BALDR on a golden-bristled boar. In a more elaborate account of the giving of Gullinborsti (at this point unnamed) to Frey by the dwarf BROKK at the same time as ODIN was given the spear DRAUPNIR and THOR was given the hammer MJÖLLNIR, Snorri states that:

[Brokk] gave the boar to Frey and said that it could run across sky and sea day or night faster than any horse, and it never grew so dark at night, nor in any place of darkness, that it was not bright enough wherever it travelled, so much light was shed from its bristles.

B24, 28, 35, 40, 50; C5, 9, 48

Gullintanni ('golden-toothed')

According to the thirteenth-century Icelander SNORRI STURLUSON, another name for the god HEIMDALL. Quite apart from his golden teeth, Heimdall was also supposed to ride on a horse called Gulltopp ('golden top').

B24, 28, 35, 40, 50; C5, 9, 48

Gullnir

In the course of the abusive exchange or FLYTING in which the legendary warriors GUDMUND and SINFJÖTLI indulge before the battle of FREKASTEIN, according to the eddic poem HELGAKVIDA HUNDINGSBANA I, Gudmund accuses Sinfjötli (or perhaps vice versa) of 'milking Gullnir's goats'. The allusion is undoubtedly intended as obscene, while the context appears to suggest that Gullnir was a giant.

B12, 30, 56, 73, 87, 90; C2, 17, 24, 33, 46

Gullrönd

According to the eddic poem GUDRÚNARKVIDA I, a daughter of the legendary king GJÚKI, who acts as a kind of chorus on the dramatic events of the poem. To her sister, the tragic heroine GUDRÚN, she says (of Gudrún's marriage to the mighty hero Sigurd):

'I know that your love was greater
than any man's or woman's in the world;
you were never happy outside or in,
my sister, except by Sigurd.'

To BRYNHILD, her sister's great rival, she is equally forthright:

'Don't say such words, you hateful woman!
You have always proved poisonous to princes:
the whole world sees you steeped in wickedness,
a source of sorrow for seven kings,
a mighty widow-maker of wives.'

B12, 30, 56, 73, 87, 90; C2, 17, 24, 33, 46

Gulltopp see ÆSIR; GULLINTANNI.

Gullveig ('gold-draught')

An extremely perplexing figure, named only in a single stanza of the eddic poem VÖLUSPÁ, immediately preceding the war that erupts between the divine races of the ÆSIR and the VANIR. The relevant passage of the poem reads as follows:

Then [the sibyl] remembered the first great war in
   the world,
when they stabbed at Gullveig with spears,
and they burned her in ODIN's hall;
thrice they burned the thrice-born girl,
often, not once, but still she lived.

They called her HEID, when she came to the house,
a sibylline witch, who knew the skill of wands,
she practised SEID where she could, practised *seid* in
   a trance;
she was always a delight to wicked women.

Gullveig is sometimes held to be a personification of gold, purified through repeated smelting, or perhaps one of the Vanir ill-treated. Her coming among the Æsir clearly foments discord. It has even been suggested that Gullveig is another name for the goddess

FREYJA, who is certainly of the Vanir, is associated with gold (for example through the gold tears she shed for her beloved husband ÓD, and through her daughters, GERSEMI and HNOSS, who may, however, be one and the same) and is particularly linked with the form of magic known as *seid*.

B12, 30, 56, 59, 73, 87, 90; C2, 17, 24, 33, 46; D156, 182, 306, 406

Gungnir ('swaying one')

The mighty spear owned by the god ODIN. According to the thirteenth-century Icelander SNORRI STURLUSON, Gungnir was a gift of the dwarfs known as ÍVALDI'S SONS. In Snorri's YNGLINGA SAGA both Odin and the god NJÖRD mark themselves with a spear to dedicate themselves to Odin, and similar dedications are widely witnessed in the sources. Odin's practice of dedicating himself to himself is echoed in the account of his acquisition of the RUNES, as described in the eddic poem HÁVAMÁL, while the association of Odin and the spear seems genuinely old. From the earliest skaldic poetry of BRAGI BODDASON, Odin is described as 'Gungnir's shaker', and although such a description does not of itself guarantee the antiquity of the name (the term could simply be a poetic term for 'spear'), the link is clear. Runic inscriptions are commonly found on spears from the fourth century on, and, according to the eddic poem SIGRDRÍFUMÁL, similar runes are found at the tip of Odin's spear. Still earlier Bronze Age carvings depict a figure clutching a spear whom some have identified with Odin.

B12, 14, 23, 24, 28, 30, 335, 40, 50, 56, 59, 73, 87, 90; C2, 5, 9, 17, 24, 33, 46, 48

Gunn see VALKYRIES.

Gunnar ('warrior')

One of the best attested of legendary heroes, the eldest son of GJÚKI and GRÍMHILD, and the brother of GUDRÚN, HÖGNI GJÚKASON and GUTTHORM; a princely figure who appears in numerous poems of the POETIC EDDA, as well as, for example, in the legendary VÖLSUNGA SAGA. Gunnar becomes embroiled in the tragic events of the VÖLSUNG-cycle when the mighty hero SIGURD comes to visit Gjúki, after his first encounter with the Valkyrie BRYNHILD (in the guise of SIGRDRÍFA). Gunnar and his brother Högni take the dashing Sigurd as their blood-brother, and, after he has been given a magic potion by Queen Grímhild, Sigurd forgets his love for Brynhild and marries Gudrún. Grímhild now urges Gunnar to win Brynhild, but when first his own horse, GOTI, and then Sigurd's, GRANI, refuse to leap the flickering flames that surround Brynhild, Gunnar is forced to turn to Sigurd for help. Grímhild has taught the pair how to exchange forms, which they duly do, and Sigurd (in Gunnar's shape) rides Grani through the flames and wins Brynhild, who duly marries Gunnar. Only when Gudrún reveals to Brynhild the deception by which she was won do events begin to unravel, and Brynhild plots a grim revenge. *Völsunga saga* offers an emotionally charged description of relations between Gunnar and his wife, who has in the meantime vented her spleen on Sigurd:

> After that, Brynhild went out and sat under the wall of her chamber, and she grieved bitterly. She said that everything, property and power, were detestable to her, if she did not have Sigurd. Then Gunnar came to her. Brynhild said: 'You shall lose power and possessions, your life and wife, and I shall go back to my family and stay there in sorrow unless you kill Sigurd and his son. Don't bring up a wolf cub.' Then Gunnar became very depressed; it seemed to him he didn't know what was the best thing to do, since he was bound to Sigurd by his oath; different thoughts passed through his mind, but it seemed to him that the worst disgrace would be if his wife left him. Gunnar said: 'Brynhild is dearer to me than anything else, and she is the most distinguished of all women. I would rather lose my life than surrender her love'.

The notion that Gunnar is a careful, thoughtful prince is supported by the description of his mental turmoil offered in BROT AF SIGURDARKVIDU:

> It was late in the evening, the drinking had been heavy;
> every kind of friendly word had been said;
> everyone went to their beds and slept,
> but Gunnar lay waking long after the rest.
>
> His legs moved, his lips muttered,
> the troop-wrecker began to ponder
> what was the meaning of that pair in the wood,
> a raven and eagle, as they rode home.

The result of all this mental anguish is that Sigurd is duly despatched by Gutthorm and Brynhild flings herself upon his pyre. The bereaved brother and sister are reconciled only after Grímhild has administered another draught of her magic potion to Gudrún, and when Gudrún is married off to Brynhild's brother, ATLI BUDLASON, Gunnar conducts a passionate affair with Atli's other sister, ODDRÚN. When Atli invites Gunnar and Högni to visit him, it is clear that he means no good. At this point, the eddic poem ATLAKVIDA depicts Gunnar as a proud and powerful prince, keenly aware of his superior status; as he says to his brother:

> 'We two own seven buildings full of swords;
> every one has a hilt of gold.
> I know my mount is best, my blade keenest;

> bows deck my halls and mail-coats of gold,
> the brightest helmets and shields, brought from KJÁR's hall;
> one of mine is better, than those of all the Huns.'

Despite (or because of) the warning of Gudrún and the misgivings of others, Gunnar views the invitation as a challenge to his honour which he is happy to accept:

> No kinsman pushed Gunnar on, nor any near-relation,
> no counsellor nor confidant, nor any noble.
> But Gunnar spoke, as a king should,
> magnificent in the mead-hall, out of mighty spirit:
>
> 'Rise up now, Fjörnir, make the golden cups of warriors,
> flow around the benches in the hands of men.
>
> 'The wolf shall possess the Niflung inheritance,
> old guardians in grey, if Gunnar disappears.
> Black-coated bears shall chew with fearsome fangs
> delight the dog-stud, if Gunnar does not return.'

When he and Högni are captured, Gunnar displays remarkable equanimity in demanding his brother's heart, before being thrust into the snake-pit. The author of *Atlakvida* leaves him with an admiring glance: 'So must a brave distributor of rings guard his gold against men.' ATLAMÁL gives a still more spectacular account of Gunnar's demeanour when thrust into the snake-pit:

> Gunnar took a harp,
> strummed it with foot-twigs,
> he knew how to play,
> so that women wept,
> and men sobbed,
> who could hear it clearly.
> He announced the affair to the powerful lady:
> the rafters burst apart.

The scene is an arresting one, and it is hardly surprising that it should have attracted so many sculptors and artists. A particularly fine example is found among a series of splendid twelfth-century wood-carvings from the church of Hylestad, Setesdal, in Norway.

Gunnar is also found in the name-lists or THULUR as one of the many names of ODIN, although it is possible that in this case it is simply an error for Ginnar, which is elsewhere attested as one of Odin's names.

B12, 20, 25, 30, 31, 32, 42, 56, 65, 68, 73, 79, 87, 90; C1–3, 6, 17, 24, 33, 46; D60, 304, 431

Gunnlöd ('war-invitation')

A giantess, daughter of SUTTUNG, who is set by her father to guard the MEAD OF POETRY in a place called HNITBJÖRG, in the midst of a mountain. The god ODIN, calling himself Bölverk, prevails on her uncle, BAUGI, to bore a hole through the mountain with an auger and enters in the form of a snake. He sleeps with her for three nights, in return for which he is granted a single sip from each in turn of the three containers, Bodn, Són and ÓDRERIR, which he duly drains. Immediately afterwards he escapes in the form of an eagle. The thirteenth-century Icelander SNORRI STURLUSON gives the fullest account of the tale, much of which he derives from a brief section of the eddic poem HÁVAMÁL, which, however, differs in a number of details. The poetic account pays most attention to Gunnlöd herself, who is simply presented as another of Odin's sexual conquests. As Odin himself describes it:

'I sought the ancient giant; now I have returned,
I got little there by being silent.
With many words I wove my own fame
in Suttung's halls.

'Gunnlöd gave me, on the golden throne,
a drink of the dear-won mead.
In return I gave her bad recompense,
for her whole heart,
for her sorrowful soul.

'With the mouth of RATI, I made myself room,
and nibbled my way through the rock;
above and beneath were the giants' paths;
in this way I hazarded my head.

'I took advantage of my disguise:
wise men want for little;
and now Ódrerir has emerged
inside the sacred boundaries of men.

'I doubt I would have returned
back from the giants' domain,
if I hadn't had Gunnlöd, that fine woman
whom I laid in my arms.

'The following day the frost-giants came
and found Odin already in Hávi's [Odin's] hall;
they asked if Bölverk had gone to the gods
or Suttung had slain him.

'I reckon that Odin swore a ring-oath:
how can his truth be trusted?
He left Suttung deceived, without drink,
and Gunnlöd grieving.'

B12, 14, 23, 24, 28, 30, 35, 40, 50, 56, 69, 73, 87, 90; C2, 5, 9, 17, 24, 33, 46, 48

Gunther see NIBELUNGENLIED.

Gunnthrá, Gunnthráin, Gunnthró see HVERGEL-MIR.

Gust
According to the eddic poem REGINSMÁL, a previous

owner of the huge treasure-hoard guarded by the dragon FÁFNIR.

B12, 30, 56, 73, 87, 90; C2, 17, 24, 33, 46

Gut(t)horm

A legendary warrior, royal son of GJÚKI and GRÍMHILD, and brother of GUNNAR, HÖGNI GJÚKASON and GUDRÚN; together with his siblings, a pivotal figure in the events of the so-called VÖLSUNG-cycle. Since Gunnar and Högni are blood-brothers of the mighty hero SIGURD, they refuse to act against him and instead persuade Gutthorm to kill Sigurd for supposedly violating his sometime beloved, BRYNHILD, who had later become Gunnar's wife. According to the legendary VÖLSUNGA SAGA, supported by a verse, the brothers offer Gutthorm not only wealth and gold but also a magic potion made from the flesh of a snake and a wolf. As the saga continues:

Gutthorm came in to Sigurd the next morning, while he lay on his bed, but when Sigurd looked at him, Gutthorm did not dare attack, but turned away and

Gutthorm *Detail of the portal from the church at Hylestad, Setesdal, Norway, showing how Gutthorm murdered the mighty hero Sigurd, who was suspected of an illicit love-match with Brynhild, the wife of Gutthorm's brother, Gunnar.*

went back out. So it went on a second time. Sigurd's eyes were so piercing that few dared to look into them. But the third time Gutthorm entered, he found Sigurd asleep. Gutthorm drew his sword, and thrust it into Sigurd, so that the sword point pierced the bolster underneath. Sigurd awoke with the wound, and Gutthorm went off towards the door. But Sigurd took the sword GRAM, and threw it after him, and it entered his back, cutting him in half through the middle, so that his feet and legs fell one way, and his head and arms the other, back into the room.

B12, 20, 25, 30, 32, 42, 56, 65, 68, 73, 79, 87, 90; C1–3, 6, 17, 24, 33, 46

Gylfaginning ('the beguiling of Gylfi')

One of the four principal parts of the thirteenth-century Icelandic SNORRA EDDA, composed by SNORRI STURLUSON. Three of the ÆSIR, described in a spirit of EUHEMERISM as deriving from Asia, are questioned by the legendary Swedish king, GYLFI, who has come upon them in the guise of a wanderer, calling himself Gangleri. Snorri presents in the words of these three mysterious figures, who call themselves 'High', 'Just-as-high' and 'Third', a complete account of the history of the world, from the emergence of the first GIANT to the apocalyptic events of RAGNARÖK, drawing freely on a number of eddic poems, especially GRÍMNISMÁL, VAFTHRÚDNISMÁL, SKÍRNISMÁL and VÖLUSPÁ, stanzas from each of which stud the text. After they have explained how a new world will emerge after Ragnarök, the three enigmatic speakers refuse to answer any further questions and suddenly disappear, rather in the manner of the hall of the giant ÚTGARDALOKI, in an account of his beguiling of the god THOR that is found later in *Snorra Edda* itself:

> Then Gangleri heard mighty sounds from every direction, and he looked to one side; and when he looked around, he saw that he was standing outside in the open, and could see no hall or castle.

The basic question and answer structure of *Gylfaginning* recalls that of a number of versified wisdom contests, notably *Vafthrúdnismál*, ALVÍSSMÁL and *Gestumblindagátur*. A similar prose structure is apparent later in *Snorra Edda*, when in SKÁLDSKAPARMÁL a character called ÆGIR visits the Æsir, and engages the god BRAGI in a series of questions about the activities of the gods. In each of these cases (including *Gylfaginning*) the didactic conversations take place between creatures of different kinds: gods and giants (*Vafthrúdnismál* and, perhaps, *Skáldskaparmál*); gods and dwarfs (*Alvíssmál*);

and gods and humans (*Gestumblindagátur*, *Gylfaginning* and, perhaps, *Skáldskaparmál*). Typically, Snorri addresses his material in a playful fashion. Gylfi himself adopts a disguise (and name, Gangleri) usually associated with the god ODIN, while his three interlocutors also carry recognizable Odin-names. It is far from clear, moreover, both from the title ('the beguiling of Gylfi') and the contents of *Gylfaginning*, just who is beguiling whom. In the same spirit, in *Skáldskaparmál* Snorri has Ægir, who as a sea-giant is usually the host of the gods' feasting, playing the role of inquisitive guest. Snorri seems to intend Ægir to be identified both with the amiable sea-giant, in which case *Skáldskaparmál* represents a precise reversal of the structure of god questioning wise giant found in *Vafthrúdnismál*, and as a purely human figure, like Gylfi.

B12, 14, 23, 24, 28, 30, 35, 40, 50, 51, 56, 59, 73, 87, 90; C2, 5, 9, 17, 24, 33, 46, 48; D32, 370, 413

Gylfi ('wave', 'sea')

(1) According to the thirteenth-century Icelander SNORRI STURLUSON, the legendary king who took over Sweden from the ÆSIR and whose 'beguiling' (GYLFAGINNING) provides the narrative framework for much of Snorri's main account of Norse mythology. (2) The name appears in the name-lists or THULUR as the name of a sea-king, and this is clearly the role of Gylfi in Snorri's YNGLINGA SAGA, in which he grants the goddess GEFJON plough-land, and, aided by her monstrous sons, she ploughs out the island of Zealand.

B24, 28, 35, 40, 50; C5, 9, 48; D32, 370, 476

Gyllir ('yeller')

(1) According to the thirteenth-century Icelander SNORRI STURLUSON, one of the horses belonging to the ÆSIR. (2) According to the name-lists or THULUR the name of a giant.

B24, 28, 35, 40, 50; C5, 9, 48

Gymir ('sea'?, 'engulfer')

A giant, according to the eddic poems SKÍRNISMÁL and HYNDLULJÓD, the father of GERD, the beloved of FREY. The thirteenth-century Icelander SNORRI STURLUSON broadly agrees, but in addition makes Gymir an alternative name for ÆGIR, an identification that accords both with the prose introduction to the eddic poem LOKASENNA and with a skaldic verse of the eleventh-century Icelandic poet Ref Gestsson.

B12, 14, 23, 24, 28, 30, 35, 40, 50, 56, 59, 73, 87, 90; C2, 5, 9, 17, 24, 33, 46, 48

H

Hábrók ('high-breeches')

According to a verse from the eddic poem GRÍMNISMÁL, cited by the thirteenth-century Icelander SNORRI STURLUSON, the best of hawks.

B12, 14, 23, 24, 28, 30, 35, 40, 50, 56, 59, 73, 87, 90; C2, 5, 9, 17, 24, 33, 46, 48

Haddingjar

A pair of legendary brothers, the youngest of twelve, who were perhaps twins and were held to be so close that only together were they able to fight effectively. They appear in two legendary sagas, ÖRVAR-ODDS SAGA and HERVARAR SAGA OK HEIDREKS KONUNGS, as well as in one eddic poem, HYNDLULJÓD. The early thirteenth-century Danish historian SAXO GRAMMATICUS concentrates on only one of the pair, whom he dubs HADDINGUS.

B64, 80; C7, 8, 21, 35, 38; D119

Haddingus

According to the early thirteenth-century Danish historian SAXO GRAMMATICUS, a heroic king whose foster-father is a giant and who dedicated his life to the god ODIN. After many spectacular victories in battle apparently granted by Odin, Haddingus similarly dedicates his death to him, by hanging himself in the sight of all his troops.

B64; C7, 8; D119

Hæming *see* HUNDING.

Hænir *see* HŒNIR.

Hagal

According to the eddic poem HELGAKVIDA HUNDINGSBANA II, the foster-father of the eponymous hero HELGI SIGMUNDARSON HUNDINGSBANI. When King HUNDING's men come upon his home unawares, Hagal disguises Helgi as his slave-girl and sets him to grind barley. When one of Hunding's men expresses surprise at how mightily the 'girl' grinds, Hagal answers coolly:

'Little wonder though the mill-stand screams,
when a king's daughter turns the handle;
above the clouds she used to sweep,

she dared to slaughter like a Viking,
before Helgi held her captive;
she is the sister of HÖGNI and SIGAR,
the Ylfing maid has a dreadful gaze.'

Hagal has a son, Hamal, who also plays a minor role in the poem.

B12, 30, 56, 73, 87, 90; C2, 17, 24, 33, 46

Hagbard *see* HELGI SIGMUNDARSON HUNDINGSBANI.

Hagbard Hámundarson

A legendary warrior, named in VÖLSUNGA SAGA by the Valkyrie BRYNHILD, together with his brother Haki, as the foremost of kings.

B25, 42, 65, 68, 79; C1, 6

Hagen *see* NIBELUNGENLIED.

Haki Hámundarson *see* HAGBARD HÁMUNDARSON.

Hákon, king of Denmark *see* THÓRA.

Hákonarmál ('the song of Hákon')

A panegyric composed by the tenth-century Norwegian poet EYVIND FINNSSON SKÁLDASPILLIR ('the plagiarist') on his dead lord, Hákon gódi, who died in 961 in battle against the sons of Eirík Bloodaxe, his brother and former rival. Eyvind's nickname may well be exemplified by his practice here; the mid-thirteenth-century manuscript Fagrskinna states baldly that Eyvind borrowed the idea for the poem from an earlier panegyric in praise of Hákon's dead brother, EIRÍKSMÁL, while the final stanza of the poem clearly alludes to a passage found repeated in the eddic poem HÁVAMÁL. *Hákonarmál* itself is split into three sections, partly distinguished by a change in metre. The first section describes how the god ODIN sends two VALKYRIES into the battle to pick out Hákon and bring him to VALHALL; a second section tells of his being met on the way to Valhall by BRAGI and HERMÓD; the closing section ends with fulsome praise of the dead king, concluding with a sentiment closely parallel to what is found in general terms in *Hávamál*:

Cattle die, kinsman die:
land and people laid waste;

since Hákon departed with the heathen gods,
many a host is destroyed.

B87; D238, 347, 619

Hal *see* RÍGSTHULA.

Háleygjatal

Along with HÁKONARMÁL, one of the most celebrated poems of the tenth-century Norwegian poet EYVIND FINNSSON SKÁLDASPILLIR. Composed for Earl Hákon at some point after 985, *Háleygjatal* traces Hákon's ancestry back to the gods and specifically to the son of the god ODIN and the giantess SKADI, who is usually held to be the wife of the god NJÖRD.

B39, 45, 62, 83, 87; C16; D552, 553

Hálf

A legendary king of Denmark, at whose court, according to both the eddic poem GUDRÚNARKVIDA II and the legendary VÖLSUNGA SAGA, the tragic heroine GUDRÚN took refuge after the death of her husband, SIGURD.

B12, 20, 25, 30, 32, 42, 56, 65, 68, 73, 79, 87, 90; C1–3, 6, 17, 24, 33, 46

Halfdan

A common name in the literary sources. (1) According to the eddic poem HELGAKVIDA HUNDINGSBANA II, the father of the Valkyrie KÁRA. (2) Elsewhere in the POETIC EDDA, in GROTTASÖNGR, Halfdan is the name of the brother of the bountiful king, FRÓDI. (3) The thirteenth-century Icelander SNORRI STURLUSON names yet another Halfdan as the father of the legendary King DAG.

B12, 30, 56, 73, 87, 90; C2, 17, 24, 33, 46

Hallfred Óttarsson vandrædaskáld ('the troublesome poet')

A late tenth-century Icelandic poet, whose career spans the period of the conversion to Christianity. The skaldic poetry attributed to him neatly illustrates the difficulties faced by poets accustomed to using pagan mythological references routinely in their verse. Two stanzas describing Hallfred's painful change of allegiance amount to a catalogue of the major figures of the ÆSIR:

All our kin has composed
poems to praise ODIN;
I recall the precious feat
of those people, our ancestors;
but, grudging, because Odin's rule
has pleased the poet well,
I send spite against FRIGG's spouse:
for now we follow Christ.

May FREY and FREYJA scorn me,
as well as mighty THOR:
I've surely spurned NJÖRD's deceit;
let fiends fawn over Odin.
On Christ alone and on God
shall I call for all favour;
I'm loath to face the wrath of the Son,
who rules glorious under the world's Father.

In the much later Icelandic HALLFREDAR SAGA, which preserves much of his poetic corpus, the prose narrative presents a parallel account of how Hallfred and his two sons are approached by the pagan family-spirit or FYLGJA, in the form of a mighty woman who, having been spurned by Hallfred, offers her services to his sons. One refuses, but the other accepts, neatly illustrating the reluctance with which some Icelanders, according to the rather romantic view of the saga's author, at least, turned from the old beliefs.

B39, 45, 62, 75, 83, 87; C3, 16; D152, 165–7, 194–6, 308, 620

Hallfredar saga

An Icelandic saga, probably composed in the thirteenth or fourteenth century and purporting to give the life-history of the celebrated late tenth-century poet HALLFRED OTTARSSON VANDRÆDASKÁLD. Hallfred's life and poetry are of particular interest in that they span the period of the conversion, and Hallfred's progressive shunning of the poetic diction and trappings of the pagan past are carefully chronicled. One episode in particular depicts how the pagan family-spirit or FYLGJA appears to Hallfred and his sons in the form of a mighty woman, not unlike the personified luck or HAMINGJA that appears to the eponymous hero of VÍGA-GLÚMS SAGA, and is turned away by Hallfred himself and one of his sons, but is accepted by the other son. Much of the saga, however, is devoted to the depiction of Hallfred in the role of love-struck swain so familiar from other poets' sagas, such as KORMÁKS SAGA.

B47, 75, 81; C3, 16, 18

Hallinskidi ('asymmetrically horned'?)

(1) According to the thirteenth-century Icelander SNORRI STURLUSON, another name for the god HEIMDALL. (2) Found in the name-lists or THULUR as the name of a ram (as is Heimdali), so fostering a persistent association between Heimdall and rams.

B24, 28, 35, 40, 50; C5, 9, 48

Hamal *see* HAGAL.

Hamdir

The son of the tragic heroine GUDRÚN and her third

husband, JÓNAK, and brother of the doomed warri-
or SÖRLI. Together with his brothers, and incited by
Gudrún, he sets off on the ill-fated mission to avenge
the death of SVANHILD, the beautiful daughter of
the hero SIGURD. The entire episode is described in
the eddic poem HAMDISMÁL and alluded to in some
surviving skaldic verses by BRAGI BODDASON. Before
sending her sons off to their doom, Gudrún had given
them impenetrable mail-coats, whence Hamdir often
appears in poetic periphrases or KENNINGS for armour
or mail-shirt.

B12, 20, 30, 32, 39, 45, 56, 62, 73, 83, 87, 90; C2, 13, 16, 17, 24, 33, 46; D350, 521

Hamdismál ('the lay of Hamdir')

More properly known as *Hamdismál in forna* ('the old
lay of Hamdir') – although a younger lay is no longer
extant – an eddic poem in mixed metre preserved
in the CODEX REGIUS manuscript. The poem begins
with the inciting by the tragic heroine GUDRÚN of her
two sons, HAMDIR and SÖRLI, to avenge their sister
SVANHILD, whose husband JÖRMUNREKK had caused
to be trampled to death by horses on suspicion of
adultery. The same act of incitement forms the main
theme of the eddic poem GUDRÚNARHVÖT, with which
Hamdismál also shares considerable parallels of diction.
The brothers agree but foretell that they will not return,
a possibility that they themselves render more likely by
snubbing the offer of help made to them *en route* by
their half-brother ERP JÓNAKRSSON, whom they kill for
his perceived presumption. Jörmunrekk is undaunted
by their appearance and threatens them with death, but
after they have cut off his hands and feet, the maimed
king is said to growl like a bear and command his men
to stone the brothers, since they appear invulnerable to
weapons. As they fall, the brothers acknowledge their
folly in killing their half-brother on the way:

> 'Now the head would be off,
> if Erp were alive.'

Hamdismál mixes scenes of elegiac sadness and grim
heroism with considerable skill. So, for example,
Gudrún describes her desolation at Svanhild's death:

> 'Solitary I stand,
> as an aspen in a wood,
> bereft of kin
> as a pine tree of branches,
> shorn of pleasure
> as a tree of leaves,
> when that branch-stripping girl,
> passes one warm day.'

No less striking is the heroic defiance of the poem's
end, when one of the brothers (presumably Sörli), says:

> 'Great glory we have gained
> though we die now or tomorrow;
> no man survives a single dusk
> beyond the NORNS' decree.'

The poem concludes with great narrative simplicity:

> There Sörli fell
> at the hall's gable;
> and Hamdir slumped
> at the rear of the house.

B12, 20, 30, 32, 56, 73, 79, 87, 90; C2, 17, 24, 33, 46; D257, 350, 518, 521, 524, 526

hamingja ('luck')

The embodiment of personal or family luck, often
described in the same manner as the better attested FYLGJA. Perhaps the most striking description
of the way in which the *hamingja* might pass from
one family-member to another is that found in the
thirteenth-century Icelandic VÍGA-GLÚMS SAGA, which
describes how the hero, Glúm, inherits the *hamingja* of
his Norwegian grandfather, Vígfús:

> It is said that one night Glúm had a dream. He thought
> he was standing outside the house and gazing towards
> the fjord. He thought he saw a woman striding across
> the countryside and coming towards Thverá; she was
> so large that her shoulders reached the mountains on
> either side. He thought he went out of the home-field
> to meet her and invited her to his home. Then he woke
> up. Everyone thought it was an odd dream, but he said:
> 'This is a great and noteworthy dream, which I would in-
> terpret as follows: my grandfather Vígfús must be dead,
> and the woman who walked taller than the mountains
> must be his *hamingja*, for he was almost always greater
> than other men in honour; now his *hamingja* must be
> seeking to dwell where I am'.

The scene is paralleled in HALLFREDAR SAGA, in which,
however, it is the family *fylgja* (again in the form of a
huge and stately woman), who offers her allegiance to
the sons of the poet and Christian convert, HALLFRED
OTTARSSON VANDRÆDASKÁLD.

B47, 75, 81; C3, 16; D408, 563

Hamskerpir

According to a verse cited by the thirteenth-century
Icelander SNORRI STURLUSON, the stallion who sired
Hófvarpnir, the horse ridden by the goddess GNÁ.

B24, 28, 35, 40, 50; C5, 9, 48

Hámund

According to the legendary VÖLSUNGA SAGA, the son of
the hero SIGMUND and BORGHILD, and brother of the
hero HELGI SIGMUNDARSON HUNDINGSBANI.

B25, 42, 65, 68, 78; C1, 6

Hár

Hár ('high one')

(1) One of the many names of the god ODIN; the god adopts another version of the name, Hávi, in the eddic poem HÁVAMÁL. (2) According to the catalogue in the eddic poem VÖLUSPÁ, a dwarf. (3) The thirteenth-century Icelander SNORRI STURLUSON gives the names Hár, Jafnhár and Thridi ('high', 'just-as-high' and 'third') to the three interrogators of the legendary Swedish king GYLFI in GYLFAGINNING.

B12, 14, 23, 24, 28, 30, 35, 40, 50, 56, 59, 73, 87, 90; C2, 5, 9, 17, 24, 33, 46, 48

Haraldskvædi see HRAFNSMÁL.

Hárbardsljód ('the lay of Hárbard')

An eddic poem preserved in the CODEX REGIUS manuscript, as well as (in part) in another manuscript, AM 748 I 4to, and describing a lively battle of words between the gods ODIN and THOR. Odin, assuming the disguise of a cantankerous ferryman named Hárbard ('grey-beard'), refuses to convey Thor, who has apparently just returned from one of his giant-slaying expeditions, across a narrow stretch of water. The bad-tempered exchange degenerates into a formal contest of insults or FLYTING (Old Norse *senna*) of the kind also seen in other eddic poems, notably LOKASENNA, but also has the serious purpose of providing a basis for comparison of the feats and deeds (Old Norse *mannjafnaðr*) of these two most important ÆSIR. While Thor boasts about killing giants, Odin matches him by bragging of his sexual conquests and appears to make a distinction between his own aristocratic followers and the commoners that are Thor's lot:

> 'Odin gets the noblemen, who fall in slaughter,
> but Thor gets the kin of slaves.'

B12, 30, 56, 73, 87, 90; C2, 17, 24, 33, 46; D24, 78, 79, 225, 227, 261, 339, 494

Hardgreip ('hard-grip')

According to the early thirteenth-century Danish historian SAXO GRAMMATICUS, who gives her name as Harthgrepa, the daughter of the giant Vagnophtus, who is the foster-father of the hero HADDINGUS. Hardgreip's role develops as Haddingus grows up. She becomes in turn his wet-nurse, his lover and, in male garb, his faithful companion on the road. In one episode she incites a dead man into prophecy by placing a rune-stick under his tongue, and in another she is able to fend off a gigantic hand that enters the hut where she and Haddingus are sleeping. The latter incident is presumably the source of her name, which also appears in the name-lists or THULUR as that of both a giant and a giantess.

B64; C7, 8

Hardvéur ('the strong defender')

According to the name-lists or THULUR, one of the many titles of the god THOR. The simple form, Véur, is the one found (no fewer than three times) in the eddic poem HYMISKVIDA.

B12, 14, 23, 24, 28, 30, 35, 40, 50, 56, 59, 73, 87, 90; C2, 5, 9, 17, 24, 33, 46, 48

Harthgrepa see HARDGREIP.

Hati

According to the eddic poem HELGAKVIDA HJÖRVARDS-SONAR, a giant and father of HRÍMGERD, who proudly proclaims of herself:

> 'My name is Hrímgerd, my father's name Hati,
> whom I knew as the most mighty of giants,
> many a bride he had snatched from their homes,
> till Helgi hewed him down.'

B12, 30, 56, 73, 87, 90; C2, 27, 24, 33, 46

Hati Hródvitnisson

According to the thirteenth-century Icelander SNORRI STURLUSON, the wolf that will eventually swallow MÁNI, the moon, during the cataclysmic events of RAGNARÖK.

B24, 28, 35, 40, 50; C5, 9, 48

Háttatal ('tally of metres')

The last of the four main sections of SNORRA EDDA, the major treatise on the art of poetry composed by the thirteenth-century Icelander SNORRI STURLUSON. Probably the first of those sections to have been composed, *Háttatal* consists of three lengthy series of verses eulogizing King Hákon Hákonarson and Earl Skúli, the two main players in Norwegian politics of the time. Snorri produced no fewer than 102 stanzas in the course of *Háttatal*, interspersed with a detailed prose commentary of his own, explaining the metrical and rhetorical points being illustrated in the verse. As such, *Háttatal* offers a large number of examples of the mythological and legendary diction that Snorri went on to explain in the remainder of *Snorra Edda*.

B24, 28, 35, 40, 50; C5, 9, 48; D40, 41, 102–4, 118, 148, 149, 170, 224, 249, 266, 368, 382, 384, 476, 478, 479, 483–5, 487, 626

haugbúi see DRAUGAR.

Haustlöng ('autumn-long')

A shield-poem apparently composed (to judge from the title) over the course of an autumn by the Norwegian poet THJÓDÓLF OF HVÍN, at some time around the turn of the tenth century. Evidently the shield being celebrated depicted two principal tales, namely that in which the goddess IDUN and her youth-bringing apples were snatched from the ÆSIR by the giant THJAZI and that in which the god THOR defeats the giant HRUNGNIR in single combat. The thirteenth-century Icelander SNORRI STURLUSON makes copious use of *Haustlöng* in his versions of these tales and in illustrating some technical features of skaldic diction. Indeed, *Haustlöng* entirely owes its preservation to the inclusion of extracts from it in manuscripts of Snorri's work.

B24, 28, 35, 39, 40, 45, 50, 62, 83, 87; C5, 9, 16, 48; D264

Hávamál ('the song of Hávi (Odin)')

The second eddic poem in the CODEX REGIUS manuscript, a composite work consisting of as many as six sections, composed in a variety of metres. Many of the poem's 164 stanzas are spoken in the person of the god ODIN or describe various of his adventures. The poem opens with the wheedling address of an anonymous travelling poet newly arrived in a strange hall and begging a warm welcome. The poet offers a series of commonplace observations on human existence and experience, culminating in some famous lines about the nature of fame:

Cattle die, kinsmen die,
you yourself die.
But words of glory never die
for the man who achieves a good name.

Cattle die, kinsmen die,
you yourself die.
I know one thing that never dies:
the fame of each man dead.

Other stanzas of this section stress the value of life and companionship, and the grim fate of those who have no family or friends:

The fir tree fades
that stands in the grove;
its bark and needles give no shelter:
so it is for a man,
whom nobody loves,
why must he live for long?

Towards the end of this section detailing commonsense values, there is above all a call for caution in all things, especially when dealing with women, whose relationships with men form a constant link through the following stanzas:

Praise the day at evening;
a wife, when she's been burned;
a sword, when it's been tested;

a maid, when she's been married;
ice, when it's crossed over;
ale, when it's drunk down.

Cut wood on a windy day,
row to sea in fine weather,
murmur to friends in the darkness:
many are the eyes of day;
ask swiftness of a ship, protection from a shield,
sharpness from a sword, kisses from a girl.

Drink ale by the fireside, slide on ice,
buy a mount lean, and a sword-blade bloody,
fatten a horse at home, and a hound in the house.
Never trust the words of a maid,
nor whatever a woman says:
on a whirling wheel their hearts are thrown,
fickleness fills their breasts.

A creaking bow, a crackling flame,
a gaping wolf, a croaking crow,
a squealing swing, a rootless tree,
a swelling wave, a bubbling pot,
a flying dart, a falling surge,
overnight ice, a snake tight-sprung,
a bride's bed-talk or a broken blade,
a bear's play or a king's young boy,
a sick calf, a self-willed slave,
a soothsayer's smooth talk, a fresh-killed corpse,
a field sown early: let no one trust them,
nor a son too soon;
weather creates crops, but wit a son,
each of them is in doubt.

Your brother's bane, if you pass him in the street,
a house half-burned, a horse too frisky –
a steed is useless, if it breaks a leg –
none is so assured as to trust all these.

The love of women whose hearts are false,
is like driving an unshod steed over slippery ice,
a two-year-old, frolicsome, badly broken;
or like being in a rudderless boat in a storm,
or a cripple trying to catch reindeer on a thawing slope.

Now I speak plainly: since I know both sides:
Men's minds are fickle to women;
the fairer we speak, the falser we think,
that trips up any sensible soul.

Fair speaking and fine gifts
will win the love of a lass;
praise the figure of the fine-looking girl:
the one who woos will win.

No man must ever reproach

another man for their love;
they often snare the wise,
what cannot catch the fool:
the loveliest looks of all.

No one should reproach in any way
what comes to many a man;
almighty love takes the sons of men,
and makes of wise men fools.

The mind alone knows what lives near the heart;
alone it sees into the soul.
Worse for the wise than any disease:
to find nothing left to love.

Such melancholy thoughts lead naturally into a further section that describes one of Odin's sexual adventures, this time with the otherwise unidentified 'BILLING's girl', whose deception Odin deplores. In the following section Odin celebrates his more successful seduction of the giantess GUNNLÖD, in the course of his acquisition of the MEAD OF POETRY. The fourth section introduces a character called LODDFÁFNIR, who may be a travelling minstrel of the kind whose speech opens the poem and who is offered gnomic advice on a variety of topics. The final two sections of the poem address more arcane topics, RUNES and spells respectively. In the first of these Odin tells how he acquired the runes by sacrificing himself to himself:

'I know that I hung on that windy tree,
spear-wounded, nine full nights,
given to Odin, myself to myself,
on that tree that rose from roots
that no man knows.

'They gave me neither bread nor drink from horn
I peered below.
I clutched the runes, screaming I grabbed them,
and then sank back.

'I had nine mighty songs from that famed
son of Bölthor, father of BESTLA,
and one swig I snatched of that glorious mead
drained from ÓDRERIR.

'Then I quickened and flourished
sprouted and throve.
From a single word, another sprung:
from a single deed, another sprung.'

The final section of the poem provides a catalogue of some eighteen spells, which some have related to the 'nine mighty songs' mentioned in the previous speech or even to the nine spells that are described in the eddic

poem GRÓAGALDR. The concluding stanza of the poem may well be the work of the poet who has cobbled the whole piece from such disparate sources:

Now are the words of the High One uttered
within the High One's hall.
Very useful to the sons of men
no use at all to the sons of giants.
Good luck to whoever recited them,
good luck to whoever knows them!
Use them well, if you learn them:
Good luck to all who have heard them!

B12, 14, 23, 30, 56, 73, 87, 90; C2, 17, 24, 33, 46; D2, 33, 147, 186, 224, 273, 274, 334, 449, 522, 523, 611

Hávard *see* HUNDING.

Hávi *see* HÁR.

Hedin Hjarrandason

The abductor of the legendary heroine HILD, the daughter of HÖGNI, and one of the protagonists in the grim events leading up to the endless battle of the HJADNINGAVÍG.

B24, 28, 35, 40, 50; C5, 9, 48; D345

Hedin Hjörvardsson

According to the eddic poem HELGAKVIDA HJÖRVARDSSONAR, the son of King HJÖRVARD and ÁLFHILD. After snubbing the advances of a giantess, Hedin swears a fatal vow to win the Valkyrie SVÁVA, the beloved of his brother HELGI; naturally, the vow has dreadful consequences:

Hedin was at home with his father, King Hjörvard, in Norway. Hedin was going home on his own through the woods one yule-eve, when he met a troll-wife; she was riding a wolf with snakes for reins, and she offered her company to Hedin. 'No,' said Hedin. She said: 'You'll pay for this at the BRAGAFUL.' In the evening they were making vows. A sacrificial boar was led forwards, and men placed their hands on it and swore a vow with the *bragaful*. Hedin swore a vow to have Sváva, the daughter of EYLIMI, although she was the beloved of Helgi, his brother, and he regretted it so much that he went off, travelling unknown paths south by land until he found Helgi, his brother. Helgi said:

'Welcome, Hedin. What news
from Norway can you tell?
What has driven you out,
prince, to travel alone to find me?'

'I have done a dreadful deed:

I have chosen the child of a king,
your own bride, at the *bragaful*.'

'You've done nothing wrong; it may turn out
that your ale-talk, Hedin, comes true for us both.
A prince has challenged me to a duel
in three nights' time, and I must go;
I doubt I shall return again:
then let it turn out for the best.'

'Helgi, you have said that Hedin was,
worthy of good and fine gifts from you;
It's more seemly for you to redden your sword,
than to give peace to your foes.'

B12, 30, 56, 73, 87, 90; C2, 17, 24, 33, 46

Hefring *see* ÆGIR.

Heid ('brightness', 'fame')

The name given to the wicked GULLVEIG in the eddic
poem VÖLUSPÁ, in her role as a travelling seer and
witch. Outside *Völuspá*, several other witches are also
called Heid, notably in LANDNÁMABÓK, as well as in
the legendary sagas HRÓLFS SAGA KRAKA and ÖRVAR-
ODDA SAGA.

B6, 12, 30, 42, 56, 59, 68, 73, 74, 86, 87, 90; C2, 17, 20, 21, 24, 33, 35, 36, 38, 46;
D156, 182, 306, 406

Heiddraupnir

An isolated form which is found in the eddic poem
SIGRDRÍFUMÁL, where it is presumably another name
for the wise giant MÍMIR.

B12, 30, 56, 59, 73, 87, 90; C2, 17, 24, 33, 46

Heidrek ('heath-ruler'?)

(1) According to the eddic poem ODDRÚNARGRÁTR,
the father of the legendary princess BORGNÝ. (2) In
the late tenth-century skaldic poem, THÓRSDRÁPA, the
name of a giant. (3) One of the protagonists of the
legendary HERVARAR SAGA OK HEIDREKS KONUNGS.

B12, 30, 56, 73, 80, 87, 90; C2, 17, 21, 24, 33, 46

Heidreks saga see HERVARAR SAGA OK HEIDREKS
KONUNGS.

Heidrún

A mythical goat, which, standing on the roof of the

Heidrún *Seventeenth-century manuscript illustration,*
offering a rather imaginative depiction of the mighty
hall of Valhall, with the mythical goat Heidrún on
the roof.

mighty hall VALHALL, provides the fighting and feasting EINHERJAR with their mead. In the thirteenth century the Icelander SNORRI STURLUSON, drawing on a description in the eddic poem GRÍMNISMÁL, describes Heidrún succinctly:

> There is a goat called Heidrún, standing on top of Valhall, feeding on the leaves of the branches of that famed tree call LÆRAD, and from the udders of the goat there flows mead, whereby it fills a vat every day. The vat is so big that all the Einherjar can drink their fill from it.

B12, 14, 23, 24, 28, 30, 35, 40, 50, 56, 59, 73, 87, 90; C2, 5, 9, 17, 24, 33, 46, 48

Heidthornir *see* VINDBLÁIN.

Heimdall ('world-brightener')

Heimdall is the watchman of the gods, whose hearing, according to the thirteenth-century Icelander SNORRI STURLUSON, is keen enough to sense grass grow and whose vision extends more than a hundred miles, day or night. According to the account of the end of the world at RAGNARÖK in the eddic poem VÖLUSPÁ, it is Heimdall who, like the angel Gabriel, blows the mighty GJALLARHORN, the horn that summons the ÆSIR to their doom. In the eddic poem RÍGSTHULA he is named as the progenitor of mankind, and in *Völuspá* both gods and men alike are described as the 'greater and lesser kinsmen of Heimdall'. Snorri depicts him as a somewhat mysterious figure with golden teeth – whence his alternative name, GULLINTANNI ('golden teeth') – who rides the horse Gulltopp ('golden top'). Heimdall is especially hostile to LOKI, with whom he is said once to have fought in the shape of a seal, and this marine association may also be echoed in the tradition that he is the son of nine mothers, all sisters, perhaps the daughters of the sea-giant ÆGIR. Elsewhere, Heimdall is associated with the figure of a ram, whence his other title, HALLINSKIDI, although this may be an extension of his traditional role as possessor of the Gjallarhorn. Another of his titles, Vindhlér ('wind-shield'), attests to Heimdall's function as a watchman, out in all weathers. Heimdall, who is involved in some way with recovery of the necklace BRÍSINGAMEN, is an essentially mythological figure, of whose cult and worship there is little evidence, and it is clear that even by the time Snorri was compiling his SNORRA EDDA many of the legends concerning Heimdall were already obscure: there is no explanation of why one poetic term or KENNING for 'sword' is 'the head of Heimdall' and another for 'head' is 'the sword of Heimdall', although it is possible that his identification with rams and horns may have something to do with it. After all, according to Snorri, the fertility-god FREY killed the giant BELI with an antler.

The mysterious origin of Heimdall is described in still greater detail in the eddic poem HYNDLULJÓD:

> One was born in ancient days,
> much imbued with strength, of the race of gods;
> nine bore him, a point-glorious man,
> giant's maid, on the edge of the earth . . .

> GJÁLP bore him, Greip bore him,
> Eistla bore him, and Eyrgjafa.
> Úlfrún bore him, and Angeyja,
> Imd and Atla, and JÁRNSAXA.

> He was imbued with the strength of the earth,
> with the chill-cold sea, and the blood of a swine[?].

All of the nine female figures named occur elsewhere as giantesses, mostly in the name-lists or THULUR; rather confusingly, however, Gjálp and Greip are also named as the daughters of the giant GEIRRÖD, who try to hinder the god THOR in his expedition against their father, while Járnsaxa is named as the mother of Thor's son, MAGNI.

B12, 14, 23, 24, 28, 30, 35, 40, 50, 56, 59, 73, 87, 90; C2, 5, 9, 17, 24, 33, 46, 48; D125, 435, 496, 500, 517, 600

Heimdalargaldr ('Heimdall's spell')

An otherwise unknown poem, of which fragments are cited by the thirteenth-century Icelander SNORRI STURLUSON.

B24, 28, 35, 40, 50; C5, 9, 48

Heimir

Foster-father of the legendary Valkyrie BRYNHILD, to whose sister, BEKKHILD BUDLADÓTTIR, he is married. The legendary VÖLSUNGA SAGA describes how he directs the heroes GUNNAR and SIGURD to Brynhild's mountain-top dwelling, where she is surrounded by a wall of flame. Among the poems of the POETIC EDDA, only GRÍPISSPÁ names Heimir. In an ominous passage, GRÍPIR prophesies to Sigurd:

> 'You will be robbed of all delight
> by the beauty Heimir fosters;
> you will be deprived of sleep and peace,
> care for nothing else, except that girl.'

B12, 25, 30, 42, 56, 65, 68, 73, 79, 87, 90; C1–3, 6, 17, 24, 33, 46

Heimskringla

A lengthy historical work attributed to the thirteenth-century Icelander SNORRI STURLUSON and consisting of a prologue and sixteen sagas concerning the kings of Norway from their semi-legendary origins before the ninth century down to Magnús Erlingsson in 1177.

Heimskringla contains large numbers of skaldic verses, which offer insights into the myths and legends of the North. The first saga, YNGLINGA SAGA, is an especially valuable repository of information about Norse beliefs and customs, including an extraordinarily vivid EUHEMERISTIC account of the origins of the gods.

B1; C22, 23; D30, 585, 613

heiti

A word used as a poetic alternative to the simple noun, occasionally an archaic, borrowed or dialect form. So, for example, among the various *heiti* for 'shield' listed by the thirteenth-century Icelander SNORRI STURLUSON are words that could be translated as follows:

> 'Shield', 'narrow-hall', 'cover', 'hall-binder', 'bender', 'protecting-edge' and 'buckler', 'fight-bend', 'targe', 'storm-bright' and 'protection', 'wide-pale', 'engraved', 'battle-bright' and 'linden'.

Often *heiti* are preserved in mnemonic lists known as THULUR, and an individual *heiti* might well be employed as part of a wider poetic periphrasis or KENNING.

B24, 28, 35, 40, 50; C5, 9, 48; D77, 169, 278, 308

Hel

Both the place of the dead, specifically of those who perish of sickness or old age, and the goddess who presides over the Underworld. The topography of Hel is complex, developing over time, and has undoubtedly been influenced by Christian sources at several points. According to the thirteenth-century Icelander SNORRI STURLUSON, the path to Hel lies north and down, and other sources describe a mighty river, generally freezing cold and filled with blocks of ice or, in some cases, weapons. The name of the river is variously given as Geirvimul, GJÖLL or Slíd, and access is possible over a bridge, GJALLARBRÚ, which Snorri claims is guarded by a giantess called MÓDGUD. Elsewhere, Hel is described as fenced in by a protective barrier known descriptively as Helgrind ('Hel-gate'), Nágrind ('corpse-gate') or Valgrind ('corpse-gate'). The entrance to Hel is guarded by a mighty dog, according to BALDRS DRAUMAR, similar to the Graeco-Roman Cerberus and perhaps to be identified with the huge mythical dog GARM.

The female figure of Hel, who rules the Underworld down in NIFLHEIM, is named as one of the three offspring of LOKI and the giantess ANGRBODA; her brothers are FENRIR and the MIDGARD-SERPENT. Snorri gives the fullest (if most fanciful account) of her fate at the hands of ODIN, in a passage filled with allegorical significance and self-conscious identification with the Christian concept of hell:

> Hel [the god Odin] cast into Niflheim and granted her dominion over nine worlds, so that she had to grant board and lodging to those sent to her, which were those that die of sickness or old age. She has mighty halls there, and her walls are hugely high, and the gates great. Her hall is called ELIÚDNIR ['damp'], her dish Hungr ['hunger'], her knife Sultr ['famine'], servant Ganglati ['lazy walker'], serving-maid Ganglöt ['lazy walker'], her threshold at the entrance Fallanda Forad ['stumbling-block'], her bed Kör ['sick-bed'], her drapes Blíkjanda Böl ['shining-harm']. She is half black and half the colour of flesh, and so she is easily recognized, and rather sad and grim-looking.

The journeys to Hel of both the legendary Valkyrie BRYNHILD and the mythical figures of both BALDR and HERMÓD are described in the sources, notably in the eddic poem HELREID BRYNHILDAR and in Snorri's account of the death of Baldr, although it seems likely that there has been some external influence on the descriptions offered.

B12, 14, 23, 24, 28, 30, 35, 40, 50, 56, 59, 73, 87, 90; C2, 5, 9, 17, 24, 33, 46, 48; D137

Helblindi ('Helblind')

(1) One of the many names of the god ODIN, found in the eddic poem GRÍMNISMÁL. (2) According to the thirteenth-century Icelander SNORRI STURLUSON, the name of one of the brothers of the mischievous LOKI.

B12, 14, 23, 24, 28, 30, 35, 50, 56, 59, 73, 87, 90; C2, 5, 9, 17, 24, 33, 46, 48

Helgakvida Hjörvardssonar

A mixed composition of prose and verse in different metres found in the CODEX REGIUS manuscript and consisting of at least three quite distinct sections. In the first of these we are introduced to the legendary King HJÖRVARD, who has four wives but still seeks the fairest of women. In a scene strongly reminiscent of the passage in the eddic poem FÁFNISMÁL in which the talking birds reveal the whereabouts of the legendary Valkyrie BRYNHILD to the mighty hero SIGURD, the beauty of a woman called SIGRLINN is celebrated by a bird in a tree, and overheard by ATLI IDMUNDSSON, who presumably passes on the information to Hjörvard. A prose passage describes how Atli wins Sigrlinn for Hjörvard, and together they have a splendid if laconic son who grows up and one day is sitting on a gravemound when he sees nine Valkyries riding past. They dub him Helgi and tell him about a miraculous sword. One of the Valkyries in particular, SVÁVA, adopts him as her own and oversees his victories. The second sec-

Helgakvida Hundingsbana I and II

tion of the poem concerns an abusive battle of words or FLYTING that Helgi and Atli have with the giantess HRÍMGERD, whose father had been slain by Helgi. In recompense, Hrímgerd seeks to have sex with Helgi, who, along with Atli, simply delays her until the break of day when (like the dwarf ALVÍS in the eddic poem ALVÍSSMÁL) the giantess turns to stone. After this rather self-contained section, the poem returns to the love between Helgi and Sváva. A prose passage describes how they exchange vows, and then tells how HEDIN HJÖRVARDSSON, Helgi's brother has a nocturnal yuletide encounter in the woods with a troll-wife, who rides a wolf with snakes for reins and offers to spend the night with him. When he refuses, she promises revenge when he drinks that night from the sacred cup. The curse comes true when Hedin finds himself vowing to have Sváva, his brother's beloved, and in remorse he travels to find Helgi and confess. Helgi, who is on the point of fighting a battle with a king called ÁLF HRODMARSSON, takes the news circumspectly, seeing in it a prophecy of his impending death. Sure enough, he is fatally wounded in the battle, and with his dying words he commends his bride to accept his brother. The poem ends with an enigmatic sentence in prose: 'It has been said that Helgi and Sváva were born again', and this REINCARNATION serves to connect *Helgakvida Hjorvardssonar* with two other eddic poems in the Codex Regius, namely HELGAKVIDA HUNDINGSBANA I and II.

B12, 30, 56, 73, 87, 90; C2, 17, 24, 33, 46; D14, 353, 354, 602

Helgakvida Hundingsbana I and II

Two eddic poems found in the CODEX REGIUS manuscript, relating the life of the legendary hero HELGI SIGMUNDARSON HUNDINGSBANI, whom the poet makes a half-brother of SIGURD. These poems are separated in the manuscript by the eddic poem HELGAKVIDA HJÖRVARDSSONAR, and together the three texts have come to be known as the 'Helgi-lays' because of the sometimes rather self-conscious parallels of content and diction that connect them.

Helgakvida Hundingsbana I, the first of the so-called Helgi-lays in the manuscript, is in many ways the most tightly structured of the three. For an eddic poem, *Helgakvida Hundingsbana* I contains a large number of poetic periphrases or KENNINGS. The opening stanza sets the heroic tone:

> In days of yore when eagles screamed,
> holy streams fell from Himinfjöll,
> at that time was Helgi the mighty-hearted
> born to BORGHILD in Brálund.

Others of the trappings of the heroic life are immediately introduced: the NORNS approach to settle the new-born's fate, and a raven in a tree salutes the youngster. At the age of fifteen, Helgi slays the powerful King HUNDING, and similarly despatches Hunding's four sons, who come seeking compensation. Soon afterwards, Helgi is sitting outside at ARASTEIN when he sees Valkyries riding past. Helgi invites them to come back with him and his warriors. One of the Valkyries, later identified as SIGRÚN, says that they have other things on their mind: her father means her to marry one HÖDBRODD, whom she despises. Helgi promises to help and assembles his host. As Helgi approaches, a ritualized slanging match or FLYTING takes place between SINFJÖTLI, half-brother to both Helgi and the still mightier hero Sigurd and GUDMUND, brother to Hödbrodd. The flyting, which focuses on charges of unmanliness and sexual transgression, matches similar contests elsewhere in eddic verse, notably in HÁRBARDSLJÓD and LOKASENNA. Hödbrodd is summoned and the two armies clash. As the poem ends, Sigrún salutes Helgi for killing Hödbrodd, and promises him wealth, prosperity and her own hand.

Like *Helgakvida Hjörvardssonar*, with which both the other Helgi-lays share many parallels of content and diction, *Helgakvida Hundingsbana* II is a composite work in which verse that may derive from several different sources and periods is interspersed with prose passages. The opening prose narrative explains how Helgi is the son of SIGMUND and Borghild, and introduces Hunding and his sons, sworn enemies of Helgi and his father. Next is outlined a curious episode in which Helgi sets out to spy on Hunding's court, is pursued and has to disguise himself as a bondmaid grinding barley. After Helgi has killed Hunding, and so earned his nickname, a prose passage explicitly links Helgi Sigmundarson Hundingsbani with Helgi Hjorvardsson by stating of the beloved of Helgi Hundingsbani that:

> King HÖGNI had a daughter called Sigrún; she was a Valkyrie, and rode across the sea and sky: she was SVÁVA reborn.

In a verse exchange, Sigrún describes her support for Helgi and promises more. A prose passage tells how, after Helgi had defeated the four sons of Hunding, Sigrún comes to him at Arastein and explains how her father has betrothed her to Hödbrodd. Helgi sets off to assemble his troops and, as in *Helgakvida Hundingsbana* I (albeit rather more briefly), Sinfjötli, Helgi and Gudmund have a brief and vicious exchange of words, Gudmund rides off to summon Hödbrodd's army, which includes Högni, Sigrún's own father, and BRAGI and DAG, her brothers. In a dramatic series of verses, Sigrún triumphantly addresses the dying Hödbrodd, and comes the side of Helgi, who confesses that he has killed her father and one of her brothers. Sigrún marries him nonetheless, and they have sons. But, as another prose passage explains:

Helgi did not live to grow old. Dag, son of Högni, sacrificed to [the god] ODIN for help in avenging his father. Odin lent Dag his spear; Dag met Helgi, his sister's husband, at a place called Fjöturlund: he ran Helgi through with his spear. Helgi died there.

When Dag approaches his sister with the news, she curses him, and he blames Odin for sowing such dissension among kin. Sigrún praises her lost husband in words which closely parallel some of those which the tragic heroine GUDRÚN uses of her dead husband, Sigurd, in the eddic poem GUDRÚNARHVÖT:

'So much fear did Helgi incite in the hearts
of all his foes and their kin,
as before a wolf, running mad,
mountain goats scatter in terror.

'So much did Helgi rise above heroes
as the well-formed ash above the thorn,
or that noble stag dripping with dew,
who lives higher than all beasts.'

The latter comparison, with its mention of ash tree, stag, thorn and dew, is presumably a reference to the mythical stag EIKTHYRNIR, which stands on top of the mighty hall VALHALL, nibbling at the branches of the cosmic ash tree YGGDRASIL, and from whose horns drops the moisture from which mighty rivers flow. After Helgi's death, he is observed riding to his own burial mound with many men, and in a grisly scene Sigrún goes and, finding the mound open, joins her blood-stained husband for the night in his barrow. The next day he rides away, never to return, and, as the final prose passage has it: 'grief and mourning made Sigrún die young'. The cycle of rebirth is set to go on, and the prose concludes by saying that:

Helgi and Sigrún are said to have been reborn; he was called Helgi Haddingsbanni, and she KÁRA Halfdansdóttir, as is told in the [now-lost] *Káraljód*, and she was a Valkyrie.

B12, 30, 56, 73, 87, 90; C2, 17, 24, 33, 46; D226, 265, 276, 353, 602

Helgi

An otherwise unknown character who is mentioned once in the eddic poem GRÍPISSPÁ, in which the wise GRÍPIR says to his foster-son, the hero SIGURD that:

'A prince's daughter sleeps on the fell,
bright, in a mail-coat, after Helgi's death.

You shall slice, with your sharp blade,
cut that mail-coat with FÁFNIR's bane.'

The evident allusion to the Valkyrie Sigrdrífa (usually identified with BRYNHILD), would seem to make Helgi the same figure elsewhere called HJÁLMGUNNAR. At all events, this Helgi is quite distinct from HELGI HJÖRVARDSSON and HELGI SIGMUNDARSON HUNDINGSBANI.

B12, 30, 56, 73, 87, 90; C2, 17, 24, 33, 46

Helgi Haddingsbani *see* HELGAKVIDA HUNDINGSBANA I and II; KÁRA.

Helgi Hjörvardsson

The eponymous hero of the eddic poem HELGAKVIDA HJÖRVARDSSONAR, which offers a graphic account of his life and love for the Valkyrie SVÁVA.

B12, 30, 56, 73, 87, 90; C2, 17, 24, 33, 46; D14

Helgi-lays *see* HELGAKVIDA HUNDINGSBANA I and II.

Helgi Sigmundarson Hundingsbani ('the holy one')

Son of SIGMUND and BORGHILD, brother of HÁMUND and the eponymous hero of two eddic poems, HELGAKVIDA HUNDINGSBANA I and II. The legendary VÖLSUNGA SAGA, drawing freely on both poems, provides a thumbnail account of his early life:

Sigmund now became a rich and splendid king, wise and enterprising. He married a woman called Borghild; they had two sons, one named Helgi and the other Hámund. When Helgi was born, NORNS came and gave him his destiny: he would become the most renowned of all kings. Sigmund had then returned from battle, and approached his son with the gift of a leek. Alongside that he gave the boy the name Helgi, and gave him Hringstead ['ring-place'], Sólfell ['sun fell'] and a sword as naming-gifts. He called for the boy to grow up well, and take after the VÖLSUNG-race. Helgi grew up to be great-hearted and popular, and he surpassed most other people in every attainment. It is said that he first went to war at the age of fifteen.

The account of Helgi's birth that is given in *Helgakvida Hundingsbana* I, from which the account in *Völsunga saga* is partly derived, is still more spectacular:

In days of yore when eagles screamed,
holy streams fell from Himinfjöll,
at that time was Helgi the mighty-hearted
born to Borghild in Brálund.

Helgrind

That night there came Norns to the house,
they who would set the princeling's fate.
Great fame, they said, would be his lot,
and he would be called the best of kings.

Helgi's reputation soars when, at the age of fifteen, he kills the mighty King HUNDING and then goes on to slaughter four of Hunding's sons, Álf, Eyjólf, Hagbard and Hervard. When he falls in love with the Valkyrie SIGRÚN, he fights a successful battle at FREKASTEIN against her unwanted suitor, HÖDBRODD, but in the process kills both her brother BRAGI and her father HÖGNI. Their deaths are eventually avenged by DAG, her only surviving brother, who kills Helgi with a spear ostensibly given him by ODIN himself. Sigrún keeps a grisly tryst with the dead Helgi in his grave-mound, and as the prose epilogue to *Helgakvida Hundingsbana* II has it: 'grief and sorrow made Sigrún die young.'

B12, 25, 30, 42, 56, 65, 68, 73, 79, 87, 90; C1 – 3, 6, 17, 24, 33, 46

Helgrind *see* HEL.

Helreid Brynhildar ('the Hel-ride of Brynhild')

An eddic poem interspersed with prose passages, found in the CODEX REGIUS manuscript as well as, in part, in NORNAGESTS THÁTTR; the poem provides the opportunity for the Valkyrie BRYNHILD, who often appears as the villain of the VÖLSUNG-cycle in other eddic verse, to state her case. The prose introduction states that after Brynhild died of grief at the death of her beloved SIGURD, two pyres were built, one for Sigurd, and the other, rather after the fashion of the OSEBERG burial, containing a chariot and costly cloth. Brynhild is said to have travelled in this chariot along the road to HEL, and there to have been stopped by a giantess, who blames her for all the misfortunes of the sons of GJÚKI and reproaches her for chasing Sigurd, who was, after all, the husband of another woman, GUDRÚN. In reply, Brynhild describes her childhood and early life as a Valkyrie, explaining how she was punished by the god ODIN for granting victory to the wrong side in battle and describing how she was fell into an enchanted sleep in a hall protected by a ring of flame, to await the hero bold enough to claim her. When Sigurd did so, she says, they spent eight nights together in the one bed 'like brother and sister'. Her wrath had been roused only when the hero GUNNAR, her husband, had accused her of sleeping with Sigurd, and she came to realize that she had been tricked into marrying Gunnar. The closing stanza underlines her grim determination:

'They must all too long in the face of great strife
men and women be born and raised;
we two shall share the rest of our time,

Sigurd and I together:
sink yourself, giantess-spawn!'

B12, 25, 30, 42, 56, 65, 68, 73, 79, 87, 90; C1 – 3, 6, 17, 21, 24, 33, 46; D25

Hengest ('stallion')

According to the early eighth-century Anglo-Saxon historian BEDE, one of two Germanic brothers with equine names – the other was Horsa ('horse') – who were invited by the Celtic king Vortigern to help defend Britain against the invading Germanic hordes in 449. Hengest and Horsa not only stayed on but took over. Given the evidence for an early Germanic cult of twins, such as the ALCIS attested by the first-century Roman historian TACITUS, together with an apparent interest in horse-deities, it has been suggested that Hengest and Horsa represent just such a divine pair.

B2, 15; C29, 41; D558, 606

Hengikjöpt ('hang-jaw')

According to the thirteenth-century Icelander SNORRI STURLUSON, the figure, presumably a giant, who gave the legendary and bountiful King FRÓDI the magic mill GROTTI.

B24, 28, 35, 40, 50; D5, 9, 48

Hengjankjapta ('hang-jaw')

According to a verse by the Icelandic poet THORBJÖRN DÍSARSKÁLD cited by the thirteenth-century Icelander SNORRI STURLUSON, a giantess killed by the god THOR.

B24, 28, 35, 40, 50; C5, 9, 48

Heorot ('hart')

The mighty hall built by the Danish King Hrothgar at the start of the Old English poem BEOWULF, and the scene of the nocturnal depredations of the monster GRENDEL. Apparently so called because of its horned gables, it is possible that the hart-imagery may be connected to the figure of the stag EIKTHYRNIR, which, according to the thirteenth-century Icelander SNORRI STURLUSON, stands above VALHALL.

B44; C4

Herborg

According to the eddic poem GUDRÚNARKVIDA I, a queen of the Huns, who tells the tragic heroine GUDRÚN of her own grief to try to alleviate her pain over her husband SIGURD's death:

Then said Herborg, queen of Hunland,
'I have a still greater grief to tell:
in the south of the land my seven sons,
my husband too, all fell slain;

likewise father and mother, my four brothers,
when the wind got up on the sea,
were all wave-battered within their boats.

'With my own hands I laid them,
with my own hands I buried them,
with my own hands I arranged things
for their trip to the dead;
I went through all this in a single season,
and no one came to show me comfort.

'Then I was caught and taken captive
the same season after that happened;
I had to dress and bind the shoes
of my master's wife every morning.

'She hated me from jealousy,
and beat me with heavy blows;
I never knew a better master,
or a mistress who was worse.'

B12, 30, 56, 73, 87, 90; C2, 17, 24, 33, 46

Herfjötur *see* VALKYRIES.

Herkja ('dearth')
(1) According to the eddic poem GUDRÚNARKVIDA
III, the mistress of ATLI BUDLASON. Rather ironically,
Herkja wrongly accuses Atli's wife, the tragic heroine
GUDRÚN, of adultery and suffers the consequences. (2)
In the name-lists or THULUR, the name of a troll-wife
or giantess.

B12, 30, 56, 73, 87, 90; C2, 17, 24, 33, 46

Hermanaric *see* JÖRMUNREKK.

Herminones *see* TUISTO.

Hermód ('war-spirit')
According to the thirteenth-century Icelander SNORRI
STURLUSON, the son of the god ODIN and the brother of
BALDR, after whose death Hermód undertook a journey
to HEL, riding Odin's horse SLEIPNIR. The omission
of any mention of Hermód in the one eddic poem
that deals with Baldr's death in any detail, BALDRS
DRAUMAR, together with the appearance of a human
hero called Hermód in the eddic poem HYNDLULJÓD
suggests that Hermód's affiliation with the ÆSIR is a
fiction of Snorri's, who calls him 'Hermód the Brave,
Odin's boy'. It is certainly striking that Hermód
appears alongside BRAGI, who seems to have been a
human figure originally, likewise elevated into the pantheon, welcoming the dead Hákon into VALHALL in the
tenth-century poem HÁKONARMÁL, while elsewhere he
figures as part of a poetic periphrasis or KENNING for

'warrior'. A legendary (human) figure called Heremod
features in the Anglo-Saxon poem BEOWULF, and also
appears in a number of Anglo-Saxon genealogies.

B12, 14, 23, 24, 28, 30,, 35, 40, 50, 56, 59, 73, 87, 90; C2, 5, 9, 17, 24, 33, 46, 48;
D37, 285

Hersir *see* RÍGSTHULA.

Heruli
Wandering Germanic warrior-bands, widely attested in
classical sources, whose name has become associated
with a term used in early inscriptions to signify the
rune-master. The same root lies behind Old English
eorl ('noble', 'warrior').

B44; D424

Hervarar saga ok Heidreks konungs
A legendary saga composed in the middle of the thirteenth century and surviving in three quite separate
versions, which is based on the lives of Hervör and her
son King Heidrek. The latter eventually engages in a
riddle contest – the so-called *Gestumblindagátur* – with
one GESTUMBLINDI, who turns out to be the god ODIN
in disguise. The saga as a whole is distinctly episodic
but contains a number of motifs, such as the sword,
Tyrfing, which (like DÁINSLEIF) must kill every time it
is unsheathed, that can be paralleled closely in other
sources.

B80; C21

Hervard Hundingsson *see* HELGI SIGMUNDARSON
HUNDINGSBANI.

Hervör alvitr ('all-wise'?, 'strange creature'?)
(1) According to the prose introduction to the eddic
poem VÖLUNDARKVIDA, the daughter of King
HLÖDVER, sometime wife of the legendary smith,
VÖLUND, and a Valkyrie. The meaning of the second
element of her name is the subject of some dispute: current suggestions include 'all-wise' or, on the pattern of
Old English *ælwiht*, 'strange creature'. (2) A quite separate, if equally legendary, figure called Hervör is the
eponymous heroine of HERVARAR SAGA OK HEIDREKS
KONUNGS.

B12, 30, 31, 56, 73, 80, 87, 90: C2, 17, 21, 24, 33, 46

Hild ('battle')
(1) According to the eddic poem VÖLUSPÁ, a Valkyrie.
(2) In the POETIC EDDA, in HELREID BRYNHILDAR, the
legendary heroine BRYNHILD says that she herself was
known as Hild when she was a Valkyrie. (3) The name
of the beautiful daughter of the legendary King HÖGNI,

Hildi

whose abduction by HEDIN HJARRANDASON sparks off the endless battle of the HJADNINGAVÍG.

B12, 30, 56, 59, 73, 87, 90; C2, 17, 24, 33, 46

Hildi *see* VALKYRIES.

Hildisvíni ('battle-boar')

According to the eddic poem HYNDLULJÓD, the boar on which the goddess FREYJA rides, described as 'golden-bristled' (*gullinborsti*), and therefore having an evident connection with the better attested boar GULLINBORSTI, which belonged to the god FREY, Freyja's brother.

B12, 30, 56, 73, 87, 90; C2, 17, 24, 33, 46

Hildólf ('battle-wolf')

In the eddic poem HÁRBARDSLJÓD, the god ODIN, disguised as the cantankerous boatman Hárbard ('grey beard'), tells the god THOR that he works as a ferryman for an otherwise unknown Hildólf; it seems likely that Hildólf is simply another of Odin's many names. Such a supposition is supported by the inclusion of the name in a list preserved in the thirteenth-century SNORRA EDDA, where, however, Hildólf is given as one of the sons of Odin.

B12, 30, 565, 73, 87, 90; C2, 17, 24, 33, 46

Himinbjörg ('heaven-protection')

According to the thirteenth-century Icelander SNORRI STURLUSON, a place situated where the rainbow-bridge BIFRÖST enters ÁSGARD. The watchman-god HEIMDALL lives there.

B24, 28, 35, 40, 50; C5, 9, 48

Himinfjöl *see* HELGAKVIDA HUNDINGSBANA I.

Himinglæva *see* ÆGIR.

Himinhrjód ('heaven-destroyer')

According to the thirteenth-century Icelander SNORRI STURLUSON, the huge ox, belonging to the giant HYMIR, whose head the god THOR tore off and used as bait when he went fishing for the MIDGARD-SERPENT.

B24, 28, 35, 40, 50; C5, 9, 48

Hinda(r)fjall ('hind mountain')

The mountain where the legendary heroine BRYNHILD slept behind a wall of flame, before being visited by the mighty hero SIGURD; Sigurd's approach to the mountain is summarized in the prose preface to the eddic poem SIGRDRÍFUMÁL and repeated practically verbatim in the legendary VÖLSUNGA SAGA:

Ahead of him on the mountain he saw a mighty light, as if a fire was blazing there, and its flames reached the heavens. When he approached, there stood ahead of him a barrier of shields, and above it a banner. Sigurd went through the barrier of shields and saw someone lying there asleep in full armour.

B12, 25, 30, 42, 56, 65, 68, 73, 79, 87, 90; C1–3, 6, 17, 24, 33, 46

Historia ecclesiastica gentis Anglorum *see* BEDE.

Hjadningavíg ('the battle of the Hjadnings')

According to both the thirteenth-century Icelander SNORRI STURLUSON and (in a slightly different form) the later SÖRLA THÁTTR, a never-ending battle that takes place between two kings, HÖGNI and HEDIN HJARRANDASON, after Hedin abducts Högni's beautiful daughter, HILD. When the battle-lines are drawn and Hedin's initial offer of recompense, made to her father by Hild, has been turned down, Hedin increases his offer, but too late. As Högni says:

> 'Your offer has come too late, if you want to make amends, for I have now drawn (the sword) DÁINSLEIF, which the dwarfs made, which must kill someone every time it is unsheathed, and whose stroke never fails, and whose wound never heals.'

They fight all day, and at night Hild visits the battlefield and tends the sick and dead, and renders men and weapons fit to fight the next morning; and so they must fight on till the end of the world at RAGNARÖK. Snorri quotes some skaldic verses of RAGNARSDRÁPA as illustration.

B24, 28, 35, 39, 40, 50, 62, 83, 87; C5, 9, 16, 21, 48; D345

Hjalli

The unfortunate and cowardly cook whose heart, according to both ATLAKVIDA and ATLAMÁL in the POETIC EDDA, is cut out and presented to the legendary hero GUNNAR as that of his brother HÖGNI GJÚKASON. *Atlamál* presents the fullest version of Hjalli's pathetic predicament:

> The saucepan-keeper panicked,
> he didn't hang around:
> he knew how to blub,
> and climbed into every cranny.
> He called himself a victim of their war
> to pay for all his effort:
> it was a sad day for him,
> to die and leave the pigs,
> all the resources,
> which he had owned before.

The legendary VÖLSUNGA SAGA, clearly drawing on the

description in *Atlamál*, presents a curiously staccato account, in which Hjalli is first spared at the insistence of Högni, but then has his heart cut out anyway:

> The slave, hearing this, screamed loudly and scampered off to wherever he thought he could hide. He said he had a raw deal from their hostility, and paying for their problems; he said it was a bad day when he had to leave his fine life and the care of the pigs. They grabbed him and drew their knives. He screamed loudly, before he felt the knife point. Then Högni spoke, as it befits few who come into such a trial; he interceded for the slave and said that he did not want to hear such shrieking. He said that it was easier for him to play that game. The slave was granted his life . . . then they seized the slave a second time, and cut out his heart.

B12, 20, 25, 30, 31, 42, 56, 65, 68, 73, 79, 87, 90; C1–3, 6, 17, 24, 33, 46

Hjálmgunnar

According to a prose passage in the eddic poem SIGRDRÍFUMÁL and incorporated into the legendary VÖLSUNGA SAGA, a king struck down by the Valkyrie BRYNHILD (using the name SIGRDRÍFA), after the god ODIN had promised him victory in his battle against AGNAR AUDABRÓDIR. Odin's revenge is swift:

> Brynhild said that two kings had fought each other. One, called Hjálmgunnar, was old and a mighty warrior, and Odin had promised him the victory, and the other was called Agnar or Audabródir. 'I struck down Hjálmgunnar in battle. Then Odin stabbed me with a sleep-thorn in revenge for this, and said that I should never have a victory afterwards, and said that I had to marry. In return, I vowed that I would never marry anyone who knew fear.'

B25, 42, 65, 68, 79; C1, 6

Hjálprek

Legendary king of Denmark, the father of ÁLF HJÁLPREKSSON and foster-father of the mighty hero SIGURD, whom, according to the eddic poem REGINSMÁL, he provides with a manned ship to avenge his natural father, SIGMUND.

B12, 30, 56, 73, 87, 90; C2, 17, 24, 33, 46

Hjördís

Daughter of the legendary King EYLIMI, and, according to the eddic poem GRÍPISSPÁ, brother of GRÍPIR, wooed by both the hero SIGMUND (as his second wife) and by LYNGVI. After Sigmund's death, when she is already pregnant with their son, the hero SIGURD, she is captured on a raid by ÁLF HJÁLPREKSSON, who marries her. According to the legendary VÖLSUNGA SAGA, which describes her as 'the fairest and wisest of all

women', she presents Sigurd with the broken pieces of Sigmund's sword, re-forged by the devious REGIN as the mighty sword GRAM.

B12, 25, 30, 42, 56, 65, 68, 73, 79, 87, 90; C1–3, 6, 17, 24, 33, 46

Hjörleif

According to the eddic poem HELGAKVIDA HUN-DINGSBANA I, one of the warriors (unattested elsewhere) who fought alongside the eponymous hero, HELGI SIGMUNDARSON HUNDINGSBANI.

B12, 30, 56, 73, 87, 90; C2, 17, 24, 33, 46

Hjörvard

The father of a number of heroes, notably HELGI HJÖRVARDSSON and HEDIN. According to the prose introduction to the eddic poem HELGAKVIDA HJÖR-VARDSSONAR:

> There was a king named Hjörvard; he had four wives. One was called ÁLFHILD, and their son was called Hedin; the second was called SÆREID, and their son was called HUMLUNG; the third was called SINRÖD, and their son was called HYMLING. King Hjörvard had sworn a vow to marry the fairest woman he could find.

It is the account of King Hjörvard's wooing by proxy of his fourth bride, SIGRLINN, the beautiful mother of Helgi, that takes up the first part of the poem.

B12, 30, 56, 73, 87, 90; C2, 17, 24, 33, 46

Hjörvard Hundingsson

Son of the legendary King HUNDING, sliced in two by the mighty hero SIGURD in his battle against LYNGVI, according to the legendary VÖLSUNGA SAGA.

B25, 42, 65, 68, 79; C1, 6

Hjúki *see* MÁNI.

Hladgud svanhvít ('swan-white')

According to the eddic poem VÖLUNDARKVIDA, the beloved of SLAGFID, the brother of the legendary smith, VÖLUND. In the prose introduction to *Völundarkvida* Hladgud svanhvít is described, alongside HERVÖR ALVITR and ÖLRÚN, as possessing a cloak of swan-feathers, presumably to aid flight. All three are said to be VALKYRIES.

B12, 30, 31, 56, 73, 87, 90; C2, 17, 24, 33, 46

hlauttein ('sacrificial twig')

A twig apparently used at heathen SACRIFICES to spatter blood on the temple walls and on the congregation; the thirteenth-century Icelander SNORRI

Hlébard

STURLUSON mentions the use of a *hlauttein* in his HEIMSKRINGLA, and similar references are included in the mid-thirteenth-century EYRBYGGJA SAGA (in the course of detailed description of a temple) and *Kjalnesinga saga*. The opening stanza of the eddic poem HYMSIKVIDA appears to imply that similar twigs could be used for DIVINATION:

> The ÆSIR were glad: they'd had a good hunt,
> and felt like feasting, because they'd found out,
> by shaking some twigs sprinkled with blood,
> that [the sea-giant] ÆGIR had everything to brew ale.

B77; C39

Hlébard ('protecting beard')

According to the eddic poem HÁRBARDSLJÓD, a giant from whom the god ODIN won a magic wand or GAMBANTEINN, which he then used to drive the giant into a frenzy.

B12, 30, 56, 73, 87, 90; C2, 17, 24, 33, 46

Hlér ('sea')

Another name for the sea-giant, ÆGIR. The early thirteenth-century Danish historian SAXO GRAMMATICUS mentions a character called Lerus, who is the father of Snjó ('snow') and who is probably to be identified with Hlér. Elsewhere, Hlér is listed as one of the children of the primordial frost-giant, FORNJÓT.

B64; C7, 8

Hlidskjálf ('gate-tower'?)

According to the thirteenth-century Icelander SNORRI STURLUSON, the seat on which the god ODIN sits in his hall, VALASKJÁLF, and from which he can observe all the worlds. The account given in the prose preface to the eddic poem GRÍMNISMÁL is slightly different, in that the name is given to the place itself rather than to the seat, and elsewhere Snorri seems to agree. Skaldic verse is of little help in deciding the precise topography. One poetic periphrasis or KENNING simply describes Odin as 'Hlidskjálf's king'. According to the prose preface to the eddic poem SKÍRNISMÁL, it is from Hlidskjálf that the fertility-god FREY first spies the beautiful giantess GERD, and it is possible that his subsequent longing was partly interpreted as a punishment for his presumption in usurping Odin's seat.

B12, 14, 23, 24, 28, 30, 35, 40, 50, 56, 59, 73, 87, 90: C2, 5, 9, 17, 24, 33, 46, 48; D292

Hlín ('protectoress')

According to the thirteenth-century Icelander SNORRI STURLUSON, one of the goddesses or ÁSYNJUR, to whom is given the responsibility of protecting the favourites of the goddess FRIGG. In the eddic poem VÖLUSPÁ, however, Hlín would appear to be simply another name for Frigg herself, while the numerous occurrences of the name in skaldic poetry in poetic periphrases or KENNINGS for women do nothing to dispel the confusion.

B12, 14, 23, 24, 28, 30, 35, 40, 50, 56, 59, 73, 87, 90; C25, 9, 17, 24, 33, 46, 48

Hljód ('howling')

According to the legendary VÖLSUNGA SAGA, a daughter of the giant HRÍMNIR, who marries VÖLSUNG. Together they have ten sons, of whom the eldest is the mighty SIGMUND, and one daughter, SIGNÝ. In the very first chapter of *Völsunga saga* it is stated that Hljód, here described as a 'wish-maiden' of the god ODIN, and so perhaps a VALKYRIE, assumed the shape of a crow and gave an apple of fertility to RERIR, Völsung's father, who had been childless until then. Her role in the conception of her own husband seems to confirm the extraordinary longevity of such beings.

B25, 42, 65, 68, 79; C1, 6

Hlöd *see* HLÖDSKVIDA.

Hlödskvida

Also known as 'The Battle of the Goths and the Huns', a poem usually included alongside others of the POETIC EDDA, although it is not found in the great manuscript collection known as the CODEX REGIUS. In the course of the poem, preserved in the legendary HERVARAR SAGA OK HEIDREKS KONUNGS, the mighty Angantýr (representing the Goths) and Hlöd (representing the Huns) clash over a fabulous inheritance, including the cursed sword Tyrfing. After Angantýr's death, his warrior-maiden daughter Hervör visits him in his burial mound to demand Tyrfing, in order to wreak vengeance on her father's killers.

B12, 30, 32, 33, 56, 73, 80, 87, 90; C2, 17, 21, 24, 33, 46; D421, 579

Hlödvard *see* HRÍMGERD.

Hlödvér

(1) According to the prose preface to the eddic poem VÖLUNDARKVIDA, the father of the swan-maidens HLADGUD SVANHVÍT and HERVÖR ALVITR, who forms liaisons with the legendary smith VÖLUND and his brother SLAGFID. (2) The name of an otherwise unknown warrior whose property, according to the eddic poem GUDRÚNARKVIDA II, is offered to the tragic heroine GUDRÚN by her mother GRÍMHILD as a peace-offering after the death of Gudrún's husband, the hero SIGURD.

B12, 30, 31, 56, 73, 87, 90; C2, 17, 24, 33, 46

Hlódyn ('the hidden one'?)

According to the eddic poem VÖLUSPÁ, Hlódyn is the mother of the god THOR, who is elsewhere given as JÖRD. Since Hlódyn appears in poetic periphrases or KENNINGS for land and rocks and in name-lists or THULUR for earth, it seems most likely that it is simply an alternative name. Several second- and third-century Latin inscriptions from Germanic areas commemorate a figure known as Hludana, who is probably to be identified with Hlódyn.

B12, 30, 56, 59, 73, 87, 90; C2, 17, 24, 33, 46

Hlökk *see* VALKYRIES.

Hlóra

The foster-mother of the god THOR, according to the thirteenth-century Icelander SNORRI STURLUSON. Presumably equivalent to the character variously named Lóra or Glóra, whom Snorri identifies as the foster-mother of TROR.

B24, 28, 35, 40, 50; C5, 9, 48

Hlór(r)idi ('loud rider')

Another name, sometimes also spelled Lóridi, for the god THOR, witnessed in the POETIC EDDA in HYMISKVIDA, LOKASENNA and THRYMSKVIDA.

B12, 30, 56, 73, 87, 90; C2, 17, 24, 33, 46

Hludana *see* HLÓDYN.

Hlymdalir ('din dales')

According to the legendary VÖLSUNGA SAGA, the home of HEIMIR, the foster-father of the heroine BRYNHILD. The name in *Völsunga saga* is almost certainly derived from Brynhild's assertion in the eddic poem HELREID BRYNHILDAR that:

> In Hlymdalir I was called HILD under helm;
> I was a VALKYRIE, devoted to war.

B12, 25, 30, 42, 56, 65, 68, 73, 79, 87, 90; C1–3, 6, 17, 24, 33, 46

Hlyrnir *see* VINDBLÁIN.

Hniflung *see* NIFLUNG.

Hnikar ('inciter')

One of the many names used by the god ODIN. According to the eddic poem REGINSMÁL, the hero SIGURD and his men, sailing to the battle in which they are to kill LYNGVI and his brothers, are caught in a storm and spot a mysterious man on the nearby cliffs, who calls himself Hnikar, Feng ('grasp') and Fjölnir ('much-wise', 'concealer'), all recognizable titles of Odin:

They turned ashore, and the man came on board; the storm ceased.

[Sigurd said]
'Tell me, Hnikar, since you know all things
in the destiny of gods and men;
what are the best, when it comes to battle,
of the omens when swords are swinging?'

Hnikar said:
'Many are good, if a warrior is aware
of the omens when swords are swinging;
I reckon that a raven's presence
bodes a warrior well.

'There's a second, when you step outside,
about to take a trip,
if you see stand in your way,
a pair of praise-eager men.

'There's a third, if you hear howl
a wolf beneath ash-boughs;
you'll get good luck from helmeted men
if you see them walking ahead.

'No fighting-man must strive in the face
of the late-shining sister of Moon;
they win the struggle, brisk of battle,
who can see to set up their wedge.

'There's great danger, if you stumble,
as you stride to war.
deceitful DÍSIR stand on each side
and wish to see you wounded.

'Combed and washed should be the wise
and fully fed each morning;
no one knows what evening brings;
it's bad to fall in the face of fate.'

B12, 30, 56, 73, 87, 90; C2, 17, 24, 33, 46

Hnitbjörg ('crashing rock')

According to the thirteenth-century Icelander SNORRI STURLUSON, the place where the giant SUTTUNG hid the MEAD OF POETRY, guarded by his daughter, GUNNLÖD.

B24, 28, 35, 40, 50; C5, 9, 48

Hnoss ('treasure')

One of the daughters of FREYJA and ÓD. According to the thirteenth-century Icelander SNORRI STURLUSON:

> She is so fair that from her name anything that is beautiful or precious is called *hnossir* ['treasures'].

B24, 28, 35, 40, 50; C5, 9, 48

Höd

Höd ('warrior')

The blind son of the god ODIN who, misled by LOKI, kills his brother BALDR with a sprig of mistletoe, and is in turn killed in vengeance by VÁLI, another of Odin's sons. In the POETIC EDDA the killing of Baldr by Höd is prophesied to Odin both in BALDRS DRAUMAR and, most chillingly, in VÖLUSPÁ; as the prophetess says:

I saw for Baldr, the blood-stained god,
Odin's son, his fate settled;
there stood blooming, above the ground,
meagre, mighty beautiful: mistletoe.

From that plant, that seemed so slender,
Höd learned to shoot a dangerous dart of harm;
Baldr's brother was quickly born:
that son of Odin learned to kill when one night old.

Later on in the poem we learn that after the apocalyptic events of RAGNARÖK both Höd and Baldr will return from the dead, to help govern the new world.

In what looks like a parallel episode in the Anglo-Saxon poem BEOWULF, a character called *Hæð*cyn (Höd?) kills his brother Here*beald* (Baldr?) with an arrow, so allowing Hygelac, Beowulf's lord, to come to the Geatish throne; the thirteenth-century Icelander SNORRI STURLUSON himself appears to tell a very similar tale in YNGLINGA SAGA, where one Hugleik (Hygelac?) becomes king after two brothers are involved in a hunting accident.

B12, 30, 56, 73, 87, 90; C2, 17, 24, 33, 46; D122

Hödbrodd

Son of the legendary warrior GRANMAR and betrothed to the unwilling Valkyrie SIGRÚN, who persuades the hero HELGI SIGMUNDARSON HUNDINGSBANI to fight and kill Hödbrodd and his troops at FREKASTEIN. Among the litany of warriors summoned by Hödbrodd to the fateful battle are the hero HÖGNI and the brothers Álf inn gamli ('the old'), Atli and Yngvi, the sons of HRING; despite such an impressive line-up, Hödbrodd and his men are doomed. The tale is told in the eddic poems HELGAKVIDA HUNDINGSBANA I and II.

B12, 30, 56, 73, 87, 90; C2, 17, 24, 33, 46

Hoddmímir ('hoard-Mímir')

According to the eddic poem VAFTHRÚDNISMÁL, it was in the wood or tree of Hoddmímir that the human beings named LÍF and Lífthrásir (elsewhere called LEIFTHRÁSIR) hid and were able to survive the apocalyptic events of RAGNARÖK. Since the wise giant MÍMIR is so closely associated with the mighty ash tree YGGDRASIL, it seems likely that 'the wood or tree of Hoddmímir' is nothing more than the world-tree itself.

B122, 30, 56, 73, 87, 90; C2, 17, 24, 33, 46

Hoddrofnir

An isolated form found in the eddic poem SIGRDRÍFUMÁL, where it is presumably another name for the wise giant MÍMIR.

B12, 30, 56, 73, 87, 90; C2, 17, 24, 33, 46

Hœnir

One of the ÆSIR, generally depicted as a companion of the god ODIN. According to the eddic poem VÖLUSPÁ, it is Hœnir (sometimes spelled Hænir), alongside Odin and LODUR, who animates the tree trunks from which the first humans, ASK and EMBLA are formed. Rather curiously, it is Hœnir who is said to have imbued the lifeless wood with *óðr* ('frenzy', 'passion'), rather than Odin, who derives his own name from the quality. Elsewhere in the POETIC EDDA, in REGINSMÁL, Hœnir is again found wandering in the company of Odin and another of the ÆSIR, in this case LOKI, when Loki kills OTR and effectively sparks off the series of tragedies that form the cycle of tales surrounding the VÖLSUNGS. The same wandering triad – Odin, Hœnir and Loki – is present when Loki first offends the giant THJAZI, as a reference in the skaldic poem HAUSTLÖNG, composed around the turn of the eleventh century, makes clear. The thirteenth-century Icelander SNORRI STURLUSON describes Hœnir's rather passive role in his retelling of all these tales, except for the first, in which he has a different triad – Odin, VILI and VÉ – involved in the activation of Ask and Embla. Snorri gives a list of appropriate designations for Hœnir, which is no more illuminating; he is described as 'Odin's table-companion, or colleague, or comrade, the swift Ás, long-legs, muddy-king'. Elsewhere, in his YNGLINGA SAGA, Snorri describes how Hœnir was given as one of two hostages, alongside MÍMIR, from the Æsir to the VANIR, but tells that the tall and good-looking Hœnir defers in all things to his companion. The only consistent image in all these accounts is that of Hœnir as a feeble figure, who cannot act alone, but whose power derives from his companionship with others.

B12, 14, 23–5, 28, 30, 35, 39, 40, 42, 45, 50, 56, 59, 62, 65, 68, 73, 79, 83, 87, 90; C1–3, 5, 6, 9, 13, 16, 17, 24, 33, 46, 48; D313

Hófvarpnir *see* GNÁ.

Högni

(1) Father of the Valkyrie SIGRÚN. He makes a brief appearance in the eddic poems HELGAKVIDA HUNDINGSBANA I and II and is described fighting against the great hero HELGI SIGMUNDARSON HUNDINGSBANI in the battle at FREKASTEIN, where he is killed, along with his son BRAGI. His other son, DAG, avenges his father and brother by killing Helgi with a

spear, supposedly lent him by the god ODIN himself. (2) The name of the father of the beautiful HILD and one of the protagonists in the never-ending battle of the HJADNINGAVÍG.

B2, 30, 56, 73, 87, 90; C2, 17, 24, 33, 46

Högni Gjúkason

A son of the legendary King GJÚKI, and brother of GUNNAR and GUTTHORM. Högni is intimately involved in the spiralling vengeance and killing depicted in the POETIC EDDA in both ATLAKVIDA and ATLAMÁL (and elaborated upon in the legendary VÖLSUNGA SAGA) as part of the VÖLSUNG-cycle. Although he takes a sub-ordinate role to Gunnar in the decision to visit the hall of the scheming ATLI BUDLASON to see their sis-ter (and Atli's wife), the tragic heroine GUDRÚN, it is Högni who is first given the chance to exhibit his steely heroism, not only in his resistance to capture but also in his grim willingness to have the heart cut out of his living flesh rather than betray his brother and reveal the whereabouts of their inherited treasure.

B12, 20, 25, 30, 31, 42, 56, 65, 68, 73, 79, 87, 90; C1–3, 6, 17, 24, 33, 46

Höld *see* RÍGSTHULA.

Hólgabrúd ('bride of Hólgi'?)

According to the name-lists or THULUR, the name of a giantess. *See also* THORGERD HÓLGABRÚD.

B24, 28, 35, 40, 50; C5, 9, 48; D66

Hölkvir

The name of the horse owned by the hero HÖGNI GJÚKASON, according to a number of sources associat-ed with the so-called VÖLSUNG-cycle.

B25, 42, 65, 68, 79; C1, 6

hörg ('altar')

A sacrificial altar, built up of stones or timbers, and witnessed in a large number of place-names. An account of such an altar is included in the mid-thirteenth-century Icelandic EYRBYGGJA SAGA, in the course of a detailed description of a temple). In the eddic poem HYNDLULJÓD, the goddess FREYJA salutes her favourite, Ottar, as follows:

> He made me a high altar
> of heaped-up stones:
> the gathered rocks
> have grown all bloody,
> and he reddened them again
> with the fresh blood of cows;
> Ottar has always
> had faith in the ÁSYNJUR.

B12, 30, 56, 73, 77, 87, 90; C2, 17, 24, 33, 39, 46

Hörn ('flaxen'?)

(1) According to the name-lists or THULUR, the name of a giantess. (2) The thirteenth-century Icelander SNORRI STURLUSON gives this as another name for the fertility-goddess FREYJA.

B24, 28, 35, 40, 50; C5, 9, 48

Horsa *see* HENGEST.

Hösvir *see* RÍGSTHULA.

Hrafnkels saga Freysgoda

A short Icelandic saga, probably composed in the late thirteenth century, giving an account of the fall from grace of the powerful and arrogant Hrafnkel, a priest – GODI – of the god FREY, and his subsequent return to fortune, once he has abandoned the service of his god. In the first part of the saga the seeds of Hrafnkel's self-destruction are sown when he makes a vow to kill anyone who rides a horse, Freyfaxi, which he has dedi-cated to Frey, and such a vow is particularly interesting given the widespread evidence of the importance of horses in the cult-practices of the north over a long period. For example, the first-century Roman histo-rian TACITUS describes various kinds of DIVINATION employed by the continental Germanic tribes, while in the eighth century, the Anglo-Saxon monk BEDE describes how pagan priests were forbidden to ride stallions.

B2, 37; C29, 42; D191, 429

Hrafnsmál ('raven-song')

A fragmentary skaldic poem, assembled by modern scholars from several sources and usually ascribed to the ninth-century poet, THORBJÖRN HORNKLOFI. The poem deals with the life and martial activities of King Harald Fairhair, and for this reason the poem is some-times called *Haraldskvædi*. After a brief invocation to listeners to be quiet, the bulk of the surviving poem consists of a dialogue between a raven and a VALKYRIE.

B39, 45, 62, 83, 87; C16

Hraudung ('destroyer')

According to the eddic poem GRÍMNISMÁL, a legendary king, and the father of AGNAR and GEIRRÖD, who spend a brief period staying with an elderly couple who turn out to have been the gods ODIN and FRIGG in disguise.

B12, 30, 56, 73, 87, 90; C2, 17, 24, 33, 46

Hreggmímir *see* VINDBLÁIN.

Hreidmar

According to a number of sources associated with the

Hreim

so-called VÖLSUNG-cycle, the shape-changing father of three equally shifty sons, FÁFNIR, REGIN and OTR. According to the eddic poem REGINSMÁL, when Otr is killed in the shape of an otter by LOKI, accompanied by the gods ODIN and HŒNIR, Hreidmar demands as compensation the cursed gold-hoard of the dwarf ANDVARI. Hreidmar is soon killed by his greedy son Fáfnir, who, in the shape of a dragon, takes over the whole hoard, while Regin, plotting vengeance, leaves to become the foster-father of the hero SIGURD, whom he eventually persuades to kill his brother.

B12, 25, 30, 42, 56, 65, 73, 79, 87, 90; C1–3, 6, 17, 24, 33, 46

Hreim see RÍGSTHULA.

Hríd see HVERGELMIR.

Hrímfaxi ('frosty-mane')

According to the eddic poem VAFTHRÚDNISMÁL, the horse of night; as the wise giant VAFTHRÚDNIR asks the god ODIN (here disguised as Gagnrád):

'Tell me, Gagnrád, since you wish from the floor,
to make a test of your talents,
what that steed is called who draws from the east
night over glorious gods.'

'He's called Hrímfaxi who draws in turn
night over glorious gods.
Foam from his bit falls each morning,
from which the dew-drops form.'

B12, 30, 51, 56, 73, 87, 90; C2, 17, 24, 33, 46

Hrímgerd ('frost-Gerd')

According to the eddic poem HELGAKVIDA HJÖRVARDSSONAR, the daughter of the giant HATI, and she engages the heroes HELGI and ATLI IDMUNDSSON in a vicious contest of abuse or FLYTING after Helgi kills her father. Among her many boasts and threats, she mentions drowning the sons of the otherwise unknown Hlödvard.

B12, 30, 56, 73, 87, 90; C2, 17, 24, 33, 46

Hrímgrímnir ('frost-masked')

According to the name-lists or THULUR, the name of a giant. In the eddic poem SKÍRNISMÁL, after the beautiful giantess GERD has initially refused his suit on the god FREY's behalf, the messenger SKÍRNIR threatens her with a curse, the first part of which involves her marriage to Hrímgímnir in HEL. Faced with such a prospect, Gerd relents soon after the curse is uttered.

B12, 30, 56, 73, 87, 90; C2, 17, 24, 33, 46

Hrímnir ('frosty')

A giant, father of the giantess HLJÓD, who, according to

the legendary VÖLSUNGA SAGA, marries VÖLSUNG and is the mother of the hero SIGMUND.

B25, 42, 65, 68, 79; C1, 6

hrímthursar ('frost-giants')

The primeval race of GIANTS, who seem (like the mighty giant YMIR) simply to have emerged from the primordial ice. The thirteenth-century Icelander SNORRI STURLUSON gives them prominence in his account of the beginning of the world, and they are equally mentioned in a number of eddic sources known to him, including GRÍMNISMÁL, HÁVAMÁL, SKÍRNISMÁL and VAFTHRÚDNISMÁL.

B12, 14, 23, 24, 28, 30, 35, 40, 50, 51, 56, 59, 73, 87, 90; C2, 5, 9, 17, 24, 33, 46, 48

Hring

According to the eddic poem HELGAKVIDA HUNDINGSBANA I, the father of a number of HÖDBRODD's warriors at the battle of FREKASTEIN.

B12, 30, 56, 73, 87, 90; C2, 17, 24, 33, 46

Hringhorni(r) ('ring-horn')

According to the thirteenth-century Icelander SNORRI STURLUSON, the ship belonging to the god BALDR, 'the biggest of all ships' and the one in which he was buried.

B24, 28, 35, 40, 50; C5, 9, 48

Hringstead see HELGI SIGMUNDARSON HUNDINGSBANI.

Hrist see VALKYRIES.

Hrjód see VINDBLÁIN.

Hródmar

According to the eddic poem HELGAKVIDA HJÖRVARDSSONAR, one of the suitors of the beautiful SIGRLINN and the slayer of SVÁFNIR, her father. Eventually Sigrlinn marries the hero HJÖRVARD, and their son, HELGI, kills Hródmar in revenge for his maternal grandfather.

B12, 30, 56, 73, 87, 90; C2, 17, 24, 33, 46

Hródvitnir ('fame-wolf')

According to the eddic poem GRÍMNISMÁL and repeated by the thirteenth-century Icelander SNORRI STURLUSON, the father of the wolf HATI HRÓDVITNISSON, who pursues, and eventually, during the apocalyptic events of RAGNARÖK, swallows the moon.

B12, 14, 23, 24, 28, 30, 35, 40, 50, 56, 59, 73, 87, 90; C2, 5, 9, 17, 24, 33, 46, 48

Hrólf kraki ('pole')

A legendary king of Denmark, son of a woman with

the suspiciously bear-like name of Yrsa ('she-bear'), eponymous hero of the legendary HRÓLFS SAGA KRAKA and the commander of a group of twelve BERSERKS. The thirteenth-century Icelander SNORRI STURLUSON describes the origin of his nickname as follows:

> There was a king in Denmark called Hrólf kraki; he was the most famous of ancient kings, mainly for generosity and bravery and humility. There is one illustration of his humility, which is very famous in ancient tales, which concerns a poor little boy called Vögg, who entered King Hrólf's hall. At that time the king was young and thin. Vögg approached him and stared at him; the king said: 'What do you want to say, lad, since you are staring at me?' Vögg said: 'When I was at home, I heard tell that King Hrólf at Lejre was the mightiest man in the north, but now there sits on the throne a beanpole (kraki), and they call it their king.' Then the king answered: 'You, lad, have given me a name, and I shall be called Hrólf kraki, and it is usual to give a gift to mark a name-giving. But I see that you haven't got any gift to mark my name-giving, so the one who has something to give had better give it.' He took a ring from his arm, and gave it to him. Then Vögg said: 'May you be blessed in your giving beyond all kings: I take a solemn vow to kill the man who kills him.' Then the king said, laughing, 'It doesn't take much to please Vögg.'

A curious episode in the late fourteenth-century Icelandic manuscript FLATEYJARBÓK bears witness to the popularity of Hrólf kraki; the god ODIN himself is said to have visited King Olaf Tryggvason in his customary guise as a mysterious traveller with a broad-brimmed hat pulled low, calling himself Gest:

> Gest asked the king: 'Lord, which ancient king would you most like to have been, if you could choose?' The king answered: 'I wouldn't want to be any heathen man at all, neither a king nor anybody else.' Gest said: 'Of course you wouldn't want to be anyone other than you are, but what I'm asking is this: which ancient king would you most like to resemble, if you had to?' 'It's the same now as before,' said the king, 'I wouldn't want to be like any ancient king. But if I had to say something about it, then I would most prefer to have the presence and leadership of Hrólf kraki, as long as I retained all the Christianity of my faith.' Gest said: 'Why would you most want to be like Hrólf kraki, who might be called a nobody compared to another king that there has been? Why would you not want to be like that king who had victory against anyone he fought in battle, and was so splendid and accomplished in skills that no one was his match in the north, and who could give victory to others in conflict as for himself, and whom poetry permeates like ordinary speech does other men?'

The unnamed king is clearly Odin himself, whose basic characteristics are often so described in various legendary sagas or FORNALDARSÖGUR.

B24, 28, 35, 40, 50, 60, 74, 85; C5, 9, 20, 48; D438

Hrólfs saga kraka

One of the most celebrated of the legendary sagas, FORNALDARSÖGUR, giving a detailed account of life of King HRÓLF KRAKI and his twelve BERSERK champions. The saga provides a veritable motif-index of supernatural elements, including references to DRAGONS, ELVES, NORNS, TROLLS and WITCHES. Among the more memorable minor characters is the bear-like hero BÖDVAR BJARKI, who is often associated with the bear-like hero of the Old English poem BEOWULF, one of whose own minor characters, Hrothulf, can be identified with Hrólf himself.

B74; C20; D438

Hrollaug

According to the eddic poem HELGAKVIDA HUNDINGSBANA II, the father of several warriors killed by the hero HELGI SIGMUNDARSON HUNDINGSBANI.

B12, 30, 56, 73, 87, 90; C2, 17, 24, 33, 46

Hrönn ('wave')

(1) According to the thirteenth-century Icelander SNORRI STURLUSON, one of the rivers that flows from the horns of the mythical stag EIKTHYRNIR, via the seething torrents of HVERGELMIR. (2) One of the daughters of the sea-giant ÆGIR.

B24, 28, 35, 40, 50; C5, 9, 48

Hrothulf see HRÓLFS SAGA KRAKA.

Hrótti

According to a prose passage in the eddic poem FÁFNISMÁL, a sword that the hero SIGURD took from the hoard of the slain dragon, FÁFNIR.

B12, 30, 56, 73, 87, 90; C2, 17, 24, 33, 46

Hrungnir ('brawler')

A giant who, true to his name, picks a quarrel with the god ODIN by challenging him to a horse-race in which his own stallion, GULLFAXI, is defeated by the eight-legged SLEIPNIR. The race, which begins in JÖTUNHEIM, does not end until both riders end up in ÁSGARD, where Hrungnir, after being offered a consoling drink, becomes so intoxicated that, in a familiar echo of drunken boasts everywhere, he threatens to smash the place up, drink the bar dry and kill everyone except the beautiful goddesses FREYJA and SIF, whom he intends to carry off for his own pleasure. At this point the ÆSIR invoke Sif's husband, THOR, who turns up and attempts to eject the unwanted guest, who

Hrym

promptly challenges him to a duel. At the appointed time and place, Thor appears with his second, THJÁLFI, and Hrungnir appears with a mighty clay figure called MOKKURKÁLFI, to whom he has given a mare's heart. At the sight of Thor, Mokkurkálfi promptly wets himself, but Hrungnir, whose heart, along with his head and shield, is apparently made of stone, is literally made of sterner stuff, and prepares to cast his weapon, a

Hrungnir *The sacred significance of the whetstone is evident not simply in a number of myths and legends, for example that of the battle between the giant Hrungnir and the god Thor, but also in the archaeological record. This illustration of the ceremonial whetstone from Sutton Hoo, shows not only the apparent importance of the stone itself, attested by its rich setting, but may also point to some cultic significance for the stag which tops the piece. According to Norse sources the stag Eikthyrnir stands atop the mighty hall Valhall, whilst the great hall celebrated in the Old English poem* Beowulf *is called Heorot ('hart').*

whetstone. Thjálfi warns him that Thor, who is, after all the son of JÖRD ('earth'), may attack from beneath the ground, at which point Hrungnir stands on his shield. Thor throws his hammer, MJÖLLNIR, Hrungnir throws his whetstone, and the weapons collide in mid-air. Hrungnir's whetstone is shattered, along with his head, but Thor is doubly wounded by a shard of whetstone lodging in his head, and, as he falls, by being trapped under one leg of the conquered Hrungnir. In the meantime Thjálfi despatches Mokkurkalfi, but neither the trapped Thor, nor Thjálfi, nor any of the Æsir is able to lift the giant's leg until MAGNI, the son of Thor and the giantess JÁRNSAXA, manages the feat; he is then three years old. As a reward, Thor gives him Gullfaxi, much to the chagrin of Odin. The attempts of the witch GRÓA to remove the whetstone through sorcery are only partially successful, and as a result there is a taboo against throwing whetstones across a room, because when that happens the whetstone still lodged in Thor's head is said to move and cause him considerable discomfort. So much is apparent from the detailed account given by the thirteenth-century Icelander SNORRI STURLUSON, which he claims to derive from the skaldic poem HAUSTLÖNG composed around the turn of the tenth century by THJÓDÓLF OF HVÍN, although the tale is only partially supported by the stanzas he cites. Nonetheless, Hrungnir's name is found as part of numerous poetic periphrases or KENNINGS for shield.

B39, 45, 62, 83, 87; C16

Hrym ('decrepit')

According to the eddic poem VÖLUSPÁ, a giant who will play a major role in the apocalyptic events of RAGNARÖK. The thirteenth-century Icelander SNORRI STURLUSON (directly contradicting *Völuspá*) makes him captain of the fearsome ship NAGLFARI at Ragnarök.

B12, 14, 23, 24, 28, 30, 35, 40, 50, 56, 59, 73, 87, 90; C2, 5, 9, 17, 24, 33, 46, 48

Hugi ('thought')

According to the thirteenth-century Icelander SNORRI STURLUSON, the personification of thought, whom the cunning giant, ÚTGARDALOKI, sets to race against the servant THJÁLFI when the god THOR comes to visit.

B24, 28, 35, 40, 50; C5, 9, 48

Hugin ('thought')

One of the two ravens belonging to the god ODIN; the other is MUNIN. As the thirteenth-century Icelander SNORRI STURLUSON explains of Odin:

> Two ravens perch on his shoulders and speak into his ear all the news they see or hear; their names are Hugin and Munin. He sends them out at daybreak to fly all

over the world, and they return in the evening; because of this he is able to find out about many things, and so he is called the raven-god.

The two ravens often appear together engraved on picture-stones, but in literary sources Hugin is mentioned far more frequently than Munin, especially in eddic poetry, and in skaldic verse regularly occurs as little more than a poetic term for 'raven'.

B24, 28, 35, 39, 40, 45, 50, 62, 83, 87; C5, 9, 16, 48

Humlung

According to the prose introduction to the eddic poem HELGAKVIDA HJÖRVARDSSONAR, the son of the legendary King HJÖRVARD and SÆREID, his second wife.

B12, 30, 56, 73, 87, 90; C2, 17, 24, 33, 46

Hunding

A number of legendary figures share this name. REGINSMÁL in the POETIC EDDA says that the hero SIGURD killed LYNGVI and three other sons of one Hunding in revenge for the mighty warrior EYLIMI. Presumably this latter Hunding is the same character who is killed by Sigurd's half-brother, HELGI SIGMUNDARSON HUNDINGSBANI, the eponymous hero of the eddic poems HELGAKVIDA HUNDINGSBANA I and II, at the precocious age of fifteen; as *Helgakvida Hundingsbana* I puts it:

Helgi grew swiftly among his friends,
a noble hero bright with joy;
freely he gave gold to warriors
nor did he spare blood-stained treasure.

He did not wait but went to war
as soon as he reached his fifteenth year;
he struck down the brave Hunding
who had ruled long both lands and men.

When Hunding's sons demand compensation, Helgi refuses, and ends up slaughtering four of them – Álf, Eyjólf, Hagbard and Hervard – in battle at ARASTEIN. The prose preface and first stanza of *Helgakvida Hundingsbana* II mention another son, the otherwise unknown Hæming, while *Helgakvida Hundingsbana* I notes yet another, Hávard.

B12, 30, 56, 73, 87, 90; C2, 17, 24, 33, 46

Hungr *see* HEL.

Húsdrápa ('house-lay')

A skaldic poem with mythological content, composed a decade or so before the year 1000 by the Icelander ÚLF UGGASON to commemorate the fine hall built at Hjardarholt by Óláf pái ('the peacock') by describing the mythological scenes carved on its panelling. A description of the circumstances surrounding the poem's composition is given in the mid-thirteenth-century LAXDŒLA SAGA, and about the same time fragments of the poem are preserved by SNORRI STURLUSON, whose SKÁLDSKAPARMÁL uses many half-stanzas from the poem to illustrate particular features of diction. The extant verses seem to focus chiefly on three mythological episodes: the battle between LOKI and the god HEIMDALL, fought in the shape of seals for a 'beautiful sea-kidney', usually identified with the splendid treasure of the BRÍSINGAMEN; the god THOR's battle against the MIDGARD-SERPENT; and the god BALDR's funeral. Each of these tales is to some extent represented elsewhere, although in some cases the other witnesses are scarcely independent. It is clear that Snorri relied on *Húsdrápa* for at least some of his material in his versions of each of these three episodes, as well as for his analysis of its poetic diction. It seems possible, therefore, that one can use Snorri to recreate lost elements of the poem. So, for example, *Húsdrápa* gives a few snapshots of various mythological beings in Baldr's funeral procession, a scene summed up by Snorri as follows:

> This burning was attended by many kinds of creatures: first to tell of ODIN, accompanied by FRIGG and VALKYRIES and his ravens, while FREY drove in a chariot with a boar called GULLINBORSTI or Slidrugtanni; Heimdall rode a horse called Gulltopp; FREYJA had her cats; there followed a mighty procession of frost-giants and mountain-giants.

B24, 28, 35, 39, 40, 45, 50, 62, 83, 87; C5, 9, 16, 28, 48; D499, 500

Hvergelmir ('bubbling boiling-spring')

According to the eddic poem GRÍMNISMÁL, the mythical source from which all the rivers of the world spring and itself fed by the liquid that drips from the antlers of the mythical stag EIKTHYRNIR. The thirteenth-century Icelander SNORRI STURLUSON develops the idea, naming Hvergelmir as the source of ÉLIVÁGAR, making it the home of the dragon NÍDHÖGG, and placing it under the world-tree YGGDRASIL. Among the many rivers that, according to Snorri, spring from Hvergelmir are Böll, Ekin, FIMBULTHUL, Fjörm, Geirvimul, Gipul, Gömul, Göpul, Grád, Gunnthrá, Gunnthráin, Gunnthró, Hríd, HRÖNN, Leipt (or Leift), Nonn, Not, Nyt, Sekin, Síd, Slíd, Svinn, Svöl(l), Thjódnuma, Thöll, Thyn, Veg, Víd, Vín, Vína and Ylg. Eleven of these rivers together form the churning streams of Élivágar.

B1, 14, 23, 24, 28, 30, 35, 40, 50, 56, 59, 73, 87, 90; C2, 5, 9, 17, 24, 33, 46, 48; D216

Hymir

According to the eddic poem HYMISKVIDA, a giant, father of the god TÝR and the person from whom the god THOR fetched a brewing-cauldron for the sea-giant

Hymiskvida

ÆGIR to enable him to hold a feast for the ÆSIR. In the course of his visit, Thor goes fishing with Hymir and manages to hook the MIDGARD-SERPENT, which he almost succeeds in landing, much to the giant's discomfort; the fishing scene is often featured on stone carvings. After a number of further tests of strength, Thor is finally permitted to take home his prize. The thirteenth-century Icelander SNORRI STURLUSON tells a much embellished version of the story, in which several comic details are developed, not least of which is the idea that Thor visits Hymir in the shape of a young boy.

B12, 14, 23, 24, 28, 30, 35, 40, 50, 56, 59, 73, 87, 90; C2, 5, 9, 17, 24, 33, 46, 48

Hymiskvida ('the lay of Hymir')

An eddic poem, preserved not only in the CODEX REGIUS but also in the manuscript AM 748 I 4to, and giving a largely narrative account of the god THOR's fishing expedition alongside the giant HYMIR to catch the MIDGARD-SERPENT. The same tale is told by the thirteenth-century Icelander SNORRI STURLUSON, although several of the narrative details differ: Snorri has Thor's legs driving through the bottom of the boat to get purchase on the sea floor and Hymir cutting Thor's line in terror that he will succeed in landing the brute, while *Hymiskvida* is silent on both these counts. By contrast, the poem (which, unlike some others of the eddic corpus, has no prose passages interspersed with the verse) provides a framework to the episode, explaining how the ÆSIR need a massive cauldron in which the sea-giant ÆGIR can brew mead for a feast and how TÝR offers to accompany Thor on an expedition to Hymir, whom Týr describes as his kinsman, to obtain such a cauldron. Other episodes from Thor's life, as recounted elsewhere, also intrude into the narrative. The story of his acquisition of his two servants, THJÁLFI and RÖSKVA is alluded to, and both before and after his fishing expedition events take place in Hymir's hall which match closely what Thor's experience in the hall of another giant, GEIRRÖD. Such apparently extraneous material makes *Hymiskvida*, with its rather baroque vocabulary and relatively free use of KENNINGS, an important source in considering the stories surrounding Thor. The central point of the story, when Thor actually catches the Midgard-serpent, is briskly told:

> Deed-brave Thor mightily dragged
> the venom-stained serpent up to the gunwale;
> he struck from above with his hammer

Hymir *Seventeenth-century manuscript illustration, depicting the midgard-serpent which the god Thor caught with a hook baited with an ox-head, while on a fishing trip with Hymir the giant.*

the hideous hair-summit of the close brother of the wolf.

The rock-monsters groaned, the stone-fields thundered,
the ancient earth all moved together;
then there sank back that fish into the sea.

The diction of *Hymiskvida* in many ways resembles more closely that of skaldic poetry rather than the other poems of the POETIC EDDA, especially in its frequent use of poetic periphrases or kennings.

B12, 30, 56, 73, 87, 90; C2, 17, 24, 33, 46; D187, 480, 511, 540, 628

Hymling

According to the prose introduction to the eddic poem HELGAKVIDA HJÖRVARDSSONAR, the son of the legendary King HJÖRVARD and SINRJÓD, his third wife.

B12, 30, 56, 73, 87, 90; C2, 17, 24, 33, 46

Hyndluljód ('the lay of Hyndla')

A short eddic poem that is not included in the CODEX REGIUS but that is found in the late fourteenth-century manuscript FLATEYJARBÓK; *Hyndluljód* incorporates a brief imitation of VÖLUSPÁ usually known as *Völuspá in skamma* ('the short *Völuspá*').

At the opening of the poem the goddess FREYJA rouses the giantess Hyndla and accompanies her to VALHALL to discover more about the ancestors of her favourite, Ottar, who needs this information to defeat one Angantýr in a legal dispute. The bulk of the poem simply consists of a list of over almost seventy names of alleged ancestors of Ottar.

B12, 30, 56, 60, 73, 85, 87, 90; C2, 17, 24, 33, 46; D211, 552, 553

Hyrrokkin ('fire-withered')

A giantess, who, according to the thirteenth-century Icelander SNORRI STURLUSON, was summoned from JÖTUNHEIM by the ÆSIR when they were unable to launch the largest of all ships, HRINGHORNI, at the BOAT BURIAL of the god BALDR. Snorri's account, with its mention of the god ODIN and his BERSERKS and the wrath of the god THOR, is full of delicate narrative touches. After explaining that the Æsir were unable to budge the vessel, he continues:

They sent to Jötunheim for a giantess called Hyrrokkin, and when she arrived riding a wolf with vipers for reins, she dismounted from her steed, and Odin called four berserks to take care of the mount, but they were unable to contain it without knocking it down. Then Hyrrokin went to the prow of the vessel, and with her first touch she pushed it out so that flame flew from the rollers, and the whole ground shook. Then Thor became enraged, and gripped his hammer, and was about to smash her head until all the Æsir begged for mercy for her.

B24, 28, 35, 40, 50; C5, 9, 483

I

Ibn Fadlan

Arab traveller and diplomat who has provided the most vivid eyewitness account of Scandinavian merchants, called Rus, on the Volga. In particular he offers a spectacular description of the BOAT BURIAL cremation rites of one of their chiefs, involving the human SACRIFICE of a slave-girl with whom his associates have sex at the funeral, before burning her on the pyre, a combination of the elements of SUTTEE and human sacrifice witnessed elsewhere in the written record.

C40; D3, 538

Idavöll ('splendour-plain')

According to the eddic poem VÖLUSPÁ, the plain, situated near ÁSGARD, where those who survive the apocalyptic events of RAGNARÖK will meet after the end of the old world. The thirteenth-century Icelander SNORRI STURLUSON places Idavöll at the very heart of Ásgard, where the ÆSIR meet to determine the destinies of men.

B12, 14, 23, 24, 28, 30, 35, 40, 50, 56, 59, 73, 87, 90; C2, 5, 9, 17, 24, 33, 46, 48; D268, 315

Idmund *see* ATLI IDMUNDSSON.

Idun ('rejuvenator')

One of the goddesses or ÁSYNJUR. According to the thirteenth-century Icelander SNORRI STURLUSON, she was the wife of the god BRAGI and custodian of the apples that the ÆSIR eat to maintain their youth. In a tale recounted in the skaldic poem HAUSTLÖNG, composed around the turn of the tenth century by THJÓDÓLF OF HVÍN and retold by Snorri, both Idun and her apples are lured away by the giant THJAZI with the connivance of LOKI. After the Æsir have begun to feel the effects of age in the absence of Idun and her apples, they enjoin

Ilm

Loki to make good his wrong-doing, which he does by transforming himself into a falcon and making off with Idun, who is, according to Snorri, in the shape of a nut. Thjazi, who pursues Loki all the way to ÁSGARD in the form of an eagle, is promptly killed, and in compensation for his death, his daughter SKADI is permitted to marry NJÖRD. Beyond Snorri and *Haustlöng*, Idun makes a brief appearance in the eddic poem LOKASENNA, where she attempts to intervene between Loki and Bragi, and in return is accused by Loki of having slept with her brother's killer.

B12, 14, 23, 24, 28, 30, 35, 39, 40, 45, 50, 56, 59, 62, 73, 83, 87, 90; C2, 5, 9, 13, 16, 17, 24, 33, 46, 48; D62, 264

Ilm

According to a list preserved by the thirteenth-century Icelander SNORRI STURLUSON, the name of one of the goddesses or ÁSYNJUR.

B24, 28, 35, 40, 50; C5, 9, 48

Ím

According to the eddic poem VAFTHRÚDNISMÁL, a giant, apparently the son of the wise giant VAFTHRÚDNIR himself.

B12, 30, 51, 56, 73, 87, 90; C2, 17, 24, 33, 46

Imd ('ogress')

According to the name-lists or THULUR, the name of a troll-wife or giantess. In the contest of ritualized abuse or FLYTING in the eddic poem HELGAKVIDA HUNDINGSBANA I, SINFJÖTLI accuses GUDMUND (or perhaps vice versa) that he once acted the part of 'Imd's daughter'.

B12, 30, 56, 73, 87, 90; C2, 17, 24, 33, 46

Ing

Ing occurs only in the Anglo-Saxon *Rune Poem*, both as the name of an individual rune and as that of a mysterious figure who travels in a chariot. There is a strong temptation to identify Ing with YNGVI-FREY, given the numerous descriptions from various sources of the god Frey being carried in a chariot.

B29

Ingunar-Frey

A title given to the god FREY in the eddic poem LOKASENNA and also found in one version of the saga of Saint Olaf; evidently a version of his more conventional title of YNGVI-FREY.

B12, 30, 56, 73, 87, 90; C2, 17, 24, 33, 46

Ingvaeones *see* TUISTO.

Irminsûl ('mighty pillar')

In various documents relating to the campaign that Charlemagne waged against the Saxons in the last quarter of the eighth century, Irminsûl is described as a huge pillar, venerated by the Saxons, which Charlemagne destroyed. It has been suggested that the cult of Irminsûl is reflected in the north in the mythic status of the world-tree YGGDRASIL, while the first element of the name is echoed in such formations as JÖRMUNGAND, another name for the mighty MIDGARD-SERPENT.

D598

Istvaeones *see* TUISTO.

Ísung

In the eddic poem HELGAKVIDA HUNDINGSBANA I, the eponymous hero HELGI describes his rival HÖDBRODD to the Valkyrie SIGRÚN, as 'Ísung's bane'. One can only assume that Ísung is an otherwise unattested warrior.

B12, 30, 56, 73, 87, 90; C2, 17, 24, 33, 46

Ívaldi's sons

The name given to a group of dwarfs who, according to the thirteenth-century Icelander SNORRI STURLUSON, following in part the eddic poem GRÍMNISMÁL, created the ship SKÍDBLADNIR for the god FREY, the spear GUNGNIR for the god ODIN and a new head of golden hair for the goddess SIF, the wife of THOR. When LOKI foolishly wagers with another dwarf named BROKK that the treasures cannot be bettered, the ÆSIR gain still greater gifts, and Loki has to use considerable cunning to escape with his head.

B12, 14, 23, 24, 28, 30, 35, 40, 50, 56, 59, 73, 87, 90; C2, 5, 9, 17, 24, 33, 46, 48

J

Jafnhár *see* HÁR.

jardarmen ('turf-strip')
The strip of raised turf, cut with its ends still attached and supported in the middle by an upright spear, under which men passed to mingle their blood in the performance of the rite of blood-brotherhood. Several literary sources provide references to the practice, notably the Icelandic GÍSLA SAGA, which describes how Gísli and three others of his immediate family circle carry out a doomed ceremony of blood-brotherhood:

> They went out to [the point called] Eyrarhválsoddi and raised up a strip of earth from the ground, so that both ends were fixed in the earth, and set up under it a pattern-bladed spear, with a shaft so long that one could just reach the nails of the socket with outstretched arms. All four of them had to go underneath it there, Thorgrím, Gísli, Thorkel and Véstein; and then they each drew their own blood and let the gore mingle in the soil that had been disturbed under the strip of earth, and mix it all together, soil and blood; and then they all fell to their knees and swore an oath, that each should avenge the other like his brother, and they name all the gods as witness.

B78; C19; D180

Jarisleif
According to the legendary VÖLSUNGA SAGA, one of the noble characters who are said to accompany the heroes GUNNAR and HÖGNI GJÚKASON on their mission to the court of King HÁLF, to reconcile themselves with their sister GUDRÚN after the killing of her husband, the mighty hero SIGURD. Jarisleif is sometimes (somewhat anachronistically) identified with King Jaroslav the Great of Russia (1015–54).
B25, 42, 65, 68, 79: C1, 6

Jarl *see* RÍGSTHULA.

Járnsaxa ('iron-sax')
(1) According to the name-lists or THULUR, the name of a giantess. (2) Named in the eddic poem HYNDLULJÓD as one of the nine mothers of the god HEIMDALL. (3) The thirteenth-century Icelander SNORRI STURLUSON confuses the picture still further,

making Járnsaxa the name of a giantess on whom the god THOR begets his son MAGNI.
B12, 14, 23, 24, 28, 30, 35, 40, 50, 56, 59, 73, 87, 90; C2, 5, 9, 17, 24, 33, 46, 48

Járnvid ('iron wood')
According to the eddic poem VÖLUSPÁ, in a verse which is cited by the thirteenth-century Icelander SNORRI STURLUSON, the home of the giantess who fosters the wolf that will devour the sun at the end of the world, at RAGNARÖK. Snorri gives an even more vivid description:

> A certain giantess lives east of MIDGARD in a wood called Járnvid; in that wood dwell the troll-wives called JÁRNVIDJUR. This ancient giantess breeds as her sons many giants, all in wolf form, and it is from them that wolves are descended. It is said that from this race will arise one most mighty, called MÁNAGARM; he will fill himself with the life-blood of everyone who dies, and swallow heavenly bodies, and spatter the sky and all heaven with blood. Because of this the sun will lose its brightness, and winds will rage and buffet to and fro.

B24, 228, 35, 40, 50; C5, 9, 48

Járnvidja ('iron hag')
According to the name-lists or THULUR, the name of a troll-wife or giantess. The plural form, *Járnvidjur*, is connected by the thirteenth-century Icelander SNORRI STURLUSON with the mythical wood of JÁRNVID.
B24, 228, 35, 40, 50; C5, 9, 48

Járnvidjur *see* JÁRNVIDJA.

Jelling
A royal site in Jutland in Denmark, and the setting for a series of mounds and monuments that together document the conversion of Denmark. Two large, now empty, mounds flank a church on its northern and southern sides, and two rune stones are situated between the church and the southern mound. The oldest of these is a monument erected by the pagan king, Gorm, to the memory of his wife, Thyri. The other, and larger, monument was erected by their son, King Harald Bluetooth, in memory of both his parents and as a memorial to his own conversion of the Danes. It seems that the northern mound was built over an

Jód

Jelling *A replica of King Harald Bluetooth's stone at Jelling, decorated in the so-called Mammen style.*

earlier burial mound, the first resting-place of the pagan Gorm, who died around 958 at the age of forty or fifty. He was apparently re-interred in a church newly built by his son after the conversion, and at the same time Harald erected his own rune stone, and raised both southern and northern mounds.

B4, 54, 57; C70, 312, 355, 437

Jód *see* RÍGSTHULA.

Jökul *see* FORNJÓT.

Jónak

A king, third husband of the tragic heroine GUDRÚN and father of the doomed heroes HAMDIR, SÖRLI and ERP JÓNAKRSSON. The legendary VÖLSUNGA SAGA gives the fullest account of how Gudrún, wishing to kill herself, presumably after she has murdered her second husband, ATLI BUDLASON, and their two sons, falls into Jónak's hands:

> One day Gudrún went to the sea, picked up rocks in her arms and strode out into the water, intending to kill herself. But mighty waves carried her out over the sea, and with their help she floated at last to the fortress of King Jónak, a mighty ruler with many men. He married Gudrún. Their children were Hamdir, Sörli and Erp; SVANHILD [Gudrún's daughter by an earlier marriage] was brought up there.

Eddic sources, notably HAMDISMÁL, make Erp Jónakrsson a half-brother of Hamdir and Sörli, attributing to him a different mother.

B25, 42, 65, 68, 79; C1, 6

Jörd ('earth')

A giantess, the mother of the god THOR, a product of Jörd's union with the god ODIN. Jörd is also called FJÖRGYN. According to the thirteenth-century Icelander SNORRI STURLUSON, she was the daughter of NÓTT ('night'), and as such he reckons her among the goddesses or ÁSYNJUR, alongside other giantesses, such as RIND, who gave birth to ÆSIR. Her name is often invoked in skaldic poetry, both as a poetic term for land or the earth, and in poetic periphrases or KENNINGS for the same concepts and for Thor.

B24, 28, 35, 40, 50; C5, 9, 48

Jordanes

A sixth-century historian, whose *Getica* is an invaluable source for the customs and beliefs of contemporary Goths. So, for example, writing about the methods by which the Goths worshipped their god of battle, 'Mars' (presumably to be equated with the god ODIN), Jordanes notes that:

> They thought that he who is lord of battle should be placated by the shedding of human blood. To him they used to offer the first share of the spoil, and in his honour the weapons stripped from enemy corpses were hung from trees.

The interest of the passage lies in the fact that similar descriptions of human sacrifice and the suspension of offerings on trees is recorded of UPPSALA by ADAM OF BREMEN, writing some five centuries later.

B55; C31

Jörmungand ('mighty wand')

Another name for the MIDGARD-SERPENT, found in the earliest skaldic verse of BRAGI BODDASON, and repeated in various other sources, including the eddic poem VÖLUSPÁ and a number of the works of the thirteenth-century Icelander SNORRI STURLUSON.

B12, 14, 23, 24, 28, 30, 35, 40, 50, 56, 59, 73, 87, 90; C2, 5, 9, 17, 24, 33, 46, 48; D598

Jörmunrekk ('mighty ruler')

The Norse name for Ermanaric (also attested as Hermanaric), king of the Ostrogoths, a historical figure who died in 375 and who features prominently as a cruel tyrant in Germanic legend. Old English poems castigate him for his 'wolf-like mind' and describe him (in language elsewhere used of the devil) as a 'cruel breaker of faith'. According to the legendary VÖLSUNG-cycle he is responsible for having the beautiful SVANHILD, the daughter of the tragic GUDRÚN and the hero SIGURD (and his own intended bride), trampled to death by horses for suspected adultery. When Gudrún sends her sons HAMDIR and SÖRLI to avenge their half-sister, Jörmunrekk kills them both but is himself horribly maimed. The broad outline of the tale agrees remarkably well with what is recorded by JORDANES, writing in the mid-sixth century:

> Hermanaric, king of the Goths, as we have said above, was the conqueror of many nations. Nonetheless, while he was preparing for the approach of the Huns, the treacherous nation of the Rosmoni, who, among others, owed him allegiance, seized the chance to turn against him. Stricken with rage, the king ordered that the wife of a certain chieftain of the aforementioned nation, named Sunhilda [Svanhild?], be bound to wild horses on account of her husband's treachery; she was then ripped apart by the horses galloping at full speed in opposite directions. After this killing, her brothers Sarus [Sörli?] and Ammius [Hamdir?] avenged her death by thrusting a sword into Hermanaric's side. Afflicted by this wound, Hermanaric eked out a failing existence in his sickly body. Balamber, king of the Huns, took advantage of this feebleness and moved his battle-hardened troops into the territory of the Ostrogoths, from whom the Visigoths had already separated because of some dispute. Meanwhile Hermanaric, unable to bear the pain of his wound and grief at the Hunnish incursion, died

full of days at the age of 110. As a result of his death the Huns ruled over those Goths who, as we have explained, settled in the East, and are called Ostrogoths.

B12, 25, 30, 42, 55, 56, 65, 68, 73, 79, 87, 90; C1–3, 6, 17, 24, 31, 33, 46; D7, 47, 206, 598, 627

Jöruvellir ('sandy plains')

According to the thirteenth-century Icelander SNORRI STURLUSON, the setting for AURVANGAR, the home of the DWARFS.

B24, 28, 35, 40, 50; C5, 9, 48

jötnar see JÖTUN.

jötun ('giant')

The Norse common noun for a GIANT (plural *jötnar*), perhaps related with the verb *eta* ('to eat'), a supposition strengthened by the cognate Old English term *eoten* and Middle English *ettin*.

D398, 401, 402

Jötunheim ('giant-home')

The realm of the GIANTS, generally situated to the east of MIDGARD but increasingly identified with a region in the north, perhaps as a result of the influence of Christian cosmology concerning the situation of hell. As with HEL, Jötunheim is usually described as separated from Midgard by various rivers, although mention is often made of a wood, JÁRNVID, which appears to serve a similar function.

B24, 28, 35, 40, 50; C5, 9, 48; D73

K

Kálfsvísa

A poem, named as *Alsvinnsmál* by the thirteenth-century Icelander SNORRI STURLUSON, which provides a list of mythical and legendary horses and their riders.

B24, 28, 35, 40, 50; C5, 9, 48

Kára

According to the prose epilogue of the eddic poem HELGAKVIDA HUNDINGSBANA II, the daughter of one HALFDAN, and the reincarnation of the Valkyrie SIGRÚN:

> In olden days it was believed that people could be reborn, although now that is reckoned an old wives' tale. HELGI [SIGMUNDARSON HUNDINGSBANI] and Sigrún

are said to have been reborn; he was called Helgi Haddingjaskadi, and she Kára Halfdansdóttir, as is told in the [now lost] *Káraljód*, and she was a Valkyrie.

B12, 30, 56, 73, 87, 90; C2, 17, 24, 33, 46

Káraljód see KÁRA.

Kari see FORNJÓT.

Karl ('old man', 'churl', 'freeman')

(1) One of the many names of the god ODIN. (2) The son of Afi and Amma, according to the eddic poem RÍGSTHULA, and so progenitor of the race of freemen, as opposed to slaves or nobles.

B12, 30, 56, 73, 87, 90; C2, 17, 24, 33, 46

Kefsir

Kefsir *see* RÍGSTHULA.

kenning

A form of poetic periphrasis much favoured in skaldic verse, in which a metaphorical description is substituted for a simple term. Most kennings consist of only two elements, but much more complicated periphrases could be built up. So, for example, once it is known that Heiti is the name of a sea-king or legendary Viking warrior, 'Heiti's animal' will be a kenning for 'ship', which Heiti rode as another man might ride a horse or other animal; 'the adornment of Heiti's animal' will be a kenning for 'shield', since shields adorn ships; 'the tumult of the adornment of Heiti's animal' will be a kenning for 'battle', since it is in battle that shields clash; 'the gull of the tumult of the adornment of Heiti's animal' will be a kenning for any kind of carrion bird, since they hover over battle as do gulls at sea; and, finally, 'the hunger-appeaser of the gull of the tumult of the adornment of Heiti's animal' will be a kenning for a warrior, who gives carrion birds their fill: this last kenning, with its six separate components, is actually employed by the Icelander HALLFRED OTTARSSON VANDRÆDASKÁLD. Because of its often heavily traditional content and diction, kennings may well contain much material of a mythological or legendary nature, and they are a useful source of evidence, albeit of an often tantalizing kind.

Kennings were a highly prized part of a poet's stock-in-trade, as a number of narratives demonstrate. According to a tale told by the thirteenth-century Icelander SNORRI STURLUSON, BRAGI BODDASON was travelling through a wood late at night when he came upon a troll-wife; each challenged the other to say what they were. The troll-wife said:

'Trolls call me the moon of dwelling-RUNGNIR,
giant's treasure-sucker, storm-sun's terror,
friendly accomplice of a prophetess, corpse-fjord's guardian,
swallower of heaven's wheel: what is a troll but that?'

Bragi replied:

'Poets call me Vidur's skill-smith,
Gaut's gift-getter, fulsome warrior,
bearer of YGG's ale, the mind-enrager of ÓD
skilful rhyme-smith: what is a poet but that?'

Bragi's apparently impenetrable answer includes four recognizable names of the god ODIN, and so alludes deftly to the myth of the MEAD OF POETRY, an undoubtedly suitable topic in any contest of kennings.

B24, 28, 35, 39, 40, 45, 50, 62, 75, 83, 87; C3, 5, 9, 16, 48; D3, 4, 77, 153, 169, 179, 278, 308, 349, 356, 372, 596

Kerlaug ('kettle-bath')

The name, according to the eddic poem GRÍMNISMÁL, in a verse cited by the thirteenth-century Icelander SNORRI STURLUSON, of two of the rivers through which the god THOR wades on his way to his judgement-throne; the two other rivers through which the god wades on his journey are called Körmt and Örmt.

B12, 14, 23, 24, 28, 30, 35, 40, 50, 56, 59, 73, 87, 90; C2, 5, 9, 17, 24, 33, 46, 48

Kjár

According to the eddic poem VÖLUNDARKVIDA, the father, from Valland, of the swan-maiden ÖLRÚN. Elsewhere in the POETIC EDDA, in ATLAKVIDA, the hero GUNNAR boasts of having 'the brightest helmets and shields, brought from Kjár's hall', although here, as in *Völundarkvida*, the name may be no more than a title, as it appears attached to a number of legendary kings.

B12, 30, 31, 56, 73, 87, 90; C2, 17, 24, 33, 46

Kleggi *see* RÍGSTHULA.

Klúr *see* RÍGSTHULA.

Knéfröd

According to the eddic poem ATLAKVIDA, the cool and skilful messenger of ATLI BUDLASON, and the one who brings the invitation to visit Atli and his wife, the tragic heroine Gudrún, to her brothers, the unsuspecting heroes GUNNAR and HÖGNI GJÚKASON.

B12, 20, 30, 31, 56, 73, 87, 90; C2, 17, 24, 33, 46

Kólga *see* ÆGIR.

Konung *see* RÍGSTHULA.

Kör *see* HEL.

Kormák Ögmundarson

A tenth-century Icelandic poet, many of whose verses contain mythological allusions, including, for example, the assertion that the god ODIN seduced the giantess RIND by employing the particular form of magic known as SEID. Many of Kormák's verse are preserved in the much later (thirteenth-century) KORMÁKS SAGA, which largely portrays Kormák in the rather stereotypical role of lovelorn poet, in the same mould as, say, HALLFREDAR SAGA. In some sources his name is spelled Kormak.

B75; C3, 18

Kormáks saga

Perhaps written in the early thirteenth century, the saga purports to present the life of the tenth-century poet KORMÁK ÖGMUNDARSON and contains no fewer than sixty-four stanzas attributed to him, alongside many others. Among the antiquarian material preserved by the saga is an account of a SACRIFICE to ELVES (ÁLFABLÓT), which a WITCH advises to cure a slow-healing wound.

B75; C18

Körmt *see* KERLAUG.

Kostbera

Wife of the legendary hero HÖGNI GJÚKASON and sometimes also known as Bera. According to the eddic poem ATLAMÁL, she attempted to decipher the warning runes carved by Högni's sister, the tragic heroine GUDRÚN, to keep her brothers Högni and GUNNAR from visiting her scheming husband, ATLI BUDLASON. Unfortunately, the runes had been disfigured by the malicious VINGI; nonetheless, Kostbera, like Gunnar's wife, GLAUMVÖR, has foreboding dreams, but when she tells her husband, Högni simply dismisses them:

'I had a dream, Högni, I make no mistake,
things will go wrong for you, or else I'm filled with fear.

'I thought your bedclothes were all ablaze;
the flame leapt high throughout my house.'
'There's linen here you little like:
it'll soon be burned like the bedclothes you saw.'

'I thought a bear had entered, broke up the boards,
swiped its paws, and made us scared.
Its jaws had many of us, and we were powerless;
its stomping tread did not sound soft.'

'The weather will change; it'll soon be dawn.
You imagined a white bear: there'll be snow from
    the east.'

'I thought an eagle had flown in, the length of the hall;
there'll be a mighty pay-off for us: it spattered us all
    with blood.
I thought from its threats it was Atli's form.'

'Soon we put beasts to slaughter; then we shall see
    blood.
It often means oxen, a dream of eagles.
Atli is sound of spirit whatever dreams you dream.'

Like most foreboding dreams in the myths and legends of the north, however, Kostbera's come tragically true.

B12, 20, 30, 56, 73, 87, 90; C2, 17, 24, 33, 46

Kraki *see* HRÓLF KRAKI.

Kriemhilt *see* NIBELUNGENLIED.

Kumba *see* RÍGSTHULA.

Kund *see* RÍGSTHULA.

Kvasir ('fermented berry-juice')

One of the central figures in the legend of the MEAD OF POETRY. According to the tale expounded most fully by the thirteenth-century Icelander SNORRI STURLUSON, Kvasir was created as a result of the peace made between the ÆSIR and the VANIR after their war. Both parties spat into a vessel to signify their agreement, and from the combined saliva a man was created. Snorri describes him as:

so wise that no one was able to ask him any questions to which he did not know the answer; he travelled widely throughout the world, teaching folk wisdom.

It was his blood, shed by the dwarfs FJALAR and GALAR with whom he was staying, that was fermented into the brew that became the mead of poetry. The whole tale seems indebted to myths surrounding the twin processes of fermentation, in which saliva sometimes formed a part, and intoxication, during which the singing of songs is not unknown. The various liquors known in Norwegian as *kvase* and in Russian as *kvas* seem to derive from the same etymological source. Poetry is certainly described in KENNINGS as 'Kvasir's blood' in numerous skaldic sources, but even in his own writings, Snorri is unable to offer a completely coherent explanation of Kvasir's origins, describing him variously as the wisest of the Vanir, the wisest of the Æsir and as a hostage granted by the Vanir to the Æsir alongside NJÖRD, in exchange for HŒNIR and MÍMIR.

B24, 28, 35, 39, 40, 45, 50, 62, 83, 87; C5, 9, 16, 48

L

Lærad ('root of harm'?)

The tree that, according to the eddic poem GRÍM-NISMÁL, stands beside VALHALL, and in whose branches the mythical goat HEIDRÚN and the hart EIK-THRYNIR, perching on top of Valhall, graze:

> The goat is called Heidrún, standing on Herjafödr's
> [ODIN's] hall,
> who bites off Lærad's limbs;
> she fills a vat with shining mead,
> a draught that does not diminish.

> The hart is called Eikthyrnir, standing on Herjafödr's
> hall,
> who bites off Lærad's limbs;
> from his horns there drips into HVERGELMIR
> the source from which all rivers run.

Lærad is sometimes identified with the world-tree YGGDRASIL, partly on the rather doubtful grounds that Norse sources name no other mythological tree. The thirteenth-century Icelander SNORRI STURLUSON further confuses the issue by describing Lærad, which he calls Lerad, otherwise unattested outside *Grímnismál*, as a 'tree, whose name is well known'.

B12, 14, 23, 24, 28, 30, 35, 40, 50, 56, 59, 73, 87, 90; C2, 5, 9, 17, 24, 33, 46, 48; D405

landálfar *see* LANDVÆTTIR.

Landnámabók ('Book of Settlements')

A detailed account of the Settlement of Iceland, preserved in no fewer than five redactions, the earliest of which must go back to the twelfth century. With its account of the land-taking of over 400 of the original settlers, and its register of over 5,000 personal and place names, *Landnámabók* is a valuable historical and onomastic source resource, but it also contains considerable lore pertaining to the customs and beliefs of the settlers, for example those pertaining to the LANDVÆTTIR or the oath-taking ceremonies invoking, among others, ALMÁTTKI ÁSS.

B6, 86; C36

landvættir ('land-wights')

Protective spirits of the land, recorded in several Icelandic documents and depicted on the current coinage. The earliest of these documents, the twelfth-century LANDNÁMABÓK, includes a legal provision that ships approaching Iceland had to remove the dragon-head carvings on the bows of their ships, lest the *landvættir* be frightened away. A much more fully developed – and evidently Christianized – picture of the *landvættir* is given by the thirteenth-century Icelander SNORRI STURLUSON in *Óláfs saga Tryggvassonar* in his account of how King Harald Gormsson of Denmark, intending to sail to Iceland with a hostile fleet, sends ahead a scout:

> King Harald told a wizard to go to Iceland with an altered appearance, to try and find out what he could report; and he set out in the shape of a whale, and as he approached the land, he went to the west coast of Iceland, where he saw all the mountains and fells full of *landvættir*, some big, some small. When he approached Vápnafjörd [in the east], he went in towards the shore, intending to land; but a mighty dragon rushed down the valley towards him, followed by a train of serpents, toads and vipers, spewing venom at him. Then he turned to go west around the country as far as Eyjafjörd [in the north], and he entered the fjord. Then a bird flew at him, and it was so vast that its wings stretched out over the surrounding mountains, and there were many birds, both big and small, with it. So he swam further west, and then south, into Breidafjörd [in the west]. As he entered the fjord, a huge grey bull ran towards him, wading into the sea, bellowing in a terrifying fashion, and followed by a crowd of *landvættir*. From there he went round by Reykjanes [in the southwest], intending to land at Víkarskeid [in the south], but there came down a mountain-giant towards him with an iron staff in his hands. He was a head taller than the mountains, and many other giants followed him. He then swam eastwards along the land, but, he reported, there was nothing to see except sand and vast deserts, and beyond the skerries, high-breaking surf; and the sea between the countries was so broad that no long ship could cross it. At that time Brodd-Helgi lived at Vápnafjörd, Eyjólf Valgerdsson in Eyjafjörd, Thord Gellir in Breidafjörd, and Thorodd GODI in Ölfús. Then the Danish king turned back with his fleet, and sailed back to Denmark.

Snorri's mention of the four chieftains towards the end of the passage is presumably intended to suggest that these *landvættir* were each in some sense a representation of the externalized soul or FYLGJA of each chieftain. The fact that the wizard proceeds around Iceland in an anticlockwise – widdershins – fashion only underlines his pagan intent, and it seems likely that the forms the *landvættir* adopt have been influenced to some extent by Christian representations of the four evangelists as lion, eagle, bull and man.

A not dissimilar scene, this time relating to the *landálfar* ('land-elves') is played out in the thirteenth-century EGILS SAGA SKALLA-GRÍMSSONAR, which some believe also to have been composed by Snorri, in which Egil sets up a 'pole of malice' against his enemy Eirík Bloodaxe, and against Eirík's wife, Gunnhild, on the island of Herdla:

> Then they prepared to sail, and when they were about to sail, Egil went up onto the island. He took in his hand a pole of hazel, and climbed up on a rock that stuck out towards the mainland. Then he took a horse's head, and shoved it on the pole. Then he spoke this curse, saying: 'Here I set up a pole of malice; and I direct this malice at King Eirík and Queen Gunnhild' – he pointed the horse's head towards the mainland – 'I direct this malice against the *landálfar*, so that they may all wander astray, and none can reach or find their home until they drive King Eirík and Queen Gunnhild from the land.' Then he shoved the pole into a crack in the rock and left it standing there. He turned his head towards the mainland, and carved runes on the pole, and spoke the full curse.

B6, 58, 82, 86; C10, 36, 37; D584

Laufey *see* LOKI.

laukar, laþu *see* ALU.

Laxdœla saga

An Icelandic saga probably composed in the middle of the thirteenth century and combining a number of earlier sources to offer an extended narrative spanning some two centuries, focusing on the life and loves of Gudrún Ósvifrsdóttir, an imperious and doomed figure who lives up to her namesake, the tragic heroine GUDRÚN, who is celebrated in numerous poems of the POETIC EDDA as well as in the legendary VÖLSUNGA SAGA.

B25, 42, 65, 68, 79; C1, 6, 28

Leggjaldi *see* RÍGSTHULA.

Leif

According to the legendary VÖLSUNGA SAGA, the captain of the warship of the mighty hero HELGI SIGMUNDARSON HUNDINGSBANI.

B25, 42, 65, 68, 79; C1, 6

Leift *see* HVERGELMIR.

Leifthrásir ('thriving remnant')

According to the thirteenth-century Icelander SNORRI STURLUSON, one of the two people who survive the apocalyptic events of RAGNARÖK by hiding in HODDMÍMIR's holt, usually identified with the world-tree YGGDRASIL. The equivalent character in the eddic poem VAFTHRÚDNISMÁL, a variant stanza of which Snorri cites, is called Lifthrásir.

B12, 14, 23, 24, 28, 30, 35, 40, 50, 51, 56, 59, 73, 87, 90; C2, 5, 9, 17, 24, 33, 46, 48

Leipt *see* HVERGELMIR.

Lerad *see* LÆRAD.

Léttfeti *see* ÆSIR.

Leyding

According to the thirteenth-century Icelander SNORRI STURLUSON, the first of the fetters with which the ÆSIR attempt to bind the monstrous wolf FENRIR, before finally succeeding in restraining the animal with GLEIPNIR.

B 24, 28, 35, 40, 50; C5, 9, 48

Líf ('life')

According to the eddic poem VAFTHRÚDNISMÁL, a woman, one of two people (the other is LEIFTHRÁSIR) who survive the apocalyptic events of RAGNARÖK, by being concealed in the wood of HODDMÍMIR, which is usually interpreted as the world-tree YGGDRASIL. The thirteenth-century Icelander SNORRI STURLUSON adds the details that they sustained themselves on morning dew and together propagated the new race of men.

B12, 14, 23, 24, 28, 30, 35, 40, 50, 51, 56, 59, 73, 87, 90; C2, 25, 9, 17, 24, 33, 46, 48

Lífthrásir *see* LEIFTHRÁSIR.

light elves

A race of beings, *ljósálfar*, distinct from BLACK ELVES, according to the thirteenth-century Icelander SNORRI STURLUSON, who calls them 'fairer to look at than the sun'. Elsewhere, Snorri describes the dwelling of the light elves (whom he evidently regards as essentially angelic) as being in GIMLÉ, situated in the third heaven.

B24, 28, 35, 40, 50; C5, 9, 48

Lit ('hue')

(1) A dwarf, according to the catalogue in the eddic poem VÖLUSPÁ. (2) Found in a ninth-century skaldic verse by BRAGI BODDASON, cited by the thirteenth-

century Icelander SNORRI STURLUSON, as the name of a giant. In Snorri's own account of the death of the god BALDR, however, Lit is given as the name of a dwarf inadvertently kicked onto Baldr's funeral pyre by the god THOR.

B12, 14, 23, 24, 28, 30, 35, 40, 50, 56, 59, 73, 87, 90; C2, 5, 9, 17, 24, 33, 46, 48

ljósálfar see LIGHT ELVES.

Loddfáfnir

According to the eddic poem HÁVAMÁL, a confidant of the god ODIN and the recipient of his wisdom. The etymology of the name is obscure: probably it is to be connected with a series of words in both Norse and Latin for a trickster, jester or stooge, a sense quite in keeping with the dramatic presentation of *Hávamál*.

B12, 14, 23, 30, 56, 73, 87, 90; C2, 17, 24, 33, 46; D273

Lodin ('stumpy')

A giant, with whose evidently loathsome company the hero HELGI HJÖRVARDSSON threatens the giantess HRÍMGERD in the eddic poem HELGAKVIDA HJÖRVARDSSONAR:

Lodin's the name of the one you'll wed, loathsome to
    men as you are,
the ogre who lives on the island Tholley;
the very wise giant, and worst of rock-dwellers:
he's a suitable mate for you.

B12, 30, 56, 73, 87, 90; C2, 17, 24, 33, 46

Lodur, Lódur ('fruitful'?)

According to the eddic poem VÖLUSPÁ, one of two figures – the other is HŒNIR – who accompany the god ODIN on his travels. As part of this triad, Lodur is involved in the animation of the tree trunks ASK and EMBLA who become the first human beings. Elsewhere, in two poetic periphrases or KENNINGS in skaldic verse, Odin is described as 'Lodur's friend', and such a designation is consistent with the parallel depiction of Odin as 'LOKI's friend', given Loki's appearance alongside Odin in similar triads of travelling figures. The thirteenth-century Icelander SNORRI STURLUSON, who certainly knew *Völuspá*, which he cites extensively, repeats the tale of Ask and Embla, but names Odin's brothers VILI and VÉ in place of Lodur and Hœnir.

B12, 30, 56, 59, 73, 87, 90; C2, 17, 24, 33, 46; D461

Lofn ('comforter'?)

One of the goddesses or ÁSYNJUR, according to various lists. The thirteenth-century Icelander SNORRI STURLUSON includes her among the ÆSIR, and adds with a typical etymological flourish:

She is so compassionate and good to pray to that she obtains permission from All-father [ODIN] and FRIGG for marriage, between women and men, even if it had previously been forbidden or denied. So it is from her name that permission [*lof*] is so called, as well as when something is greatly praised [*lofat*].

B24, 28, 35, 40, 50; C5, 9, 48

Lofnheid

According to the eddic poem REGINSMÁL, one of the two daughters of the shape-changer HREIDMAR (the other is Lyngheid), whom their father begs for help as he is being murdered in his bed by his son, FÁFNIR:

'Lyngheid, Lofnheid, look: my life is lost!
Necessity's a fearsome force.

Lyngheid replied:
'Few sisters, though their father is lost,
can avenge a brother's crime.'

B12, 30, 56, 73, 87, 90; C2, 17, 24, 33, 46

Loft, Lopt ('air')

Another name for LOKI, mentioned in the eddic poems LOKASENNA and HYNDLULJÓD.

B12, 30, 56, 73, 87, 90; C2, 17, 24, 33, 46

Logi ('flame')

A giant, the embodiment of flame and one of the three sons of the primeval ancestor FORNJÓT. According to the thirteenth-century Icelander SNORRI STURLUSON, when the god THOR travels to the halls of the giant ÚTGARDALOKI with his companions THJÁLFI and LOKI, each is challenged to at least one contest. Loki is set to an eating contest, but only narrowly defeated by an opponent, Logi, who has not only matched Loki in eating the meat from the bones, but, true to his name, has utterly consumed both bones and trencher, too.

B24, 28, 35, 40, 50; C5, 9, 48

Lokasenna ('the flyting of Loki')

An extraordinary eddic poem, couched in the form of a ritualized contest of abuse or FLYTING, found in the CODEX REGIUS manuscript. The simple narrative framework of the poem belies its complex structure and purpose. In the Codex Regius, *Lokasenna* immediately follows the eddic poem HYMISKVIDA, part of the purpose of which was to explain how the god THOR obtained a mighty cauldron from the giant HYMIR, so that the sea-giant ÆGIR might brew ale for the ÆSIR, and the prose preface to *Lokasenna* explains how the mischievous LOKI has appeared at the ensuing feast, while Thor is away in JÖTUNHEIM fighting giants. The prose describes how Loki killed one of Ægir's servants, FIMAFENG, then is chased away and returns, demanding entry. When he is eventually granted admittance, he saunters in among the hushed throng and takes his seat at the insistence of the god ODIN himself, who seems loath to provoke him. His diplomacy is scarcely repaid: Loki proceeds to abuse all the Æsir present, charging all the male Æsir with cowardice or other kinds of unmanly practice, and charging all the goddesses or ÁSYNJUR who attempt to intervene with adultery, often with himself. In this way he deals with BRAGI, IDUN, GEFJON, Odin, FRIGG, FREYJA, NJÖRD, TÝR, FREY, BYGGVIR, HEIMDALL, SKADI, SIF and BEYLA. At this point, the god THOR appears, and in the face of considerable abuse himself, forces Loki to leave on pain of being struck with the hammer MJÖLLNIR. A prose epilogue describes how Loki turned himself into a salmon in an attempt to escape the wrath of the Æsir, but they captured and bound him with the entrails of his own son, NARI, and left him bound with a serpent dripping venom on his face; only his wife SIGYN stayed loyal, catching the venom in a bowl which she must empty from time to time. Occasionally a drop of venom will reach his face, and his resultant writhing produces earthquakes.

Perhaps the most curious aspect of the poem is the extent to which the most powerful and wisest of the Æsir refuse to be provoked, despite the vileness of Loki's claims; the repeated references to the apocalyptic events of RAGNARÖK, which a final split between Loki and the Æsir can only hasten, perhaps explain both the reluctance of the Æsir to strike and Loki's own reckless spite, as he tries to lure the Æsir into hastening their own doom. Moreover, in so far as his accusations can be corroborated with the external evidence of other sources, it seems that Loki is speaking no more than the truth.

B12, 30, 56, 73, 87, 90; C2, 17, 24, 33, 46; D6, 24, 99, 212, 225, 227, 249, 360, 488, 509, 541, 568, 615

Loki

A wholly ambiguous figure, equally at home among the ÆSIR and among their most deadly foes, the GIANTS, capable of extracting the Æsir from terrible predicaments, albeit ones in which he is himself heavily implicated, but also famously the father of three of their most implacable enemies, namely FENRIR (who will swallow the god ODIN), the MIDGARD-SERPENT (who will kill the god THOR), and HEL (who will hold the god BALDR). These three monstrous offspring are the product of his union with the giantess ANGRBODA, but he also had a wife who was listed among the ÁSYNJUR, namely SIGYN, with whom he had perhaps two sons

Loki *Detail from a fragmentary cross from Kirkby Stephen, Cumbria, England. The so-called 'bound giant' figure, seen here in a late tenth-century Anglo-Saxon carving, is sometimes interpreted as a representation of the bound god Loki.*

variously named NARI or Narfi and VÁLI or Áli. Loki's ambiguous nature is well summed up by the thirteenth-century Icelander SNORRI STURLUSON, who notes that:

Loki is pleasant and handsome in appearance, wicked in character and very changeable in his ways. He had much more than others that kind of intelligence that is called cunning and stratagems for every eventuality. He was always placing the Æsir into the most difficult situations; and often extracted them by his wiles.

One such occasion is that celebrated in the apparently late and comic eddic poem THRYMSKVIDA, where Loki plays a crucial role not only in locating the god THOR's lost hammer, MJÖLLNIR, but also in the plans for its recovery. He it is who eventually persuades Thor to dress up as a woman and offers to accompany him in the role of a handmaid. When he and Thor arrive in JÖTUNHEIM, once again it is Loki who, by his quick thinking, heads off the giants' suspicions when Thor begins to act like his old self at the wedding-feast:

Early at evening they all arrived,
and ale was brought forth before the giants.
One guest ate a whole ox, eight salmon too,
and all of the dainties intended for the women;
then SIF's husband [Thor] drank three casks of mead.

Then Thrym spoke, the lord of ogres:
'Did you ever see bride eat more keenly;
I never saw bride eat more widely,
nor any maiden drink more mead.'

The all-cunning handmaid sat ready,
and found something to say to the giant's speech:
'She hasn't eaten at all for eight nights,
she was so desperate for the giants' domain.'

He bent down under the veil, and wished for a kiss;
and then jumped back the full length of the hall:
'Freyja's eyes! Why are they so fierce?
Fire seemed to me to flare from her eyes.'

The all-cunning handmaid sat ready,
and found something to say to the giant's speech:
'Freyja hasn't slept at all for eight nights,
she was so desperate for the giants' domain.'

According to HYNDLULJÓD:

Loki sired the wolf with Angrboda
and bore [the horse] SLEIPNIR with SVADILFŒRI:
one piece of witchcraft most wicked of all
was born of BYLEIST's brother.

Loki ate from a heart, burned with linden,
a half-charred woman's heart he'd found,
from that wicked woman LOFT [Loki] came with child,
thence in the world every ogress sprang.

In a number of sources, Loki is described as the son of the otherwise unknown Laufey ('leaf-island'), presumably a giantess, whose name is also given as Nál ('nail').

B5, 12–14, 16, 23, 24, 28, 30, 35, 40, 50, 56, 59, 73, 87, 90; C2, 5, 9, 17, 24, 33, 46, 48; D29, 122, 127, 168, 314, 325, 331, 333, 383, 473, 488, 500, 502, 509, 541, 542, 561, 594

Lopt *see* LOFT.

Lóra *see* TROR.

Loricus

According to the EUHEMERISTIC account the gods offered by the thirteenth-century Icelander SNORRI STURLUSON, the foster-father of TROR, evidently to be identified with the god THOR.

B24, 28, 35, 40, 50; C5, 9, 48

Lóridi *see* HLÓRRIDI.

Lút ('stooped')

(1) One of the children of Thræl and Thír, according to the eddic poem RÍGSTHULA. Together Lút and his siblings are the progenitors of the race of slaves. (2) According to a verse by the skaldic poet THORBJÖRN DÍSARSKÁLD, quoted by the thirteenth-century Icelander SNORRI STURLUSON, Lút is a giant slain by the god THOR.

B12, 14, 23, 24, 28, 30, 35, 40, 50, 56, 59, 73, 87, 90; C2, 5, 9, 17, 24, 33, 46, 48

Lyngheid *see* LOFNHEID.

Lyngvi

According to the legendary VÖLSUNGA SAGA, the son of the warrior HUNDING and the rival of the mighty hero SIGMUND for the hand of the beautiful HJÖRDÍS. When Hjördís chooses the older Sigmund, Lyngvi is enraged, and, together with his brothers, he wages a battle against Sigmund and his new father-in-law, EYLIMI. The account of the battle, which is going Sigmund's way until he is approached by a mysterious figure clearly intended to be identified with ODIN, is a stirring example of the kind of episode with which *Völsunga saga* is packed:

The Vikings leapt from their ships with an unbeatable force; King Sigmund and Eylimi set up their banners, and the trumpets were sounded. King Sigmund then had blown the horn that his father had owned, and egged on his men. Sigmund had a much smaller army. A hard battle began, and, although Sigmund was old, he fought hard and was always the foremost of his men. Neither shield nor mail-coat could withstand him, and time and again that day he sliced through the ranks of his foes, so that no one could tell how it would turn out. Many a spear and arrow was shot into the air. Sigmund's prophetic DÍSIR [presumably here VALKYRIES or NORNS] protected him so well that he was not wounded, and no one could count how many men fell before him. Both his arms were covered in blood to the shoulder. When the battle had been going on for a time, a figure appeared among the fighting with a broad-brimmed hat and a blue-black hooded cloak. He was one-eyed, and had a spear in his hand. This man approached Sigmund, with raised spear. When Sigmund struck firmly, his sword shattered in two against the spear. Then the tally of killing turned, and Sigmund's luck deserted him; many of his men fell. The king did not try to protect himself, but fiercely egged on his men. Now it turned out as the saying goes: no single man can prevail against many.

Even though Lyngvi wins the battle, killing both Sigmund and Eylimi, he loses the woman; Hjördís escapes and gives birth to SIGURD, Sigmund's son, who grows up to avenge his father with the very sword, GRAM, now re-forged, that Sigmund was carrying when he died. Once again *Völsunga saga* provides a stirring set-piece description of the battle, which is clearly intended as a companion to the earlier description of Sigmund's end:

King Lyngvi called men to arms throughout his kingdom. He refused to run away and called to him everyone who would offer him support. He went against Sigurd with a vast array, and his brothers with him, and then the hardest of battles began between them. Many spears and arrows could be seen flying through the air; axes swung fiercely, shields were carved, mail-coats was sliced, helmets were cut, skulls were split, and many fell to the ground. When the battle had gone on a very long time, Sigurd went forward past the banners, with the sword Gram in his hand. He cut both men and horses and went through the ranks, so that both his arms were covered in blood to the shoulder. Men fled before him as he went, and neither helmet of mail-coat could withstand him. No one thought that they had ever seen his like before. This battle went on for a long time, with great slaughter and fierce attacks. What happened there was unusual when the land-army attacks: they could not advance. So many fell on the side of the sons of Hunding that no one could reckon their number, and Sigurd was the foremost of his men. Then the sons of King Hunding attacked him. Sigurd struck at King Lyngvi, and split his helmet, his head, and his armoured trunk. Then he cut Lyngvi's brother Hjorvard into two, and afterwards killed all the sons of Hunding who were still live, together with most of their army.

B245, 42, 65, 68, 79; C1, 6

M

Magi

According to the EUHEMERISTIC account of the origin of the gods offered by the thirteenth-century Icelander SNORRI STURLUSON, a descendant of TROR (who is evidently to be identified with the god THOR); on that basis, Magi is presumably to be equated with MAGNI.

B24, 28, 35, 40, 50; C5, 9, 48

magic

Magic and witchcraft are commonplace in the literary record and are used for a variety of purposes: healing, prophecy, binding and releasing friends and foes, inducing (and curing) sickness and love, putting out fires, calming storms and even communing with the dead. The range of magical activity attested in the myths and legends is to a great extent covered by the eighteen spells or chants listed in a section of the eddic poem HÁVAMÁL, and ostensibly put into the mouth of the god ODIN himself:

'I know those spells no noble wife knows
or any son of man.
One is called 'help', and it will help you
against strife and sorrow and every grief.

'I know another, that men's sons need
who wish to live as doctors.

'I know a third, if I feel pressing need,
to hold those who hate me in check:
I blunt the blades of my enemies,
their weapons and bats won't bite.

'I know a fourth, if men bring forward
shackles for my limbs:
I utter the words, and I walk free;
the fetter springs from my leg,
the manacle from my arms.

'I know a fifth if I see fly
an arrow in the midst of fighting-men.
It won't fly so straight that I can't stop it
if I can fix it in my sight.

'I know a sixth, if someone harms me,
with the roots of a raw-green tree:
then the man who means damage to me,
himself rather gets the harm.

'I know a seventh, if I see a high hall
aflame above bench-companions;
It won't burn so briskly that I can't save it;
I know the charm to chant.

'I know an eighth, that's useful
for everyone to learn.
When hatred grows between a chieftain's sons,
I can quickly cure it.

'I know a ninth, if the need should arise
to save my ship at sea.
I quell the wind upon the wave
and soothe the face of the sea.

'I know a tenth, if I see hag-riders
stream across the sky.
I can cause them to wander
away from their proper forms,
away from their proper minds.

'I know an eleventh, if I must take
old friends to fight a battle:
I chant under shields, and they pass with power,
safely into battle,
safely out of battle,
safely wherever they walk.

'I know a twelfth, if I see in a tree
a hanged corpse dangle;
I cut and colour certain runes,
so the man walks and talks with me.

'I know a thirteenth, if it falls to me,
to sprinkle a young boy with water,
he will never fall when he walks to war,
that warrior will never sink under swords.

'I know a fourteenth, if before a host
I have to give a tally of the gods;
I know something about all the ÆSIR and ELVES:
few foolish men know the same.

'I know a fifteenth, that Thjódrœrir the DWARF
chanted before DELLING's doors:
he chanted strength to the Æsir, success to the elves,
knowledge to Hroptatýr [the god Odin].

'I know a sixteenth, if I want
all a wise girl's lust and love:
I can change the mind of a white-armed lass,
and totally turn her heart.

'I know a seventeenth, to make a young maid
slow to separate from me.
These spells, LODDFÁFNIR,
you will long be lacking,
though they bring you good, if you get them,
benefit, if you but learn them,
profit, if you procure them.

'I know an eighteenth, which I never tell
a maid or any man's wife:
much better if only one is aware
(the last it is of my chants)
except only her my arms enfold,
or perhaps my sister.'

Outside the literary record, evidence of magical activity is largely restricted to RUNES, both in the carving of particular words (such as ALU) or nonsensical letter-combinations and repetitions that were held to have magical power, or by the inscribing of runes in places where they could have had no functional value, usually because such runes would have proved invisible. A handful of grimoires, some containing material that appears to date from the medieval period, have survived, but there is little to suggest that the practice of magic was particularly widespread.

B12, 14, 23, 24, 28, 30, 35, 40, 50, 56, 59, 73, 87, 90; C2, 5, 9, 17, 24, 33, 46, 48; D96, 98, 121, 161, 162, 388, 389, 558, 564, 578

Magni ('the strong')

The son of the god THOR and the brother of MÓDI, according to numerous sources, including the late tenth-centu̵fy skaldic poem THÓRSDRÁPA and the eddic poems HÁRBARDSLJÓD and VAFTHRÚDNISMÁL. It is said that Magni and his brother will survive RAGNARÖK and inherit the mighty hammer MJÖLLNIR from their dead father. The thirteenth-century Icelander SNORRI STURLUSON names Magni's mother as the giantess JÁRNSAXA and includes a tale of the early strength of the young lad. When Thor killed HRUNGNIR, one of the legs of the falling giant had toppled Thor, pinning him to the ground. None of the ÆSIR could move the leg, except Magni, then three years old. As a reward his father gave him Hrungnir's swift horse, GULLFAXI.

B12, 14, 23, 24, 28, 30, 35, 40, 50, 51, 56, 59, 73, 87, 90; C2, 5, 9, 17, 24, 33, 46, 48

Mánagarm ('Máni's Garm')

According to the thirteenth-century Icelander SNORRI STURLUSON, the mighty wolf that will swallow the heavenly bodies during the apocalyptic events of RAGNARÖK. As he explains:

A certain giantess lives east of MIDGARD in a wood called JÁRNVID; in that wood dwell the troll-wives called JÁRNVIDJUR. This ancient giantess breeds as her sons many giants, all in wolf form, and it is from them that wolves are descended. It is said that from this race will arise one most mighty, called Mánagarm; he will fill himself with the life-blood of everyone that dies, and swallow heavenly bodies, and spatter the sky and all heaven with blood. Because of this the sun will lose its brightness, and winds will rage and buffet to and fro.

B24, 28, 35, 40, 50; C5, 9, 48

Manheim ('man-home')

The world of men, as distinct from the dwellings of the gods, according to the tenth-century skaldic poem HÁLEYGJATAL of EYVIND FINNSSON SKÁLDASPILLIR. The thirteenth-century Icelander SNORRI STURLUSON appears to agree, offering a euhemerized scheme in which Manheim is given as a name for Sweden, as opposed to Godheim, which is considered to equate to Scythia, the 'original' home of the ÆSIR. Elsewhere, however, Snorri names Manheim as the home of the god NJÖRD and the giantess SKADI.

B24, 28, 35, 393, 40, 45, 50, 62, 83, 87; C5, 9, 16, 48

Máni ('moon')

According to the eddic poem VAFTHRÚDNISMÁL, the personified moon. The son of MUNDILFARI and the brother of SÓL, the sun, Máni was said to have been pursued by the wolf HATI HRÓDVITNISSON, who will eventually devour him at RAGNARÖK. The thirteenth-century Icelander SNORRI STURLUSON gives a still more fulsome account, and apparently describes the folk myth of the Man in the Moon, explaining how:

> Máni controls the course of the moon, and governs his waxing and waning. He took two children called BIL and Hjúki from the world, when they were coming from the spring Byrgir, carrying on their shoulders the bushel Sæg and the pole SIMUL. Their father's name is Vidfinn, and these children accompany the moon, as can be seen from the earth.

Elsewhere, however, Snorri gives a somewhat more elevated view of Bil, whom he lists as one of sixteen goddesses or ÁSYNJUR.

B12, 14, 23, 24, 28, 30, 35, 40, 50, 51, 56, 59, 73, 87, 90; C2, 5, 9, 17, 24, 33, 46, 48

Mannus ('man')

According to the first-century Roman historian TACITUS, Mannus was the son of TUISTO and the father of three sons, who in turn became the progenitors of the Ingvaeones, Herminones and Istvaeones. Parallels have been pointed out with a similar descent of father, son, three grandsons in the line BÚRI and BOR, and the gods ODIN, VILI and VÉ at the beginning of the world.

B2; C29

Mardöll An alternative name for FREYJA.

master builder

The tale of the master builder, whom the ÆSIR employ to build their citadel of ÁSGARD in return for marrying the fertility-goddess FREYJA and possessing the sun and the moon is expounded in full only by the thirteenth-century Icelander SNORRI STURLUSON in the course of explaining the birth of the god ODIN's eight-legged horse, SLEIPNIR:

> It happened right at the start of the settlement of the gods, once the gods had established MIDGARD and created VALHALL, there arrived a certain builder, who

offered to make them a stronghold in three seasons so fine that it would be safe and secure against mountain-giants and frost-giants, even though they might get in over Midgard, and he asked as payment Freyja for his bride, together with the sun and moon. The Æsir had a debate and made their decision, and a bargain was struck with the builder that he could have what he asked if he managed to build the stronghold in a single winter, but if any part of the building of the stronghold remained undone on the first day of summer, then he was to forfeit payment, and he was to receive no help from any man in his work. When they made this stipulation to him, he asked if could be allowed the help of his stallion, called SVADILFARI, and on the advice of LOKI he was permitted that. He began building the stronghold on the first day of winter, and at night he brought up the stone with his stallion. The Æsir thought it amazing how much rock the stallion shifted, and the stallion performed twice the labour that the builder managed. When they struck their bargain there had been many witnesses and mighty oaths sworn, since giants didn't consider it safe to be among the Æsir without guarantees of security if THOR were to come home, although at that time he had gone east to batter trolls. As winter passed, the building of the stronghold took rapid shape, and it became so high and strong that it could not be taken. When there were only three days left until summer, he had almost reached the entrance. The gods sat on their judgement-thrones and sought a solution, and asked each other who was responsible for their agreement to marry off Freyja into JÖTUNHEIM, and to ruin the sky and the heavens by taking away the sun and moon and giving them to giants. They all agreed that the responsibility lay with the one who was responsible for most wicked advice, Loki Laufeyjarson, and they declared that he deserved a shameful death if he did not come up with a scheme to make the builder forfeit payment. They were about to assault Loki, but he grew scared and swore oaths that he would see to it that builder forfeited payment, whatever it cost him. That same evening, when the builder went of for stone with the stallion Svadilfari, a mare trotted out from a certain wood towards the stallion and whinnied at him. As soon as the stallion realized what kind of horse it was, he became aroused and burst his ropes and ran after the mare, and she off to the woods, with the builder in pursuit, trying to catch the stallion while the horses ran about all night and the building-work was delayed for that night. Next day less was built than had previously been the case, and when the builder saw that the work was not going to be finished, he flew into a giant-rage, and as soon as the Æsir saw for sure that a mountain-giant had been in their midst, they called on Thor, and he came straightaway. The next thing was that the hammer MJÖLLNIR was aloft, and he paid off the builder,

mead of poetry

not with the sun and moon, either: he put a stop to him living in Jötunheim, and at the first blow he struck him his skull shattered into tiny bits, and he sent him down into NIFLHEIM. But whatever Loki had been up to with Svadilfari, some time later he gave birth to a foal, which was grey and had eight legs; it was the finest horse among gods and men.

The supporting passage from the eddic poem VÖLUSPÁ, which Snorri quotes immediately afterwards, is far from specific, and may even allude to a quite different event. The tale of a thwarted master builder is, however, widely attested in folklore, and versions of it are even found in two Icelandic sagas; it seems possible that Snorri has simply conflated this floating folktale with the notion that Sleipnir derived from the union of Loki and Svadilfœri (a suggestion which is supported by a reference in HYNDLULJÓD) in order to produce his own account.

B12, 14, 23, 24, 28, 30, 35, 40, 50, 56, 59, 73, 87, 90; C2, 5, 9, 17, 24, 33, 46, 48; D164, 224, 394

mead of poetry

A central tale, witnessed by numerous poetic periphrases or KENNINGS, and told most fully by the thirteenth-century Icelander SNORRI STURLUSON, who traces the ultimate origins of the story back to the divine war between the ÆSIR and VANIR. According to his account, the final truce was sealed by both parties spitting in a vessel, from which liquid KVASIR, a creature of extraordinary wisdom, is created. In his wanderings Kvasir is (in every sense) taken in by two dwarfs, the brothers FJALAR and GALAR, who murder him for no apparent reason and preserve his blood in three vessels, named ÓDRERIR, Bodn and Són. From this blood, mixed with honey, they brew a mead that gives its drinkers the powers of poesy and scholarship, and they guard it jealously. Unfortunately, they are unable to restrain themselves from further unwarranted killing, despatching the hapless giant GILLING and his unnamed wife, and bringing upon themselves the vengeance of Gilling's son, SUTTUNG, who leaves the dwarfs on a skerry, below the high-water mark. The dwarfs ransom themselves with the mead, which Suttung now hoards in a place called HNITBJÖRG, guarded by GUNNLÖD, his daughter. As Snorri succinctly recaps:

> That is why we call poetry Kvasir's blood, or dwarfs' drink, or the contents or some word for liquid of ÓDRERIR, Bodn or Són, or conveyance of dwarfs, since this mead gave them an escape from the skerry, or Suttung's mead, or the liquid of Hnitbjörg.

The god ODIN – disguised as Bölverk ('evil work') –

seeking to recover the mead, causes dissension among the servants of BAUGI, Suttung's brother, bringing them to kill each other with their scythes for the sake of a wondrous whetstone. Bolverk offers his services to Baugi, and performs the work of the nine servants he has indirectly slain for an entire summer, demanding in payment a single sip of Suttung's mead. Suttung, asked by his brother, flatly refuses, and so Bölverk prevails on Baugi to help him to his goal by stealth. Bölverk persuades Baugi to bore through the mountainside where the mead is kept, using a special auger, provided by Bölverk, called RATI. As soon as Baugi is successful, Bölverk transforms himself into a snake and slips into the hole, at which point Baugi, his suspicions finally aroused, stabs after the disappearing snake with the auger but to no avail. Gunnlöd, too, seems strangely trusting of the stranger who mysteriously appears in her hiding-place and sleeps with her for three nights, in return receiving a draught from each of the three vessels in turn. Bölverk requires no more than a single draught to empty each, and then transforms himself into an eagle and heads back to the citadel of the gods in ÁSGARD, pursued by Suttung, who has also transformed himself into an eagle. Odin arrives just in front, and spews up the mead he has carried into vessels which the Æsir have set out, although Snorri also tells us that Suttung chased Odin so close that he let some mead spill out behind (it is quite possible that Snorri intends it to be understood that Odin was so frightened of capture that he wet himself); whatever the provenance of the mead that was lost, it is now known as 'the troubadour's share'.

Snorri's account, with its progressive mutation of fluids, from spittle to blood to mead to vomit and perhaps piss, appears to derive from a notion that poetry, while intoxicating, can equally appear as 'drivel'; the twin notions are (as usual) splendidly expressed in a skaldic stanza by the tenth-century poet Egil Skalagrímsson, in a saga, EGILS SAGA SKALL-GRÍMSSONAR, which some have thought to have been written by Snorri himself.

Elsewhere, the main eddic support for Snorri's version comes in a section of the eddic poem HÁVAMÁL, which describes Odin's seduction of Gunnlöd, where, however, there are a number of significant differences:

> I sought the ancient giant; now I have returned,
> I got little there by being silent.
> With many words I wove my own fame
> in Suttung's halls.
>
> Gunnlöd gave me, on the golden throne,
> a drink of the dear-won mead.
> In return I gave her bad recompense,

for her whole heart,
for her sorrowful soul.

With the mouth of Rati, I made myself room,
and nibbled my way through the rock;
above and beneath were the giants' paths;
in this way I hazarded my head.

I took advantage of my disguise:
wise men want for little;
and now Ódrerir has emerged
inside the sacred boundaries of men.

I doubt I would have returned
back from the giants' domain,
if I hadn't had Gunnlöd, that fine woman
whom I laid in my arms.

The following day the frost-giants came
and found Odin already in Hávi's hall;
they asked if Bölverk had gone to the gods
or Suttung had slain him.

I reckon that Odin swore a ring-oath:
how can his truth be trusted?
He left Suttung deceived, without drink,
and Gunnlöd grieving.

From what can be deduced from this and other passages in *Hávamál*, the name Ódrerir is given to the mead itself, rather than one of the vessels that contains it, Gunnlöd is named as the daughter of one Fjalar, not Suttung, and none of the transformations into eagle or serpent are alluded to. A kenning in another of Egil's verses, however, which describes poetry as 'the seed of the eagle's beak', together with a picture-stone which appears to show a female figure (Gunnlöd?) offering a drinking-horn to another figure in eagle form, may together suggest that Snorri's account is not wholly unsupported.

B12, 14, 23, 24, 28, 30, 35, 39, 40, 45, 50, 56, 58, 59, 62, 73, 82, 83, 87, 90; C2, 5, 9, 10, 13, 16, 17, 24, 33, 37, 46, 48; D170, 555

megingjörd ('power-belt')

The belt of power that is described by the thirteenth-century Icelander SNORRI STURLUSON as one of three main possessions of the god THOR, together with the hammer MJÖLLNIR and an iron glove:

One of them is the hammer Mjöllnir, familiar to frost-giants and mountain-giants when it is raised aloft, and little wonder: it has smashed many of their fathers' and kinsmen's skulls. He has another possession that is most precious, a *megingjörd*, that doubles his Ás-strength when he buckles it on. He has a third and most crucial

possession: a pair of iron gloves, with which he has to hold the hammer.

By contrast, in his account of Thor's visit to the court of the giant GEIRRÖD, Snorri describes how the giantess GRÍD gave him a staff called Grídarvöl, a *megingjörd*, and an iron glove.

B24, 28, 35, 40, 50; C5, 9, 48

Meili

(1) According to the eddic poem HÁRBARDSLJÓD, the brother of the god THOR. (2) Elsewhere identified as a son of the god ODIN.

B12, 30, 56, 73, 87, 90; C2, 17, 24, 33, 46

Mélnir

According to the eddic poem HELGAKVIDA HUNDINGSBANA I, one of the warriors of the legendary fighter HÖDBRODD.

B12, 30, 56, 73, 87, 90; C2, 17, 24, 33, 46

Menglöd ('gem-glad')

A beautiful female, who lives on a hill enclosed within walls of fire and clay, and guarded by the giant Fjölsvinn and his two dogs, according to FJÖLSVINNSMÁL. SVIPDAG sets out to win her hand.

B12, 30, 56, 73, 87, 90; C2, 17, 24, 33, 46

Menja *see* FENJA.

Mennon *see* MUNON.

Mercurius

The Roman god most often identified with the figure of the god ODIN, presumably deriving from their shared association with the dead and from their physical depiction as mysterious wanderers, clad in broad-brimmed hat and cloak, carrying a staff or spear. Accordingly, large numbers of votive inscriptions in Latin in Germanic territories celebrate Mercury from an early period, while several Christian authors make the same connection, enshrined in the names of the days of the week (compare English Wednesday, named for WODEN, with French *mercredi*, named for Mercury). Some of the fullest comparisons are found in late Anglo-Saxon England, where ÆLFRIC (followed by WULFSTAN) speaks of 'the heathen god Mercury, whom the Danes call Odin'. The Old English *Rune Poem* adds the tantalizing detail that the originator of letters was 'Mercurius the giant', which some have taken to allude to the role of Odin in discovering RUNES.

B29; D48

Merseburg charms

The collective name given to two pagan spells found in a tenth-century manuscript in the Cathedral Library at Merseburg. The first charm describes how a number of divine females called *idisi*, perhaps to be compared with Norse female deities called DÍSIR, have the power to release bonds and chains, ending with an invocation to jump free from chains and flee from enemies. The second charm is more complex, and includes several names, and perhaps also an honorific title. The charm explains how two characters, Phol and Wodan, 'rode into a wood', where the foreleg of the horse of one Balder (presumably another companion) becomes dislocated, and the rest of the charm concerns the efforts of two pairs of sisters, with the alliterative names Sinthgunt and Sunna, and Friia and Volla, to sing an effective healing charm before Woden himself is successful and is praised for his general efficacy as a healer. Readily recognizable are the names of the gods ODIN, FRIGG (or perhaps FREYJA) and BALDR, although it has been argued that the name Balder here signifies nothing more than the title 'lord' and that Odin's own horse is involved. The other characters are unparalleled, although the thirteenth-century Icelander SNORRI STURLUSON names one of the goddesses or ÁSYNJUR as FULLA, a name that perhaps echoes the Volla of the charm. One proposed solution even has Phol and Volla as a brother-sister pair equivalent to Frey and Freyja, although there is nothing more to sustain the suggestion.

D163, 183, 433, 510, 546

Midgard ('middle-enclosure')

According to the thirteenth-century Icelander SNORRI STURLUSON, the place where men live, as distinct from ÁSGARD, the citadel of the ÆSIR, or JÖTUNHEIM, the land of the GIANTS. Outside Snorri, the term Midgard seems to refer to the enclosing wall that encircles the dwelling of men, rather than the region itself, and the eddic poem GRÍMNISMÁL states that Midgard was created from the eyebrows of the primeval giant, YMIR. In many places in Snorri's works, however, the term Midgard appears to refer less specifically to the dwelling of men, than that of men and Æsir together, as opposed to the dwelling of the giants, and the same inference can be drawn from the use of the term *middangeard* in Old English, in which it is used to gloss *orbis uel cosmus* ('world or cosmos').

B12, 14, 23, 24, 28, 30, 35, 40, 50, 56, 59, 73, 87, 90; C2, 5, 9, 17, 24, 33, 46, 48

Midgard-serpent

According to the thirteenth-century Icelander SNORRI STURLUSON, the world-encircling serpent who lives in the ocean. Eddic and skaldic sources avoid the term and speak simply of 'the girdle of the world', 'the serpent' or 'the dragon', or employ the name JÖRMUNGAND, which Snorri also uses on occasion. The Midgard-serpent, or Midgardsorm, is described in several sources as the child of LOKI, the fruit of his union with the giantess ANGRBODA, alongside the monsters FENRIR and HEL. The particular enemy of the Midgard-serpent is the god THOR, whose specific animosity is attested in numerous sources and in several episodes. The tale of Thor's fishing expedition with the giant HYMIR, in which, using only a mighty hook baited with an ox-head, Thor almost succeeds in landing the serpent, is told not simply by Snorri, but also occurs in whole or part in the eddic poem HYMISKVIDA and in skaldic verses by BRAGI BODDASON in the ninth century and ÚLF UGGASON in the late tenth. Snorri alone describes a similar episode in which Thor, visiting the court of ÚTGARDALOKI and invited to raise his host's 'cat', almost succeeds in lifting the Midgard-serpent from the floor.

In the latter case, Thor appears as the dupe in a comic tale, and in his account of the fishing expedition Snorri is careful to exploit the humour of the situation to an extent unmatched in the poetic versions. After explaining how, invited fishing, Thor simply tore off the head of Hymir's largest ox and rowed much further out than Hymir wished. Snorri explicitly compares the encounter of Thor and the serpent with the (in Snorri's chronology) earlier contest in the hall of Útgardaloki and describes how, having hooked the serpent, Thor drove his feet through the bottom of the boat and braced himself on the ocean floor in an effort to land his catch. Snorri continues that:

> You could say that no one knows what a terrible sight is who did not see how Thor fixed his gaze on the serpent, and the serpent stared back, spewing venom. It is said that the giant Hymir changed colour, and turned pale in panic when he saw the serpent and the sea washing in and out of the boat; and just at the point that Thor was lifting his hammer aloft, the giant snatched at his fishing knife and cut Thor's line at the gunwale, and the serpent sank back into the sea. But Thor threw his hammer after it, and some say that he struck off its head on the ocean floor, but in contrast I reckon that it is true to say that the Midgard-serpent still lives and dwells in the encircling ocean. Thor swung his fist and hit Hymir on the ear, so that he plunged overboard and you could see the soles of his feet; and Thor waded ashore.

Several picture-stones depict the episode, some including the detail of Thor bracing himself against the sea floor, but others of the features of Snorri's account seem plainly included for comic relief. Snorri's expressed doubt that Thor managed to kill the Midgard-serpent in this episode is doubtless linked to his knowledge, supported by the eddic poem VÖLUSPÁ, that Thor and the Midgard-serpent were to fight each other to a mutually fatal standstill in the apocalypse of RAGNARÖK.

B12, 14, 23, 24, 38, 30, 35, 39, 40, 45, 50, 56, 59, 62, 73, 83, 87, 90; C2, 5, 9, 13, 16, 17, 24, 33, 46, 48; D205, 283, 540

Midgardsorm *see* MIDGARD-SERPENT.

Mím *see* MÍMIR.

Mímir ('wise', 'mindful')

A mystic figure of wisdom, whom the thirteenth-century Icelander SNORRI STURLUSON describes as one of the ÆSIR but whose name also occurs among lists of giants. According to Snorri, Mímir is sent, together with the taciturn HŒNIR, as a hostage from the Æsir to the VANIR at the end of their war. When the Vanir discover that Hœnir is unable to act without the advice of his companion, they decapitate Mímir (Hœnir might well have seemed the more logical candidate), and send back his head to the god ODIN, who preserves it and is said to consult the disembodied head for advice. Various poetic periphrases or KENNINGS in skaldic poetry refer to Odin as 'Mímir's friend', and seem to support the notion of some link. VÖLUSPÁ speaks of 'Mímir's well' as a source of wisdom and later describes Odin consulting 'Mím's head' about the impending crisis of RAGNARÖK. An intriguing passage in the eddic poem SIGRDRÍFUMÁL assigns to Mímir a particular power with RUNES. Snorri, as ever, appears to synthesize a number of accounts in localizing the well under one of the roots of the world-tree YGGDRASIL and claiming that Mímir derives his wisdom from the well by drinking from it daily using the horn GJALLARHORN, which elsewhere is the name given to the horn with which HEIMDALL announces the impending battle at Ragnarök.

B12, 14, 23, 24, 28, 30, 35, 40, 50, 56, 59, 73, 87, 90; C2, 5, 9, 17, 24, 33, 46, 48; D531

Mímir *Silver pendant in the form of a human head from Aska, Hagebyhöga, Östergötland, Sweden. There is little evidence for a cult of the head in Norse myth and legend (although some have suggested some connection with the wise Mímir), and it seems more likely that the pendant is in origin simply a mount for a knife-handle.*

minni ('remembrance')

According to the thirteenth-century Icelander SNORRI STURLUSON, the last of three toasts drunk at a SACRIFICE, after the toast to the ÆSIR and the so-called BRAGAFUL have been drunk. The *minni* was drunk specifically to honour the dead.

B1; C22, 23

Mirkwood *see* MYRKVID.

Miskorblindi

Also spelled Mistorblindi and, according to HYMISKVIDA, the father of the sea-giant ÆGIR. Other sources name Ægir's father as the giant FORNJÓT.

B12, 30, 56, 73, 87, 90; C2, 17, 24, 33, 46

Mist *see* VALKYRIES.

Mistorblindi *see* MISKORBLINDI.

Mithotyn ('false Odin'?)

According to the early thirteenth-century Danish historian SAXO GRAMMATICUS, a wizard who, in the absence of ODIN, usurped his position as chief of the ÆSIR and instigated the notion of sacrifice to individuals rather than to the Æsir collectively. On Odin's return he fled and was killed, but caused problems after his death in the manner of a *draugr* (*see* DRAUGAR) and was finally quelled in a similar way, when his corpse was decapitated and a stake driven through his chest.

B64; C7, 8

Mjöl

Mjöl *see* FORNJÓT.

Mjöllnir ('lightning'?, 'bright one'?)

The hammer of the god THOR and the chief weapon with which he despatches the giants who are the chief enemies of the gods. According to the thirteenth-century Icelander SNORRI STURLUSON, Mjöllnir was created by the dwarfs BROKK and EITRI, alongside other gifts for the gods FREY and ODIN. In Snorri's account, it is the special quality of Mjöllnir that, as Brokk tells Thor:

> he would be able to strike as firmly as he wanted, whatever his aim, and the hammer would never fail, and if he threw it at something, it would never miss and never fly so far from his hand that it would not find its way back, and when he wanted, it would be so small that it could be carried inside his tunic.

Mjöllnir *Silver pendant incorporating both cross and hammer motifs from Fossi, Iceland. The hammer, named Mjöllnir in the literary sources, is the symbol of the god Thor, and such pendants illustrate the way in which Christianity and paganism were not necessarily mutually exclusive; according to the sagas, for example, some Icelanders were* blandinn í trú *('mixed in faith') even after the conversion.*

This last property may well be reflected in the miniature axes and hammers that are found as AMULETS from the earliest period. Elsewhere, Snorri describes Mjöllnir as the first of Thor's three most prized possessions:

> One of them is the hammer Mjöllnir, familiar to frost-giants and mountain-giants when it is raised aloft, and little wonder: it has smashed many of their fathers' and kinsmen's skulls. He has another possession that is most precious, a belt of strength, that doubles his Ás-strength when he buckles it on. He has a third and most crucial possession: a pair of iron gloves to hold the hammer.

The notion that Mjöllnir is the bane of many a giant is certainly well attested elsewhere. In eddic sources alone, Mjöllnir despatches HYMIR, THRYM and perhaps THJAZI, while Snorri further recounts the killings of HRUNGNIR and SKRÝMIR, as well as the attempted slaying of the MIDGARD-SERPENT. It is scarcely surprising that the eddic poem THRYMSKVIDA is entirely devoted to the comic tale of Thor's attempts to recover Mjöllnir, after it is stolen by an understandably cautious giant, Thrym. Both the early thirteenth-century Danish historian SAXO GRAMMATICUS and Snorri agree that Mjöllnir is, however, a slightly blemished weapon, being shorter in the handle than it ought. Saxo attributes this to battle-damage; Snorri, more vividly, to the spiteful activities of LOKI, who, transforming himself into a gadfly, harasses the dwarf Brokk as he assists his brother, the smith Eitri, at his craft.

B12, 14, 23, 24, 28, 30, 35, 40, 50, 56, 59, 64, 73, 87, 90; C2, 5, 7–9, 17, 24, 33, 46, 48; D93, 568, 644

Móda

According to the EUHEMERISTIC account of the origin of the gods offered by the thirteenth-century Icelander SNORRI STURLUSON, a descendant of TROR (who is evidently to be identified with the god THOR); on that basis, Móda is presumably to be equated with MÓDI.

B24, 28, 35, 40, 50; C5, 9, 48

Módgud ('war-frenzy')

According to the thirteenth-century Icelander SNORRI STURLUSON, the maiden (presumably a giantess) who guards the bridge over the river GJÖLL and who, therefore, functions as a parallel figure to the watchman of the ÆSIR, HEIMDALL.

B24, 28, 35, 40, 50; C5, 9, 48

Módi

According to the eddic poems VAFTHRÚDNISMÁL and HYMISKVIDA, one of the sons of the god THOR; after the apocalyptic events of RAGNARÖK he and his brother MAGNI will both inherit their father's hammer, MJÖLLNIR.

B12, 30, 51, 56, 73, 87, 90; C2, 17, 24, 33, 46

Módir *see* RÍGSTHULA.

Modraniht (Old English: 'mothers' night')

According to the eighth-century Anglo-Saxon historian BEDE, a yule-tide sacrifice made by the Angles and evidently associated with a cult of female deities, perhaps to be identified with those later known as DÍSIR.

B15; C41

Mög *see* RÍGSTHULA.

Mögthrásir

According to the eddic poem VAFTHRÚDNISMÁL, the father of some benevolent giant maidens, who shall exert their beneficent influence on the earth after the apocalyptic events of RAGNARÖK:

> [ODIN said:]
> 'Much have I travelled, much have I tried,
> much have I tested the gods,
> who are those maidens who pass over the sea,
> travelling with wisdom of mind?'

> [VAFTHRÚDNIR said:]
> 'Three of the race of the maidens of Mögthrasir
> come to descend over dwellings;
> they alone are the guardian spirits in the world,
> though they were raised among giants.'

B12, 30, 51, 56, 73, 87, 90; C2, 17, 24, 33, 46

Móin *see* YGGDRASIL.

Mokkurkálfi ('cloud-calf')

According to the thirteenth-century Icelander SNORRI STURLUSON, the huge figure, nine leagues tall and three leagues broad across the chest, that the giant HRUNGNIR makes of clay, animates with the heart of a mare and uses as his second in his duel with the god THOR. Mokkurkálfi is matched against Thor's servant, THJÁLFI, who despatches him easily. Snorri adds the unflattering detail that, at his first sight of Thor, Mokkurkálfi was so utterly terrified that he wet himself.

B24, 28, 35, 40, 50; C5, 9, 48

Mundilfari

According to the eddic poem VAFTHRÚDNISMÁL, followed by the thirteenth-century Icelander SNORRI STURLUSON, the father of the sun, SÓL, and the moon, MÁNI.

B12, 14, 23, 24, 28, 30, 35, 40, 50, 51, 56, 59, 73, 87, 90; C25, 9, 17, 24, 33, 46, 48

Munin ('memory')

(1) One of the two ravens of the god ODIN, the other being HUGIN, who sit at his shoulder and keep him supplied with information. Munin is less well-attested in the sources than Hugin; the eddic poem GRÍMNISMÁL has Odin say of the two birds:

> 'Every day Hugin and Munin fly over the
> wide earth.
> I worry that Hugin may not return,
> but I am more worried about Munin.'

The notion that thought and memory can be expressed as birds, visiting distant places and returning, is a commonplace of early Germanic and Celtic verse. In skaldic sources Munin appears simply as a poetic term or HEITI for 'raven', as in a verse by the twelfth-century poet Einar Skúlason which describes how: 'blue-black Munin sips blood from wounds.'

(2) Munin also occurs as an isolated dwarf-name in one of the name-lists or THULUR.

B12, 30, 56, 73, 87, 90; C2, 17, 24, 33, 46

Munon

According to the EUHEMERISTIC account of the origins of the gods given by the thirteenth-century Icelander

Munin *Stone monument from Kirk Andreas, Isle of Man, depicting the god Odin being devoured by the monstrous wolf Fenrir at Ragnarök, with one of his ravens, either Hugin or Munin, at his shoulder.*

Muspel

SNORRI STURLUSON, the husband of TROAN, who was said to be the daughter of King Priam of Troy. Troan and Munon produce a mighty child, TROR, who is evidently to be identified with the god THOR. Munon is also known as Mennon.

B24, 28, 35, 40, 50; C5, 9, 48

Muspel ('world's end'?)

Evidently related to the Old High German *muspilli* ('doomsday'), Muspel occurs in several guises, even according to the normally synthesised view of the thirteenth-century Icelander SNORRI STURLUSON. Muspel is given as the name both of a fiery region, south of the gaping primeval void of GINNUNGAGAP and balancing the frosty wastes of NIFLHEIM to the north, and of the shadowy figure who presides over such a realm; one might compare the twin aspects of HEL, the name given equally to the infernal realm and its queen. The eddic sources seem to favour the interpretation of Muspel with a dread figure. VÖLUSPÁ speaks of 'Muspel's troops' waging war against the ÆSIR during the apocalyptic events of RAGNARÖK, and LOKASENNA names 'Muspel's sons' in a similar context. Even Snorri describes Muspel as the owner of the fateful ship NAGLFAR, which is used to ferry the army ranged alongside the giants at Ragnarök, and it may be that Muspel is nothing more than another designation for the other fire-giant of Ragnarök, SURT, or perhaps for the region from which Surt derives. As Snorri puts it:

> But first there was that region in the south called Muspel, which is bright and hot; the place is burning and fiery, and impassable to all those who visit and are not native there. There is a figure called Surt, stationed at the border to protect the land; he has a fiery sword,

and at Ragnarök he will go and fight and conquer all the Æsir, and burn the whole world with fire.

Although Snorri goes on to quote *Völuspá* in support of his interpretation, in fact such quotation only clouds the picture. *Völuspá* clearly distinguishes Surt (who comes from the south) from 'Muspel's troops' (who come from the east).

B12, 14, 23, 24, 28, 30, 35, 40, 50, 56, 59, 73, 87, 90; C2, 5, 9, 17, 24, 33, 46, 48

Muspilli

An Old High German poem, usually dated from around the turn of the tenth century, concerning the apocalypse, and using the term *muspilli* to refer to the blazing fire that will sweep the world at the end of time. Some connection with the Norse personal or place-name MUSPEL seems assured.

D97, 137

Mýlnir

According to the eddic poem HELGAKVIDA HUNDINGSBANA I, one of the warriors of the mighty leader HÖDBRODD.

B12, 30, 56, 73, 87, 90; C2, 17, 24, 33, 46

Myrkvid ('murky wood')

According to the eddic poem LOKASENNA, the dark forest through which the sons of MUSPEL will ride to battle at the time of the apocalyptic events of RAGNARÖK. In the heroic poems of the POETIC EDDA, Myrkvid (sometimes called Mirkwood) also appears as the name of a legendary forest, of the sort quite common in medieval literature, that both forms a barrier between the mundane world and the world of magic and myth, and is also a setting for that enchantment.

B12, 30, 56, 73, 87, 90; C2, 17, 24, 33, 46

N

Naglfar(i) ('nail-ship', perhaps originally 'corpse-ship')

According to the thirteenth-century Icelander SNORRI STURLUSON, the biggest of all ships and the one that will ferry the enemies of the ÆSIR, including the sons of MUSPEL, to battle from the east during the apocalyptic events of RAGNARÖK. Snorri also describes how, because of the thrashing of the MIDGARD-SERPENT, the world will be flooded, and on that flood Naglfar will be launched. Snorri tells further how the ship is:

> made from the nails of the dead, and it is worth taking care that no one dies with untrimmed nails, because they add much to the ship Naglfar, which both Æsir and men would wish to take a long time to complete . . . a giant called HRYM will steer Naglfar.

According to the eddic poem VÖLUSPÁ, it is the wicked (and by now unbound) LOKI who will steer the ship. Elsewhere, Snorri describes Naglfari as the husband of NÓTT, the personification of night.

B12, 14, 23, 24, 28, 30, 35, 40, 50, 56, 59, 73, 87, 90; C2, 5, 9, 17, 24, 33, 46, 48; D97

Nágrind *see* HEL.

Nál *see* LOKI.

Nanna ('mamma'?)

Wife of the god BALDR, daughter of NEP and mother of FORSETI, according to the thirteenth-century Icelander SNORRI STURLUSON, who reckoned her one of the goddesses or ÁSYNJUR. In Snorri's account of the funeral of Baldr, Nanna collapses with grief and dies as Baldr is brought out to the pyre, and she joins him there, an example of the Norse practice of SUTTEE that is far from unparalleled. By contrast, the early thirteenth-century Danish historian SAXO GRAMMATICUS makes Nanna the wife of Baldr's brother (and eventual slayer) HÖD, but beloved by Baldr, and so the cause of the conflict of the two.

B24, 28, 35, 40, 50, 64; C5, 7–9, 48

Nar(f)i ('narrow'?)

(1) Son of LOKI and his wife SIGYN, brother (or perhaps half-brother) of one VÁLI or ÁLI, and also half-brother of Loki's more monstrous offspring, the wolf FENRIR, the infernal queen HEL and the MIDGARD-SERPENT. According to the thirteenth-century Icelander SNORRI STURLUSON, when the ÆSIR wished to punish Loki for his part in the slaying of BALDR, they took three stone slabs, pierced them and laid them on their side, then turned Loki's son Áli or Váli into a wolf which then tore his brother Narfi to bits. It was with the entrails of Narfi, later turned to iron, that Loki was bound at the shoulders, knees and loins to the three pierced slabs until the end of the world at RAGNARÖK, tormented by dripping poison kept from him only by the solicitude of his long-suffering wife, Sigyn.

(2) Snorri cites Narfi as an alternative form of the name of the giant NÖRFI.

B24, 28, 35, 40, 50; C5, 9, 48

Nástrandir ('corpse strands')

According to VÖLUSPÁ, a sunless place where a hall, woven from snakes' backs, stands with north-facing doors and venom dripping from the smoke-hole. It is the abode of perjurers and murderers, who shall have to wade heavy streams, which the thirteenth-century

Icelander SNORRI STURLUSON takes to be rivers of poison.

B12, 14, 23, 24, 28, 30, 35, 40, 50, 56, 59, 73, 87, 90; C2, 5, 9, 17, 24, 33, 46, 48

Nep

According to the thirteenth-century Icelander SNORRI STURLUSON, the father of the goddess NANNA; his name also appears in a list of gods or ÆSIR.

B24, 28, 35, 40, 50; C5, 9, 48

Neri

According to the eddic poem HELGAKVIDA HUNDINGS-BANA I, it was 'Neri's sister', presumably one of the NORNS, who fastened the thread of fate for the hero HELGI SIGMUNDARSON HUNDINGSBANI.

B12, 30, 56, 73, 87, 90; C2, 17, 24, 33, 46

Nerthus

According to the first-century Roman historian TACITUS, the Germanic fertility-goddess whom no fewer than seven tribes gather to worship on an island in the Baltic. Tacitus describes a sacred cart drawn by cattle in a grove and guided by a priest in procession. At the end of the festival a ritual bathing of the cart and the goddess is conducted in a hidden lake by slaves who are then drowned to preserve its secrecy. The name Nerthus readily recalls that of the god NJÖRD, albeit with a change of gender, and his close association with fertility strengthens the association. Given the pairing of the siblings FREY and FREYJA, Njörd's children by

Nerthus *The wagon from the burial mound at Oseberg, Vestfold, Norway. Wagons are often depicted with cultic significance, such as that which, according to the Roman historian Tacitus, draws the goddess Nerthus.*

an unnamed mother, and the apparent propensity for sex and marriage between brother and sister among the VANIR, it is possible that Nerthus and Njörd together represented just such a sacred union.

B2; C29; D460, 463, 519

Nibelungenlied ('the lay of the Nibelungs')

A vast epic poem, composed around the turn of the thirteenth century for performance in Austria and recounting the tragic legendary events surrounding the death of the great hero SIGURD (here called Siegfried) and the doomed race of Nibelungs (or NIFLINGS). Many of the characters and incidents from the poem are familiar from their depiction elsewhere, notably in the heroic poems of the POETIC EDDA, the legendary VÖLSUNGA SAGA and THIDREKS SAGA. The cast of major characters in each case is more or less identical, but whereas the other sources tend to focus on the actions of Sigurd, GUNNAR (here called Gunther) and the imperious BRYNHILD (here called Brunhild), the *Nibelungenlied* increasingly centres on the activities of GUDRÚN (here called Kriemhilt) and HÖGNI GJÚKASON (here called Hagen). Despite its courtly setting, the poem maintains all the raw elements of murder and vengeance that so distinguish the grim events associated with the so-called VÖLSUNG-cycle.

B8, 25, 42, 65, 68, 71, 79, 84; C1, 6, 14, 15, 21, 25, 44; D9 – 11, 17

Nidafjöll

According to the thirteenth-century Icelander SNORRI STURLUSON, the place where the hall SINDRI is situated, and where the righteous will dwell after the end of the world at RAGNARÖK.

B24, 28, 35, 40, 50; C5, 9, 48

Nidhögg ('vicious blow')

The serpent that, according to the eddic poem VÖLUSPÁ, torments the bodies of the dead. Earlier in the poem, Nidhögg is also described as one of the tormentors of the world-tree YGGDRASIL. In the version recounted by the thirteenth-century Icelander SNORRI STURLUSON, Nidhögg inhabits the Underworld of NIFLHEIM and gnaws away at the root of Yggdrasil that extends to the seething streams of HVERGELMIR. The squirrel RATATOSK conveys messages of hatred between Nidhögg and the eagle that perches in the topmost branches of the tree. Elsewhere the term Nidhögg is given simply as a poetic term or HEITI for serpent and even as the name of a sword.

B12, 14, 23, 24, 28, 30, 35, 40, 50, 56, 59, 73, 87, 90; C2, 5, 9, 17, 24, 33, 46, 48

Nid, Nidjung *see* RÍGSTHULA.

Nídud

According to the eddic poem VÖLUNDARKVIDA, the king of the Njars, father of the tragic princess BÖDVILD, and persecutor of the legendary smith VÖLUND. After Nídud captures Völund, has him hamstrung and sets him to work for him at the island smithy of SÆVARSTAD, Völund wreaks his terrible revenge, slaughtering Nídud's two young sons, creating treasures for the king from his own sons' corpses and raping his daughter. Völund's vengeance is complete when he describes to the shattered king exactly what he has done, before apparently flying off on some wings he has crafted for himself.

B12, 30, 31, 56, 73, 87, 90; C2, 17, 24, 33, 46

Niflheim ('dark world')

A place of freezing mists that, according to the thirteenth-century Icelander SNORRI STURLUSON, existed before the earth was created. In its midst is the boiling spring HVERGELMIR, from which the eleven rivers usually identified as the ÉLIVÁGAR sprang. Niflheim is understood to be in the north, separated from the fiery world of MUSPEL to the south by the gaping void of GINNUNGAGAP, where the contrasting fluids from north and south meet, congeal and eventually combine to form the primordial beings. Eventually, one of the roots of the world-tree YGGDRASIL is understood to spread across Niflheim, and it is there to which the infernal queen HEL is condemned, along with, ultimately, all evil-doers. Here, there is some confusion with NIFLHEL, and indeed some manuscripts consistently confuse the terms.

B24, 28, 35, 40, 50; C5, 9, 48

Niflhel ('dark Hel')

The lowest and darkest pit of the infernal region of HEL, to which, according to the eddic poem VAFTHRÚDNISMÁL, go the dead of Hel. In the version offered by the thirteenth-century Icelander SNORRI STURLUSON they are joined there by evil-doers, although there is some confusion in the sources as to whether Niflhel or the equally dreadful NIFLHEIM is intended.

B12, 14, 23, 24, 28, 30, 35, 40, 50, 51, 56, 59, 73, 87, 90; C2, 5, 9, 17, 24, 33, 46, 48

Niflung

According to the legendary VÖLSUNGA SAGA, a son of the mighty hero HÖGNI GJÚKASON, who aids Högni's sister, the tragic GUDRÚN, in killing her cruel second husband, ATLI BUDLASON. In the POETIC EDDA the term Niflung (also spelled Hniflung) is practically synonymous with Gjúking, the term used to describe the descendants of King GJÚKI, principally the family of Gudrún, Högni and their brother, the celebrated hero GUNNAR. As such, the activities of the Niflungs are inseparable from those associated with the so-called VÖLSUNG-cycle, recounted not only in the heroic poems of the Poetic Edda and *Völsunga saga* but also in other sources, notably THIDREKS SAGA and the NIBELUNGENLIED.

B8, 25, 42, 65, 68, 71, 79, 84; C1, 6, 14, 15, 21, 25, 44; D9–11

Njáls saga

Also known as *Brennu-Njáls saga*, the longest and, for many, the greatest of all the Icelandic sagas. Probably composed towards the end of the thirteenth century, *Njáls saga* focuses on the relations between two families, those of the ageing and cunning lawyer, Njál, and the young and dynamic hero Gunnar Hámundarson, who are firm friends. Despite their own best efforts, both men are drawn into a spiral of murder and revenge that eventually leaves Gunnar outlawed and dead and Njál burned to death in his own home. Quite apart from its outstanding literary merits, *Njáls saga* is also extremely valuable for its depiction of the events leading up the conversion of Iceland, and it preserves a number of extraordinary vignettes relating to beliefs surrounding the pagan period. Njál himself is depicted as prescient, able to interpret not only dreams but also the appearance of a man's externalized soul or FYLGJA, while the great hero Gunnar is presented singing in his BURIAL MOUND after death. In a saga so intimately concerned with the mechanisms of fate it is hardly surprising that much space is given to otherworldly or supernatural happenings, and in its preservation of the extraordinary poem DARRADARLJÓD, in which supernatural women, probably VALKYRIES, are depicted weaving the bloody destinies of doomed men on a loom strung with entrails weighted with heads, as a prelude to battle, *Njáls saga* simply makes explicit the concerns of an author evidently familiar with the customs and traditions of the far past.

B76; C26; D263, 303

Njörd

A god, father of FREY and FREYJA, and, like them, one of the fertility-gods or VANIR, who was left as hostage among the ÆSIR at the end of the great war between the two kinds of deity. His dwelling in NÓATÚN, and his association with fertility and growth mark him as typical of the Vanir; as the thirteenth-century Icelander SNORRI STURLUSON says:

> He governs the movement of the winds, and controls sea and flame; it is to him you should pray for voyages and fishing. He is so rich and prosperous that he can grant

prosperity of land or property to those who pray to him for them.

His association with the sea is presumably the root of the extraordinary assertion by LOKI in the eddic poem LOKASENNA that the daughters of the giant HYMIR used Njörd's mouth as a piss-pot. Because giants are associated with rocks and mountains, their daughters might figuratively be interpreted as rivers, which, naturally, discharge into the sea; such a solution seems greatly preferable to any alternative explanation. Ironically, Njörd is given as husband to the giantess SKADI in compensation for the killing of her father THJAZI by the god THOR. Selected solely (as it were) on the basis of his beautiful feet, his marriage to Skadi is not without its problems: neither party can bear to live with the other, Skadi despising his seaside home, Njörd loathing the mountains. Some connection with the Germanic goddess NERTHUS, described by the first-century Roman historian TACITUS seems assured, although the precise relationship is open to interpretation.

B2, 12, 14, 23, 24, 28, 30, 35, 40, 50, 56, 59, 73, 87, 90; C2, 5, 9, 17, 24, 29, 33, 46, 48; D102

Njörún

According to a list attached to SNORRA EDDA, one of the goddesses or ÁSYNJUR, although nothing else of this mysterious (and possibly fictitious) figure is known.

B24, 28, 35, 40, 50; C5, 9, 48

Nóatún ('ship-enclosure')

The seaside home of the god NJÖRD, according to the eddic poem GRÍMNISMÁL, the deep loathing of which by the giantess SKADI, Njörd's wife, is vividly depicted by the thirteenth-century Icelander SNORRI STURLUSON.

B12, 14, 23, 24, 28, 30, 35, 40, 50, 56, 59, 73, 87, 90; C2, 5, 9, 17, 24, 33, 46, 48

Nonn *see* HVERGELMIR.

Nör *see* NÖRFI.

Nordri *see* AUSTRI.

Nörfi

According to the thirteenth-century Icelander SNORRI STURLUSON, who is apparently basing his account on a verse in the eddic poem VAFTHRÚDNISMÁL, itself borrowed elsewhere in the POETIC EDDA in ALVÍSSMÁL, the father of NÓTT, the personification of night; as Snorri says:

> Nörfi or Narfi was the name of a giant who lived in

Nornagests tháttr

JÖTUNHEIM; he had a daughter called Nótt. She was dark and black, in accordance with her descent.

In the eddic poems the alternative name-forms Nör and Nörvi are used.

B12, 14, 23, 24, 28, 30, 35, 40, 50, 51, 56, 59, 73, 87, 90; C2, 5, 9, 17, 24, 33, 46, 48

Nornagests tháttr

A legendary tale, probably written no earlier than the fourteenth century and preserved in two manuscripts, including FLATEYJARBÓK. The tale describes how a mysterious stranger, calling himself Gest ('guest'), much after the fashion of the god ODIN, regales the court of King Olaf Tryggvason with an account of his 300-year life, in the course of which he has witnessed and learned of many great and legendary deeds, including a number associated with the events of the so-called VÖLSUNG-cycle. Gest's great age is attributed to the actions of the NORNS at his birth. When the youngest of their number prophesied that he should live no longer than the candle burning by his cradle lasted, an older Norn immediately snuffed it out and preserved it unburned. Eventually King Olaf persuades his visitor to submit to baptism, and the candle is lit and allowed to burn down, so releasing Gest from the troubles of his long life.

B25, 42, 60, 65, 68, 79, 85; C1, 6, 21

Norns

Mysterious female figures, often, like the Graeco-Roman Fates, three in number, who determine the fates of men. They are most fully described by the thirteenth-century Icelander SNORRI STURLUSON, drawing on a verse of the eddic poem FÁFNISMÁL, who describes their dwelling in the gods' citadel of ÁSGARD, under the world-tree YGGDRASIL:

> There stands a fair hall under the ash, by the well, and out of this hall there come three maidens, who are called URD, VERDANDI and SKULD. These maidens shape the lives of men; we call them Norns. But there are other Norns who visit every child that is born, to shape its life, and they are descended from the ÆSIR, others still are descended from ELVES, and a third kind from the race of DWARFS . . . good Norns, from a noble line, shape good lives, but wicked Norns are to blame for those whose lives are miserable.

The notion of three races of Norns, descended from Æsir, elves and dwarfs, derives directly from the eddic verse cited and would appear to echo the three named figures, Urd, Verdandi and Skuld, whose names apparently signify past, present and future. The Norns are often depicted at the birth of great heroes, and their role in determining the course of an individuals destiny is celebrated in numerous poems of the POETIC EDDA, such as HELGAKVIDA HUNDINGSBANA I, as well as in other legendary narratives, such as NORNAGESTS THÁTTR.

B12, 14, 23, 24, 28, 30, 35, 40, 50, 56, 59, 73, 87, 90; C2, 5, 9, 17, 21, 24, 33, 46, 48; D561, 608

Nörvi *see* NÖRFI.

Not *see* HVERGELMIR.

Nótt ('night')

According to the eddic poems ALVÍSSMÁL and VAFTHRÚDNISMÁL, the personification of night, and, according to the thirteenth-century Icelander SNORRI STURLUSON, the daughter of a giant named NÖRFI or Narfi. Snorri goes on to state that Nótt was married three times. First to one Naglfari, with whom she had a son called Aud ('wealth'), second to an otherwise unattested figure with the suspicious name of ANNAR ('second'), with whom she has a daughter called Iörd, and third to one DELLING, alleged to be of the race of the ÆSIR, with whom she has a son called DAG ('day'). Snorri describes how the god ODIN set Nótt and her son Dag into two chariots, to ride around the earth and so bring night and day.

B12, 14, 23, 24, 28, 30, 35, 40, 50, 51, 56, 59, 73, 87, 90; C2, 5, 9, 17, 24, 33, 46, 48

Nyt *see* HVERGELMIR.

O

Oaths

A number of oaths are recorded in the literary record. One, apparently sworn on a TEMPLE RING and quoted in both LANDNÁMABÓK and *Ólafs saga tryggvasonar*, appeals as witnesses to the gods FREY, NJÖRD and the ALMÁTTKI ÁSS, while others are rather more complex. In the eddic poem ATLAKVIDA, the tragic heroine GUDRÚN reminds her cruel husband ATLI BUDLASON of his broken promises to her brother GUNNAR:

'May it go with you, Atli, according to those oaths
you often swore to Gunnar, and invoked long ago:
by the sun in the south, and by ODIN's rock;
by the horse of sleep's bedding, and by ULL's ring.'

A quite different oath is extracted by the legendary smith VÖLUND from his captor, King NÍDUD in the eddic poem VÖLUNDARKVIDA before he will reveal the dreadful fate of the king's sons:

'First you must swear solemn oaths:
by a ship's sides and a shield's rim,
by a steed's shoulder and a sword's edge,
that your hand will never harm a wife of mine,
that you will not slaughter Völund's bride,
though you know well the one I wed,
and we have a baby born in your halls.'

Ironically enough, in view of his invocation in some oath formulae, the eddic poem HÁVAMÁL points out that in his acquiring of the MEAD OF POETRY, Odin himself bore false witness on a ring, before deceiving the giants SUTTUNG and GUNNLÖD:

I reckon that Odin swore a ring-oath:
how can his truth be trusted?
He left Suttung deceived, without drink,
and Gunnlöd grieving.

Oaths found in prose have a similar formalized and rhythmic quality to those found in verse. A good example is that found in VÍGA-GLÚMS SAGA in which through a clever use of antiquated diction the hero, Víga-Glúm, is able to extricate himself from a difficult situation by swearing an ambiguous oath. Traces of similarly ancient and formulaic language are probably preserved in an extraordinary truce-formula recorded in GRETTIS SAGA ÁSMUNDARSONAR, and repeated elsewhere, with minor variants:

A traitor is one who breaks the peace . . . and he must be driven out . . . and must be spurned everywhere like a wolf, where Christians go to church, where heathens sacrifice, where fire burns, where earth makes anything grow, where a child cries out for its mother or a mother bears a son, where men make fire, ships sail, shields gleam, sun shines, snow falls, Finns ski, firs grow, a falcon flies on a long spring day, carried by a light breeze under both wings, where the skies are curved above, where houses are inhabited, where the wind directs the waters on their way to the sea, where men sow seed. He must avoid churches and Christians and sacrifices made by the heathens, house and cave, every dwelling except for the Underworld.

B6, 12, 30, 31, 41, 47, 56, 73, 81, 86, 87, 90; C2, 12–17, 24, 30, 33, 36, 46; D324, 342

Ód ('Frenzy')

Husband of the fertility-goddess FREYJA, father of HNOSS and, according to the thirteenth-century Icelander SNORRI STURLUSON, one of the ÆSIR. Ód is an essentially shadowy figure, and the extent to which his role has been entirely subsumed into that of his wife can clearly be seen in Snorri's account of Freyja, where the fullest (if still patchy) picture of Ód can be found:

- Freyja is highest in rank next to FRIGG; she was married to someone called Ód, and their daughter is called Hnoss . . . Ód disappeared on long travels, and Freyja stayed behind in tears, and her tears are red gold. Freyja has many names, because she took on different names when she journeyed among foreign peoples searching for Ód.

The apparent contradiction of the last two sentences cited here underlines the difficulty of sketching out a function for Ód; it has even been suggested that his name simply denotes an aspect of the god ODIN (and one might compare the similar name-pair ULL/Ullin), who was well known for his wanderings, a notion to some extent supported by the way in which the roles

Ódáinsakr

of Freyja and Frigg are occasionally confused and conflated.

B24, 28, 35, 40, 50; C5, 9, 48; D251, 599

Ódáinsakr ('field of the undying')

A paradisal plain where the dead still live, according to a number of descriptions all but restricted to a few fourteenth-century Icelandic legendary sagas. The notion cannot be dismissed entirely as a borrowing from around that date, and its closest parallel is undoubtedly the classical Elysium. The early thirteenth-century Danish historian SAXO GRAMMATICUS mentions a field called Undensake (or perhaps Undersakre), with apparently the same function. Nonetheless, there is no literary evidence for Ódáinsakr from earlier than the twelfth century.

B64; C7–9

Oddrún

Apparently a sister (or perhaps half-sister) of the cruel ATLI BUDLASON and the imperious BRYNHILD, who together play such pivotal roles in the tragic events of the so-called VÖLSUNG-cycle. Oddrún's own small part in these events is described in the eddic poem ODDRÚNARGRÁTR.

B12, 25, 30, 42, 56, 65, 68, 73, 79, 87, 90; C1–3, 6, 17, 24, 33, 46

Oddrúnargrátr ('the lament of Oddrún')

An eddic poem, preserved in the CODEX REGIUS manuscript, which attempts to offer a different perspective on the cycle of tragic events surrounding the hero SIGURD and his wife GUDRÚN by giving the viewpoint of the otherwise almost unknown ODDRÚN, described here as the sister (or perhaps half-sister) of ATLI BUDLASON, Gudrún's second husband, and BRYNHILD, Gudrún's great rival for Sigurd's affections, and the wife of her brother, GUNNAR. In keeping with the outlandish nature of her kin, Oddrún is depicted as a witch, who travels to help BORGNÝ, the daughter of King HEIDREK, to give birth. Borgný's lover, and the father of her children, is named as one VILMUND, who is said to have slain HÖGNI GJÚKASON, the brother of Gunnar and Gudrún. Oddrún herself is said to have been Gunnar's mistress, although he married her sister, Brynhild. As Oddrúnargrátr puts it: 'I gave my love to Gunnar, the noble lord, in Brynhild's place.' The occasion of Borgný's child-bearing provides her with the opportunity for an extended lament on her lost love, slain by Atli after he discovered that she and Gunnar were lovers. She recalls how she had remained powerless when Gunnar was cast into the snake-pit, where Atli's mother (though not, we assume, hers) had sunk her teeth into Gunnar's heart, presumably in the shape of a snake. Her final refrain is suitably poignant:

'Each man lives according to his loves;
now is ended Oddrún's lament.'

The legendary VÖLSUNGA SAGA, which at this point is paraphrasing the eddic poem *Sigurdakvida in skamma*, includes Gunnar's love for Oddrún as one of a number of events prophesied to Gunnar by Brynhild before she dies:

Now I shall swiftly say what lies in store. Through the advice of the witch GRÍMHILD, you will shortly be reconciled with Gudrún. The daughter of Sigurd and Gudrún will be called SVANHILD, and she will be the most beautiful of any woman born. Gudrún will marry Atli against her will. You will want to marry Oddrún, but Atli will forbid it. You and Oddrún will then meet in secret, and she will love you. Atli will betray you and place you in a snake-pit, and then Atli and his sons will be slain; Gudrún will kill them. Then mighty waves will carry Gudrún to the stronghold of King JÓNAK, and she will give birth to fine sons. Svanhild will be sent out of the country and married to King JÖRMUNREKK. The counsels of BIKKI will cause her harm. Then all your kin will perish, and the sorrows of Gudrún will increase.

The original verse in *Sigurdakvida in skamma* is still more succinct and chilling:

'You will want to have Oddrún,
but Atli will not allow it.
You two will yield together in secret.
She will love you as I should have done
if the gods had made things better for us.'

B12, 25, 30, 42, 56, 65, 68, 73, 79, 87, 90; C1–3, 6, 17, 24, 33, 46

Odin ('frenzy')

According to the thirteenth-century Icelander SNORRI STURLUSON, the most important of all the ÆSIR and among the most ambiguous in character and attributes. As Snorri says:

Odin is the highest and most venerable of the Æsir; he governs everything, and although the other Æsir are powerful, they defer to him like children to their father . . . Odin is called Alfödr ['all-father'], because he is the father of all the Æsir. He is also called Valfödr ['father of the slain'], because everyone who falls in battle is his foster-son; he allots them places in VALHALL and VINGÓLF, and they are known as EINHERJAR. He is also called Hangagud ['god of the hanged'], Haptagud ['god of the bound'] and Farmagud ['god of cargoes'].

The number of Odin's names is indeed legion (see

Odin Copper alloy figure from Lindby, Svenstorp, Skåne, Sweden, often interpreted as that of the one-eyed god Odin.

Appendix A), but Snorri's explanation carries the whiff of bookishness:

> Most names have been given to him because, with all the branches of languages in the world, every people finds it necessary to adapt his name to their language, for their prayers and invocations, but some events that have happened to him on his travels have given rise to stories and have produced these names, and no one can claim to be wise unless they can recount these important events.

Snorri names Odin, alongside his brothers VILI and VÉ, as the first of the Æsir to be born, the sons of the giants BESTLA and BOR. Snorri also makes Odin and his brothers responsible for creating the first human beings, ASK and EMBLA, in sharp contrast to the witness of the eddic poem VÖLUSPÁ, which Snorri clearly plunders as his source. A similar expansion of Odin's role by Snorri is evident in his claim that Odin is the father of all the Æsir. Skaldic tradition gives Odin three sons among the Æsir – albeit three of the most important – BALDR, THOR and VÁLI, but Snorri adds BRAGI, HEIMDALL, HÖD, TÝR and VÍDAR, often in the face of conflicting evidence. Of the six remaining Æsir in Snorri's own list of twelve (from which Baldr and Höd are naturally omitted, given the inclusion of Váli, Baldr's avenger and the slayer of Höd), NJÖRD and FREY are well attested as VANIR (and therefore cannot be Odin's sons), FORSETI is named as Baldr's son (and so substituted in this list), ULL's origins are obscure, and LOKI and HŒNIR

are explicitly listed as Odin's companions rather than his sons.

Among the main physical attributes of Odin are the hat and cloak of his wandering, his spear, GUNGNIR, and his single eye. Such attributes enable Odin to be recognized easily in a number of appearances among legendary kings and heroes in the so-called FORNALDARSÖGUR – for example, when the great hero SIGMUND draws a mighty sword from the tree BARNSTOKK in the legendary VÖLSUNGA SAGA and again in the same tale when Sigmund meets his end. Several themes recur in the course of the many tales and stories that are associated with Odin's name, most notably the quest for wisdom and knowledge, together with an eager passion for using sex and deception in the pursuit of his aims. In some narratives – for example, that of the MEAD OF POETRY, in which Odin plays a central role – all these characteristics are exhibited. Odin is often found in the sources engaged in a battle of wits, whether with giants (such as in the eddic poem VAFTHRÚDNISMÁL), with humans (for example, in the eddic poem GRÍMNISMÁL and in the so-called *Gestumblindagátur*), and even with others of the Æsir – as in the eddic poem HÁRBARDSLJÓD, in which he clashes with Thor. His close association with the dead is also apparently connected with this thirst for knowledge, which extends to speaking with the hanged and maimed, and raising the dead to seek wisdom that is otherwise unavailable. In the eddic poem HÁVAMÁL, Odin himself acknowledges the lengths to which he goes to acquire wisdom, in this case in the form of RUNES, sacrificing himself to himself by hanging on a mighty wind-swept tree (presumably YGGDRASIL), pierced by a spear (presumably Gungnir).

Faithfulness at any level is not a feature of Odin's actions. Even in *Hávamál* itself, which is largely devoted to a celebration of a number of his aspects, the question is posed as to how anyone can trust him. His long-suffering wife FRIGG bears him Baldr but is frequently deserted in a string of sexual peccadilloes with a variety of female creatures, notably giantesses, including GUNNLÖD, JÖRD and RIND. The argument that in each case Odin was acting with a noble purpose, given that these liaisons produce the mead of poetry, Thor and Váli respectively, is less easy to sustain with regard to the attempted seduction of BILLING's maid, as recorded in the eddic poem *Hávamál*, nor does it square with Odin's boastfulness about his many conquests to Thor in *Harbardsljód*, which he explicitly compares to Thor's own martial conquests.

In a number of sources, a specific rivalry is apparent between Odin and Thor, perhaps reflecting a tension between their differing supporters. Such rivalry

Odin

is particularly evident, for example, in *Hárbardsljód*, in which Odin taunts and frustrates Thor at every turn and clearly regards his own domain as essentially more aristocratic than Thor's plebeian constituency:

> 'Odin gets the noblemen, who fall in slaughter,
> but Thor gets the kin of slaves.'

A somewhat similar notion lies behind the speech of one of Odin's heroes, BÖDVAR BJARKI, according to the late twelfth-century Danish historian SAXO GRAMMATICUS:

> War springs from the noble-born; famous lineages are the makers of war, because the dangerous deeds that noblemen attempt are not to be achieved by the acts of common men ... no inconspicuous and humble kin, no ignoble dead, no lowly souls are Pluto's prey, but he weaves the dooms of the mighty, and fills Phlegethon with noble forms.

Another tale, this time preserved in FLATEYJARBÓK, illustrates not only the rivalry between Odin and Thor, but also the practice of dedicating entire opposing armies to him. According to the account in Flateyjarbók, when the Swedish King Eirík fights against Styrbjörn the Mighty at the Battle of Fyrisvellir in 960, Styrbjörn asks Thor for help, but Eirík makes a dedication to Odin:

> Eirík dedicated himself to [Odin] in exchange for victory, and pledged to die in ten years' time. He had already made many sacrifices, since it seemed likely that he would come off worst. Shortly afterwards, he saw a tall man with a hood over his face [presumably Odin]. He gave Eirík a thin stick, and told him to cast it over Styrbjörn's host, and to say: 'Let Odin take you all.' But when he had thrown it, it seemed to him like a javelin in flight and soared over Styrbjörn's host. Instantly a blindness fell over Styrbjörn's men, and then over Styrbjörn himself. Then a great miracle occurred, because an avalanche took hold on the mountain and collapsed on Styrbjörn's host, and all his men were killed.

A similar form of dedication is made by Odin himself in *Völuspá*, and even in the synthetic and antiquarian atmosphere of EYRBYGGJA SAGA, the Icelander Steinthór Thorlaksson casts a spear over his enemies in a minor skirmish at Alptafjörd just before the conversion, 'for good luck, according to ancient custom'.

At RAGNARÖK, when the old world ends, Odin will be swallowed by the wolf FENRIR, and much of his wandering in search of wisdom (even to the point of communing with the dead) appears to be devoted to ascertaining the precise circumstances that will lead to these apocalyptic events. In other ways, too, his activities would appear to focus on the mighty battle to be fought at the end of the world. In particular one might mention his association with all aspects of warfare (although he never fights), his particular connection with BERSERKS and VALKYRIES and his role as chief patron in VALHALL of the warriors who form the EINHERJAR. *Grímnismál* contains one of the most vivid descriptions of Odin in his majestic splendour in Valhall, feeding carrion to his two wolves, FREKI and Geri, while he himself survives sipping wine; and all the time his two ravens, HUGIN and MUNIN, fly throughout the worlds, collecting news.

Odin's interest in knowledge and wisdom is not limited to Ragnarök, however. As already noted, he plays a central role in the acquisition of the mead of poetry and has a strong connection not simply with runes, but with magic lore of all kinds. In contrast to others of the Æsir (notably Thor), Odin appears as a complex and often contradictory character with a wide range of attributes, which are carefully summarized by Snorri in his EUHEMERISTIC account of the gods in YNGLINGA SAGA:

> Odin was the cleverest of all, and from him all the others learned their arts and skills. But he knew them first, and more than other folk. But in order to say why he is so respected, we should mention the various reasons for it. When he sat among his friends, his face was so fair and dignified, that the spirits of all were uplifted by it, but when he went to war he seemed fearsome to his foes. This was because he could change his skin and appearance in any fashion he chose; another reason was that he spoke so cunningly and readily that everyone listening believed him. He uttered everything in verse, of the kind we now call poetic craft, and both he and the priests of his temple were called songsmiths, since it was through them that the art of song came into the lands of the north. Odin could make his enemies in battle blind or deaf, or paralysed with fear, and their weapons so blunt that had no more cutting-power than a willow-wand, while his own men dashed ahead with no armour, frenzied as dogs or wolves, and bit their shields, and were as strong as bears or wild bulls, killing folk at a blow, whereas neither fire nor iron could touch them. This was called the berserk-rage. Odin knew how to alter his shape: his body would lie as if dead or sleeping, while he would be in the form of a fish or snake or bird or beast, and be off in a moment to distant lands, on business of his own or other folk's. With only a word or two he knew how to put out fire, calm the stormy sea or change the wind to any direction he wanted. Odin had a ship called SKÍDBLADNIR, in which he sailed over the wide oceans and which he could roll up like a cloth; he carried with

him MÍMIR's head, which told him all the news of other lands. Sometimes he even summoned the dead from the ground or sat beside hanged men; because of that he was called lord of the DRAUGAR and god of the hanged. He owned two ravens and had taught them human speech; they flew far and wide throughout the land, bringing him news. Because of all this he was extremely wise. He taught all these arts in runes, and songs that are called *galdrar*, and because of that the Æsir are called GALDR-smiths. Odin was skilled in the art in which the greatest power is vested and which he himself practised, namely what is called SEID. Through this he was able to know beforehand the fate of men and what had not yet come to pass, and he could bring death, bad luck and sickness to people, and take the strength or wisdom from one person and give it to another. But after such sorcery there followed such weakness and worry that it was not reckoned proper for men to practise it, and so priestesses were taught this craft. Odin knew precisely where all hidden treasure was buried in the ground and knew the incantations whereby the earth, the hills, the stone and the mounds opened up to him, and he bound those who dwell therein through the power of his word, and entered and took what he wanted. Through these arts he became very famous: his enemies feared him, and his friends put their faith in him and trusted in him and his power.

B5, 12–14, 16, 17, 23–5, 28, 30, 35, 39, 40, 42, 45, 50, 51, 56, 59, 60, 62, 64, 65, 68, 73, 77, 79, 83, 85, 87, 90; C1–3, 5–9, 13, 16, 17, 24, 33, 39, 46, 48; D20, 48, 64, 71, 95, 121, 141, 145, 158, 159, 186, 203, 204, 215, 222, 233, 235, 275, 297, 298, 379, 435, 488, 505, 565, 585, 595, 599, 604

Ódrerir, Ódrœrir ('frenzy-stirrer')

According to the thirteenth-century Icelander SNORRI STURLUSON, one of three vessels – the others are Bodn and Són – in which the dwarfs FJALAR and GALAR collected the blood of KVASIR and brewed the MEAD OF POETRY. In other sources, Ódrerir, which is also spelled Ódrœrir, clearly refers to the mead itself rather than to the vessel that contains it.

B24, 28, 35, 40, 50; C5, 9, 48; D336

Öflugbardi ('mighty striker')

According to a skaldic verse by the ninth-century poet BRAGI BODDASON cited by the thirteenth-century Icelander SNORRI STURLUSON, a giant killed by the god THOR.

B24, 28, 35, 40, 50; C5, 9, 48

Ófnir ('weaver', 'inciter')

(1) One of the many names of the god ODIN. (2) According to the eddic poem GRÍMNISMÁL, in a verse cited by the thirteenth-century Icelander SNORRI

STURLUSON, one of the snakes that slither at the foot of the world-tree YGGDRASIL.

B12, 14, 23, 24, 28, 30, 35, 40, 50, 56, 59, 73, 87, 90; C2, 5, 9, 17, 24, 33, 46, 48

Ökkvinkálfa *see* RÍGSTHULA.

Öku-Thor An alternative name for THOR.

Olaf Geirstadaálf *see* REINCARNATION.

Ölrún ('ale-rune')

According to the eddic poem VÖLUNDARKVIDA, a VALKYRIE, the daughter of KJÁR and the wife of EGIL, the brother of the legendary smith, VÖLUND. In the prose introduction to *Völundarkvida* Ölrún is described, alongside HLADGUD SVANHVÍT and HERVÖR ALVITR, as possessing a cloak of swan feathers, presumably in order to aid flight. All three are said to be Valkyries.

B12, 30, 31, 56, 73, 87, 90; C2, 17, 24, 33, 46

Ölvaldi An alternative form of ALVALDI.

öndvegissúlur ('high-seat pillars')

Ornately carved pillars that supported the house and that form the main supports for the seat of honour. Several Icelandic sagas, as well as LANDNÁMABÓK, describe a practice employed by a number of the first settlers, who cast their *öndvegissúlur* overboard when in sight of land and settled wherever the pillars were washed ashore. EYRBYGGJA SAGA gives a slightly more detailed picture of a particular set of such pillars that came from a Norwegian temple, on one of which was inscribed a carving of the god THOR.

B6, 77, 86; C36, 39

Or

According to the eddic poem HELGAKVIDA HUNDINGSBANA I, one of the warriors of the fierce fighter HÖDBRODD.

B12, 30, 56, 73, 87, 90; C2, 17, 24, 33, 46

oracles *see* DIVINATION.

Orkning

According to the eddic poem ATLAMÁL, the brother of KOSTBERA. He accompanies his brother-in-law HÖGNI GJÚKASON on his fatal trip to visit the cruel ATLI BUDLASON, who is married to Högni's sister, the tragic heroine GUDRÚN. The legendary VÖLSUNGA SAGA, clearly drawing on *Atlamál* for information, describes Orkning as 'a renowned champion'.

B12, 20, 25, 30, 42, 56, 65, 68, 73, 79, 87, 90; C1–3, 6, 17, 24, 33, 46

Oseberg The ship from the burial mound at Oseberg, Vestfold, Norway. Such boat burials are well-attested in both the literary and the archaeological evidence.

Örmt *see* KERLAUG.

Orosius *see* PAULUS OROSIUS.

Örvar-Odds saga

A legendary saga, one of the most celebrated of the FORNALDARSÖGUR, probably composed no earlier than the fourteenth century, and now extant in two versions. The saga has much in common with others of the genre, particularly HERVARAR SAGA OK HEIDREKS KONUNGS, with which it shares some details of its narrative. It broadly concerns the Viking- and monster-slaying exploits of its eponymous hero and his sometimes strained relationship with his patron, the god ODIN.

B42, 68; C21, 35, 38

Oseberg

A Viking Age BOAT BURIAL from Vestfold in Norway, generally dated round 850. The ship contained two female corpses, the elder of which is between fifty and sixty, and the younger of which is between twenty and thirty. The ship itself is sumptuously appointed and considerably less robust than, for example, the GOKSTAD ship. The Oseberg vessel is often interpreted as a variety of luxury yacht for strictly inshore sailing. The richness of the objects found in the grave suggests that at least one of the women had some connection with the YNGLING dynasty, and they include a highly carved wagon, four sledges and a large number of wooden objects such as buckets, chests, troughs and shovels. Elegant tapestries and other textiles attest to the refined tastes of an aristocratic woman of the mid-ninth century.

D55, 138, 536

Otr ('otter')

Son of the shape-changer HREIDMAR and brother of the wicked FÁFNIR and REGIN, all of whom play major parts in the developing tragedy of the so-called VÖLSUNG-cycle. It is Otr's slaying at the hands of the god LOKI that requires the compensation of the dwarf ANDVARI's marvellous treasure-hoard to be paid to Hreidmar, who is consequently murdered by his greedy son, Fáfnir. The fabulous nature of the treasure hoard is such that a common poetic periphrasis or KENNING for 'gold' is 'Otr's ransom'. The killings of Otr and then Hreidmar begin the spiral of murder, kin-slaying and revenge that constitutes the Völsung-cycle. In the legendary VÖLSUNGA SAGA, the task of explaining the background to the initial killing is given to Regin himself, in his role as foster-father to the mighty hero, SIGURD. He describes his own family in chilling terms:

> This story begins with my father, who was called Hreidmar, and who was a rich and powerful man. One of his sons was called Fáfnir, the second Otr, and I was the third. I was the least talented and the least respected. I knew how to work iron, and I was able to fashion something useful out of silver or gold or anything. My brother Otr had a different pastime and demeanour: he was a mighty fisherman,

surpassing other men; he took on the shape of an otter in the daytime and was forever in the river, fetching up fish in his mouth. He brought his fishing catch to his father and so was a great support to him. He resembled an otter in many ways; he came home late and ate on his own with his eyes shut, because he could not bear to watch his food grow less. Fáfnir was by far the biggest and grimmest of the sons, and wanted everything there was to be called his.

Strife in such a dysfunctional family did not take long to break out. Only Fáfnir's subsequent metamorphosis into a dragon, and the slaying of both Fáfnir and Regin by Sigurd put an end to the family's strife, transferring the curse of Andvari's treasure to the VÖLSUNGS, with tragic results.

B24, 25, 28, 35, 40, 42, 50, 65, 68, 79; C1, 5, 6, 9, 48

Ottar *see* HYNLULJÓD.

P

Paul the Deacon *see* PAULUS DIACONUS.

Paulus Diaconus

A Langobard cleric of noble stock who spent several years at the court of Charlemagne and whose *Historia Langobardorum* ('History of the Langobards'), completed around 790, provides, alongside the anonymous and earlier *Origo gentis Langobardorum* ('Origin of the Langobard People'), the fullest contemporary account of their customs and beliefs. The account offered by Paulus Diaconus is particularly interesting when it supports or illuminates other witnesses, although in some cases it is difficult to be sure that Paulus is providing a completely independent account. So, for example, the Roman historian TACITUS, writing in the first century AD, had noted a particular form of DIVINATION employed by the Germanic peoples:

> There is still another sort of divination used to predict the outcome of serious wars. They devise a way of taking a prisoner from the tribe against which they are fighting, and match him against their own champion, while each of them is armed with his national weapons; the victory of one or the other is considered to predict the outcome of the war.

The description by Paulus Diaconus of one such encounter is all the more vivid in that he puts the rationale behind such a practice into the mouth of one of the protagonists:

> 'See how many people there are on both sides: what need is there for so many to die? Let him and me join in single combat, and may whichever of us the god had granted victory keep and hold together all these people unharmed.'

B2, 9, 21; C11, 29

Paulus Orosius

A highly influential fifth-century historian, whose *Historiae adversus paganos* ('History Against the Pagans') contains much useful material on the beliefs and customs both of contemporary and much earlier Germanic peoples. So, for example, writing of the behaviour of the Cimbri, whose sacrificial practices were also the subject of scrutiny by the first-century Greek geographer STRABO, Orosius notes the barbarity of their actions after a great victory in a battle which has been dated to 105BC:

> They captured both camps, and took a huge amount of booty. In accordance with a strange and peculiar vow, they began to destroy everything that they had captured. Clothing was ripped to shreds and thrown away, silver and gold were chucked in the river, men's armour was cut to pieces, horses' trappings were smashed and the horses drowned in swift eddies, and men were hanged from trees with nooses round their necks. In this way there was booty for the conquerors and no mercy for the conquered.

D419, 495, 533

Phol *see* MERSEBURG CHARMS.

Poetic Edda

The generic name given to the heterogeneous body of verse texts dealing with a range of mythological and legendary material, also known as the Elder or Verse Edda (and as Sæmundar Edda in older commentary), to distinguish it from the Younger or SNORRA EDDA, composed by the thirteenth-century Icelander SNORRI STURLUSON. In very general terms, such poems are distinguished from skaldic verse by their subject matter, metre, diction and attribution: none of the poems

Procopius

in the Poetic Edda can be attributed to any named author. The great majority of the texts that form the Poetic Edda are preserved in the CODEX REGIUS manuscript, but other important poems from elsewhere – for example, RÍGSTHULA and GROTTASÖNGR – are usually included in the tally on the grounds of metre and content.

B12, 30, 56, 73, 87, 90; C2, 17, 24, 33, 46; D12, 18, 21, 112, 13, 120, 121, 126, 144–6, 197, 209, 219, 220, 228, 229, 253, 258, 259, 289, 290, 295, 311, 319, 322, 323, 327–9, 364, 366, 374, 414, 420, 458, 465, 466, 482, 528, 539, 543, 590, 597

Procopius

A sixth-century Greek historian, whose account of the Gothic wars contains much useful material on the beliefs and customs of contemporary Germanic peoples. So, for example, speaking of the men of 'Thule', usually identified with modern Norway and Sweden, he notes that:

> The sacrifice most esteemed is that of the first man captured in battle. They offer this sacrifice to Ares, since they reckon him the mightiest of the gods. They sacrifice the prisoner not merely by killing him, but by hanging him from a branch, or thrusting him among thorns, or putting him to death by some other dreadful means.

The notion of a sacrifice involving hanging or piercing (or both) is frequently met with in the later sources – for example, GAUTREKS SAGA or the eddic poem HÁVAMÁL – as a method of dedicating the victim to the god ODIN, who, in his role as god of battle is presumably the deity identified here as Ares.

B69; C35, 38

R

Rádgríd see VALKYRIES.

Rævil

A sea-king, mentioned in poetic periphrases or KENNINGS for ships or the sea. So, for example, in the eddic poem REGINSMÁL, a mysterious figure who calls himself HNIKAR, a recognized name of the god ODIN, spies from a cliff-top the legendary hero SIGURD's ship setting out to avenge his father SIGMUND and asks:

> 'Who rides there on Rævil's steeds [ships],
> the towering waves and roaring seas?
> The sail-chargers are drenched in spume,
> the wave-steeds won't withstand the wind.'

B12, 30, 56, 73, 87, 90; C2, 17, 24, 33, 46

Ragnarök ('the doom of the gods')

The end of the old world, when all its mythic powers are destroyed in a mighty flood, battle and conflagration. Both the thirteenth-century Icelander SNORRI STURLUSON and the eddic poem LOKASENNA employ the more vivid form Ragnarökk ('twilight of the gods'), which has influenced many modern authors and commentators. The fullest description of Ragnarök is that given by Snorri, who quotes from, and elaborates on, sections of his main source, the eddic poem VÖLUSPÁ. Ragnarök will be preceded by cataclysmic events: a mighty winter, the FIMBUL-WINTER, lasting three years, will be preceded by a season of kin-slaying and moral decay:

> Brothers will struggle and slaughter each other,
> and sisters' sons spoil kinship's bonds.
> It's hard on earth: great whoredom;
> axe-age, blade-age, shields are split;
> wind-age, wolf-age, before the world crumbles:
> no man shall spare another.

Wolves will swallow the sun and moon, stars will go out, the earth will tremble, and all bonds will break. The monstrous wolf FENRIR and his father LOKI will be set free, and another of Loki's children, the MIDGARD-SERPENT, will move ashore. The ship NAGLFAR, filled with the enemies of the ÆSIR, will set sail, and from the torn sky the sons of the MUSPEL will ride in their flaming panoply, with the fire-giant SURT at their head. All the opponents of the Æsir will approach the battlefield of VÍGRÍD, and the rainbow-bridge BIFRÖST will shatter under their weight. The watchman of the gods, HEIMDALL, will warn the Æsir of the approaching conflict by sounding GJALLARHORN, and ODIN will consult with the wise head of MÍMIR, before arming the Æsir and the fallen heroes of the EINHERJAR and setting off to fight. Within the general conflict, a number of individual scores are settled: Fenrir devours Odin and is in turn slain by Odin's son, VÍDAR; the god THOR and the Midgard-serpent kill each other; Surt slaughters the fertility-god FREY; the huge dog GARM and the god TÝR battle to the death, as do Loki and Heimdall. The earth will sink under fire and flood, to rise again anew.

Similar descriptions to those of Ragnarök are found

in many different contexts. For example, the early thirteenth-century Danish historian SAXO GRAMMATICUS echoes much of the imagery in his account of the fall of King Harald of Denmark:

> The sky seemed to fall suddenly to the earth, and fields and forests to sink to the ground; all things were disturbed, and the ancient chaos came again; earth and heaven confused in one stormy tempest, and the world rushing to universal destruction.

The apocalyptic themes of Ragnarök appear to have attracted numerous sculptors and carvers. Several scenes are depicted in wood and stone carvings from a number of areas. The close parallels to be observed between some literary descriptions of the cosmological trauma of Ragnarök and the Christian Apocalypse almost certainly indicate that some Norse authors were influenced by Christian accounts, although it is often difficult to be dogmatic – for example, the quoted passage from *Völuspá* above has been seen to have close parallels with a section of a sermon by the eleventh-century Anglo-Saxon Archbishop WULFSTAN, although a direct link is far from assured.

B5, 12–14, 6, 23, 24, 28, 30, 35, 40, 50, 56, 59, 64, 73, 87, 90; C2, 5, 7–9, 17, 24, 33, 46, 48; D29, 110, 111, 351

Ragnarökk *see* RAGNARÖK.

Ragnarsdrápa ('the lay of Ragnar')

A skaldic poem, thought to have been composed by the ninth-century poet BRAGI BODDASON in honour of the legendary Danish Viking Ragnar loðbrók ('hairy-breeches') to commemorate a shield, decorated with mythological and legendary images that Ragnar had presented to him. Most of the stanzas attributed to *Ragnarsdrápa* are preserved by the thirteenth-century Icelander SNORRI STURLUSON in the course of his works. Among the subjects depicted are the battle fought by the brothers HAMDIR and SÖRLI against the wicked King JÖRMUNREKK, a conflict that provides the theme for the eddic poem HAMDISMÁL; the ploughing by the giantess GEFJON and her giant oxen of land from the Swedish king, GYLFI; the god THOR's fishing expedition against the MIDGARD-SERPENT; and the incitement by the beautiful HILD of her father HÖGNI and her abductor HEDIN HJARRANDASON to fight in the never-ending battle known as the HJADNINGAVÍG. A stray half-stanza describes how the god Thor cast the eyes of the giant THJAZI into the sky and turned them into stars.

B24, 28, 35, 39, 40, 45, 50, 62, 83, 87; C5, 9, 16, 48; D384, 367, 475

Rán ('plunder')

The wife of the sea-giant ÆGIR, mother of the waves, and the figure consistently blamed in skaldic poetry as responsible for drownings; to be drowned is to 'seek Rán's embrace'. According to the prose introduction of the eddic poem REGINSMÁL, adapted and developed in the legendary VÖLSUNGA SAGA, it is with Rán's net that the mischievous LOKI catches the dwarf ANDVARI in the shape of a salmon.

B12, 25, 30, 42, 56, 65, 68, 73, 79, 87, 90; C1–3, 6, 17, 24, 33, 46

Randgríd *see* VALKYRIES.

Randvér

The son of the despotic King JÖRMUNREKK, sent by his father on a mission to woo the beautiful SVANHILD, daughter of the tragic heroine GUDRÚN and her first husband, the mighty hero SIGURD. Unfortunately, he is accompanied by the evil counsellor BIKKI, who first urges Randvér to take Svanhild for himself, and then informs Jörmunrekk, who, in his wrath, has both of them killed. The legendary VÖLSUNGA SAGA describes Randvér's dignified response as he is led off to be hanged:

> [Jörmunrekk] could not assuage his anger and commanded that Randvér be taken and hanged on a gallows. As he was being led to the gallows, Randvér took a hawk, plucked off all its feathers and said that it should be shown to his father. When the king saw it, he said: 'It is clear that he reckons that I am deprived of honour, just as this hawk is deprived of feathers,' and commanded that he be taken down from the gallows. But meanwhile Bikki had been busy, and Randvér was dead.

B25, 42, 65, 68, 79; C1, 6

Ratatosk ('drill-tooth')

The squirrel that, according to the eddic poem GRÍMNISMÁL, carries messages of hatred between the eagle that lives in the upper branches of the world-tree YGGDRASIL and the serpent, NÍDHÖGG, that gnaws away at its roots.

B12, 30, 56, 73, 87, 90; C2, 17, 24, 33, 46

Rati ('drill')

According to the thirteenth-century Icelander SNORRI STURLUSON, Rati was the name of the drill that the god ODIN, calling himself Bölverk, persuaded the giant BAUGI, the brother of SUTTUNG, to use to drill through to the rock chamber where GUNNLÖD, Suttung's daughter, sat guarding the MEAD OF POETRY. The whole episode is also alluded to by Odin himself in the eddic poem HÁVAMÁL, where he seems to assert that it was he who used Rati.

B12, 14, 23, 24, 28, 30, 35, 40, 50, 56, 59, 73, 87, 90; C2, 5, 9, 17, 24, 33, 46, 48

Refil

Refil

According to the thirteenth-century Icelander SNORRI STURLUSON, the sword owned by REGIN, the wicked foster-father of the mighty hero SIGURD.

B24, 28, 35, 40, 50; C5, 9, 48

Regin ('the powerful one')

(1) A skilful figure, sometimes reckoned a dwarf, brother of FÁFNIR and OTR, son of the shape-changer HREIDMAR and a key player in the events surrounding the VÖLSUNG-cycle. It is Regin who, dispossessed by Fáfnir of the treasure of the father he has murdered, becomes the foster-father of the mighty hero SIGURD, for whom he forges the sword GRAM. According to the legendary VÖLSUNGA SAGA, Regin teaches Sigurd all the necessary accomplishments of a young noble, including sports, a form of chess, RUNES and several languages. After egging Sigurd on to kill Fáfnir, who has by now assumed the shape of dragon, Regin, too, falls at his foster-son's hands, after Sigurd, who has licked the blood from the dragon's heart and can understand the language of animals, is warned of Regin's plans to kill him by some birds.

(2) The name of a dwarf, according to the catalogue in the eddic poem VÖLUSPÁ.

B12, 13, 23–5, 28, 30, 35, 40, 42, 50, 56, 59, 65, 68, 73, 79, 87, 90; C1–3, 5, 6, 9, 17, 24, 33, 46, 48

Reginleif *see* VALKYRIES.

reginnaglar ('nails of power')

Nails hammered into the high-seat pillars, decorated with the image of the god THOR, of the Icelandic settler Thorólf Mostrarskegg, according to the mid-thirteenth-century EYRBYGGJA SAGA. Their precise function is unknown.

B77; C39

Reginsmál ('the lay of Regin')

An eddic poem interspersed with prose, closely associated with FÁFNISMÁL, the eddic poem that immediately follows it in the CODEX REGIUS manuscript. It seems likely that both poems were originally intended to be read together, and they offer a detailed account of how SIGURD, the mightiest of all the heroes of the North, came to slay the dragon FÁFNIR at the instigation of his foster-father, REGIN, who was Fáfnir's own brother.

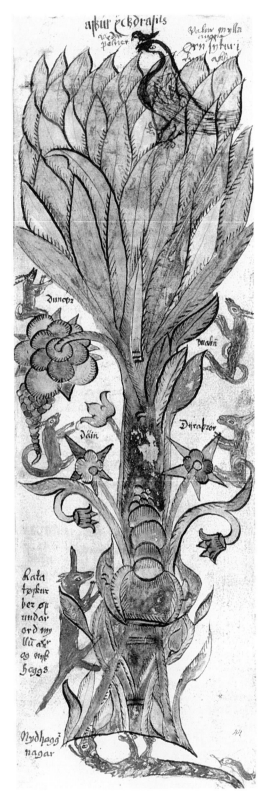

Ratatosk *An illustration from the manuscript AM 738 4to of* Snorra Edda, *dated c. 1680, depicting the world-tree Yggdrasil; the mythical squirrel Ratatosk is depicted in the lower left-hand corner.*

Regin *Detail of the Rasmundsberget runestone from Jäder, Södermanland, Sweden, depicting the wicked Regin, decapitated by the mighty hero Sigurd after he learns about his evil intentions.*

The prose introduction to *Reginsmál* describes how, in his youth, Sigurd selected his famous steed GRANI and was fostered by Regin, described as 'a dwarf in stature, wise, cruel, and skilled in magic'. Regin recounts the origins of Fáfnir's fabulous hoard of treasure, and the poem includes descriptions of the roles of the god LOKI and the dwarf ANDVARI in the acquisition of the hoard. A further prose passage describes how Regin forged the mighty sword GRAM for his foster-son, and the poem ends with a series of verses giving an account of how Sigurd, with the help of the disguised god ODIN, was able to avenge his murdered father, SIGMUND.

B12, 30, 56, 73, 87, 90; C2, 17, 24, 33, 46; D301, 436, 466

reincarnation

Only scattered references in the literary record seem to support the notion of a belief in reincarnation, the most celebrated of which cluster around the so-called 'Helgi-lays' (HELGAKVIDA HUNDINGSBANA I and II and HELGAKVIDA HJÖRVARDSSONAR), in which a pair of doomed lovers repeat their passion over three lifetimes. At the end of the eddic poem *Helgakvida Hjörvardssonar*, a terse comment in prose asserts that 'it is said of HELGI (HJÖRVARDSSON) and SVÁVA (the Valkyrie) that they were reborn,' while a pair of equally brief comments in *Helgakvida Hundingsbana* II state that the hero HELGI SIGMUNDARSON HUNDINGSBANI was named after Helgi Hjörvardsson, and that his beloved Sigrún 'was a Valkyrie, who rode across the sea and sky; she was Sváva reborn'. A somewhat longer prose passage at the end of *Helgakvida Hundingsbana* II completes the cycle:

In olden days it was believed that people could be reborn, although now that is reckoned an old wives' tale. Helgi and Sigrun are said to have been reborn; he was called Helgi Haddingjaskadi, and she KÁRA Halfdansdóttir, as is told in the [now lost] *Káraljóð*, and she was a Valkyrie.

FLATEYJARBÓK tells a not dissimilar tale about Saint Olaf of Norway, who was supposed to have been named after an earlier king called Olaf Geirstadaálf ('Geirstad-elf'), at whose barrow the common folk are said to have sacrificed in times of famine. At the time of his naming, Saint Olaf was given the sword and ring of his namesake, apparently taken from his tomb, and people believed that Saint Olaf was his predecessor reincarnate, although the Christian king was quick to quash such suggestions:

Olaf rode with his bodyguard past the barrow of Olaf Geirstadaálf and one of his men, who is not named, said 'Tell me, lord . . . were you buried here?' The king answered: 'My soul has never had two bodies; and cannot, either now or on the day of resurrection. If I said anything different, there would be no common truth or honesty in me.' The man said: 'It is said that when you came to this place before, you said: "Here we were once, and here we pass now"'. 'I have never said such a thing,' said the king, 'and I shall never say it.' The king was greatly agitated, and struck spurs to his horse at once, and fled the place as quickly as he could.

B12, 30, 56, 60, 73, 85, 87, 90; C2, 17, 24, 33, 46; D237

Rerir

Son of SIGI, grandson of the god ODIN and father of the

Ridil

hero VÖLSUNG. According to the legendary VÖLSUNGA SAGA, Rerir and his wife were unable to have children until HLJÓD, the daughter of the giant HRÍMNIR and described as one of Odin's 'wish-maids', visits Rerir and gives him an apple of fertility. Völsung is conceived soon after, but before he can be born Rerir, off on a campaign to subdue his land, dies of sickness and intends 'to go to Odin'.

B25, 42, 65, 68, 79; C1, 6

Ridil

According to a prose passage in the eddic poem FÁFNISMÁL, the sword with which REGIN cuts out the heart of his brother, the dragon FÁFNIR. The legendary VÖLSUNGA SAGA, which clearly depends on *Fáfnismál*, has the hero SIGURD wielding Ridil instead.

B12, 30, 56, 73, 87, 90; C2, 17, 24, 33, 46

Ríg ('king')

According to the eddic poem RÍGSTHULA, the progenitor of the three social classes of men: slaves, freemen and nobles. The prose preface in one manuscript explicitly identifies Ríg with the god HEIMDALL, an association that some have seen strengthened by the description of both ÆSIR and men together as 'greater and lesser kinsmen of Heimdall'.

The name Ríg seems related to the Irish word for 'king' (*ri*; *rig* in oblique cases) and is but one of several features that can be paralleled in Irish sources. In general, one might compare the Irish term DÍAR, which also occurs in Norse.

B12, 30, 56, 73, 87, 90; C2, 17, 24, 33, 46; D373

Rígsthula ('the lay of Ríg')

An incomplete poem, found only in one manuscript of SNORRA EDDA and describing how the three classes of society (slaves, freemen and nobles) all descend from a single progenitor, a wanderer named RÍG. A prose preface identifies Ríg with the god HEIMDALL, an identification to some extent supported by the opening of the eddic poem VÖLUSPÁ, which describes both ÆSIR and men together as 'greater and lesser kinsmen of Heimdall' but which finds no echo in the poem itself, in which Ríg is simply described as a 'wise Ás'. According to *Rígsthula*, Ríg comes in his travels to the humble home of ÁI ('great grandfather') and Edda ('great grandmother'), and spends three nights sharing a bed and sleeping between the couple; Edda subsequently gives birth to a boy named Thræl ('slave'). Thræl marries a girl called (appropriately enough) Thír ('slave-girl'), and together they propagate the generation of slaves, all with suitably evocative names: Ambát ('serving-girl'), Arinnefja ('hook-

nose'), Digraldi ('fatso'), Drött ('backward'), Drumb ('stumpy'), Drumba ('stumpy'), Eikintjasna ('oaken-pegged'), Fjósnir ('byre-boy'), Fúlnir ('smelly'), Hösvir ('grizzled'), Hreim ('shriek'), Kefsir ('bedmate'), Kleggi ('horse-fly'), Klúr ('stomp'), Kumba ('dumpy'), Leggjaldi ('thick-limbed'), LÚT ('stooped'), Ökkvinkálfa ('stocky-calves'), Tötrughypja ('tatty-coat'), Trönubeina ('crane-legs') and Ysja ('screamer'). The same thing happens when Ríg stays with a second couple in his travels, Afi ('grandfather') and Amma ('grandmother'), to whom is born KARL ('freeman'), who weds Snør ('daughter-in-law'), from whom are bred the class of freemen, with their rather more up-market names: Boddi ('homeowner'), Bóndi ('farmer'), Brattskegg ('trimmed beard'), Breid ('stout fellow'), Brúd ('bride'), Búi ('landowner'), Bundinskeggi ('neat beard'), Dreng ('splendid fellow'), Feima ('shy maid'), Fljód ('mistress'), Hal ('fine fellow'), Höld ('good fellow'), Ristil ('sharp maid'), Segg ('chap'), Smid ('smith'), Snót ('girl'), Sprakki ('miss'), Sprund ('lady'), Svanni ('lass'), Svarri ('damsel'), Thegn ('thegn') and Víf ('wife'). Still Ríg continues his travels and enjoys the generous hospitality of Fadir ('father') and Módir ('mother'), to whom is born Jarl ('noble'). In the fullness of time, Jarl marries Erna ('brisk'), the daughter of Hersir ('lord'), and together they breed fine and noble sons, with lofty names reflecting their station: Adal ('noble'), Arfi ('heir'), Barn ('child'), Bur ('born'), Jód ('offspring'), Kund ('child'), Mög ('kinsman'), Nid ('kin'), Nidjung ('kinsman'), Son ('son'), Svein ('boy') and the youngest son, Konung ('young kin', 'king'). As the incomplete poem ends rather abruptly, Ríg returns to teach Jarl's youngest son, Konung, how to be a king (Old Norse *konungr*).

It seems likely that *Rígsthula* reflects a degree of Irish influence at some level, since Ríg's very name seems connected with the Old Irish word for 'king', *rí* (in oblique cases *rig*), and the custom of allowing important visitors the right to sleep with the woman of the house is attested in Irish literature.

B12, 30, 56, 73, 87, 90; C2, 17, 24, 33, 46; D114, 123, 245, 373, 423, 498, 520, 617, 625

Rind

The mother of VÁLI, seduced by the god ODIN, according to numerous poetic periphrases or KENNINGS in skaldic verse, the eddic poem BALDRS DRAUMAR and the thirteenth-century Icelander SNORRI STURLUSON, who, presumably because of her relationship with both Odin and Váli, counts her among the ÆSIR. It seems likely that she was, in fact, a giantess. According to a skaldic verse by the tenth-century poet KORMÁK

ÖGMUNDARSON, Odin used magic to entrap her, and the same is true in the much expanded version of the tale given by the early thirteenth-century Danish historian SAXO GRAMMATICUS, who describes all the various shapes and disguises assumed by Odin in his attempted seduction, before, appearing in the guise of a medicine-woman, he is finally able to force her.

B12, 14, 23, 24, 28, 30, 35, 39, 40, 45, 50, 56, 59, 62, 64, 73, 75, 83, 87, 90; C2, 5, 7–9, 13, 16–18, 24, 33, 46, 48

ring-oath *see* OATHS.

Ristil *see* RÍGSTHULA.

Röskva ('mature')

The serving-maid of the god THOR, daughter of an un-named peasant and sister of THJÁLFI, according to both the thirteenth-century Icelander SNORRI STURLUSON and his source, the late tenth-century skaldic poem THÓRSDRÁPA by EILÍF GODRÚNARSON. She accompanies her brother, together with the gods THOR and LOKI, on the trip to the hall of the cunning giant, ÚTGARDALOKI.

B24, 28. 35. 39, 40, 45, 50, 62, 83, 87; C5, 9, 16, 48

Róta *see* VALKYRIES.

runes

The archaic letters of the Germanic peoples, in part derived from the Roman alphabet, in which curved and horizontal lines are largely avoided, perhaps to facilitate carving on wood. Around 6,000 inscriptions are extant, of which more than half derive from Sweden, 1,600 from Norway and 800 from Denmark. The runic alphabet is called the *fuþark* or FUTHARK after its first six letters, and it evolved considerably over the centuries and in different geographical areas. The earliest Germanic *futhark*, of twenty-four runes, is found in some 350 inscriptions dating from around the mid-second to mid-eighth centuries, of which more than half derive from inscribed BRACTEATES. A variant version, incorporating additional characters, was widely used in Anglo-Saxon England, while in the Scandinavian homelands a much-simplified, so-called younger *futhark* of only sixteen characters prevailed widely from the eighth to the eleventh centuries, by which time a more sophisticated, so-called medieval *futhark* had evolved. Alongside the younger *futhark*, moreover, there had developed in Scandinavia a variant version, in which several of the characters were carved with simplified or truncated forms. The superficially attractive suggestion that such 'short-twig' runes, which were inevitably quicker to carve, acted as a kind of shorthand for the mercantile classes is not, unfortu-

runes *Detail from an Anglo-Saxon manuscript, St John's College, Oxford, MS 17, which offers a table of differing forms and names of runes alongside other arcane lore.*

nately, sustained by the extant evidence. It is possible that the 'short-twig' runes were simply variants on the more usual pattern.

From the earliest runic inscriptions, it is clear that orthographic conventions were flexible with regard to the direction of writing, the orientation of individual runes and the possibility of merging consecutive runes – if both required a vertical stroke, for example, they might share the same stave (and are then usually described as 'bind runes'), or a single rune is often inscribed for two, even where the two required runes belong to different words (because words are regularly run together in runic inscriptions). Later evidence indicates that each rune had its own meaningful name, and could be used as shorthand for the word in question. Manuscript sources, including a variety of so-called rune-poems in various languages, spell out the significance of each character in detail.

The notion that the god ODIN invented runes is alluded to in several sources, and the eddic poem HÁVAMÁL contains an extremely vivid account of how the knowledge was gained through Odin's pained SAC-RIFICE of himself to himself, hanging from a mighty tree (presumably YGGDRASIL) and pierced by a fearsome spear (presumably GUNGNIR). Two Old English texts likewise attribute the invention of letters to *Mercurius se gigant* ('Mercury the giant'), while both ÆLFRIC and WULFSTAN preserve the traditional identification with the Roman MERCURIUS and Odin. Despite this connection, however, there is little written evidence to suggest that in Anglo-Saxon England there was any necessary connection between runes and MAGIC, as is often asserted. A passing allusion by Ælfric and a doubtful reference by BEDE (and his Old English trans-lator), both referring to the same episode, are all that survive from the post-conversion period. By contrast, there is a much more secure link to be made from the Norse material, especially with regard to the (much later) literary evidence. Both GRETTIS SAGA and EGILS SAGA (to cite but two examples) allude in almost casual terms to a tradition of runic magic. In the first case, a witch carves runes reddened in her own blood to bring Grettir to his doom, while in the second, Egil himself carves runes, which he reddens in his own blood, on a suspicious horn of ale, which turns out to be poisoned and so shatters. Later in the same saga Egil visits a farm where the daughter of the household is sick and, after discovering the cause of the illness to be some badly carved runes intended to make the girl fall in love with the carver, carves further runes to cure her. Both the POETIC EDDA and SNORRA EDDA likewise contain refer-ences to the magical power of runes. In particular, both

Hávamál and SIGRDRÍFUMÁL contain lengthy passages devoted to the notion.

The archaeological evidence with regard to the magi-cal significance (or otherwise) of runic inscriptions is less easy to assess. There can be a tendency among commentators simply to label as 'magical' any in-scription not readily understood. Certainly, however, a number of particular words or phrases with an appar-ently mystical significance – ALU, for example – appear often in the runic record, as do seemingly nonsensical or repetitive strings of characters with no evident prac-tical purpose. Likewise, the carving of individual runes on weapons or in places where they could not readily be seen, such as on the underside of grave-markers, seems to attest to some magical significance. The later literary evidence for magical practices involving runes is often used to support the notion of mystical significance in individual cases, but it is quite clear that in the vast majority of surviving inscriptions the runes have been carved with a determinedly mundane and practical purpose.

A20, 88; B4, 18, 19, 29, 36, 46, 49, 54, 57, 66, 89; D48, 151, 161, 241, 326, 348, 386–8, 411, 445–7, 453, 577

Rungnir

According to a poetic periphrasis or KENNING in a verse of the ninth-century poet BRAGI BODDASON INN GAMLI cited by the thirteenth-century Icelander SNORRI STURLUSON, a giant, most likely the same as HRUNGNIR, whom the god THOR slew.

B24, 28, 35, 40, 50; C5, 9, 48

Rym ('roaring')

(1) According to the name-lists or THULUR, the name of a troll-wife or giantess. (2) Perhaps surprisingly, giv-en his deep antagonism to giants, an alternative name for the god THOR.

D396

S

sacral kingship

From the earliest period it would appear that Germanic rulers attempted to legitimize their power by tracing it back to the gods, and the extant genealogies of many of the royal houses stretch back to a handful of divine figures such as the gods ODIN (or, in Anglo-Saxon

England, WODEN) and FREY. More striking are those cases where the life and livelihood of the king were held to affect the fertility of his land. The historian Ammianus Marcellinus describes how the fourth-century Burgundians deposed a king after a series of failed harvests, while the thirteenth-century Icelander

SNORRI STURLUSON, building on poetic descriptions in YNGLINGATAL (composed around the turn of the tenth century by THJÓDÓLF OF HVÍN), describes in his YNGLINGA SAGA how a series of Swedish kings was sacrificed in the interests of a fertile land. The death of one such, DÓMALDI, is described as follows:

> Dómaldi took up his inheritance from his father, Vísbur, and ruled the country. During his period there was a famine and hunger in Sweden. Then the Swedes made preparations for a mighty sacrifice at Uppsala. The first autumn they sacrificed oxen, but the crops did not improve. The second autumn they started sacrificing people, but the harvest was as bad as before or worse. When the third autumn arrived, a large number of Swedes gathered at Uppsala, where the sacrifice was to be held. Then the chieftains held their meeting, and came to an agreement that the problem must have arisen from Dómaldi, their king, and also that they should sacrifice him for better crops by attacking him, killing him and reddening the altars with his blood. As Thjódólf says:

> 'It happened before,
> that sword bearers
> reddened the earth
> with their lord,
> and the land's war-band
> made weapons bloody
> in Dómaldi, bereft of life,
> when, eager for crops,
> the race of Swedes,
> were forced to slaughter
> the enemy of the Jutes.'

Other aspects of the symbolic significance of Scandinavian kingship are evident in, for example, several of the poems of the tenth-century Norwegian poet EYVIND FINNSSON SKÁLDASPILLIR, who describes the relationship between King Hákon the Good (c.920–60) and his land as a kind of symbolic marriage, praising his lord, 'under whose arms Val-Týr's bride (ODIN's bride; JÖRD, the earth), all the way east to the dwelling of the Agderman, now lies'. When Hákon is killed in battle by the sons of Eirík Bloodaxe, who take over the country, Eyvind bewails how the land suffers at the hands of Eirík's sons, who, having been baptized in England, have destroyed a number of pagan temples:

> It snows in midsummer
> on the mistress of Svölnir [Odin, whose mistress is Jörd, the earth];
> like the Lapps we tie up indoors
> the gnawing-hind of buds [sheep or goats].

In this and verses like it, Eyvind implicitly draws a link between the prosperity of the land and the relationship of its ruler with the gods, which reflects in the third quarter of the tenth century a Germanic belief traceable through the words of Ammianus Marcellinus back to the fourth.

B1; C22, 23; D337, 357, 363, 559, 561

sacrifice

Sacrifices among Germanic peoples are recorded from the earliest periods and do not always imply the shedding of blood. The sinking of weapons in bogs is attested by the first-century Roman historian TACITUS. Tacitus also speaks of human sacrifice as reserved for Mercury, the chief god of the Germanic tribes, where other gods are offered animals:

> Of the gods, they worship Mercury in particular, and on certain days they even reckon it legitimate to sacrifice human victims to him; they placate Hercules and Mars with permitted animals. Some of the Suebi even sacrifice to Isis; the reason and origin of this foreign worship I have not wholly discovered, except that the very emblem, which takes the form of a Liburnian galley, demonstrates that the custom has been imported.

The precise identities of the gods named can only be guessed at: 'Hercules' may well represent the god THOR, with the club of the monster-slaying Hercules being equated with the hammer of the giant-killer; 'Mars', the Roman god of war, may represent the god TÝR, at least to judge from the identity of Germanic-derived names for the days of the week with those from a Roman background (one might compare English 'Tuesday' with French mardi); Isis could represent either the goddess FRIGG or FREYJA, although neither of the latter is particularly associated with a boat. Mercury is elsewhere identified with the god ODIN (and again one might compare English 'Wednesday' with French mercredi), and in the eddic poem HÁVAMÁL Odin himself appears to confirm the notion of human sacrifice to Odin, in his account of his acquisition of the RUNES. The same notion is implicit in the well-known description of the sacrifice of King VÍKAR carried out by the legendary figure of STARKAD in GAUTREKS SAGA. When King Víkar's army is becalmed, it learns through DIVINATION that Odin expects a human sacrifice, the victim to be determined by lot. When the lot falls to King Víkar himself, his counsellors decide to stage a mock sacrifice, to be presided over by Starkad:

> Close by there was a pine tree, and next to it a large tree trunk; the pine tree had a thin branch not far from the ground, that stretched up into the leaves. Just then the servants were making breakfast; a calf had been killed,

and its innards cleaned out. Starkad asked for its guts, climbed up the tree, bent down the thin branch, and tied the calf's guts to it. 'Your gallows are ready for you now, sire,' he said to King Víkar, 'and it doesn't seem too dangerous. Come here, and I'll place the noose around your neck.' 'As long as that contraption isn't more dangerous than it looks,' said the king, 'it won't cause me much harm. But if it turns out not to be the case, then it's all in the hands of fate.' So he mounted up onto the tree stump. Starkad put the noose around his neck and climbed down. Then he stabbed the king with a reed stalk, saying: 'Now I give you to Odin.' Then Starkad let go of the branch: the reed stalk turned into a spear and pierced the king, the tree stump slipped from under his feet, the calf's guts turned into a strong withy, the branch sprang upwards with the king into the leaves, and he died there. Ever since, the place has been called Víkarshólm ['Víkar's island'].

A quite different form of sacrifice to Odin may lie behind the extraordinary account of the family cliff or ÆTTERNISSTAPI, from which family members leap in dedicating themselves to the god, described earlier in *Gautreks saga*. In YNGLINGA SAGA the thirteenth-century Icelander SNORRI STURLUSON offers a systematic account of the appropriate times for sacrifice and implies that the legislation surrounding sacrifice had been laid down by Odin himself:

> On the first day of winter there should be a blood-sacrifice for a good year, and in midwinter for a good crop, and the third sacrifice should be on the first day of summer, for victory in war.

Similar notions of the possibility of sacrificing the king for the fertility of the land are closely linked to the concept of sacral kingship. The fifth-century bishop SIDONIUS APOLLINARIS alludes to the practice among continental Saxons of sacrificing as many as one in ten prisoners when they return from a raiding expedition, presumably to ensure a fair wind home. In medieval Scandinavia other named sacrifices (albeit ones about which detailed knowledge is rather limited) include one for elves (ÁLFABLÓT) and another for the supernatural female figures known as DÍSIR (DÍSABLÓT).

B2, 12, 30, 56, 69, 73, 87, 90; C2, 17, 24, 29, 33, 35, 38, 46; D158, 159, 419, 495, 505, 533, 559–61

Sæg *see* MÁNI.

Sæhrímnir ('sooty sea-beast')
The 'best of meats', which, according to the eddic

poem GRÍMNISMÁL, is cooked by the mythical chef ANDHRÍMNIR in the pot ELDHRÍMNIR. The thirteenth-century Icelander SNORRI STURLUSON interprets the verse, making Sæhrímnir a boar that is cooked and consumed every night in the mighty hall of VALHALL by the hungry EINHERJAR, but, like the equally self-rejuvenating goats of the god THOR, appears whole the next day to be eaten again. Snorri makes his assertion despite the fact that the very verse from *Grímnismál* that he cites in support says plainly: 'but there are few who know the food of the Einherjar.'

B12, 14, 23, 24, 28, 30, 35, 40, 50, 56, 59, 73, 87, 90; C2, 5, 9, 17, 24, 33, 46, 48

Sæmundar Edda *see* POETIC EDDA.

Særeid ('sea-riding')
According to the prose preface to the eddic poem HELGAKVIDA HJÖRVARDSSONAR, the second wife of the mighty hero HJÖRVARD and the mother of the legendary warrior HUMLUNG.

B12, 30, 56, 73, 87, 90; C2, 17, 24, 33, 46

Sævarstad ('sea-stead')
The place where, according to the eddic poem VÖLUNDARKVIDA, the wicked King NÍDUD imprisons the maimed and legendary smith VÖLUND. It is to Sævarstad that Völund lures Nídud's young sons and his daughter BÖDVILD in order to wreak his terrible revenge.

B12, 30, 31, 56, 73, 87, 90; C2, 17, 24, 33, 46

Sága ('seeress'?)
According to the thirteenth-century Icelander SNORRI STURLUSON, one of the goddesses or ÁSYNJUR, although little further information is offered. Snorri simply says that 'she lives at SÖKKVABEKK, and that is a big place'. In so doing, Snorri is simply elaborating on a brief allusion to Sága in the eddic poem GRÍMNISMÁL, where it says that she drinks in Sökkvabekk alongside the god ODIN.

B12, 14, 23, 24, 28, 30, 35, 40, 50, 56, 59, 73, 87, 90; C2, 5, 9, 17, 24, 33, 46, 48

Salgófnir
According to the eddic poem HELGAKVIDA HUNDINGSBANA II, a cock who rouses warriors from sleep, presumably including those in the mythical hall of VALHALL. As the dead hero HELGI SIGMUNDARSON HUNDINGSBANI says to his beloved, the Valkyrie SIGRÚN:

> 'It's time for me to ride the reddened roads,
> let my pale charger tread the paths of flight;

I must pass west of the rainbow-bridge
before Salgófnir wakes the victory-host.'

B12, 30, 56, 73, 87, 90; C2, 17, 24, 33, 46

Saxi ('the Saxon')

According to the eddic poem GUDRÚNARKVIDA III, the 'southerners' king', called on by the tragic heroine GUDRÚN to bless the boiling cauldron before she submits herself to ordeal after being accused of adultery.

B12, 30, 56, 73, 87, 90; C2, 17, 24, 33, 46

Saxnôt

A divine figure who appears in a ninth-century Old Saxon baptismal pledge alongside figures usually identified with the gods THOR and ODIN. The person taking the pledge was expected to say the following:

> I renounce all the works and words of devil, Thunær and WODEN and Saxnôt, and all those demons who are their companions.

Various forms of the name S(e)axn(e)(a)t are found in royal genealogies from Anglo-Saxon England, and one Seaxnet is given as the progenitor of the line of the East Saxon King Offa, who abdicated in 709.

D424

Saxo Grammaticus

Author of the compendious *Gesta Danorum* ('Deeds of the Danes'), a history divided into some sixteen books of unequal length, and most likely composed at some point in the period 1216 to 1223. These sixteen books can themselves be divided into four groups of four books each, describing the Danes up to the birth of Christ (books 1–4), up to the conversion (books 5–8), up to the promotion of Lund as metropolitan see (books 9–12), and up to recent history (books 13–16, ending in 1187). Book 1–9 in particular are a veritable treasure-trove of legendary and mythological lore, presented as history.

B64; C7, 8, 13; D43, 174, 175, 298, 325, 344, 483, 537

Sceaf (Old English: 'sheaf')

One of the ancestors of the Anglo-Saxon royal house of Wessex, according to a genealogy of Æthelwulf, the father of King Alfred the Great, which is given in the Anglo-Saxon Chronicle for 855. As such, Sceaf is listed as one of the ancestors of WODEN and also appears in the mythical genealogy of the kings of Denmark offered by the Anglo-Saxon poem BEOWULF, which describes how Sceaf's son SCYLD appeared mysteriously from across the sea as a child. In the tenth-century *Chronicon*

of Æthelweard, it is Sceaf himself who appears in this way; as Æthelweard says:

> And this Sceaf arrived on a small boat at the island in the ocean called Skåney, surrounded by weapons; he was a very young child, unknown to the inhabitants of that land, but he was accepted by them, and they kept him as one of their own with careful attention, and afterwards they chose him as king. From his line King Æthelwulf descends.

B44; C4; D244

Scyld (Old English: 'shield')

In the Anglo-Saxon poem BEOWULF, the son of SCEAF, and mythical ancestor of the Danish royal line, who appears mysteriously as a child from across the sea. In Norse sources one SKJÖLD appears as the eponymous ancestor of the Skjoldung dynasty in Denmark, while Scyld is also found in the royal genealogies of a number of Anglo-Saxon lines, most notably that of Æthelwulf, the father of Alfred the Great, which is given in the Anglo-Saxon Chronicle for 855; here, however, Scyld (who appears as Sceldwea) is not given as the son of Sceaf.

B44; C4; D27, 177, 244

S(e)axn(e)(a)t *see* SAXNÔT.

Segg *see* RÍGSTHULA.

seid ('sorcery', 'magic')

A particular form of magic especially associated with the god ODIN, according to the description offered by the thirteenth-century Icelander SNORRI STURLUSON:

> Odin governed and practised that art which is most powerful of all, called *seid*, and through it he knew the fate of men and future pitfalls, as well as how to bring death on someone, or bring bad luck or cause illness, and how to deprive someone of power and wisdom, and give it to someone else. But such dishonour was associated with this skill that men believed that they could not practise it without dishonour, and so they taught this art to the priestesses.

A skaldic verse from the mid-tenth century by the Icelandic poet KORMÁK ÖGMUNDARSON, cited by Snorri, blankly asserts of Odin's seduction of the giantess, RIND, that 'Odin won Rind by *seid*'. Elsewhere, however, Snorri claims that it was FREYJA who was responsible for bringing *seid* from the VANIR to the ÆSIR, and the practice of *seid*, with the exception of Odin, seems particularly restricted to women. Of the mysterious female figure of GULLVEIG or Heid, who

Sekin

may be Freyja in another form, and whose appearance among the Æsir seems to sow such discord, the eddic poem VÖLUSPÁ says simply:

> They called her Heid, when she came to the house,
> a sibylline witch, who knew the skill of wands,
> she practised *seid* where she could, practised *seid* in a trance;
> she was always a delight to wicked women.

In the Icelandic sagas, particularly the FORNAL-DARSÖGUR, *seid* is clearly the preserve of witches, who can perform transformations and prophecies through its agency, for example the transformation of SIGNÝ described in the legendary VÖLSUNGA SAGA.

B25, 39, 42, 45, 62, 65, 68, 75, 79, 83, 87; C1, 6, 16, 18; D564

Sekin *see* HVERGELMIR.

Semnones

According to the first-century Roman historian TACITUS, the Semnones are the oldest tribe of the Suebi, and they are responsible for a great festival of human sacrifice held in a sacred grove that could only be approached by those in fetters. Some connection has been suggested with the place Fjöturlund ('fetter-grove') mentioned in the eddic poem HELGAKVIDA HUNDINGSBANA I.

B2, 12, 30, 56, 73, 87, 90; C2, 17, 24, 29, 33, 46; D

senna *see* FLYTING.

Sessrumnir ('seat-room')

According to the thirteenth-century Icelander SNORRI STURLUSON, the dwelling of the fertility-goddess FREYJA, which he describes as 'large and fair'. Elsewhere, Sessrumnir appears, equally without elaboration (but equally plausibly), among a list of ship-names.

B24, 28, 35, 40, 50; C5, 9, 48

shamanism

The practice of inducing a ritual frenzy, often for the purposes of DIVINATION, communing with the dead or acquiring mantic wisdom. A number of aspects of the cults and myths surrounding the god ODIN in particular have been related to the practice of attested shamans in the north, whether through ritual hanging or piercing (as seems to be described in the eddic poem HÁVAMÁL, with respect to Odin's discovery of the runes) or a fire-ordeal (as in Odin's torture between fires in GEIRRÖD's hall, as outlined in the eddic poem GRÍMNISMÁL). Odin's general association with frenzy is enshrined in the etymology of his name, as well as in

his close links with BERSERKS and their ilk, but a more specific connection with the practices elsewhere associated with shamanism remains to be demonstrated to the satisfaction of all commentators.

B12, 30, 56, 73, 87, 90; C2, 17, 24, 33, 46; D54, 134, 158–60, 190

ship burial *see* BOAT BURIAL.

Sibyl

According to the EUHEMERIZED account of the gods offered by the thirteenth-century Icelander SNORRI STURLUSON, the wife of the legendary TROR; given that Tror is clearly to be equated with the god THOR, Sibyl is presumably equivalent to SIF.

B24, 28, 35, 40, 50; C5, 9, 48

Síd *see* HVERGELMIR.

Sidonius Apollinaris

A fifth-century bishop of Clermont, several of whose surviving works record his impressions of the neighbouring pagan Germanic tribes. For example, one of his letters seems to indicate that at least part of the Saxons' confidence in their sea-faring skill lay in a practice of human SACRIFICE:

> Moreover, when the Saxons set sail from the continent and are about to drag their firmly secured anchors from a hostile coast, it is their practice on the voyage home to sacrifice every tenth prisoner to a watery grave, casting lots in absolute fairness among the doomed in pursuit of this deplorable condemnation to death. The custom is all the more heinous for its being prompted by plain superstition; these people are bound by vows that have to be discharged in victims, and so they reckon it a religious duty to carry out their terrible killing: what is a foul sacrilege is, according to them, an absolving sacrifice.

D419, 495, 533

Sif ('relation')

Mother of the archer-god ULL and (apparently later) wife of the god THOR and mother of THRÚD. Despite her evident closeness to the gods, she is a notable omission from the lists of goddesses or ÁSYNJUR given by the thirteenth-century Icelander SNORRI STURLUSON. Sif appears in numerous poetic periphrases or KENNINGS, usually with reference to either Thor or Ull, or in the form 'Sif's hair', evidently a kenning for gold. Snorri alone explains the kenning, at first glance little more than a compliment to a famous beauty, in literal terms, relating a tale of the mischief of LOKI, and the ingenuity of the BLACK ELVES:

Loki Laufeyarson, out of sheer malice, once cut off all of Sif's hair, and when Thor heard of it, he grabbed Loki and was about to break every bone in his body until he promised to have the black elves make a head of hair for Sif from gold, one that would grow like real hair.

Snorri adds that in the course of Loki's dealing with the black elves other gifts are made for the ÆSIR, including the spear GUNGNIR, the ship SKÍDBLADNIR, the ring DRAUPNIR, the boar GULLINBORSTI and, most valuable of all, the hammer MJÖLLNIR. The emotionally charged triangle of Sif, Loki and Thor is all the more evident in the eddic poem LOKASENNA, when Sif tries to placate Loki in the midst of his malicious wrangling:

Then Sif approached, offered Loki mead from a crystal cup, and said:
'Hail now, Loki, accept this crystal cup,
full of antique mead.
Better find one woman, among the Æsir's sons,
who is without fault.'

He accepted the horn and drank it down:
'You'd be the one, if only you were
wary and cautious with men;
but I know someone, it seems to me,
who made you unfaithful to Thor,
and that one was crafty-wise Loki.'

B12, 14, 23, 24, 28, 30, 35, 40, 50, 56, 59, 73, 87, 90; C2, 5, 9, 17, 24, 33, 46, 48

Sigar

A fairly common name given to an uncertain number of bit-part players in the myths and legends of the north. It is difficult to discern from the scattered allusions quite how many characters may be involved. According to the eddic poem HELGAKVIDIA HJÖRVARDSSONAR, HELGI HJÖRVARDSSON, on the point of death, sends Sigar to visit his beloved, the Valkyrie SVÁVA, with the bad news:

Helgi sent Sigar to ride
after EYLIMI's only daughter,
to tell her quickly to come prepared
if she wished to find her lord alive.

[Sigar said:]
'Helgi has sent me here,
to speak to you, Sváva, yourself,
the prince said he would see you
before the noble one loses his life.'

[Sváva said:]
'What has happened to Helgi, Hjörvard's son?
I am called to heavy sorrows;
if the sea took him, or a sword cut him,
I shall make someone pay.'

[Sigar said:]
'He fell this morning at FREKASTEIN,
the best prince under the sun.
Álf must win the whole victory;
would that this time never was!'

It is possible that the Sigar who appears briefly in the eddic poem HELGAKVIDA HUNDINGSBANA II as the uncle of the beautiful SIGRÚN, who is said to be Sváva reborn, is the same figure, although this seems incapable of definite proof. The eddic poem GUDRÚNARKVIDA II also mentions a character named Sigar, whose battle against SIGGEIR at Fjón was apparently the subject of an embroidery made by the tragic heroine GUDRÚN when she was staying with THÓRA. The legendary VÖLSUNGA SAGA, certainly drawing on *Gudrúnarkvida* II, mentions the same notion but also has Gudrún name Sigar as the character who humiliated the warriors Haki and HAGBARD HÁMUNDARSON, the sons of HÁMUND, by snatching one of their sisters and burning another in her house, after the imperious heroine BRYNHILD has named the brothers as the most outstanding of kings.

B12, 25, 30, 42, 56, 65, 68, 73, 79, 87, 90; C1 – 3, 6, 17, 24, 33, 46

Sigemund

A dragon-slayer, celebrated briefly in the Old English poem BEOWULF and evidently to be identified with the Scandinavian hero SIGMUND. The account of Sigemund's dragon-slaying is inserted into a description of the elaborate praise showered by an individual poet who 'remembered a great multitude of ancient tales' on Beowulf after he has killed Grendel:

[The poet] told almost everything
that he had heard tell of Sigemund's
glorious deeds, many an unfamiliar thing:
the struggles and wide wanderings of the son of Wæls;
feuds and outrages, things of which the sons of men
scarcely knew, except for his companion, Fitela,
when he wanted to tell something,
an uncle to his nephew, since they were always,
in every encounter, close companions;
they had silenced with swords large number
of the race of giants. To Sigemund there accrued
after his death-day, no little glory,
once the war-hard one killed the serpent,
the guardian of the hoard; he alone,
under the grey rock, the prince's child,
dared the perilous deed: Fitela was not with him;
yet it was granted to him that the sword penetrated
the wondrous serpent, so that it stuck in the wall,
the noble iron; the dragon perished in death.
The awesome one had accomplished through his might
that he could enjoy the ring-hoard

Siggeir

on his own terms; he loaded up the sea-vessel,
bore into the bosom of the ship bright ornaments,
the son of Wæls; the hot serpent melted.

A number of the figures mentioned here have direct parallels in the Scandinavian tradition: Fitela, named here as Sigemund's nephew, can be identified with SINFJÖTLI, who is both Sigmund's nephew and his son, while Wæls, whom the Old English describes as Sigemund's father, is surely the same figure as the Scandinavian VÖLSUNG. The comparison between Sigemund and Beowulf effectively foreshadows Beowulf's own fatal encounter with a dragon towards the end of the poem.

B44; C4; D46, 285, 571

Siggeir

(1) According to the fullest account, found in the legendary VÖLSUNGA SAGA, the king of Gautland, who marries the reluctant SIGNÝ. At their wedding-feast the mighty hero SIGMUND manages to draw the sword embedded in the great tree BARNSTOKK, after Siggeir himself has failed. When Sigmund refuses to sell the sword to Siggeir at any price, Siggeir plots revenge. He invites Sigmund's father, VÖLSUNG, and his ten sons to a feast, which they attend against the advice of Signý, where he attacks and kills Völsung and all his men, and captures the ten brothers. At the encouragement of Signý, he has them all put in stocks in the woods to be devoured by a she-wolf, but Signý contrives the escape of the youngest, Sigmund, who makes himself an underground lair in the forest. Signý sends Sigmund two of hers sons by Siggeir, one after the other, and when each in turn fails a test of valour set by Sigmund, Signý tells him to kill them; he is happy to oblige. Later, when Sigmund and Signý have an incestuous child of their own, SINFJÖTLI, he too is brought up to help Sigmund and his sister revenge themselves on Siggeir. First, Sinfjötli slaughters two (more?) of Siggeir's sons, before he and Sigmund are captured by Siggeir and entombed in a great mound of rock and turf to die. Fortunately, Signý has managed to smuggle in Sigmund's sword, and together they quite literally saw through the rocks with the sword and escape, burning Siggeir to death in his own hall.

(2) The eddic poem GUDRÚNARKVIDA II mentions a character named Siggeirr, whose battle against SIGAR (Sigarr) at Fjón was apparently the subject of an embroidery made by the tragic heroine GUDRÚN when she was staying with THÓRA, a notion that is also echoed in *Völsunga saga*.

B12, 25, 30, 42, 56, 65, 68, 73, 79, 87, 90; C1–3, 6, 17, 24, 33, 46

Sighvat Thórdarson

An Icelandic poet, born around the turn of the eleventh century and author of over 160 extant skaldic stanzas and half-stanzas. Closely allied to Saint Olaf, he was not present at the death of his lord at the Battle of Stiklestad in 1030, because he was on a pilgrimage to Rome. Presumably because of his Christian patron and standpoint, Sighvat in general avoids the mythological poetic periphrases or KENNINGS that were the stock in trade of other Norse poets, but provides in the course of one of his longer verse-sequences, *Austfararvísur*, an account of travelling through west Gautland and being refused lodging because a particular SACRIFICE to the elves (ÁLFABLÓT) was taking place.

B39, 45, 62, 83, 87; C16; D166

Sigi

According to both the thirteenth-century Icelander SNORRI STURLUSON and the legendary VÖLSUNGA SAGA, a son of the god ODIN and father of RERIR. Sigi can, therefore, be regarded as the progenitor of the doomed dynasty of VÖLSUNGS.

B24, 25, 28, 35, 40, 42, 50, 65, 68, 79; C1, 5, 6, 9, 48

Sigmund

Son of VÖLSUNG, brother (and lover) of SIGNÝ, father of the great heroes SIGURD, HELGI SIGMUNDARSON HUNDINGSBANI, HÁMUND and SINFJÖTLI, and a leading figure in the tragic events of the VÖLSUNG-cycle. The figure named SIGEMUND in the Old English poem BEOWULF is clearly the same character, although there he is credited with the kind of dragon-slaying usually associated in the Scandinavian sources with his son. The fullest account of his life is given in the legendary VÖLSUNGA SAGA, which describes how as a young man he drew the sword embedded in the great tree BARNSTOKK, so earning the enmity of SIGGEIR, who has married Signý, Sigmund's sister, against her will. When Sigmund, together with his nine brothers, plans to accompany their father Völsung on a trip to visit Siggeir, Signý, rather in the manner of the tragic heroine GUDRÚN, attempts to warn her father and brothers away, but, again like Gudrún, her solicitude only strengthens their resolve. Völsung is duly killed, and his sons taken captive and submitted to a particularly terrible form of death:

A mighty tree-trunk was brought and made into stocks for the feet of the ten brother at a certain place in the forest; they sat there throughout the day until night. Then at midnight an ancient she-wolf approached them from the forest as they sat in the stocks: she was both huge and grim. She bit one of the brothers to death, and then swallowed him all up; then she went away. In the morning Signý sent her most faithful servant to her brothers to find out what had happened. When he returned, he told her that one of them was dead, and she thought it would be awful if they all went the same way, but she was unable to help them. What happened next can be swiftly said: for nine nights in succession the same she-wolf approached at midnight, and every time killed and ate one of the brothers, until all except Sigmund were dead. But before the tenth night Signý sent her faithful servant to her brother Sigmund, gave him some honey, and told him to smear it on Sigmund's face, and put some in his mouth. Her servant did as he was told and came home. The she-wolf came in the night as before, intending to bite Sigmund to death, as she had his brothers; but then she detected the smell of the honey that had been smeared on him. She licked him all over his face and put her tongue in his mouth; he stayed calm, and bit into the she-wolf's tongue. She wrenched back, and tugged hard, forcing her feet against the tree trunk so that it split. But Sigmund kept so tight a grip that the she-wolf's tongue was ripped out by the roots, and that was the death of her; some say that the she-wolf was Siggeir's mother, who had taken on the shape through witchcraft and magic.

Sigmund's connection with wolves is strengthened still further when he and Sinfjötli, his son by an incestuous relationship with Signý, don wolf-skins and behave like WEREWOLVES, before revenging themselves upon Siggeir. Later, Sigmund marries BORGHILD, and together they have two sons, Helgi and Hámund, before Sigmund drives her out to die after she poisons Sinfjötli for killing her brother. Afterwards, Sigmund, now a venerable warrior, woos the beautiful HJÖRDÍS, the daughter of EYLIMI, and wins her in the opposition of the younger LYNGVI, the son of HUNDING. Lyngvi and his brothers collect together an army in response to the perceived threat, and kill in battle both Sigmund and Eylimi. But Hjördís is already pregnant by Sigmund, and bears a son, SIGURD, who goes on to avenge his father against all the sons of Hunding.

Sigmund is also found as one of the many names of ODIN.

B25, 42, 65, 68, 79; C1, 6; D46, 275, 285, 416, 571

Sigmund Sigurdarson

According to the legendary VÖLSUNGA SAGA, the son of the mighty hero SIGURD and his wife, the tragic heroine GUDRÚN. The imperious BRYNHILD, Sigurd's beloved, realizing that she has been betrayed, brings about Sigurd's death, then that of his three-year-old son, before joining them both on the funeral pyre.

B25, 42, 65, 68, 79; C1, 6

Signý

Daughter of VÖLSUNG, sister (and lover) of the great hero SIGMUND, mother of SINFJÖTLI and wife of SIGGEIR. She is extremely unwilling to be married off to Siggeir and, rightly, predicts a disastrous outcome. When Siggeir kills her father and nine of her brothers in battle, Signý manages to save the tenth brother, Sigmund, whom she hides in an underground lair in the forest. She sends two of her sons by Siggeir to their deaths at Sigmund's hands, and herself has an incestuous relationship with her brother, described in detail in the legendary VÖLSUNGA SAGA:

> It is now told that once while Signý was sitting in her chamber, a witch, very highly skilled in [the kind of magic called] SEID, approached her. Signý said to her: 'I want us two to swap shapes.' The witch said: 'Just as you wish,' and she used her tricks, so that they swapped shapes. Now, as Signý wished, the witch took Signý's place: she slept with the king that night, and he did not notice that it was not Signý beside him. Now, it is to be said of Signý that she went to her brother's underground lair, and asked him to give her shelter for the night, 'because I have lost my way in the woods, and I don't know where I am going'. He said that she could stay and that he would not turn away a lone woman, since she would not repay his fine hospitality by betraying him. She entered his lair, and they sat down to eat. He looked at her often and thought her a fine and lovely woman. And when they had eaten, he told her that he wanted the two of them to share a bed that night. She did not shrink from it, and he kept her beside him for three nights together. Then she went back home, met the witch, and asked that they swap shapes again; the witch did so.

The product of this union, Sinfjötli, grows up in the forest alongside Sigmund, who as both father and maternal uncle maintains an extraordinarily influential position, and together they avenge themselves on Siggeir, eventually burning him in his hall. Even then Signý plays a prominent, even heroic part, as she refuses her brother's offer to come out from the burning hall and be saved:

> [Sigmund] asked his sister to come out and receive great honour and much respect at his hands, since he wanted by so doing to cure her grief. She answered: 'Now you will see whether I have remembered how King Siggeir slew King Völsung. I had our children slain when I thought them too slow to avenge our father, and I came to you in the woods in the shape of a witch, and Sinfjötli is our son. That is why he has so much manly vigour: he was born of both a son and a daughter of King Völsung. I have tried in every way to bring about the killing of

Sigrdrífa

King Siggeir; I have spent so much effort on vengeance that I no longer wish to live. Now I shall die with King Siggeir willingly, though unwillingly I wed him.' Then she kissed her brother Sigmund and Sinfjötli, walked into the flames, and bade them farewell. She perished there alongside King Siggeir and all his men.

Similar examples of SUTTEE are certainly found in the written record, albeit rarely.

B25, 42, 65, 76, 79; C1, 6, 26

Sigrdrífa ('victory-urger')

A VALKYRIE, mentioned briefly in the eddic poems SIGRDRÍFUMÁL and FÁFNISMÁL, and evidently identified (even in *Sigrdrífumál* itself) with BRYNHILD.

B12, 25, 30, 42, 56, 65, 68, 73, 79, 87, 90; C1–3, 6, 17, 24, 33, 46; D11, 469, 470

Sigrdrífumál ('the lay of Sigurdrífa')

An eddic poem, interspersed with prose, found in the CODEX REGIUS immediately following FÁFNISMÁL and continuing the poetic account of the life of the mighty hero SIGURD. The end of the poem is lost, at the start of a gap in the manuscript usually known as 'the great lacuna', the basic contents of which have to be inferred from outside sources such as the legendary VÖLSUNGA SAGA. A prose introduction picks up the narrative at the point, detailed in *Fáfnismál*, where Sigurd, having eaten the dragon's heart, is able to understand the language of birds; they advise him to ride to HINDAFJALL, where he will find a sleeping warrior-maiden in a hall on a mountain, surrounded by flames. In *Fáfnismál*, the maiden is called Sigrdrífa, although the name, which literally means 'victory-urger', may simply be a description appropriate to any VALKYRIE; in other accounts of the legend BRYNHILD plays the same role. The prose introduction to *Sigrdrífumál* offers a slightly different picture and describes Sigurd riding to Hindafjall, from the top of which he sees a great light on another mountain, which turns out to be flames and a shield-wall, topped with a banner. Behind the shield-wall he sees a reclining figure, but (despite what is said in *Fáfnismál*), he does not realize that the figure is that of a woman until he removes her helmet. He tries to remove her mail-coat (an action that might well seem at the very least a little ungallant), but it is so skin-tight that he has to resort to cutting it off with his sword, GRAM. It is the removal of the mail-coat that apparently rouses the sleeping figure, at the commencement of the verse.

The sleeping woman wakes, asks who Sigurd is and salutes her surroundings. In an intervening piece of prose she identifies herself as the Valkyrie Sigrdrífa, and explains that the god ODIN had caused her to slumber as punishment for allowing his favourite to fall in battle. When he further proclaims that she will no longer be a Valkyrie but will have to marry, she says that she has vowed never to marry any man who knows what fear is. At this point Sigurd asks her to teach him the wisdom she has acquired. She offers him a drink to help him remember, before embarking on a versified exposition of RUNES, charms and advice that takes up the whole of the rest of the poem that survives.

B12, 25, 30, 42, 56, 65, 68, 73, 79, 87, 90; C1–3, 6, 17, 24, 33, 46; D422, 469, 470

Sigrlinn

According to the eddic poem HELGAKVIDA HJÖRVARDSSONAR, the daughter of SVÁFNIR, the fourth wife of the hero HJÖRVARD and the mother of the famed warrior HELGI HJÖRVARDSSON.

B12, 30, 51, 56, 73, 87, 90; C2, 17, 24, 33, 46

Sigrún

A Valkyrie, daughter of King HÖGNI, and wife of the great warrior HELGI SIGMUNDARSON HUNDINGSBANI. A prose passage in the eddic poem HELGAKVIDA HUNDINGSBANA II introduces her as follows:

> There was a king called Högni, his daughter was Sigrún; she was a Valkyrie, and rode across the sea and sky: she was SVÁVA reborn.

Although she figures briefly in the eddic poem *Helgakvida Hundingsbana* I, it is in *Helgakvida Hundingsbana* II that her sorry tale is most vividly recalled. She was betrothed to one HÖDBRODD, the son of GRANMAR, but was unwilling to wed him. When she tells Helgi of her predicament, he tries to save her by entering into a fateful battle at FREKASTEIN not only with Hödbrodd, but with Sigrún's father, Högni, and her two brothers, BRAGI and DAG. Although he wins the battle and kills Hödbrodd, Helgi is also responsible for the deaths of Högni and Bragi, and, as another prose passage has it:

> Helgi married Sigrún, and they had sons. Helgi did not grow old. Dag, son of Högni, made a SACRIFICE to ODIN for help in avenging his father. Odin loaned Dag his spear; Dag met Helgi, his kinsman by marriage, at a place called Fjöturlund: he ran Helgi through with the spear. Helgi died there.

When Dag tells his sister the news, she curses him and mourns her lost husband in words that closely parallel some of those that the tragic heroine GUDRÚN uses of her first husband, the mighty hero SIGURD:

> 'I shall never sit happy at Sefafells,
> from dawn till night-time I shall loathe my life

until a brightness dawns from the prince's troops
where VÍGBLÆR gallops beneath the ruler,
the steed with golden bit and I can welcome the warrior.

'So much fear did Helgi incite in the hearts
of all his foes and their kin,
as before a wolf, running mad,
mountain goats scatter in terror.

'So much did Helgi rise, above heroes
as the well-formed ash above the thorn,
or that noble stag dripping with dew,
who lives higher than all beasts.'

As the subsequent prose passage fantastically asserts:

A BURIAL MOUND was made for Helgi; what is more,
when he came to VALHALL, Odin bid him govern everything at his side.

When Helgi and his ghostly following are observed
riding near the barrow, Sigrún sets out for a gruesome
reunion with her dead beau:

Sigrún went into the burial mound to Helgi and said:
'Now I am as keen for us to meet
as Odin's hawks, eager to eat,
when they scent the slain, the warmth of flesh,
or, dew-bright see the glint of the day.

'First I will kiss the lifeless king
before you cast off your bloody mail.
Helgi, your hair is heavy with hail;
wholly is the warrior drenched in bloody dew,
ice-cold the arms of Högni's kin.
How, lord, can I make this better?'

'You alone, Sigrún of Sefafells,
drench Helgi in sorrow's dew;
with bitter tears you grieve, gold-wrapped girl,
sun-bright southerner, before you sleep;
each one drops like blood on the leader's breast,
ice-cold, piercing [?], heavy with pain.

'Let us drink up costly draughts,
though we have lost both love and lands;
no man must make a dirge for me,
though wounds gape upon my breast,
now that my bride lies buried in the barrow
the longed-for woman, at this dead man's side.'

Some have seen in Sigrún's willingness to be interred
beside her husband's corpse a reflection of an ancient practice of SUTTEE, and *Helgakvida Hundingsbana
II* concludes with a final piece of prose echoing
the notion earlier expressed, that Sigrún was Sváva
reborn:

From grief and sorrow, Sigrún's life was brief. There
was a belief in olden days, that people were reborn,
though nowadays that is reckoned an old wives' tale.
Helgi and Sigrún are said to have been reborn. He was
then known as Helgi Haddingjaskadi, and she KÁRA,
Hálfdan's daughter, as is mentioned in *Káraljód*, and she
was a Valkyrie.

B12, 30, 56, 73, 87, 90; C2, 17, 24, 33, 46

Sigurd

The dragon-slayer, son of the hero SIGMUND, husband
of the tragic heroine GUDRÚN, sometime betrothed to
the imperious BRYNHILD and a leading figure in the
doom-laden events of the VÖLSUNG-cycle. Sigurd is the
quintessential Norse hero and plays a prominent role
in numerous eddic poems. The fullest prose account
of his adventures is found in the legendary VÖLSUNGA
SAGA, which draws heavily on a wide range of earlier
verse, and this saga also offers the most comprehensive

Sigurd *Detail of the portal from the church at Hylestad,
Setesdal, Norway, depicting the mighty hero Sigurd
roasting the dragon Fáfnir's heart, whilst the wicked
Regin looks on. As soon as he sucks his thumb, burnt on
the dragon's blood, he finds he can understand the
language of birds, who warn him of Regin's evil intent.*

version of Sigurd's early life. Sigurd's mother, HJÖRDÍS, was already pregnant with Sigurd when his father, Sigmund, was killed in battle by the warrior LYNGVI and his brothers. The dying Sigmund entrusts his broken sword to Hjördís and predicts that the son she is carrying will 'accomplish great deeds, which will never be forgotten, while the world lasts, and his name will be remembered, while the world lasts'. Hjördís, attempting to escape from Lyngvi's clutches, is captured by Álf, the son of King HJÁLPREK of Denmark, who looks after her honourably, intending to marry her after she has given birth to her child. As *Völsunga saga* continues:

It is now said that Hjördís gave birth to a little boy, and the boy was brought to King Hjálprek. The king was delighted when he saw the boy's piercing eyes, that he had in his head, and he said that no one would turn out to be his like or equal. He was sprinkled with water and named Sigurd. Everyone says a single thing about him: no one was his match in size and demeanour. He was brought up by King Hjálprek, with much love. And when all the most splendid men and kings in the ancient sagas are named, Sigurd must be reckoned the greatest in strength and talents, in vigour and bravery; he had more of these qualities than any other person in the northern world.

According to the eddic poem GRÍPISSPÁ, Sigurd's maternal uncle, GRÍPIR, makes a similarly positive pronouncement to his young nephew, in the course of a lengthy prophecy concerning the course of his future life:

'You will be of men the mightiest under the sun
the highest born of any prince;
giving of gold, a stranger to flight
glorious to gaze on, and wise in words.'

Everything turns out as Grípir predicts, as the unfolding narrative both in the POETIC EDDA and in *Völsunga saga* reveals. The wicked REGIN becomes Sigurd's foster-father, and teaches him all the skills and accomplishments appropriate to a prince. Among other things, Regin helps Sigurd acquire his famed horse, GRANI (in which choice Sigurd is also aided by the god ODIN, according to *Völsunga saga*), and forges his wondrous sword, GRAM, from the broken pieces of Sigmund's shattered weapon. The first thing Sigurd does is to avenge his father, Sigmund, on Lyngvi and the other sons of Hunding, as is described in the eddic poem REGINSMÁL. Immediately before the battle, Sigurd has been given advice by one HNIKAR, a recognizable pseudonym of Odin. After vengeance is complete, Sigurd turns to killing the dragon FÁFNIR

at the insistence of Fánir's own brother, Regin. This episode, depicted numerous times on monuments and carvings, is described in several literary sources, notably the eddic poem FÁFNISMÁL and in *Völsunga saga*. The prose preface to *Fáfnismál* gives the bare outline of the killing:

Sigurd and Regin went up onto GNITAHEID and came upon the trail by which Fáfnir slithered to the water. Then Sigurd dug a large hole in the path, and Sigurd entered into it. When Fáfnir slithered away from his gold, he spewed poison, which spurted from above onto Sigurd's head. When Fáfnir slithered over the hole, Sigurd pierced him to the heart with his sword. Fáfnir twisted about, smashing his head and tail. Sigurd jumped out of the hole, and each of them gazed at the other.

The opening stanzas of *Fáfnismál* detail the extraordinary conversation which takes place between the dying dragon and Sigurd. Among other things, the dragon warns Sigurd that he too will be betrayed by Regin, and then expires. Regin, who has been absent while the killing has taken place, reappears, cuts out his brother's heart with the sword RIDIL, and drinks his blood. As Sigurd roasts Fáfnir's heart on a spit for Regin to eat, he burns his fingers on the dragon's hot blood, and when he puts his finger in his mouth, he finds that he can understand the speech of seven nuthatches in the branches above, each of whom warns of Regin's wicked intentions. When Sigurd duly despatches Regin, and drinks his blood alongside that of Fáfnir, whose heart he has wholly consumed, the birds offer further advice:

'Sigurd, load up the red rings;
it is not princely to mourn many things;
I know a maid, the fairest by far,
decked with gold, if you can gain her.

'Green paths lead to GJÚKI's home,
fates point forth for a brave warrior;
the rich king there has raised a daughter,
she can be bought for a dowry, Sigurd.

'A high hall stands on HINDAFJALL,
entirely fenced about with flame;
wise men have made it
from the undark brightness of dread.

'I know that a Valkyrie sleeps on the fell,
and there plays over her the peril of wood;
YGG stabbed her with a thorn: she slew other men,
that woman, than he had wished.

'You can see, lad, that helmeted maid,

who rode from battle on VINGSKORNIR;
You can rouse Sigrdrífa from sleep,
child of princes, by the NORNS' decree.'

After looting Fáfnir's hoard, removing from it two chests of gold, together with other treasures, including the sword HRÓTTI, a 'helmet of terror' and a golden mail-coat, Sigurd sets off to face the next stage of his destiny, described in the eddic poem SIGRDRÍFUMÁL.

Sigurd duly travels to Hindafjall, passes through the flickering flames and wakes the sleeping Valkyrie, Sigrdrífa, who duly offers the young prince a comprehensive programme of runic instruction. At this point in the CODEX REGIUS there is a significant loss of material, now known as 'the great lacuna', the supposed contents of which have to be deduced from *Völsunga saga*, whose author appears to have had access to the complete texts of the relevant poems. *Völsunga saga* explicitly identifies Sigrdrífa with Brynhild and describes how after she has imbued him with wisdom, they exchange solemn vows to wed each other and no one else. At this crucial point in the narrative, *Völsunga saga* includes the most comprehensive description of Sigurd, and one that is in many ways indebted to a tradition of heroic description alien to the north, as the use of the word *kurteisi* ('courtesy'):

Now Sigurd rode away. His shield many layered, covered with red gold and inscribed with a dragon. Its upper half was dark brown and its lower pale red, and his helmet, saddle and topcoat were marked in the same manner. He had a golden mail-coat, and all his weapons were decorated with gold. The dragon was depicted on all his weapons in this fashion, so that whenever he was sighted, whoever passed of all those who had heard the news recognized that he had slain the mighty dragon that the Scandinavians call Fáfnir. All of his weapons were decorated with gold and were shining bright to look at, since he far surpassed other men in courtesy, in all fit behaviour, and in almost every way. When all the mightiest champions and the most celebrated leaders are reckoned, he will always be reckoned the greatest, and his name is known in all the languages north of the Greek Ocean [the Mediterranean]. And so it must be, while the world lasts. His hair was brown in colour and fair to look at, falling in great locks. His beard was the same colour, thick and short. He had a high nose, and a broad, fine-lined face. His eyes were so piercing that few dared to gaze on his face. His shoulders were as broad as if you were looking at two men. His body was beautifully proportioned in height and breadth, and in every respect, most handsome. It is an indication of his great height, that when he strapped on the sword Gram, which is seven spans long, and waded through a field of fully ripened rye, the tip of the sword's scabbard just grazed the top of the upright field. And his might exceeded his height. He was well able to handle a sword, cast a spear, throw a javelin, hold a shield, bend a bow, and ride a horse. Sigurd had also learned much courtesy in his youth; he was a learned man, aware of things before they occurred, and he knew the language of birds. Because of these talents, few things came on him unawares. He could speak for a long time, and eloquently, so that when he took it on himself to argue some case, everyone agreed even before he finished talking that there could be no option other than that he proposed. He took pleasure in supporting his men, testing himself through mighty deeds, depriving his enemies of treasure, and bestowing it on his friends. He never lacked courage, and he knew no fear.

Sigurd comes to the court of HEIMIR, who is married to BEKKHILD BUDLADÓTTIR, the sister of Brynhild, and there makes a renewed acquaintance with the Valkyrie he has awoken. According to *Völsunga saga*:

Then she arose, with her four handmaids, and went towards him with a golden goblet, and bid him drink. He reached out his hand towards the goblet, and took her hand, and she sat next to him; he put his arms around her neck, and kissed her, saying: 'No woman was ever born more beautiful than you.' Brynhild said: 'Better for you not to put your faith in a woman, because they always break their promises.' Sigurd said: 'Best for us the day when we can take our pleasure from each other.' Brynhild said: 'We are not fated to live together. I am a Valkyrie; I wear a helmet alongside fighting kings. I have to give them help, and I don't mind fighting.' Sigurd replied: 'Our lives will be richest if we live as one. If we don't, the pain will be harder to bear than a sharp blade.' Brynhild answered: 'I must offer help to fighting men, and you must marry Gudrún, the daughter of Gjúki.' Sigurd answered: 'No princess shall persuade me. I am determined in this: I swear by the gods I shall marry you, and no one else.' She said the same. Sigurd thanked her for saying so, and gave her a golden ring; they made their vows again.

Everything unravels when Sigurd goes to the court of King Gjúki, where GRÍMHILD, Gjúki's queen, gives Sigurd a draught of forgetfulness so that Brynhild will disappear from his thoughts and he will marry their daughter Gudrún. Sigurd duly does so, and Grímhild decides that her son GUNNAR should wed Brynhild instead. She has already brought about by her witchcraft that Sigurd and Gunnar, by now his sworn-brother, have the ability to exchange shapes, so that when Gunnar's horse, GOTI, refuses to leap through the flickering flames surrounding Brynhild's bower, and when Sigurd's horse, Grani, refuses to respond to

Sigurdarkvida Fáfnisbana in fyrsta

Gunnar, Sigurd himself adopts Gunnar's shape, and, riding Grani, penetrates the flames. Brynhild is duly persuaded to marry 'Gunnar', but at the wedding-feast, according to *Völsunga saga*, Sigurd regains his memory of the vows that the two of them had once exchanged, although he keeps things to himself. Matters come to a head when Gudrún and Brynhild vie for superiority, and Gudrún reveals the truth about what happened. Brynhild, incensed, urges Gunnar to slay Sigurd, who had slept with her long before Gunnar, and who had given her a child, ÁSLAUG. Neither Gunnar nor his brother HÖGNI GJÚKASON can bring themselves to kill their sworn-brother, Sigurd, but they persuade another of King Gjúki's sons, GUTTHORM, to slay Sigurd in his bed. As he lies dying, Sigurd manages to avenge himself on the fleeing Gutthorm by throwing Gram at him and slicing him in two. Sigurd's funeral is a poignant affair, stage-managed by Brynhild herself, according to the account in *Völsunga saga*, which is itself largely derived from the final stanzas of the eddic poem *Sigurdarkvida in skamma*:

[Brynhild said]: 'Gunnar, now I make you a last request: have a single huge pyre built on the flat plain for all of us: me, and Sigurd, and those killed alongside him. Have the tents there reddened with human blood, and burn me on one side of the Hunnish king, and on his other side my people, two at his head, two at his feet, and two hawks, in a symmetrical pattern. Lay between us a drawn sword, like before, when we went into the same bed and vowed to be man and wife. The door [of HEL] will not shut on his heels if I follow him, and our funeral rites will not be stingy, if five slave-girls and eight serving-maids given me by my father follow him. Also burn there those, who were killed alongside Sigurd. I would say more if I were unwounded, but now my cut bubbles, and the wound gapes; but what I said was true.' Sigurd's corpse was then prepared in the ancient manner, and a mighty pyre was built. When it was wholly kindled, the body of Sigurd Fáfnir's bane was laid on top, along with that of his three-year-old son [SIGMUND SIGURDARSON], whom Brynhild had caused to be slain, and that of Gutthorm. When the pyre was entirely ablaze, Brynhild went out onto it and told her serving-maids to take the gold she wished to give them. Then Brynhild died, and burned alongside Sigurd, and in this way their lives came to an end. Everyone who heard the news said that no man the match of Sigurd would ever come into the world and that never again would a man be born like Sigurd was in every kind of thing, and his name would never be forgotten in the Germanic language and in the lands of the north, as long as the world lasts.

A number of the poems in the poetic Edda consist of la-ments for Sigurd; typical is the way Gudrún mourns in *Gudrúnarkvida* I, when GULLRÖND, her sister, sweeps the covering from Sigurd's corpse:

Gudrún gave a single glance:
she saw the prince's hair drip blood
the warrior's keen eyes dimmed
the chieftain's mighty chest sword-rent.

Leaning, Gudrún bent low to the pillow
her hair came loose, her cheeks grew red,
raindrop tears ran down her knees.

The Gudrún, Gjúki's daughter, grieved
and tears streamed through her tresses;
out in the yard, the geese began honking,
those famous fowl the lady owned.

Then said Gullrönd, Gjúki's daughter,
'I know that your love was greater
than any man's or woman's in the world;
you were never happy outside or in,
my sister, except by Sigurd.'

[Gudrún spoke:]
'Next to Gjúki's sons my Sigurd towered
like a leek that stands among grass,
or a dazzling gem on a string of beads,
a precious jewel among the princes.'

B12, 25, 30, 42, 56, 65, 68, 73, 79, 87, 90; C1–3, 6, 17, 24, 33, 46; D46, 58, 60, 128, 136, 185, 214, 248, 250, 275, 293, 318, 346, 416, 436, 459

Sigurdarkvida Fáfnisbana in fyrsta see GRÍPISSPÁ.

Sigurdarkvida in meiri ('the longer lay of Sigurd')
The editorial title given to the now-lost eddic poem that apparently followed the truncated SIGRDRÍFUMÁL in the CODEX REGIUS manuscript and occupied much of the fifth gathering of eight manuscript pages, which has now disappeared and is usually termed 'the great lacuna'. Immediately following the lacuna is the fragmentary BROT AF SIGURDARKVIDU, of which the opening has been lost. The contents of *Sigurdarkvida in meiri* have to be inferred from the parallel treatment of the narrative material in the legendary VÖLSUNGA SAGA.
D15

Sigurdarkvida in skamma ('the shorter lay of Sigurd')
Despite its name, one of the longest extant eddic poems in the CODEX REGIUS manuscript, so called to distin-guish the poem from the now-lost SIGURDARKVIDA IN MEIRI. While offering a general survey of the events

surrounding the VÖLSUNG-cycle, the poem provides a particular focus on the character and motivation of the tragic heroine BRYNHILD, whose love for the hero SIGURD led to both their deaths. Much of the last part of the poem is taken up with Brynhild's prophecy of the grim events that are to overtake GUDRÚN, Sigurd's widow, together with their daughter, SVANHILD, and her brothers, GUNNAR and HÖGNI GJÚKASON. Although *Sigurdarkvida in skamma* contains long passages of decidedly inferior quality, it also contains some memorable vignettes, not least that of the blood-spattered Gudrún woken from sleep at her murdered husband's side. As the poem closes, Brynhild perishes on the pyre of her beloved Sigurd.

B12, 30, 56, 73, 87, 90; C2, 17, 24, 33, 46; D260, 299, 547, 621

Sigyn ('victorious girl-friend')

One of the goddesses or ÁSYNJUR, wife of the mischievous LOKI and mother of NARI or Narfi. As early as the ninth-century skaldic verses of THJÓDÓLF OF HVÍN, Sigyn is linked with Loki, who is referred to in a poetic periphrasis or KENNING as 'the burden of Sigyn's arms'. Her loyalty to her husband's remains firm even after he has been finally punished by the rest of the ÆSIR, bound with the entrails of his own son to three slabs of rock, and left with a snake hanging over him, dripping venom onto his face. According to the thirteenth-century Icelander SNORRI STURLUSON:

His wife Sigyn stands near him, holding a bowl under the drops of venom; when the bowl is full, she goes and pours the venom away, but then the venom drips on his face, and he writhes so much that all the world shakes: it is called an earthquake.

The eddic poem VÖLUSPÁ presents a similar picture, as the sibyl sees a scene she briefly describes to the god ODIN:

She saw a prisoner prostrate
under Hveralund,
in Loki's likeness,
ever eager for harm;
there sits Sigyn,
over her husband,
but she feels little glee:
do you know yet, or what?

B12, 14, 23, 24, 38, 30, 35, 39, 40, 45, 56, 59, 62, 73, 83, 87, 90; C2, 5, 9, 13, 16, 17, 24, 33, 46, 48; D331

Silfr(in)topp *see* ÆSIR.

Simul ('eternal'?)

(1) According to the name-lists or THULUR, the name of a troll-wife or giantess. (2) The name of the pole that the children Bil and Hjúki were carrying from the well when they were abducted by MÁNI, the personified moon, according to the thirteenth-century Icelander SNORRI STURLUSON.

B24, 28, 35, 40, 50; C5, 9, 48

Sindri ('sparky')

According to the thirteenth-century Icelander SNORRI STURLUSON, the hall on NIDAFJÖLL in which virtuous folk will dwell after RAGNARÖK. The eddic poem VÖLUSPÁ speaks instead in this context of a 'golden hall of Sindri's kin'. It is possible that Snorri has misconstrued the term, and it may be that Sindri was a dwarf, especially since a later hand annotating one of the manuscripts of SNORRA EDDA names Sindri as the brother of dwarf BROKK, and therefore as the creator of a number of the gods' most prized possessions, notably the ring DRAUPNIR, the boar GULLINBORSTI and especially the hammer MJÖLLNIR.

B12, 13, 23, 24, 28, 30, 35, 40, 50, 56, 59, 73, 87, 90; C2, 5, 9, 17, 24, 33, 46, 48

Sinfjötli

The product of the incestuous union between the mighty hero SIGMUND and his sister, SIGNÝ. The fullest account of his birth and upbringing is found in the legendary VÖLSUNGA SAGA:

After a while, Signý gave birth to a baby boy. This boy was called Sinfjötli, and when he grew up he was both big and strong, handsome to look at, and very like the Völsung breed; when he was not yet ten years old, Signý sent him to Sigmund in his underground lair. Before she sent her first sons to Sigmund, she had tested them by sewing the sleeves of their shirts to their hands, forcing the needle through both skin and flesh. They handled the test badly and screamed. She also did the same thing to Sinfjötli; he never flinched. Then she tore the shirt off him, so that the skin came off with the sleeves. She said that it must surely hurt; he replied that: 'pain like that seems little to a Völsung.' Then the boy came to Sigmund. Sigmund asked him to knead the dough [as he had done Signý's other sons], while he went looking for firewood. He put a sack in his hand, and went off for wood. When he came back, Sinfjötli had finished baking. Sigmund asked if he had found anything in the dough. 'I'm not completely positive,' said the boy, 'that there wasn't something alive in the dough when I first started to knead, but whatever it was, I kneaded it in.' Then Sigmund said, with a laugh: 'I don't think you should eat this bread tonight, because you have kneaded into it a huge and poisonous serpent.' Sigmund was so robust that he could consume poison with no ill effects, but Sinfjötli, even though he could

Singastein

survive venom from the outside, could neither eat nor drink it.

Such a weakness is eventually to prove his downfall, for after an eventful period as Sigmund's companion, part of which time the father and son live as WERE-WOLVES, he wreaks vengeance on SIGGEIR, Signý's husband, joins his half-brother, HELGI, on an expedition against the warrior HÖDBRODD, in the course of which he engages in a contest of ritualized abuse or FLYTING against GRANMAR, before being poisoned by his stepmother, BORGHILD, after he kills her brother in a dispute over a woman. Sinfjötli's death and his funeral, where he is borne away by mysterious figure presumably to be identified as the god ODIN, are described in detail in *Völsunga saga*, drawing on a legend also alluded to in the prose passage FRÁ DAUDA SINFJÖTLA found in the CODEX REGIUS manuscript:

> [Borghild] then arranged her brother's funeral feast with the king's consent. She prepared the banquet with the finest provisions, and invited many important people. Borghild served the drink herself. She approached Sinfjötli with a large horn, saying: 'Drink this, stepson.' He accepted the horn, looked into it, and said: 'The drink is tainted.' Sigmund said: 'Give it to me then.' He drank it. The queen said: 'Why should other men drink your ale for you?' She came back with the horn. 'Drink this.' And she made many taunts. He accepted the horn, and said: 'The drink is spoiled.' Sigmund said: 'Give it to me then.' A third time she came, and told him to drink it, if he had a Völsung's heart. Sinfjötli accepted the horn, and said: 'This drink is poisoned.' Sigmund replied: 'Let your moustache sort it out, son.' The king was rather drunk to have said this. Sinfjötli drank and immediately fell down. Sigmund got up and his grief almost killed him. He took the body in his arms, and walked out into the forest, until finally he came to a fjord. There he saw a man in a small boat. The man asked if he would take a passage from him across the fjord. Sigmund agreed. The boat was so small that it could not take them all, so the body went first, and Sigmund walked along the fjord. Then the boat and the man vanished before Sigmund's eyes.

B25, 42, 65, 68, 79; C1, 6

Singastein

According to a verse from the late tenth-century skaldic poem HÚSDRÁPA, cited by the thirteenth-century Icelander SNORRI STURLUSON, the place where the god HEIMDALL battled against his hated rival, LOKI.

B24, 28, 35, 40, 50; C5, 9, 48

Sinir *see* ÆSIR.

Sinrjód

According to the prose preface to the eddic poem HELGAKVIDA HJÖRVARDSSONAR, the third wife of King HJÖRVARD, and the mother of the warrior HYMLING.

B12, 30, 56, 73, 87, 90; C2, 17, 24, 33, 46

Sinthgunt *see* MERSEBURG CHARMS.

Sjofn *see* ÁSYNJUR.

Skadi

(1) The daughter of the giant THJAZI, wife of the god NJÖRD and inhabitant of Thrymheim. The eddic and skaldic sources are relatively reticent about Skadi, but the thirteenth-century Icelander SNORRI STURLUSON gives a much fuller picture, tracing her presence among the ÁSYNJUR to her threatened vengeance over the killing of her father by the god THOR. According to Snorri:

> Skadi . . . took her helmet and mail-coat and all her weapons, and went to ÁSGARD to avenge her father. The ÆSIR offered her recompense and compensation, the first part of which was that she could choose a husband from among the Æsir, judging by the feet, without seeing anything else of them. Then she saw that one person's feet were particularly fair, and said: 'I choose him; not much is ugly about BALDR'. But it was Njörd of NÓATÚN. The second part of her settlement was that the Æsir had to do something she thought they could not, namely make her laugh. So LOKI tied a piece of string around the beard of a nanny-goat, and the other end around his balls, and they tugged each other to and fro, squealing loud. Then Loki collapsed into Skadi's lap, and she laughed. Then the settlement of the Æsir was complete; but it is said that in compensation to her ODIN took Thjazi's eyes, and cast them into the sky, and made two stars from them.

Skadi's dealings with the Æsir do not seem to have been entirely successful; after her marriage to Njörd he wishes to remain in his seaside home of Nóatún, she in her father's windy mountain-halls at Thrymheim. As Snorri observes, quoting stanzas from the eddic poem GRÍMNISMÁL:

> They agreed that they would stay nine nights in Thrymheim, and the next nine in Nóatún. But when Njörd returned to Nóatún from the mountain he said: 'I loathe the mountains (I wasn't there long, just nine nights); the howling of wolves seemed harsh to me after the singing of swans.' Then Skadi said: 'I couldn't sleep on the sea-bed, because of the screaming of birds; the gull that returns from the sea every morning keeps me awake.'

Skadi seems to retire to the hills, becoming associated with skiing, archery and the hunting of game. According to Snorri's YNGLINGA SAGA, she also becomes the lover of the god Odin, while in the eddic poem LOKASENNA, Loki accuses her (along with almost every other of the Ásynjur present) of taking him to her bed. Snorri depicts Skadi as taking a special part in the revenge of the Æsir against Loki, for it is she who places the serpent over his face, dripping venom.

(2) The name Skadi is also given to a (male) character in the opening chapter of VÖLSUNGA SAGA, a large and powerful figure, whose thrall, Bredi, is killed by SIGI, the son of Odin, so causing his outlawry.

B12, 14, 23–5, 28, 30, 35, 40, 42, 50, 56, 59, 65, 68, 73, 78, 87, 90; C1–3, 5, 6, 9, 17, 24, 33, 46, 48; D102, 333, 481

Skáldskaparmál ('the language of poetry')

The third of the four major sections of SNORRA EDDA, cast in the beginning in the form of a dialogue between BRAGI, the god of poetry, and ÆGIR, the sea-giant. Bragi describes a number of the major myths, culminating (most appropriately) in the most detailed account extant of the acquisition of the MEAD OF POETRY. Following that tale is a full discussion of the language of poetry, set against a learned and Latinate context that views the gods in a spirit of EUHEMERISM, equating them with well-known characters from the Trojan War. The language of poetry is divided into two general areas, concerning on the one hand the poetic periphrases or KENNINGS employed and on the other the poetic synonyms or HEITI of which kennings may occasionally be composed. In the course of the discussion large numbers of skaldic verses are cited as illustrative examples, and several myths and legends that have not been discussed elsewhere in the course of *Snorra Edda* are outlined. Many manuscripts of *Skáldskaparmál* conclude with long series of THULUR, or versified and mnemonic lists of such *heiti*, presumably to help potential poets in the composition of verses and any potential audience to appreciate what had been preserved.

B24, 28, 35, 40, 50; C5, 9, 48; D40, 41, 102–4, 118, 148, 149, 170, 224, 249, 266, 368, 382, 384, 476, 478, 479, 483–5, 487, 626

Skatýrnir ('fee-wetter')

According to the thirteenth-century Icelander SNORRI STURLUSON, the ninth heaven, above VINDBLÁIN, 'higher than the clouds, beyond all worlds'.

B24, 28, 35, 40, 50; C5, 9, 48

Skeggjöld *see* VALKYRIES.

Skeidbrimir *see* ÆSIR.

Skídbladnir

The magical ship of the god FREY or, according to a variant account in YNGLINGA SAGA, of the god ODIN. Elsewhere, the thirteenth-century Icelander SNORRI STURLUSON, who composed *Ynglinga saga*, is unequivocal:

> It was some dwarfs, ÍVALDI'S SONS, who made Skídbladnir and gave the ship to Frey; it is large enough for all the ÆSIR to board it fully armed, and it takes a fair wind as soon as the sail is hoisted, wherever is has to go. When it is not at sea, it is constructed so skilfully and of so many parts that it can be folded up like a cloth and put in a pocket.

B24, 38, 35, 40, 50; C5, 9, 48; D529

Skínfaxi ('shining-mane')

According to the eddic poem VAFTHRÚDNISMÁL, the horse who pulls the chariot of day. As the giant VAFTHRÚDNIR asks the god ODIN, who is at this point disguised as a traveller calling himself Gagnrád:

> 'Tell me, Gagnrád, since you wish from the floor,
> to make a test of your talents,
> what's the name of the horse who always draws
> each day over troops of men?'

> 'He's called Skínfaxi who always draws
> each day over troops of men.
> The glorious Goths think him the best horse:
> his mane shines always aflame.'

B12, 30, 51, 56, 73, 87, 90; C2, 17, 24, 33, 46

Skírnir ('bright one')

Servant of the god FREY and his go-between to the beautiful giantess GERD, as recounted in detail in the eddic poem SKÍRNISMÁL. In return, Frey gives Skírnir his sword and, as the thirteenth-century Icelander SNORRI STURLUSON records, has to kill the otherwise unknown BELI with a stag's antler, while in the apocalypse of RAGNARÖK, when facing the fire-giant SURT, Frey again feels the loss of his weapon. According to Snorri, the god ODIN also uses Skírnir to run errands for him, including a trip to the DARK ELVES to have the fetter GLEIPNIR made for the wolf FENRIR.

B12, 14, 23, 24, 28, 30, 35, 40, 50, 56, 59, 73, 87, 90; C5, 9, 7, 24, 33, 46, 48

Skírnismál ('the lay of Skírnir')

An eddic poem, preserved in the CODEX REGIUS, where it is entitled *För Scírnis* ('Skírnir's journey'), as well as in the manuscript AM 748 I 4to, and used by the thirteenth-century Icelander SNORRI STURLUSON in his account of the wooing of the beautiful giantess GERD by

Skjálf

FREY. The prose introduction provides the background to the tale:

> Frey, the son of NJÖRD, had sat himself on HLIDSKJÁLF and was looking over all the worlds. He looked into JÖTUNHEIM and saw there a beautiful girl, as she walked from her father's halls to her bower. From then on, he grew very sick at heart.

Frey's father, Njörd, asks SKÍRNIR, Frey's servant, to find out what ails his son, and Frey confesses readily, taking on the sullen tones of a love-lorn swain:

> 'In GYMIR's yards I saw wander
> a maiden dear to me: her arms were bright,
> and from their light all sea and sky seemed to gleam.
>
> 'A girl dearer to me than to any lad
> in all the days of old; but none of them wish
> of the ÆSIR and ELVES the two of us to be at one.'

The alleged antipathy to the match, presumably deriving from the deep hostility between GIANTS and Æsir, is swept aside by Skírnir, who simply asks for Frey's horse, that can ride through encircling flames (a curious echo of events in the VÖLSUNG-cycle, where the mighty hero SIGURD rides through encircling flames to woo the imperious VALKYRIE BRYNHILD on behalf of his friend, the brave warrior GUNNAR), and also for his magic sword, which can fight on its own. Despite the grim warnings of a giant herdsman seated, according to a prose passage, on a grave mound at the entrance to Gymir's court, Skírnir succeeds in meeting Gerd, whom he first of all tries to bribe with the promise of eleven golden apples, then with a gold ring, presumably DRAUPNIR, which self-replicates every ninth night. Nothing avails him, so he changes his tone abruptly, threatening to slice off her head, then her father's, before launching into a chain of abuse and curses (in a different metre), which would condemn her to a night-mare existence at the hands of frenzied giants, with only goat's piss to drink and all food tasting of snakes. In order to accomplish this, Skírnir is prepared to resort to runes and magic. As he finishes his vile threats, the speed of Gerd's response is striking:

> 'Your health, rather, young man:
> take this white-topped cup
> full of vintage mead; I never thought
> that I would love one of the VANIR so well.'

A meeting is fixed, nine nights hence, at a secluded place called BARRI, and Skírnir returns home to tell Frey. As the poem ends, Frey is impatient for their tryst:

> 'A night is long; two are longer:
> how can I bear three?
> Often to me a month has seemed less
> than half a night of such craving.'

B12, 30, 56, 73, 87, 90; C2, 17, 24, 33, 46; D31, 34, 108, 223, 320, 397, 403, 442, 551–3

Skjálf An alternative name for FREYJA.

Skjöld ('shield')

According to the thirteenth-century Icelander SNORRI STURLUSON, a son of the god ODIN and the eponymous founder of the Danish dynasty of the Skjoldungs. Earlier in his work, Snorri had named one Skjaldan, 'whom we call Skjöld', as an ancestor of Odin, in line with the appearance of a character named SCYLD in Anglo-Saxon royal genealogies as an ancestor of WODEN. The early thirteenth-century Danish historian SAXO GRAMMATICUS gives an account of Skjold's life, which compares with that of Scyld in the Old English BEOWULF, stating that he first appeared mysteriously from across the sea as a child, and was adopted by the Danish people, and eventually made their king.

B24, 28, 35, 40, 50, 64; C5, 7–9, 47; D27

Skögul see VALKYRIES.

Sköll ('treachery')

According to the thirteenth-century Icelander SNORRI STURLUSON, the name of the wolf that pursues SÓL, the sun. Eventually, in the course of the apocalyptic events of RAGNARÖK, Sköll will devour her prey.

B24, 28, 35, 40, 50; C5, 9, 48

Skrýmir ('braggart')

A mighty giant who, according to the thirteenth-century Icelander SNORRI STURLUSON, first meets the god THOR and his companions on their trip to the court of the giant ÚTGARDALOKI, and who indeed is later revealed as Útgardaloki himself in disguise. As a mark of his scale, Snorri recounts a number of details designed, quite literally, to belittle Thor, who sleep in a huge hall that turns out to have been Skrýmir's glove. The following day the giant offers them the hospitality of the food in his knapsack, and settles down to sleep. Thor is quite unable to undo the giant's bag and, infuriated at his lack of success, strikes the giant on the head. The giant merely wakes and asks if a leaf has fallen on him. Two further blows with the hammer MJÖLLNIR are similarly dismissed as the dropping of an acorn and of bird-shit. It is a much deflated Thor and his companions who finally approach the court of ÚTGARDALOKI. Only after a series of similarly humiliating escapades does Útgardaloki reveal the extent to which Thor has been deceived: far from diminishing his stature, he has terrified his enemies.

B24, 28, 35, 40, 50; C5, 9, 48

Skuld ('debt', 'future'?)

One of the three NORNS, according to the eddic poem VÖLUSPÁ, whose testimony is repeated by the thirteenth-century Icelander SNORRI STURLUSON; the others are URD and VERDANDI. Elsewhere in *Völuspá*, however, Skuld appears as the name of a VALKYRIE, and Snorri attempts to rationalize the discrepancy by describing Skuld as the youngest Norn, who rides to battle alongside the Valkyries, to help choose the slain.

B12, 14, 23, 24, 28, 30, 35, 40, 50, 56, 59, 73, 87, 90; C2, 5, 9, 17, 24, 33, 46, 48

Slagfid ('beating-Finn')

According to the eddic poem VÖLUNDARKVIDA, the brother of the legendary smith, VÖLUND, and the husband of the swan-maiden HLADGUD SVANHVÍT, whom he pursues after she and her companions abandon Slagfid and his brothers. Slagfid's name, with its suggestion both of smith-craft and of the magical abilities traditionally assigned to the Finns or Lapps, appears to combine elements of the legendary activities of Völund himself

B12, 30, 31, 56, 73, 87, 90; C2, 17, 24, 33, 46

Sleipnir ('slippy')

The eight-legged grey horse of the ODIN, described as the best of all horses in the eddic poem GRÍMNISMÁL. According to the thirteenth-century Icelander SNORRI STURLUSON, Sleipnir is the product of the union between LOKI, playing the part of a mare, and the mighty stallion SVADILFARI, who was assisting the anonymous GIANT BUILDER who fortified ÁSGARD. Odin is later said to have lent Sleipnir to HERMÓD, so that he can travel to HEL after the death of BALDR. A number of picture-stones depict an eight-legged horse, usually identified as Sleipnir.

B12, 14, 23, 24, 28, 30, 35, 40, 50, 56, 59, 73, 87, 90; C2, 5, 9, 17, 24, 33, 46, 48

Slíd *see* HVERGELMIR.

Slídrugtanni An alternative name for GULLINBORSTI.

Smid *see* RÍGSTHULA.

Snær *see* FORNJÓT.

Snævar

Son of the mighty hero HÖGNI GJÚKASON and broth-

er of the warrior Sólar. According to ATLAMÁL, both brothers accompany their father, together with their uncle, the doomed hero GUNNAR, on his fateful trip to the stronghold of ATLI BUDLASON, the husband of their aunt, the tragic heroine Gudrún.

B12, 20, 30, 56, 73, 87, 90; C2, 17, 24, 33, 46

Snjó *see* HLÉR.

Snør *see* RÍGSTHULA.

Snorra Edda ('Snorri's Edda')

An Icelandic treatise on poetry composed by the thirteenth-century Icelander SNORRI STURLUSON in four separate sections, as distinct from the collection of eddic poems formerly known as *Sæmundar Edda* ('Sæmund's Edda'). The attribution of this latter verse collection to Sæmund inn fródi ('the wise') is no longer accepted, and the collection is more commonly known as the Elder or Poetic Edda. *Snorra Edda*, by contrast, is also called the Younger or Prose Edda. The name 'Edda' itself is a matter of debate. The common noun *edda* is found both in *Snorra Edda* itself and in the

Snorra Edda *An illustration from the fourteenth-century manuscript, Uppsala University Library, Delagardie 11, depicting the deluding of Gylfi from* Snorra Edda.

Snorri Sturluson

eddic poem RÍGSTHULA as a word meaning 'great-grandmother', while connections with the place Oddi in southern Iceland where Snorri was raised and with the Old Norse noun *óðr* ('poetry', 'inspiration') have been suggested. Perhaps the most plausible suggestion is that the word is itself Snorri's own self-deprecating coinage, based on the Latin word *edo* ('I proclaim'), just as the Icelandic formation *kredda* ('a foolish belief') is based on the Latin word *credo* ('I believe'). The sense would then seem to be 'scribblings', 'jottings' or some such. A humorous or ironic title of this kind would be in keeping with Snorri's style and temperament, which tends easily to comedy or farce.

Snorra Edda is clearly divided into four self-contained sections: *Prologue*, GYLFAGINNING, SKÁLDSKAPARMÁL and HÁTTATAL. Snorri's plan seems to have been nothing less than a handbook of Norse poetics, describing metre, diction and (finally) imagery. He claimed that such a scheme was necessary to preserve a knowledge of the Icelandic poetry of the past, which was becoming progressively more difficult to understand as knowledge of the underlying myths and legends became less common; indeed, there are clear cases where Snorri himself has been unable to understand a verse or where his solution has seemed unlikely to modern scholars. Necessarily, such a scheme involves the retelling of myths and legends of the pagan past, some of which Snorri excused and others of which he appears to have transformed, according to his own Christian beliefs.

Of the four sections of *Snorra Edda*, it seems likely the last, *Háttatal*, was, in fact, the first to have been composed. *Háttatal* consists of little more than a series of three poems of 102 stanzas in total, exemplifying a wide variety of skaldic metres and practices, together with a prose commentary explaining the salient features of alliteration, diction or prosody being demonstrated. The introduction is couched in the question-and-answer format that is common in grammatical treatises in Latin from the fourth century on.

B24, 28, 35, 40, 50; C5, 9, 48; D40, 41, 102–4, 118, 148, 149, 170, 224, 249, 266, 368, 382, 384, 476, 478, 479, 483–5, 487, 626

Snorri Sturluson

Undoubtedly the most important and influential of all authors from medieval Iceland and the source of much mythological and legendary lore. Snorri's life (1178/9–1241) coincided with a crucial period in Icelandic history, as the commonwealth was collapsing and the threat from the Norwegian crown was constantly increasing. Snorri, as part of the influential Sturlung clan, played a full part in the endless scheming and vicious machinations that followed; his role as law-speaker, chieftain and political fixer is described in detail in the remarkable *Íslendinga saga*, which was composed by his nephew Sturla Thordarson (1214–84) and preserved as part of the massive *Sturlunga saga*. In such an essentially political history, it is perhaps not surprising that Snorri's role as a man of letters is but rarely mentioned. It is sobering to consider that this most refined of men was slaughtered alone in his cellar at Reykholt on 23 September 1241, at the instigation of his own son-in-law.

Snorri was the author of a vast history of Norway, HEIMSKRINGLA, and is often credited with the authorship of EGILS SAGA SKALL-GRÍMSSONAR, although convincing proof has not been brought forward. But it is the remarkable composite work now known as SNORRA EDDA, and consisting of four sections (*Prologue*, GYLFAGINNING, SKÁLDSKAPARMÁL and HÁTTATAL) for which he is perhaps best known.

B24, 28, 35, 40, 50, 58, 82; C5, 9, 10, 37, 48; D76, 170, 218, 266, 325, 328, 375, 382, 384, 409, 427, 428, 449, 478, 479, 483–5, 487, 530, 545

Snót *see* RÍGSTHULA.

Snotra ('clever')

According to the thirteenth-century Icelander SNORRI STURLUSON, one of the goddesses or ÁSYNJUR, although little more about her is known. Snorri's assertion that she is 'clever and well-behaved' derives directly from her name, and it seems that he had access to no further information, if indeed she is not an invention of his own.

B24, 28, 35, 40, 50; C5, 9, 48

Sökkvabekk ('sunken bank')

According to the thirteenth-century Icelander SNORRI STURLUSON, the dwelling of the goddess SÁGA and 'a big place'.

B24, 28, 35, 40, 50; C5, 9, 48

Sól ('sun')

Personification of the sun, often reckoned among the goddesses or ÁSYNJUR. The thirteenth-century Icelander SNORRI STURLUSON, basing his account on the eddic poems GRÍMNISMÁL and VAFTHRÚDNISMÁL, provides a full narrative, describing how Sól and her brother MÁNI ('moon') were the beautiful children of one MUNDILFARI, who betrothed her to a figure called Glen. Outraged at such arrogance, the ÆSIR set Sól to drive the chariot of the sun and Máni to drive the chariot of the moon; each of them is pursued by wolves, named SKÖLL and HATI HRÓDVITNISSON respectively, who will catch and devour them during the apocalyptic events of RAGNARÖK. Another name given to Sól in *Vafthrúdnismál* is Álfrödul ('elf-beam'), while the eddic poem ALVÍSSMÁL contains a number of other poetic circumlocutions for the sun.

B12, 14, 23, 24, 28, 30, 35, 40, 50, 51, 56, 59, 73, 87, 90; C2, 5, 9, 17, 24, 33, 46, 48

Sólar *see* SNÆVAR.

Sólfell *see* HELGI SIGMUNDARSON HUNDINGSBANI.

Són *see* ÓDRERIR.

Son *see* RÍGSTHULA.

Sönnung An alternative name for THOR.

Sörla tháttr

A tale, preserved only in the late fourteenth-century Icelandic manuscript FLATEYJARBÓK, that combines a large number of elements of mythical and legendary history. Part of the tale is given over to an account of the theft by the cunning LOKI of the fabulous BRÍSINGAMEN from the goddess FREYJA and its subsequent recovery. Having established the pattern of the theft and recovery of a valuable treasure in the mythological sphere, the narrative goes on to recount the story of the events leading up to the everlasting battle of the HJADNINGAVÍG.

B60, 85; C21; D85

Sörli

A son of the tragic heroine GUDRÚN and her third husband, King JÓNAK, brother of HAMDIR and half-brother of ERP JÓNAKRSSON, whose combined tale forms part of the doom-laden events of the VÖLSUNG-cycle. Together with Hamdir (and incited by Gudrún), he sets off on the ill-fated mission of avenging the death of his half-sister SVANHILD, the beautiful daughter of Gudrún and her first husband, the mighty hero SIGURD. The entire episode is described in the eddic poem HAMDISMÁL, alluded to in some surviving skaldic verses by BRAGI BODDASON and sketched out in the legendary VÖLSUNGA SAGA. Before sending her sons off to their doom, Gudrún had given them impenetrable mail-coats, whence Hamdir and Sörli often appear in poetic periphrases or KENNINGS for armour or mail-shirt. It is presumably Sörli who utters the final defiant words of the brothers in *Hamdismál*, before they are stoned to death:

'Great glory we have gained
though we die now or tomorrow;
no man survives a single dusk
beyond the NORNS' decree.'

There Sörli fell

at the hall's gable;
and Hamdir slumped
at the rear of the house.

The eponymous hero of SÖRLA THÁTTR is a quite separate figure.

B12, 25, 30, 39, 42, 45, 56, 62, 65, 68, 73, 79, 83, 87, 90; C1–3, 6, 13, 16, 17, 24, 33, 46; D350, 521

soul *see* FYLGJA; HAMINGJA.

spells *see* MAGIC.

Sporvitnir

According to the evidence of the eddic poem HELGAKVIDA HUNDINGSBANA I, one of the warriors of the fierce war-leader HÖDBRODD.

B12, 30, 56, 73, 87, 90; C2, 17, 24, 33, 46

Sprakki *see* RÍGSTHULA.

Sprund *see* RÍGSTHULA.

Starkad

(1) According to the legendary GAUTREKS SAGA, a long-lived hero with a particular devotion to the god ODIN. At his birth and in front of a company of twelve judges, ostensibly from the ÆSIR, the gods THOR and Odin, apparently playing the part of the NORNS, bestow their competing gifts:

Then Thor spoke, and said: 'Since Starkad's grandmother, Álfhild, preferred a wise giant to Thor himself as the father of her son, I decree that Starkad himself shall have neither a son or a daughter, and that his line shall end with him.' Odin said: 'I decree that he shall live for three life-spans.' Thor said: 'And he shall commit a most terrible deed in each.' Odin said: 'I decree that he shall have the finest weapons and clothes.' Thor said: 'I decree that he shall have neither land nor estates.' Odin said: 'I give him this: he shall have great wealth.' Thor said: 'I put a curse on him, so that he shall never be satisfied with what he has.' Odin said: 'I grant him victory and glory in every battle.' Thor said: 'I put a curse on him, that he shall be terribly wounded in every battle.' Odin said: 'I grant him the art of poetry, so that he shall compose verses as fast as he speaks.' Thor said: 'He shall never remember what he composes.' Odin said: 'I decree that he shall be very highly thought of by all the noblest and best.' Thor said: 'All the common people shall hate him.' Then the judges decided that everything that had been decreed should happen.

Starkad's story is also told by the early thirteenth-

Strabo

century Danish historian SAXO GRAMMATICUS. Thor's animosity towards Starkad may be reflected in a tenth-century skaldic verse by Vetrlidi Sumarlidason, who invokes Thor's defeat of several giants, apparently including one named Starkad; moreover, Starkad's legendary abilities as a poet may be commemorated in the fact that he seems to have given his name to a specific metre.

(2) According to the eddic poem HELGAKVIDA HUNDINGSBANA II, the name of one of the warrior GRANMAR's sons, who is killed by the hero HELGI SIGMUNDARSON HUNDINGSBANI, who appears to suggest that Starkad's body fought on after Helgi had cut his head off.

B12, 30, 56, 64, 69, 73, 87, 90; C2, 7, 8, 17, 24, 33, 35, 38, 46; D74, 199, 377, 537, 542

Strabo

A first-century Greek geographer, many of whose descriptions of Celtic and Germanic tribes survive. For example, when writing of the Cimbri, who may perhaps have been of Celtic origin but who were certainly in close contact with Germanic peoples, many of whose customs they appear to have shared, Strabo notes that in performing their human SACRIFICES they hanged their victims over huge bowls, while their presiding priestesses, who were old women in white, climbed ladders and slit their throats, so that their blood dripped into the bowls below. Aspects of this practice seem reflected in much later accounts, for example those of IBN FADLAN or PAULUS OROSIUS.

B9, 21; C11

Sudri *see* AUSTRI.

Sultr *see* HEL.

Sumr ('summer')

The personification of summer, and, according to the thirteenth-century Icelander SNORRI STURLUSON, the son of the giant SVÁSUD.

B24, 28, 35, 40, 50; C5, 9, 48

Sunna *see* MERSEBURG CHARMS.

Surt ('black')

The mighty fire-demon or giant, who, according to the thirteenth-century Icelander SNORRI STURLUSON, stands guard with a flaming sword at the border of the fiery region of MUSPEL:

> There is a figure called Surt, stationed at the border to protect the land; he has a fiery sword, and at RAGNARÖK

he will go and fight and conquer all the ÆSIR, and burn the whole world with fire.

Snorri's description appears to owe something to biblical and patristic notions of the angel with a flaming sword who expelled Adam and Eve from paradise and who stands guard over the Garden of Eden. Surt's particular role in the apocalyptic events of Ragnarök, when he leads a band of troops against the Æsir and kills the god FREY, is outlined in the eddic poem VÖLUSPÁ, and Snorri, building on the description found there, depicts the advent of the sons of Muspel after the sky has been torn as follows:

> Surt will ride in the vanguard, and both before and behind him there will be burning flame; his sword will be splendid, and light will blaze from it more brightly than the sun.

According to the name-lists or THULUR, Surt is simply listed as a giant.

B24, 28, 35, 40, 50; C5, 9, 48; D456

suttee

The name given to the practice of a wife burning on her husband's funeral pyre. Echoes of the practice are widespread in Norse literature. According to the thirteenth-century Icelander SNORRI STURLUSON, NANNA, the wife of the god BALDR, died of grief and was burned at his side, while in eddic verse BRYNHILD organizes her own death, alongside a number of other human sacrifices, at the pyre of her beloved, the mighty hero and dragon-slayer SIGURD. That episode is also recorded in the legendary VÖLSUNGA SAGA, where a still more curious case is attested, when SIGGEIR is burned alive in his house by the heroes SIGMUND and SINFJÖTLI, in revenge for the killing of VÖLSUNG, Sigmund's father. Völsung's daughter, SIGNÝ, the reluctant wife of Siggeir, who has acted throughout to hasten his death, is offered an escape by her brother (and lover), Sigmund, and by Sinfjötli, their son by an incestuous union, but prefers instead to die alongside her hated husband. The early thirteenth-century Danish historian SAXO GRAMMATICUS tells a still more touching story about another Signý, the betrothed of the warrior Hagbard, who when she believed her beloved had been captured and hanged, had her serving-maids set fire to their house, and hanged herself as it burned around her. Hagbard, however, had delayed his own execution precisely to find out if Signý would act as she should. When he sees the flames rise from her house, he goes to his death happy, proclaiming:

> Now . . . a sure hope remains of a love renewed; and

even death shall have its own delight. Both worlds have their own pleasure.

In a similar vein, the late fourteenth-century FLATEYJARBÓK manuscript records the salutary tale of Sigrid the Proud, later the wife of King Svein of Denmark, who left her first husband, King Eirík of Sweden, after he dedicated his life to the god ODIN:

> Then at this point Sigrid the Proud abandoned King Eirík, and it was said by everyone that he felt humiliated by her behaviour. For in fact it was the custom in Sweden that if a king died his queen should lie beside him in the barrow; but she knew that he had dedicated his life to Odin [for ten years] in exchange for victory when he fought against his kinsman Styrbjörn, and that he had not many years to live.

The late thirteenth-century NJÁLS SAGA includes what is perhaps the most touching and vivid account of the practice in the literary record, albeit one that involves Christians. When the aged Njál and his sons are surrounded in their home by their enemies, who are about to burn them in their house, both Njál and his elderly wife Bergthóra are offered safe passage from the house by Flósi, the leader of the burners:

> Flósi came up to the door and said that Njál and Bergthóra should come to speak to him. Njál did so. Flósi said: 'I want to offer you a way out, because you don't deserve to burn inside.' Njál said: 'I don't want to come out, because I am an old man, and I am scarcely equipped to avenge my sons, and I don't want to live in shame.' Flósi spoke to Bergthóra: 'Come out, you lady of the house, for I wouldn't wish you to burn inside for anything.' Bergthóra said: 'I was young when I married Njál, and I promised him that one fate should affect us both.'

Bergthóra and her husband retire to their bed, lie under the covers, and are duly burned; when the burners inspect the corpses afterwards, they are amazed that their bodies appear unharmed, an outcome considered a mark of especial divine favour.

B25, 42, 60, 64, 65, 68, 76, 79, 85; C1, 6–8, 20; D525

Sutton Hoo

The most celebrated of Anglo-Saxon burial sites, consisting of a large number of BURIAL MOUNDS. The main mound contains a substantial BOAT BURIAL with rich treasures, including a helmet, purse-cover, ceremonial whetstone and shield, all of which incorporate traditional motifs. Alongside the trappings of a pagan burial, however, there are also a number of items, including baptismal spoons, that may suggest that the occupant was a recent convert. No human remains were recovered from the mound, and it is possible that the entire construction was intended as a cenotaph, although given the condition of the soil it is still feasible that no remains have survived. It seems most likely that the mound was built as part of the funerary rites of a member of East Anglian royal dynasty. Rædwald remains the most plausible person to be associated with the site, although it has recently been suggested that the mound and its contents were intended as a cenotaph to King Sæberht of Essex. Both the contents of the main mound itself, and a number of individual items recovered from it are routinely associated with events and descriptions in the Old English poem BEOWULF, although no definite link has ever been demonstrated beyond doubt.

B44; C3; D52, 53, 61, 424

Suttung ('sup-heavy')

A giant, sometime owner of the MEAD OF POETRY, which he extorted from the dwarfs FJALAR and GJALAR, in compensation for their murder of his parents. His name occurs in a number of eddic poems simply as that

Sutton Hoo *The helmet from the boat burial at Sutton Hoo.*

of a giant, but only in HÁVAMÁL is he linked directly with the tale of the mead of poetry.

B12, 14, 23, 24, 38, 30, 35, 40, 50, 56, 59, 73, 87, 90; C2, 5, 9, 17, 24, 33, 46, 48

Svadilfari ('unlucky traveller')

According to the eddic poem HYNDLULJÓD, the stallion who impregnated LOKI, transformed into a mare, with the eight-legged SLEIPNIR. The thirteenth-century Icelander SNORRI STURLUSON incorporates Svadilfari into his own account of the GIANT BUILDER, describing in detail both Svadilfari's tremendous powers of endurance and his 'seduction' by Loki.

B12, 14, 23, 24, 28, 30, 35, 40, 50, 56, 59, 73, 87, 90; C2, 5, 9, 17, 24, 33, 46, 48

Sváfnir ('sleep-bringer')

(1) According to the eddic poem HELGAKVIDA HJÖRVARDSSONAR, the father of the beautiful SIGRLINN. (2) One of the many names of the god ODIN. (3) Elsewhere in the POETIC EDDA, in GRÍMNISMÁL, in a verse cited by the thirteenth-century Icelander SNORRI STURLUSON, the name of one of the snakes who slither at the foot of the world-tree YGGDRASIL.

B12, 14, 23, 24, 28, 30, 35, 40, 50, 56, 59, 73, 87, 90; C2, 5, 9, 17, 24, 33, 46, 48

Svafrlöd

According to the legendary VÖLSUNGA SAGA, one of GUDRÚN's serving-maids. When, after Gudrún's rival BRYNHILD has discovered the truth of the deception of her husband GUNNAR's wooing, she is asked by Gudrún what is troubling her and her colleagues, she replies (with some understatement): 'This is a dreadful day: our hall is full of grief.'

B25, 42, 65, 68, 79; C1, 6

Svanhild ('swan-battle')

Doomed daughter of the mighty hero SIGURD and the tragic heroine GUDRÚN. The legendary VÖLSUNGA SAGA describes her as follows:

> Gudrún and Sigurd had a daughter called Svanhild; she was the most beautiful of all women, and had piercing eyes like her father's, so that few dared look her in the face. She far surpassed other women in her beauty as the sun does other heavenly bodies.

This physical trait is recalled in the saga in its account of her death, which comes about at the instigation of BIKKI, the wicked counsellor of King JÖRMUNREKK. After Jörmunrekk sends his son RANDVÉR to woo Svanhild on his behalf, Bikki, who is accompanying Randvér, first urges the young prince to take Svanhild for himself, and then informs the elderly king, who has both

young people put to death. Randvér is hanged, but Svanhild's fate is far less prosaic:

> Bikki spoke another time: 'No one has earned worse from you than Svanhild; have her die in disgrace.' The king replied: 'I'll take your advice.' So Svanhild was tied up at the gate to the stronghold, and horses stampeded towards her. But when she turned her eyes on them, the horses shied from trampling her. When Bikki saw this, he had a bag pulled over her head. That was done, and she died.

These dreadful events lead directly on to the vengeance Gudrún prepares for Jörmunrekk through her sons, HAMDIR and SÖRLI, as described in the eddic poem HAMDISMÁL. The normally passive Gudrún has clearly been provoked beyond endurance. In the eddic poem GUDRÚNARHVÖT, which was clearly one of the sources used by the compiler of *Völsunga saga*, Gudrún describes her daughter's fate as follows:

> 'All round Svanhild sat serving-maids,
> she it was I loved best of all my bairns.
> Such was Svanhild in my chamber:
> like a glorious gleam of sun.

> 'I decked her with gold and gorgeous gowns,
> before I gave her away to the Goths.
> For me the hardest of all my griefs
> is for the fair head of Svanhild,
> that they trod in the mud under horses' hooves.'

B12, 20, 25, 30, 32, 42, 56, 65, 68, 73, 79, 87, 90; C1–3, 6, 17, 24, 33, 46

Svanhvít *see* HLADGUD SVANHVÍT.

Svanni *see* RÍGSTHULA.

Svarri *see* RÍGSTHULA.

Svartálfaheim *see* BLACK ELVES.

Svarthöfdi ('black head')

According to a verse that appears in the eddic poem HYNDLULJÓD, quoted by the thirteenth-century Icelander SNORRI STURLUSON, the progenitor of all sorcerers.

B12, 14, 23, 24, 28, 30, 35, 40, 50, 56, 59, 73, 87, 90; C2, 5, 9, 17, 24, 33, 46, 48

Svásud ('delightful')

According to the name-lists or THULUR, the name of a GIANT; the thirteenth-century Icelander SNORRI STURLUSON names him as the father of SUMR, the personified summer.

B24, 28, 35, 40, 50; C5, 9, 48

Sváva ('sleep-maker')

A VALKYRIE, the daughter of the legendary King EYLIMI and, according to the eddic poem HELGAKVIDA HJÖRVARDSSONAR, the beloved of the hero HELGI HJÖRVARDSSON. In the eddic poem HELGAKVIDA HUNDINGSBANA I, the Valkyrie SIGRÚN is said to be the reincarnation of Sváva.

B12, 30, 56, 73, 77, 90; C2, 17, 24, 33, 46

Svebdeg *see* SVIPDAG.

Sveggjud

According to the eddic poem HELGAKVIDA HUNDINGSBANA I, echoed in VÖLSUNGA SAGA, the horse of the hero HÖDBRODD.

B12, 25, 30, 42, 56, 65, 68, 73, 79, 87, 90; C1–3, 6, 17, 24, 33, 46

Svein *see* RÍGSTHULA.

Sveipud *see* SVIPUD.

Svinn *see* HVERGELMIR.

Svipdag ('sudden day')

A hero, whose wooing of the beautiful MENGLÖD is recounted in the eddic poem SVIPDAGSMÁL. Other sources, including the early thirteenth-century Danish historian SAXO GRAMMATICUS and the legendary HRÓLFS SAGA KRAKA, also chronicle various deeds of derring-do performed by legendary heroes named Svipdag. The thirteenth-century Icelander SNORRI STURLUSON names Svipdag, whom he gives alternatively as Svebdeg, as a descendent of the god ODIN's son Veggdegg, who ruled over the East Saxons; the occurrence of a character called Swæfdæg in the royal genealogies of Anglian houses in Anglo-Saxon England strengthens the association. Elsewhere the association between Svipdag and his god is still more explicit: according to Snorri's YNGLINGA SAGA, the god Odin travels under the name Svipdag the Blind.

B12, 30, 56, 64, 73, 74, 87, 90; C2, 7, 8, 17, 20, 24, 33, 46; D139, 140, 566, 567

Svipdagsmál ('the lay of Svipdagr')

A composite work, consisting of the two poems usually known as GRÓAGALDR and FJÖLSVINNSMÁL, together recounting the education and deeds of the legendary hero SVIPDAG.

B12, 30, 56, 64, 73, 87, 90; C2, 7, 8, 17, 24, 33, 46; D139, 140, 393, 516

Svipud

According to the eddic poem HELGAKVIDA HUNDINGSBANA I, echoed in the legendary VÖLSUNGA SAGA (which uses the form Sveipud), the horse of the hero GRANMAR.

B12, 25, 30, 42, 56, 65, 68, 73, 79, 87, 90; C1–3, 6, 17, 24, 33, 46

Svívör ('shame-goddess')

According to a verse by the poet THORBJÖRN DÍSARSKÁLD, cited by the thirteenth-century Icelander SNORRI STURLUSON, a giantess who was killed by the god THOR.

B24, 28, 35, 40, 50; C5, 9, 48

Svöl(l) *see* HVERGELMIR.

Swæfdæg *see* SVIPDAG.

Sylg ('sucking')

According to the thirteenth-century Icelander SNORRI STURLUSON, one of the rivers that flows from the horns of the mythical stag EIKTHYRNIR, via the seething torrents of HVERGELMIR.

B24, 28, 35, 40, 50; C5, 9, 48

Syn ('refusal')

According to the thirteenth-century Icelander SNORRI STURLUSON, one of the goddesses or ÁSYNJUR.

B24, 28, 35, 40, 50; C5, 9, 48

Sýr An alternative name for FREYJA.

T

Tacitus

A Roman historian (AD55–118), whose GERMANIA, written to contrast the clean simplicity of the life of the Germanic tribes with the moral degeneracy of con-temporary Rome, nonetheless remains an important source for the beliefs and customs of Germanic peoples in the first century.

B2; C29

Tanngnjóst

Tanngnjóst ('gnash-tooth')

According to the thirteenth-century Icelander SNORRI STURLUSON, one of the two goats – the other is Tanngrísnir ('snarl-tooth') – who pull THOR 's chariot. Both goats could be (and were) slaughtered one evening for food and would reappear whole the next day as long as their bones were unharmed. Similar magical powers of self-renewal are attributed to the boar SÆHRÍMNIR, which feeds the hungry warriors of the EINHERJAR. Snorri gives a typically lively description of the process and incidentally explains how Thor acquired his two servants THJÁLFI and RÖSKVA, in his account of the journey of Thor and LOKI to the hall of the giant ÚTGARDALOKI:

> They came at evening to the house of a peasant, and took lodgings for the night there; in the evening Thor took his goats and slaughtered both. Then they were flayed and put in the pot. When it had boiled, Thor and his companion settled down to supper, and Thor invited the peasant his wife and their children to eat with them; the peasant's son was called Thjálfi and the daughter Röskva. Then Thor placed the goat-skins on the far side of the fire, and said that the peasant and his family should throw the bones onto the goat-skins. Thjálfi, the peasant's son, picked up a goat's thigh-bone and split it with his knife to get at the marrow. Thor stayed there the night and arose before dawn, and dressed himself and took his hammer Mjöllnir and raised it up and hallowed the goat-skins; the goats got up, but one of them was lame in a hind leg. Thor noticed this, and declared that the peasant or one of his household must not have behaved properly with the goat's bones; he could see that the thigh-bone was broken. There is no need to describe at length, since everyone can imagine how terrified the peasant must have been, when he saw how Thor let his brows sink down over his eyes; as for what he could see of the eyes themselves, he thought he would collapse just from the sight of them. Thor gripped his hammer-shaft with his hands, so that his knuckles whitened, while the peasant and his family did as one would expect: they cried out earnestly and begged for mercy, and offered in compensation everything they owned. When he saw their terror, his anger left him and he calmed down, and took from them in settlement their children, Thjálfi and Röskva, and they became his bond servants and have attended him ever since.

B24, 28, 35, 40, 50; C5, 9, 48

Tanngrísnir *see* TANNGNJÓST.

temple ring

A large ring, evidently kept within the TEMPLE or, according to some sources, worn by the priest or GODI, upon which the most solemn OATHS were sworn. Literary descriptions of such rings are relatively widespread in the sagas and in a handful of eddic poems (notably ATLAKVIDA and HÁVAMÁL). The Anglo-Saxon Chronicle for 876 recalls how a peace settlement was made between the Danes and the Angles *on þam halgan beage* ('on the holy ring').

B12, 14, 20,, 23, 30–2, 56, 73, 87, 90; C2, 17, 24, 33, 46

temples

The earliest Germanic sacred sites appear to have been special groves or enclosures, each of which might be described by the generic term VÉ, found widely in place-names. Each such sacred site might well contain an altar or HÖRG, as well as representations of the gods, and the trappings of sacrifice. According to the Roman historian TACITUS, describing the practice of the continental Germanic tribes in the first century:

> They do not consider it to be compatible with the majesty of the heavenly beings to enclose their gods within walls, or to depict them in the image of any human face; they consecrate groves and woods, and they call with names of gods that secret thing, which they see only with the eye of faith.

The most extensive description of such a sacred site, including a temple complex, is that of UPPSALA, given by the eleventh-century chronicler ADAM OF BREMEN, in his *Gesta Hammaburgensis ecclesiae pontificum* ('Deeds of the Bishops of the Church of Hamburg-Bremen'), composed after he arrived in Bremen in 1066 or 1067 to act as adviser to Archbishop Adalbert (1043–72), and purporting to be a contemporary depiction. By contrast, the fullest description of a temple (Old Norse *hof*) is that found in a mid-thirteenth-century Icelandic saga, EYRBYGGJA SAGA, but it too can scarcely be considered a reliable account. Although the author of the saga elsewhere amply demonstrates considerable antiquarian interest, it seems likely that in this case he is simply embellishing an only marginally earlier description by the thirteenth-century Icelander SNORRI STURLUSON in his *Hákonar saga góða*. Nonetheless, the description might be cited in full, as providing, at worst, an imaginative reconstruction of the thirteenth century of a supposed temple from the time of the settlement of Iceland. The saga tells how the settler Thórólf Mosturskegg has brought high-seat pillars (Old Norse ÖNDVEGISSÚLUR) from his temple in Norway, one of which is carved with an image of the god THOR; he has also brought soil from under Thor's seat. After casting his high-seat pillars overboard when in sight of land, he determines to settle and build where the pillars are washed ashore:

Thorólf built a large farm at Hofsvag, which he called Hofstadir, and had a big temple erected there with its door in one of the side-walls by the gable. Just inside the door were the high-seat pillars with the so-called 'sacred nails' embedded in them, and beyond that point the building was held to be hallowed. Within the temple proper there was a construction built much like the choir in present-day churches, and in the midst of it a raised platform like an altar. On this platform lay a solid ring of some twenty ounces, on which folk had to swear all their OATHS. It was the duty of the temple GODI to wear this ring on his arm at every public gathering. Also on the platform was a sacrificial bowl, with a sacrificial twig (Old Norse HLAUTTEIN) shaped like a priest's aspergillum for the blood of animals sacrificed to the gods to be sprinkled from the bowl. Within the choir-like part of the building were arranged the images of the gods, in a circle right around the platform. Every farmer had to pay tax to the temple, and another of their duties was to support the temple *godi* in his duties, just as farmers these days have to support their chieftains. It was the duty of the temple *godi* to look after the temple and see to its proper upkeep at his own expense, as well as to hold sacrifices.

Excavations carried out at Hofstadir in Mývatnssveit in Iceland at the beginning of the century to some extent confirm the picture offered in *Eyrbyggja saga*; attached to a turf long-house was a stone-built extension containing a pit filled with charcoal, ashes and the remains of various animal-bones, presumably all that was left of sacrificial offerings. To judge from Norwegian place-name evidence, where the element *hof* is used either alone or in combination with the name of a god in over a hundred locations, it would seem that such temples form an annexe to the domestic buildings of particular homesteads (presumably those of priests) who would preside over ceremonies for neighbouring homesteads as well as their own.

B2, 77; C29, 39; D105, 181, 280, 457

Thakrád

According to the eddic poem VÖLUNDARKVIDA, one of the servants of the wicked King NÍDUD; it is to Thakrád that Nídud turns to summon his hapless daughter BODVÍLD, after she has been seduced by the legendary smith, VÖLUND.

B12, 30, 31, 56, 73, 87, 90; C2, 17, 24, 33, 46

Thegn *see* RÍGSTHULA.

Thekk ('clever')

(1) A DWARF, according to the catalogue in the eddic poem VÖLUSPÁ. (2) Found as one of the many names

of the god ODIN in the eddic poem GRÍMNISMÁL.

B12, 30, 56, 59, 73, 87, 90; C2, 17, 24, 33, 46

Thidreks saga

A work, also known as *Thikdreks saga af Bern*, probably first compiled in the first half of the thirteenth century, that gives a detailed account of the lives and genealogies of a number of heroes and legendary figures widely celebrated in Old English, German and Norse literature, including (to use the Norse forms of their names) ATLI BUDLASON, GUNNAR, HÖGNI GJÚKASON, JÖRMUNREKK, SIGURD and VÖLUND. All of these heroes are celebrated according to their relationships, whether by blood, marriage or simply acquaintance, with the central character of Thidrek of Bern, who is therefore presented as something of a King Arthur figure, presiding over a court of champions. Within the purview of this grand plan, chronology is (necessarily) widely flouted, with heroes from utterly distinct generations and even centuries placed together. The prologue, which purports to offer an unusually detailed account of the process of saga-composition, claims to have assembled material from many diverse sources, including venerable oral sources finally preserved in written form, such as German lays. Recent research suggests a much simpler picture: the composer may well have done little more than translate an already existing Low German compilation, adding orally transmitted material of his own.

B8, 31, 42, 71, 84; C15, 21, 25, 44; D16, 84, 88, 362, 410, 557, 627

Thír *see* RÍGSTHULA.

Thjálfi ('serving-elf'?)

Servant of the god THOR, and brother of RÖSKVA. According to the thirteenth-century Icelander SNORRI STURLUSON, it was Thjálfi who lamed one of the two goats who pulled Thor's chariot, TANNGNJÓST and Tanngrísnir, after Thor and LOKI had come to stay at the house of Thjálfi's father *en route* to Thor's meeting with the giant ÚTGARDALOKI. Thor slaughtered his goats and cooked them, and everyone enjoyed a meal, but after he had collected the bones into the skins and blessed the goat-skins with MJÖLLNIR, the goats apparently became whole again, although one was lame because Thjálfi had split its thigh-bone to get at the marrow. To compensate Thor, Thjálfi and his sister are handed over to accompany the two Æsir on their journey. At the court of Útgardaloki, Thjálfi becomes embroiled in a contest of his own and is humiliated in a race against the personification of thought, HUGI. In another episode recounted by Snorri, Thjálfi acquits himself well when he accompanies Thor in his duel

Thjassi

against the giant HRUNGNIR and has to face the mighty clay giant with a mare's heart, MOKKURKÁLFI, that Hrungnir has created; just as Thor defeats Hrungnir, so Thjálfi conquers his giant foe.

B24, 28, 35, 40, 50; C5, 9, 48

Thjassi *see* THJAZI.

Thjazi

A giant, father of SKADI and, according to the eddic poem HÁRBARDSLJÓD, son of one ALVALDI. Thjazi, whose name appears as Thjassi in some sources, is responsible for the abduction of the goddess IDUN, and is slain by the god THOR in an episode recounted in both skaldic poetry, at the turn of the tenth century by poet THJÓDÓLF OF HVÍN, and in prose by the thirteenth-century Icelander SNORRI STURLUSON. According to Snorri, three of the gods or ÆSIR – ODIN, HŒNIR and LOKI – kill an ox on their travels but cannot cook it, despite repeated attempts. A large eagle, observing them from a nearby tree, offers to help, if he is given his share. After they agree, the eagle quickly despatches two hams and both shoulders of the ox, leaving the three Æsir to divide the rest. Loki, indignant, aims a blow at the eagle with a rod, but the eagle flies off, with the rod still attached to it, and with Loki still attached to the rod. As Snorri puts it:

> The eagle flew at such a height that Loki's feet crashed against rocks and stones and trees, and he thought that his arms would be wrenched from their sockets; he called out, and begged persistently for a way out, but the eagle said he would never be free unless he swore solemnly to lure Idun outside ÁSGARD with her apples, and Loki agreed. He was set free, and returned to his companions.

At the agreed time Loki duly entices Idun to a certain wood outside Ásgard, on the pretext that he has found apples more splendid than her own, which she should bring along for comparison. Thjazi arrives in eagle shape and snatches her off to his home in THRYMHEIM. The Æsir soon miss Idun and her apples and begin to age and fade. After holding a council, they threaten to kill or torture Loki, the last one to see Idun, unless he can recover her. Loki promises to do so only if the goddess FREYJA will lend him her falcon cloak. Then he flies to JÖTUNHEIM, turns Idun into a nut and flies back to Ásgard as fast as he can, pursued by Thjazi in the shape of an eagle. The waiting Æsir build a great fire on Ásgard's walls, which the clumsier eagle is unable to avoid. Thjazi is killed by the waiting Æsir, chiefly by Thor. When his daughter, Skadi, comes seeking revenge, she is bought off, mainly by being married to

NJÖRD, although the match does not prove a happy one.

In contrast to *Hárbardsljód*, Snorri gives the name of Thjazi's father as Ölvadi and speaks of his enormous wealth, which his sons divided among themselves by taking equal numbers of mouthfuls of gold in turn.

B12, 14, 23, 24, 38, 40, 35, 40, 50, 56, 59, 73, 87, 90; C2, 5, 9, 17, 24, 33, 46, 48; D264

Thjódmar

According to the eddic poem GUDRÚNARKVIDA III, the father of the legendary hero THJÓDREK, with whom the tragic heroine GUDRÚN is (wrongly) accused of having an affair.

B12, 30, 56, 73, 87, 90; C2, 17, 24, 33, 46

Thjódnuma *see* HVERGELMIR.

Thjódólf of Hvín

A Norwegian poet who flourished at the turn of the tenth century, and is chiefly remembered as one of the court-poets of King Harald Fair Hair. Two extant skaldic poems, HAUSTLÖNG and YNGLINGATAL, are attributed to him from a relatively early period, while a third, HRAFNSMÁL (also known as *Haraldskvædi*), is ascribed to him by no less an authority than the thirteenth-century Icelander SNORRI STURLUSON, who also preserves many of his other verses. Recent opinion prefers the attribution given in other manuscripts of *Hrafnsmál*, which is now usually thought to have been composed by another of Harald's court-poets, THORBJÖRN HORNKLOFI.

B24, 28, 35, 39, 40, 45, 50, 62, 83, 87; C5, 9, 16, 48; D264

Thjódrek

According to the eddic poem GUDRÚNARKVIDA III, the son of THJÓDMAR, and the prince with whom the tragic heroine GUDRÚN is alleged by the vindictive HERKJA to have had an affair. Gudrún's second husband, ATLI BUDLASON, is naturally unhappy when he hears this. As the poem has it:

> Gudrún said:
> 'What ails you Atli? Always, BUDLI's son,
> your heart seems heavy; why never laugh?
> To your noblemen it would seem better
> to talk to men and look at me.'

> 'I am grieved, Gudrún, GJÚKI's daughter:
> in my hall Herkja told me,
> that you and Thjódrek had slept under sheets,
> and lightly lingered under linen.'

> 'I shall swear my most solemn oath,

160

on the white and holy stone,
I never did so with Thjódmar's son,
what man and woman might do.

'I only embraced the leader of hosts,
the warrior brave, a single time;
other conversations were otherwise
when we two sank sadly into solitary talk.

'Thjódrek came here with thirty men,
of all those thirty not one yet lives:
you robbed me of brothers and mail-clad men,
you robbed me of every close relation.'

Thjódrek would appear to be identical with the character Thidrek or Dietrich of Bern, well attested elsewhere, who appears at the centre of the extraordinary compilation of legendary material entitled THIDREKS SAGA.

B8, 12, 42, 30, 56, 71, 73, 84, 87, 90; C2, 13, 15, 17, 21, 24, 25, 33, 44, 46

Thökk ('thanks')

A giantess, assumed to be LOKI in disguise, who refused to weep for the dead god BALDR and so liberate him from HEL. Her rather ironic name is recorded by the thirteenth-century Icelander SNORRI STURLUSON, who cites a supporting verse:

Thökk will weep with dry tears
at Baldr's funeral: alive or dead
I had no benefit from the old man's son.
Let Hel keep what she has.

B24, 28, 35, 40, 50; C5, 9, 48

Thöll *see* HVERGELMIR.

Thor

Son of the god ODIN and the giantess JÖRD, who is also known as HLÓDYN or FJÖRGYN. The mightiest of the ÆSIR and the chief giant-killer, Thor is among the best attested of all the figures of northern myth and legend, and a large number of tales are attached to his name. As the thirteenth-century Icelander SNORRI STURLUSON puts it:

Thor is the most outstanding of the Æsir ... he is the mightiest of all the Æsir and men. His dominion is a place called THRÚDVANGAR, and his hall is called BILSKÍRNIR, where there are 540 rooms: it is the largest building ever built ... Thor has two goats, called TANNGNJÓST and Tanngrísnir, and a chariot in which he drives, drawn by these goats; from this he is called Öku-Thor ['charioteer-Thor']. He has three special possessions; one of them is the hammer MJÖLLNIR, familiar

Thor *Copper alloy figure from Eyrarland, Iceland, of a seated figure, holding a hammer (or perhaps his beard); although usually interpreted as a depiction of Thor, the figure may be a gaming-piece instead.*

to frost-giants and mountain-giants when it is raised aloft, and little wonder: it has smashed many of their fathers' and kinsmen's skulls. He has another possession that is most precious, a belt of strength, that doubles his Ás-strength when he buckles it on. He has a third and most crucial possession: a pair of iron gloves, with which he has to hold the hammer. But there is no one so knowledgeable that they can describe all his adventures, but I can tell you so many tales about him, that it will take much time before every tale I know is told.

Thor's wife is SIF of the golden hair, and his children all have suitably mighty names: his two sons, who will inherit the hammer Mjöllnir after the apocalyptic events of RAGNARÖK, are called MAGNI and MÓDI, and his daughter is THRÚD.

Physical descriptions of him are few. Snorri, in a EUHEMERISTIC account that identifies him with one TROR, a grandson of King Priam of Troy (and a forefather of Odin) says that he was outstandingly beautiful, with hair fairer than gold. According to the eddic poem THRYMSKVIDA, however, he has a bristling red beard, piercingly frightening eyes when roused and a vast appetite. His drinking-prowess is similarly attested in accounts of his journey to the court of ÚTGARDALOKI when he begins to drain the ocean, and in the tale of the giant HRUNGNIR, who has to be entertained in ÁSGARD from Thor's drinking-horn.

Thor's main role in the literary record is as a killer of giants; some skaldic verses simply consist of lists of his victims, among the most celebrated of whom are undoubtedly GEIRRÖD, HYMIR, Hrungnir, THJAZI, THRÍVALDI and THRYM, and the giant builder of Ásgard. A verse by the Icelander Vetrlidi Sumarlidason, who was himself killed by Christian missionaries in the course of the conversion, simply celebrates Thor's prowess against his (mostly) giant foes:

You broke the limbs of Leikn,
you thumped Thrívaldi,
you struck down STARKAD,
you dealt a death-blow to GJÁLP.

A still longer list is provided by THORBJÖRN DÍSARSKÁLD, also composed about the time of the conversion in Iceland, in which no fewer than eight of Thor's victims among the giants are given. But his special wrath is reserved for the MIDGARD-SERPENT, which he will eventually kill at Ragnarök, in a mighty conflict in which he himself is slain. Before that, however, he almost succeeds in hauling the Midgard-serpent from the ocean, with a hook baited with an ox-head, in his fishing-trip with the giant Hymir, as well as nearly raising it from the ground in the course of his journey to the court of ÚTGARDALOKI. In the latter expedition, of course, he is accompanied by LOKI, father of the Midgard-serpent, along with his customary servants THJÁLFI and his sister RÖSKVA. Thor's relationship with Loki is deeply ambiguous. At times the two are seen, as in the trip to the courts of Útgardaloki or Thrym, as travelling-companions, but at other times their antagonism is deep. In the eddic poem LOKASENNA it is only the physical threats of Thor that finally silence Loki. Presumably on the occasions when Loki is included as Thor's companion, his sharp wits are expected to balance Thor's physical prowess. Thor's interventions are seldom subtle, and often, as in his first meeting with Hrungnir or the giantess HYRROKKIN, he has to be dissuaded by the other Æsir from immediately escalating conflicts to violence. A more intellectual side to Thor's nature is perhaps seen in the eddic poem ALVÍSSMÁL, in which he is seen to question and eventually outwit a dwarf, ALVÍS, whose very name suggests that he is 'all-wise'. But in another eddic dialogue-poem, HÁRBARDSLJOD, Thor finds himself matched against Odin, the more usual protagonist in these wisdom contests, and clearly comes off worst. In *Hárbardsljód*, Odin's jibe about their relative constituencies may well reflect the fact that Thor's chief popularity lay among the common folk:

Odin gets the noblemen, who fall in slaughter,
but Thor gets the kin of slaves.

Thor was clearly much worshipped throughout the period. Even if we discount the elaborate description of a TEMPLE to Thor in EYRBYGGJA SAGA, there are plenty of similar accounts. In FLATEYJARBÓK, for example, there is a detailed description of a statue of Thor in a temple in Thrandheim, to which one Skeggi brings King Olaf Tryggvason:

Thor sat in the middle; he was the most highly venerated. He was vast, and entirely decorated with gold and silver. Thor was positioned sitting in a chariot; he was extremely fine. There were two goats harnessed in front of him, splendidly made. Both the chariot and the goats ran on wheels. The rope around the goats' horns was made of twisted silver, and the entire piece was made with extremely sumptuous skill.

Apart from the statue of the god, it is clear that temples might also contain other items. The early thirteenth-century Danish historian SAXO GRAMMATICUS reports on the sacking of a pagan temple of Thor in Sweden by Magnus Nilsson in 1125 as follows:

He made sure that he brought home some hammers of an unusual weight, which they call Jupiter's, used by the people of the island in the ancient religion. For the men of old, seeking to understand the causes of thunder and lightning through the equation of things, took huge heavy hammers of bronze, by which they thought the crashing in the sky might have been caused, reckoning that the mighty and powerful noise might (at it were) very possibly be imitated by the labour of a smith. But Magnus, in his zeal for Christian doctrine and his hatred of paganism, determined to rob the temple of its accoutrements, and Jupiter of his symbols in his very sanctuary. As a result, to this day the Swedes reckon him guilty of sacrilege, and a plunderer of sacred property.

Among the many honorific titles attested for Thor are Ásabrag ('prince of the Æsir'; found in SKÁLDSKAPARMÁL), Ása-Thor ('Thor of the Æsir'), Atli ('the fearsome one'; found in *Skáldskaparmál*), HLÓR RIDI ('loud rider'), Öku-Thor ('charioteer Thor'), Sönnung ('the true one'); Véur ('the holy one', witnessed only in the eddic poem HYMISKVIDA, although Snorri uses the related title Véud), VINGNIR ('swinger'?) and VINGTHÓR ('tumult-Thór').

B12, 14, 23, 24, 28, 30, 35, 40, 50, 56, 59, 60, 64, 73, 77, 85, 87, 90; C2, 5, 7–9, 17, 24, 33, 39, 46, 48; D69, 93, 133, 205, 283, 296, 332, 348, 464, 477, 480, 486, 512, 515, 540, 565, 628

Thóra

Daughter of King Hákon of Denmark. According to the eddic poems GUDRÚNARKVIDA I and II, echoed by the legendary VÖLSUNGA SAGA, it was with Thóra that the tragic heroine GUDRÚN stayed for seven seasons after the killing of the mighty hero SIGURD, while she and Thóra made an elaborate embroidery. As *Gudrúnarkvida* II has Gudrún explain:

'I sat with Thóra for seven seasons,
Hákon's daughter, in Denmark;
to give me joy she embroidered in gold
southern halls and Danish swans.

'We two portrayed the play of warriors,
the leader's troops with delicate toil,
red shields, and ranks of Huns,
a sword-band, a helm-band, a leader's train.

'SIGMUND's ships, slipped from shore,
with gilded beaks and graven stems;
on the cloth we embroidered the battle
of SIGAR and SIGGEIR south at Fjón.'

B12, 25, 30, 42, 56, 65, 68, 73, 79, 87, 90; C1–3, 6, 17, 24, 33, 46

Thorbjörg lítilvölva

A prophetess, according to EIRÍKS SAGA RAUDA, which offers a strikingly vivid description of both Thorbjörg and her methods, when the settlement in Greenland seek her help in the midst of a devastating famine:

There was a woman in the settlement called Thorbjörg; she was a prophetess, and was known as *lítilvölva* ('little sibyl'). She had nine sisters, who had all been prophetesses, but she was the only one left alive. In the winter it was Thorbjörg's custom to attend feasts; people invited her to their houses, especially those who were curious about their own futures or the prospects for the harvest. Since Thorkel of Herjólfsness was the chief farmer in the district, it was thought to be up to him to find out when the current difficulties would cease. Thorkel invited the prophetess to his house, and a good reception was prepared for her, as was normal when women of that kind were being received. A high-seat was prepared for her with a cushion, which had to be filled with hen's feathers. When she arrived in the evening, accompanied by the man who had been sent to fetch her, she was dressed in a blue cloak with a strap, and with stones all the way down to the hem. On her neck she wore glass beads, and on her head she wore a hood of black lamb-skin, lined with white cat-skin. She carried a staff in her hand, with a knob on top; it was made of brass, and just below the knob the staff was set round with stones. She wore a belt made of crumbling wood, from which hung a large skin pouch, where she kept the charms she needed for her craft. She wore shaggy calf-skin shoes on her feet, and huge long laces with big tin buttons on the end. She wore cat-skin gloves, white inside and furry. When she entered the room everyone thought they ought to offer her warm greetings, which she received according to her opinion of whoever bestowed them. Farmer Thorkel took the wise woman by the hand and escorted her to the seat that had been prepared for her. Thorkel asked her to run her eyes over his herds and home and household; she said little about anything. The tables were set up that evening, and the meal of the prophetess went as follows: a kid's-milk gruel was made for her, and prepared for her food were the hearts of every kind of living creature available. She had a brass spoon and an ivory-handled knife bound with two copper rings, the tip of which was broken. When the tables were cleared, farmer Thorkel approached Thorbjörg and asked her how she liked his home and everyone's behaviour, and how soon she would know the answer to his question, which everyone wanted to know. She said that she would reveal nothing until the morning, after she had slept there that night. Late the next day she was supplied with necessary preparations for performing [the form of magic known as] SEID. She asked to be provided with women who knew the incantation necessary for performing *seid* called *Varðlokkur* ['guardian songs']; no such women could be found, so people on the farm were asked if anyone knew the incantation. Then Gudríd said: 'I am neither a witch nor a wise-woman, but Halldís, my foster-mother taught me an incantation in Iceland called *Varðlokkur*.' Thorbjörg answered: 'Then you are wiser than I thought.' Gudríd said: 'This is the sort of knowledge and activity that I want no part of, because I am a Christian woman.' Thorbjörg answered: 'It may turn out that you shall give help to others here, and be no worse a woman for it. But I look to Thorkel to provide what is necessary.' Thorkel put pressure on Gudríd, and she said she would do what he wanted. The women made a circle, and in the middle sat Thorbjörg on a special raised platform [Old Norse: *seiðhjallr*]. Gudríd recited the chants so beautifully and well that no one present thought they had ever heard more beautiful chanting. The prophetess thanked her for the chant; many spirits who thought the chanting beautiful had turned up: 'They had previously avoided us and refused to give us any help; now many of those things are clear to me which had previously baffled both me and others. I can say that this famine will not last longer than the winter, and that matters will improve with the spring; the sickness that has lain here long shall also improve more quickly than expected. As for you,

Thorbjörn dísarskáld

Gudríd, I shall reward for the help you have given us, since now your future is entirely clear to me. You will make a most distinguished marriage here in Greenland, although it will not last long, since your paths point abroad towards Iceland, and there will arise there a great and splendid line, and over your family will shine a bright beam. But now, farewell and be happy, my daughter.' Then people approached the wise-woman, and each of them asked whatever they most wanted to know. She gave replies readily, and few things did not follow in accord with what she said.

B38; C27; D292

Thorbjörn dísarskáld ('poet of the DÍSIR')

An Icelandic poet of the late tenth century, composing around the time of the conversion. His nickname implies that he composed verses of the female divinities known as DÍSIR, but only one and a half stanzas of his work survive, evidently part of a longer poem on the god THOR, celebrating his defeat of a number of named giantesses:

[MJÖLLNIR] struck on Keila's skull,
Kjallandi you battered in full;
LÚT and Leida you'd already killed,
Búseyra's blood you let flow;
HENGJANKJAPTA you finished off,
HYRROKKIN died at an earlier stage,
and similarly SVÍVÖR, earlier still,
was likewise deprived of her life.

B39, 45, 62, 83, 87; C16

Thorbjörn hornklofi ('horn-claw')

A court-poet of King Harald Fairhair. The reason behind Thorbjörn's nickname, which also appears as a poetic term or HEITI for 'raven', is all the more intriguing given that he is principally associated with the skaldic poem HRAFNSMÁL (also known as *Haraldskvædi*).

B39, 45, 62, 83, 87; C16

Thorgerd Hölgabrúd ('Thorgerd, bride of Hölgi')

According to the thirteenth-century Icelander SNORRI STURLUSON:

it is said that there was a king called Hölgi, after whom Hálogaland was named; he is the father of Thorgerd Hölgabrúd. SACRIFICES were made to both of them, and the BURIAL MOUND which was piled up over Hölgi was made of alternate layers of sacrificial coins of gold and silver, and layers of earth and stones.

Apart from the implicitly incestuous suggestion that Thorgerd's father was called Hölgi, the notion that she

is the object of cult of veneration local to Hálogaland seems supported by other sources, including *Færeyinga saga* and *Jómsvíkinga saga*. NJÁLS SAGA adds the detail that the temple to Thorgerd Hölgabrúd also contained a statue of the Thor in his chariot. Hölgabrúd also occurs in lists of poetic words or THULUR for troll-wife or giantess.

B11, 24, 28, 35, 40, 50, 76; C5, 9, 26, 48; D66

Thorri see FORNJÓT.

Thórsdrápa

A fragmentary late tenth-century composition of the poet EILÍF GODRÚNARSON, generally considered to be one of the most allusive and difficult of all skaldic poems. *Thórsdrápa* is preserved by the thirteenth-century Icelander SNORRI STURLUSON in the course of his retelling of the mythical content, which concerns the god THOR's expedition to the court of the giant GEIRRÖD, an episode that contains a number of parallels with others of Thor's expeditions to the courts of other giants, notably HYMIR and ÚTGARDALOKI. The problem for modern interpreters of the poem lies partly in the fiercely difficult diction and poetic periphrases or KENNINGS of the poem, but also in the extent to which Snorri's own interpretation can be trusted.

B24, 28, 35, 39, 40, 45, 50, 62, 83, 87; C5, 9, 16, 48; D172, 291

Thræl see RÍGSTHULA.

Thridi see HÁR.

Thrívaldi ('thrice-mighty')

According to the thirteenth-century Icelander SNORRI STURLUSON, who quotes a skaldic verse in support, a giant who battled against the god THOR and was killed. The ninth-century poet BRAGI BODDASON specifies that Thrívaldi had nine heads.

B24, 28, 35, 40, 50; C5, 9, 48

Thröng An alternative name for FREYJA.

Thrór ('burgeoning')

(1) A DWARF, according to the catalogue in the eddic poem VÖLUSPÁ. (2) One of the many names of the names ODIN.

B12, 30, 56, 59, 73, 87, 90; C2, 17, 24, 33, 46

Thrúd ('power')

(1) A daughter of the god THOR, sister of the mighty offspring MAGNI and MÓDI. It is possible that she is the figure that the dwarf ALVÍS wishes to wed in the eddic

poem ALVÍSSMÁL, and it is intriguing to note that the giant HRUNGNIR is described by the ninth-century BRAGI BODDASON as 'the abductor of Thrúd', but otherwise the sources are silent. (2) The name Thrúd also appears in the eddic poem GRÍMNISMÁL as that of one of the thirteen VALKYRIES to offer ale to the warriors of the EINHERJAR in VALHALL.

B24, 28, 35, 40,4 50; C5, 9, 48

Thrúdgelmir ('power-yeller')
According to the name-lists or THULUR, presumably drawing on the eddic poem VAFTHRÚDNISMÁL, the name of a GIANT.

B12, 14, 23, 24, 28, 30, 35, 40, 50, 51, 56, 59, 73, 87, 90; C2, 5, 9, 17, 24, 33, 46, 48

Thrúdheim ('power-home')
According to the eddic poem GRÍMNISMÁL, the home of the god THOR. In his EUHEMERIZED account of the gods, however, the thirteenth-century Icelander SNORRI STURLUSON distinguishes between Thor's residence in ÁSGARD (which he calls THRÚDVANGAR), and the kingdom of TROR, the grandson of King Priam of Troy, whom he identifies with Thor. Tror rules over Thrace, 'which we call Thrúdheim'.

B12, 30, 56, 73, 87, 90; C2, 17, 24, 33, 46

Thrúdi *see* VALKYRIES.

Thrúdvangar ('power-plain')
According to the thirteenth-century Icelander SNORRI STURLUSON, the home of the god THOR; the eddic poem GRÍMNISMÁL calls the place THRÚDHEIM.

B12, 14, 23, 24, 28, 30, 35, 40, 50, 56, 59, 73, 87, 90; C2, 5, 9, 17, 24, 33, 46, 48

Thrungva An alternative name for FREYJA.

Thrym ('crash')
The giant, unattested outside the eddic poem THRYMSKVIDA, who stole the god THOR's hammer MJÖLLNIR in order to gain the goddess FREYJA as his bride. The plan backfires badly, however, when Thor himself turns up in Freyja's place, dressed in women's clothing. After eating and drinking his (considerable) fill, Thor waits for the wedding to be hallowed with Mjöllnir. Once it is back in his hands he puts the hammer to customary use, striking the love-lorn Thrym dead.

B12, 30, 56, 73, 87, 90; C2, 17, 24, 33, 46

Thrymheim ('crash-home')
According to the thirteenth-century Icelander SNORRI STURLUSON, who is drawing on the eddic poem

GRÍMNISMÁL, the home of the giant THJAZI and his daughter SKADI. After her marriage to the god NJÖRD in compensation for the killing of her father, Skadi tries to persuade the god to live with her in Thrymheim, but he cannot abide it, preferring his own seaside home in NÓATÚN.

B12, 14, 23, 24, 28, 30, 35, 40, 50, 56, 59, 73, 87, 90; C2, 5, 9, 17, 24, 33, 46, 48; D264

Thrymgjöll ('mighty crash')
According to the eddic poem FJÖLSVINNSMÁL, the gate to the hall of the giantess MENGLÖD, guarded by dogs and a wall of flame; apparently the gate was built for Menglöd by some dwarfs, the sons of the otherwise unknown Sólblindi ('sun-blind').

B12, 30, 56, 73, 87, 90; C2, 17, 24, 33, 46

Thrymskvida ('the poem of Thrym')
An eddic poem, preserved in the CODEX REGIUS manuscript, that offers a comic account of an otherwise unattested episode of mythical history, namely that in which the giant THRYM steals the god THOR's hammer MJÖLLNIR in a vain attempt to gain the goddess FREYJA as his bride. The poem seems to go much further than other comic poems in the eddic corpus, such as the eddic poems HYMISKVIDA or LOKASENNA, both of which appear to have been known to the poet. Indeed, *Thrymskvida* derives much of its diction from other eddic and skaldic poems, including BALDRS DRAUMAR, HÚSDRÁPA, *Hymiskvida*, *Lokasenna* and VÖLUSPÁ, and appears to have been a relatively late composition, perhaps of the early thirteenth century. Just as *Thrymskvida* appears to lean on the diction of earlier poems, so, too, does it seem to exploit (and invert) a number of perceived stereotypes for comic effect. The manly Thor, for example, is depicted in full bridal dress, as a result of the rather coy refusal of the normally sexually voracious Freyja to comply with the giant's request. Thrym himself is portrayed as a fairly naïve and sympathetic character, far removed from the kind of rough, violent or grandiosely wise giant who appears elsewhere.

Thrymskvida tells a relatively straightforward tale in a brisk, repetitive style close to that of a ballad. Thor awakes to find his hammer stolen, and (rather curiously, given their usual relationship) rushes to tell LOKI, who borrows Freyja's feather-cloak and flies off to JÖTUNHEIM, where he discovers that the culprit, Thrym, demands Freyja as ransom. When Loki returns, Thor barges into Freyja's chamber to tell her to get ready and her refusal is magisterial:

Freyja was enraged, and gave a snort,

so that all the gods' hall trembled,
and the great BRÍSINGAMEN burst:
'You'd think I'd become the most desperate for men,
if I drove with you to the giants' domain.'

The ÆSIR hold council, and, again rather curiously, it is the taciturn watchman of the gods HEIMDALL who suggests that Thor dress up as a woman and travel in Freyja's place:

Then Heimdall spoke, the brightest of gods:
he saw far ahead, like the other VANIR.
'Let us put Thor in the bridal gown,
let him wear the great Brísings' neck-ring!

Let us have keys jangling beneath him,
and women's clothes falling round his knees,
and broad gems sitting on his chest,
let us top out his head with style.'

Then Thor spoke, the strapping god:
'The gods will call me an effeminate wretch,
if I let myself be put in a bridal gown.'

Then Loki spoke, the son of Laufey:
'Shut up, Thor, and don't say such things;
Giants will soon dwell within the gods' borders
unless you have your hammer back.'

Then they put Thor into a bridal gown,
had him wear the great Brísings' neck-ring;
they had keys jangling beneath him,
and women's clothes falling round his knees,
and broad gems sitting on his chest,
and they topped out his head with style.

When Thor is finally persuaded to agree, Loki gleefully accompanies him, dressed as his handmaid. There follows a splendidly comic set-piece scene at the wedding banquet at Thrym's court, where the 'bride' alone consumes an entire ox, eight salmon, all the delicate tit-bits intended for the women and three casks of mead. Loki explains that 'Freyja', wild with longing, has fasted for eight days. When Thrym peeks under the veil for a kiss, he is so startled by the fierce eyes of his intended that he leaps back the whole length of the room; Loki explains that 'Freyja' has had eight sleepless nights in anticipation:

Early at evening they all arrived,
and ale was brought forth before the giants.
One guest ate a whole ox, eight salmon too,
and all of the dainties intended for the women;
then SIF's husband drank three casks of mead.

Then Thrym spoke, the lord of ogres:
'Did you ever see bride eat more keenly;
I never saw bride eat more widely,
nor any maiden drink more mead.'

The all-cunning handmaid sat ready,
and found something to say to the giant's speech:
'Freyja hasn't eaten at all for eight nights,
she was so desperate for the giants' domain.'

He bent down under the veil, and wished for a kiss;
and then jumped back the full length of the hall:
'Freyja's eyes! Why are they so fierce?
Fire seemed to me to flare from her eyes.'

The all-cunning handmaid sat ready,
and found something to say to the giant's speech:
'Freyja hasn't slept at all for eight nights,
she was so desperate for the giants' domain.'

Apparently as part of the marriage ceremony, Mjöllnir is brought in to hallow the bride 'in the name of [the goddess] VÁR', who is listed elsewhere as one of the ÁSYNJUR. Once Thor finds his hammer back in his hands, the fate of the giants is sealed; the hapless Thrym is the first to be slain.
B12, 30, 56, 73, 87, 90; C2, 17, 24, 33, 46; D91, 93, 107, 212, 216, 239, 249, 277, 316, 340, 454, 455, 472, 515, 534, 576, 592, 617

thulur

The name given to versified and mnemonic lists of poetic synonyms or HEITI; the singular form is *thula*. Common subjects for such lists are ÆSIR, ÁSYNJUR, GIANTS, DWARFS, sea-kings and VALKYRIES, as well as the trappings of the Viking life, such as shields, swords, ships, sea and battle. Several eddic poems incorporate such lists, for example VÖLUSPÁ, which contains a catalogue of dwarfs, and GRÍMNISMÁL, which contains a list of names for the god ODIN, and others, such as ALVÍSSMÁL, are themselves apparently structured around similar mnemonic principles.
B12, 14, 23, 24, 28, 30, 35, 40, 50, 56, 59, 73, 87, 90; C2, 5, 9, 17, 24, 33, 46, 48; D210, 272, 310

Thunær *see* SAXNÔT; THUNOR.

Thunor (Old English: 'thunder')

The Anglo-Saxon god of thunder, identified with THOR. Thunor is witnessed in Anglo-Saxon sources almost exclusively in place-names, and in the term *Thunresdæg* ('thursday'). When describing the activities of the pagan Danes, the Christian Anglo-Saxon commentators such as ÆLFRIC or WULFSTAN almost invariably use the Norse name Thor. In a ninth-century Old Saxon baptismal pledge, the form given is Thunær.

B67; C45

thurs ('giant')

A term (plural *thursar*) for GIANT, used alongside (and apparently almost interchangeably with) such terms as JÖTUN and TROLL. Also the name of a RUNE.

D398, 401, 402

Thviti

According to the thirteenth-century Icelander SNORRI STURLUSON, the rock used by the ÆSIR to help bind the wolf FENRIR to the stone slab GJÖLL.

B24, 28, 35, 40, 50; C5, 9, 48

Thyn *see* HVERGELMIR.

Tiw

An Anglo-Saxon deity, presumably derived from the Germanic *Tiwaz*, and identified with the Norse battle-god TÝR; in Old English verse the cognate word *tir* means 'glory'. Tiw's appearance in the Anglo-Saxon written record is largely confined to the term *Tiwesdæg* ('Tuesday'), and the warlike characteristics of the god are deduced from the parallel position of the Roman god of war Mars in the weekly calendar in, say, French *mardi*.

B67; C45

Tötrughypja *see* RÍGSTHULA.

Troan

According to the EUHEMERISTIC account of the gods offered by the thirteenth-century Icelander SNORRI STURLUSON, the daughter of King Priam of Troy, and mother of TROR, who is identified with the god THOR.

B24, 28, 35, 40, 50; C5, 9, 48

troll ('giant', 'monster')

A term for GIANT, alongside JÖTUN and THURS. Trolls and troll-wives are seldom depicted as helpful or beneficent, and they tend to live in remote rocks, caves and mountains. Often they appear alone, but sometimes trolls are depicted in cosy family groups, usually consisting of mother-and-son or father-and-daughter combinations; the troll Thórir and his daughters, who take in the outlaw Grettir in GRETTIS SAGA ÁSMUNDARSONAR, are a case in point, as are GRENDEL and his mother in the Old English BEOWULF.

B41; C12

Trönubeina *see* RÍGSTHULA.

Tror

According to the EUHEMERISTIC account of the gods offered by the thirteenth-century Icelander SNORRI STURLUSON, the son of MUNON and TROAN, and so the grandson of King Priam of Troy. As Snorri explains:

> We call him THOR. He was brought up in Thrace by a duke called LORICUS, and when he was ten he inherited his father's weapons. He was as beautiful to gaze upon when he walked among others as ivory inlaid in oak. His hair is more beautiful than gold. When he was twelve he had his full strength: he lifted from the ground twelve bear-skins at once, and killed his foster-father Loricus and his wife Lóra or Glóra, and took control of the whole kingdom of Thrace, which we call THRÚDHEIM. Then he travelled through many lands and explored every corner of the world and alone defeated all berserks and giants, one of the greatest dragons and many wild animals. In the northern part of the world he met a prophetess called SIBYL, whom we call SIF, and married her. No one can tell Sif's ancestry. She was the fairest of all women, and her hair was like gold.

B24, 28, 35, 40, 50; C5, 9, 48; D296

Tuisto

The first-century Roman historian TACITUS gives an account of the belief of the continental Germanic tribes in the first century in his GERMANIA:

> In the traditional poems, which form their only chronicle of the past, the Germans celebrate a deity born from the earth called Tuisto, whose son MANNUS is thought to be the source of their race and himself to have begotten three sons who have given their names to three groups of tribes: the Ingvaeones, closest to the sea; the Herminones, in the interior; and the Istvaeones, who comprise all the rest.

B2; C29

Týr ('god')

One of the ÆSIR, associated with battle and war. According to the thirteenth-century Icelander SNORRI STURLUSON he placed his right hand in the mouth of the wolf FENRIR as a pledge when the Æsir were trying to bind him with the magical fetter GLEIPNIR, and lost it when the wolf realized he had been deceived. As Snorri puts it:

> He is the bravest and most daring and he has much power over victory in battles; it is good for bold men to pray to him. A man who does not flinch and surpasses others is said to be 'as brave as Týr'. He was so clever that a clever man is called 'as wise as Týr'. One demonstration of his bravery is that when the Æsir were enticing Fenrir

to place the fetter Gleipnir on him, he did not trust them to release him until they placed Týr's hand in the wolf's mouth as a pledge; and when the Æsir would not release him he bit off the hand at the wolf-joint [wrist], and so Týr is one-handed and is not considered a promoter of settlements between people.

During the apocalyptic events of RAGNARÖK, rather confusingly, he faces the huge dog GARM rather than Fenrir, and each slays the other. Further confusion surrounds his ancestry. The eddic poem HYMISKVIDA makes him the son of the giant HYMIR, while Snorri calls him the god ODIN's son. In the eddic poem LOKASENNA, LOKI claims to have fathered a son on Týr's wife, but nothing more is known of either the woman or the child.

Týr's very name, of course, is apt to sow confusion, being derived from Germanic *Tiwaz* as a simple noun for 'god' and related to both Greek Zeus and Latin *deus*. The singular form of his name often occurs in poetic periphrases or KENNINGS for the other Æsir, while the plural form, *tivar*, simply means 'gods'. Týr is also the name of a RUNE associated, according to the eddic poem SIGRDRÍFUMÁL, with victory.

B12, 14, 23, 24, 28, 30, 35, 40, 50, 56, 59, 73, 87, 90; C2, 5, 9, 17, 24, 33, 46, 48; D95, 129, 56

Tyrfing *see* HLÖDSKVIDA.

U

Úlf Uggason

An Icelandic poet, who flourished at the time of the conversion, around the year 1000, best known for his composition of the skaldic poem HÚSDRÁPA, which celebrates the mythological scenes depicted on the hall that Oláf pái had caused to be built at Hjardarholt. Among the myths depicted are the procession of mythological beings who attended the funeral of the god BALDR, the conflict between the god THOR and the MIDGARD-SERPENT, and the battle apparently fought by the gods HEIMDALL and LOKI in the shape of seals.

B39, 45, 62, 83, 87; C16; D499, 500

Úlfdalir ('wolf-dales')

The place inhabited by the legendary smith VÖLUND and his brothers, according to the eddic poem VÖLUNDARKVIDA. It is from Úlfdalir that Völund is abducted by the warriors of the wicked King NÍDUD, as he waits alone for the return of his beloved HERVÖR ALVITR.

B12, 310, 31, 56, 73, 87, 90; C2, 17, 24, 33, 46

Úlfhednar ('wolf-skins')

Like the bear-like BERSERKS, with whom they are often conflated and confused, frenzied warriors who appear to have fought in animal guise, in this case that of wolves, and often in teams. In later sources, such warriors, like the berserks, seem to have become linked to those characters, invariably pagans, who are said to have the power to change shape, notably into WEREWOLVES.

D87

Ull

According to the thirteenth-century Icelander SNORRI STURLUSON, one of the ÆSIR, son of the goddess SIF and so step-son of the god THOR. Numerous poetic periphrases or KENNINGS in skaldic verse attest to his association with archery and hunting, as well as with skating and skiing. As Snorri puts it:

> He is such a fine archer and skier that no one can match him; he is also handsome in appearance, with the talents of warrior: he is good to pray to in single combat.

Other kennings suggest that he used a shield as a boat on at least one occasion, and similar tales can be inferred about characters such as the Norse SKJÖLD and the Anglo-Saxon SCYLD. Although the literary evidence for Ull is sparse, there is plentiful place-name evidence, some based on the variant form of his name, Ullin, to suggest a widespread cult.

B24, 28, 35, 39, 40, 45, 50, 62, 83, 87; C5, 9, 16, 48; D35

Ullin *see* ULL.

Unn *see* ÆGIR.

Uppsala

An important cult centre and supposedly the site of a huge temple complex, named Ubsola, described in great detail by the eleventh-century chronicler ADAM OF BREMEN, in his *Gesta Hammaburgensis ecclesiae pontificum* ('Deeds of the Bishops of the Church of Hamburg-Bremen'), composed after he arrived in Bremen in 1066 or 1067 to act as adviser to Archbishop Adalbert (1043–72). His account deserves full quotation, including his own added notes:

> Now I shall say something about the superstition of the Swedes. That people have a very famous TEMPLE called Ubsola, not far from the town of Sigtuna. In that temple, which is wholly adorned with gold, the people worship the statues of three gods, of which the mightiest, THOR, sits in the middle of a triple throne. Wodan [WODEN] and Fricco [FREY?] sit on either side. The following are the meanings of the three: Thor, they reckon, rules the sky; he governs thunder and lightning, winds and storms, fine weather and fertility. The second is Wodan, that is, 'frenzy'. He rules war and gives people strength against the enemy. The third is Fricco, who grants peace and sensual delight to mortal men; they depict his image with a huge erect penis, but they carve Wodan in armour, as our people depict Mars, and Thor, with his mace, looks like Jupiter. They also worship gods who were once men, whom they reckon to be immortal because of their heroic acts ... For each of their gods they have appointed priests to offer up the SACRIFICES of the people. If plague or famine threatens, there is a sacrifice to the image of Thor; if war, to Odin; if a marriage is to be held, to Fricco. Moreover, every nine years there is a communal festival of every province in Sweden held at Ubsola, and no one is granted an exemption from the ceremony. Everyone, including commoners and kings, sends their offerings to Ubsola; and (what is crueller than any punishment) those already converted to Christianity have to buy themselves off from the ceremonies. The sacrifice proceeds as follows: nine males of every living creature are offered up, and it is customary to placate the gods with their blood: their corpses are hung in the grove next to the temple. That grove is so sacred to the heathens that every single tree is considered to be divine, thanks to the death or rotting carcass of the sacrificed; they hang dogs and horses there alongside men. One Christian told me that he had seen seventy-two corpses of various kinds hanging there. In addition, the empty songs with which they conduct this sacrificial rite are so many and disgusting that it is best to pass over them in silence.
>
> Close to the temple there is a vast tree, with its branches spreading far and wide, evergreen both in summer and winter. There is also a spring there, where pagan sacrifices are held. A man is flung into the spring alive; if he fails to resurface, the wish of the people will be fulfilled.
>
> The temple is surrounded by a golden chain, hanging from the building's gables, and plainly visible from far away to those approaching, since the shrine itself is found on a level plain surrounded by hills, like an amphitheatre.
>
> These feasts and sacrifices last nine days. Each day they sacrifice a man with the other animals, so that in nine days a total of seventy-two creatures are sacrificed; the sacrifice takes place about the time of the spring equinox.

The accuracy of Adam's vivid account has been questioned on several levels, not least since Bishop Thietmar of Merseburg offers a much less detailed version of a similar sacrifice offered at Lejre a few generations earlier. Extensive archaeological investigations at Uppsala itself have failed to reveal anything on the scale proposed for the temple, although three large royal burial mounds testify to the importance of the site.

B48, 70; C47; D280, 334

Urd ('fate')

One of the NORNS, who are said to live at URDARBRUNN. Together with her sisters, SKULD and VERDANDI, she is said by the thirteenth-century Icelander SNORRI STURLUSON to determine the fates of men.

B24, 28, 35, 40, 50; C5, 9, 48; D22, 608

Urdarbrunn ('Urd's well', 'fate's well')

A holy spring in ÁSGARD, under one of the roots of the world-tree YGGDRASIL, close to the place where the ÆSIR hold their council. According to the thirteenth-century Icelander SNORRI STURLUSON, two birds, from whom all swans are descended, live at Urdarbrunn.

B24, 28, 35, 40, 50; C5, 9, 48; D22, 23

Útgard ('the world outside')

The area inhabited by GIANTS and TROLLS, as distinct from the parts (generally called MIDGARD, but sometimes divided as ÁSGARD and Midgard) that are inhabited by the ÆSIR and by men. Often located in the east, Utgard was presumably thought to encircle the known world. In the tale of ÚTGARDALOKI, as told by the thirteenth-century Icelander SNORRI STURLUSON, Útgard has become localized still further, and appears simply as the castle of Útgardaloki.

B24, 28, 35, 40, 50; C5, 9, 48

Útgardaloki ('Útgard-Loki')

The giant who beguiles the god THOR and his companions in a number of tests of strength and ability, according to a tale most fully expounded by the thirteenth-century Icelander SNORRI STURLUSON. The story bears certain similarities to that relating to a journey made by Thor to the home of the giant GEIRRÖD, as is clear from parallel accounts of both episodes in the writings of the early thirteenth-century historian SAXO GRAMMATICUS, and it may be that both versions ultimately derive from one original. According to Snorri, Thor is accompanied on his travels by his servants, THJÁLFI and his sister RÖSKVA, together with LOKI. They meet a huge giant who calls himself SKRÝMIR and who proceeds to humiliate the travellers, notably Thor, in a number of ways, before directing them to the castle of Útgardaloki, where he claims they will face still sterner tests. Loki faces an eating contest with a character called LOGI, and is narrowly defeated, while Thjálfi is equally made to look foolish in a race against someone called HUGI. Both these contests are, however, merely the prelude to a series of trials of strength faced by Thor himself. First he is challenged to a drinking contest, using a horn that Snorri describes as 'not all that big, but rather long'; as Útgardaloki is made to explain:

> It is considered well drunk from this horn if it is drained at a single draught, but some drain it in two; no one is so poor a drinker that they cannot manage it in three.

After three hefty pulls, Thor makes only a moderate impression on the level of liquid. Next, much chastened, he is invited to lift up Útgardaloki's cat from the floor, a feat that is reckoned child's play; nonetheless, Thor succeeds in raising only a single paw. Finally, Thor is asked to wrestle Útgardaloki's aged nurse, but fails to throw her, and is indeed himself brought to one knee before his genial host calls a halt. When they leave the next day, Thor and his companions, utterly humiliated, are accompanied by Útgardaloki, who at parting reveals the extent of the deception he has played upon them.

He was Skrýmir, and all their frustrations were due to his tricks. In the various contests, they were up against opponents they could not hope to beat: Thjálfi had run against *hugi* (thought'), which outpaces all, and Loki had eaten against *logi* ('fire'), which consumes everything. Thor's performance had shocked the giants, for the horn from which he drank was connected to ocean, which had ebbed visibly: henceforth the tides would commemorate his feat; the cat had been the MIDGARD-SERPENT, whose mighty bulk he had caused to stir; he had wrestled against *elli* ('old age'), which none could conquer and which had brought even the mightiest men low. As Thor vows vengeance, both Útgardaloki and his castle melt away.

Apart from the general resemblances to others of Thor's giant-slaying expeditions already noted, specific details of Thor's trip to the hall of Útgardaloki are hard to parallel. The notion that one of the humiliations heaped upon Thor and his companions was that they hid in the thumb of Skrýmir's glove, convinced that it was a hall, is, however apparently alluded to in two eddic poems; in LOKASENNA Loki (who, in Snorri's version at least, was present at the time) taunts Thor not only with hiding in the thumb of the glove but also with being unable to undo the straps of the knapsack tied by Skrýmir, and in HÁRBARDSLJÓD the god ODIN (disguised as Hárbard) seems to refer to the same episode, although here the giant in question is called FJALAR:

> 'Thor has strength aplenty, but not heart:
> in fear and cravenness you cowered in a glove,
> you wouldn't then have seemed to be Thor;
> you didn't then dare, because of your fear,
> to sneeze or fart, in case Fjalar heard.'

B24, 28, 35, 40, 50, 64; C5, 7–9, 48; D325, 415, 395

V

Vafthrúdnir ('mighty weaver')
A wise giant, whom the god ODIN engages in a deadly battle of wits in the eddic poem VAFTHRÚDNISMÁL. After initially testing his guest, the giant is submitted to a detailed series of mythological queries, culminating in a series of questions about the apocalyptic events of RAGNARÖK, ending with an inquiry about Odin's own death. Apparently satisfied, Odin then asks the giant an unanswerable question about what he himself had whispered into the ear of his dead son, BALDR, on the

funeral pyre. Vafthrúdnir ruefully concedes defeat at this point and, we surmise, consequently forfeits his own life.

B12, 30, 51, 56, 73, 87, 90; C2, 17, 24, 33, 46

Vafthrúdnismál ('the lay of Vafthrúdnir')
An eddic poem, preserved in the CODEX REGIUS and much used as source by the thirteenth-century Icelander SNORRI STURLUSON, who quotes a number of stanzas. The core of the poem depicts a wisdom

contest between the god ODIN and the wise giant VAFTHRÚDNIR, introduced by a series of stanzas in which the goddess FRIGG implores her husband not to undertake a proposed trip to the Vafthrúdnir's hall. Odin duly arrives, calling himself Gagnrád, belittles the giant's wisdom and is asked four questions concerning cosmology. When he successfully answers these, the giant invites Odin to join him on the bench for a more serious contest, in which the loser's head is at stake. Odin proceeds to ask twelve questions about the past and the present, ending with one about where Vafthrúdnir acquired his own wisdom; Vafthrúdnir replies that part of his knowledge comes from the dead. The contest proceeds, with Odin asking four questions relating to the future and specifically to the end of the world at RAGNARÖK. Up to this point there has been a certain patterning in the questioning, based on multiples of four (four questions for Odin, twelve for Vafthrúdnir on the past and the present, four for Vafthrúdnir on the future), but now Odin adds a further question about Ragnarök, asking about his own fate; Vafthrúdnir duly answers that Odin will be swallowed by the wolf, FENRIR, and avenged by VÍDAR. Having apparently satisfied himself as to his own fate (which logically precludes failure in the current wisdom contest), Odin ends the match by asking a question about BALDR's funeral to which the giant cannot know the answer:

'Much have I travelled,
Much have I tried,
Much have I tested the powers.
What did Odin himself say
into the ear of his son
before he mounted the pyre?'

Vafthrúdnir's reply, the final stanza of the poem, is a dignified acceptance at once of the identity of his opponent, and of defeat:

'No man knows
what you said long ago
into the ear of your son;
with a doomed mouth
did I tell my ancient lore
and speak of Ragnarök.
It was with Odin I traded my wit:
you will always be wisest of all.'

B12, 30, 51, 56, 73, 87, 90; C2, 17, 24, 33, 46; D131, 548

Valaskjálf

An ancient home of the ÆSIR, decked in silver, according to the eddic poem GRÍMNISMÁL. The thirteenth-century Icelander SNORRI STURLUSON assigns it to the

Valhall Picture stone from Tjängvide, Gotland, Sweden, usually interpreted as depicting a warrior's welcome into Valhall. The warrior is shown riding an eight-legged horse, like Sleipnir, the horse of the god Odin; the dead warrior is being welcomed by a female figure (perhaps a Valkyrie) carrying a horn.

god ODIN, and says that it is the site of his panoramic seat of HLIDSKJÁLF.

B24, 28, 35, 40, 50; C5, 9, 48

Valdamar of Denmark

According to the legendary VÖLSUNGA SAGA, one of the noble characters who are said to accompany the doomed heroes GUNNAR and HÖGNI GJÚKASON on their mission to the court of King HÁLF, to reconcile themselves with their sister GUDRÚN after the killing of her first husband, the mighty hero SIGURD.

B25, 42, 65, 68, 79; C1, 6

Valgrind *see* HEL.

Valhall ('hall of the slain')

The mighty hall, also known as Valhöll or Valhalla, where the god ODIN gathers about him those slain in battle. The thirteenth-century Icelander SNORRI STURLUSON gives a full account, describing how these warriors, the EINHERJAR, are waited upon by VALKYRIES, eat boar's flesh provided by the ever-renewed SÆHRÍMNIR and drink the mead that is given by the mythical goat HEIDRÚN. Odin joins the feast but does not share in it: he only drinks wine and, requiring no food, offers instead morsels to two wolves, FREKI and Geri, who sit at his feet. Physical details of Valhall can be gleaned from the eddic poem GRÍMNISMÁL and other sources. It has 540 gates, through which 800 warriors can pass at a time, and is thatched with spears; mail and shields bedeck the interior. Clearly the conception is that of a paradise for warriors training for the final battle at RAGNARÖK. An example of the extraordinary zeal with which some characters, in fiction at least, might face the prospect of a trip to Valhall is found in the so-called death song attributed to the mighty Danish Viking, Ragnar loðbrók:

> It pleases me to know that BALDR's father [Odin] prepares the benches for a feast; soon we shall drink ale from those curved horns. A champion who enters Odin's dwelling-place does not bemoan his death; I shall not enter his hall with words of fear on my lips. The ÆSIR will welcome me, death comes without grief . . . I am keen to be away. The DÍSIR summon me home, those whom Odin sends for me from the halls of the Lord of Hosts. Gladly shall I drink ale in the high-seat alongside the Æsir. The days of my life are over; I laugh as I die.

B24, 28, 35, 40, 50; C5, 9, 48; D347, 417

Valhalla, Valhöll *see* VALHALL.

Váli

(1) Also known as ÁLI, the son of the god ODIN and the giantess RIND, and, by killing the god HÖD, the avenger of the god BALDR. According to the eddic poem VÖLUSPÁ, the vengeance was carried out when he was only one day old. The thirteenth-century Icelander SNORRI STURLUSON describes him as 'brave in battle and an excellent shot'. As one of the younger generation of ÆSIR, he is destined to survive the apocalyptic events of RAGNARÖK, and live on in the reborn world.

(2) The name Váli is also given in some sources as that of a son of LOKI, and in some versions of *Völuspá* as that of a dwarf.

B12, 14, 23, 24, 28, 30, 35, 40, 50, 56, 59, 73, 87, 90; C2, 5, 9, 17, 24, 33, 46, 48

Valkyries ('choosers of the slain')

Female figures, closely associated with the god ODIN, whose function it was to select those slain in battle for VALHALL. GRÍMNISMÁL records the names of thirteen Valkyries who would serve ale to the EINHERJAR there:

> I want Hrist and Mist to bring me a horn
> Skeggjöld and Skögul,
> Hildi and Thrúdi, Hlökk and Herfjötur,
> Göll and Geirölul,
> Randgríd and Rádgríd and Reginleif:
> they bring the *einherjar* ale.

The thirteenth-century Icelander SNORRI STURLUSON, who cites the relevant verse, describes the Valkyries

Valkyries *Silver figures from Birka, Björkö, Uppland, Sweden, of women bearing drinking horns; such figures are often interpreted as Valkyries.*

immediately after the goddesses or ÁSYNJUR, and says:

> There are still other women, whose task is to wait in Valhall, serve drink and take care of the tableware and drinking-vessels . . . these are called Valkyries. Odin sends them to every battle; they allot death to men and decide on victory. Gunn and Róta and the youngest Norn, who is called SKULD, always ride and choose the slain and decide on the killing.

In the heroic poems of the POETIC EDDA, several of the female protagonists are depicted as Valkyries, notably BRYNHILD, KÁRA, SIGRÚN and SVÁVA, although in many of these cases the necessary identification is only made in the prose that accompanies the verse.

B12, 14, 23, 24, 28, 30, 35, 40, 50, 56, 59, 73, 87, 90; C2, 5, 9, 17, 24, 33, 46, 48; D106, 232, 302, 303, 561

Ván ('hope')

According to the rather allegorical account of the thirteenth-century Icelander SNORRI STURLUSON, the river that was formed from the dribbling saliva of the bound wolf FENRIR.

B24, 28, 35, 40, 50; C5, 9, 48

Vanadís An alternative name for FREYJA.

Vanaheim ('the home of the Vanir')

According to the eddic poem VAFTHRÚDNISMÁL, the home of the fertility-gods or VANIR.

B12, 30, 51, 56, 73, 87, 90; C2, 17, 24, 33, 46

Vánargand ('wand of hope')

According to the thirteenth-century Icelander SNORRI STURLUSON, another name for the wolf FENRIR.

B24, 28, 35, 40, 50; C5, 9, 48

Vanir

Fertility figures, who fought a war against the ÆSIR, and exchanged hostages. The god NJÖRD was one of those who was given to the Æsir, and he and his two children, the gods FREY and FREYJA, although formally counted among the Æsir, maintain their affiliation with their former kin. The Vanir are also indirectly involved in the myth of the MEAD OF POETRY, since KVASIR, from whose blood the mead was made, was himself first created from the shared spittle of Æsir and Vanir with which the truce was formally concluded. The longest account of the war between the Æsir and the Vanir is given by the thirteenth-century Icelander SNORRI STURLUSON in YNGLINGA SAGA:

> ODIN took his troops to battle against the Vanir, but they soon became aware of it and defended their land so that neither side could win. Each despoiled the other's territory and did much damage; when they both grew weary of this, they agreed a peace meeting, made a truce and exchanged hostages. The Vanir offered their most distinguished men, Njörd the Wealthy and his son Frey, but the Æsir took someone named HŒNIR, whom they called a splendid chieftain: he was a large and handsome man. They sent MÍMIR with him, a very wise man, and the Vanir offered the cleverest of their number, who was called Kvasir.

Aside from the discrepancy over the origin of Kvasir here, Snorri's account also conflicts with the highly allusive version of the tale given in the eddic poem VÖLUSPÁ, in stanzas that Snorri actually quoted:

> She remembers the war,
> the first in the world,
> when they stabbed GULLVEIG with many spears,
> and in HÁR's [Odin's] hall
> they burned her.
> Three times they burned
> the one thrice born,
> often, over again;
> but she still lives.
>
> They called her Heid,
> when she came to the house,
> a witch who could foretell;
> she knew the skill of wands,
> she practiced SEID where she could,
> she practiced *seid* in a trance;

> she was always a delight
> to wicked women.
>
> Then all the powers
> went to their judgement-thrones,
> the greatly hallowed gods,
> and held debate,
> whether the Æsir were obliged
> to render tribute,
> or all the gods were obliged,
> to pay the price.
>
> Odin flung his spear,
> cast it into the host,
> still that was the war,
> the first in the world;
> the shield-wall was shattered
> of the fortress of the Æsir,
> the Vanir with their war-spells
> trampled the battlefield.

B12, 14, 23, 24, 28, 30, 35, 40, 50, 56, 59, 73, 87, 90; C2, 5, 9, 17, 24, 33, 46, 48; D49, 115, 120, 439, 443, 504

Vár ('pledge')

According to the thirteenth-century Icelander SNORRI STURLUSON, one of the goddesses or ÁSYNJUR:

> She hears people's oaths and the private contracts men and women make between them. So contracts are called *várar*; she likewise punishes those who break them.

In the eddic poem THRYMSKVIDA she is invoked as part of the marriage ceremony conducted between the giant THRYM, and his 'bride' (the god THOR in disguise), although the antiquity of such a ritual is far from clear.

B12, 14, 23, 24, 28, 30, 35, 40, 50, 56, 59, 73, 87, 90; C2, 5, 9, 17, 24, 33, 46, 48

Varg ('wolf', 'outlaw')

A wolf or outlaw. Sometimes the two concepts are combined, and there is evidence to suggest that some *vargar* were WEREWOLVES.

D87

Vartari *see* BROKK.

Vásad *see* VETR.

Vé ('sacred enclosure')

Brother of the gods ODIN and VILI. According to the eddic poem LOKASENNA, both he and his brother Vili became lovers of Odin's wife, FRIGG.

B12, 30, 56, 73, 87, 90; C2, 17, 24, 33, 46

vé ('sacred enclosure')

The sacred enclosure surrounding a TEMPLE or often, apparently, simply a marked-out open space

Vedrfölnir

where worship could take place. The Roman historian TACITUS, describing the practice of the continental Germanic tribes in the first century, makes a particular point about the fact that, unlike the Romans, the Germanic tribes did not seek to contain their deities within temple walls.

B2; C29; D437, 457, 508

Vedrfölnir ('wind-witherer')

According to the thirteenth-century Icelander SNORRI STURLUSON, the hawk that sits between the eyes of the eagle perched on top of the world-tree YGGRDRASIL.

B24, 28, 35, 40, 50; C5, 9, 48

Veg see HVERGELMIR.

Veg(g)deg(g) see SVIPDAG.

Vegtamskvida see BALDRS DRAUMAR.

Veleda

According to the first-century Roman historian TACITUS, a Germanic seeress, worshipped by the local tribe as a goddess. No one was permitted to approach her directly. She dwelt in a high tower, and questions (and her responses) were conveyed by a member of her family. The notion of a magical or revered female figure dispensing mantic wisdom from a raised platform finds a curious echo some twelve centuries later in the account of THORBJÖRG LÍTILVÖLVA from EIRÍKS SAGA RAUDA.

B2; C29

Verdandi ('happening', 'present'?)

According to the thirteenth-century Icelander SNORRI STURLUSON, basing his account in part on the eddic poem VÖLUSPÁ, one of the three NORNS, whose sisters are URD ('past') and SKULD ('future').

B12, 14, 23, 24, 28, 30, 35, 40, 50, 56, 59, 73, 87, 90; C2, 5, 9, 17, 24, 33, 46, 48

Verse Edda see POETIC EDDA.

Vestri see AUSTRI.

Vetmímir see VINDBLÁIN.

Vetr ('winter')

The personification of winter. According to the thirteenth-century Icelander SNORRI STURLUSON:

> Vetr's father is called either Vindlóni or VINDSVAL; he is Vásad's son, and members of that family are grim and cold-hearted, and Vetr takes after them.

B24, 28, 35, 40, 50; C5, 9, 48

Véud, Véur. Alternative names for THOR.

Víd see HVERGELMIR.

Vídar ('wide-ruler'?)

Slayer of the wolf FENRIR during the apocalyptic events of RAGNARÖK, and so the avenger of his father, the god ODIN. The eddic poem VÖLUSPÁ, followed by the name-lists or THULUR, confirms him as Odin's son, while the thirteenth-century Icelander SNORRI STURLUSON names the giantess GRÍD as his mother.

Vídar *Detail from the late tenth-century Gosforth Cross, Cumbria, England, depicting the god Vídar ripping open the mouth of the monstrous wolf Fenrir at Ragnarök, in order to avenge the killing of his father, the god Odin.*

Elsewhere, Snorri describes Vídar as: 'the silent; he has a thick shoe, and is almost equal in strength to [the god] THOR. He is a great help to the ÆSIR in all perils.' His thick shoe plays a crucial role in his killing of Fenrir, as Snorri notes:

> The wolf will swallow Odin, and that will be his death; straight afterwards Vídar will approach and step with one foot on the wolf's lower jaw. On this foot he will wear a shoe made of material collected throughout all the ages: waste pieces cut from the toes and heels of people's shoes (so anyone who wants to help the Æsir should throw these bits away). With one hand he will seize the wolf's upper jaw, and tear its mouth apart: and that will be the wolf's death.

In the Epilogue to SKÁLDSKAPARMÁL, Snorri, in a typical piece of classicizing EUHEMERISM, goes so far as to identify Vídar with Aeneas, the hero of Virgil's Latin epic, the *Aeneid*.

B12, 14, 23, 24, 28, 30, 35, 40, 50, 56, 59, 73, 87, 90; C2, 5, 9, 17, 24, 33, 46, 48

Vídbláin, Vídfadmir *see* VINDBLÁIN.

Vidfinn *see* MÁNI.

Vidólf ('wood-wolf')

According to a verse from HYNDLULJÓD, quoted by the thirteenth-century Icelander SNORRI STURLUSON, the progenitor of all WITCHES.

B12, 14, 23, 24, 28, 30, 35, 40, 50, 56, 59, 73, 87, 90; C2, 5, 9, 17, 24, 33, 46, 48

Víf *see* RÍGSTHULA.

Víga-Glúms saga

An Icelandic saga, probably composed in the mid-thirteenth century, offering biographical information about the difficult and troublesome tenth-century figure Víga-Glúm Eyjólfsson. Unlike the equally re-calcitrant hero of the comparable EGILS SAGA, whose problematic relationship with his god, ODIN, forms a sub-plot throughout the saga, Víga-Glúm is to some extent presented as a man at odds with the fertility-god, FREY, to whom his enemy makes a specific SACRIFICE and appeal after he has been deprived by Víga-Glúm of land, including the remarkably fertile field VITAZGJAFI. Despite inheriting the family luck or HAMINGJA of his Norwegian grandfather Vígfús, Víga-Glúm is unable to withstand the displeasure of the god and is himself eventually driven from all the land he has acquired.

B47, 58, 81, 82; C10, 30, 37; D114, 262

Vígblær ('killing-breeze')

According to the account given in eddic poem

HELGAKVIDA HUNDINGSBANA II, the horse ridden into battle with a golden bit by the hero HELGI SIGMUNDARSON HUNDINGSBANI.

B12, 30, 35, 56, 73, 87, 90; C2, 17, 24, 33, 46

Vígríd ('battle-surge')

According to the eddic poem VAFTHRÚDNISMÁL, in a verse repeated by the thirteenth-century Icelander SNORRI STURLUSON, the battlefield of RAGNARÖK at the end of the world; as the wise giant VAFTHRÚDNIR says:

> 'The place is called Vígríd, where battle will join between [the fire-giant] SURT and the splendid gods; a hundred leagues in every direction it spreads, as all who know can tell.'

B12, 14, 23, 24, 28, 30, 35, 40, 50, 51, 56, 59, 73, 87, 90; C2, 5, 9, 17, 24, 33, 46, 48

Víkar ('sacred hair'?)

According to the legendary GAUTREKS SAGA, the blood-brother of the long-lived and legendary hero STARKAD. When the blood-brothers are becalmed and decide to offer a human sacrifice, the lot falls to Víkar. A mock-sacrifice is staged, involving a 'rope' made from gut, a 'gallows tree' consisting of a thin twig and a 'spear' made from a reed, but everything goes horribly wrong: the gut becomes a thick cord, the twig a branch, the reed a spear. Víkar dies, pierced and hanged in the typical manner of a sacrifice offered to the god ODIN. The early thirteenth-century Danish historian SAXO GRAMMATICUS tells substantially the same story, albeit with a rationalizing gloss.

B64, 69; C7, 8, 35, 38

Vili(r) ('will')

Son of the giant BOR, and brother of the gods ODIN and VÉ. Together, the three brothers are accounted the first of the ÆSIR, according to the thirteenth-century Icelander SNORRI STURLUSON, who also makes them responsible for animating the first humans, ASK and EMBLA (the eddic poem VÖLUSPÁ has two others accompanying Odin at this time). In YNGLINGA SAGA Snorri adds the detail that during the period of Odin's exile his brothers took over and shared not only his dominion, but his wife, FRIGG. In the eddic poem LOKASENNA, LOKI makes much the same accusation to her face, a charge supported by the early thirteenth-century Danish historian SAXO GRAMMATICUS.

B12, 14, 23, 24, 28, 30, 35, 40, 50, 56, 59, 64, 73, 87, 90; C2, 5, 7–9, 17, 24, 33, 46, 48

Vilmeid ('wish-granter')

According to a verse from the eddic poem HYNDLULJÓD, quoted by the thirteenth-century

Vilmund

Icelander SNORRI STURLUSON, the progenitor of all warlocks.

B12, 14, 23, 24, 28, 30, 35, 40, 50, 56, 59, 73, 87, 90; C2, 5, 9, 17, 24, 33, 46, 48

Vilmund

According to the eddic poem ODDRÚNARGRÁTR, the lover of BORGNÝ, the lonely princess, as the serving-maid tells ODDRÚN, who has been summoned to assist at the ensuing pregnancy:

> 'Vilmund is the name of the valiant lover,
> who kept the maid in a warm bed
> for five years, and her father never knew.'

B12, 30, 56, 73, 87, 90; C2, 17, 24, 33, 46

Vimur

According to the thirteenth-century Icelander SNORRI STURLUSON, the most powerful of all rivers, and the one that the god THOR has to cross to reach the stronghold of the giant GEIRRÖD.

B24, 28, 35, 40, 50; C5, 9, 48

Vín, Vína see HVERGELMIR.

Vindbláin ('wind-dark')

According to the thirteenth-century Icelander SNORRI STURLUSON, one of the names of the lowest heaven; other names for the same heaven are Heidthornir ('cloudy-bright') and Hreggmímir ('storm-MÍMIR'). The other eight heavens are called Andlang ('extremely long'), Vídbláin ('wide-dark'), Vídfedmir ('wide embracer'), Hrjód ('cloaker'), Hlýrnir ('double-lit'), Gimir ('be-gemmed'), Vetmímir ('winter-Mímir') and SKATÝRNIR ('fee-wetter'), which stands 'higher than the clouds, beyond all worlds'.

B24, 28, 35, 40, 50; C5, 9, 48

Vindhlér An alternative name for the god HEIMDALL.

Vindlóni see VINDSVAL.

Vindsval ('wind-chill')

According to the name-lists or THULUR, the name of a GIANT. The thirteenth-century Icelander SNORRI STURLUSON adds that Vindsval, who is also known as Vindlóni, is the father of VETR, the personified winter.

B24, 28, 35, 40, 50; C5, 9, 48

Vingenir

According to the EUHEMERIZED account of the origin of the gods offered by the thirteenth-century Icelander SNORRI STURLUSON, one of the descendants of TROR, the evident equivalent of the god THOR; Vingenir is therefore presumably to be identified with VINGNIR, an attested honorific title of the god, in the same way that the name of another supposed descendant, Vingethór, corresponds with the title VINGTHÓR.

B24, 28, 35, 40, 50; C5, 9, 48

Vingethór see VINGENIR.

Vingi

According to the eddic poem ATLAMÁL, the treacherous messenger of the wicked King ATLI BUDLASON. When Atli's wife, the tragic heroine GUDRÚN send RUNES to her brothers, GUNNAR and HÖGNI GJÚKASON, warning of the peril that they face in visiting her, Vingi distorts the message. When Gunnar's wife, GLAUMVÖR, questions him on this, he swears a false (if perhaps ambiguous) OATH:

> Glaumvör said a word,
> Gunnar's wife;
> she spoke to Vingi
> about what she thought fit:
> 'I don't know that you'll repay us
> suitably, as we would want.
> A guest's arrival is wicked
> if anything arises from it.'

> Then Vingi took a vow
> he scarcely spared himself:
> 'Let giants take the man
> that with you speaks a lie;
> let the gallows have him wholly
> if he plots about your peace.'

When Gunnar and Högni arrive at Atli's stronghold, Vingi finally tells them the truth about the trap they have just sprung, and receives rough justice:

> They shoved Vingi away,
> sent him to HEL,
> laid at him with axes,
> while he struggled for breath.

Vingi's sorry tale is repeated, with a few minor additions, in the legendary VÖLSUNGA SAGA.

B12, 20, 25, 30, 42, 56, 65, 68, 73, 78, 87, 90; C1–3, 6, 17, 24, 33, 46

Vingnir ('swinger')

(1) According to the name-lists or THULUR, the name of a GIANT. (2) Also found as one of the many names of both the god ODIN and the god THOR.

B24, 28, 35, 40, 50; C5, 9, 48

Vingólf ('friend-hall', 'wine-hall'?)

According to the thirteenth-century Icelander SNORRI

STURLUSON, the dwelling of the righteous souls in ÁSGARD. Elsewhere, however, he makes Vingólf the beautiful sanctuary of the goddesses or ÁSYNJUR, and says that the god ODIN assigns places to the slain both in VALHALL and Vingólf.

B24, 28, 35, 40, 50; C5, 9, 48

Vingskornir

According to the eddic poem FÁFNISMÁL, the horse of the Valkyrie Sigrdrífa.

B12, 30, 56, 73, 87, 90; C2, 17, 24, 33, 46

Vingthór ('tumult-Thór')

An alternative name for the god THOR, employed in the POETIC EDDA only in ALVÍSSMÁL and THRYMSKVIDA.

B12, 30, 56, 73, 87, 90; C2, 17, 24, 33, 46

Vitazgjafi ('sure-giver')

According to VÍGA-GLÚMS SAGA, a particularly fertile field, evidently sacred to FREY. When Víga-Glúm sheds blood on the field, he immediately loses the favour of Frey, after a SACRIFICE to the god by one of his priests, whom Víga-Glúm has dispossessed.

B47, 81; C30

Vögg see HRÓLF KRAKI.

Volla see MERSEBURG CHARMS.

Völsi ('penis')

A horse-penis, worshipped as part of a cult practice described in the so-called *Völsa tháttr*, as part of the saga of Saint Olaf. When a pagan farmer's horse dies, they eat the flesh, which was held to be taboo to Christians, and preserved the penis, which becomes the object of veneration, after the farmer's son has first waved it in front of the ladies, saying:

> Here you can see,
> a rather big plonker,
> one sliced off
> the horse's dad.
> Slave-girl, for you
> this *völsi* will be
> none too sluggish
> between your thighs.

The housewife takes the *völsi*, preserves it with herbs and chants over it. Eventually, as a result of her veneration, the *völsi* becomes so big and strong that it can stand beside the housewife as she worships. When Saint Olaf hears about these activities, he acts with customary vigour to stamp them out.

B60, 85; D242, 554

Völsung

Father of the mighty hero SIGMUND and his sister (and sometime lover) SIGNÝ, grandfather of the legendary heroes SIGURD, HELGI and SINFJÖTLI, and eponymous founder of the doomed line of VÖLSUNGS. The fullest account of Völsung's own life is found in the legendary VÖLSUNGA SAGA. Völsung is conceived after his father, RERIR, who has remained childless until then, receives an apple of fertility from HLJÓD, daughter of the giant HRÍMNIR; she is described as one of the 'wish-maids' (probably VALKYRIES) of the god ODIN. After a six-year confinement, during which period Rerir has died, Völsung's mother asks that her son be cut from her body:

> It was done as she asked; the baby was a boy, and he was born already well-grown, as could be expected. It is said that the boy kissed his mother before she died. Then he was given a name and called Völsung. He was king over the land of the Huns after his father, and quickly grew up to be big, strong and brave in all that were reckoned tests of manhood and ability. He became the mightiest of warriors, unbeaten in the battles he fought on his expeditions.

When Völsung came to maturity, the giant Hrímnir sent him his daughter, Hljód, who had been instrumental in Völsung's own birth, and together they had ten sons, of whom the eldest and best was Sigmund, and a single daughter, Signý. Völsung has Signý betrothed to King SIGGEIR of Gautland, much against her will, and Siggeir becomes enraged at the wedding feast when Sigmund is able to draw an enchanted sword from the mighty tree BARNSTOKK, a feat that Siggeir himself had been unable to do. He leaves Völsung's stronghold the next day, and invites the king and his sons to visit him in Gautland three months later. Völsung accepts, and attends despite the warnings of Signý, who (like the tragic heroine GUDRÚN) suspects her husband of treachery. Völsung's response is (like that of Gudrún's brother GUNNAR in parallel circumstances) characteristic of his rash bravery:

> All nations can testify that even before I was born I made a single speech, and vowed to flee in fear from neither fire nor iron, and that is what I have done till now. Why should I not keep my vow in old age? Young girls shall not tease my sons in play that they were scared of death, since everyone has to die some time. No one can escape their death, and it is my decision that we do not flee, but for ourselves be as brave as we can. I have fought six score battles, sometimes with the bigger force, sometimes with the smaller. Every time I won, and it shall not be said either that I fled, or that I asked for a truce.

Völsunga saga

So Völsung fights and duly dies. Of his ten captured sons, only Sigmund escapes, and, after an incestuous union with him, Signý produces Sinfjötli, who, together with Sigmund, manages to avenge Völsung's death.

B25, 42, 65, 68, 79; C1, 6; D154

Völsunga saga

One of the so called 'legendary sagas' – FORNALDARSÖGUR – providing a detailed account of the events of the VÖLSUNG-cycle, largely in prose, but with thirty stanzas of verse interspersed. The narrative content overlaps considerably with a number of eddic poems, which have evidently been freely plundered as source. The focus of the first part of the tale is the mighty hero SIGURD, whose ancestry is traced back to the god ODIN and whose slaying of the dragon FÁFNIR and his brother REGINN, Sigurd's own foster-father, provide an early point of focus in the narrative. Afterwards, Sigurd finds and becomes betrothed to the Valkyrie BRYNHILD, but when he visits the court of King GJÚKI, he is given a magic potion by Gjúki's queen, GRÍMHILD, which makes him forget Brynhild and instead he marries their daughter, GUDRÚN. When Gudrún's brother GUNNAR tries unsuccessfully to woo Brynhild it is Sigurd who, taking on the shape of Gunnar, wins her, and the unsteady family peace is shattered when Gudrún and Brynhild quarrel and the truth is revealed. Brynhild suggests that Sigurd slept with her before she married Gunnar, and the allegation leads to his death at the hands of GUTTHORM, Gunnar's youngest brother, who, unlike Gunnar himself or HÖGNI GJÚKASON, their other brother, is not tied to Sigurd by bonds of blood-brotherhood. Before he expires, Sigurd manages to avenge himself on Gutthorm, and it is the remaining two brothers, Gunnar and Högni, who takes possession of Sigurd's fabulous treasure-hoard, which he himself had acquired after slaying the dragon Fáfnir. At Sigurd's funeral Brynhild declares his innocence and, after killing herself, joins him on the pyre.

The next stage of the saga concerns the marriage of Gudrún to ATLI BUDLASON, Brynhild's brother, who lures Gunnar and Högni to his court to gain their treasure. When he seizes them, Gunnar refuses to disclose the whereabouts of the treasure while his brother lives, but when Högni's heart is presented to him he laughs in Atli's face, and says that now he alone knows the secret, and will never tell. Atli casts him into a snake-pit, and in revenge for her two brothers Gudrún kills the two sons she has had by Atli and feeds them to him unawares. Then she kills him, aided by her nephew NIFLUNG, Högni's son, and sets fire to Atli's hall.

The third phase of the saga concerns Gudrún's third marriage, to JÓNAK, and the vengeance of their sons HAMDIR, SÖRLI and ERP JÓNAKRSSON for their half-sister, SVANHILD, Gudrún's daughter by Sigurd. When the aged JÖRMUNREKK sends his son RANDVÉR to woo Svanhild on his behalf, he is only too willing to believe the malicious rumours spread by BIKKI about the relationship between the young pair, and so he has his

Völsunga saga Detail of the portal from the church at Hylestad, Setesdal, Norway, depicting the mighty hero Sigurd piercing the belly of the dragon Fáfnir, an episode described in detail in Völsunga saga.

son hanged and Svanhild trampled to death by horses. Gudrún incites her three sons to revenge, and they all perish.

B25, 42, 65, 68, 79; C1, 6; D154, 155, 275, 346, 616

Völsungs

The illustrious and doom-laden line of kings and heroes descended from the eponymous progenitor VÖLSUNG, and including SIGMUND, SIGNÝ, SIGURD, HELGI HJÖRVARDSSON and SINFJÖTLI. The account of their activities can be gleaned from numerous eddic verses and from the derivative and legendary VÖLSUNGA SAGA. Since RERIR, Völsung's father, was himself a son of ODIN, and since HLJÓD, Völsung's wife, was the daughter of a giant, it follows that the line of Völsung carried the blood of both the giant-race and the ÆSIR, a factor that perhaps helps to explain the pre-eminence of their kin. A potted account 'about the Völsungs' is provided in the prose introduction to the eddic poem HELGAKVIDA HUNDINGSBANA II:

> King Sigmund, Völsung's son, married BORGHILD from Brálund. They called their son Helgi, after Helgi Hjörvardsson. Hagal was Helgi's foster-father. There was a powerful king called Hunding; Hundland is named after him. He was a mighty warrior, and had many sons who went out on raiding expeditions. There was antagonism and spite between King HUNDING and King Sigmund; each killed the other's kinsmen. King Sigmund and his male descendants were called Völsungs or Ylfings ('wolflings').

B25, 42, 65, 68, 79; C1, 6; D346

Völund

The legendary smith, whose name occurs elsewhere in Germanic myth and legend in a variety of forms, including Wayland, Weland and Welund. According to the prose introduction to the eddic poem VÖLUNDARKVIDA, Völund and his two brothers, SLAGFID and EGIL, are the sons of the Finnish king, and each of them marries a VALKYRIE bride. When their women disappear, Slagfid and Egil, set off in pursuit, but Völund, mourning the disappearance of his own beloved, is captured by the cruel King NÍDUD. Nídud's daughter BÖDVILD is given one of the golden rings that Völund has made, perhaps that which his wife had once owned, while Nídud wears the sword that Völund himself had owned. Völund's reaction is vividly described by Nídud's queen:

> 'He bares his teeth, when he's shown the sword,
> or catches sight of Bödvild's ring.
> His gaze is as piercing as a gleaming snake:
> sever him from his mighty strength,
> and then set him up in some seaside spot.'

Völund is duly hamstrung and placed on the island-refuge of SÆVARSTAD to plot his revenge. Eventually, he persuades Nídud's two young sons to come to visit him alone, whereupon he slaughters them and makes from their eyes and teeth baubles for Bödvild and her mother, and from their skulls drinking-vessels for Nídud. His next victim is Bödvild herself, who appears to have conceived a fascination for the mysterious stranger and whom he plies with beer when she visits him, before violating her in a chillingly cold-blooded fashion:

> He overbore her with beer, since he knew better,
> so that on the seat she dropped off to sleep.

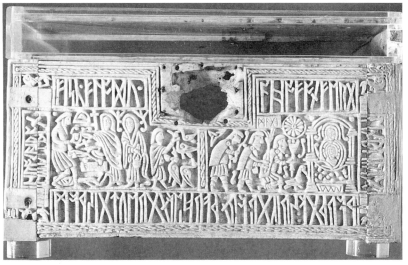

Völund The Franks casket, showing Völund, the legendary crippled smith, being visited by the doomed and love-struck princess Bödvild and her maid.

'Now I have avenged my grievances
all except one, most malicious.

'If only', said Völund, 'I could get properly to my feet,
of which Nídud's warriors have deprived me.'
Laughing, Völund raised himself aloft;
weeping, Bödvild departed the island:
she loathed her lover's leaving and her father's wrath.

His vengeance complete, Völund flies off, using a pair
of wings which, according to other sources, notably the
legendary THIDREKS SAGA, he had fashioned himself.
Before disappearing utterly, however, Völund allows
himself the spiteful pleasure of announcing to the
anguished Nídud precisely what he has done.

B8, 12, 30, 31, 42, 53, 56, 71, 73, 84, 87, 90; C2, 13, 15, 17, 21, 24, 25, 33, 44, 46;
D26, 56, 90, 94, 200, 286, 318, 399, 400, 418, 610, 614

Völundarkvida ('the lay of Völund')

An eddic poem, preserved in the CODEX REGIUS manuscript, which gives the fullest account in verse of the
life of the legendary smith VÖLUND, whose tale is also
told in the legendary THIDREKS SAGA. The occurrence
of *Völundarkvida* in the Codex Regius sandwiched
between two mythological poems, THRYMSKVIDA and
ALVÍSSMÁL, is curious – one might more naturally expect it to have been placed after *Alvíssmál*, at the head
of the heroic and legendary poems that follow; most
likely it is his designation early in the poem as 'lord of
elves' that has led to the inclusion of the poem among
the 'mythological section' of the manuscript.

A prose introduction describes how Völund and his
two brothers, SLAGFID and EGIL, came across three
VALKYRIES who had removed their swan-cloaks to spin
flax by a lake. Each of three brothers took a Valkyrie
to wife, and when, after seven years, the Valkyries
flew away, Völund remained waiting behind when his
two brothers went off in search of their wives. The
verses allude to the same tale, and continue by relating
how King NÍDUD captured Völund, who was extremely
skilful with his hands, hamstrung him and set him on
an island to make him treasures. A gold ring, which
Völund had made for his wife, now sits on the finger of
the king's daughter, BÖDVILD. Völund's vengeance is
grim: he lures the king's two young sons to visit him at
his island smithy, kills them and fashions jewels for the
king and queen from their skulls, teeth and eyes. Likewise, when the young Bödvild, who appears to have
conceived a fascination for the mysterious smith, asks
him to fix a gold ring (presumably the same ring that
had once belonged to Völund's wife), he plies her with
beer and seduces her. Although he is hamstrung and
unable to walk, it appears from the poem that he has
acquired the power of flight; *Thidreks saga* states that

he fashioned wings for himself. At any rate, he is able
to escape from his island-prison, pausing *en route* to
tell Nídud precisely what has happened to his children;
the poem closes with an uneasy conversation between
Nídud and Bödvild, in which she confirms the truth of
what Völund has said:

'It's true, Nídud, what he told you:
Völund and I spent time together the two of us on
   the island
a single tide's turn: it should never have been.
I didn't have the wits to struggle against him;
I didn't have the strength to struggle against him.'

B8, 12, 30, 31, 42, 53, 56, 71, 73, 84, 87, 90; C2, 13, 15, 17, 21, 24, 25, 33, 44, 46;
D42, 56, 101, 200, 232, 361, 399, 400, 474, 573, 614

Völuspá ('the prophecy of the sibyl')

Perhaps the grandest and most celebrated of all eddic
poems, which opens the CODEX REGIUS manuscript
and which provided the thirteenth-century Icelander
SNORRI STURLUSON, who quotes its verses extensively,
with a large amount of his material. Besides the (sometimes quite different) versions of the text found in the
Codex Regius and in Snorri's GYLFAGINNING, *Völuspá*
is also found in a third version in the so-called *Hauksbók*
manuscript (AM 544 4to), which varies considerably
from the other two texts. The two complete versions of
Völuspá in the Codex Regius and in *Hauksbók* differ not
only in individual readings, but in the order of certain
stanzas and even in their inclusion: each version contains examples of individual stanzas entirely omitted in
the other. For this reason, notwithstanding other textu-
al difficulties, it is hazardous to outline the structure of
the text with any confidence; the discussion here draws
largely upon the Codex Regius text.

The framework of the poem seems to suggest that
the entire piece is addressed by a sibyl or prophetess, perhaps raised from the dead, to the god ODIN,
apparently engaged on precisely the same quest for
wisdom that characterizes other eddic poems such as
VAFTHRÚDNISMÁL. Like the wise giant VAFTHRÚDNIR,
the sibyl seeks to establish her credentials by first describing events from the mythological past and present,
before moving on to tell in great detail about events
surrounding the end of the old world at RAGNARÖK.
So, she recalls the gaping void of GINNUNGAGAP, before
the earth was made, and describes the role of the ÆSIR
in creating the earth, ordering the heavens and giving
life to the DWARFS and men. Even at this early stage, a
darker note creeps in, as the sibyl describes how three
giant maidens appear, followed by an appetite for gold
and a great war against the VANIR. It is in the course of
rebuilding ÁSGARD that the moral decline of the Æsir is
most in evidence, and in an allusive account of the giant

builder the sibyl implicitly points out that they proved themselves not merely oath-breakers but murderers. It is at this point, we infer, that Odin begins his quest for wisdom, and the sibyl taunts him for pledging his eye and continually asks 'do you know enough yet, or what?' The further decline of the Æsir is traced through the episode of the death of the god BALDR, and the poem builds towards an apocalyptic account of Ragnarök, introduced by a vivid set of stanzas that describe the signs that will precede it:

Brothers will struggle and slaughter each other,
and sisters' sons spoil kinship's bonds.
It's hard on earth: great whoredom;
axe-age, blade-age, shields are split;
wind-age, wolf-age, before the world crumbles:
no man shall spare another.

The sibyl goes on to describe how the various forces muster for battle, as all bonds are broken: the enemies of the Æsir approach by land and sea. At the final battle, old scores are settled: Odin is swallowed by the wolf FENRIR and avenged by VÍDAR, his son; the fire-giant SURT kills the god FREY; finally, the god THOR slays the MIDGARD-SERPENT and perishes from its poison, as the sky goes black with flame:

The sun turns black, land sinks into sea;
the bright stars scatter from the sky.

Flame flickers against the world-tree
fire flies high against heaven itself.

But the world is reborn:

She sees rising up a second time
the earth from the ocean, ever-green;
the cataracts tumble, an eagle flies above,
hunting fish on the fell.

B12, 14, 23, 24, 28, 30, 35, 38, 40, 50, 51, 56, 59, 73, 87, 90; C2, 5, 9, 17, 24, 33, 46, 48; D31, 45, 57, 111, 113, 115, 182, 279, 315, 352, 409, 430, 462, 465, 474, 497, 501, 549, 575, 622, 623

Völuspá in skamma *see* HYNDLULJÓD.

völva *see* WITCH.

Vör ('aware', 'careful')
According to the thirteenth-century Icelander SNORRI STURLUSON, one of the goddesses or ÁSYNJUR:

She is wise and inquisitive, so that nothing can be hidden from her. The saying goes that women become 'aware' (*vör*) when they find things out.

Snorri's etymologizing interpretation is scarcely profound, and may imply that he had no access to further material; certainly references to Vör in the written record are extremely scarce.
B12, 14, 23, 24, 28, 30, 35, 40, 50, 56, 59, 73, 87, 90; C2, 5, 9, 17, 24, 33, 46, 48

W

Wayland, Weland, Welund *see* VÖLUND.

werewolves

People who change into wolves; a characteristic often connected with a number of pagan heroes. Around the turn of the eleventh century belief in such creatures is recorded by Burchard of Worms, and the connection between shape-changing and the kinds of warriors known as BERSERKS or ÚLFHEDNAR is made by the thirteenth-century Icelander SNORRI STURLUSON. Werewolves feature in several sagas, most notably in EGILS SAGA SKALLA-GRÍMSSONAR, where Egil's own grandfather, Kveld-Úlf ('evening wolf'), is held to have been such a shape-changer:

He generally got up early . . . he was able to offer good advice in all cases, for he was very wise; but every

day as it approached evening he became sullen, so that hardly anyone could speak to him; he was sleepy in the evening, and it was said that he must be a mighty shape-changer.

Later in the saga, Kveld-Úlf goes berserk in battle, and we are told:

It is said of those who were shape-changers or who went berserk, that while they were affected they were so strong that nothing could withstand them, but as soon as it left them they were weaker than normal. Kveld-Úlf was like this, and when the fury left him he was exhausted from the attack, and felt totally wrecked and collapsed in bed.

Egil, his grandson, displays considerable violence and

on at least one occasion distinctly lupine and ursine tendencies when dealing with an enemy, Atli, in a duel:

> A big old bull was brought forward; this was called the sacrificial animal, and whoever won was to kill it. Sometimes it was one animal, sometimes both men in the duel had one brought. When they were ready to fight they dashed at each other, and first cast their spears; but neither spear hit a shield: both landed in the ground. Then both of them turned to their swords. They attacked each other, fiercely trading blows. Atli stood his ground. They struck swiftly and hard, and soon the shields were useless. When Atli's shield was redundant he threw it away, clasped his sword in both hands, and struck as hard as he could. Egil swung at his shoulder, but the sword did not bite: he swung a second and a third time. It was easy for him to pick a spot to strike Atli, because he had no protection. Egil swung the sword with all his might, but wherever he struck it would not bite. Then Egil realized that nothing could be done as things stood, for at this point his shield was becoming useless. Egil let his sword and shield drop, and jumped at Atli, grabbing him with both hands. Then the difference in their strength was apparent, and Atli fell backwards on to the ground. Egil bent over and bit through his windpipe; Atli died there. Egil leapt up swiftly and went over to where the sacrificial animal stood; he grabbed its jaw in one hand and its horn in the other, and wrenched it so that its feet pointed up and its neck-bone shattered.

A particular connection with wolves is also imputed to the legendary hero SIGMUND and to SINFJÖTLI, the son he had by an incestuous relationship with his sister, SIGNÝ, according to the legendary VÖLSUNGA SAGA. Sigmund is thus both father and maternal uncle to Sinfjötli, both positions of enormous influence and importance, and the two live together in an underground lair in the forest:

> Once, when they went back to the forest to get some booty for themselves. They found a house and, inside, two sleeping men, wearing fat gold rings. They had been bewitched: wolf-skins hung over them in the house, and they could shed their skins only every tenth day. They were kings' sons. Sigmund and Sinfjötli donned the skins, and could not take them off. The strange power was with them as previously: they howled like wolves, and both understood the howling. Then they went out into the woods, each his own way. They agreed that they would dare to fight with up to seven men, but no more, and that the one who was attacked by more should howl like a wolf. 'Don't break this vow,' said Sigmund, 'because you are young and rash, and people will reckon it a good idea to hunt you.' Then they both went their own way. When they had separated, Sigmund found seven men, and howled like a wolf; Sinfjötli heard him, came immediately and killed them all. Then they parted. Before he had wandered very far into the woods, Sinfjötli met eleven men and attacked them; at last he killed them all. Terribly wounded, Sinfjötli went to rest under an oak tree. Then Sigmund came and said: 'Why didn't you call?' Sinfjötli answered: 'I didn't want to call for your help. You took help to kill seven men. In age I am like a child compared to you, but I didn't ask for help to kill eleven men.' Sigmund jumped at him so savagely that Sinfjötli stumbled and fell; Sigmund bit him in the throat. They could not get out of the wolf-skins that day. Sigmund put Sinfjötli over his shoulder, took him back to the hut, and sat over him; he cursed the wolf-skins and bade the trolls have them. One day Sigmund looked where two weasels were; one bit the other in the throat. Then he scurried into the woods, took a leaf, and placed it on the wound. The second weasel jumped up whole. Sigmund went out and saw a raven flying with a leaf. The raven brought the leaf to Sigmund, who placed it on Sinfjötli's wound; immediately Sinfjötli jumped up whole, as if he had never been wounded. Then they went to an underground lair, and remained there until they were able to take off the wolf-skins. They took the skins and burned them on the fire, hoping that they would cause no more harm.

It is from their lupine associations, we are given to understand, that the descendants of Sigmund, are known not only as Völsungs but as Ylfings ('wolflings').
B25, 42, 58, 65, 68, 79, 82; C1, 6, 10, 37; D98, 184, 489

wild hunt

A phenomenon, common in later folktale, in which a frenzied host, often including ghosts or spectres is seen, generally held to presage some portentous event. Instances in Norse myth and legend tend to be restricted to visions of wild female riders. Some such notion appears to lie behind the *túnriður* ('enclosure-riders', 'hag-riders'), against whom the god ODIN claims that the tenth of the spells he lists in the *Ljódatal* section of the eddic poem HÁVAMÁL is effective:

> 'I know a tenth, if I see hag-riders
> stream across the sky.
> I can cause them to wander
> away from their proper forms,
> away from their proper minds.'

A further example is the *gandreið* ('wand-ride', 'witch-ride') which Hildiglúm sees, as described in NJÁLS SAGA, boding ill for the doomed Flósi:

> He heard a mighty crash, and both heaven and earth seemed to her to shake. Then she gazed out in the direction of the west, and she thought she saw a circle,

and in the circle a man on a grey horse. He passed swiftly over, and he was riding hard; he had a burning brand in his hand. He rode so close to him that he could clearly see him; he seemed to him as black as pitch, and he could hear, how he spoke a verse with great zeal:

'I ride a horse
frost-battered,
ice-topped,
boding ill.
Fire at the ends
poison in the middle,
so it is with Flósi's state
as the roller goes,
and so it is with Flósi's state
as the roller goes.'

It seemed to him that he shot the brand east to the mountains, and there seemed to him to spring up a fire so great, that he thought he could not see the mountains in front. The man appeared to ride east under the fire and there he disappeared.

B76; C26; D271, 604

witch

A convenient general term under which to discuss a variety of prophetic and wise women, as well as those who engage in sorcery and MAGIC. The longest and most detailed account of such a wandering figure is that of THORBJÖRG LÍTILVÖLVA in EIRÍKS SAGA RAUDA, but the Roman historian TACITUS, writing in the first century, is the first to note the importance of such women, focusing in particular on the veneration of such wise women as VELEDA and ALBRUNA. As the much later account of NORNAGESTS THÁTTR in FLATEYJARBÓK has it:

In those days wise women, called prophetesses, used to travel about the countryside, and they foretold people's lives. Because of that, many people invited them to their homes, made feasts in their honour, and gave them gifts when they left.

A not dissimilar picture is offered by the description of GULLVEIG in the eddic poem VÖLUSPÁ:

They called her Heid,
when she came to the house,
a witch who could foretell;
she knew the skill of wands,
she practised SEID where she could,
she practised *seid* in a trance;
she was always a delight
to wicked women.

The legendary FORNALDARSÖGUR contains numerous accounts of the activities of witches, often called Heid, but it is clear that such figures, while often commanding reverence and respect, were also liable after the conversion to severe punishments. An Anglo-Saxon charter of between 963 and 975, detailing a land transaction between Bishop Æthelwold of Winchester and a certain Wulfstan Uccea, describes in a casual way the treatment that suspected witches might expect:

Here it is declared in this document that Bishop Æthelwold and Wulfstan Uccea have exchanged estates with the knowledge of King Edwin and his councillors. The bishop gave Wulfstan the estate at Washington [Sussex], and Wulfstan gave him the estates at Yaxley [Huntingdonshire] and at Ailsworth [Northamptonshire]. Then the bishop gave the estate at Yaxley to Thorney [Thorney Abbey, Cambridgeshire], and the one at Ailsworth to Peterborough. The estate at Ailsworth had been forfeited by a widow and her son because they stuck an iron pin into [a model of] Wulfstan's father, Ælfsige; and it was discovered, and they took the deadly object from her closet. Then they seized the woman, and drowned her at London Bridge, but her son escaped and became an outlaw. The estate passed into the hands of the king, and later the king gave it to Ælfsige, and then his son, Wulfstan Uccea, gave it to Bishop Æthelwold, just as it says above.

B2, 12, 30, 38, 56, 59, 60, 73, 85, 87, 90; C2, 17, 21, 24, 27, 29, 33, 45, 46; D3, 44, 307, 385, 389, 448

witchcraft *see* WITCH.

Wodan *see* WODEN.

Woden

The Anglo-Saxon name of the god ODIN, witnessed in numerous place-names and in *Wodnesdæg* ('Wednesday'). A number of Anglo-Saxon royal houses trace their lineage back to Woden, but his occurrence in the literary record is relatively sparse. The so-called *Nine Herbs Charm* attributes to Woden the passing on of the knowledge of the pharmaceutical efficacy of the nine herbs in question, and says:

A worm came sneaking, it slew nothing;
then Woden took nine twigs of glory,
and struck the snake so it scattered in nine bits.

B72; C45; D145, 246, 371, 490, 535, 565

Wulfstan

Bishop of London (996–1002) and archbishop of both Worcester (1002–16) and York (1002–23), and an important and influential cleric and statesman, responsible not only for a number of sermons and public addresses, but also as a framer of legislation. His most famous address is undoubtedly the so-called *Sermo Lupi* ('Sermon of the Wolf'), an apocalyptic vision of the impending end of the world, which survives in no fewer than three different versions in five manuscripts. Wulfstan's diatribe, which in one version is dated to the year 1014, is of interest in the context of a study of Germanic and Scandinavian myth and legend because he links the moral decline of the English specifically to the wave of Viking attacks in the period and, indeed, contrasts the degenerate behaviour of contemporary Christians with the comparative respect paid by heathens:

> Among heathen peoples no one dares to withhold in small or great part what is laid down for the worship of false gods, but everywhere we withhold God's dues all too frequently; and among heathen peoples no one dares to diminish inside or out any of those things which are brought to the false gods, and are designated as offerings, but we have stripped God's house clean inside and out; and God's servants are everywhere deprived of respect and protection, but no one dares to mistreat the servants of false gods in any way among heathen peoples, just as is done too widely to the servants of God, where Christians ought to keep God's laws and protect God's servants.

Other commentators have noticed a general resemblance between the language used to describe the end of the world in Wulfstan's *Sermo Lupi* and in the eddic poem VÖLUSPÁ, although few have gone so far as to argue for direct influence of the former on the latter. The Norse poem describes how:

> Brothers will struggle and slaughter each other,
> and sisters' sons spoil kinship's bonds.
> It's hard on earth: great whoredom;
> axe-age, blade-age, shields are split;
> wind-age, wolf-age, before the world crumbles:
> no man shall spare another.

Wulfstan describes the decline in moral standards in very similar terms:

> Now very often a kinsman does not protect a kinsman any more than a stranger, nor a father his child, nor sometimes a child his own father, nor one brother another; nor has any of us regulated his life as he should, neither the clerics according to the rule, nor laymen according to the law, but we have all too frequently made lust our law, and neither hold the teachings or laws of God or men as we should.

Later in the sermon, more specifically, Wulfstan includes in his list of signs of sinful behaviour a reference both to WITCHES and, more surprisingly, to VALKYRIES, whom the context implies are viewed as purely human agents of wickedness:

> Here, so it might seem, too many in the land are sorely injured by the wounds of sin: here are man-slayers, and killers of kinsmen, and murderers of priests, and enemies of monasteries, and here are cruel perjurers and murderers, and here are whores and child-killers, and many foul fornicating adulterers, and here are witches and Valkyries, and here are robbers and plunderers, and mighty despoilers, and, to speak briefly, numberless kinds of crime and every misdeed.

Still clearer evidence of Wulfstan's implacable opposition to all things pagan is found in his remarkable tract *De falsis deis* ('On False Gods'), clearly adapted from the earlier work on the same theme by his contemporary, ÆLFRIC. The bulk of the piece is taken up with a detailed consideration of pagan gods, both from the classical past and, more intriguingly, from the contemporary heathen present of the invading Danes:

> In days of yore there was a certain man who was called Saturn, dwelling on that island which is called Crete, and he was so cruel and fierce that he did away with all his own children except one, and in an unfatherly manner destroyed their lives in early youth. Reluctantly he let one live, although he had otherwise done away with its brothers, and that one was called Jove, and he became a hostile fiend. He afterwards drove his own father out of that same aforesaid island called Crete, and would readily have killed him if he could, and that Jove was so lecherous that he took his own sister, who was called Juno, as a wife, and she became reckoned a very lofty goddess according to heathen reckoning. Their two daughters were Minerva and Venus. These wicked people about whom we speak were reckoned as the most splendid gods in those days, and the heathens worshipped them greatly through the devil's teaching. But the son was more greatly worshipped according to heathen practice than the father was, and he is reckoned indeed the most venerable of all those gods that the heathens in those days took for gods in their folly. And he is called THOR by another name among some nations, and the Danish peoples favour him most, and in their folly they worship him most earnestly. His son is called Mars, who has always promoted strife and conflict, and has frequently stirred up argument and contention. After his death the heathens also worshipped this wretch as a lofty god, and as often as they went to war or wanted to fight, they offered their sacrifices beforehand to honour this false god, and they believed that he could help them greatly in battle, because he loved battle and strife while he lived. There was also a certain man who was called

Mercury in his lifetime, who was very deceptive, and even though he was very wise in speech, he was tricky in his deeds and deceptions. The heathens also made him a splendid god according to their reckoning, and often and frequently made offerings to him at crossroads through the devil's teaching, and often brought him various sacrificial offerings on high mountains. This false god was venerated among all the heathens in those days, and he is called ODIN by another name in the Danish manner. Now, some Danish men say in their folly, that Jove, whom they call Thor, was the son of Mercury, whom they call Odin, but they are wrong, because we read in books, both heathen and Christian, that the hateful Jove is in fact the son of Saturn. And a certain woman was called Venus, who was Jove's daughter, and she was so foul and depraved in lechery that her own brother screwed her, so they say, through the devil's teaching, and the heathens worship that wicked creature as a lofty woman. Many other heathen gods were variously devised, and also heathen goddesses held in great worship throughout the world to the detriment of mankind, but these are reckoned the most important in paganism, though they lived foully in the world.

Such a EUHEMERIZED account of the heathen deities is not unusual. Similar descriptions are offered, for example, by both the thirteenth-century Icelander SNORRI STURLUSON and the early thirteenth-century Danish historian SAXO GRAMMATICUS.

Saxo, indeed, not only gives a very similar account of the gods of the Scandinavian pagan past, but also effectively answers Wulfstan's somewhat pedantic difficulty with the exact identification of classical and Scandinavian deities:

At one time certain individuals, skilled in the magic arts, namely Thor, Odin, and several others who were skilful at conjuring up wondrous illusions, confused the minds of simple men, and began to take on the venerated rank of godhead. Norway, Sweden, and Denmark, were caught up in a baseless belief, moved to a fawning veneration of these impostors, and tainted by their wicked fraud. The impact of their trickery spread, so that all other kingdoms came to honour some kind of divine authority in them, believing that they were gods or the confidants of gods. They offered up earnest prayers to these sorcerers, and gave the respect due to true religion to a wicked heresy. One result of this is that the days of the week, in their due series, are reckoned under the names of these 'gods', whereas the ancient Romans are known to have given them separate titles, from the names of their gods, or from the seven planets. It can clearly be deduced from the very names of the days that those who were worshipped by our people were not the same as those the early Romans called Jupiter and Mercury, or those to whom Greece and Italy granted all the obeisance of superstition. What we call Thor's or Odin's day [i.e. Thursday or Wednesday] is termed by them Jove's or Mercury's day [cf. French *jeudi* or *mercredi*]. If we accept that Thor is Jupiter and Odin Mercury, following the change in the day's names, then it is a clear demonstration that Jupiter was the son of Mercury, if we accept the assertions of our compatriots, who generally consider that Thor was the child of Odin. Since the Romans hold the opposite opinion, namely that Mercury was born of Jupiter, if follows that, unless their assertion is disputed, we must accept that Thor and Jupiter, and Odin and Mercury, are different figures.

B10, 12, 30, 56, 59, 64, 67, 73, 87, 90; C2, 7, 8, 12, 17, 24, 33, 46; D57

Y

Ýdalir ('yew-dales')

According to the thirteenth-century Icelander SNORRI STURLUSON, drawing on a reference in the eddic poem GRÍMNISMÁL, the aptly named dwelling-place of the archer-god, ULL.

B12, 14, 23, 24, 28, 30, 35, 40, 50, 56, 59, 64, 73, 87, 90; C2, 5, 7–9, 17, 24, 33, 46, 48

Ygg ('terrible one')

A frequent name for the god ODIN, widely witnessed both in skaldic sources and the POETIC EDDA, and intimately connected with the designation of the world-tree as YGGDRASIL. The early thirteenth-century Dan-

ish historian SAXO GRAMMATICUS describes a venerable prophet called Uggerus, 'a man whose unknown years stretched beyond human span', and who undoubtedly reflects an aspect of Odin's character.

B39, 45, 62, 64, 83, 87; C7, 8, 16

Yggdrasil ('Ygg's horse', 'Odin's steed')

The world-tree, apparently so-called because it was the tree upon which the god ODIN rode when he hanged himself in sacrifice to himself, in the episode described in the eddic poem HÁVAMÁL in which he acquired the RUNES. According to the eddic poems GRÍMNISMÁL and VÖLUSPÁ, Yggdrasil is an ash tree, a designation made the more interesting given that the first man, fashioned from a tree trunk, is himself called ASK. The fullest description is given by the thirteenth-century Icelander SNORRI STURLUSON, who describes Yggdrasil as the 'holy place of the ÆSIR', the place where the Æsir hold their daily courts. He continues:

> The ash is the biggest and best of all trees; its branches extend over the whole world, and spread out over the sky. Three roots support the tree, and they spread extremely far: one is among the Æsir, the second among the frost-giants, and the third spreads over NIFLHEIM, and under that root lies HVERGELMIR, where NÍDHÖGG gnaws at the root-bottom. But under the root that spreads towards the frost-giants lies MÍMIR'S WELL, containing wisdom and knowledge . . . the third root of the ash spreads to ÁSGARD, and under that root is a very sacred well, called URDARBRUNN, where the Æsir hold their court.

Later in his account Snorri gives further details of all the mythical creatures who inhabit Yggdrasil:

> An eagle sits in the branches of the ash, and he is very knowledgeable, and between his eyes there sits the hawk called VEDRFÖLNIR; a squirrel called RATATOSK scampers up and down throughout the ash and carries vicious words between the eagle and Nídhögg. Four stags wander in the branches of the ash and browse on the foliage; they are called Dáin, Dvalin, Dúneyr and Durathrór, and there are so many snakes in Hvergelmir with Nídhögg that no tongue can count them.

Elsewhere, the alternative name Dvalar is found in place of Dvalin as that of one of the four stags who browse on Yggdrasil, while a stanza from *Grímnismál*, which Snorri actually cites, names the snakes who inhabit Hvergelmir as Góin and Móin (who are named as the sons of one Grafvitnir), Grábak, Grafvöllud, ÓFNIR (2) and SVÁFNIR (3).

A6; B12, 14, 23, 24, 28, 30, 35, 40, 50, 56, 59, 73, 87, 90; C2, 5, 9, 17, 24, 33, 46, 48; D23, 341, 405

Ylfings *see* VÖLSUNGS.

Ylg *see* HVERGELMIR.

Ymir ('groaner')

The primordial giant, whom some sources name AURGELMIR, from whom the world was created. Numerous poetic periphrases or KENNINGS and references in both skaldic and eddic poetry describe the sea as his blood, the sky as his skull or the mountains as his bones. The thirteenth-century Icelander SNORRI STURLUSON

describes in detail the circumstances surrounding his emergence from the coming together of primeval heat and frost in the gaping void of GINNUNGAGAP, and of his role as the progenitor of the frost-giants, cautioning against regarding him as a god:

> In no way do we recognize him as a god; he was wicked, as were all his descendants, whom we call frost-giants. It is said that while he slept, he sweated, and there grew under his left arm a male and a female, and one of his legs got a son on the other, and descendants sprang from them, that are called frost-giants. We call the ancient frost-giant Ymir.

After describing how Ymir was sustained by the primeval cow AUDHUMLA, who eventually licked into shape (quite literally) the ancestor of the first of the ÆSIR, namely the god ODIN and his brothers VILI and VÉ. They it was who killed Ymir, and, as Snorri says:

> They took Ymir and brought him into the middle of Ginnungagap, and from him they fashioned the earth, from his blood the sea and lakes. The earth was made of his flesh, and the rocks from his bones; stones and gravel they made from his teeth and molars, and from the broken bones . . . they also took his skull and from it made the sky.

B24, 28, 35, 39, 40, 45, 50, 62, 83, 87; C5, 9, 16, 48

Ynglinga saga

The first part of HEIMSKRINGLA, composed by the thirteenth-century Icelander SNORRI STURLUSON and describing the mythical and legendary history of the YNGLING dynasty of Sweden. Like most Germanic royal houses, the Ynglings traced their lineage back to a divine ancestor, in this case YNGVI-FREY, and Snorri presents a euhemerized account, based on a variety of sources including skaldic poems, such as YNGLINGATAL or BRAGI BODDASON's RAGNARSDRÁPA, and prose sources, including *Skjöldunga saga*, the original form of which is now lost. The view that he adopts closely parallels his EUHEMERISTIC perspective in the preface to his prose Edda, where the ÆSIR are 'men of Asia', ultimately tracing their ancestry back to Troy. Several of the Æsir feature prominently in *Ynglinga saga*, notably the gods ODIN, THOR and FREY.

B39, 45, 62, 83, 87; C16; D75, 300, 468

Ynglingatal ('the tally of the Ynglings')

A poem, composed around the turn of the tenth century by THJÓDOLF OF HVIN for his patron, Rognvald heidumhæri, celebrating no fewer than twenty-seven of Rognvald's ancestors and providing a versified history of his line. The thirteenth-century Icelander

SNORRI STURLUSON makes much use of *Ynglingatal* in the course of his own YNGLINGA SAGA. Although it is entirely composed in an eddic metre, *Ynglingatal* contains a striking proportion of poetic periphrases or KENNINGS, in line with its quirky blend of legend and history. Notwithstanding the potential dryness of its theme, the poem includes a number of passages of lyrical beauty, for example that in which the poet employs a kenning concerning the sea-giant GYMIR to lament the fall of King Yngvar on the coast of Estonia:

> And the Eastern sea
> sings the song of Gymir
> to bring some pleasure
> to Sweden's prince.

B1, 39, 45, 87; C16, 22, 23; D1, 300, 468, 552, 553, 589

Ynglings

The royal dynasty of Sweden, from which the first king of Norway, Harald Fairhair (who died in 933) descended, when the Norwegian royal line of Ynglings traced their ancestry until the fourteenth century. Among the documentary sources describing the origins of the line in semi-mythological terms are YNGLINGATAL and YNGLINGA SAGA.

D1, 300, 468, 552, 553, 589

Yngvi-Frey

The name which the thirteenth-century Icelander SNORRI STURLUSON gives to the god FREY in his YNGLINGA SAGA to explain the eponymous origin of the Swedish royal line of the YNGLINGS. The first element of the name is evidently connected not only with the primordial ancestor of the tribe of Ingvaeones mentioned by the first-century Roman historian TACITUS, but also with the figure ING who appears in Anglo-Saxon sources and who gave his name to a RUNE.

B2, 24, 28, 35, 40, 50; C5, 9, 29, 48

Yngvi *see* HÖDBRODD.

Younger Edda *see* SNORRA EDDA.

Yrsa *see* HRÓLF KRAKI.

Ysja *see* RÍGSTHULA.

yule

Germanic midwinter festival, progressively subsumed into the Christian festivities surrounding Christmas. The name yule, or a variant form of it, is attested from the earliest times as that of a month or some similar period of time, corresponding to the end of the modern calendar year. In practice, it is difficult to specify the yule-tide period more accurately than at some point between about mid-November and the beginning of January. In fourth-century Gothic the period is called *fruma jiuleis*, while, according to the contemporary historian BEDE, it was known in eighth-century Anglo-Saxon England as *geola* or *giuli*. The period evidently coincided with a fertility festival, but also appears to have carried associations of the supernatural; in Icelandic sagas – for example GRETTIS SAGA ÁSMUNDARSONAR – DRAUGAR are routinely said to increase their activity around yule-tide, when, moreover, other ghostly manifestations such as the WILD HUNT are said to appear.

B3, 15, 41; C12, 41; D36

Appendices

The following appendices are included to offer some insight into the extraordinarily rich tradition of meaningful name-giving that is found throughout Norse myths and legends. All the names are given in their attested Norse form, without employing the simplified system of spellings used elsewhere in the book (except in the case of cross-references, where a comparison of the spellings may prove instructive). Many of the names recorded here are little more than that, and represent on the one hand tantalizing and often impenetrable glimpses of traditions now lost, and on the other hand a later caricaturing of such traditions. While in the case of the god Odin the plethora of his names and titles undoubtedly reflects in some measure his complex and multivalent nature, there may also be an element of taboo in avoiding his mention too transparently. The other appendices provide a much more jumbled assemblage of lore, some of which is undoubtedly old, but much of which seems derived from a streak of antiquarian stereotyping to be found in the medieval sources. None of the lists provided here is intended to be exhaustive, and indeed all can be supplemented from material noted in the bibliography; still further information can be obtained from the individual entries on dwarfs, giants, Valkyries and Odin, together with the bibliographical references given there.
A29, 94, 108; D141, 193, 203, 213, 391, 396, 402

Appendix A: Odin's Names and Titles

Aldafǫðr ('father of men')
Aldagautr ('GAUTR of men')
Aldingautr ('the ancient GAUTR')
Alfǫðr ('father of all')
Arnhǫfði ('eagle-head')
Atriði, Atriðr ('attacking rider')
Auðun ('wealth-friend'?)
Báleygr ('blaze-eye')
Biflindi ('shield-shaker')
Bileygr ('feeble eye')
Bjǫrn ('bear')
Blindi, Blindr ('blind')
Bǫlverkr ('evil-doer') *see* MEAD OF POETRY
   (Bölverk)
Bragi ('chieftain')
Brúni, Brúnn ('the brown one')
Darraðr, Dǫrruðr ('spearman')
Draugadróttin ('lord of the dead')
Ennibrattr ('the one with a straight forehead')
Eylúðr ('island-vessel'?, 'ever-booming'?)
Farmaguð, Farmatýr ('cargo-god')
Farmǫgnuðr ('journey-empowerer')
Fengr ('snatch')

Fimbultýr ('mighty god')
Fimbulþulr ('mighty þulr', 'mighty poet')
Fjǫlnir ('much-wise'?, 'concealer'?) *see* FJÖLNIR
Fjǫlsviðr, Fjǫlsvinnr ('much-wise') *see* FJÖLSVID
Forni ('the ancient one')
Fornǫlvir ('ancient Ǫlvir')
Fráríðr ('one who rides forth')
Fundinn ('the found')
Gagnráðr ('contrary advisor') *see* VAFTHRÚDNISMÁL
   (Gagnrád)
Gangleri ('wanderer')
Gangráðr ('journey-advisor')
Gapþrosnir ('one in gaping frenzy'?)
Gauti, Gautr ('one from Gotland', 'Gaut', 'Goth')
Geiguðr ('dangler')
Geirlǫðnir ('spear-inviter')
Geirtýr ('spear-god')
Geirvaldr ('spear-master')
Geirǫlnir ('spear-charger')
Gestr ('guest')
Gestumblindi ('the blind guest') *see* GESTUMBLINDI
Ginnarr ('deceiver')
Gizurr ('riddler'?)

Glapsviðr ('seducer')
Goðjaðarr ('god-protector')
Gǫllnir, Gǫllor, Gǫllungr ('yeller')
Gǫndlir ('wand-wielder')
Grímnir, Grímr ('the masked one')
Grímr ('grim')
Gunnar ('warrior'?)
Gunnblindi ('battle-blinder')
Hagvirkr ('skilful worker')
Hangaguð, Hangatýr ('hanged-god')
Hangi ('hanged one')
Haptaguð ('fetter-god')
Haptsœnir ('fetter-loosener')
Hár ('high one') *see* HÁR
Hárbarðr ('grey-beard') *see* HÁRBARDSLJÓD (Hárbard)
Hárr ('one-eyed')
Hávi ('high one') *see* HÁVAMÁL (Hávi)
Helblindi ('Helblind')
Hengikeptr ('hang-jaw')
Herblindi ('host-blind')
Herfǫðr, Herjafǫðr ('host-father')
Hergautr ('host-Gautr')
Herjan(n), Herran ('the one of the host')
Herteitr ('host-glad')
Hertýr ('host-god')
Hildólf ('battle-wolf')
Hjalmberi ('helm-bearer')
Hjarrandi ('screamer')
Hléfreyr ('famous lord'?, 'mound-lord')
Hnikarr, Hnikuðr ('inciter') *see* HNIKAR
Hóarr ('one-eyed')
Hóvi ('high one')
Hrafnáss ('raven-god')
Hrammi ('fetterer'?, 'ripper'?)
Hrani ('blusterer')
Hrjótr ('roarer')
Hroptatýr ('lord of gods'?, 'tumult-god'?)
Hroptr ('god'?, 'tumult'?)
Hrosshársgrani ('horse-hair moustache')
Hvatmóðr ('whet-courage')
Hveðrungr ('roarer')
Ítreker ('splendid ruler')
Jafnhár ('just as high') *see* HÁR
Jalfaðr, Jalfǫðr ('yellow-brown back')
Jalgr, Jalkr ('gelding')
Járngrímr ('iron-grim')
Jólfr ('horse-wolf', 'bear')
Jólnir ('yule-figure')
Jǫrmunr ('mighty one')
Karl ('old man')
Kjalarr ('nourisher')
Langbarðr ('long-beard')
Loðungr ('shaggy cloak wearer')
Njótr ('user', 'enjoyer')
Óðinn ('frenzied one') *see* ODIN
Óðr ('frenzy')

Ófnir ('weaver', 'inciter')
Olgr ('protector'?, 'hawk'?)
Ómi ('boomer')
Óski ('wished-for')
Rauðgrani ('red moustache')
Reiðartýr ('wagon-god')
Sanngetall ('truth-getter')
Sannr, Saðr ('truth')
Síðgrani ('drooping moustache')
Síðhǫttr ('drooping hat')
Síðskeggr ('drooping beard')
Sigðir ('victory-bringer')
Sigfaðir ('victory-father')
Siggautr ('victory-Gautr')
Sigmundr ('victory-protection')
Sigrhǫfundr ('victory-author')
Sigrunnr ('victory-tree')
Sigþrór ('victory-successful')
Sigtryggr ('victory-sure')
Sigtýr ('victory-god')
Skollvaldr ('treachery-ruler')
Sváfnir ('sleep-bringer')
Sveigðir ('reed-bringer'?)
Sviðrir, Sviðurr ('calmer'?, 'spear-god'?)
Svipall ('fleeting')
Svǫlnir ('cooler'?, 'sweller'?)
Þekkr ('clever')
Þrasarr ('quarreler')
Þriði ('third') *see* HÁR (Thridi)
Þriggi ('triple')
Þrór ('burgeoning')
Þróttr ('strength')
Þrundr ('sweller')
Þundr ('rumbler')
Þunnr, Þuðr ('lean', 'pale')
Tveggi ('double')
Tvíblindi ('twice-blind')
Unnr, Uðr ('lover'?, 'beloved'?, 'striver'?)
Váfǫðr, Váfuðr ('dangler')
Vakr ('vigilant')
Valfǫðr ('father of the slain')
Valgautr ('slaughter-Gaut')
Valkjósandi ('chooser of the slain')
Valtamr ('slain-tame')
Valtýr ('slain-god')
Valþǫgnir ('slain-receiver')
Vegtamr ('way-tame') *see* BALDRS DRAUMAR (Vegtam)
Veratýr ('god of men')
Viðrir ('stormer')
Víðfrægr ('wide-famed')
Við(h)rímnir ('contrary-screamer')
Viðurr ('killer'?)
Vingnir ('swinger')
Vǫfuðr ('dangler')
Yggr ('terrible') *see* YGG
Ýrungr ('stormy')

Appendix B: Dwarf Names

Ái ('great-grandfather') *see* ÁI
Álfr ('elf')
Álfrigg ('elf-king')
Alíus ('other') *see* ANNAR
Alþjófr ('all-thief')
Alvíss ('all-wise') *see* ALVÍS
Án(n), Ánarr ('pal'?; 'sword-part'?)
Andvari ('careful one') *see* ANDVARI
Annarr ('second', 'other') *see* ANNAR
Aurvangr ('soily') *see* AURVANGAR (Aurvang)
Aurvargr ('muddy wolf')
Austri ('east') *see* AUSTRI
Bari ('feisty')
Barri ('clumsy') *see* BARRI
Bávǫrr ('grumbler'?)
Berlingr ('handspike')
Bifurr, Bivǫrr ('trembler')
Bíldr ('spike')
Billingr ('twin') *see* BILLING
Bláinn ('corpse-blue')
Blávǫrr, Blǫvurr ('shiner')
Blindviðr ('hidden tree')
Bǫmburr, Bumburr ('tubby'; 'swollen')
Brísingr ('sparkle')
Brokkr ('trotter'?) *see* BROKK
Brúni ('brown')
Búinn ('laid out')
Buri, Burinn ('son')
Dagfinnr ('day-Finn')
Dáinn, Dáni ('dead')
Darri, Dǫrri ('spearman')
Dellingr ('glowing')
Dolgr ('foe')
Dolgþrasir ('strife-keen')
Dolgþvari ('strife-spear')
Dori ('borer')
Draufnir, Draupnir ('dripper')
Dúfr ('snoozy'?)
Dúri, Durinn, Dúrnir ('sleepy')
Dvalinn ('dawdler') *see* DVALIN
Eggmóinn ('sword-mown')
Eikinskjaldi ('oaken-shield')
Eitri ('poisonous') *see* EITRI
Fáinn ('stained')
Falr ('spear-socket'?)
Fár ('stained')

Farli ('wanderer')
Fíli ('file')
Finnr, Fiðr ('Finn', 'magician')
Fjalarr ('hider', 'deceiver'; 'plank-maker'?) *see* FJALAR
Fjǫlsviðr, Fjǫlsvinnr ('much-wise') *see* FJÖLSVID
Fornbogi ('ancient bow')
Frægr ('famous')
Frár ('swift')
Frosti ('frosty')
Fullangr ('tall enough')
Fundinn ('found')
Galarr ('screamer') *see* GALAR
Gandálfr ('wand-elf')
Gin(n)arr ('gaper', 'deceiver')
Glói, Glóinn, Glóni ('glowing')
Gustr ('wind')
Han(n)arr ('skilful'; 'cock')
Hár ('high')
Haugspori ('grave-treader')
Hepti ('grip')
Heptifíli ('file with handle')
Heri ('hare'; 'fighter')
Hildingr ('warrior')
Hleðjólfr ('protecting wolf'?)
Hléþjófr ('protecting thief')
Hlévangr ('shelter-plain'?)
Hlévargr ('protecting wolf')
Hljóðjólfr ('howling wolf')
Hornbori ('horn-carrier')
Ingi ('lordly'?)
Ívaldi ('bowman')
Jari ('fighter')
Kíli ('wedge')
Litr ('hue')
Liðskjálfr ('limb-shaker')
Ljómi ('brightness')
Lofarr ('praiser'; 'stooper')
Lóinn ('dawdler')
Lóni ('dawdler'; 'muddy')
Miðviðr ('middle log')
Mjǫðvitnir ('mead seeker')
Móðsognir ('frenzy-roarer')
Móðvitnir ('frenzy seeker')
Mótsognir ('battle-roarer')
Mǫndull ('mill-handle')
Næfr ('clever')

Náinn ('corpse')
Náli ('bodkin'; 'corpse')
Nár ('corpse')
Narr ('fool')
Nefi ('nephew')
Niði ('fading moon'?; 'kinsman')
Nífengr ('craggy'?)
Nípingr ('pinch')
Nóri ('little scrap')
Norðri ('northerly') *see* AUSTRI (Nordri)
Nýi, Nýr ('growing'?, 'new')
Nýráðr ('cunning')
Óinn, Ónni ('shy')
Ǫlnir ('lucky')
Ónarr ('gawper')
Óri, Órr ('raving')
Patti ('little scrap')
Ráðspakr ('counsel-wise')
Ráðsviðr ('counsel-wise')
Reginn ('mighty') *see* REGIN
Rekkr ('warrior')
Sindri ('sparky') *see* SINDRI
Sjárr ('sparky')
Skáfiðr ('crooked Finn')
Skáviðr ('slanting board')
Skáværr ('crooked'; 'good-natured')
Skirvir ('craftsman')
Sólblindi ('sun-blind')

Suðri ('south') *see* AUSTRI
Sviðr ('wise')
Svíurr, Svíarr ('waner')
Tóki ('fool')
Þekkr ('clever')
Þjóðrœrir ('mighty cairn-dweller'?)
Þjórr ('bull')
Þorinn ('daring')
Þráinn ('craver')
Þrasir ('raving')
Þrór ('burgeoning')
Þulinn ('chanter', 'mumbler')
Uni ('calm')
Úri ('smith')
Vali ('foreign'?)
Varr ('careful')
Vegdrasill ('glory-horse')
Veggr ('wedge')
Veigr ('brew')
Vestri ('west') *see* AUSTRI
Viðr ('wood')
Vífir ('fornicator')
Viggr ('horse'; 'axe-bit')
Víli ('drudge')
Vindálfr ('wind-elf')
Virvir ('dyer')
Vitr ('smart')
Yngvi ('lordly'?; 'FREYR'?)

Appendix C: Giant Names

Ægir ('sea') *see* ÆGIR
Alfarinn ('well-travelled')
Alsvartr ('all black')
Alsviðr, Alsvinnr ('all-swift') *see* ALSVID
Alvaldi ('all-powerful') *see* ALVALDI
Ámr ('tub'; 'dark')
Anduðr ('opponent')
Arngrímr ('eagle-masked')
Aurgelmir ('gravel-yeller') *see* AURGELMIR
Aurgrímnir ('gravel-masked')
Aurnir ('muddy')
Aurrekr ('gravel-lord')
Baugi ('bowed')
Beinviðr ('bone-wood')
Beli ('roarer') *see* BELI
Bergelmir ('mountain-roarer'?, 'bare yeller'?) *see*
  BERGELMIR
Bergfinnr ('mountain-Finn')

Bergþórr ('mountain-THOR')
Björgólfr ('protecting elf')
Blapþvari ('smiter'?)
Bölþorn ('evil-thorn') *see* BÖLTHORN
Brandingi ('burner')
Brimir ('sea')
Brúni ('brown')
Brúsi ('he-goat')
Byleistr ('wind-lightning'?) *see* BYLEIST
Dofri ('sluggard'; 'mountain-man')
Dumbr ('dumb')
Dúrnir ('sleepy')
Eimgeitir ('vapour-giant'?)
Eitill ('chilly'?)
Eldr ('fire')
Farbauti ('sudden-striker') *see* FARBAUTI
Fenrir ('fen-dweller') *see* FENRIR
Fjalarr ('hider', 'deceiver') *see* FJALAR

Appendices

Fjǫlsviðr, Fjǫlsvinnr ('much-wise') *see* FJÖLSVID
Fjǫlverkr ('worker')
Fleggr ('troll')
Fornjótr ('destroyer'?; 'ancient giant'?) *see* FORNJÓT
Fyrnir ('crumbly')
Galarr ('screamer') *see* GALAR
Ganglati ('walk-slacker') *see* HEL
Gangr ('traveller') *see* ALVALDI (Gang)
Gapi ('gaper')
Gaulnir ('yeller')
Gautr ('Gaut')
Geirhamðir ('spear-man')
Geirrǫðr ('spear-reddener')
Geitir ('butt')
Gillingr ('yeller') *see* GILLING
Glámr ('gleaming')
Glaumr, Glaumarr ('yeller')
Gljúfrageirr ('chasm-spear')
Gǫlnir ('screamer')
Grimlingr ('savage')
Grímr ('masked one')
Grímúlfr ('wolf-masked')
Grímnir ('masked one')
Guðlaugr ('god-protected')
Guðmundr ('god-protected')
Gusir ('gusty')
Gyllingr, Gyllir ('yeller')
Gymir ('sea'?, 'engulfer') *see* GYMIR
Hallmundr ('stone-protection')
Harðgreipr ('hard-grip')
Harðverkr ('hard-worker')
Hástigi ('high-stepper')
Hati ('hateful')
Heiðr ('hawk'?; 'honour'?)
Helreginn ('HEL-power')
Hengikjaftr, Hengikjǫptr ('hang-jaw')
Hergrímr ('battle-mask')
Herkir ('enduring')
Hildir ('battle')
Hlébarðr ('protecting-beard')
Hlói ('roarer')
Hræsvelgr ('corpse-swallower')
Hrauðnir, Hrauðungr ('spoiler')
Hrímgrímnir ('frost-masked')
Hrímnir ('frosty')
Hrímþurs ('frost-giant')
Hripstǫðr ('leaky'?)
Hróarr ('famed')
Hróðr ('famed')
Hrǫkkvir ('whipper')
Hrǫngviðr ('noisy tree')
Hrólfr ('famed wolf')
Hrossþjófr ('horse-thief')
Hrungnir ('brawler') *see* HRUNGNIR
Hrymr ('decrepit')
Hundálfr ('hound-elf')

Hvalr ('whale')
Hveðrungr ('flapper'?)
Hymir ('creeper') *see* HYMIR
Iði ('eager'?) *see* ALVALDI (Idi)
Ímr ('strife')
Járngrímr ('iron-mask')
Járnhauss ('iron skull')
Járnnefr ('iron nose')
Járnskjǫldr ('iron shield')
Kaldgrani ('cold-moustache')
Kálfr ('calf')
Kǫttr ('tom-cat')
Kyrmir ('screamer')
Leiði ('loathed; fair-wind')
Leifi ('inheritor')
Loðinn ('stumpy')
Lundr ('grove')
Lútr ('stooping')
Miði ('middle-man')
Miðjungr ('middle-man')
Miðvitnir ('mid-wolf')
Mímir ('wise', 'mindful') *see* MÍMIR
Mǫgþrasir ('kin-fighter')
Nati ('keen')
Nǫrfi, Nǫrr, Nǫrvi ('narrow') *see* NÖRFI
Ǫflugbarði ('mighty striker')
Ófóti ('footless')
Óglaðnir ('ungladdener')
Ǫlvaldi ('mighty-ruler') *see* ALVALDI (Ölvaldi)
Ǫnduðr ('dead'?)
Ǫrnir ('eagle')
Ǫskruðr ('bellower')
Ǫsgrúi ('mouth-crowder')
Óskrúðr ('unshrouded')
Rangbeinn ('bent-bone')
Rauðfeldr ('red-cloak')
Reginn ('power') *see* REGIN
Rǫndólfr ('shield-elf')
Rungnir ('brawler') *see* HRUNGNIR
Sækarlsmúli ('seaman's snout'?)
Salfangr ('bargain-grasper')
Sámendill ('swarthy'; 'Finn')
Sámr ('swarthy'; 'Finn')
Selr ('seal')
Skærir ('cutter')
Skalli ('baldy')
Skelkingr ('scary')
Skerkir ('noisy')
Skorir ('crag')
Skrámr ('scary')
Skratti ('guffawing')
Skrýmir ('brawler'?) *see* SKRÝMIR
Sǫkkmímir ('sinking-MÍMIR')
Sómr ('seemly'?)
Sprettingr ('spurter')
Starkaðr ('bold'?) *see* STARKAD

Stígandi ('strider')
Stórverkr ('mighty worker')
Stumi ('dumb')
Surtr ('black') *see* SURT
Suttungr ('sup-heavy') *see* SUTTUNG
Svaði ('slippery')
Svalfangr ('cool catch')
Svalr ('cool')
Svárangr ('stodgy'?)
Svartr ('black')
Svásuðr ('delightful') *see* SVÁSUD
Þistillbarði ('thistle-beater'?)
Þjazi (etymology unknown) *see* THJAZI
Þorn ('thorn')
Þrásir ('stormer')
Þrígeitir ('thrice-butt')
Þrívaldi ('thrice-powerful')
Þrúðgelmir ('power-yeller') *see* THRÚDGELMIR
Þrymr ('crash') *see* THRYM

Tindr ('peak')
Tjǫsnir ('peg')
Úlfheðinn ('wolf-cloaked')
Úlfr ('wolf')
Útgarðaloki ('wilderness-LOKI') *see* ÚTGARDALOKI
Vafþrúðnir ('mighty weaver'?) *see* VAFTHRÚDNIR
Vagnhǫfði ('whale-head')
Valdi ('powerful')
Vasuðr ('wetness')
Viðblindi ('blind')
Vindlóni ('gentle wind') *see* VINDSVAL
Vindr ('windy')
Vindsvalr ('chill wind') *see* VINDSVAL
Vingripr ('clutcher')
Viparr ('whipper')
Vǫrnir ('defensive')
Ylfingr ('wolf')
Ymir ('groaner') *see* YMIR

Appendix D: Names of Troll-wives, Giantesses and Valkyries

Áma, Ámma ('black')
Ámgerðr ('black-GERD')
Angeyja ('barker')
Angrboða ('harm-bidder') *see* ANGRBODA
Arinnefja ('eagle-nose')
Atla ('grim')
Aurboða ('gravel-bidder') *see* AURBODA
Bakrauf ('arse-hole') *see* BAKRAUF
Bara, Bára ('wave') *see* ÆGIR
Bergdís ('rock-DÍS')
Bestla ('wife', 'bark') *see* BESTLA
Blátǫnn ('black tooth')
Blóðughadda ('bloody hair') *see* ÆGIR (Blódughadda)
Brana ('spurt')
Brók ('breeches')
Bryja ('chewer'?)
Brynhildr ('bright battle') *see* BRYNHILD
Búseyra ('muddy-dwelling'?, 'big ears'?, 'house-starver'?)
Bylgja ('billow') *see* ÆGIR
Drífa ('drifting snow')
Drǫfn ('foaming sea') *see* ÆGIR (Dröfn)
Dúfa ('dipping') *see* ÆGIR
Eimyrja ('embers')
Eisa, Eistla ('spurt')
Eisurfála ('ember lass'?)
Eydís ('island-DÍS')
Eyrgjafa ('gravel-giver')

Fála ('lass')
Feima ('young girl')
Fenja ('swampy') *see* FENJA
Fjǫlvǫr ('great care')
Flannhildr ('battle-prick')
Flaumgerðr ('din-GERD')
Flegða ('ogress')
Forað ('abyss'?; 'danger'?)
Fríðr ('beautiful')
Fǫnn ('snow')
Gála ('shrew')
Geirahöð ('spear-fight')
Geirnefja ('spear-nose')
Geirǫlul ('spear-waver') *see* VALKYRIES (Geirölul)
Geirríðr ('spear-rider')
Geirskǫgul ('spear-shaker')
Geit ('she-goat')
Geitla ('butt')
Gerðr ('enclosure') *see* GERD
Gestilja ('hostess'?)
Geysa ('spouter')
Gjálp ('yelper') *see* GJÁLP
Gjǫlp ('shrieker')
Glumra ('rattler')
Gneip ('spike'?)
Gnepja ('spiky'?)
Gnípa ('peak')

Appendices

Gnissa ('spectre')
Gǫll ('tumult') *see* VALKYRIES (Göll)
Gǫndul ('wand-wielder')
Greip ('gripper') *see* GJÁLP
Gríðr ('peace')
Gríma ('masked one')
Grímhildr ('mask-battle')
Grísla ('young sow')
Grottintanna ('grit-teeth')
Grýla ('bug-bear')
Guðrún ('battle-rune')
Guma ('fussy')
Gunnr ('war')
Gunnlǫð ('war-summons')
Hadda ('hair')
Hæra ('tall')
Hála ('tail')
Hallkatla ('boulder-kettle'?)
Harðgreip ('hard-grip') *see* HARDGREIP
Hefring ('goat') *see* ÆGIR
Hel ('HEL') *see* HEL
Helga ('hallowed')
Hengikepta, Hengjankjapta ('hang-jaw')
Herfjötur ('host-fetter') *see* VALKYRIES (Herfjötur)
Hergerðr ('war-GERD')
Hergunnr ('war-battle')
Herkja ('dearth')
Hetta ('hood')
Hildi, Hildr ('battle') *see* VALKYRIES
Hildigunnr ('war-battle')
Hildiríðr ('war-rider')
Himinglæva ('heaven-reacher') *see* ÆGIR
Hljóð ('sound')
Hlǫkk ('noise', 'battle') *see* VALKYRIES (Hlökk)
Hǫdd ('hair')
Hǫlgabrúðr ('bride of Hǫlgi'?) *see* THORGERD
   HÖLGABRÚD
Hǫrgatroll ('altar-troll')
Hǫrn ('flaxen'?)
Hornnefja ('horn-nose')
Hrafnborg ('raven-rock')
Hrafnhildr ('raven-battle')
Hremsa ('clutcher')
Hrímgerðr ('frost-GERD')
Hrist ('shaker') *see* VALKYRIES
Hrǫnn ('wave') *see* ÆGIR (Hrönn)
Hrund ('pricker')
Hrúga ('heap')
Hrygða ('sorrowful')
Hrǫnn ('wave') *see* ÆGIR (Hrönn)
Huld ('hidden')
Hveðra ('roaring one')
Hyndla ('little bitch')
Hyrja ('fiery')
Hyrrokkin ('fire-steamer')
Íma ('embers'; battle'?)

Ímð(r) ('ogress'; 'battle'?)
Ímgerðr ('ember-GERD'?; 'battle-GERD'?)
Íviðja ('hag')
Járnglumra ('iron-rattle')
Járnsaxa ('iron-sax') *see* JÁRNSAXA
Járnviðja ('iron hag')
Jǫrð ('earth') *see* JÖRD
Keila ('strait')
Kleima ('smear')
Kólga ('cool wave') *see* ÆGIR
Kráka ('crow')
Kúla ('knob')
Leikn ('trickery')
Leirvǫr ('muddy lips')
Ljóta ('ugly')
Loðinfingra ('stumpy fingers')
Mána ('moon')
Margerðr ('sea-Gerd')
Mella ('noose')
Menglǫð ('necklace-glad') *see* MENGLÖD
Menja ('necklace')
Mist ('cloud') *see* VALKYRIES
Mjǫll ('powdered snow')
Molda ('clay')
Mǫrn ('nightmare')
Munnharpa ('mouth cramp')
Munnriða ('mouth rider')
Myrkriða ('dark rider')
Nál ('needle')
Nefja ('nosey')
Nípa ('peak')
Nótt ('night')
Qflugbarða ('mighty striker')
Ráðgríð ('counsel-truce') *see* VALKYRIES (Rádgrid)
Randgríð ('shield-truce') *see* VALKYRIES (Randgrid)
Reginleif ('power-trace') *see* VALKYRIES
Rúna ('confidante')
Rýgr ('lady')
Rymr ('roaring')
Sigrdrífa ('victory-urger') *see* SIGRDRÍFA
Sigrún ('victory-RUNE') *see* SIGRÚN
Simul ('eternal'?)
Sívǫr ('continual caution')
Skaði ('harm') *see* SKADI
Skeggjǫld ('axe-age')
Skellinefja ('clatter-nose')
Skinnbrók ('skin-breeches')
Skinnefja ('skin-nose')
Skinnhetta ('skin-hood')
Skinnhúfa ('skin-cloak')
Skjalddís ('shield-DÍS')
Skjaldgerðr ('shield-GERD')
Skjaldvǫr ('shield-caution')
Skögul ('shaker')
Skríkja ('shrieker')
Skrukka ('sea-urchin')

Skuld ('debt', 'future'?)

Sleggja ('sledge-hammer')

Sváva ('sleep-maker')

Sveipinfalda ('swooping hood')

Þórdís ('THOR-DÍS')

Þúfa ('mound')

Þrúðr ('power')

Þurborð ('dry board')

Torfa ('turf')

Torfar-Kolla ('turf-beast')

Trana ('crane')

Uðr, Unnr ('wave') *see* ÆGIR
   (Ud, Unn)

Úlfrún ('wolf-rune')

Unngerðr ('wave-Gerd')

Varðrún ('secret-keeper')

Vargeisa ('wolf-fire')

Vígglǫð ('battle-glad')

Bibliography and Further Reading

The bibliography below offers a notion of the vast and extensive range of material, including both primary and secondary sources, which has been written on the myths and legends of the North. While far from exhaustive, the bibliography is intended to provide the more adventurous reader with the opportunity to explore the issues raised here in more detail than the scope of this book would allow. To that end, the bibliography is divided into four sections of unequal length: reference tools and general surveys (section A); editions of primary texts (section B); translations of primary texts (section C); and secondary references (section D). Given that the relevant (and more specific items) from sections B to D are noted in the lists of references that follow each main entry in the Dictionary, it may be helpful briefly to consider the more general items listed in section A.

Most of the general historical surveys of the period focus on the events and personalities of the so-called Viking Age (c.800–1100), although few (despite their titles) can be considered as exclusive to that period (A21, 22, 25, 31–3, 38, 48–50, 73, 83, 91, 97, 104, 105). A number of more specific historical studies concentrate on the Christianization of the North, and in particular on the undoubtedly profound impact of Christianity on the myths and legends that have been preserved, often by Christian authors (A1, 38, 103, 107, 123, 127, 139). Knowledge of such a historical and cultural background is vital to the interpretation and understanding of much of the extant literary evidence in particular, not only in Norse, but also in other languages, notably Old English and Latin. For the pre-Christian period, by contrast, we rely heavily on the surviving cultural artefacts, as well as on a variety of linguistic and literary evidence, from both Scandinavia and beyond.

In the field of language, there has been a steady stream of fascinating studies in the specific area of onomastics, including detailed work on what can be deduced about the myths and legends of the North from surviving personal and place-names (A24, 29, 44, 46, 64, 71, 94, 108, 112). Other linguistic (and art-historical) scholarship has focused on the numerous surviving runic inscriptions and picture-stones (A19, 47, 55, 56, 70, 88, 134), while other more general surveys have concentrated on other kinds of material evidence in the wider areas of art and archaeology (A32, 33, 59, 70, 83, 87, 99, 135–7). Such evidence needs to be weighed carefully against that of the surviving literary sources, which in almost all general surveys (including this one) has tended to prevail.

Modern readers of the primary literary material from Scandinavian sources have access to a range of dictionaries and concordances (A8, 18, 27, 52, 61, 72, 94, 132), as well as to various bibliographies of more or less specialist interest (A4, 5, 9, 26, 35, 36, 39–43, 67, 68). Each of the literary genres germane to a study of the myths and legends of the North has a vigorous tradition of scholarly study and debate. This is particularly true of skaldic verse, which includes some of the earliest literary material extant in Norse, but which also offers many of the most difficult problems of interpretation (A10, 26, 28, 34, 43, 45, 54, 57, 58, 60, 66, 74, 84, 85, 92, 93, 96, 100, 109, 110, 116, 122, 126, 127, 130, 133). Eddic verse, while (generally) less opaque, nonetheless has attracted an impressive range of general discussion (A10, 30, 34–6, 41, 46, 52–4, 57, 58, 61, 79, 84, 92, 110, 113, 126, 127, 133); likewise, the later ballad tradition has been scanned for its relevance to earlier tales and beliefs (A85, 138). The extant prose literature, composed long after the conversion (but often incorporating much earlier material, especially in verse), offers its own particular problems of interpretation. Many of the sagas, including the so-called *fornaldarsögur* ('sagas of bygone days'), have been thought to contain echoes of earlier myth and legend, and have consequently been studied in detail for the often inscrutable evidence they appear to offer (A7, 9, 39, 40, 57, 58, 86, 110, 124, 126, 127, 133). The superficially more straightforward compositions of the thirteenth-century Icelander Snorri Sturluson likewise raise many questions about the ways in which the literary evidence can be interpreted, and several studies have focused on the problems and difficulties of interpreting his work (A3, 57, 58, 102, 110, 126, 127, 133). Indeed, modern scholars have been so prolific in their interpretation of the extant literary evidence that it is possible to identify within the more general field a number of still more specialized areas of research which have become popular in recent years: on the range of roles played by women in the surviving texts (A48, 62, 79, 80), for example, or on the extent of Irish influence to be detected in the sources (A113, 125).

Modern readers of the myths and legends of the North also have recourse to large numbers of reference tools and resources drawing together all of the various kinds of evidence discussed above, including in particular both various encyclopedias (A63, 95, 115), and a large number of general overviews (A6, 11–17, 22, 23, 51, 62, 65, 67–9, 75–8, 81, 82, 90, 102, 106, 107, 111, 114, 119–121, 128, 129, 131, 133). The theoretical background to such overviews is minutely considered in a bewildering array of discussions of the very nature of Norse myth and legend, including anthropological, sociological, and feminist approaches (A2, 13–15, 17, 65, 76–8, 82, 89, 98, 101, 111, 113, 117, 118). It will be clear that much work had already been done on describing and explaining the myths and legends of the North, and that each generation has favoured specific areas and approaches to their study. But it will also be evident that much remains unsettled, and that if not every problem can be solved, there can still be much wonder and delight in the search.

For the purposes of alphabetization the following equivalencies have been observed for upper and lower case forms: ä, æ = ae; ð = d; ö, œ = oe; þ = th; ü=ue. All other diacritics have been ignored. Icelandic authors are given under their patronymics.

A. Reference Books and General Surveys

A1. AÐALSTEINSSON, Jón Hnefill, *Under the Cloak: The Acceptance of Christianity in Iceland with Particular Reference to the Religious Attitudes Prevailing at the Time*, Studia Ethnologica Upsaliensia 4 (Stockholm: Almqvist and Wiksell, 1978)

A2. AÐALSTEINSSON, Jón Hnefill, 'Folk Narrative and Norse Mythology', *Arv* (1990), 115–22

A3. BAETKE, W., *Die Götterlehre der Snorra-Edda*, Berichte über die Verhandlungen der sächsischen Akademie der Wissenschaften zu Leipzig, phil.-hist. Klasse 97.3 (1950), pp. 1–68; rptd in his *Kleine Schriften: Geschichte, Recht und Religion in germanischem Schrifttum*, ed. Kurt Rudolph and Ernst Walter (Weimar: Böhlaus, 1973), pp. 206–46

A4. BEKKER-NIELSEN, Hans, *Bibliography of Old Norse-Icelandic Studies* (Copenhagen: Munksgaard, 1964–)

A5. BEKKER-NIELSEN, Hans, *Old Norse-Icelandic Studies. A Select Bibliography* (Toronto: Toronto University Press, 1967)

A6. BOYER, Régis, *Yggdrasill: la religion des anciens scandinaves* (Paris: Payot, 1981)

A7. BYOCK, Jesse L., *Medieval Iceland: Society, Sagas, and Power* (Berkeley, CA: University of California Press, 1988)

A8. CLEASBY, Richard, and Guðbrandur Vigfusson, *An Icelandic-English Dictionary*, 2nd edn rev. by Sir William A. Craigie (Oxford: Oxford University Press, 1957)

A9. CLOVER, Carol J., 'Icelandic Family Sagas (*Íslendinga sögur*)', in *Old Norse-Icelandic Literature: a Critical Guide*, ed. Carol J. Clover and John Lindow, Islandica 45 (Ithaca: Cornell University Press, 1985), pp. 239–315

A10. CRAIGIE, W.A., *The Art of Poetry in Iceland* (Oxford: Oxford University Press, 1900)

A11. DAVIDSON, H.R. Ellis, *Gods and Myths of Northern Europe* (Harmondsworth: Penguin, 1964)

A12. DAVIDSON, H.R. Ellis, *Pagan Scandinavia* (London: Thames & Hudson, 1967)

A13. DAVIDSON, H.R. Ellis, *Scandinavian Mythology* (London: Hamlyn, 1969)

A14. DAVIDSON, H.R. Ellis, *Myths and Symbols in Pagan Europe* (Manchester: Manchester University Press, 1988)

A15. DAVIDSON, H.R. Ellis, *The Lost Beliefs of Northern Europe* (London and New York: Routledge, 1993)

A16. DRONKE, Ursula, *Myth and Fiction in Early Norse Lands* (Aldershot: Variorum, 1996)

A17. DUMÉZIL, Georges, *Gods of the Ancient Northmen*, ed. Einar Haugen, Publications of the UCLA Center for the Study of Comparative Folklore and Mythology 3 (Berkeley, CA: University of California Press, 1973)

A18. EGILSSON, Sveinbjörn, *Lexicon Poeticum Antiquae Linguae Septentrionalis*, 2nd edn by Finnur Jónsson (Copenhagen: Møller 1966)

A19. EINARSSON, Stefán, *A History of Icelandic Literature* (New York: Johns Hopkins Press for American-Scandinavian Foundation, 1957)

A20. ELLIOTT, Ralph W.V., *Runes* (Manchester: Manchester University Press, 1959)

A21. FARRELL, R.T. (ed.), *The Vikings* (Chichester: Phillimore, 1982)

A22. FELL, C.E., 'From Odin to Christ', in *The Viking World*, ed. J. Graham-Campbell (London: Weidenfeld & Nicolson, 1980), pp. 172–93

A23. FELL, C.E., 'Gods and Heroes of the Northern World', in *The Northern World: The History and Heritage of Northern*

Europe, AD400–1100, ed. D.M. Wilson (London: Thames and Hudson, 1980), pp. 33–46

A24. FELLOWS-JENSEN, Gillian, 'Place-Name Research in Scandinavia 1960–82, with a Select Bibliography', *Names* 32 (1984), 267–324

A25. FOOTE, P.G., and D.M. Wilson, *The Viking Achievement*, 2nd edn (London: Sidgwick & Jackson, 1979)

A26. FRANK, Roberta, 'Skaldic Poetry', in *Old Norse-Icelandic Literature: a Critical Guide*, ed. Carol J. Clover and John Lindow, Islandica 45 (Ithaca: Cornell University Press, 1985), pp. 157–96

A27. FRITZNER, Johan, *Ordbog over Det gamle norske sprog*, 4 vols, 4th edn (Oslo: Møller, 1973)

A28. GABRIELI, Mario, *La poesia scaldica norrena: Introduzione e testi* (Rome: Ateneo, 1962)

A29. GILLESPIE, George T., *A Catalogue of Persons Named in German Heroic Literature (700–1600), including Named Animals and Objects and Ethnic Names* (Oxford: Clarendon, 1973)

A30. GLENDINNING, Robert J., and Haraldur Bessason (ed.), *Edda: A Collection of Essays*, University of Manitoba Icelandic Studies 4 (Winnipeg: University of Manitoba Press, 1983)

A31. GRAHAM-CAMPBELL, J., *The Viking World* (London: Weidenfeld & Nicolson, 1980)

A32. GRAHAM-CAMPBELL, J., *Viking Artefacts: a Select Catalogue* (London: British Museum Publications, 1980)

A33. GRAHAM-CAMPBELL, J., and D. Kidd, *The Vikings* (London: British Museum Publications, 1980)

A34. HALLBERG, Peter, *Old Icelandic Poetry: Eddic Lay and Skaldic Verse*, trans. Paul Schach and Sonja Lindgrenson (Lincoln: University of Nebraska Press, 1975)

A35. HANNESSON, Jóhann S., *Bibliography of the Eddas: A Supplement to Bibliography of the Eddas (Islandica 13)*, Islandica 37 (Ithaca, NY: Cornell University Press, 1955)

A36. HARRIS, Joseph, 'Eddic Poetry', in *Old Norse-Icelandic Literature: A Critical Guide*, ed. Carol J. Clover and John Lindow. Islandica 45 (Ithaca, NY: Cornell University Press, 1985), pp. 157–96

A37. HAYWOOD, John, *The Penguin Historical Atlas of the Vikings* (Harmondsworth: Viking, 1995)

A38. HEINRICHS, Anne, 'The Search for Identity: a Problem after the Conversion', *Alvíssmál* 3 (1994), 43–62

A39. HERMANNSSON, Halldór, *Bibliography of Icelandic Sagas and Minor Tales*, Islandica 1 (Ithaca, NY: Cornell University Press, 1908)

A40. HERMANNSSON, Halldór, *Bibliography of the Mythical-Heroic Sagas*, Islandica 5 (Ithaca, NY: Cornell University Press, 1912)

A41. HERMANNSSON, Halldór, *Bibliography of the Eddas*, Islandica 13 (Ithaca, NY: Cornell University Press, 1920)

A42. HERMANNSSON, Halldór, *The Sagas of the Kings and the Mythical-Heroic Sagas: Two Bibliographical Supplements*, Islandica 26 (Ithaca, NY: Cornell University Press, 1937)

A43. HOLLANDER, Lee M., *A Bibliography of Skaldic Studies* (Copenhagen: Munksgaard, 1958)

A44. HOLMBERG, Bente, 'Om sakrale sted- og personnavne', in *Nordisk Hedendom. Et Symposium*, ed. Gro Steinsland (Odense: Odense University Press, 1991), pp. 149–60

A45. HOLTSMARK, Anne, *Studier i norrøn diktning* (Oslo: Gyldendal, 1956)

A46. HORNBY, R., *et al.*, *Danmarks gamle Personnavne*, 2 vols (Copenhagen: Gad, 1936–64)

A47. JACOBSEN, L., and E. Moltke, *Danmarks Runeindskrifter: Atlas* (Copenhagen: Munksgaard, 1941)

A48. JESCH, Judith, *Women in the Viking Age* (Woodbridge: Boydell, 1991)

A49. JÓHANNESSON, Jón, *Íslendinga saga. A History of the Old Icelandic Commonwealth*, trans. Haraldur Bessason (Winnipeg: University of Manitoba Press, 1974)

A50. JONES, Gwyn, *A History of the Vikings* (Oxford: Oxford University Press, 1968; repr. London, 1973)

A51. JONES, Gwyn, *Kings, Beasts, and Heroes* (Oxford: Oxford University Press, 1972)

A52. KELLOGG, R. L., *A Concordance to Eddic Poetry* (East Lansing, MI: Colleagues, 1988)

A53. KLINGENBERG, Heinz, *Edda – Sammlung und Dichtung*, Beiträge zur nordischen Philologie 3 (Basel: Kohlhammer, 1974)

A54. KOCK, Ernst A., *Notationes norrænæ: Anteckningar till Edda och skaldediktning* (Lund: Gleerup, 1923–44)

A55. KOLSTRUP, Inger-Lise, 'Ikonografi og religion', in *Nordisk Hedendom. Et Symposium*, ed. Gro Steinsland (Odense: Odense University Press, 1991), pp. 181–204

A56. KRAUSE, Wolfgang, *Bibliographie der Runeninschriften nach Fundorten*, 2 vols (Göttingen: Vandenhoeck & Ruprecht, 1973)

A57. KRISTJÁNSSON, Jónas, *Eddas and Sagas: Iceland's Medieval Literature* (Reykjavik: Hið Íslenzka Bókmenntafélag, 1988)

A58. KRISTJÁNSSON, Jónas, 'Heiðin trú í fornkvæðum', in *Snorrastefna. 25.–27. júli 1990*, ed. Úlfar Bragason, Rit Stofnunar Sigurðar Nordals 1 (Reykjavik: Stofnun Sigurðar Nordals, 1992), pp. 99–112

A59. KRISTJÁNSSON, Jónas, *Icelandic Manuscripts: Sagas, History and Art*, trans. Jeffrey Cosser (Reykjavík: Hið Íslenzka Bókmenntafélag, 1993)

A60. KUHN, Hans, *Das Dróttkvætt* (Heidelberg: Winter, 1983)

A61. LA FARGE, Beatrice, and P. Tucker, *Glossary to the Poetic Edda* (Heidelberg: Winter, 1992)

A62. LARRINGTON, Carolyne, 'Scandinavia', in *The Feminist Companion to Mythology*, ed. Carolyne Larrington (London: Pandora, 1992), pp. 137–61

A63. LÁRUSSON, Magnús Már, Jakob Benediktsson, *et al.* (ed.), *Kulturhistorisk leksikon for nordisk middelalder*, 22 vols. (Reykjavik, 1956–78)

A64. LIND, E.H., *Norsk-isländska dopnamn och fingerade namn från meideltiden* (Uppsala, 1905–14; suppl. Oslo: Dybwad, 1931)

A65. LINDOW, John, *Swedish Legends and Folktales*, (Berkeley, CA: University of California Press, 1978)

A66. LINDOW, John, 'Narrative and the Nature of Skaldic Poetry', *Arkiv för nordisk filologi* 97 (1982), 94–121

A67. LINDOW, John, 'Mythology and Mythography', in *Old Norse-Icelandic Literature: a Critical Guide*, ed. Carol J. Clover and John Lindow, Islandica 45 (Ithaca: Cornell University Press, 1985), pp. 21–67

A68. LINDOW, John, *Scandinavian Mythology: an Annotated Bibliography*, Garland Folklore Bibliographies 13 (New York and London: Garland, 1988)

A69. LINDOW, John, 'Bloodfeud and Scandinavian Mythology', *Alvíssmál* 4 (1994), 51–68

A70. LINDQVIST, Sune, *Gotlands Bildsteine*, Kungl. Vitterhets historie och antikvitets akademien, monografier 28, 2 vols. (Stockholm: Wahlström & Widstrand, 1941–2)

A71. LUNDGREN, M.F., and M.F. Brate, *Personnamn från medeltiden* (Uppsala: Almqvist & Wiksell, 1892–1934)

A72. MAGNÚSSON, Ásgeir Blöndal, *Íslenzk Orðsifjabók* (Reykjavík: Orðabók Háskolans, 1989)

A73. MAGNUSSON, Magnus, *Vikings!* (London: BBC Publications, 1980)

A74. MAROLD, Edith, 'Skaldendichtung und Mythologie', in *Poetry in the Scandinavian Middle Ages*, ed. Teresa Pàroli, The Seventh International Saga Conference, Atti del XII Congresso internazionale di studi sull' alto medioevo (Spoleto: Presso la sede del centro studi, 1990), pp. 107–30

A75. MCKINNELL, John, *Both One and Many: Essays on Change and Variety in Late Norse Heathenism* (Rome: Il Calamo, 1994) [with an Appendix by M.E. Ruggerini]

A76. MELETINSKIJ, Eleazar M., 'Scandinavian Mythology as a System I', *Journal of Symbolic Anthropology* 1 (1973), 43–587

A77. MELETINSKIJ, Eleazar M., 'Scandinavian Mythology as a System II', *Journal of Symbolic Anthropology* 2 (1973), 57–78

A78. MELETINSKIJ, Eleazar M., 'Scandinavian Mythology as a System of Oppositions', in *Patterns in Oral Literature*, ed. Dimitri Segal and Heda Jason (The Hague: Mouton, 1977), pp. 252–60

A79. MOTZ, Lotte, 'Sister in the Cave: The Stature and the Function of the Female Figures of Eddas', *Arkiv för nordisk filologi* 99 (1984), 175–87

A80. MOTZ, Lotte, *The Beauty and the Hag: Female Figures of Germanic Faith and Myth*, Philologica Germanica 15 (Vienna: Fassbaender, 1993)

A81. MUNCH, Peter Andreas, *Norse Mythology: Legends of Gods and Heroes*, trans. Sigurd Bernhard Hustvedt, Scandinavian Classics (New York: American-Scandinavian Foundation, 1963)

A82. MUNDAL, Else, 'Forholdet mellom myteinnhald og myteform', in *Nordisk Hedendom. Et Symposium*, ed. Gro Steinsland (Odense: Odense University Press, 1991), pp. 229–44

A83. MYHRE, Bjørn, 'The Beginning of the Viking Age–Some Current Archaeological Problems', in *Viking Revaluations. Viking Society Centenary Symposium 14–15 May 1992*, ed. Anthony Faulkes and Richard Perkins (London: Viking Society for Northern Research, 1993), pp. 182–203

A84. NOREEN, E., *Den norsk-isländska poesien* (Stockholm: Norstedt & Söners, 1926)

A85. ÓLASON, Vésteinn, *The Traditional Ballads of Iceland* (Reykjavík: Stofnun Árna Magnússonar, 1982)

A86. ÓLASON, Vesteinn, 'The Sagas of Icelanders', in *Viking Revaluations. Viking Society Centenary Symposium 14–15 May 1992*, ed. Anthony Faulkes and Richard Perkins (London: Viking Society for Northern Research, 1993), pp. 26–42

A87. OLSEN, O., *Hørg, Hov og Kirke: Historiske of Arkæologiske Vikingetidsstudier* (Copenhagen: Lynge & Søn, 1966)

A88. PAGE, R.I., *An Introduction to English Runes* (London: Methuen, 1973)

A89. PAGE, R.I., 'Dumézil Revisited', *Saga-Book of the Viking Society* 20 (1978–9), 49–69

A90. PAGE, R.I., *Norse Myths* (London: British Museum Press, 1990)

A91. PAGE, R.I., *Chronicles of the Vikings: Records, Memorials and Myths* (London: British Museum Press, 1995)

A92. PÁLSSON, Heimir, *Frasagnarlist fyrri alda: Íslensk bókmenntasaga frá landnámsöld til siðskipti* (Reykjavik: Forlagið, 1985)

A93. POOLE, Russell G., *Viking Poems on War and Peace: A Study in Skaldic Narrative* (Toronto: University of Toronto Press, 1991)

A94. PORTER, Mary Gray, 'A Dictionary of the Personal Names in the Eddic Poems (Elder Edda and Eddica minora)' (unpublished PhD dissertation, Chapel Hill, 1980)

A95. PULSIANO, Phillip, Kirsten Wolf, *et al.* (ed.), *Medieval Scandinavia: an Encyclopedia*, Garland Encyclopedia of the Middle Ages 1 (New York and London: Garland, 1993)

A96. REICHARDT, Konstantin, *Studien zu den Skalden des 9. und 10. Jahrhunderts*, Palaestra 159 (Leipzig: Mayer & Müller, 1929)

A97. ROESDAHL, Else, *The Vikings*, trans. Susan Margeson and Kirsten Williams (London: Lane, 1991)

A98. ROESDAHL, Else, 'Nordisk førkristen religion. Om kilder og metoder', in *Nordisk Hedendom. Et Symposium*, ed. Gro Steinsland (Odense: Odense University Press, 1991), pp. 293–302

A99. ROESDAHL, Else, 'Pagan Beliefs, Christian Impact and Archaeology–a Danish View', in *Viking Revaluations. Viking Society Centenary Symposium 14–15 May 1992*, ed. Anthony Faulkes and Richard Perkins (London: Viking Society for Northern Research, 1993), pp. 128–36

A100. ROSS, Margaret Clunies, 'Style and Authorial Presence in Skaldic Mythological Poetry', *Saga-Book of the Viking Society* 20 (1981), 276–304

A101. ROSS, Margaret Clunies, 'Pseudo-Procreation Myths in Old Norse: an Anthropological Approach', in *Social Approaches to Viking Studies*, ed. Ross Sampson (Glasgow: Cruithne Press, 1991), pp. 35–44

A102. ROSS, Margaret Clunies, *Prolonged Echoes: Old Norse Myths in Medieval Northern Society. Volume 1: The Myths*, The Viking Collection 7 (Odense: Odense University Press, 1994)

A103. SAWYER, B., P. Sawyer, and I. Wood (ed.), *The Christianization of Scandinavia. Report of a Symposium held at Kungälv, Sweden 4–9 August 1985* (Alsingås: Viktoria bokforlag, 1987)

A104. SAWYER, P.H., *The Age of the Vikings*, 2nd edn (London: Methuen, 1971)

A105. SAWYER, P.H., *Kings and Vikings* (London: Methuen, 1982)

Bibliography and Further Reading

A106. SCHJØDT, Jens Peter, 'Recent Scholarship in Old Norse Mythology', *Religious Studies Review* 14 (1988), 104–10

A107. SCHOMERUS, Rudolf, *Die Religion der Nordgermanen im Spiegel christlicher Darstellung* (Borna: Noske, 1926)

A108. SCHÖNFIELD, Markus, *Wörterbuch der altgermanischen Personen- und Völkernamen*, 2nd edn (Heidelberg: Winter, 1965)

A109. SEE, Klaus von, *Skaldendichtung: Eine Einführung* (Munich: Artemis, 1980)

A110. SEE, Klaus von, *Edda, Saga, Skaldendichtung. Aufsätze zur skandinavischen Literatur des Mittelalters* (Heidelberg: Winter, 1981)

A111. SEE, Klaus von, *Mythos und Theologie im skandinavischen Hochmittelalter* (Heidelberg: Winter, 1988)

A112. SIGMUNDSSON, Svavar, 'Átrúnaður og örnefni', in *Snorrastefna. 25.–27. júli 1990*, ed. Úlfar Bragason, Rit Stofnunar Sigurðar Nordals 1 (Reykjavik: Stofnun Sigurðar Nordals, 1992), pp. 241–54

A113. SIGURÐSSON, Gísli, *Gaelic Influence in Iceland: Historical and Literary Contacts. A Survey of Research*, Studia Islandica 46 (Reykjavík: Bókaútgáfa menningarsjóðs, 1988)

A114. SIMEK, Rudolf, *Altnordische Kosmographie: Studien und Quellen zu Weltbild und Weltbeschreibung in Norwegen und Island vom 12. bis zum 14. Jahrhundert*, Ergänzungsbände zum Reallexikon der germanischen Altertumskunde 4 (Berlin: de Gruyter, 1990)

A115. SIMEK, Rudolf, *Dictionary of Northern Mythology*, trans. Angela Hall (Cambridge: D.S. Brewer, 1993)

A116. SMIRNICKAJA, Olga A., 'Mythological Nomination and Skaldic Synonymics', in *Snorrastefna. 25.–27. júli 1990*, ed. Úlfar Bragason, Rit Stofnunar Sigurðar Nordals 1 (Reykjavik: Stofnun Sigurðar Nordals, 1992), pp. 217–25

A117. SØRENSEN, Preben Meulengracht, *The Unmanly Man. Concepts of Sexual Defamation in Early Northern Society*, trans. Joan Turville-Petre, The Viking Collection 1 (Odense: Odense University Press, 1983)

A118. SØRENSEN, Preben Meulengracht, 'Historical Reality and Literary Form', in *Viking Revaluations. Viking Society Centenary Symposium 14–15 May 1992*, ed. Anthony Faulkes and Richard Perkins (London: Viking Society for Northern Research, 1993), pp. 172–81

A119. STEBLIN-KAMENSKIJ, M.I., *Myth: The Icelandic Sagas and Eddas*, trans. Mary P. Coote (Ann Arbor, MI: Karoma, 1982)

A120. STEFFENSEN, J., 'Aspects of Life in Iceland in the Heathen Period', *Saga-Book of the Viking Society* 17 (1967–8), 177–205

A121. STRÖM, Folke, *Nordisk hedendom: Tro och sed i förkristen tid*, 2nd ed., (Gothenburg: Gumpert, 1967)

A122. STRÖM, Folke, 'Poetry as an Instrument of Propaganda. Jarl Hákon and his Poets', in *Speculum Norroenum: Norse Studies in Memory of Gabriel Turville-Petre*, ed. Ursula Dronke, Guðrún P. Helgadóttir, Gerd Wolfgang Weber, and Hans Bekker-Nielsen (Odense: Odense University Press, 1981), pp. 440–58

A123. STRÖMBÄCK, Dag, *The Conversion of Iceland: a Survey* (London: Viking Society for Northern Research, 1975)

A124. SVEINSSON, Einar Ól., *Dating the Icelandic Sagas* (London: Viking Society for Northern Research, 1958)

A125. SVEINSSON, Einar Ól., 'Celtic Elements in Icelandic Tradition', *Béaloideas* 15 (1959), 3–24

A126. SVEINSSON, Einar Ól., *Íslenzkar bókmenntir í fornöld I* (Reykjavik: Almenna bókafélagið, 1962)

A127. TURVILLE-PETRE, E.O.G., *Origins of Icelandic Literature* (Oxford: Clarendon, 1953)

A128. TURVILLE-PETRE, E.O.G., *The Heroic Age of Scandinavia* (London: Hutchinson, 1958)

A129. TURVILLE-PETRE, E.O.G., *Myth and Religion of the North: The Religion of Ancient Scandinavia* (London: Weidenfeld & Nicolson, 1964)

A130. TURVILLE-PETRE, E.O.G., 'Scaldic Poetry: History and Literature', *Bibliography of Old Norse-Icelandic Studies* (1969), 7–20

A131. VRIES, Jan de, *Altgermanische Religionsgeschichte*, 2 vols, 2nd edn (Berlin: Walter de Gruyter, 1956)

A132. VRIES, Jan de, *Altnordisches etymologisches Wörterbuch*, 2nd edn (Leiden: Brill, 1962)

A133. VRIES, Jan de, *Altnordische Literaturgeschichte*, 2 vols, 2nd edn (Berlin: Walter de Gruyter, 1964–7)

A134. WILSON, David M., 'Manx Memorial Stones of the Viking Period', *Saga-Book of the Viking Society* 18 (1970–1), 1–18

A135. WILSON, David M., *The Viking Age in the Isle of Man: The Archaeological Evidence*, C.C. Rafn Lecture 3 (Odense: Odense University Press, 1974)

A136. WILSON, David M., *Anglo-Saxon Paganism* (London: Routledge, 1992)

A137. WILSON, David M., and Ole Klindt-Jensen, *Viking Art*, 2nd edn (London: George Allen & Unwin, 1980)

A138. WOLF, Alois, 'Medieval Heroic Traditions and their Transitions from Orality to Literacy', in *Vox intexta. Orality and Literacy in the Middle Ages*, ed. A.N. Doane and Carol Braun Pasternack (Madison, WI: University of Wisconsin Press, 1991), pp. 67–88

A139. WOOD, Ian, 'Christians and Pagans in Ninth-Century Scandinavia', in *The Christianization of Scandinavia. Report of a Symposium held at Kungälv, Sweden 4–9 August 1985*, ed. B. Sawyer, B., P. Sawyer, and I. Wood (Alsingås: Viktoria bokforlag, 1987), pp. 36–67

B. Primary Sources

B1. AĐALBJARNASON, Bjarni (ed.), *Heimskringla I–III*, Íslenzk fornrit 26–8 (Reykjavík: Hið íslenzka fornritafélag, 1941–51)

B2. ANDERSON, J.G.C. (ed.), *Cornelii Taciti De Origine et Situ Germanorum* (Oxford: Clarendon, 1938)

B3. ÁRNASON, Jón, ed. *Íslenzkar þjóðsögur og ævintýri*, ed. Árni Böðvarsson and Bjarni Vilhjálmsson, 6 vols, 2nd edn (Reykjavík, Prentsmiðjan Hólar, 1961)

B4. BÆKSTED, A., *Målruner og Troldruner* (Copenhagen: Gyldendal, 1952)

B5. BAILEY, R.N., *Viking Age Sculpture in Northern England* (London: Collins, 1980)

B6. BENEDIKTSSON, Jakob (ed.), *Landnámabók*, Íslenzk fornrit 1 (Reykjavík: Hið íslenzka fornritafélag, 1968)

B7. BENEDIKTSSON, Jakob (ed.), *Íslendingabók*, Íslenzk fornrit 1 (Reykjavík: Hið íslenzka fornritafélag, 1968)

B8. BERTELSEN, H. (ed.), *Þiðreks saga af Bern*, Samfund til udgivelse af gammel nordisk litteratur, 2 vols. (Copenhagen: Møller, 1905–11)

B9. BETHMANN, L., and G. Waitz (ed.), *Paulus Diaconus: 'Historia Langobardorum'*, Monumenta Germaniae Historica, Scriptores Rerum Langobardicarum et Italicarum (Hannover: Hahn, 1878)

B10. BETHURUM, Dorothy (ed.), *The Homilies of Wulfstan* (Oxford: Clarendon, 1957)

B11. BLAKE, N.F., ed. and trans., *Jómsvikinga saga: The Saga of the Jomsvikings* (London: Nelson, 1962)

B12. BOER, R.C. (ed.), *Die Edda mit historisch-kritischem Commentar I: Einleitung und Text* (Haarlem: Willink & Zoon, 1922)

B13. CALVERLEY, W.S., *Notes on the Early Sculptured Crosses, Shrines, and Monuments in the Present Diocese of Carlisle*, ed. W.G. Collingwood (Kendal: Wilson, 1899)

B14. CLARKE, D.E. Martin, ed. and trans., *The Hávamál, with selections from other Poems of the Edda, Illustrating the Wisdom of the North in Heathen Times* (Cambridge: Cambridge University Press, 1929)

B15. COLGRAVE, Bertram, and R.A.B. Mynors, ed. and trans., *Bede, 'Historia Ecclesiastica'* (Oxford: Clarendon, 1969; repr. 1991)

B16. COLLINGWOOD, W.G., *Northumbrian Crosses of the Pre-Norman Age* (London, 1927; repr. Lampeter: Llanerch, 1989)

B17. CUBBON, A.M., *The Art of the Manx Crosses* (Douglas, 1977)

B18. DEROLEZ, R. (ed.), *Runica Manuscripta: The English Tradition* (Bruges: de Tempel, 1954)

B19. DICKINS, Bruce (ed.), *Runic and Heroic Poems of the Old Teutonic Peoples* (Cambridge: Cambridge University Press, 1915)

B20. DRONKE, Ursula (ed.), *The Poetic Edda I: Heroic Poems* (Oxford: Clarendon, 1969)

B21. DROYSEN, H. (ed.), *Pauli Diaconi Historia Langobardorum*, Monumenta Germaniae Historica, Rerum Langobardicarum II (Berlin: Weidmann, 1879)

B22. EBEL, Uwe (ed.), *Vǫlsunga saga* (Frankfurt: Haag & Herchen, 1983)

B23. EVANS, D. A. H. (ed.), *Hávamál* (London: Viking Society, 1987)

B24. FAULKES, Anthony, *Snorri Sturluson, Edda. Prologue and Gylfaginning* (Oxford: Clarendon, 1982)

B25. FINCH, R.G., ed. and trans., *Vǫlsunga saga: The Saga of the Volsungs* (London: Nelson, 1965)

B26. FOOTE, Peter (ed.), and Quirk, Randolph, trans., *The Saga of Gunnlaug Serpent-Tongue* (London: Nelson, 1957)

B27. GUÐMUNDSSON, Finnbogi (ed.), *Orkneyinga saga*, Íslenzk fornrit 34 (Reykjavík: Hið íslenzka fornritafélag, 1965)

B29. HALSALL, Maureen (ed.), *The Old English Rune Poem: a Critical Edition* (Toronto: Toronto University Press, 1981)

B28. HÁNY, Arthur, ed. and trans., *Snorri Sturluson, Prosa-Edda: Altisländische Göttergeschichten*, Manesse Bibliothek der Weltliteratur (Zurich: Manesse, 1989)

B30. HELGASON, Jón (ed.), *Eddadigte*, Nordisk filologi A: 4 and 7–8 (Copenhagen: Munksgaard, 1951–2)

B31. HELGASON, Jón (ed.), *Tvær kviður fornar: Vǫlundarkviða og Atlakviða*, 2nd edn (Reykjavík: Heimskringla, 1962)

B32. HELGASON, Jón (ed.), *Kviður af Gotum og Húnum: Hamðismál, Guðrúnarhvöt, Hlöðskviða* (Reykjavík: Heimskringla, 1967)

B33. HEUSLER, Andreas, and Willhelm Ranisch (ed.), *Eddica Minora: Dichtungen eddischer Art aus den Fornaldarsögur und anderen Prosawerken* (Dortmund: Ruhfus, 1903)

B34. HILL, Joyce (ed.), *Old English Minor Heroic Poems*, Durham and St Andrews Medieval Texts 4 (Durham: University of Durham, 1983)

B35. HOLTSMARK, Anne, and Jón Helgason (ed.), *Snorri Sturluson: Edda. Gylfaginning og prosafortællingene av Skáldskaparmál*, 2nd edn (Copenhagen: Gad, 1956)

B36. JANSSON, Sven B.F., *Runes in Sweden*, trans. Peter Foote (Stockholm: Gidlunds, 1987)

B37. JÓHANNESSON, Jón (ed.), *Austfirðinga sǫgur*, Íslenzk fornrit 11 (Reykjavík: Hið íslenzka fornritafélag, 1950)

B38. JÓNSSON, Eiríkur, and Finnur Jónsson (ed.), *Hauksbók* (Copenhagen: Gyldendal, 1892–6)

B39. JÓNSSON, Finnur (ed.), *Den norsk-islandske skjaldedigtning*, 4 vols (Copenhagen: Gyldendal, 1912–15)

Bibliography and Further Reading

B40. JÓNSSON, Finnur (ed.), *Edda Snorra Sturlusonar* (Copenhagen: Gyldendal, 1931)

B41. JÓNSSON, Guðni (ed.), *Grettis saga Ásmundarsonar*, Íslenzk fornrit 7 (Reykjavík: Hið íslenzka fornritafélag, 1936)

B42. JÓNSSON, Guðni, (ed.), *Fornaldar Sögur Norðurlanda* 4 vols. (Reykjavík: Íslendingasagnaútgáfan, 1950)

B43. KERSHAW, N. (ed.), *Anglo-Saxon and Norse Poems* (Cambridge: Cambridge University Press, 1922)

B44. KLAEBER, F. (ed.), *Beowulf and the Fight at Finnsburg*, 3rd edn (Lexington, MA: D.C. Heath, 1950)

B45. KOCK, Ernst A. (ed.), *Den norsk-isländska Skaldediktningen*, 2 vols (Lund: Gleerup, 1946–50)

B46. KRAUSE, Wolfgang, *Die Runeninschriften im älteren Futhark*, with a supplement by Herbert Jankuhn, Abhandlung der Akademie der Wissenschaften in Göttingen 65 (Göttingen: Vandenhoeck & Ruprecht, 1966)

B47. KRISTJÁNSSON, Jónas (ed.), *Viga-Glúms saga*, Íslenzk fornrit 9 (Reykjavík: Hið íslenzka fornritafélag, 1956)

B48. LAPPENBERG, J.M. (ed.), *Adam of Bremen, 'Gesta Hammaburgenis Ecclesiae Pontificum'*, Monumenta Germaniae Historica, Scriptores Rerum Germanicarum (Hannover: Hahn, 1876)

B49. LINDQVIST, S., *Gotlands Bildsteine*, 2 vols (Uppsala: Almqvist & Wiksell, 1941–2)

B50. LORENZ, Gottfried, ed. and trans., *Snorri Sturluson, Gylfaginning: Texte, Übersetzung, Kommentar*, Texte zur Forschung 48 (Darmstadt: Wissenschaftliche Buchgesellschaft, 1984)

B51. MACHAN, T.W. (ed.), *Vafþrúðnismál*, Durham and St Andrews Medieval Texts 6 (Durham: Durham Medieval Texts, 1989)

B52. MALONE, Kemp (ed.), *Widsith*, 2nd edn (Copenhagen: Rosenkilde & Bagger, 1977)

B53. MALONE, Kemp (ed.), *Deor*, rev. edn (Exeter: University of Exeter Press, 1977)

B54. MOLTKE, E., *Runes and their Origins: Denmark and Elsewhere*, trans. Peter Foote (Copenhagen, 1981)

B55. MOMMSEN, T. (ed.), *Jordanes: Getica* (Berlin: Weidmann, 1882)

B56. NECKEL, Gustav (ed.), *Die Lieder des Codex Regius nebst verwandten Denkmälern I: Text*, rev. Hans Kuhn, 5th ed. (Heidelberg: Winter, 1983)

B57. NIELSEN, N.A., *Danske Runeindskrifter* (Copenhagen: Hernov, 1983)

B58. NORDAL, Sigurður (ed.), *Egils saga Skallagrímssonar*, Íslenzk fornrit 2 (Reykjavik: Hið íslenzka fornritafélag, 1933)

B59. NORDAL, Sigurður (ed.), *Völuspá*, trans. B. Benedikz and J. McKinnell, Durham and St Andrews Medieval Texts 1 (Durham: Durham Medieval Texts, 1978)

B60. NORDAL, Sigurður, *et al.* (ed.), *Flateyjarbók*, 4 vols. (Akranes: Flateyjarútgáfan, 1944–5)

B61. NORDAL, Sigurður, and Guðni Jónsson (ed.), *Gunnlaugs saga ormstungu*, Íslenzk fornrit 3 (Reykjavík: Hið íslenzka fornritafélag, 1938)

B62. NOREEN, E., *Den norsk-isländska poesien* (Stockholm, 1926)

B63. OLRIK, A. (ed.), *Danmarks heltedigtning*, 2 vols (Copenhagen: Gad, 1903–10)

B64. OLRIK, J., and H. Ræder (ed.), *Saxonis Gesta Danorum*, 2 vols (Copenhagen: Munksgaard, 1931–7)

B65. OLSEN, Magnus (ed.), *Völsunga saga ok Ragnars saga loðbrókar* (Copenhagen: Møller, 1906–8)

B66. OLSEN, M.B., *Norges Innskrifter med de Yngre Runer I–VI* (Oslo: Dybwad, 1941–80)

B67. POPE, John C. (ed.), *Homilies of Ælfric. A Supplementary Collection*, 2 vols, Early English Texts Society, OS 259–60 (London: Oxford University Press, 1967–8)

B68. RAFN, C.C. (ed.), *Fornaldar sögur Nordrlanda*, 3 vols (Copenhagen: Popp, 1829–30)

B69. RANISCH, Wilhelm (ed.), *Die Gautreks saga in zwei Fassungen* (Berlin, 1900)

B70. SCHMEIDLER, Bernhard (ed.), *Magistri Adami Bremensis Gesta Hammaburgensis Ecclesiae Pontificum*, Monumenta Germaniae Historica, Scriptores Rerum Germanicarum 2 (Hannover: Hahn, 1917)

B71. SCHNEIDER, H. (ed.), *Germanische Heldensage*, 2 vols (Berlin and Leipzig: de Gruyter, 1928–34)

B72. SHIPPEY, T.A., ed. and trans., *Poems of Wisdom and Learning in Old English* (Cambridge: Brewer, 1976)

B73. SIJMONS, B., and Hugo Gering, ed. *Die Lieder der Edda* 3 vols (Halle, 1903–31)

B74. SLAY, Desmond (ed.), *Hrólfs saga kraka* (Copenhagen: Munksgaard, 1960)

B75. SVEINSSON, Einar Ól. (ed.), *Vatnsdæla saga*, Íslenzk fornrit 8 (Reykjavík: Hið íslenzka fornritafélag, 1939)

B76. SVEINSSON, Einar Ól. (ed.), *Brennu-Njáls saga*, Íslenzk fornrit 12 (Reykjavík: Hið íslenzka fornritafélag, 1954)

B77. SVEINSSON, Einar Ól., and Mattías Þórðarson (ed.), *Eyrbyggja saga*, Íslenzk fornrit 4 (Reykjavík: Hið íslenzka fornritafélag, 1935)

B78. ÞÓRÓLFSSON, Björn K., and Guðni Jónsson (ed.), *Gísla saga Súrssonar*, Íslenzk fornrit 6 (Reykjavík: Hið íslenzka fornritafélag, 1943)

B79. THORSSON, Örnólfur (ed.), *Völsunga saga* (Reykjavik, 1985)

B80. TOLKIEN, Christopher (ed.), *Saga Heiðreks konungs ins vitra. The Saga of King Heidrek the Wise* (Edinburgh and London: Nelson, 1960)

B81. TURVILLE-PETRE, E.O.G. (ed.), *Viga-Glúms saga* (Oxford: Clarendon, 1960)

B82. TURVILLE-PETRE, E.O.G. (ed.), 'The Sonatorrek', in *Iceland and the Mediaeval World. Studies in Honour of Ian Maxwell*, ed. E.O.G. Turville-Petre and J.S. Martin (Melbourne, 1974), 33–55

B83. TURVILLE-PETRE, E.O.G., *Scaldic Poetry* (Oxford: Oxford University Press, 1976)

B84. UNGER, C.R. (ed.), *Saga Þiðriks konungs af Bern* (Christiania: Feilberg & Landmarks Forlag, 1853)

B85. VÍGFÚSSON, Guðbrandur, and C.R. Unger, ed. *Flateyjarbók*, 3 vols (Christiania: Malling, 1860–80)

B86. VÍGFÚSSON, Guðbrandur, and F. York Powell, ed. and trans., *Origines Islandicae: a Collection of the More Important Sagas and Other native Writings relating to the Settlement and Early History of Iceland*, 2 vols (Oxford: Oxford University Press, 1905)

B87. VÍGFÚSSON, Guðbrandur, and F. York Powell, ed. and trans., *Corpus Poeticum Boreale. The Poetry of the Old Northern Tongue*, 2 vols (Oxford: Oxford University Press, 1883; repr. New York: Russell & Russell, 1965)

B88. VILMUNDARSON, Þórhallur, and Bjarni Vilhjálmsson (ed.), *Harðar saga*, Íslenzk fornrit 13 (Reykjavík: Hið íslenzka fornritafélag, 1991)

B89. WESSÉN, Elias, and Sven B.F. Jansson, *Upplands Runinskrifter*, 4 vols (Stockholm, 1940–58)

B90. WIMMER, F.A., and Finnur Jónsson (ed.), *Håndskriftet Nr 2365 4to gl. kgl. samling på det store Kgl. bibliothek i København (Codex regius af den ældre Edda) i fototypisk og diplomatisk gengivelse*, Copenhagen: Samfund til udgivelse af gammel nordisk litteratur, 1891)

C. Translations of Primary Sources

C1. ANDERSON, George K., *The Saga of the Völsungs, together with Excerpts from the 'Nornageststháttr' and Three Chapters from the 'Prose Edda'* (East Brunswick: Associated University Presses, 1982)

C2. AUDEN, W.H., and Paul B. Taylor, trans., *Norse Poems* (London: Athlone, 1981)

C3. BOUCHER, Alan, *The Saga of Hallfred the Troublesome Scald* (Reykjavík: Iceland Review, 1981)

C4. BRADLEY, S.A.J., trans., *Anglo-Saxon Poetry* (London: Dent, 1982)

C5. BRODEUR, A.G., trans., *The Prose Edda by Snorri Sturluson* (New York, 1916)

C6. BYOCK, Jesse L., trans., *The Saga of the Volsungs: The Norse Epic of Sigurd the Dragon Slayer* (Berkeley, LA: University of California Press, 1990)

C7. DAVIDSON, Hilda Ellis, and Peter Fisher, *Saxo Grammaticus, The History of the Danes, Books I–IX*, 2 vols. (Cambridge: D.S. Brewer, 1979–80)

C8. ELTON, Oliver, trans., *The First Nine Books of the Danish History of Saxo Grammaticus*, with some considerations on Saxo's sources, historical methods and folklore by F. York Powell, Folklore Society Publications 33 (London: Nutt, 1894)

C9. FAULKES, Anthony (ed.), *Snorri Sturluson: Edda* (London: Dent, 1987)

C10. FELL, Christine, trans., *Egils saga*, rev. ed. (London: Dent, 1993)

C11. FOULKE, W.D., trans., *Paul the Deacon: Historia Langobardorum* (New York: Longmans, 1907)

C12. GARMONSWAY, G.N., Simpson, Jacqueline, and H.R. Ellis Davidson, trans., *Beowulf and its Analogues* (London: Dent, 1968)

C13. HALLBERG, Peter, *Old Icelandic Poetry: Eddic Lay and Skaldic Verse*, trans. Paul Schach (Nebraska: University of Nebraska Press, 1975)

C14. HATTO, A.T., trans., *The Nibelungenlied* (Harmondsworth: Penguin, 1969)

C15. HAYMES, Edward R., trans., *The Saga of Thidrek of Bern*, Garland Library of Medieval Literature 56 (New York: Garland, 1988)

C16. HOLLANDER, Lee M., *The Skalds: A Selection of their Poems, with Introductions and Notes* (New York: Ann Arbor, 1945)

C17. HOLLANDER, Lee M., trans., *The Poetic Edda, with Introduction and Explanatory Notes* (Austin, TX: University of Texas Press, 1962)

C18. HOLLANDER, Lee M., trans., *The Sagas of Kormák and the Sworn Brothers* (Princeton: Princeton University Press, 1949)

C19. JOHNSTON, George, trans., *The Saga of Gisli* (London: Dent, 1963)

C20. JONES, Gwyn, trans., *Eirik the Red and Other Icelandic Sagas*, World's Classics Series (London: Oxford University Press, 1961)

C21. KERSHAW, N., trans., *Stories and Ballads of the Far Past* (Cambridge: Cambridge University Press, 1921)

C22. LAING, Samuel, trans., *The Olaf Sagas*, 2 vols (London: Dent, 1915)

C23. LAING, Samuel, trans., *Heimskringla: Sagas of the Norse Kings* (London: Dent, 1930)

C24. LARRINGTON, Carolyne, trans., *The Poetic Edda*, Oxford World's Classics (Oxford: Oxford University Press, forthcoming)

C25. LARSON, L.M., trans., *The King's Mirror: Speculum Regale, Konungs Skuggsjá*, Scandinavian Monographs 3 (New York, 1917)

C26. MAGNUSSON, Magnus, and Hermann Pálsson, trans., *Njal's Saga* (Harmondsworth: Penguin Classics, 1960)

C27. MAGNUSSON, Magnus, and Hermann Pálsson, trans., *The Vinland Sagas: The Norse Discovery of America. Grænlendinga Saga and Eirik's Saga* (Harmondsworth: Penguin Classics, 1965)

C28. MAGNUSSON, Magnus, and Hermann Pálsson, trans., *Laxdæla Saga* (Harmondsworth: Penguin Classics, 1969)

C29. MATTINGLEY, H., trans., *Tacitus: The Agricola and the Germania*, rev. S.A. Handford (Harmondsworth: Penguin Classics, 1970)

C30. MCKINNELL, John, trans., *Viga-Glúm's saga, with the Tales of Ögmund Bash and Thorvald Chatterbox* (Edinburgh: Canongate, 1987)

C31. MIEROW, C.C., *The Gothic History of Jordanes* (Princeton: Princeton University Press, 1915)

C32. OLRIK, A., *The Heroic Legends of Denmark*, trans. L.M. Hollander (New York: American Scandinavian Foundation, 1919)

Bibliography and Further Reading

C33. ORCHARD, Andy, trans., *The Poetic Edda* (Harmondsworth: Penguin Classics, forthcoming)

C34. PÁLSSON, Hermann, trans., *Hrafnkels Saga and Other Icelandic Stories* (Harmondsworth: Penguin Classics, 1971)

C35. PÁLSSON, Hermann, and Paul Edwards, trans., *Gautreks Saga and Other Medieval Tales* (London: University of London Press, 1968)

C36. PÁLSSON, Hermann, and Paul Edwards, trans., *The Book of Settlements: Landnámabók* (Manitoba: University of Manitoba Press, 1972)

C37. PÁLSSON, Hermann, and Paul Edwards, trans., *Egil's saga* (Harmondsworth: Penguin Classics, 1976)

C38. PÁLSSON, Hermann, and Paul Edwards, trans., *Seven Viking Romances* (Harmondsworth: Penguin Classics, 1985)

C39. PÁLSSON, Hermann, and Paul Edwards, trans., *Eyrbyggja saga* (Harmondsworth: Penguin Classics, 1989)

C40. PRITSAK, O., *The Origin of Rus', I: Old Scandinavian Sources other than the Sagas* (Cambridge, MA: Harvard University Press, 1981)

C41. SHERLEY-PRICE, Leo, trans., *Bede's Ecclesiastical History of the English People*, rev. ed. (Harmondsworth: Penguin Classics, 1965)

C42. SIMPSON, Jacqueline, trans., *The Northmen Talk: a Choice of Tales from Iceland* (London: Dent, 1965)

C43. SMITH-DAMPIER, E.M., trans., *Sigurd the Dragon-Slayer* (Oxford: Blackwell, 1934; repr. New York: Kraus, 1969)

C44. SMYSER, H.M., and F.P. Magoun, Jr, trans., *Survivals in Old Norwegian of Medieval English, French, and German Literature, together with the Latin Versions of the Heroic Legend of Walter of Aquitaine*, Connecticut College Monograph 1 (Baltimore: Waverly, 1941)

C45. SWANTON, Michael, trans., *Anglo-Saxon Prose* (London: Dent, 1993)

C46. TERRY, Patricia, trans., *Poems of the Elder Edda*, rev edn (Philadelphia, PA: University of Pennsylvania Press, 1990)

C47. TSCHAN, F.J., trans., *Adam of Bremen: History of the Archbishops of Hamburg-Bremen*, Columbia University Department of History, Records of Civilization, Sources and Studies 53 (New York: Columbia University Press, 1959)

C48. YOUNG, J.I., *The Prose Edda of Snorri Sturluson* (Cambridge: Bowes & Bowes, 1954)

D. Secondary Works

D1. ÅKERLUND, W., *Studier över Ynglingatal* (Lund: Gleerup, 1939)

D2. ALBERTSSON, Kristján, 'Hverfenda hvel', *Skírnir* 151 (1977), 57–8

D3. ALLEN, W.E.D., 'The Poet and the Spae-Wife: An Attempt to Reconstruct al-Ghazal's Embassy to the Vikings', *Saga-Book of the Viking Society* 15 (1958–61), 149–258

D4. AMORY, Frederic, 'Towards a Grammatical Classification of Kennings as Compounds', *Arkiv för nordisk filologi* 97 (1982), 67–80

D5. AMORY, Frederic, 'Kennings, Referentiality and Metaphors', *Arkiv för nordisk filologi* 103 (1988), 87–101

D6. ANDERSON, Philip N., 'Form and Content in the *Lokasenna*: A Re-Evaluation', *Edda* 81 (1981), 215–25

D7. ANDERSSON, Theodore M., 'Cassiodorus and the Gothic Legend of Ermanaric', *Euphorion* 57 (1963), 28–43

D8. ANDERSSON, Theodore M., 'An Alemannic *Atlakviða*', in *Studies for Einar Haugen: Presented by Friends and Colleagues*, ed. Evelyn Scherabon Firchow, Kaaren Grimstad, Nils Hasselmo, and Wayne A. O' Neil (The Hague: Mouton, 1972), pp. 31–45

D9. ANDERSSON, Theodore M., 'The Epic Source of *Niflunga saga* and the *Nibelungenlied*', *Arkiv för nordisk filologi* 88 (1973), 1–54

D10. ANDERSSON, Theodore M., '*Niflunga saga* in the Light of German and Danish Materials', *Mediaeval Scandinavia* 7 (1974), 22–30

D11. ANDERSSON, Theodore M., *The Legend of Brynhild*, Islandica 43 (Ithaca, NY: Cornell University Press, 1980)

D12. ANDERSSON, Theodore M., 'The Lays of the Lacuna of *Codex Regius*', in *Speculum Norroenum: Norse Studies in Memory of Gabriel Turville-Petre*, ed. Ursula Dronke, Guðrún P. Helgadóttir, Gerd Wolfgang Weber, and Hans Bekker-Nielsen (Odense: Odense University Press, 1981), pp. 7–26

D13. ANDERSSON, Theodore M., 'Did the Poet of *Atlamál* know *Atlaqviða*?', in *Edda: A Collection of Essays*, ed. R.J. Glendinning and Haraldur Bessason, University of Manitoba Icelandic Studies 4 (Winnipeg: University of Manitoba Press, 1983), pp. 243–57

D14. ANDERSSON, Theodore M., '"Helgakviða Hjǫrvarðssonar" and European Bridal-Quest Narrative', *Journal of English and Germanic Philology* 84 (1985), 51–73

D15. ANDERSSON, Theodore M., 'Beyond Epic and Romance: *Sigurðarkviða in meiri*', in *Sagnaskemmtun: Studies in Honour of Hermann Pálsson*, ed. Rudolf Simek, Jónas Kristjánsson, and Hans Bekker-Nielsen (Vienna: Böhlau, 1986), pp. 1–11

D16. ANDERSSON, Theodore M., 'An Interpretation of *Þiðreks saga*', in *Structure and Meaning in Old Norse Literature*, ed. John Lindow, Lars Lönnroth, and Gerd Wolfgang Weber (Odense: Odense University Press, 1986), pp. 347–77

D17. ANDERSSON, Theodore M., *A Preface to the Nibelungenlied* (Stanford: Stanford University Press, 1987)

D18. ANDREWS, A. LeRoy, 'The Criteria for Dating the Eddic Poems', *Publications of the Modern Language Association* 42 (1927), 1044–54

D19. ARENT, Margaret, 'The Heroic Pattern: Old Germanic Helmets, *Beowulf*, and *Grettis saga*', in *Old Norse Literature and Mythology*, ed. Edgar C. Polomé (Austin, TX: University of Texas Press, 1969), pp. 130–99

D20. AULD, 'The Psychological and Mythic Unity of the God "Oðinn"', *Numen* 23 (1976), 145–60

D21. BAETKE, Walter, 'Die Götterlieder der Edda und ihre Deutungen', in his *Kleine Schriften: Geschichte, Recht und Religion in germanischem Schrifttum*, ed. Kurt Rudolph and Ernst Walter (Weimar: Böhlaus, 1973), pp. 195–205

D22. BAUSCHATZ, Paul, 'Urth's Well', *Journal of Indo-European Studies* 3 (1975), 53–86

D23. BAUSCHATZ, Paul, *The Well and the Tree: World and Time in Early Germanic Culture* (Amherst: University of Massachusetts Press, 1982)

D24. BAX, Marcel, and Tineke Padmos, 'Two Types of Verbal Duelling in Old Icelandic: The Interactional Structure of the *senna* and the *mannjafnaðr* in *Hárbarðsljóð* ', *Scandinavian Studies* 55 (1983), 149–74

D25. BEARD, D.J., 'The Berserkr in Icelandic Literature', in *Approaches to Oral Literature*, ed. Robin Thelwell (Ulster: New University of Ulster Press, 1978), pp. 99–114

D26. BECK, Heinrich, 'Der kunstfertige Schmied – ein ikonographisches und narratives Thema des frühen Mittelalters', in *Medieval Iconography and Narrative: A Symposium*, ed. Flemming G. Andersen *et al.* (Odense: Odense University Press, 1980), pp. 15–37

D27. BENEDIKTSSON, Jakob, 'Icelandic Traditions of the Scyldings', *Saga-Book of the Viking Society* 15 (1957), 48–66

D28. BENEDIKZ, Benedikt S., 'Bede in the Uttermost North', in *Famulus Christi*, ed. Gerald Bonner (London: SPCK, 1976), pp. 334–41

D29. BERG, K., 'The Gosforth Cross', *Journal of the Warburg and Courtauld Institutes* 21 (1958), 27–43

D30. BERMAN, Melissa A., '*Egils saga* and *Heimskringla*', *Scandinavian Studies* 54 (1982), 21–50

D31. BESSASON, Haraldur, 'Myth and Literary Technique in Two Eddic Poems', in *Snorrastefna. 25.–27. júlí 1990*, ed. Úlfar Bragason, Rit Stofnunar Sigurðar Nordals 1 (Reykjavík: Stofnun Sigurðar Nordals, 1992), pp. 70–81

D32. BEYSCHLAG, Siegfried, 'Die Betörung Gylfis', *Zeitschrift für deutsches Altertum* 85 (1954), 163–81

D33. BEYSCHLAG, Siegfried, 'Zur Gestalt der Hávamál: zu einer Studie Klaus von Sees', *Zeitschrift für deutsches Altertum* 103 (1974), 1–19

D34. BIBIRE, Paul, 'Freyr and Gerðr: The Story and its Myths', in *Sagnaskemmtun: Studies in Honour of Hermann Pálsson*, ed. Rudolf Simek, Jónas Kristjánsson, and Hans Bekker-Nielsen (Vienna: Böhlau, 1986), pp. 19–40

D35. BING, J., 'Ull', *Maal og Minne* (1916), 107–24

D36. BJÖRNSSON, Árni, *Jól á Íslandi*, Sögurit 31 (Reykjavík: Ísafoldarprentsmiðja, 1963)

D37. BLAKE, N. F., 'The Heremod Digressions in *Beowulf*', *Journal of English and Germanic Philology* 61 (1962), 278–87

D38. BLANEY, Benjamin, 'The Berserkr: his Origin and Development in Old Norse Literature' (unpublished PhD dissertation, University of Colorado, 1972)

D39. BLANEY, Benjamin, 'The Berserk Suitor: The Literary Application of a Stereotyped Theme', *Scandinavian Studies* 54 (1982), 279–94

D40. BOER, R.C., 'Studier over Snorra Edda', *Aarbøger for nordisk oldkyndigeid og historie* (1924), 145–272

D41. BOER, R.C., 'Studien über die Snorra Edda: Die Geschichte der Tradition bis auf den Archetypus', *Acta Philologica Scandinavica* 1 (1926–7), 54–150

D42. BONSACK, Edwin, *Dvalinn: The Relationship of the Friedrich von Schwaben, Vǫlundarkviða and Sǫrla þáttr* (Wiesbaden: Steiner, 1983)

D43. BOSERUP, Ivan (ed.), *Saxostudier. Saxo-kollokvierne ved Københavns Universitet*, Opuscula Graecolatina 2 (Copenhagen: Institut för Klassisk filologi, 1975)

D44. BOYER, Régis, 'Paganism and Literature: The So-Called "Pagan Survivals" in the Samtíðarsögur', *Gripla* 1 (1975), 135–67

D45. BOYER, Régis, 'On the Composition of *Vǫlospá*', in *Edda: A Collection of Essays*, ed. R.J. Glendinning and Haraldur Bessason, University of Manitoba Icelandic Studies 4 (Winnipeg: University of Manitoba Press, 1983), pp. 117–33

D46. BOYLE, J.A., 'Historical Dragon-Slayers', in *Animals in Folklore* (ed.), J.R. Porter and W.M.S. Russell, Folklore Society Mistletoe Series (Ipswich: Brewer, 1978), pp. 23–32

D47. BRADY, C.A. von E., *The Legends of Ermaneric* (Berkeley, CA: University of California Press, 1943)

D48. BREMMER, Rolf H., 'Hermes-Mercury and Wodan-Odin as Inventors of Alphabets: A Neglected Parallel', in *Old English Runes and their Continental Background*, ed. Alfred Bammesberger, Anglistische Forschungen 217 (Heidelberg: Winter, 1991), pp. 409–19

D49. BRIEM, Ólafur, *Vanir og Æsir*, Studia Islandica 21 (Reykjavík, 1963)

D50. BRØGGER, A.W., H. Falk, and H. Schetelig, *Osebergfundet*, 5 vols (Oslo, 1917–27)

D51. BRØNSTED, Johannes, 'Danish Inhumation Graves of the Viking Age', *Acta Archaeologica* 7 (1936), 81–228

D52. BRUCE-MITFORD, Rupert (ed.), *The Sutton Hoo Ship-Burial*, 3 vols. (London: British Museum Publications, 1975–82)

D53. BRUCE-MITFORD, Rupert, 'The Sutton Hoo Ship Burial: Some Foreign Connections', *Settimane di studio del centro italiano di studi sull' alto medioevo* (1986 for 1984), 143–218

D54. BUCHHOLZ, Peter, 'Shamanism: The Testimony of Old Icelandic Tradition', *Mediaeval Scandinavia* 4 (1971), 7–20

D55. BUGGE, Sophus, 'Iduns æbler', *Arkiv för nordisk filologi* 4 (1889), 1–45

D56. BURSON, Ann C., 'Swan Maidens and Smiths: A Structural Study of the *Vǫlundarkvida*', *Scandinavian Studies* 55 (1983), 222–35

Bibliography and Further Reading

D57. BUTT, Wolfgang, 'Zur Herkunft der Voluspá', *Beiträge zur Geschichte der deutschen Sprache und Literatur* (Tübingen) 91 (1969), 82–103

D58. BYOCK, Jesse L., 'Sigurðr Fáfnisbani: An Eddic Hero Carved on Norwegian Stave Churches', in *Poetry in the Scandinavian Middle Ages*, ed. Teresa Pàroli, The Seventh International Saga Conference, Atti del XII Congresso internazionale di studi sull' alto medioevo (Spoleto: Presso la sede del centro studi, 1990), pp. 619–28

D59. CALDWELL, James Ralston, 'The Origin of the Story of Boðhvar-Bjarki', *Arkiv för nordisk filologi* 55 (1940), 223–75

D60. CAPLES, Cynthia B., 'The Man in the Snakepit and the Iconography of the Sigurd Legend', *Rice University Studies* 62 (1976), 1–16

D61. CARVER, M.O.H. (ed.), *The Age of Sutton Hoo* (Woodbridge: Boydell, 1992)

D62. CASSIDY, Vincent H. de P., 'The Location of Ginnungagap', in *Scandinavian Studies: Essays Presented to Dr Henry Goddard Leach on the Occasion of his Eighty-Fifth Birthday*, ed. Carl F. Bayerschmidt and Erik J. Friis (Seattle: University of Washington Press, 1965), pp. 27–38

D63. CAWLEY, F. Stanton, 'An Eddic Parallel in Tennyson's "Princess"', *Scandinavian Studies* 8 (1924–5), 210–24

D64. CHADWICK, Hector Munro, *The Cult of Othin: An Essay in the Ancient Religion of the North* (Cambridge: Cambridge University Press, 1899)

D65. CHADWICK, Nora K., 'Norse Ghosts: A Study in the *draugr* and the *haugbúi*', *Folk-Lore* 57 (1946), 50–65 and 106–27

D66. CHADWICK, Nora K., 'Þorgerðr Holgabrúðr and the Trollaþing', *The Early Cultures of North-West Europe: H.M. Chadwick Memorial Studies*, ed. Cyril Fox and Bruce Dickins (Cambridge: Cambridge University Press, 1950), pp. 397–417.

D67. CHADWICK, Nora K., 'Dreams in Early European Tradition', in *Celtic Studies – Essays in Honour of Angus Matheson*, ed. J. Carney and D. Greene (New York: Barnes & Noble, 1968), pp. 33–50

D68. CHAMBERS, R.W., *Widsith: A Study in Old English Heroic Legend* (Cambridge: Cambridge University Press, 1912)

D69. CHESNUTT, Michael, 'The Beguiling of Þórr', in *Úr Dölum til Dala: Guðbrandur Vigfússon Centenary Essays*, ed. Rory McTurk and Andrew Wawn, Leeds Texts and Monographs, n.s. 11 (Leeds: Leeds Studies in English, 1989), pp. 35–64

D70. CHRISTENSEN, Askel E., 'The Jelling Monuments', *Medieval Scandinavia* 8 (1975), 7–20

D71. CIKLAMINI, Marlene, 'Óðinn and the Giants', *Neophilologus* 46 (1962), 145–57

D72. CIKLAMINI, Marlene, 'Grettir and Ketill Hængr, the Giant-Killers', *Arv* 22 (1966), 136–55

D73. CIKLAMINI, Marlene, 'Journeys to the Giant-Kingdom', *Scandinavian Studies* 60 (1968), 95–110

D74. CIKLAMINI, Marlene, 'The Problem of Starkaðr', *Scandinavian Studies* 43 (1971), 169–88

D75. CIKLAMINI, Marlene, '*Ynglinga saga*: its Function and its Appeal', *Mediaeval Scandinavia* 8 (1975), 86–99

D76. CIKLAMINI, Marlene, *Snorri Sturluson*, Twayne's World Author Series 493 (Boston: Twayne, 1978)

D77. CLOVER, Carol J., 'Skaldic Sensibility', *Arkiv för nordisk filologi* 93 (1978), 63–81

D78. CLOVER, Carol J., '*Hárbarðsljóð* as Generic Farce', *Scandinavian Studies* 51 (1979), 124–45

D79. CLOVER, Carol J., 'The Germanic Context of the Unferþ Episode', *Speculum* 55 (1980), 444–68

D80. COFFIN, R. N., '*Beowulf* and its Relationship to Norse and Finno-Uguric Beliefs and Narratives' (unpublished PhD dissertation, Boston University, 1962)

D81. CONDO, Sela Ann, 'The *Atlamál*: A Study of Multiple Authorship' (unpublished PhD dissertation, Yale University, 1972)

D82. CRONAN, Dennis, 'A Reading of Guðrúnarkviða onnor', *Scandinavian Studies* 57 (1985), 174–87

D83. CROZIER, Alan, 'Ørlygis draugr and ørlog drýgja', *Arkiv för nordisk filologi* 102 (1987), 1–12

D84. CURSCHMANN, Michael, 'The Prologue of Þiðreks saga: Thirteenth-Century Reflections on Oral Tradition', *Scandinavian Studies* 56 (1984), 140–51

D85. DAMICO, Helen, 'Sorlaþáttr and the Hama Episode in *Beowulf*', *Scandinavian Studies* 55 (1983), 222–35

D86. DAMICO, Helen, *Beowulf's Wealtheow and the Valkyrie Tradition* (Madison, WI: University of Wisconsin Press, 1984)

D87. DANIELLI, Mary, 'Initiation Ceremonial from Norse Literature', *Folklore* 56 (1945), 229–45

D88. DAVIDSON, Andrew R., 'The Legends of Þiðreks saga af Bern' (unpublished PhD thesis, University of Cambridge, 1995)

D89. DAVIDSON, Hilda R. Ellis, 'The Hill of the Dragon: Anglo-Saxon Burial Mounds in Literature and Archaeology', *Folklore* 61 (1950), 169–85

D90. DAVIDSON, Hilda R. Ellis, 'Weland the Smith', *Folklore* 69 (1958), 145–59

D91. DAVIDSON, Hilda R. Ellis, 'The Sword at the Wedding', *Folklore* 71 (1960), 1–18

D92. DAVIDSON, Hilda R. Ellis, *The Sword in Anglo-Saxon England: its Archaeology and Literature* (Oxford: Clarendon, 1962)

D93. DAVIDSON, Hilda R. Ellis, 'Thor's Hammer', *Folklore* 76 (1965), 1–15

D94. DAVIDSON, Hilda R. Ellis, 'The Smith and the Goddess: Two Figures on the Franks Casket from Auzon', *Frühmittelalterliche Studien* 3 (1969), 216–26

D95. DAVIDSON, Hilda R. Ellis, *The Battle God of the Vikings*, G.N. Garmonsway Memorial Lecture, University of York, Medieval Monographs 1 (York: University of York Press, 1972)

D96. DAVIDSON, Hilda R. Ellis, 'Hostile Magic in the Icelandic Sagas', in *The Witch Figure*, ed. V. Newall (London: Routledge, 1973), pp. 20–41

D97. DAVIDSON, Hilda R. Ellis, 'The Ship of the Dead', in *The Journey to the Other World*, ed. Hilda R. Ellis Davidson (Ipswich: Brewer, 1975), pp. 73–87

D98. DAVIDSON, Hilda R. Ellis, 'Shape-Changing in the Old Norse Sagas', in *Animals in Folklore* (ed.), J.R. Porter and W.M.S. Russell, Folklore Society Mistletoe Series (Ipswich: Brewer, 1978), pp. 126–42

D99. DAVIDSON, Hilda R. Ellis, 'Insults and Riddles in the Poetic Edda', in *Edda: A Collection of Essays*, ed. R.J. Glendinning and Haraldur Bessason, University of Manitoba Icelandic Studies 4 (Winnipeg: University of Manitoba Press, 1983), pp. 25–46

D100. DIETERLE, Richard L., 'The Song of Baldr', *Scandinavian Studies* 58 (1986), 285–307

D101. DIETERLE, Richard L., 'The Metallurgical Code of the *Vǫlundarkviða* and its Theoretical Import', *History of Religions* 27 (1987), 1–31

D102. DILLMANN, François-Xavier, 'Les nuits de Njǫrðr et de Skaði. Notes critiques sur un chapitre de la *Snorra Edda*', in *Festskrift til Ottar Grønvik på 75–årsdagen den 21. oktober 1991*, ed. John Ole Askedal *et al.* (Oslo: Universitetslaget, 1991), pp. 174–82

D103. DILLMANN, François-Xavier, 'Textafræði og goðafræði. Um Þórfina á betri útgáfu á *Snorra-Eddu*', in *Snorrastefna. 25.–27. júlí 1990*, ed. Úlfar Bragason, Rit Stofnunar Sigurðar Nordals 1 (Reykjavík: Stofnun Sigurðar Nordals, 1992), pp. 9–18

D104. DILLMANN, François-Xavier, 'Frigg, Baldr et les serpents venimeux–Note de critique textuelle sur un passage de l' *Edda* de Snorri', in *Sagnaþing helgað Jónasi Kristjánssyni sjötugum, 10. apríl 1994*, ed. Gísli Sigurðsson, Guðrún Kvaran, and Sigurgeir Steingrímsson, 2 vols. (Reykjavik: Hið íslenska bókmenntafélag, 1994), pp. 131–6

D105. DOMMASNES, Liv Helga, 'Arkeologi og religion', in *Nordisk Hedendom. Et Symposium*, ed. Gro Steinsland (Odense: Odense University Press, 1991), pp. 47–64

D106. DONAHUE, C., 'The Valkyries and the Irish War-Goddesses', *Publications of the Modern Language Association* 56 (1941), 1–12

D107. DRONKE, Peter, 'Learned Lyric and Popular Ballad in the Early Middle Ages', *Studi Medievali*, ser. 3, 17 (1976), 1–40

D108. DRONKE, Ursula, 'Art and Tradition in *Skírnismál*', in *English and Medieval Studies Presented to J.R.R. Tolkien on the Occasion of his Seventieth Birthday*, ed. Norman Davies and C.L. Wrenn (London: Allen & Unwin, 1962), pp. 250–68

D109. DRONKE, Ursula, 'The Lay of Attila', *Saga-Book of the Viking Society* 16 (1963), 1–21

D110. DRONKE, Ursula, '*Beowulf* and Ragnarǫk', *Saga-Book of the Viking Society* 17 (1969), 302–25

D111. DRONKE, Ursula, 'Classical Influences on Early Norse Literature', in *Classical Influences on European Culture* AD 500–1500: Proceedings of an International Conference Held at King's College, Cambridge, ed. R.R. Bolgar (Cambridge: Cambridge University Press, 1971), pp. 143–49

D112. DRONKE, Ursula, 'Le caractère de la poésie germanique héroïque', in *Barbara et Antiquissima Carmina*, ed. U. Dronke and P. Dronke (Barcelona, 1978), pp. 7–26

D113. DRONKE, Ursula, '*Vǫluspá* and Satiric Tradition', *Annali dell' Universitario Orientale, Napoli, Sezione Germanica* 22 (1979), 57–86

D114. DRONKE, Ursula, '*Sem jarlar forðum*: The Influence of *Rigsþula* on Two Saga-Episodes', in *Speculum Norroenum: Norse Studies in Memory of Gabriel Turville-Petre*, ed. Ursula Dronke, Guðrún P. Helgadóttir, Gerd Wolfgang Weber, and Hans Bekker-Nielsen (Odense: Odense University Press, 1981), pp. 56–72

D115. DRONKE, Ursula, 'The War of the Æsir and the Vanir in *Vǫluspá*', in *Idee, Gestalt, Geschichte. Festschrift Klaus von See. Studien zur europäischen Kulturtradition. Studies in European Cultural Tradition*, ed. G.W. Weber (Odense: Odense University Press, 1988), pp. 223–38

D116. DRONKE, Ursula, 'The Scope of the *Corpus Poeticum Boreale*', in *Úr Dölum til Dala: Guðbrandur Vigfússon Centenary Essays*, ed. Rory McTurk and Andrew Wawn, Leeds Texts and Monographs, n.s. 11 (Leeds: Leeds Studies in English, 1989), pp. 93–111

D117. DRONKE, Ursula, 'The Contribution of Eddic Studies', in *Viking Revaluations. Viking Society Centenary Symposium 14–15 May 1992*, ed. Anthony Faulkes and Richard Perkins (London: Viking Society for Northern Research, 1993), pp. 121–7

D118. DRONKE, Ursula, and Peter Dronke, 'The Prologue of the Prose Edda: Explorations of a Latin background', in *Sjötíu Ritgerðir helgaðar Jakobi Benediktssyni*, ed. Einar G. Pétursson and Jónas Kristjánsson, 2 vols. (Reykjavik: Stofnun Árna Magnússonar, 1977), II, 153–76

D119. DUMÉZIL, Georges, *From Myth to Fiction: The Saga of Hadingus*, trans. D. Coltman (Chicago: University of Chicago Press, 1973)

D120. DUMÉZIL, Georges, 'The Gods: Æsir and Vanir', trans. John Lindow, in *Gods of the Ancient Northmen*, ed. Einar Haugen (Berkeley: University of California Press, 1973), pp. 3–25

D121. DUMÉZIL, Georges, 'Magic, War, and Justice: Odin and Tyr', trans. John Lindow, in *Gods of the Ancient Northmen*, ed. Einar Haugen (Berkeley: University of California Press, 1973), pp. 26–48

D122. DUMÉZIL, Georges, 'The Drama of the World: Balder, Hoder, Loki', trans. A. Toth, in *Gods of the Ancient Northmen*, ed. Einar Haugen (Berkeley: University of California Press, 1973), pp. 49–65

D123. DUMÉZIL, Georges, 'Two Minor Scandinavian Gods: Byggvir and Beyla', trans. John Lindow, in *Gods of the Ancient Northmen*, ed. Einar Haugen (Berkeley: University of California Press, 1973), pp. 89–117

D124. DUMÉZIL, Georges, 'The *Rigsþula* and Indo-European Social Structure', trans. John Lindow, in *Gods of the Ancient Northmen*, ed. Einar Haugen (Berkeley: University of California Press, 1973), pp. 118–25

D125. DUMÉZIL, Georges, 'Comparative Remarks on the Scandinavian God Heimdallr', trans. F. Charat, in *Gods of the Ancient Northmen*, ed. Einar Haugen (Berkeley: University of California Press, 1973), pp. 126–40

D126. DUMÉZIL, Georges, 'Notes on the Cosmic Bestiary of the Edda and the Rig Veda', trans. F. Charat, in *Gods of the Ancient Northmen*, ed. Einar Haugen (Berkeley: University of California Press, 1973), pp. 141–50

D127. DUMÉZIL, Georges, *Loki*, 3rd edn (Paris, 1986)

Bibliography and Further Reading

D128. DÜWEL, Klaus, 'On the Sigurd Representations in Great Britain and Scandinavia', in *Languages and Cultures: Studies in Honor of Edgar C. Polomé*, ed. Mohammed Ali Jazayery and Werner Winter (Berlin: de Gruyter, 1988), pp. 133–56

D129. EINARSSON, Bjarni, '*De Normannorum Atrocitate*, or on the Execution of Royalty by the Aquiline Method', *Saga-Book of the Viking Society* 22 (1986–8), 79–82

D130. EIS, Gerhard, 'Das alte Atlilied', *Germanisch-romanische Monatsschrift*, n.s. 15 (1965), 430–4

D131. EJDER, Bertil, 'Eddadikten Vafþrúðnismál', *Vetenskaps-societen i Lund årsbok* (1960), 5–20

D132. ELDJÁRN, Kristján, *Kuml og Haugfé* (Reykjavík, 1956)

D133. ELDJÁRN, Kristján, 'The Bronze Image from Eyrarland', in *Speculum Norroenum: Norse Studies in Memory of Gabriel Turville-Petre*, ed. Ursula Dronke, Guðrún P. Helgadóttir, Gerd Wolfgang Weber, Hans Bekker-Nielsen (Odense: Odense University Press, 1981), pp. 73–84

D134. ELIADE, Mircea, *Shamanism: Archaic Techniques of Ecstasy*, trans. W.R. Trask (Princeton: Princeton University Press, 1972)

D135. ELLIS, H. R., 'Fostering by Giants in Old Norse Saga Literature', *Medium Ævum* 10 (1941), 70–85

D136. ELLIS, H. R., 'Sigurd in the Art of the Viking Age', *Antiquity* 16 (1942), 216–36

D137. ELLIS, H. R., *The Road to Hel: A Study of the Conception of the Dead in Old Norse Literature* (Cambridge: CUP, 1943)

D138. ETTLINGER, Ellen, 'The Mythological Relief of the Oseberg Wagon found in Southern Norway', *Folklore* 87 (1976), 81–8

D139. FALK, Hjalmar, 'Om Svipdagsmál I', *Arkiv för nordisk filologi* 9 (1893), 31–62

D140. FALK, Hjalmar, 'Om Svipdagsmál II', *Arkiv för nordisk filologi* 10 (1894), 26–82

D141. FALK, Hjalmar, *Odensheite*, Skrifter und Afhandlunger der Norske Videnskaps Akademie 10 (Christiania: Dybwad, 1924)

D142. FARRELL, R.T., *Beowulf, Swedes, and Geats* (London: Viking Society for Northern Research, 1972)

D143. FARRELL, R.T., '*Beowulf* and the Northern Heroic Age', in *The Vikings*, ed. R.T. Farrell (Chichester: Phillimore, 1982), pp. 180–216

D144. FAULKES, Anthony, 'Edda', *Gripla* 2 (1977), 32–9

D145. FAULKES, Anthony, 'Descent from the Gods', *Mediaeval Scandinavia* 11 (1979), 92–125

D146. FAULKES, Anthony, 'Pagan Sympathy: Attitudes to Heathendom in the Prologue to *Snorra Edda*', in *Edda: A Collection of Essays*, ed. R.J. Glendinning and Haraldur Bessason, University of Manitoba Icelandic Studies 4 (Winnipeg: University of Manitoba Press, 1983), pp. 283–314

D147. FAULKES, Anthony, *Hávamál: Glossary* (London: Viking Society for Northern Research, 1987)

D148. FAULKES, Anthony, 'The Use of Snorri's Verse-Forms by Earlier Poets', in *Snorrastefna. 25.–27. júli 1990*, ed. Úlfar Bragason, Rit Stofnunar Sigurðar Nordals 1 (Reykjavík: Stofnun Sigurðar Nordals, 1992), pp. 35–51

D149. FAULKES, Anthony, 'Snorri's Rhetorical categories', in *Sagnaþing helgað Jónasi Kristjánssyni sjötugum, 10. april 1994*, ed. Gísli Sigurðsson, Guðrún Kvaran, and Sigurgeir Steingrímsson, 2 vols. (Reykjavik: Hið íslenska bókmenntafélag, 1994), pp. 167–76

D150. FELL, C.E., '*Víkingarvísur*', in *Speculum Norroenum: Norse Studies in Memory of Gabriel Turville-Petre*, ed. Ursula Dronke, Guðrún P. Helgadóttir, Gerd Wolfgang Weber, and Hans Bekker-Nielsen (Odense: Odense University Press, 1981), pp. 106–22

D151. FELL, Christine, Peter Foote, and James Graham-Campbell, and Rodney Thomson (ed.), *The Viking Age in the Isle of Man* (London: Viking Society for Northern Research, 1983)

D152. FIDJESTØL, Bjarne, 'Skaldediktinga og trusskiftet. Med tanker om litterær form som historisk kjelde', in *Nordisk Hedendom. Et Symposium*, ed. Gro Steinsland (Odense: Odense University Press, 1991), pp. 113–32

D153. FIDJESTØL, Bjarne, 'The Contribution of Scaldic Studies', in *Viking Revaluations. Viking Society Centenary Symposium 14–15 May 1992*, ed. Anthony Faulkes and Richard Perkins (London: Viking Society for Northern Research, 1993), pp. 100–20

D154. FINCH, R.G., 'The Treatment of Poetic Sources by the Compiler of *Vǫlsungasaga*', *Saga-Book of the Viking Society* 16 (1965), 315–53

D155. FINCH, R.G., '*Atlakviða, Atlamál* and *Vǫlsunga Saga*: A Study in Combination and Integration', in *Speculum Norroenum: Norse Studies in Memory of Gabriel Turville-Petre*, ed. Ursula Dronke, Guðrún P. Helgadóttir, Gerd Wolfgang Weber, and Hans Bekker-Nielsen (Odense: Odense University Press, 1981), pp. 123–38

D156. FISCHER, Rudolf W., 'Gullveigs Wandlung: Versuch einer läuternden Deutung des Kultes in Hars Halle', *Antaios* 4 (1963), 581–96

D157. FLECK, Jere, 'Drei Vorschläge zur *Baldrs draumar*', *Arkiv för nordisk filologi* 84 (1969), 19–37

D158. FLECK, Jere, 'Óðinn's Self-Sacrifice–A New Interpretation I: The Ritual Inversion', *Scandinavian Studies* 43 (1971), 119–42

D159. FLECK, Jere, 'Óðinn's Self-Sacrifice–A New Interpretation II: The Ritual Landscape', *Scandinavian Studies* 43 (1971), 385–413

D160. FLECK, Jere, 'The 'Knowledge-Criterion' in the *Grímnismál*: The Case against Shamanism', *Archiv för nordisk Filologi* 87 (1972), 97–118

D161. FLOWERS, Stephen E., *Runes and Magic: Magical Formulaic Elements in the Older Runic Tradition*, American University Studies, series 1: Germanic Languages and Literature 53 (New York: Lang, 1986)

D162. FLOWERS, Stephen E., *The Galdrabók: An Icelandic Grimoire* (Maine, MA: Samuel Weiser, 1989)

D163. FÖRSTER, Leonard, 'Zum 2. Merseburger Zauberspruch', *Archiv* 192 (1956), 155–9

D164. FONTENROSE, Joseph, 'The Building of the City-Walls: Troy and Asgard', *Journal of American Folklore* 96 (1983), 53–63

D165. FOOTE, Peter, 'On the Conversion of the Icelanders', in his *Aurvandilstá. Norse Studies*, ed. Michael Barnes,

Hans Bekker-Nielsen, and Gerd Wolfgang Weber, Viking Collection 2 (Odense: Odense University Press, 1984), pp. 56–64

D166. FOOTE, Peter, 'Nafn guðs hins hæsta', in his Aurvandilstá. Norse Studies, ed. Michael Barnes, Hans Bekker-Nielsen, and Gerd Wolfgang Weber, Viking Collection 2 (Odense: Odense University Press, 1984), pp. 121–39

D167. FOOTE, Peter, 'Historical Studies: Conversion Moment and Conversion Period', in Viking Revaluations. Viking Society Centenery Symposium 14–15 May 1992, ed. Anthony Faulkes and Richard Perkins (London: Viking Society for Northern Research, 1993), pp. 137–44

D168. FRAKES, Jerold C., 'Loki's Mythological Function in the Tripartite System', Journal of English and Germanic Philology 86 (1987), 473–86

D169. FRANK, Roberta, Old Norse Court Poetry; the Dróttkvætt Stanza, Islandica 42 (Ithaca, Cornell University Press, 1978)

D170. FRANK, Roberta, 'Snorri and the Mead of Poetry', in Speculum Norroenum: Norse Studies in Memory of Gabriel Turville-Petre, ed. Ursula Dronke, Guðrún P. Helgadóttir, Gerd Wolfgang Weber, Hans Bekker-Nielsen (Odense: Odense University Press, 1981), pp. 155–70

D171. FRANK, Roberta, 'Viking Atrocity and Skaldic Verse: The Rite of the Blood-Eagle', English Historical Review 99 (1984), 332–43

D172. FRANK, Roberta, 'Hand Tools and Power Tools in Eilífr's Þórsdrápa', in Structure and Meaning in Old Norse Literature, ed. John Lindow, Lars Lönnroth, and Gerd Wolfgang Weber (Odense: Odense University Press, 1986), pp. 94–109

D173. FRANK, Roberta, 'The Blood-Eagle Again', Saga-Book of the Viking Society 22 (1986–8), 79–82

D174. FRIIS-JENSEN, Karsten (ed.), Saxo Grammaticus: A Medieval Author between Norse and Latin Culture (Copenhagen: Museum Tusculanum, 1981)

D175. FRIIS-JENSEN, Karsten, Saxo Grammaticus as Latin Poet: Studies in the Verse Passages of the Gesta Danorum, Analecta Romana Instituti Danici, Supplementum 14 (Rome: Bretschneider, 1987)

D176. FUGLESANG, Signe Horn, 'Viking and Medieval Amulets in Scandinavia', Fornvännen 84 (1989), 15–25

D177. FULK, R.D., 'An Eddic Analogue to the Scyld Scefing Story', Review of English Studies 40 (1989), 117–38

D178. GADE, Kari Ellen, 'Skjalf', Arkiv för nordisk filologi 100 (1985), 59–71

D179. GARDNER, T., 'The Application of the Term Kenning', Neophilologus 56 (1972), 464–68

D180. GARMONSWAY, G.N., 'Old Norse jarðarmen', in The Early Cultures of North-West Europe: H.M. Chadwick Memorial Studies, ed. Cyril Fox and Bruce Dickins (Cambridge: Cambridge University Press, 1950), pp. 421–5

D181. GEHL, Walther, 'Das Problem des germanischen Tempels', Zeitschrift für deutsches Altertum 78 (1941), 37–49

D182. GEHRTS, Heino, 'Die Gullveig-Mythe der Vǫluspá', Zeitschrift für deutsche Philologie 88 (1969), 321–78

D183. GENZMER, Felix, 'Die Götter des zweiten Merseburger Zauberspruchs', Arkiv för nordisk filologi 63 (1948), 55–72

D184. GERSTEIN, M., 'Germanic Warg: The Outlaw as Werewolf', in Myth in Indo-European Antiquity, ed. G.J. Larson (Berkeley, CA, 1974), pp. 131–56

D185. GILLESPIE, George T., 'Heroic Lays: Survival and Transformation in Ballad', Oxford German Studies 9 (1978), 1–18

D186. GÍSLASON, Tryggvi, 'Óðinn og Salómon–Kristin áhrif í Gestaþætti Hávamála', in Sagnaþing helgað Jónasi Kristjánssyni sjötugum, 10. apríl 1994, ed. Gísli Sigurðsson, Guðrún Kvaran, and Sigurgeir Steingrímsson, 2 vols. (Reykjavik: Hið íslenska bókmenntafélag, 1994), pp. 805–14

D187. GLENDINNING, Robert J., 'The Archetypal Structure of Hymisqviða', Folklore 91 (1980), 92–110

D188. GLENDINNING, Robert J., 'Guðrúnarqviða forna: A Reconstruction and Interpretation', in Edda: A Collection of Essays, ed. R.J. Glendinning and Haraldur Bessason, University of Manitoba Icelandic Studies 4 (Winnipeg: University of Manitoba Press, 1983), pp. 27–41

D189. GLOB, P.V., The Bog-People: Iron Age Man Preserved, trans. R. Bruce-Mitford (London: Faber, 1969)

D190. GLOSECKI, Stephen O., Shamanism and Old English Poetry (New York: Garland, 1989)

D191. GORDON, E.V., 'On Hrafnkels Saga Freysgoða', Medium Ævum 8 (1939), 1–32

D192. GOTTZMANN, Carola L., Das alte Atlilied: Untersuchungen der Gestaltungsprinzipien seiner Handlungsstruktur, Germanische Bibliothek 3 (Heidelberg: Winter, 1973)

D193. GOULD, Chester Nathan, 'Dwarf-Names: A Study in Old Icelandic Religion', Publication of the Modern Language Association 44 (1929), 939–67

D194. GRÄSLUND, Anne-Sofie, 'Pagan and Christian in the Age of the Conversion', in Proceedings of the Tenth Viking Congress, ed. J.E. Knirk (Oslo: Universitetets Oldsaksamling, 1987)

D195. GRÄSLUND, Anne-Sofie, 'Some Aspects of Christianization in Central Sweden', in Social Approaches to Viking Studies, ed. Ross Sampson (Glasgow: Cruithne Press, 1991), pp. 45–52

D196. GRÄSLUND, Anne-Sofie, 'Arkeologi som källa för religionsvetenskapen. Några reflektioner om hur gravmaterialet från vikingatiden kan användas', in Nordisk Hedendom. Et Symposium, ed. Gro Steinsland (Odense: Odense University Press, 1991), pp. 141–8

D197. GRAZI, Vittoria, 'Die "Götterlieder" der Edda und die "Indogermanische Dichtersprache"', in Poetry in the Scandinavian Middle Ages, ed. Teresa Pàroli, The Seventh International Saga Conference, Atti del XII Congresso internazionale di studi sull' alto medioevo (Spoleto: Presso la sede del centro studi, 1990), pp. 545–70

D198. GRIENBERGER, Theodor von, Über germanische Götternamen auf Inschriften des Niederrheins mit besonderer Berücksichtigung der Matronensteine (Vienna, 1890)

D199. GRIMSTAD, Karen, 'The Giant as Heroic Model: The Case of Egill and Starkaðr', Scandinavian Studies 48 (1976), 284–98

D200. GRIMSTAD, Karen, 'The Revenge of Vǫlundr', in Edda:

Bibliography and Further Reading

A Collection of Essays, ed. R.J. Glendinning and Haraldur Bessason, University of Manitoba Icelandic Studies 4 (Winnipeg: University of Manitoba Press, 1983), pp. 187–209

D201. GRINSELL, Lynne V., 'Barrow Treasure in Fact, Tradition and Legislation', *Folklore* 78 (1967), 1–38

D202. GRUBER, Loren C., 'The Rites of Passage: *Hávamál*, stanzas 1–5', *Scandinavian Studies* 49 (1977), 330–40

D203. GRUNDY, Stephan, *Miscellaneous Studies towards the Cult of Óðinn* (Everett, WA: Vikar, 1994)

D204. GRUNDY, Stephan Scott, 'The Cult of Óðinn: God of Death?' (unpublished PhD thesis, University of Cambridge, 1995)

D205. GSCHWANDTLER, Otto, 'Christus, Thor und die Midgardschlange', in *Festschrift für Otto Höfler zum 65. Geburtstag*, ed. H. Birkhan and O. Gschwandtler (Vienna: Österreichische Akademie der Wissenschaften, 1968), pp. 145–68

D206. GSCHWANDTLER, Otto, 'Ermanrich, sein Selbstmord und die Hamdirsage: Zur Darstellung von Ermanrichs Ende in Getica 24, 129f', in *Die Völker an der mittleren und unteren Donau im fünften und sechsten Jahrhundert: Berichte des Symposiums der Kommission für Frühmittelalterforschung, 24. bis 27. Oktober 1978*, ed. Herwig Wolfram and Falko Daim (Vienna: Osterreichische Akademie der Wissenschaften, 1980), pp. 187–204

D207. GSCHWANDTLER, Otto, 'Die Überwindung des Fenriswolfs und ihr christliches Gegenstück bei Frau Ava', in *Poetry in the Scandinavian Middle Ages*, ed. Teresa Pàroli, The Seventh International Saga Conference, Atti del XII Congresso internazionale di studi sull' alto medioevo (Spoleto: Presso la sede del centro studi, 1990), pp. 509–34

D208. GÜNTERT, Hermann, *Vor der Sprache der Götter und Geister: Bedeutungsgeschichtliche Untersuchungen zur homerischen und eddischen Göttersprache* (Halle: Niemeyer, 1921)

D209. GUNNELL, Terry, *The Origins of Drama in Scandinavia* (Cambridge: D.S. Brewer, 1995)

D210. GUREVIČ, Elena A., 'Zur Genealogie der þula', *Alvíssmál* 1 (1992), 65–98

D211. GUREVICH, A. Ya., 'Edda and Law: Commentary upon *Hyndluljóð*', *Arkiv för nordisk filologi* 88 (1973), 72–84

D212. GUREVICH, A. Ya., 'On the Nature of the Comic in the Elder Edda: A Comment on an Article by Professor Höfler', *Mediaeval Scandinavia* 9 (1976), 127–37

D213. GUTENBRUNNER, Siegfried, *Die germanischen Götternamen der antiken Inschriften* (Halle, 1936)

D214. HAIMERL, Edgar, 'Sigurd – ein Held des Mittelalters. Eine textimmanente Interpretation der Jungsigurddichtung', *Alvíssmál* 2 (1993), 81–104

D215. HALD, K., 'The Cult of Odin in Danish Place-Names', in *Early English and Norse Studies Presented to Hugh Smith in Honour of his Sixtieth Birthday*, ed. Arthur Brown and Peter G. Foote (London: Methuen, 1963), pp. 99–109

D216. HALE, Christopher, 'The River-Names in *Grímnismál* 27–29', in *Edda: A Collection of Essays*, ed. R.J. Glendinning and Haraldur Bessason, University of

Manitoba Icelandic Studies 4 (Winnipeg: University of Manitoba Press, 1983), pp. 165–86

D217. HALLBERG, Peter, 'Om Þrymskviða', *Arkiv för nordisk filologi* 69 (1954), 51–77

D218. HALLBERG, Peter, *Snorri Sturluson och Egils saga Skalla-Grímssonar. Ett försök till språklig författerbestämning*, Studia Islandica 20 (Reykjavík: Minningarsjóður, 1962)

D219. HALLBERG, Peter, 'Elements of Imagery in the Poetic Edda', in *Edda: A Collection of Essays*, ed. R.J. Glendinning and Haraldur Bessason, University of Manitoba Icelandic Studies 4 (Winnipeg: University of Manitoba Press, 1983), pp. 47–85

D220. HALLBERG, Peter, 'Elements of Myth in the Heroic Lays of the Poetic Edda', in *German Dialects: Linguistic and Philological Investigations*, ed. Bela Brogyanyi and Thomas Krömmelbein (Amsterdam: John Benjamins, 1986), pp. 213–47

D221. HALLENCREUTZ, Carl Fredrik, *Adam Bremensis and Sueonia: A Fresh Look at Gesta Hammaburgensis Ecclesiae Pontificum*, Acta Universitatis Upsaliensis C, Organisation och Historia 47 (Uppsala: Almqvist & Wiksell, 1984)

D222. HAMEL, A.G. van, 'Óðinn Hanging on the Tree', *Acta Philologica Scandinavica* 7 (1933), 260–88

D223. HARRIS, Joseph, 'Cursing with the Thistle: *Skírnismál* 31, 6–8 and Old English *Metrical Charms* 9, 16–17', *Neuphilologische Mitteilungen* 76 (1975), 26–53

D224. HARRIS, Joseph, 'The Masterbuilder Tale in Snorri's Edda and in Two Sagas', *Arkiv för nordisk filologi* 91 (1976), 66–101

D225. HARRIS, Joseph, 'The *senna*: From Description to Literary Theory', *Michigan Germanic Studies* 5 (1979), 65–74

D226. HARRIS, Joseph, 'Satire and the Heroic Life: Two Studies (*Helgakviða Hundingsbana I*, 18 and Bjǫrn Hítdœlakappi's *Grámagaflim*)', in *Oral Traditional Literature: A Festschrift for Albert Bates Lord*, ed. John Miles Foley (Columbus, OH: Slavica, 1981), pp. 322–40

D227. HARRIS, Joseph, 'Two Types of Verbal Duelling in Old Icelandic: The International Structure of the *senna* and the *mannjafnaðr* in *Hárbarðsljóð*', *Scandinavian Studies* 55 (1983), 149–50

D228. HARRIS, Joseph, 'Eddic Poetry as Oral poetry: The Evidence of Parallel Passages in the Helgi Poems for Questions of Composition and Performance', in *Edda: A Collection of Essays*, ed. R.J. Glendinning and Haraldur Bessason, University of Manitoba Icelandic Studies 4 (Winnipeg: University of Manitoba Press, 1983), pp. 208–40

D229. HARRIS, Joseph, 'Reflections on Genre and Intertextuality in Eddic Poetry (with Special Reference to *Grottasǫngr*)', in *Poetry in the Scandinavian Middle Ages*, ed. Teresa Pàroli, The Seventh International Saga Conference, Atti del XII Congresso internazionale di studi sull' alto medioevo (Spoleto: Presso la sede del centro studi, 1990), pp. 231–44

D230. HARRIS, Richard, 'A Study of *Grípisspá*', *Scandinavian Studies* 43 (1971), 344–55

D231. HASTRUP, Kirsten, 'Tracing Tradition: An Anthropological Perspective on *Grettis saga*

Ásmundarsonar', *Structure and Meaning in Old Norse Literature*, ed. John Lindow, Lars Lönnroth, and Gerd Wolfgang Weber (Odense: Odense University Press, 1986), pp. 281–316

D232. HATTO, A.T., 'The Swan Maiden: A Folk-Tale of North Eurasian Origin?', *Bulletin of the School of Oriental and African Studies* 24 (1961), 326–52

D233. HAUCK, Karl, 'Lebensnormen und Kultmythen in germanischen Stammes- und Herrschergenealogien', *Saeculum* 6 (1955), 186–233

D234. HAUCK, Karl, *Goldbrakteaten aus Sievern: Spätantike Amulett-Bilder der Dania Saxonica und die Sachsen-Origo bei Widukind von Corvey* (Munich: Fink, 1955)

D235. HAUGEN, Einar, 'The Edda as Ritual: Odin and his Masks', in *Edda: A Collection of Essays*, ed. R.J. Glendinning and Haraldur Bessason, University of Manitoba Icelandic Studies 4 (Winnipeg: University of Manitoba, 1983), pp. 3–24

D236. HEINEMANN, Fredrik J., '*ealuscerwen -meoduscerwen*, the Cup of Death, and *Baldrs draumar*', *Studia Neophilologica* 55 (1983), 3–10

D237. HEINRICHS, Anne, *Der 'Oláfs þáttr Geirstaðaálfs': Eine Variantenstudie* (Heidelberg: Winter, 1989)

D238. HEINRICHS, Anne, '*Hákonarmál* im literarischen Kontext', in *Poetry in the Scandinavian Middle Ages*, ed. Teresa Pàroli, The Seventh International Saga Conference, Atti del XII Congresso internazionale di studi sull' alto medioevo (Spoleto: Presso la sede del centro studi, 1990), pp. 427–46

D239. HEINRICHS, Heinrich Matthias, 'Satirisch-parodistische Züge in der *Þrymskviða*', in *Festschrift für Hans Eggers zum 65. Geburtstag*, ed. Herbert Backes (Tübingen, 1972), pp. 501–10

D240. HELLQUIST, Elof, 'Om Fornjótr', *Arkiv för nordisk filologi* 19 (1903), 134–40

D241. HERTEIG, A.E., *The Bryggen Papers* (Bergen: Universitetsforlaget, 1984–)

D242. HEUSLER, Andreas, 'Die Geschichte von Völsi', *Zeitschrift von Volkskunde* 13 (1903), 25–39

D243. HILL, Joyce, *Widsið* and the Tenth Century', *Neuphilologische Mitteilungen* 85 (1984), 305–15

D244. HILL, Thomas D., 'Scyld Scefing and the *stirps regia*: Pagan Myth and Christian Kingship in *Beowulf* ', in *Magister Regis*, ed. A. Groos *et al.* (New York: Fordham University Press, 1986), pp. 37–47

D245. HILL, Thomas D., '*Rígsþula*: Some Medieval Christian Analogues', *Speculum* 61 (1986), 76–87

D246. HILL, Thomas D., 'Woden as "Ninth Father": Numerical Patterning in Some Old English Royal Genealogies', in *Germania: Studies in Old Germanic Languages and Literature*, ed. D.G. Calder and T.C. Christy (Woodbridge: Brewer, 1987), pp. 161–74

D247. HINES, John, 'Egill's *Hofuðlausn* in Time and Place', *Saga-Book of the Viking Society* 24 (1995), 83–104

D248. HÖFLER, Otto, *Siegfried, Arminius und die Symbolik: mit einem historischen Anhang über die Varusschlacht* (Heidelberg: Winter, 1961)

D249. HÖFLER, Otto, 'Götterkomik: Zur Selbstrelativierung des Mythos', *Zeitschrift für deutsches Altertum* 100 (1971), 371–89

D250. HÖFLER, Otto, *Siegfried, Arminius und der Nibelungenhort*, Sitzungsberichte der Österreichischen Akad. der Wissen. philo.-hist. Kl. 332 (Vienna: Österreichische Akademie der Wissenschaften, 1978)

D251. HOLLANDER, Lee M., 'The Gautland Cycle of Sagas', *Journal of English and Germanic Philology* 9 (1912), 61–81

D252. HOLLANDER, Lee M., 'The Relative Age of the *Gautreks saga* and the *Hrólfs saga Gautrekssonar*', *Arkiv för nordisk filologi* 29 (1913), 120–34

D253. HOLLANDER, Lee M., 'Were the Mythological Poems of the Edda Composed in the Pre-Christian Era?', *Journal of English and Germanic Philology* 26 (1927), 98–105

D254. HOLLANDER, Lee M., 'Is the Lay of Eric a Fragment?', *Acta Philologica Scandinavica* 7 (1932–3), 249–57

D255. HOLLANDER, Lee M., 'The Old Norse God Óðr', *Journal of English and Germanic Philology* 49 (1950), 304–8

D256. HOLLANDER, Lee M., 'Notes on Two Eddic Passages: *Helreið Brynhildar*, stanza 14, and *Baldrs draumar*, stanza 12', *Scandinavian Studies* 22 (1950), 166–75

D257. HOLLANDER, Lee M., 'The Legendary Form of *Hamðismál*', *Arkiv för nordisk filologi* 77 (1962), 56–62

D258. HOLLANDER, Lee M., 'Recent Work and Views on the Poetic Edda', *Scandinavian Studies* 35 (1963), 101–9

D259. HOLLANDER, Lee M., 'For Whom Were the Eddic Poems Composed?', *Journal of English and Germanic Philology* 62 (1963), 136–42

D260. HOLLANDER, Lee M., '*Sigurðarkviða in skamma*, stanzas 62–63', *Arkiv för nordisk filologi* 81 (1966), 338

D261. HOLM, Gösta, '*Hárbarðsljóð* och Lappland', *Maal og minne* (1969), 93–103

D262. HOLTSMARK, Anne, 'Vitazgjafi', *Maal og Minne* (1933), pp. 111–33

D263. HOLTSMARK, Anne, 'Vefr Darraðar', *Maal og Minne* (1939), 74–96

D264. HOLTSMARK, Anne, 'Myten om Idun og Tjatse i Tjodolvs Haustlǫng', *Arkiv för nordisk filologi* 64 (1949), 1–73

D265. HOLTSMARK, Anne, 'Kattar sonr', *Saga-Book of the Viking Society* 16 (1962–5), 144–55

D266. HOLTSMARK, Anne, *Studier i Snorres mytologi*, Skrifter udgitt av det norske videnskabsakademi i Oslo 2, hist.-filos. kl., n.s. 4 (Oslo: Universitetsforlag, 1964)

D267. HOLTSMARK, Anne, 'Heroic Poetry and Legendary Sagas', *Bibliography of Old Norse-Icelandic Studies* (1966), 9–21

D268. HOLTSMARK, Anne, 'Iðavǫllr', in *Festschrift für Konstantin Reichardt*, ed. C. Gellinek (Bern: Francke, 1969), pp. 98–102

D269. HOUGEN, Bjørn, *Studier i Gokstadfunnet*, Universitets Oldsaksamlings Årbok, 1931–2 (Oslo: Universitets Oldsaksamling, 1934)

D270. HUME, Kathryn, 'From Saga to Romance: The Use of Monsters in Old Norse Literature', *Studies in Philology* 77 (1980), 1–25

D271. HUTH, Ott, 'Der Durchzug des Wilden Heeres', *Archiv für Religionswissenschaft* 32 (1935), 193–210

D272. JACKSON, Elizabeth, 'Some Contexts and Characteristics of Old Norse Ordering Lists', *Saga-Book of the Viking Society* 23 (1991), 112–40

D273. JACKSON, Elizabeth, 'A New Perspective on the Final Three Sections of *Hávamál* and on the Role of Loddfáfnir', *Saga-Book of the Viking Society* 24 (1994), 33–57

D274. JACKSON, Elizabeth, 'Eddic Listing Techniques and the Coherence of *Rúnatal*', *Alvíssmál* 5 (1995), 81–106

D275. JACKSON, Jess H., 'Oðinn's Meetings with Sigmundr and Sigurðr in the *Vǫlsungasaga*', *Modern Language Notes* 43 (1928), 307–8

D276. JAKOBSEN, Alfred, 'Et problem i *Helgakviða Hundingsbana* I', *Maal og minne* (1966), 1–10

D277. JAKOBSEN, Alfred, 'Þrymskviða som allusjonsdikt', *Edda* 84 (1984), 75–80

D278. JESCH, Judith, 'Scaldic Verse and Viking Semantics', in *Viking Revaluations. Viking Society Centenary Symposium 14–15 May 1992*, ed. Anthony Faulkes and Richard Perkins (London: Viking Society for Northern Research, 1993), pp. 160–71

D279. JOCHENS, Jenny, '*Vǫluspá*: Matrix of Norse Womanhood', in *Poetry in the Scandinavian Middle Ages*, ed. Teresa Pàroli, The Seventh International Saga Conference, Atti del XII Congresso internazionale di studi sull' alto medioevo (Spoleto: Presso la sede del centro studi, 1990), pp. 257–77

D280. JOHANNESSON, Kurt, 'Adam och hednatemplet i Uppsala', in Carl Fredrik Hallencreutz, *et al.* (ed.), *Adam av Bremen. Historien om Hamburgstiftet och dess biskopar* (Stockholm: Proprius, 1984), pp. 379–407

D281. KABELL, Aage, *Balder und die Mistel*, Folklore Fellows Communications 196 (Helsinki, 1965)

D282. KABELL, Aage, 'Baugi und der Ringeid', *Arkiv för nordisk filologi* 90 (1975), 30–40

D283. KABELL, Aage, 'Der Fischfang Þórs', *Arkiv för nordisk filologi* 91 (1976), 123–9

D284. KARLSSON, Stefán, 'Íviðjur', *Gripla* 3 (1979), 227–8

D285. KASKE, R. E., 'The Sigemund-Heremod and Hama-Hygelac Passages', *Publications of the Modern Language Association* 74 (1959), 489–94

D286. KASKE, R. E., 'Weland and *wurmas* in *Deor*', *English Studies* 44 (1963), 190–1

D287. KASKE, R. E., 'The *eotenas* in *Beowulf*', in *Old English Poetry: Fifteen Essays*, ed. R.P. Creed (Providence, RI: Brown University Press, 1967), pp. 285–310

D288. KAUFFMANN, Friedrich, *Balder: Mythus und Sage nach ihren dichterischen und religiösen Elementen untersucht* (Strassburg: Trübner, 1902)

D289. KELLOGG, Robert L., 'The Prehistory of Eddic Poetry', in *Poetry in the Scandinavian Middle Ages*, ed. Teresa Pàroli, The Seventh International Saga Conference, Atti del XII Congresso internazionale di studi sull' alto medioevo (Spoleto: Presso la sede del centro studi, 1990), pp. 187–200

D290. KELLOGG, Robert L., 'Literacy and Orality in the Poetic Edda', in *Vox intexta. Orality and Textuality in the Middle Ages*, ed. A.N. Doane and Carol Braun Pasternack (Madison, WI: University of Wisconsin Press, 1991), pp. 89–101

D291. KIIL, Vilhelm, 'Eilífr Goðrúnarson's *Þórsdrápa*', *Arkiv för nordisk filologi* 71 (1956), 89–167

D292. KIIL, Vilhelm, 'Hliðskjalf og seiðhallr', *Arkiv för nordisk filologi* 75 (1960), 84–112

D293. KING, K.C., 'Siegfried's Fight with the Dragon in the Edda and the Hürnen Seyfrid', in his *Selected Essays on Medieval German Literature*, ed. John L. Flood and A.T. Hatto, Publications of the Institute of Germanic Studies 20 (London, 1975), pp. 7–13

D294. KLINGENBERG, Heinz, '*Alvíssmál*: Das Lied vom überweisen Zwerg', *Germanisch-romanische Monatsschrift* 48 (1967), 113–42

D295. KLINGENBERG, Heinz, 'Types of Eddic Mythological Poetry', in *Edda: A Collection of Essays*, ed. R.J. Glendinning and Haraldur Bessason, University of Manitoba Icelandic Studies 4 (Winnipeg: University of Manitoba Press, 1983), pp. 134–64

D296. KLINGENBERG, Heinz, 'Trór Þórr (Thor) wie Trós Aeneas: *Snorra Edda* Prolog, Vergil-Rezeption und Altisländische Gelehrte Urgeschichte', *Alvíssmál* 1 (1992), 17–54

D297. KLINGENBERG, Heinz, 'Odin und die Seinen: Altisländischer Gelehrter Urgeschichte anderer Teil', *Alvíssmál*, 2 (1993), 31–80

D298. KLINGENBERG, Heinz, 'Odins Wanderzug nach Schweden: Altisländische Gelehrte Urgeschichte und mittelalterliche Geographie', *Alvíssmál* 3 (1994), 19–42

D299. KOCH, Karl-Heinz, 'Altes Sigurdlied und Altes Atlilied im Unterricht', *Der Deutschunterricht* 8 (1956), 62–74

D300. KRAG, C., *Ynglingatal og Ynglingesaga: En Studie i Historiske Kilder*, Studia Humaniora 2 (Oslo: Universitetsforlag, 1991)

D301. KRAGERUD, Alf, 'De mytologiske spørsmål i *Fáfnismál*', *Arkiv för nordisk filologi* 96 (1981), 9–48

D302. KRAPPE, Alexander Haggerty, 'The Valkyries', *Modern Language Review* 21 (1926), 55–73

D303. KRAPPE, Alexander Haggerty, 'The Valkyrie Episode in the *Njáls saga*', *Modern Language Notes* 43 (1928), 471–4

D304. KRAPPE, Alexander Haggerty, 'Snake Tower', *Scandinavian Studies* 16 (1940–1), 22–33

D305. KRAUSE, Arnulf, *Die Dichtung des Eyvindr skáldaspillir: Edition–Kommentar–Untersuchungen*, Altnordische Bibliothek 10 (Leverkusen: Reinhardt, 1990)

D306. KRAUSE, Wolfgang, 'Gullveig und Pandora', *Skandinavistik* 5 (1975), 1

D307. KRESS, Helga, 'The Apocalypse of a Culture: *Vǫluspá* and the Myth of the Sources/Sorceress in Old Icelandic Literature', in *Poetry in the Scandinavian Middle Ages*, ed. Teresa Pàroli, The Seventh International Saga Conference, Atti del XII Congresso internazionale di studi sull' alto medioevo (Spoleto: Presso la sede del centro studi, 1990), pp. 279–302

D308. KREUTZER, Gert, *Die Dichtungslehre der Skalden: Poetologische Terminologie und Autorenkommentare als Grundlage einer Gattungspoetik*, 2nd edn (Meisenheim am Glan: Hain, 1977)

D309. KRIJN, Sophia, 'Halfred Vandrædaskald', *Neophilologus* 16 (1931), 46–55 and 121–31

D310. KRIJN, Sophia, 'Om Gíslasaga Súrssonar', *Arkiv för nordisk filologi* 51 (1935), 69–84

D311. KRISTJÁNSSON, Jónas, 'Stages in the Composition of Eddic Poetry', in *Poetry in the Scandinavian Middle Ages*, ed. Teresa Pàroli, The Seventh International Saga Conference, Atti del XII Congresso internazionale di studi sull' alto medioevo (Spoleto: Presso la sede del centro studi, 1990), pp. 201–18

D312. KROGH, Knud, 'The Royal Viking-Age Monuments at Jelling in the Light of the Recent Archaeological Excavations: A Preliminary Report', *Acta Archaeologica* 53 (1982), 183–216

D313. KROGMAN, Willy, 'Hœnir', *Acta Philologica Scandinavica* 6 (1932), 311–27

D314. KROGMAN, Willy, 'Loki', *Acta Philologica Scandinavica* 12 (1937–8), 59–70

D315. KROGMAN, Willy, 'Neorxnawang und Íðavǫllr', *Archiv* 191 (1954), 30–43

D316. KVILLERUD, Reinert, 'Några anmärkingar till Þrymskviða', *Arkiv för nordisk filologi*, 80 (1965), 64–86.

D317. LAMM, J.P., and H.-Å. Nordström (ed.), *Vendel Period Studies: Transactions of the Boat-Grave Symposium in Stockholm, February 2–3, 1981* (Stockholm: Statens historiska museum, 1983)

D318. LANG, James T., 'Sigurd and Weland in Pre-Conquest Carving from Northern England', *Yorkshire Archaeological Journal* 48 (1976), 83–94

D319. LANGE, Wolfgang, 'Zahlen und Zahlenkomposition in der Edda', *Beiträge zur Geschichte der deutschen Sprache und Literatur* 77 (1955), 306–48

D320. LARRINGTON, Carolyne, '"What Does Woman Want?" *Mær* and *munr* in *Skírnismál*', *Alvíssmál* 1 (1992), 3–16

D321. LEAKE, J.A., *The Geats of 'Beowulf': A Study in the Geographical Mythology of the Middle Ages* (Madison, WI: University of Wisconsin Press, 1967)

D322. LEHMANN, Winfred P., '*Lin* and *laukr* in the Edda', *Germanic Review* 30 (1955), 163–71

D323. LEHMANN, Winfred P., 'The Composition of Eddic Verse', in *Studies in Germanic Languages and Literatures in memory of Fred O. Nolte: A Collection of Essays Written by his Colleagues and Friends*, ed. E. Hofacker and Liselotte Dieckman (St Louis: Washington University Press, 1963), pp. 7–14

D324. LIBERMAN, Anatoly, 'Beowulf-Grettir', in *German Dialects: Linguistic and Philological Investigations*, ed. Bela Brogyanyi and Thomas Krömmelbein (Amsterdam: John Benjamins, 1986), pp. 353–91

D325. LIBERMAN, Anatoly, 'Snorri and Saxo on Útgarðaloki, with Notes on Loki Laufeyjarson's Character, Career, and Name', in *Saxo Grammaticus. Tra storiografia e letteratura*, ed. Carlos Santini, I Convegni di Classiconorroena 1 (Rome: Il Calamo, 1992), pp. 91–158

D326. LIESTØL, A., 'The Viking Runes: The Transition from the Older to the Younger Fuþark', *Saga-Book of the Viking Society* 20 (1981), 247–66

D327. LINDBLAD, Gustaf, *Studier i Codex Regius av äldre Eddan*, Lundastudier i nordisk språkvetenskap 10 (Lund: Gleerup, 1954)

D328. LINDBLAD, Gustaf, 'Snorre Sturlasson och eddadiktningen', *Saga och Sed* (1978), 17–34

D329. LINDBLAD, Gustaf, 'Poetiska eddans förhistoria och skrivskicket i Codex Regius', *Arkiv för nordisk filologi* 95 (1980), 142–67

D330. LINDOW, John, *Comitatus, Individual and Honor: Studies in North Germanic Institutional Vocabulary*, University of California Publications in Linguistics 83 (Berkeley, CA: University of California Press, 1975)

D331. LINDOW, John, 'A Mythic Model in *Bandamanna saga* and its Significance', *Michigan Germanic Studies* 3 (1977), 1–12

D332. LINDOW, John, 'Addressing Thor', *Scandinavian Studies* 60 (1988), 119–36

D333. LINDOW, John, 'Loki and Skaði', in *Snorrastefna. 25.–27. júlí 1990*, ed. Úlfar Bragason, Rit Stofnunar Sigurðar Nordals 1 (Reykjavík: Stofnun Sigurðar Nordals, 1992), pp.130–42

D334. LINDQVIST, Ivar, *Die Urgestalt der Hávamál: ein Versuch zur Bestimmung auf synthetischem Wege*, Lundastudier i nordisk språkvetenskap 11 (Lund: Gleerup, 1956)

D335. LINDQVIST, S., *Uppsala Högar och Ottershögen* (Stockholm: Wahlström, 1936)

D336. LINDROTH, Hjalmar, 'Boðn, Són, och Óðrœrir', *Maal og minne* (1915), 174–7

D337. LÖNNROTH, Lars, 'Dómaldi's Death and the Myth of Sacral Kingship', in *Structure and Meaning in Old Norse Literature*, ed. John Lindow, Lars Lönnroth, and Gerd Wolfgang Weber (Odense: Odense University Press, 1986), pp. 73–93

D338. LÜTJENS, August, *Der Zwerg in der deutschen Heldendichtung*, Germanistische Abhandlungen 38 (Breslau: Marcus, 1911)

D339. LUNDBERG, Oskar, *Ön Allgrön. Är Eddans Harbardsljod ett norskt kväde?*, Arctos Svecica 2 (Stockholm: Geber, 1944)

D340. MAGERØY, Hallvard, 'Þrymskviða', *Edda*, 58 (1958), 256–70

D341. MAGNÚSSON, Eiríkur, *Yggdrasill: Óðins hestr* (Reykjavík: Félagsprentsmiðjunni, 1895)

D342. MAGOUN, Francis Peabody, 'On the Old Germanic Altar or Oath Ring', *Acta Philologica Scandinavica* 20 (1949), 277–93

D343. MAJOR, A.F., 'Ship-Burials in Scandinavian Lands and the Beliefs that Underlie them', *Folklore* 35 (1924), 113–50

D344. MALM, M., 'The Otherworld Journeys of the Eighth Book of *Gesta Danorum*', in *Saxo Grammaticus. Tra storiografia e letteratura*, ed. Carlos Santini, I Convegni di Classiconorroena 1 (Rome: Il Calamo, 1992), pp. 159–73

D345. MALONE, Kemp, 'An Anglo-Latin Version of the Hjaðningavíg', *Speculum* 39 (1964), 35–44

D346. MARGESON, Sue, 'The Vǫlsung Legend in Medieval Art', in *Medieval Iconography and Narrative: A Symposium*, ed. Flemming G. Anderson *et al.* (Odense: Odense University Press, 1980), pp. 183–211

D347. MAROLD, Edith, 'Das Walhallbild in den *Eiríksmál* und den *Hákonarmál*', *Medieval Scandinavia* 5 (1972), 19–33

D348. MAROLD, Edith, '"Thor weihe diese Runen"', *Frühmittelalterliche Studien* 8 (1974), 195–222

D349. MAROLD, Edith, *Kenningkunst: eine Beitrag zu einer Poetik der Skaldendichtung* (Berlin: de Gruyter, 1983)

D350. MAROLD, Edith, '"Nagellose Masten" – Die Sage von Hamðir und Sǫrli in der *Ragnarsdrápa*', in *Sagnaþing helgað Jónasi Kristjánssyni sjötugum, 10. apríl 1994*, ed. Gísli Sigurðsson, Guðrún Kvaran, and Sigurgeir Steingrímsson, 2 vols. (Reykjavik: Hið íslenska bókmenntafélag, 1994), pp. 565–80

D351. MARTIN, John Stanley, *Ragnarǫk: An Investigation into Old Norse Concepts of the Fate of the Gods*, Melbourne Monographs in Germanic Studies 3 (Assen: van Gorcum, 1972)

D352. MARTIN, John Stanley, '*Ár vas alda*: Ancient Scandinavian Creation Myths Reconsidered', in *Speculum Norroenum: Norse Studies in Memory of Gabriel Turville-Petre*, ed. Ursula Dronke, Guðrún P. Helgadóttir, Gerd Wolfgang Weber, and Hans Bekker-Nielsen (Odense: Odense University Press, 1981), pp. 357–69

D353. MARTIN, John Stanley, 'Some Thoughts on Kingship in the Helgi Poems', in *Poetry in the Scandinavian Middle Ages*, ed. Teresa Pàroli, The Seventh International Saga Conference, Atti del XII Congresso internazionale di studi sull' alto medioevo (Spoleto: Presso la sede del centro studi, 1990), pp. 369–82

D354. MARTíNEZ-PIZARRO, Joaquín, 'Woman-to-Man *Senna*', in *Poetry in the Scandinavian Middle Ages*, ed. Teresa Pàroli, The Seventh International Saga Conference, Atti del XII Congresso internazionale di studi sull' alto medioevo (Spoleto: Presso la sede del centro studi, 1990), pp. 339–50

D355. MARXEN, I., and E. Moltke, 'The Jelling Man: Denmark's Oldest Figure-Painting', *Saga-Book of the Viking Society* 20 (1978–81), 267–75

D356. MASTRELLI, Carlo Alberto, 'Reflections of Germanic Cosmogony in the *kenningar* for "Man/Woman"', in *Poetry in the Scandinavian Middle Ages*, ed. Teresa Pàroli, The Seventh International Saga Conference, Atti del XII Congresso internazionale di studi sull' alto medioevo (Spoleto: Presso la sede del centro studi, 1990), pp. 535–44

D357. MAZO, Jeffrey Alan, 'Sacred Knowledge, Kingship and Christianity: Myth and Cultural Change in Medieval Scandinavia', in *The Sixth International Saga Conference 28/7–2/8 1985. Workshop Papers*, 2 vols. (Copenhagen: Det arnamagnæanske Institut, 1985), 2, 751–62

D358. MCCONCHIE, R., 'Grettir Ásmundarson's Fight with Kárr the Old: A Neglected *Beowulf* Analogue', *English Studies* 63 (1982), 481–6

D359. MCCREESH, Bernadine, 'Structural Patterns in the *Eyrbyggja saga* and Other Sagas of the Conversion', *Mediaeval Scandinavia* 11 (1978–9), 271–80

D360. MCKINNELL, John, 'Motivation in *Lokasenna*', *Saga-Book of the Viking Society* 22 (1987–88), 234–62

D361. MCKINNELL, John, 'The Context of *Vǫlundarkviða*', *Saga-Book of the Viking Society* 22 (1990), 1–27

D362. MCLINTOCK, David, 'Dietrich und Theoderich – Sage und Geschichte', in *Geistliche und weltliche Epik des Mittelalters in Österreich*, ed. David McLintock, *et al.*, Göppinger Arbeiten zur Germanistik 446 (Göppingen: Kümmerle, 1987), pp. 99–106

D363. MCTURK, Rory W., 'Sacral Kingship in Ancient Scandinavia: A Review of Some Recent Writings', *Saga-Book of the Viking Society* 19 (1974–7), 139–69

D364. MCTURK, Rory W., 'Variation in *Beowulf* and the *Poetic Edda*: A Chronologial Experiment', in *The Dating of Beowulf*, ed. Colin Chase (Toronto: University of Toronto Press, 1981), pp. 141–60)

D365. MCTURK, Rory W., 'Approaches to the Structure of *Eyrbyggja saga*', in *Sagnaskemmtun: Studies in Honour of Hermann Pálsson*, ed. Rudolf Simek, Jónas Kristjánsson, and Hans Bekker-Nielsen (Cologne: Böhlau, 1986), pp. 223–38

D366. MCTURK, Rory W., 'The Poetic Edda and the Appositive Style', in *Poetry in the Scandinavian Middle Ages*, ed. Teresa Pàroli, The Seventh International Saga Conference, Atti del XII Congresso internazionale di studi sull' alto medioevo (Spoleto: Presso la sede del centro studi, 1990), pp. 321–38

D367. MCTURK, Rory W., *Studies in 'Ragnars saga loðbrókar' and its Major Scandinavian Analogues*, Medium Ævum Monographs, n.s. 15 (Oxford: Society for the Study of Mediaeval Languages and Literature, 1991)

D368. MCTURK, Rory W., 'Ytri og innri frásögn í *Snorra-Eddu*', in *Snorrastefna. 25.–27. júlí 1990*, ed. Úlfar Bragason, Rit Stofnunar Sigurðar Nordals 1 (Reykjavík: Stofnun Sigurðar Nordals, 1992), pp. 155–62

D369. MCTURK, Rory W., 'Blóðörn eða blóðormur?', in *Sagnaþing helgað Jónasi Kristjánssyni sjötugum, 10. apríl 1994*, ed. Gísli Sigurðsson, Guðrún Kvaran, and Sigurgeir Steingrímsson, 2 vols. (Reykjavik: Hið íslenska bókmenntafélag, 1994), pp. 539–42

D370. MCTURK, Rory W., 'Fooling Gylfi: Who Tricks Whom?', *Alvíssmál* 3 (1994), 3–18

D371. MEANEY, A.L., 'Woden in England: A Reconsideration of the Evidence', *Folklore* 77 (1966), 105–15

D372. MEISSNER, Rudolf, *Die Kenningar der Skalden: Ein Beitrag zur skaldischen Poetik* (Bonn: Schroeder, 1921)

D373. MEISSNER, Rudolf, 'Rígr', *Beiträge zur Geschichte der deutschen Sprache und Literatur* 57 (1933), 109–30

D374. MELETINSKIJ, Eleazar M., 'Commonplaces and Other Elements of Folkloric Style in Eddic Poetry', in *Structure and Meaning in Old Norse Literature*, ed. John Lindow, Lars Lönnroth, and Gerd Wolfgang Weber (Odense: Odense University Press, 1986), pp. 15–31

D375. MEYER, Richard Moritz, 'Snorri als Mythograph', *Arkiv för nordisk filologi* 28 (1911), 109–21

D376. MILROY, James, 'The Story of Ætternisstapi in *Gautreks saga*', *Saga-Book of the Viking Society* 17 (1967–8), 206–23

D377. MILROY, James, 'Starkaðr: An Essay in Interpretation', *Saga-Book of the Viking Society* 19 (1974–7), 118–38

D378. MITCHELL, Stephen A., '*Fǫr Scírnis* as Mythological Model: *frið at kaupa*', *Arkiv för nordisk filologi* 98 (1983), 108–22

D379. MITCHELL, Stephen A., '"Nú gef ek þik Óðni": Attitudes towards Odin in the Mythical-Heroic sagas', in *The Sixth*

International Saga Conference 28/7–2/8 1985. Workshop Papers, 2 vols. (Copenhagen: Det arnamagnæanske Institut, 1985), II, 777–91

D380. MITCHELL, Stephen A., Heroic Sagas and Ballads (Ithaca, NY: Cornell University Press, 1991)

D381. MOBERG, Lennart, 'The Languages of Alvíssmál', Saga-Book of the Viking Society 18 (1970–3), 299–323

D382. MOGK, Eugen, Novellistische Darstellung mythologischer Stoffe Snorris und seiner Schule, Folklore Fellows Communications 51 (Helsinki: Suomalainen Tiedeakatemia, 1923)

D383. MOGK, Eugen, Lokis Anteil an Balders Tode, Folklore Fellows Communications 57 (Helsinki: Suomalainen Tiedeakatemia, 1924)

D384. MOGK, Eugen, Zur Bewertung der Snorra-Edda als religionsgeschichtliche Quelle des nordgermanischen Heidentums (Leipzig: Hirzel, 1932)

D385. MOISL, H., 'Anglo-Saxon Royal Genealogies and Germanic Oral Tradition', Journal of Medieval History 7 (1981), 215–48

D386. MOLTKE, E., 'The Origins of the Runes', Michigan Germanic Studies 7 (1981), 3–7

D387. MOLTKE, E., Runes and their Origin: Denmark and Elsewhere (Copenhagen: National Museum of Denmark, 1985)

D388. MORGENROTH, W., 'Zahlenmagie in Runeninschriften. Kritische Bemerkungen zu einigen Interpretationsmethoden', Wissenschaftliche Zeitschrift der Ernst-Moritz-Arndt Universität Greifswald, gesellschafts- und sprachwissenschaftliche Reihe 3 (1961), 279–83

D389. MORRIS, Katherine, Sorceress or Witch? The Image of Gender in Medieval Iceland and Northern Europe (Lanham, MD: University Press of America, 1991)

D390. MOSHER, Arthur D., 'The Story of Baldr's Death: The Inadequacy of Myth in the Light of Christian Faith', Scandinavian Studies 55 (1983), 305–15

D391. MOTZ, Lotte, 'New Thoughts on Dwarf-Names in Old Icelandic', Frühmittelalterliche Studien 7 (1973), 100–15

D392. MOTZ, Lotte, 'Of Elves and Dwarfs', Arv 29–30 (1973–4), 93–127

D393. MOTZ, Lotte, 'The King and the Goddess: An Interpretation of the Svipdagsmál', Arkiv för nordisk filologi 90 (1975), 133–50

D394. MOTZ, Lotte, 'Snorri's Story of the Cheated Mason and its Folklore Parallels', Maal og minne (1977), 115–22

D395. MOTZ, Lotte, 'Gods and Demons in the Wilderness. A Study in Norse Tradition', Arkiv för nordisk filologi 95 (1980), 168–82

D396. MOTZ, Lotte, 'Giantesses and their Names', Frühmittelalterliche Studien 15 (1981), 495–511

D397. MOTZ, Lotte, 'Gerðr: A New Interpretation of the Lay of Skírnir', Maal og minne (1981), 121–36

D398. MOTZ, Lotte, 'Giants in Folklore and Mythology: A New Approach', Folklore 93 (1982), 70–84

D399. MOTZ, Lotte, The Wise one of the Mountain: Form, Function, and Significance of the Subterranean Smith: A Study in Folklore, Göppinger Arbeiten zur Germanistik 379 (Göppingen: Kümmerle, 1983)

D400. MOTZ, Lotte, 'New Thoughts on Völundarkviða', Saga-Book of the Viking Society 22 (1986), 50–68

D401. MOTZ, Lotte, 'The Families of Giants', Arkiv för nordisk filologi 102 (1987), 216–36

D402. MOTZ, Lotte, 'Old Icelandic Giants and their Names', Frühmittelalterliche Studien 21 (1987), 295–317

D403. MOTZ, Lotte, 'The Sacred Marriage–A Study in Norse Mythology', in Languages and Cultures: Studies in Honor of Edgar C. Polomé, ed. Mohammed Ali Jazayery and Werner Winter (Berlin: de Gruyter, 1988), pp. 449–59

D404. MOTZ, Lotte, 'The Goddess Freyja', in Snorrastefna. 25.–27. júli 1990, ed. Úlfar Bragason, Rit Stofnunar Sigurðar Nordals 1 (Reykjavík: Stofnun Sigurðar Nordals, 1992), pp. 163–79

D405. MOTZ, Lotte, 'The Cosmic Ash and other Trees of Germanic Myth', Arv (1992), 127–41

D406. MOTZ, Lotte, 'Gullveig's Ordeal; a New Interpretation', Arkiv för nordisk filologi 108 (1993), 80–92

D407. MÜLLER-WILLIE, M., 'Boat-Graves in Northern Europe', The International Journal of Nautical Archaeology and Underwater Exploration 3 (1974), 187–204

D408. MUNDAL, Else, Fylgjemotiva i norrøn litteratur, Skrifter fra instituttene for nordisk språk og litteratur ved universitetene i Bergen, Oslo, Trondheim og Tromsø 5 (Oslo: Universitetsforlaget, 1974)

D409. MUNDAL, Else, 'Snorri og Vǫluspá', in Snorrastefna. 25.–27. júli 1990, ed. Úlfar Bragason, Rit Stofnunar Sigurðar Nordals 1 (Reykjavík: Stofnun Sigurðar Nordals, 1992), pp. 180–92

D410. MUNDT, Maria, 'Observations on the Influence of Þiðriks saga on Icelandic Saga-Writing', in Proceedings of the First International Saga Conference, ed. Peter Foote, Hermann Pálsson, and Desmond Slay (London: Viking Society for Northern Research, 1973), pp. 335–59

D411. MUSSET, Lucien, Introduction à la Runologie (Paris, 1965)

D412. NÄSSTRÖM, Britt-Mari, 'Freyjas funktioner. En spegling av den ideala kvinnan', in Nordisk Hedendom. Et Symposium, ed. Gro Steinsland (Odense: Odense University Press, 1991), pp. 261–72

D413. NÄSSTRÖM, Britt-Mari, 'The Goddesses in Gylfaginning', in Snorrastefna. 25.–27. júli 1990, ed. Úlfar Bragason, Rit Stofnunar Sigurðar Nordals 1 (Reykjavík: Stofnun Sigurðar Nordals, 1992), pp. 193–203

D414. NECKEL, Gustav, Beiträge zur Eddaforschung mit Excursen zur Heldensage (Dortmund: Ruhfus, 1908)

D415. NECKEL, Gustav, 'Altnordisch draugr in Mannkenningar', Beiträge zur Geschichte der deutschen Sprache und Literatur 39 (1914), 189–200

D416. NECKEL, Gustav, 'Sigmunds Drachenkampf', Edda 13 (1920), 122–40 and 204–29

D417. NECKEL, Gustav, Walhall: Studien über germanischen Jenseitsglauben (Dortmund: Ruhfus, 1931)

D418. NEDOMA, Robert, 'The Legend of Wayland in Deor' Zeitschrift für Anglistik und Amerikanistik 38 (1990), 129–45

D419. NEFF, Mary, 'Germanic Sacrifice: An Analytical Study Using Linguistic, Archaeological, and Literary Data' (unpublished PhD dissertation, University of Austin, TX, 1980)

Bibliography and Further Reading

D420. NERMAN, Birger, *The Poetic Edda in the Light of Archaeology* (Coventry: Curtis & Beamish, 1931)

D421. NERMAN, Birger, 'Hlǫðskviðas ålder', in *Folkloristica: Festschrift til Dag Strömbäck* (Uppsla: Almqvist & Wiksell, 1960), pp. 79–86

D422. NERMAN, Birger, 'Runpartiet i *Sigrdrifumál*', *Arkiv för nordisk filologi* 76 (1961), 61–4

D423. NERMAN, Birger, 'Rígsþulas ålder', *Arkiv för nordisk filologi* 84 (1969), 15–18

D424. NEWTON, Sam, *The Origins of 'Beowulf' and the Pre-Viking Kingdom of East Anglia* (Cambridge: Brewer, 1993)

D425. NICHOLSON, Lewis E., '*Beowulf* and the Pagan Cult of the Stag', *Studi Medievali* 27 (1986), 637–69

D426. NILES, J.D., and M. Ammodio (ed.), *Anglo-Scandinavian England: Norse-English Relations in the Period before the Conquest* (Lanham, MD: University Press of America, 1989)

D427. NORDAL, Guðrún, 'Skáldið Snorri Sturluson', in *Snorrastefna. 25.–27. júli 1990*, ed. Úlfar Bragason, Rit Stofnunar Sigurðar Nordals 1 (Reykjavík: Stofnun Sigurðar Nordals, 1992), pp. 52–69

D428. NORDAL, Sigurður, *Snorri Sturluson* (Reykjavik, 1920)

D429. NORDAL, Sigurður, *Hrafnkels Saga Freysgoða: A Study*, trans. R.G. Thomas (Cardiff: Cardiff University Press, 1958)

D430. NORDAL, Sigurður, 'Three Essays on *Vǫluspá*', tr. B. S. Benedikz and J. S. McKinnell, *Saga-Book of the Viking Society* 18 (1971), 79–135

D431. NORDLAND, O., 'Ormegarden', *Viking* 13 (1949), 77–126

D432. NORTH, Richard, 'The Pagan Inheritance of Egill's *Sonatorrek*', in *Poetry in the Scandinavian Middle Ages*, ed. Teresa Pàroli, The Seventh International Saga Conference, Atti del XII Congresso internazionale di studi sull' alto medioevo (Spoleto: Presso la sede del centro studi, 1990), pp. 147–68

D433. NORTHCOTT, Kenneth, 'An Interpretation of the Second Merseburg Charm', *Modern Language Review* 54 (1959), 45–50

D434. NYLÉN, E., *Stones, Ships, and Symbols: The Picture Stones of Gotland from the Viking Age and Before* (Stockholm: Gidlunds, 1988)

D435. OHLMARKS, Åke, *Heimdalls Horn und Odins Auge* (Lund, 1937)

D436. ÓLAFSSON, Ólafur M., 'Sigurðr duldi nafns síns', *Andvari*, n.s. 12 (1970), 182–9

D437. OLSEN, Olaf, 'The "Sanctuary" in Jelling', *Mediæval Scandinavia* 7 (1974), 226–34

D438. OLSON, O., *The Relationship of the Hrólfs saga Kraka and the Bjarkarímur to Beowulf*, Publications of the Society for the Advancement of Scandinavian Study (Urbana, IL, 1916)

D439. OOSTEN, Jarich G., *The War of the Gods: The Social Code in Indo-European Mythology* (London: Routledge, 1985)

D440. OPLAND, Jeff, 'A *Beowulf* Analogue in *Njálssaga*', *Scandinavian Studies* 45 (1973), 54–8

D441. ORCHARD, Andy, *Pride and Prodigies: Studies in the Monsters of the 'Beowulf'-Manuscript* (Ipswich: Brewer, 1995)

D442. ORTON, P.R., '*The Wife's Lament* and *Skírnismál*: Some Parallels', in *Úr Dǫlum til Dala: Guðbrandur Vigfússon*

D443. ÖSTVOLD, Torbjörg, 'The War of the Æsir and the Vanir–a Myth of the Fall in Nordic Religion', *Temenos* 5 (1969), 169–202

D444. OTTÓSSON, Kjartan G., *Fróðarundur í Eyrbyggju*, Studia Islandica 42 (Reykjavik: Menningarsjóður, 1983)

D445. PAGE, R.I., *Runes* (London: British Museum Press, 1987)

D446. PAGE, R.I., 'Scandinavian Society, 800–1100: The Contribution of Runic Studies', in *Viking Revaluations. Viking Society Centenary Symposium 14–15 May 1992*, ed. Anthony Faulkes and Richard Perkins (London: Viking Society for Northern Research, 1993), pp. 145–59

D447. PAGE, R.I., *Runes and Runic Inscriptions: Collected Essays on Anglo-Saxon and Viking Runes*, ed. David Parsons (Woodbridge: Boydell, 1995)

D448. PÁLSSON, Gísli, 'The Name of the Witch: Sagas, Sorcery, and Social Context', in *Social Approaches to Viking Studies*, ed. Ross Sampson (Glasgow: Cruithne Press, 1991), pp. 157–68

D449. PÁLSSON, Heimir, 'Þekkti Snorri Hávamál?', in *Sagnaþing helgað Jónasi Kristjánssyni sjötugum, 10. april 1994*, ed. Gísli Sigurðsson, Guðrún Kvaran, and Sigurgeir Steingrímsson, 2 vols. (Reykjavik: Hið íslenska bókmenntafélag, 1994), pp. 365–76

D450. PÁLSSON, Hermann, 'Áss hin almáttki', *Skírnir* 130 (1956), 187–92

D451. PÁLSSON, Hermann, and Paul Edwards, *Legendary Fiction in Medieval Iceland* (Reykjavik, 1971)

D452. PÀROLI, Teresa, '*Baldr's Dreams*: A Poet Awaiting Vision', *Rendiconti della Classe di Scienze morali storiche e filologiche della Accademia Nazionale dei Lincei* 9.3 (1992), 137–61

D453. PARSONS, David N., 'Anglo-Saxon Runic Inscriptions on Portable Objects' (unpublished PhD thesis, University of Cambridge, 1995)

D454. PERKINS, Richard, '*Þrymskviða* Stanza 20, and a Passage from *Viglundar saga*', *Saga-Book of the Viking Society* 22 (1988), 279–84

D455. PERKINS, Richard, 'The Eyrarland Image–*Þrymskviða*, stanzas 30–31', in *Sagnaþing helgað Jónasi Kristjánssyni sjötugum, 10. April 1994*, ed. Gísli Sigurðsson, Guðrún Kvaran, and Sigurgeir Steingrímsson, 2 vols. (Reykjavik: Hið íslenska bókmenntafélag, 1994), pp. 653–64

D456. PHILPOTTS, Bertha S., 'Surt', *Arkiv för nordisk filologi* 17 (1905), 14–30

D457. PHILPOTTS, Bertha S., 'Temple-Administration and Chieftainship in Pre-Christian Norway and Iceland', *Saga-Book of the Viking Society* 8 (1913–14), 264–84

D458. PHILPOTTS, Bertha S., *The Elder Edda and Ancient Scandinavian Drama* (Cambridge: Cambridge University Press, 1920)

D459. PLOSS, Emil, *Siegfried-Sigurd der Drachenkämpfer*, Landschaftsverband Rheinland, Rheinisches Landesmuseum (Cologne: Böhlau, 1966)

D460. POLOMÉ, E.C., 'A propos de la déesse Nerthus', *Latomus* 13 (1954), 167–200

D461. POLOMÉ, E.C., 'Quelques notes à propos de l'énigmatique dieu scandinave Lóðurr', *Revue Belge de Philologie* 33 (1955), 493–4

D462. POLOMÉ, E.C., 'Comments on *Vǫluspá*, stanzas 17–18', in *Old Norse Literature and Mythology*, ed. E.C. Polomé (Austin, TX: University of Texas Press, 1969), pp. 265–90

D463. POLOMÉ, E.C., 'Some Aspects of the Cult of the Mother Goddess in Western Europe', *Vistas and Vectors. Festschrift H. Rehder* (Austin, TX: University of Texas Press, 1980), 493–4

D464. PUHVEL, Martin, 'The Deicidal Otherworld Weapon in Celtic and Germanic Mythic Tradition', *Folklore*, 83 (1972), 210–19.

D465. QUINN, Judith E., '*Vǫluspá* and the Composition of Eddic Verse', in *Poetry in the Scandinavian Middle Ages*, ed. Teresa Pàroli, The Seventh International Saga Conference, Atti del XII Congresso internazionale di studi sull' alto medioevo (Spoleto: Presso la sede del centro studi, 1990), pp. 303–20

D466. QUINN, Judith E., 'Verseform and Voice in Eddic Poems: The Discourses of *Fáfnismál*', *Arkiv för nordisk filologi* 107 (1992), 100–30

D467. RALPH, Bo, 'The Composition of the *Grímnismál*', *Arkiv för nordisk filologi* 87 (1972), 97–118

D468. RAUSING, Gad, '*Beowulf, Ynglingatal*, and the *Ynglinga saga*', *Fornvännen* 80 (1985), 163–78

D469. REICHERT, Hermann, 'Zum Sigrdrífa-Brünhild Problem', in *Antiquitates Indogermanicae: Studien zur indogermanischen Altertumskunde und zur Sprach- und Kulturgeschichte der indogermanischen Völker. Gedenkschrift für Hermann Güntert*, ed. Manfred Mayrhofer *et al.*, Innsbrucker Beiträge zur Sprachwissenschaft 12 (Innsbruck: Institut für Sprachwissenschaft der Universität Innsbruck, 1974), pp. 252–65

D470. REICHERT, Hermann, 'Die Brynhild-Lieder der *Edda* im europäischen Kontext', in *Poetry in the Scandinavian Middle Ages*, ed. Teresa Pàroli, The Seventh International Saga Conference, Atti del XII Congresso internazionale di studi sull' alto medioevo (Spoleto: Presso la sede del centro studi, 1990), pp. 571–96

D471. REUSCHEL, H., *Untersuchungen über Stoff und Stil der Fornaldarsagas* (Bühl-Baden, 1933)

D472. RIEGER, Gerd Enno, '*Þrk*. 20 *við scolom aka tvau*', *Skandinavistik* 5 (1975), 7–10

D473. ROOTH, A.B., *Loki in Scandinavian Mythology*, Skrifter utgivna af Kungl. Humanistiska Vetenskapssamfundet i Lund 61 (Lund: Gleerup, 1961)

D474. ROSENFELD, Hellmut, 'Wielandlied, Lied von Frau Helchen Söhnen und Hunnenschlachtlied: Historische Wirklichkeit und Heldenlied', *Beiträge zur Geschichte der deutschen Sprache und Literatur* 77 (1955), 204–48

D475. ROSS, Margaret Clunies, 'An Edition of the *Ragnarsdrápa* of Bragi Boddason' (Unpublished DPhil. dissertation, University of Oxford, 1973)

D476. ROSS, Margaret Clunies, 'The Myth of Gefjon and Gylfi and its Function in *Snorra Edda* and *Heimskringla*', *Arkiv för nordisk filologi* 93 (1978), 149–65

D477. ROSS, Margaret Clunies, 'An Interpretation of the Myth of Þórr's Encounter with Geirrøðr and his Daughters',

in *Speculum Norroenum: Norse Studies in Memory of Gabriel Turville-Petre*, ed. Ursula Dronke, Guðrún P. Helgadóttir, Gerd Wolfgang Weber, and Hans Bekker-Nielsen (Odense: Odense University Press, 1981), pp. 370–91

D478. ROSS, Margaret Clunies, 'Snorri Sturluson's Use of the Norse Origin-Legend of the Sons of Fornjótr in his *Edda*', *Arkiv för nordisk filologi* 98 (1983), 47–66

D479. ROSS, Margaret Clunies, *Skáldskaparmál. Snorri Sturluson's Ars Poetica and Medieval Theories of Language*, The Viking Collection 4 (Odense: Odense University Press, 1987)

D480. ROSS, Margaret Clunies, 'Two of Þórr's Great Fights according to *Hymiskviða*', *Leeds Studies in English*, n.s. 20 (1989), 7–27

D481. ROSS, Margaret Clunies, 'Why Skaði Laughed. Comic Seriousness in an Old Norse Mythic Narrative', *Maal og Minne* (1989), 1–14

D482. ROSS, Margaret Clunies, 'Voice and Voices in Eddic Poetry', in *Poetry in the Scandinavian Middle Ages*, ed. Teresa Pàroli, The Seventh International Saga Conference, Atti del XII Congresso internazionale di studi sull' alto medioevo (Spoleto: Presso la sede del centro studi, 1990), pp. 219–30

D483. ROSS, Margaret Clunies, 'Mythic Narrative in Saxo Grammaticus and Snorri Sturluson', in *Saxo Grammaticus tra storiografia e letteratura. Bevegna, 27.–29. settembre 1990*, ed. Carlo Santini (Rome: Il Calamo, 1992), pp. 47–59

D484. ROSS, Margaret Clunies, 'Snorri's *Edda* as Medieval *Religionsgeschichte*', in *Germanische Religionsgeschichte: Quellen und Quellenprobleme*, ed. H. Beck, Detlev Ellmers, and Kurt Schier (Berlin: de Gruyter, 1992), pp. 633–55

D485. ROSS, Margaret Clunies, 'The Mythological Fictions of *Snorra Edda*', in *Snorrastefna. 25.–27. júlí 1990*, ed. Úlfar Bragason, Rit Stofnunar Sigurðar Nordals 1 (Reykjavík: Stofnun Sigurðar Nordals, 1992), pp. 204–16

D486. ROSS, Margaret Clunies, 'Þórr's Honour', in *Studien zum Altgermanischen. Festschrift Heinrich Beck*, ed. Heiko Uecker (Berlin: de Gruyter, 1994)

D487. ROSS, Margaret Clunies, and B.K. Martin, 'Narrative Structures and Intertextuality in *Snorra Edda*: The Example of Þórr's Encounter with Geirrøðr', in *Structure and Meaning in Old Norse Literature*, ed. John Lindow, Lars Lönnroth, and G.W. Weber (Odense: Odense University Press, 1986), 56–72

D488. RUGGERINI, Maria Elena, *Le invettive di Loki*, Testi e studi di filologia 2 (Rome: Istituto di glottologia, 1979)

D489. RUSSELL, W.M.S., and C. Russell, 'The Social Biology of Werewolves', in *Animals in Folklore*, ed. J.R. Porter and W.M.S. Russell (Cambridge: Brewer, 1978), pp. 143–82

D490. RYAN, J.S., 'Othin in England. Evidence from the Poetry for a Cult of Woden in Anglo-Saxon England', *Folklore* 74 (1963), 460–80

D491. SALUS, Peter H., 'More "Eastern Echoes" in the *Edda*? An Addendum', *Modern Language Notes* 79 (1964), 426–8

D492. SALUS, Peter H., and Paul Beekman Taylor, '*Eikinskjaldi, Fjalarr*, and *Eggþér*: Notes on Dwarves and Giants in the *Vǫluspá*', *Neophilologus* 53 (1969), 76–81

Bibliography and Further Reading

D493. SANDBACH, Mary, 'Grettir in Thorisdal', *Saga-Book of the Viking Society* 12 (1937–8), 93–106

D494. SANTINI, Carlo, 'Die Frage der *Hárbarðzlióð* in Bezug auf die klassische literarische Tradition', in *Poetry in the Scandinavian Middle Ages*, ed. Teresa Pàroli, The Seventh International Saga Conference, Atti del XII Congresso internazionale di studi sull' alto medioevo (Spoleto: Presso la sede del centro studi, 1990), pp. 487–508

D495. SAUVÉ, James L., 'The Divine Victim: Aspects of Human Sacrifice in Viking Scandinavia and Vedic India', in *Myth and Law among the Indo-Europeans: Studies in Indo-European Comparative Mythology*, ed. Jaan Puhvel, Publications of the UCLA Center for the Study of Comparative Folklore and Mythology 1 (Berkeley, CA: University of California Press, 1970), pp. 173–91

D496. SAYERS, William A., 'Irish Perspectives on Heimdallr', *Alvíssmál* 2 (1993), 3–30

D497. SCHACH, Paul, 'Some Thoughts on Völuspá', in *Edda: A Collection of Essays*, ed. R.J. Glendinning and Haraldur Bessason, University of Manitoba Icelandic Studies 4 (Winnipeg: University of Manitoba Press, 1983), pp. 86–116

D498. SCHER, Steven P., '*Rígsþula* as Poetry', *Modern Language Notes* 78 (1963), 397–407

D499. SCHIER, Kurt, 'Die *Húsdrápa* von Úlfr Uggason und die bildliche Überlieferung altnordischer Mythen', *Minjar og menntir. Afmælisrit helgað Kristjáni Eldjárn* (Reykjavík, 1976), pp. 425–43

D500. SCHIER, Kurt, '*Húsdrápa* 2: Heimdall, Loki und die Meerniere', in *Festgabe für Otto Höfler zum 75. Geburstag* (Vienna, 1976), 577–88

D501. SCHJØDT, Jens Peter, '*Vǫluspá*: Cyclisk tidsopfattelse i gammelnordisk religion', *Danske Studier* 76 (1981), 91–5

D502. SCHJØDT, Jens Peter, 'Om Loke endnu engang', *Arkiv för nordisk filologi* 96 (1981), 49–86

D503. SCHJØDT, Jens Peter, 'The "fire ordeal" in the *Grímnismál*–Initiation or Annihilation?', *Mediaeval Scandinavia* 12 (1988), 29–43

D504. SCHJØDT, Jens Peter, 'Relationen mellem aser og vaner og dens ideologiske implikationer', in *Nordisk Hedendom. Et Symposium*, ed. Gro Steinsland (Odense: Odense University Press, 1991), pp. 303–20

D505. SCHJØDT, Jens Peter, 'The Relation between the two Phonemenological Categories Initiation and Sacrifice as exemplified by the Norse Myth of Óðinn on the Tree', in *The Problem of Ritual*, ed. Tore Ahlbäck (Åbo: Donner Institute, 1993), pp. 261–74

D506. SCHLAUCH, Margaret, *Romance in Iceland* (London: Allen & Unwin, 1934)

D507. SCHÖNBÄCK, B., 'The Custom of Burial in Boats', in *Vendel Period Studies*, ed. J.P. Lamm and H.-Å. Nordström (Stockholm: Statens historiska museum, 1983)

D508. SCHRADER, Richard J., 'Sacred Groves, Marvellous Waters, and Grendel's Abode', *Florilegium* 5 (1983), 76–84

D509. SCHRÖDER, Franz Rolf, 'Das Symposion der *Lokasenna*', *Arkiv för nordisk filologi* 67 (1952), 1–29

D510. SCHRÖDER, Franz Rolf, 'Balder und der zweite Merseburger Spruch', *Germanisch-romanische Monatsschrift* n.s. 3 (1953), 161–83

D511. SCHRÖDER, Franz Rolf, 'Das Hymirlied: zur Frage verblasster Mythen in den Götterliedern der Edda', *Arkiv för nordisk filologi* 70 (1955), 1–40

D512. SCHRÖDER, Franz Rolf, 'Indra, Thor, und Herakles', *Zeitschrift für deutsche Philologie* 76 (1957), 1–41

D513. SCHRÖDER, Franz Rolf, '*Grimnismál*', *Beiträge zur Geschichte der deutschen Sprache und Literatur* 80 (1958), 341–78

D514. SCHRÖDER, Franz Rolf, 'Die eddischen "Baldrs Träume"', *Germanisch-romanische Monatsschrift*, n.s. 14 (1964), 329–37

D515. SCHRÖDER, Franz Rolf, 'Thors Hammerholung: Otto Höfler zugeeignet', *Beiträge zur Geschichte der deutschen Sprache und Literatur* 87 (1965), 3–42

D516. SCHRÖDER, Franz Rolf, '*Svipdagsmál*', *Germanisch-romanische Monatsschrift*, n.s. 16 (1966), 113–19

D517. SCHRÖDER, Franz Rolf, 'Heimdall', *Beiträge zur Geschichte der deutschen Sprache und Literatur* 89 (1967), 1–41

D518. SCHRÖDER, Franz Rolf, 'Die Eingangsszene von *Guðrúnarhvǫt* und *Hamðismál*', *Beiträge zur Geschichte der deutschen Sprache und Literatur* 98 (1976), 430–6

D519. SCHÜTTE, Gudmund, 'The Cult of Nerthus', *Saga-Book of the Viking Society* 8 (1913–14), 29–43

D520. SEE, Klaus von, 'Das Alter der *Rigsþula*', *Acta Philologica Scandinavica* 24 (1957–61), 1–12

D521. SEE, Klaus von, 'Die Sage von Hamdir und Sörli', in *Festschrift Gottfried Weber zu seinem 70. Geburtstag überreicht von Frankfurter Kollegen und Schülern*, ed. Heinz Otto Burger and Klaus von See, Frankfurter Beiträge zur Germanistik 1 (Bad Homburg: Gehlen, 1967), pp. 47–75

D522. SEE, Klaus von, '*Sonatorrek* und *Hávamál*', *Zeitschrift für deutsches Altertum* 99 (1970), 26–33

D523. SEE, Klaus von, *Die Gestalt der Hávamál: Eine Studie zur eddischen Spruchdichtung* (Frankfurt: Athenäum, 1972)

D524. SEE, Klaus von, '*Guðrúnarhvǫt* und *Hamðismál*', *Beiträge zur Geschichte der deutschen Sprache und Literatur* 99 (1977), 250–8

D525. SHETELIG, Haakon, 'Traces of the Custom of "Suttee" in Norway during the Viking Age', *Saga-Book of the Viking Society* 6 (1908–9), 180–208

D526. SHIPPEY, T.A., 'Speech and the Unspoken in *Hamðismál*', in *Prosody and Poetics in the Early Middle Ages: Essays in Honour of C.B. Hieatt*, ed. M.J. Toswell (Toronto: University of Toronto Press, 1995), 180–96

D527. SIGURÐARDÓTTIR, Arnheiður, 'Guðrúnarkviða II og fornar hannyrðir á Norðurlöndum', *Skírnir* 143 (1969), 27–41

D528. SIGURÐSSON, Gísli, 'On the Classification of Eddic Heroic Poetry in View of the Oral Theory', in *Poetry in the Scandinavian Middle Ages*, ed. Teresa Pàroli, The Seventh International Saga Conference, Atti del XII Congresso internazionale di studi sull' alto medioevo (Spoleto: Presso la sede del centro studi, 1990), pp. 245–56

D529. SIMEK, Rudolf, 'Skíðblaðnir. Some Ideas on Ritual Connections between Sun and Ship', *Northern Studies* 9 (1977), 31–9

D530. SIMON, John, 'Snorri Sturluson: his Life and Times', *Parergon* 15 (1976), 3–15

D531. SIMPSON, Jacqueline, 'Mímir: Two Myths or One?', *Saga-Book of the Viking Society* 16 (1962), 41–53

D532. SIMPSON, Jacqueline, 'Otherworld Adventures in an Icelandic Saga', *Folklore* 77 (1966), 1–20

D533. SIMPSON, Jacqueline, 'Some Scandinavian Sacrifices', *Folklore* 78 (1967), 190–202

D534. SINGER, Samuel, 'Die Grundlagen der Thrymskvidha', *Neophilologus*, 17 (1932), 47–8.

D535. SISAM, Kenneth, 'Anglo-Saxon Royal Genealogies', *Proceedings of the British Academy* 39 (1953), 287–348

D536. SJØVOLD, T., *The Viking Ships in Oslo* (Oslo, 1979)

D537. SKOVGAARD-PETERSEN, Inge, *Starkad in Saxo's Gesta Danorum: History and Heroic Tale* (Odense: Odense University Press, 1985)

D538. SMYSER, H.M., 'Ibn Fadlān's Account of the Rūs', *Medieval and Linguistic Studies in Honour of Francis Peabody Magoun Jr*, ed. J.B. Bessinger and R.P. Creed (London: Allen & Unwin, 1965), pp. 92–119

D539. SÖDERBORG, Barbro, 'Formelgods och Eddakronologi', *Arkiv för nordisk filologi* 101 (1986), 50–86

D540. SØRENSEN, Preben Meulengracht, 'Thor's Fishing Expedition', in *Words and Objects: towards a Dialogue between Archaeology and the History of Religion*, ed. Gro Steinsland (Oslo: Norwegian University Press, 1986), 257–78

D541. SØRENSEN, Preben Meulengracht, 'Loki's *senna* in Ægir's Hall', in *Idee, Gestalt, Geschichte. Festschrift Klaus von See. Studien zur europäischen Kulturtradition. Studies in European Cultural Tradition*, ed. G.W. Weber (Odense: Odense University Press, 1988), pp. 239–59

D542. SØRENSEN, Preben Meulengracht, 'Starkaðr, Loki and Egill Skallagrímsson', in *Sagas of the Icelanders. A Book of Essays*, ed. J. Tucker (New York and London: Garland, 1989), pp. 146–59

D543. SØRENSEN, Preben Meulengracht, 'Om edda digtenes alder', in *Nordisk Hedendom. Et Symposium*, ed. Gro Steinsland (Odense: Odense University Press, 1991), pp. 217–28

D544. SØRENSEN, Preben Meulengracht, 'Freyr in den Isländersagas', in *Germanische Religionsgeschichte: Quellen und Quellenprobleme*, ed. H. Beck, Detlev Ellmers, and Kurt Schier (Berlin: de Gruyter, 1992), pp. 720–35

D545. SØRENSEN, Preben Meulengracht, 'Snorris frœði', in *Snorrastefna. 25.–27. júli 1990*, ed. Úlfar Bragason, Rit Stofnunar Sigurðar Nordals 1 (Reykjavík: Stofnun Sigurðar Nordals, 1992), pp. 270–83

D546. SPAMER, A., 'P(h)ol ende Uodan. Zum zweiten Merseburger Spruch', *Deutsches Jahrbuch für Volkskunde* 3 (1957), 347–65

D547. SPERBERG-MACQUEEN, C. Michael, 'The Legendary Form of *Sigurðarkviða in skamma*', *Arkiv för nordisk filologi* 100 (1986), 16–40

D548. SPRENGER, Ulrike, '*Vafðrúðnismál* 10, 3: Der Kaltgerippte', *Arbeiten zur Skandinavistik* 6, ed. H. Beck (Frankfurt am Main, 1985), 185–210

D549. STEINSLAND, Gro, 'Antropogonimyten i *Vǫluspá*. En tekst-

og tradisjonskritisk analyse', *Arkiv för nordisk filologi* 98 (1983), 80–107

D550. STEINSLAND, Gro, 'Giants as Recipients of Cult in the Viking Age?', in *Words and Objects: towards a Dialogue between Archaeology and the History of Religion*, ed. Gro Steinsland (Oslo: Norwegian University Press, 1986), pp. 212–22

D551. STEINSLAND, Gro, 'Pagan Myth in Confrontation with Christianity: *Skírnismál* and *Genesis*', in *Old Norse and Finnish Religions and Cultic Place-Names*, ed. T. Ahlbäck (Åbo: Donner Institute, 1990), pp. 316–28

D552. STEINSLAND, Gro, *Det hellige bryllup og norrøn kongeideologi: en analyse av hierogami-myten i 'Skírnismál', 'Ynglingatal', 'Háleygjatal', og 'Hyndluljóð'* (Oslo: Solum, 1991)

D553. STEINSLAND, Gro, 'Myte og ideologi–Bryllupsmyten i eddadiktningen og hos Snorri–Om det mytologiske grunnlaget for norrøn kongeideologi', in *Snorrastefna. 25.–27. júli 1990*, ed. Úlfar Bragason, Rit Stofnunar Sigurðar Nordals 1 (Reykjavík: Stofnun Sigurðar Nordals, 1992), pp. 226–40

D554. STEINSLAND, Gro, and Kari Voight, 'Aukinn ertu Volse ok vpp vm tekinn', *Arkiv för nordisk filologi* 91 (1981), 87–106

D555. STEPHENS, John, 'The Mead of Poetry: Myth and Metaphor', *Neophilologus* 56 (1972), 259–68

D556. STEPHENS, John, 'The Poet and *Atlakviða*: Variation on Some Themes', in *Iceland and the Mediaeval World: Studies in Honour of Ian Maxwell*, ed. G. Turville-Petre and John Stanley Martin (Melbourne, 1974), pp. 56–61

D557. STEPHENS, W.E.D., 'An Examination of the Sources of the Thidrekssaga' (unpublished MA dissertation, University of London, 1937)

D558. STORMS, Gustav, *Anglo-Saxon Magic* (The Hague: Nijhoff, 1948)

D559. STRÖM, Åke V., 'The King-God and his Connection with Sacrifice in Old Norse Religion', in *Sacral Kingship* (Leiden, 1959), pp. 702–15

D560. STRÖM, Folke, *On the Sacral Origin of the Germanic Death Penalties* (Stockholm, 1942)

D561. STRÖM, Folke, *Diser, nornor, valkyrjor: Fruktbarhetskult och sakralt kungadöme i Norden* (Stockholm: Almqvist & Wiksell, 1954)

D562. STRÖM, Folke, *Loki. Ein mythologisches Problem*, Göteborgs Universitets Årsskrift 62.8 (Göteborg: Almqvist & Winksell, 1956)

D563. STRÖMBÄCK, Dag, 'The Concept of Soul in Nordic Tradition', *Arv* 31 (1975), 5–22

D564. STRÖMBÄCK, Dag, *Sejd* (Lund: Blom, 1951)

D565. STRUTYNSKI, Udo, 'Germanic Divinities in Weekday Names', *Journal of Indo-European Studies* 3 (1975), 363–84

D566. STURTEVANT, Albert Morey, 'The Old Norse Proper Name *Svipdagr*', *Scandinavian Studies* 30 (1958), 30–4

D567. SVEINSSON, Einar Ól., 'Svipdag's Long Journey: Some Observations on *Gróagaldr* and *Fjölsvinnsmál*', in *Hereditas: Essays and Studies Presented to Professor Séamus Ó Duilearga*, ed. Bo Almqvist et al (= *Béaloideas* 39–41) (Dublin: Folklore of Ireland Society, 1971–3), pp. 298–319

D568. SWENSON, Karen, *Performing Definitions: Two Genres of*

Bibliography and Further Reading

Insult in Old Norse Literature, Studies in Scandinavian Literature and Culture 3 (Columbia, SC: Camden House, 1991)

D569. SZKLENAR, Hans, 'Anmerkungen zu einer neuen Interpretation des alten Atliliedes', *Literaturwissenschaftliches Jahrbuch der Görres-Gesellschaft* 22 (1981), 337–44

D570. TALBOT, Annelise, 'The Withdrawal of the Fertility God', *Folklore* 93 (1982), 31–46

D571. TALBOT, Annelise, 'Sigemund the Dragon-Slayer', *Folklore* 94 (1983), 153–62

D572. TAYLOR, A.R., '*Hauksbók* and Ælfric's *De Falsis Diis*', *Leeds Studies in English* n.s. 3 (1969), 101–9

D573. TAYLOR, Paul Beekman, 'The Structure of Völundarkviða', *Neophilologus* 47 (1963), 228–36

D574. TAYLOR, Paul Beekman, 'Heorot, Earth, and Asgard: Christian Poetry and Pagan Myth', *Tennessee Studies in Literature* 11 (1966), 119–30

D575. TAYLOR, Paul Beekman, 'The Rhythm of *Völuspá*', *Neophilologus* 55 (1971), 45–57

D576. TAYLOR, Paul Beekman, '*Völundarkviða*, *Þrymskviða* and the Function of Myth', *Neophilologus* 78 (1994), 263–81

D577. THOMPSON, Claibourne W., 'The Runes in *Bósa saga ok Herrauðs*', *Scandinavian Studies* 50 (1978), 50–6

D578. THUN, Nils, 'The Malignant Elves. Notes on Anglo-Saxon Magic and Germanic Myth', *Studia Neophilologica* 41 (1969), 378–69

D579. TOLKIEN, Christopher, 'The Battle of the Goths and the Huns', *Saga-Book of the Viking Society* 14 (1955–6), 141–63

D580. TOLLEY, Clive, 'The Mill in Norse and Finnish Mythology', *Saga-Book of the Viking Soviety* 24 (1995), 63–82

D581. TOORN, M.C. van den, 'Über die Ethik in den Fornaldarsaga', *Acta Philologica Scandinavica* 26 (1963–4), 19–26

D582. TULINIUS, Torfi H., *La Matière du Nord: Sagas légendaires et fiction dans la littérature islandaise en prose du XIIIe siècle* (Paris: Presses de l' Université de Paris-Sorbonne, 1984)

D583. TURVILLE-PETRE, E. O. Gabriel, 'The Cult of Freyr in the Evening of Paganism', *Proceedings the Leeds Philosophical and Literary Society* 3 (1935), 317–33

D584. TURVILLE-PETRE, E. O. Gabriel, 'A Note on the Landdisir', in *Early English and Norse Studies Presented to Hugh Smith in Honour of his Sixtieth Birthday*, ed. Arthur Brown and Peter G. Foote (London: Methuen, 1963), pp. 196–201

D585. TURVILLE-PETRE, E. O. Gabriel, 'The Cult of Óðinn in Iceland', in his *Nine Norse Studies* (London: Viking Society for Northern Research, 1972), pp. 1–19

D586. TURVILLE-PETRE, E. O. Gabriel, 'Gísli Súrsson and His Poetry: Traditions and Influences', in his *Nine Norse Studies* (London: Viking Society for Northern Research, 1972), pp. 118–53

D587. TURVILLE-PETRE, E. O. Gabriel, '*Liggja fylgjur þinar til Íslands*' in his *Nine Norse Studies* (London: Viking Society for Northern Research, 1972), pp. 52–7

D588. TURVILLE-PETRE, J.E., 'Hengest and Horsa', *Saga-Book of the Viking Society* 14 (1958), 273–90

D589. TURVILLE-PETRE, J.E. 'On *Ynglingatal*', *Medieval Scandinavia* 11 (1978–9), 47–67

D590. ULVESTAD, Bjarne, 'How Old are the Mythological Eddic Poems?', *Scandinavian Studies* 26 (1954), 49–69

D591. VESTERGAARD, Elisabeth, 'Dværgenes Skat', in *Nordisk Hedendom. Et Symposium*, ed. Gro Steinsland (Odense: Odense University Press, 1991), pp. 349–58

D592. VRIES, Jan de, 'Over de dateerung van Þrymskviða', *Tijdschrift voor nederlandse taal- en letterkunde* 47 (1928), 251–372

D593. VRIES, Jan de, 'Ginnungagap', *Acta Philologica Scandinavica* 5 (1930–1), 41–66

D594. VRIES, Jan de, *The Problem of Loki* (Helsinki, 1933)

D595. VRIES, Jan de, 'Contributions to the Study of Othin especially in his Relation to Agricultural Practices in Modern Popular Lore', *Folklore Fellows Communications* 94 (1931), 3–79

D596. VRIES, Jan de, *De Skaldenkenningen met mythologischen Inhoud*, Nederlandsche Bijdragen op het Gebied van germaansche Philologie en Linguistiek 4 (Haarlem: Tjeenk, 1934)

D597. VRIES, Jan de, 'Über die Datierung der Eddalieder', *Germanisch-romanische Monatsschrift* 22 (1934), 253–63

D598. VRIES, Jan de, 'La valeur religieuse du mot germanique *irmin*', *Cahiers du sud* 36 (1952), 18–37

D599. VRIES, Jan de, 'Über das Verhältnis von Óðr und Óðinn', *Zeitschrift für deutsche Philologie* 73 (1954), 337–53

D600. VRIES, Jan de, 'Heimdall, dieu énigmatique', *Études germaniques* 10 (1955), 257–68

D601. VRIES, Jan de, 'Der Mythos von Baldrs Tod', *Arkiv för nordisk filologi* 70 (1955), 41–60

D602. VRIES, Jan de, 'Die Helgilieder', *Arkiv för nordisk filologi* 72 (1957), 123–54

D603. VRIES, Jan de, 'Das zweite Gudrunlied', *Zeitschrift für deutsche Philologie* 77 (1959), 176–99

D604. VRIES, Jan de, 'Wodan und die Wilde Jagd', *Nachbarn: Jahrbuch für vergleichende Volkskunde* (1963), pp. 31–59

D605. VRIES, Jan de, *Heroic Song and Heroic Legend*, trans. B.J. Timmer (London: Oxford University Press, 1963)

D606. WARD, Donald, *The Divine Twins: An Indo-European Myth in Germanic Tradition* (Berkeley, CA: University of California Press, 1968)

D607. WATKINS, Calvert, 'Language of Gods and Language of Men: Remarks on Some Indo-European Metalinguistic Traditions', in *Myth and Law among the Indo-Europeans: Studies in Indo-European Comparative Mythology*, ed. Jaan Puhvel (Berkeley: University of California Press, 1970), pp. 1–17

D608. WEBER, Gerd Wolfgang, *Wyrd. Studien zum Schicksalsbegriff der altenglischen und altnordischen Literatur*, Frankfurter Beiträge zur Germanistik 8 (Bad Homburg: Gehlen, 1969)

D609. WEBER, Gerd Wolfgang, 'Die Christus-Strophe des Eilífr Goðrúnarson', *Zeitschrift für deutsches Altertum und deutsche Literatur* 99 (1970), 87–90

D610. WEBSTER, Leslie, 'Stylistic Aspects of the Franks Casket', in *The Vikings*, ed. R.T. Farrell (London and Chichester: Phillimore, 1982), pp. 20–31

D611. WESSÉN, Elias, *Hávamál: Några stilfrågor*, Filologiskt arkiv 8 (Stockholm: Almqvist & Wiksell, 1959)

D612. WEXELSEN, Einar (ed.), *Centenary of a Norwegian Viking Find: The Gokstad Excavations*, trans. Karin C. Jenssen (Sandefjord: Sandefjordmuseene, 1981)

D613. WHALEY, Diana, *'Heimskringla': An Introduction*, Viking Society for Northern Research, Text Series 8 (London: Viking Society for Northern Research, 1991)

D614. WHITBREAD, L., 'The Binding of Weland', *Medium Ævum* 35 (1956), 13–19

D615. WIEDEN, Helge bei der, 'Einige Bemerkungen zum religionsgeschichtlichen Ort der *Lokasenna*', *Zeitschrift für deutsche Philologie* 83 (1964), 266–75

D616. WIESELGREN, Per, *Quellenstudien zur Vǫlsungasaga*, Acta et Commentationes Universitatis Tartuensis, 34.3, 37.5, 38.2 (Tartu: Mattiesen, 1935–6)

D617. WIKMAN, Karl Robert V., *Om de fornnordiska formerna för äktenskpets ingående: med särskild hänsyn till Eddadikterna Rigsþula och Þrymskviða*, Societas Scientiarum Fennica: Årsbok/ Vuosikirja 34B, no. 3 (Helsingfors, 1959)

D618. WISNIEWSKI, Roswitha, *Kudrun Heldendichtung* III (Stuttgart: Metzler, 1963)

D619. WOLF, Alois, 'Zitat und Polemik in den *Hákonarmál* Eyvinds', *Germanistische Studien*, ed. J. Erben and E. Thurnher, Innsbrucker Beiträge zur Kulturwissenschaft 15 (Innsbruck, 1969), pp. 9–32

D620. WOOD, Cecil, 'The Reluctant Christian and the King of Norway', *Scandinavian Studies* 31 (1959), 65–72

D621. WOOD, Cecil, '*Sigurðarkviða en skamma* 69', *Scandinavian Studies* 35 (1963), 29–36

D622. WOOD, Frederic T., 'The Transmission of the *Vǫluspá*', *Germanic Review* 34 (1959), 247–61

D623. WOOD, Frederic T., 'The Age of the *Vǫluspá*', *Germanic Review* 36 (1961), 94–107

D624. WÜRTH, Stephanie, *Elemente des Erzählens: die þættir der Flateyjarbók*, Beiträge zur nordischen Philologie 20 (Basel: Helbing & Lichtenhahn, 1991)

D625. YOUNG, Jean I., 'Does *Rígsþula* Betray Irish Influence?', *Arkiv för nordisk filologi* 49 (1933), 97–107

D626. ZETTERHOLM, D.O., *Studier i en Snorre-Text* (Stockholm: Geber, 1949)

D627. ZINK, G., *Les légendes héroïques de Dietrich et d' Ermrich dans les littératures germaniques* (Lyon: IAC 1950)

D628. ZOTTO, Carla del, *La 'Hymskviða' e la pesca di Þórr nella tradizione nordica*, Testi e studi di filologia 1 (Rome: Istituto di glottologia, 1979)

Index of Passages
and Authors Cited in the Text